Using Java 1.2

Mike Morgan

Contents at a Glance

Using Java 1.2

International Standard Book Number: 0-7897-1627-5

Library of Congress Catalog Card Number: 98-84331

Printed in the United States of America

First Printing: June, 1998

00 99 98   4 3 2 1

Trademarks

Executive Editor
Tim Ryan

Senior Acquisitions Editor
Jeff Taylor

Development Editor
Jon Steever

Managing Editor
Patrick Kanouse

Senior Project Editor
Elizabeth A. Bruns

Copy Editors
Patricia Kinyon
Tonya Maddox
Sean Medlock

Indexer
Bruce Clingaman

Technical Editor
Billy Barron

Production
Michael Henry
Linda Knose
Tim Osborn
Staci Somers
Mark Walchle

Contents

About the Author

Michael Morgan is a professional Java software developer and founder and president of DSE, Inc., a full-service Web presence provider and software development shop. The DSE team has developed software for such companies as Intelect, Magnavox, DuPont, the American Biorobotics Company, and Satellite Systems Corporation, as well as for the Government of Iceland and the Royal Saudi Air Force. DSE's Web sites are noted for their effectiveness—one of the company's sites generated sales of over $100,000 within 30 days of being announced.

During Academic Year 1989-1990 Mike was invited by retired Navy admiral Ron Hays to serve as the first Fellow of the Pacific International Center for High Technology Research (PICHTR) in Honolulu. PICHTR is a spin-off of the University of Hawaii, and bridges the gap between academic research and industrial applications. Mike directed the first technology transfer initiatives at PICHTR, and helped PICHTR win its first industrial contract. Mike assisted Admiral Hayes in presenting PICHTR and its mission to the Hawaii research community, the Hawaii legislature, and Hawaii's representatives to Congress.

Mike is a frequent speaker at seminars on information technology, and has taught computer science and software engineering at Chaminade University (the University of Honolulu) and in the graduate program of Hawaii Pacific University. He has given seminars for the IEEE, National Seminars, the University of Hawaii, Purdue University, and the University of Notre Dame.

He holds a Master of Science in Systems Management from Florida Institute of Technology, and a Bachelor of Science in Mathematics from Wheaton College, where he concentrated his studies on computer science. He has taken numerous graduate courses in computer science through the National Technological University. Mike is currently a student in the doctoral program at the Center for Leadership Studies at Regent University, where he is exploring the relationship between software processes and organizational theory.

Mike can usually be found in his office at DSE, drinking Diet Pepsi and writing Java. He lives in Virginia Beach with his wife, Jean, and their six children.

Dedication

To my son, Glenn. I love you.

Acknowledgments

While my name appears on the cover of this book, many people worked together to produce the manuscript, and to turn the manuscript into the book. If you find this book useful, you have them to thank.

As with all my books, I am again indebted to my colleague, Christopher Kepilino, and to my wife, Jean. Chris and Jean attended to the myriad of details that are needed to turn an idea into a book. They produced screen shots, reviewed the manuscript, and made sure that files and email moved smoothly between my desk and the publisher's.

As always, the folks at Que have been capable and professional. Jon Steever reviewed the entire manuscript, providing insight into many new technology topics. Elizabeth Bruns and Pat Kinyon edited the entire manuscript—a monumental task calling for incredible patience. Thanks, guys.

I am also indebted to the readers of this and my previous books for your feedback. Please feel free to visit my Web site (`http://www.dse.com/Company/mike.html`) or send me email at `Mike.Morgan@mail.dse.com`. I look forward to hearing from you.

As always, any errors or omissions are my responsibility.

Mike Morgan

Virginia Beach

May 26, 1998

Tell Us What You Think!

As the reader of this book, *you* are our most important critic and commentator. We value your opinion and want to know what we're doing right, what we could do better, what areas you'd like to see us publish in, and any other words of wisdom you're willing to pass our way.

As the Executive Editor for the Web development team at Macmillan Computer Publishing, I welcome your comments. You can fax, email, or write me directly to let me know what you did or didn't like about this book—as well as what we can do to make our books stronger.

Please note that I cannot help you with technical problems related to the topic of this book, and that due to the high volume of mail I receive, I might not be able to reply to every message.

When you write, please be sure to include this book's title and author as well as your name and phone or fax number. I will carefully review your comments and share them with the author and editors who worked on the book.

Fax: [317-817-7070]

Email: java@mcp.com

Mail: Executive Editor
Web Publishing
Macmillan Computer Publishing
201 West 103rd Street
Indianapolis, IN 46290 USA

There's a rumor circulating that Java programmers make $400 per hour, and that if you study Java for six months, all you need to do to get a new job is to pull into a different driveway one morning. Well, that rumor may be a bit of an exaggeration, but, like most rumors, there's some truth to it. Tom Paulk of Snelling Personnel (a major technical recruiting firm) reports that Java is one of the most sought after—and lucrative—skills in the market. To see what job offers Java programmers are really getting, visit Tom's Web site at `http://www.snelling.com/chesapeake/`.

Who Should Read This Book?

Java is a platform-neutral, object-oriented programming language well-suited for use on the Internet. Unlike its cousin, JavaScript, Java is designed for professional programmers.

If you're a C or C++ programmer, this book is for you; in the section entitled "Building on the Strengths of C++" in Appendix B, "Java for C++ Programmers," you'll learn why Java may well be a better C++ than C++.

Perhaps you program in one of the so-called "legacy" languages such as COBOL or RPG. You can use Java to build a front-end to your existing applications, so that users on PCs, Macintoshes, or UNIX workstations can all access your application. You may want to consider migrating some of your existing code into Java in order to begin the process of distributing it to other machines on the network. You might even want to learn Java so you have another set of skills, hedging against the day when the demand for legacy programmers decreases.

If you're new to programming, welcome! Java is a great first language. You may need to work a bit harder than someone with more programming experience, but it's worth it—the ability to program is a valuable skill, so learning Java will reward you in many ways. If you've already had some experience with HTML and JavaScript, you can begin to use Java right away on your Web pages. See Appendix E, "Building Java Applets in an IDE." You should also plan to read Appendix A, "Introduction to Programming" to learn some of the basics.

How Is This Book Organized?

This book is organized into eight parts (not counting the appendixes). In general, foundational material comes before more advanced topics, so start skimming until you get to material that's new to you. (In the next section, I'll give you more detailed recommendations about how to read this book.)

Part I, "Getting Started," introduces you to Java. In Chapter 1, "What Is Java and Why Is It Important?" we'll see how Java fits into the rest of the programming world. Unlike programs written in nearly all other languages, programs written in Java can run easily on almost any computing platform. If you're using Java to enhance your Web site, you'll be glad for the security features that make Java *applets* an unlikely carrier for a computer virus.

Chapter 2, "A Tour of the Java World," introduces you to applets and applications. Applets are Java programs that run with the help of another program, such as a Web browser. Applications are complete programs in their own right. If you're new to programming and are mostly interested in using Java on your Web site, be sure to read "Java Applet Examples" in this chapter. That section introduces LiveConnect, a Netscape technology that allows you to integrate HTML forms, JavaScript, and Java applets. If you're considering Java as an alternative to an older programming language, be sure to read the section titled "Java Application Examples." That section shows you some of what is possible when you write a complete application in Java.

In order to write Java you need the Java Development Kit, or JDK, from Sun Microsystems. Chapter 3, "Getting Started Fast," tells you how to get the JDK and how to install it on your machine. Then we'll walk through the process of building a small application and converting it into an applet. We'll also go through the components of the JDK together, so you know what each one is supposed to do.

By the time we finish Part I, you'll have an idea of when you might want to use Java in your programming projects and how to get started. You'll know how to install an existing applet on your Web page and how to get started writing your own applets and applications.

Part II is entitled, "The Java Language." This part of the book assumes that you have installed the JDK on your computer, and that you're ready to write some programs. Chapter 4, "Understanding Java Data Types and Operators," describes the primitive data types—integers, characters, and floating point numbers—available to all Java programs. This chapter also introduces *classes*, the foundation of object-oriented programming. Chapter 5, "Using Branches and Loops," continues the discussion of the nuts and bolts of the language. Nicolas Wirth, inventor of the language Pascal, says, "Algorithms plus data structures equals programs." By the time you've finished Chapters 4 and 5, you'll know how to build algorithms and manipulate simple data structures in Java.

Today, one of the most sophisticated kinds of data structure is the class. In order to use a class, you call its *methods*—messages defined to be accessible to the class's clients. Even before you start writing much of your own code, you have access to hundreds of classes and thousands of methods built into the JDK. Chapter 6, "Methods: Adding Code to Your Objects," introduces the concept of code reuse and shows you how to avoid writing code by calling methods in existing classes. (While writing your own classes may be fun and educational, as a professional programmer you should use every opportunity to save money by reusing existing code.)

Chapter 6 serves as the jumping-off point in Part III, "Thinking in Objects." Once you've learned the basics of data structures and you've learned how to use methods defined for the JDK's classes, you'll want to start writing classes of your own. Chapter 7 ("Object-Oriented Analysis: A New Way of Looking at Software") and Chapter 8 ("Object-Oriented Design and Programming") show you how to look at your application as a collection of related objects, and how to convert those objects into class definitions. Analysis is the process of identifying the requirements of an application. Much of an analyst's time is spent talking to users, learning about the task they want the computer to solve for them. We'll look at use-case analysis—a fast way to get users to help you "write a book" on the application. Then we'll look at how you can use the parts of speech (nouns, verbs, and adjectives) to translate the use cases into a top-level design. In Chapter 8 we'll learn how to refine the top-level design into a detailed design, just one step short of an actual program. We'll introduce some coding idioms that will make your Java programs more readable for those who come after you. By the time you finish Part III, you'll be on your way to becoming a qualified object-oriented programmer.

In order for a program to qualify as a product, it should have a rich set of features and be resistant to programming errors. Part IV, "Beyond the Basics," addresses these two topics. Chapter 9, "Increasing Program Sophistication by Using Interfaces," introduces a way for classes in your Java program to behave as though they are part of more than one classification hierarchy. Chapter 10, "Simplifying Code with Exceptions," describes a problem with the "old style" of programming—from the days before C++. C++ includes a powerful way of dealing with errors, called *exceptions*. Chapter 10 shows you how to use them in Java.

By the time you reach the end of Part IV, you'll have touched on many of the elements typically covered in the first two years of an undergraduate computer science degree. Yet the programs you're writing would scarcely be recognized by most end users as an application. That's because, today, programs are more than data structures and algorithms—there's one more piece. The last essential piece of a program is the user interface. While you can write applications that work entirely with the command line, most users today demand a graphical interface, with buttons, scroll bars, and fields of all sorts. Section V, "Building a User Interface," addresses these demands.

We'll start out in Chapter 11, "Building the User Interface with the AWT," describing the classic Java graphical interface. That interface, the Abstract Windowing Toolkit, or AWT, is now embedded in a larger set of classes called the Java Foundation Classes, or JFC. The JFC's graphical components are called *Swing components*, and are described in Chapter 12, "Building the User Interface with JFC Swing Components," Chapter 13, "Designing for a JFC Interface," and Chapter 14, "Advanced User Interface Design with the JFC."

The last core information on Java programming is in Part VI, "Completing the Project." While you can write programs without using the techniques described in this part of the book, professional applets and applications will want to take advantage both of packages (the subject of Chapter 15, "Understanding Packages") and the Java debugger (described in Chapter 16, "Testing and Debugging Java Code"). This section also includes Chapter 17, "Concurrent Programming with Threads," and Chapter 18, "Communicating in Java: Streams and Sockets." In Chapter 17 you'll learn how to have the computer run several independent control paths at once—a technique called multi-threading. Chapter 18 shows you how to write clients and servers—the two essential ingredients of an Internet-based application.

Starting with Part VII, "Building Beans," we take up advanced topics. Chapter 19, "Building Components with JavaBeans," and Chapter 20, "Designing Good Beans," show how to use Java to build components. Non-programmers can drop these components into a visual development environment and build a program without typing code. This visual programming methodology is the key to many rapid application development environments used by people who need to develop applications without writing a lot of code.

Part VIII, "Advanced Java," closes the book by exploring some of the "leading edge" techniques available to Java programmers. Chapter 21, "Using the Java Database Connectivity Package," shows you how to connect to relational databases from inside a Java program. Chapter 22, "Improving Your Java Program's Performance," shows how Sun and others are defeating Java's reputation as a slow-running language. If you're considering writing a program in Java but your users are worried about performance, read this chapter to learn how to ensure that you build a high-speed solution.

When you're ready to ship your multi-class, multi-file applet or application to end users, you'll want to make a new Java archive (also known as a JAR file). Chapter 23, "Making and Using Java Archives," tells you how to prepare your files for distribution.

As you progress in your career as a Java programmer, you'll need to ensure that your code is reusable and maintainable. In this effort, code complexity is your opponent—you must learn to manage code complexity in order to build maintainable software. Read Chapter 24, "Organizing and Reusing Your Code," to learn how to defend against creeping complexity (and consequent maintenance costs).

The appendixes contain information that certain readers will find useful. Read Appendix A, "Introduction to Programming," if you're new in this business and need a grounding in fundamentals. Appendix B, "Java for C++ Programmers," is for experienced C++ programmers who need to "pick up" Java as a second language. All readers should see Appendix C, "Java Resources," to learn where to look online for additional information about the topics in this book.

Appendix D, "Java Language Reference," summarizes the syntax of the language—this resource is useful if you're tracking down a compiler error message. Appendix E, "Building Java Applets in an IDE," gives you an idea of what can be done with Java when you use an Integrated Development Environment (IDE) such as Visual Café for Java from Symantec.

Appendix F is the Glossary—turn here for any technical words you may not recognize. New glossary terms are set *like this* when they are first introduced.

How Do I Read This Book?

Whatever your programming background, I recommend that you start by reading Chapters 1 and 2. If you already know a modern structured language such as C, C++, Ada, or Pascal, dive right into Chapter 3. Much of the syntax of Java was deliberately modeled on C and C++, but if you're familiar with any programming language, you'll be able to read the simple application and applet shown in that chapter.

For New Programmers

If you're new to programming, read Chapters 1 and 2, and then go directly to Appendix A. After you've read Appendix A, go to Chapter 3 and follow the instructions there to download and install the JDK. Use a text editor and type in the simple examples (or download them from the Web site. See the section later in this introduction titled "Conventions Used in This Book" for information on how to find the Web site.) Proceed through the book at your own pace, taking time to learn the material in Chapters 4 through 11. I recommend that you skip the advanced material in Chapters 12, 13, and 14 the first time through, and go directly to Chapters 15 and 16.

Once you've read this material you're on your way to being a competent Java programmer. Continue to develop programs on your own, drawing from the material in Chapters 12 through 14 or 17 through 24 only as you need it and feel you are ready.

For Experienced C/C++ Programmers

As a programmer, you don't need to read Chapters 4, 5, or 6 (which cover the Java language) in depth. Skim them to get familiar with Java syntax, then refer back to them as needed in order to understand the other Java programs shown in this book.

If you're already familiar with the object-oriented methods, you can just skim Chapters 7 and 8 on object-oriented analysis and design. You should read Chapters 9 and 10 in depth, however—these aspects of Java are quite different from their counterparts in other languages.

C++ programmers will also benefit from Appendix B.

You'll want to read Chapter 11 to learn how to build a graphical user interface to your program. If you want to use the advanced features of the Swing components, read Chapters 12, 13, and 14 as well.

You'll need the information in Chapter 15 to build large programs, or programs that you'll distribute beyond your own machine. Packages serve to organize the folders in your development directory and separate Java classes in the same way the namespace directive does in C++.

If you're working strictly with the JDK (as opposed to using an IDE), you should read Chapter 16. If you're planning to use the debugger in an IDE, you should still read at least the first section of Chapter 16, entitled "Writing Self-Testing Classes."

Once you've finished Chapter 16, you're on your own. Select from the remaining chapters (17 through 24) as necessary to get the information you need to write your program. I particularly recommend Chapter 24. Here you'll learn how to measure your code's complexity and estimate the amount of work required to develop a new program. These two topics, perhaps more than any other, distinguish professional software engineers from amateur programmers.

For Programmers of Other Languages

If your programming experience is not in the structured languages such as C or C++, you'll want to read Chapters 4, 5, and 6 in detail. These chapters introduce the fundamentals of the Java language. Then read Chapters 7 and 8 to learn about the object-oriented techniques. Finally, proceed the same way a C or C++ programmer would (as described earlier in this section.)

Conventions Used in This Book

Commands, directions and explanations in this book are presented in the clearest format possible. The following items are some of the features that will make this book easier for you to use:

- Information that you are to enter is set in `monospace font`. For example, you can learn more about Java at `http://java.sun.com/`. If you need to fill in some information yourself, that information is set in monospace italics:
  `print theNameOfTheFile`

- Code snippets are set in fixed-point type. For example, you can write to the screen in Java by using the `System.out.println()` method, as shown here:
  ```
  System.out.println("The current message is " +
  ➥theMessage);
  ```

  Complete programs are given in numbered listings and appear on the companion Web site. To get to the site, go to the following URL in your browser: `http://www.quecorp.com/info`. Enter the ISBN (0-7897-1627-5) in the space provided under the heading Book Information and click the search button.

- Cross references. If there's a related topic that is prerequisite to the section or steps you are reading, or a topic that builds further on what you are reading, you'll find the cross reference to it after the steps or at the end of the section like this:

SEE ALSO

➢ *Learn more about interfaces, page 230*

- Glossary terms. For all the terms that appear in the glossary, you'll find the first appearance of that term in the text in italics along with its definition.

- Sidebars. Information related to the task at hand, or "inside" information from the author is offset in sidebars as not to interfere with the task at hand and to make it easy to find this valuable information. Each of these sidebars has a short title to help you quickly identify the information you'll find there. You'll find the same kind of information in these sidebars that you might find in notes, tips, or warnings in other books, but here the titles are more informative.

You can use Java to write both applets and applications. In general, I'll use the word "program" to describe a complete solution written in Java (whether it's implemented as an applet or an application). We'll reserve the word "application" for programs that run without help from a supporting program (such as a Web browser).

Bulleted lists are used when the order of the items is not important. The items represent related concepts that are explained in the list.

Numbered lists are used when the numbering, or sequence, is important. Steps in a procedure appear in numbered lists. Follow the steps from beginning to end. Make sure you understand each step—don't just skip one because you do not understand it.

The chapters also contain figures, which are often screen shots, showing you what to expect on your computer, and code listings, which contain complete programs to illustrate a technique. Your screen may look slightly different from some of the examples in this book. This is due to differences between various Web browsers, HTML editors, and hardware configurations.

Code fragments are contained in the text and are set in `monospace` font. These fragments illustrate a technique, but they are not a complete program by themselves. For code lines that exceed the margin, a code continuation character ➥ is inserted to show where the line breaks.

In many of the chapters of this book you'll see a common set of examples, drawn from a medical application. These examples are based on an actual set of Java programs and are used here to illustrate good design and programming. All of the listings in this book are available on the book's Web site.

This is a big book, and Java is a big topic. Even in a book this size, we can only cover the most popular features. As you become an accomplished Java programmer, consider reading

Special Edition Using Java 1.2, the next step in Que's family of Java books. After that book (or perhaps at the same time) read *Java 1.2 Unleashed*, a comprehensive description of the features in this new version of the JDK.

A Word About JDK 1.2

Using Java 1.2 was published shortly before the final release of JDK 1.2, so there might be some last-minute adjustments to the JDK that you need to be aware of.

As you read through this book, be sure to visit Que's Java Resource Center from time to time to check for any late-breaking information to help you stay on top of any last minute JDK changes.

You can find Que's Java Resource Center by going to the main Resource Center page at:

`http://www.mcp.com/resources`

From there, choose the link titled Programming. From the Programming Resource Center page, follow the Java Resource Center link.

Getting Started

What Is Java, and Why Is It Important?

Learn how to write applications in Java

Find out how to scale up your applications so they'll run on a Web page

See why end users are safer when downloading Java applets than with any other form of downloadable software

Find out how the newest version of Java differs from its predecessors

What Is Java?

When you write in most programming languages, you need to decide which processor and operating system your finished program is intended to run on. Then you include specific function calls to a library associated with the operating system of that target platform. For example, if you're writing for a Windows environment, you might make reference to the Microsoft Foundation Classes. If your target machine is a Macintosh, you'll call functions in the Mac OS Toolbox. Figure 1.1 illustrates this process.

FIGURE 1.1

In most programming languages you make calls directly to the native operating system.

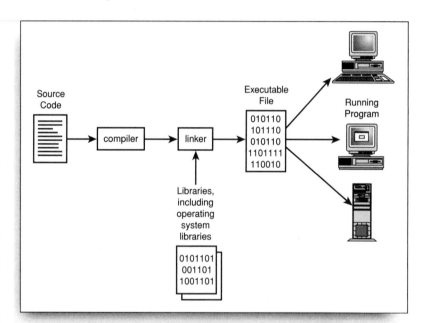

When you're ready to test your program, you send your source code through a *compiler* that transforms your code into a set of native instructions for whatever processor your target machine uses. For example, Windows is usually run on an Intel processor such as a Pentium, while Macintoshes use the Motorola 680×0 or PowerPC processors.

When you write Java, you don't need to think about calls to Windows, the Mac OS, or other operating system libraries. Java contains its own libraries—called *packages*—that are platform-independent.

Similarly, you aren't concerned with whether the finished product will run on an Intel Pentium, an IBM PowerPC, or a Sun SPARC processor. The Java compiler doesn't generate native instructions. Instead, it writes *bytecodes* for a machine that doesn't really exist—the *Java Virtual Machine*, or JVM.

Since the JVM doesn't really exist in the physical sense, how does the Java code run? Sun (and others) have implemented a software version of the JVM for most common platforms. When you load the file of bytecodes (called a *class file*) onto the target machine, it runs on the JVM on that machine. The JVM reads the class file and does the work specified by the original Java. Figure 1.2 illustrates how the Java compiler, the class file, and the JVM interact.

Understanding bytecodes

The Java compiler generates files of bytecodes–instructions for the Java Virtual Machine. Since the JVM has been ported to nearly every kind of computer, these files of bytecodes will serve as cross-platform applications.

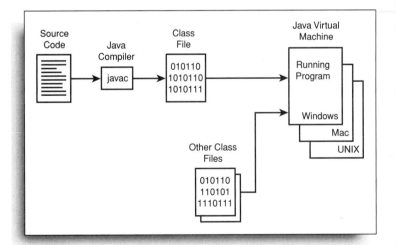

FIGURE 1.2

The output of the Java compiler is interpreted by the JVM on each specific platform.

Since the JVM is easy to port from one machine to another, you can expect that any new processor or operating system will soon have an implementation of the JVM. Once you've written Java code that runs on one machine, you can run it on any common platform.

What's the Java Runtime Environment?

The JVM is part of a larger collection of software on the end user's machine that's called the *Java Runtime Environment*, or JRE. Browser vendors, such as Microsoft and Netscape, include a JRE in their Web browsers. If you want end users to be able to run Java applications, you need to make sure they have a JRE. You get a JRE in your Java Development Kit; end users can download the JRE separately.

Running applications on a Macintosh

The Mac OS doesn't have a command prompt. To run an application on the Macintosh, drag the icon of the class file onto the icon of the Java interpreter.

Hiding the Java interpreter from the end user

If you want to deliver an application to an end user, don't ask them to go to the command prompt. Write a batch file that launches the Java interpreter and starts the application. Have the end user double-click the batch file, just as they would any other application.

Understanding Applications

If all you could do with Java was write portable applications, it would still be an important development. In 1993, however, Sun noticed that the Internet was gaining in popularity, and began to position Java to run inside *Web browsers*. Standalone Java programs are known as *applications*, while programs that run with the help of another program (typically a Web browser) are known as *applets*. I'll talk about applications in this section; we'll get to applets later in this chapter.

In most languages the "finished product" is an executable file of native binary instructions. In the DOS and Windows environments we can recognize these files because they have the suffix `.exe`. In a graphical user environment such as Mac OS or Windows, we can double-click the application's icon to run the program.

Java is a little different. Because the class files contain bytecodes for the JVM, we have to launch an implementation of the JVM in order to run the application. The Java Development Kit (JDK) includes a Java interpreter called `java` that implements the JVM. To run an application named `myApp` from the JVM you go to the command prompt and type

```
java myApp
```

SEE ALSO
➤ *For more information about downloading the JDK, page 68*

Who Needs Applets?

Modern Web browsers, such as Netscape Navigator and Microsoft Internet Explorer, are highly capable programs with a rich set of features. Why would anyone need to extend the browser through applets?

Many Web designers want to go beyond simple displays of static contents. They want dynamic or "live" pages that are able to interact with the user. Often the best way to add dynamic content is to write a program, yet the Hypertext Markup Language (HTML) that is used to write Web pages has no programming ability at all.

Both the Netscape and Microsoft browsers support scripting languages such as JavaScript. Those languages allow you to attach functions to HTML elements, such as buttons, but you don't have complete control over the appearance of the user interface. You also cannot use these scripting languages to connect the client machine back to the network, so you cannot write true client-server programs. Sometimes you need a solution that is more powerful than these scripting languages, or you need a solution that does not depend upon a particular browser. For those times, a Java applet is ideal.

You place a Java applet on your Web page by using the HTML <APPLET> tag. Since Java runs on any popular platform, the applet will appear and will work as expected as long as the visitor to the site is using one of the Java-capable browsers.

What Makes Java Different from Other Languages?

Java is a concurrent, object-oriented programming language with client/server capabilities. In this section we'll take that claim apart and examine each of Java's major distinctive qualities.

Java Is a Programming Language

In the late 1990s the world of software is similar in many ways to the way things were in the late 1970s. In those days PCs had just come out, and the available software lagged far behind the demand. However, nearly every model of PC shipped with a BASIC interpreter. Thousands of people who did not consider themselves professional programmers—teachers, life insurance agents, bankers—learned BASIC and began to write programs. Often they would share their programs by floppy disk or, later, by electronic bulletin boards, and the shareware industry was born.

Like SmallTalk, C, and C++ (and unlike BASIC), Java is designed for use by professional programmers. Today the Hypertext Markup Language (HTML) and the scripting languages such as Netscape's JavaScript occupy the niche formerly held by BASIC. Many people who do not consider themselves to be professional programmers cannot write Java applets, but they can use applets written by others to add life to their Web pages. Often they use Netscape LiveConnect, an integration technology based on JavaScript, to stitch Web pages, Java applets, and browser plug-ins together.

But this book is about Java. Unlike JavaScript, Java was designed for the experienced programmer. If you're a professional programmer, you should have little trouble learning Java. If you don't have prior experience with object-oriented techniques, you'll want to brush up on object-oriented concepts. Chapter 7, "Object-Oriented Analysis: A New Way of Looking at Software," and Chapter 8, "Object-Oriented Design and Programming," will help you come up to speed on the latest techniques.

If you're not a programmer, but you're prepared to work hard, you can use Java to learn how to program. You'll want to refer to some of the basic programming concepts described in Appendix A, "Introduction to Programming."

Java Is Object-Oriented

In general, software engineers engage in five activities during the development of software:

- *Analysis.* The process of identifying user requirements
- *Design.* The process of developing a solution to the user's needs and requirements
- *Implementation.* Coding the design in a computer language such as Java
- *Test.* Ensuring that the finished software satisfies the requirements
- *Maintenance.* Fixing latent defects, adding new features, and keeping the software up to date with its environment (such as operating systems and database managers)

During object-oriented analysis you are encouraged to view the application domain as a set of related classes. For example, in a transportation application there might be a class called Truck. When the application runs, it typically makes *instances* of these classes. You might build a fleet of trucks based on class Truck. Object-oriented analysis is described in detail in Chapter 7.

Learn JavaScript and LiveConnect

Once you've learned Java, you may also want to learn how non-programmers can use your applets in their Web pages. Read *Special Edition Using JavaScript,* 2nd Edition (Que, 1997) to learn this powerful scripting language. Then read *Special Edition Using Netscape LiveConnect* (Que, 1997) to see how to integrate JavaScript with Java applets.

During initial object-oriented design you identify all of the classes, typically arranging them in a hierarchy. Figure 1.3 illustrates where the class Truck might fall in a transportation hierarchy. You also identify methods and data that should be associated with each instance. Figure 1.4 illustrates one way of recording this information during the design activity. Chapter 8 examines the details of object-oriented design.

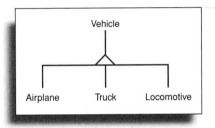

FIGURE 1.3

As designer, you will identify a hierarchy of classes in your application.

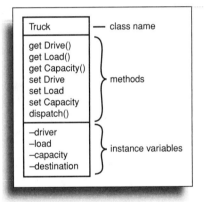

FIGURE 1.4

For each class, identify the data that each instance should store, and the methods for each class.

Once you've identified and described each class, you need to design the code for each method. Some designers prefer to write simple diagrams to show how each method should be written. Others prefer to write *pseudocode*, a loose method of coding that is intended to be read by humans rather than by the compiler. Chapter 6, "Methods: Adding Code to Your Objects," describes how to design methods for your objects.

Object-oriented languages were introduced as early as 1967. During 1983, Bjarne Stroustrup of AT&T Bell Laboratories introduced a version of the popular C programming language that supported classes. This "C with classes" went on to become

C++, the most popular object-oriented language ever—possibly the most popular computer programming language ever.

The people at Sun Microsystems who designed Java were C++ programmers. They understood the features of C++ that have made it a good language. They also understood its limitations. In designing Java, they copied C++ syntax and reused the best pieces of C++'s design, including the fact that it makes it easy to code object-oriented designs.

Java Supports the Client/Server Model

One of the design goals of C (and later, C++) was to keep platform-specific capabilities out of the core language. Thus, in C and C++ there is nothing in the language itself that allows you to output any information. Instead, you call a library routine—`printf()`.

Java has adopted this aspect of C++'s design, and has extended the standard libraries to include network communications. In Java, for example, you can open a connection to a Web page or other Internet application and read or write data, in much the same way as a C or C++ programmer reads or writes to the local terminal. This design decision makes it easy to write Internet-aware applications in Java. In fact, HotJava, the Java-aware Web browser written by Sun, is written entirely in Java.

Java Supports Concurrency

In the real world different objects do their work simultaneously. In a computer—at least, in a computer with a single processor—only one set of instructions can be executing at a time. To help programmers build applications that more accurately reflect the way the real world works, operating system developers introduced *multitasking*. In a multitasking operating system, two or more applications can share a single processor, with each having the illusion that it has the processor to itself.

Each such application (often called a *process*) has its own protected part of memory where it stores its data. In most operating systems, one process cannot accidentally interfere with another process. In fact, these operating systems include special function calls (called *Inter-Process Communication* or IPC) that allow one process to send or receive data from another.

At the operating-system level, there's a significant amount of work required to start a process, or to switch from one process to another. Programmers asked for, and got, a "lightweight process" called a *thread*. In general, threads don't offer the bullet-proof protection of processes, but they can be started and used more quickly.

The biggest problem with processes and threads is that these facilities are offered by the operating system. If you write a program to run in a Windows NT environment, you'll have to modify the parts that start and control processes and threads if you port the code to, say, UNIX. In some operating systems, such as older versions of Microsoft Windows, there may be no facilities for multitasking at all.

Sun's solution was to make threads a part of the language itself. Thus, if you write a multithreaded Java application, that application will run on any supported platform, including Windows, UNIX, and Mac OS. Further, since Java's object-oriented model restricts the way one application can communicate with another, Java threads have some of the same safeguards as processes, with little of the overhead.

SEE ALSO

➤ *Learn more about Java threads, page 454*

For example, suppose you wanted to explore what happens in a particular Web application when many users access the same page at the same time. In a multitasking operating system such as UNIX, you might write an application that makes several copies of itself. (In UNIX, such a process is called *forking*. In Windows NT, it's called *spawning*.) In older operating systems, such as Windows 3.1, you might decide to enlist the help of several friends, and have everybody press the ENTER key at once. In Java, you can write an application that reads the number of simultaneous connections from the command line, opens the specified number of threads, reads the same Web page in each thread, and reports out any errors—in just 22 lines of code.

Java Has a Strong Security Model

If you're going to design a language that makes it easy for programmers to send their work to end users, you have deal with an unpleasant reality: not all programmers are as nice as you and I. In fact, there are a few twisted people who write programs that are positively malicious.

Trojan horse programs pretend to be useful applications, but when they run they carry out some hidden (and generally malicious) operation. *Viruses* attach themselves to other programs. As part of their function, they copy themselves to still other programs. As these programs are spread around the network, more and more machines are affected. At some point the virus delivers its payload, which may be anything from a mischievous message on the screen to actually deleting data.

There are two lines of defense in preventing programs such as Trojan horses and viruses from being spread. First, you can allow the developer to "sign" the program with a signature that cannot be forged. If the signature is valid, the program does not have any viruses or other code that was added after the programmer finished the program. Second, you can design the language in such a way that certain operations, such as reading or writing the local hard drive, are prohibited. While these operations may be useful to some programs, they are also exploited by malicious programmers.

The only serious competitor to Java applets is Microsoft's ActiveX control. Both Java and ActiveX give the programmer a way to digitally sign the program, so the end user can be confident that the code he or she is downloading is actually the program the programmer wrote. Java differs from ActiveX, however, in that Java prevents the programmer from doing things on the client's machine that might be used by a virus or Trojan horse.

SEE ALSO

➤ *Learn how to digitally sign your applets, page 644*

If you have a signed program that can do anything it likes to the end user's machine, you have a serious vulnerability. Not every malicious operation is immediately obvious. If a malicious program starts deleting files off your hard drive, you'll probably notice. But will you notice if it goes through your Web browser's disk cache looking up confidential information from your intranet?

Even if you detect a malicious program at work, you may not be able to identify which program is doing the work. In fact, there's no guarantee that the problem-causing program came to you over the Internet. Some security experts have reported that more viruses are loaded from CD-ROMs than from the Internet.

So the best that an electronic signature can guarantee is that, if you detect something going wrong, and if you can determine that the problem was caused by something you downloaded, and if you can determine which downloaded program caused the problem, you now have someone to blame.

I, however, would prefer that the problem never occur in the first place. That's the Java approach—deny the malicious programmer any opportunity to write a virus or a Trojan horse in the first place.

To ensure security, Java designers implemented a mechanism called the *sandbox*. The sandbox ensures that untrusted (and possibly malicious) Java applets are only allowed access to a limited set of capabilities on the end user's machine.

This section describes the three major mechanisms that implement a sandbox:

- JVM-level checks
- Language-level safeguards
- The *JavaSecurity* interface

JVM-level Checks

Suppose you've written a Java applet and have compiled it into a class file. You use this applet on your Web page; when an end user who uses a Java-aware browser downloads this page, they also download the applet. In order to ensure that the applet cannot access system-level resources, such as the hard drive, the Java Virtual Machine (JVM) that is built into the browser performs several checks.

Use Java's security features

As an applet developer, you should become familiar with the security capabilities offered by Java. Visit the Security Frequently Asked Questions page (`http://java.sun.com/sfaq/`) to get the latest reports on Java security. Visit `http://java.sun.com/security/` for an overview of Java security.

Applets have more security restrictions than applications

The comments here about security are directed at applets, not applications. An end user can run an applet simply by downloading a Web page, so applets need tight security. End users must install applications explicitly, so applications are allowed to exercise capabilities that are denied to applets.

First, the JVM includes a *class loader*, which is responsible for finding and downloading all of the classes used by the applet. Second, before the class file is allowed to execute, the contents of the class file are tested by the *byte-code verifier*. Third, the class runs under the supervision of the JVM *Security Manager*. Figure 1.5 illustrates how these three components work together.

FIGURE 1.5

Before applet code is executed, it must pass security checks by the class loader, the byte-code verifier, and the Security Manager.

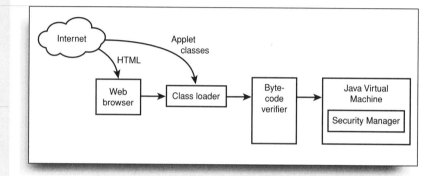

These three mechanisms work together to ensure that

- Only the proper classes are loaded
- Each class is in the proper format
- Untrusted classes are not allowed to execute dangerous instructions
- Untrusted classes are not allowed to access system resources

When a Java-aware browser sees the <APPLET> tag, it invokes the class loader and asks the class loader to load the specified applet. The class loader defines a *namespace* associated with that particular Web page. Classes loaded as part of this applet are not allowed to access other classes (though they can access classes that form part of the standard Java libraries). Figure 1.6 illustrates the class loader's namespaces.

The security provided by a class loader is only as good as the class loader itself. If the class loader was built by Sun, or is based on Sun's template, it should provide the safeguards described here. For example, Sun's model class loader contains checks to make sure the applet does not install its own class loader, or call methods that are solely used by the class loader. If the browser vendor has not followed Sun's guidelines, the class loader may have security holes.

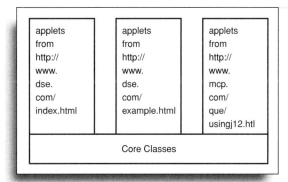

Once a class is loaded (by the class-loader) it is inspected by the byte-code verifier. The byte-code verifier includes a sophisticated theorem prover that ensures that the applet does not forge pointers, circumvent access restrictions, or convert objects illegally. Just as the class loader's namespace mechanism ensures that one applet cannot interfere with another, the byte-code verifier ensures that an applet cannot wreak havoc within its own namespace. The byte-code verifier also checks for stack overflow or underflow—a traditional way malicious programmers have breached system security.

The final set of checks at the JVM level is made by the JVM's Security Manager. The Security Manager watches out for "dangerous" operations—those that could be exploited by a malicious programmer. The Security Manager must agree any time the applet attempts to access any of the following:

- Network communications
- Protected information (including the hard drive or personal data)
- Operating-system level programs and processes
- The class loader
- Libraries of Java classes (known as packages)

Warning: Know thy class loader

Any application designer can write his or her own class loader. End users should not trust a class loader unless they trust the application developer.

The Security Manager is also responsible for preserving thread integrity. That is, code in one group of threads cannot interfere with code in another group of threads, even if the two groups have the same parent applet. (We'll talk more about threads in Chapter 17, "Concurrent Programming with Threads.")

Language-Level Safeguards

Many languages, such as SmallTalk, allow the programmer to easily convert objects of one sort to objects of another. This *loose typing* allows programmers to get code up and running quickly, but also opens opportunities for the malicious programmer (not to mention leaving opportunities for software defects).

Strongly typed languages, such as Ada, are somewhat more difficult to use, but they generally result in programs with fewer defects and tighter compiled code. For this reason, loosely typed languages are popular for prototyping, and strongly typed languages are often used for production code.

C and C++ offer a combination of typing methods. The language presents itself as being strongly typed—the compiler needs to be able to determine the type of each object—but the programmer can override a type and coerce an object of one type into a different type. This override mechanism is called *casting*. To cast an object of type Book to be of type Volume, you could write write

```
Volume myVolume = (Volume) aBook;
```

In general, much of C and C++'s strength comes from the capabilities of those languages to use *pointers*—variables that hold memory addresses of other data. While you'll sometimes see descriptions of Java that claim the language has no pointers, the fact is that everything in Java is a pointer—they're just not accessible by the user. The reason pointers are "invisible" is that the Java designers removed the ability to point a pointer to an arbitrary location. This capability, often used by C and C++ programmers, is called pointer arithmetic—the ability to modify a pointer so that it points to a new location. Pointer arithmetic allows a malicious C or C++ programmer to access anything within the program's range of allowable addresses (called the *address space*). In some operating systems and on some processors, each program has access to the entire machine's address space. On those systems, a malicious programmer can use pointer arithmetic to wreak havoc in other programs.

Another technique commonly used by malicious programmers is to deliberately overflow an array. Suppose a programmer defines an array of characters named myString to have 128 bytes. The locations myString[0] through myString[127] are reserved for use by our program. By accessing myString[128] and beyond, the program is reading and writing outside its assigned bounds. You can get away with that in C or C++, but array accesses are checked at run-time in Java. The program will not be allowed to access myString[] outside the range 0 to 127. Not only does this bounds-checking close a security hole, it also prevents one common source of program defects.

Strings are also immutable—once you've made a character string, no one can change it (though you can extract substrings and put them together to make new strings). By requiring that strings be immutable Java's designers closed another security hole and prevented still more common programming errors.

How Java Provides Security over the Internet

Because of the protection of the JVM and the language itself, most users can run most applets and be confident that the applet will "play in its own sandbox" without interfering with system resources on the end user's machine. Sometimes, however, you need to write an applet that accesses those system resources, and the end user is willing to trust you that you won't damage their system or steal confidential information.

The problem is, an end user downloading your applets over the Internet could be duped into running malicious applets written by someone else. Figure 1.7 illustrates the problem, known as the "man in the middle" attack.

In this example, Bob has connected to Alice's server. His browser downloaded a Web page that included an applet. In reality, Charlie has programmed his server to intercept the applet on its way to Bob, and substitute Charlie's version of the applet. While

Won't I miss pointer arithmetic?

If you're an experienced C or C++ programmer, you may ask, "Won't I miss pointer arithmetic?" Most pointer arithmetic is used to get efficient access to character strings or other arrays. Java supports strings and arrays as explicit classes, with efficient methods to get at their contents. If you use these built-in methods, chances are you'll never miss pointer arithmetic.

Bob thinks he's trusting Alice's applet, in reality he has opened his system to a malicious applet written by Charlie.

FIGURE 1.7

Bob thinks he's trusting the applet written by Alice, but in reality he's running an applet written by Charlie.

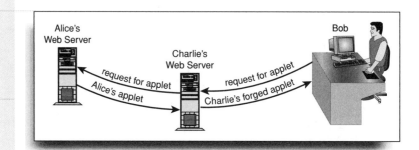

Web spoofing

For a technical description of how a man-in-the-middle attack applies to the Web, read the paper on *web spoofing* developed by the Secure Internet Programming team at Princeton University. It's available online at `http://www.cs.princeton.edu/sip/pub/spoofing.html`.

The solution to this problem is offered by an applet-level security mechanism called the JavaSecurity API. (An API is an *Application Programming Interface*—a way for a library developer to give the programmer access to some set of features.)

One of the capabilities offered in the JavaSecurity API is *digital signing*. To use this capability, bundle your Java class files and any related files that your applet needs into a *Java Archive* (JAR). You then electronically "sign" the JAR file. When the end user retrieves the JAR from your server, he or she can verify your signature. If a "man in the middle" attempts to substitute a different applet, the signature will not verify and the end user is warned about the forgery.

SEE ALSO

➤ *Learn how more about Java Archives, page 644*

Learn about the Java Archive format

Visit `http://java.sun.com/products/jdk/1.1/docs/guide/jar/jarGuide.html` to learn more about the Java Archive format. Here you'll learn how to reference a JAR in the `<APPLET>` tag instead of a class file.

Applets Versus ActiveX Controls

The only serious competitor to Java applets is offered by Microsoft, and is called ActiveX controls. ActiveX controls are an Internet version of an older standard, called OCX controls. These controls can be written in any language, and can do anything that anyone can do in that language. There's no technical reason an ActiveX programmer could not write a Trojan horse that deletes every file on your hard drive, or copies confidential information back to the Internet. Microsoft has tried to address this problem by encouraging ActiveX developers to use their code-signing facility, making ActiveX controls secure from "man in the middle" attacks.

Microsoft's approach means that every ActiveX control functions like a trusted Java applet. Since most end users will not want to download unsigned ActiveX controls, there is no equivalent to the untrusted applet, in which security is ensured by the Java sandbox.

If an end user chooses to trust all ActiveX controls, sooner or later the end user's machine may fall victim to an attack. With most attacks, it may be difficult to determine which ActiveX control was responsible. For example, an ActiveX control could replace a system file such as move.exe, and then alter itself so the malicious part of the ActiveX control was deleted. The next time the end user attempts to move a file, the Trojan horse version of move.exe runs, accomplishing the malicious programmer's objective. Even if the end user detects the problem, it will be difficult to trace the problem back to the specific ActiveX control.

Sun recommends that browser vendors limit applets by enforcing three rules. These rules are enforced by the Sun code licensed by major browser vendors such as Netscape Communications and Microsoft:

- Untrusted applets cannot access the local hard drive.

- All standalone windows put up by untrusted applets are labeled as such. Figure 1.8 shows such a window.

- Untrusted applets can only establish a network connection back to the server from which they were loaded.

The first rule closes most security holes. If an applet cannot read the local hard drive, it cannot access most confidential information. If it cannot write the hard drive, it cannot plant viruses or Trojan horses.

The second rule makes it less likely that the user will inadvertently enter confidential information (such as a credit card number) into an untrusted applet.

The third rule prevents someone from accessing non-local hard drives, such as those on a local area network or intranet. Like

In fairness to Microsoft

Microsoft's side of the applet vs ActiveX argument is that Java represents a "lowest common denominator." Microsoft casts the argument not as "Java versus ActiveX" but as "PCs versus Sun." They also point to http://www.webfayre.com/pendragon/jpr/index.html, which benchmarks Java performance on a number of different machines. (Windows NT and Windows 95 running on high-speed Pentiums outperform all other platforms.)

the first rule, this provision closes many opportunities the malicious programmer might have for stealing confidential information or for planting malicious programs.

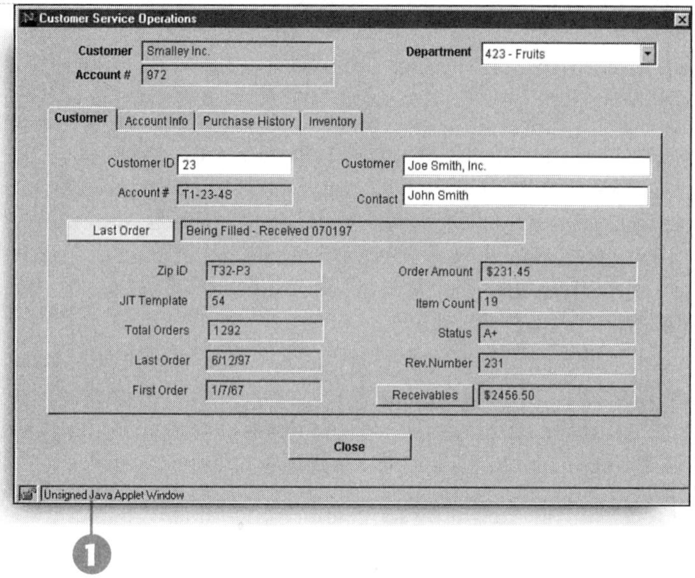

FIGURE 1.8

The browser warns the user if a window was opened by an untrusted applet.

1 Warning supplied by browser.

1

Is your browser secure?

Use the Sun examples at `http://java.sun.com/sfaq/#examples` to test your browser's behavior.

Use CERT to keep track of security issues

If you're responsible for security at your organization, you should get familiar with the services of the Computer Emergency Response Team (CERT) Coordination Center. They'll keep you up to date on known security holes and fixes. Visit their Web site at `http://www.cert.org/`.

Sun provides sample applets to test your browser's security. Your browser should catch security exceptions when you attempt to run these applets from the Internet. You shouldn't get exceptions when you run `http://java.sun.com/sfaq/examples/getOpenProperties.html`, which demonstrates the ten system properties untrusted applets are allowed to read, or `http://java.sun.com/sfaq/examples/myWindow.html`, which opens a standalone window (though you should see the "Untrusted Applet" message).

While no one has suggested that it's impossible to build malicious applets—there's probably someone working on one right now—Sun has certainly gone to great lengths to make it difficult. If someone wants to attack your system, it's far easier for them to attack through a mechanism such as an ActiveX control than through a Java applet. As long as most users are downloading both, malicious programmers will continue to favor ActiveX controls.

What's New in JDK 1.2?

In order to write Java you need an editor, a Java compiler, and a Java Runtime Environment. The easiest way to get a Java compiler and runtime environment is to download Sun's Java Development Kit (JDK). The JDK also includes a variety of tools—it's a "must-have" item for any Java developer. (You'll have to supply your own text editor.)

The first public beta release of JDK 1.2 came out in December 1997. JDK 1.2 succeeds JDK 1.1 as the current standard—it introduces a few changes to the language itself, adds a large number of new APIs, and includes some new tools.

Security Enhancements

As I pointed out earlier in this chapter, in the section entitled "The Java Security Model," tight security is one of Java's distinctives. It's not surprising that JDK 1.2 includes some major improvements in security. These changes include:

Accelerate your development with an IDE

Once you've learned Java, you may want to look at some of the Integrated Development Environments (IDEs) being offered by Microsoft, Symantec, and others. These environments typically allow you to write Java faster, though not all of them give you access to the latest Java features.

- *Policy-based access control.* The ability to grant rights to software based on an external configuration file.

- *Support for X.509v3 certificates.* You can use the latest industry-standard encryption technology to sign the Java Archives in which you distribute your classes.

- *New security tools.* Including tools to manage certificates and write your security policy file.

Policy-Based Access Control

If you've used the UNIX operating system, you're familiar with the concept of permissions. The owner of a file can grant other users (or programs) the right to read, write, or execute a file. Processes take on the rights of the person who started them—though some users will choose to restrict the rights of programs they launch. (For example, Web servers are often started by someone with root authority, but run as the non-privileged user nobody.)

Beginning in version 1.2, Java developers have similar choices with their applications and applets—though the level of control is finer-grained than that offered by many UNIX implementations.

Computer resources include files, directories, hosts, and ports. The person responsible for a computer that will be running Java can set up a *security policy* that specifies who is allowed to access each resource. Access includes read and write permission (for files and directories) and connect permission (for hosts and ports). The security policy is specified in an external security configuration file.

When a Java class is loaded, the JVM examines the security policy currently in effect. If the code is signed, permissions can be granted on the basis of the identity of the signer. Permissions can also be granted based on the location of the class file. (For example, a file loaded from the local host might be given more access than one loaded from the Internet.)

Certificate Interfaces and X.509v3 Implementation

Not so long ago, the only way for a server to identify a client was to ask the user for a username and password. If the username and password matched those stored in the password file, the server granted the user access.

There are several problems with password-based authentication. First, the password often has to travel over a non-secure network. If an adversary is able to "sniff" the username and password from the net, he or she will be able to masquerade as a valid user.

Another problem is that most users access more than one system, and have more than one username and password. Users find it difficult to keep these names and passwords straight, so they either write the names and passwords down or just use the same name and password on every system. Either solution is subject to abuse.

A better solution is for the user to generate a special kind of cryptographic key, called a public/private key pair. These keys work together—if you encrypt something with my public key, only a person with my private key can decrypt it. If I keep my private key secret, you can be sure I am the only one who can read your message.

In an ideal world, we could all post our public keys on servers somewhere, and begin to communicate securely with each other. That practice is subject to abuse, too—an opponent could put a public key on the server with my name on it. If my opponent can trick you into using the bogus key, he or she will be able to read messages intended for me. (This strategy is a variation of the "man in the middle" attack described earlier in this chapter, in the section entitled "The Java Security Model.")

The solution is simple—I generate my public/private key pair, making sure I keep my private key secret. I send my public key to a "public key certifying authority" who requires that I prove my identity. Once I've satisfied the certifying authority that I am who I say I am, they sign my key with their private key. Now anyone who wants to be sure that a public key with my name on it really belongs to me can check the signature of the certifying authority. If you find that the signature is valid, and you're satisfied with their policy for checking my identity, then you can trust my public key.

The combination of a public key, identifying information, and a certification authority's signature is called a *certificate*. The current generation of the standard for certificates is *X.509v3*.

Version 1.2 of the JDK includes new APIs for parsing certificates and maintaining local databases of X.509v3 certificates.

New Security Tools

Version 1.2 of the JDK also includes tools to help you manage X.509v3 certificates. Within your company, for example, you may decide to issue certificates to any employee. The Java *keytool*, new in version 1.2, allows each user to generate a public/private keypair. The user can also use keytool to generate his or her own certificate (though the certificate is to a slightly older standard—X.509v1).

Get your own certificate server

If you plan to issue your own certificates, you'll need a Certificate Server. Visit the Netscape site (`http://home.netscape.com/comprod/server_central/product/certificate/index.html`) and learn about Netscape's Certificate Server, part of the SuiteSpot family of servers.

javakey is now obsolete

If you've been using `javakey` from JDK 1.1 or earlier, replace it with `keytool` and `jarsigner`. The older tool, `javakey`, is now obsolete.

You use *jarsigner* in combination with your certificate to digitally sign Java Archives (JARs).

You can write an external security configuration file that specifies your machine's security policy. The easiest way to write such a file is to use Sun's *policytool*, also new in JDK 1.2.

Java Foundation Classes

Like C and C++, most of the features of Java are not in the language itself, but in the libraries (which are called packages in Java). The first releases of Java came with some simple libraries (such as the Abstract Windowing Toolkit) that served to whet developers' appetites. JDK 1.2 comes bundled with a new set of packages—the Java Foundation Classes, or JFC—that includes an improved user interface called the Swing components.

Swing Package

The first versions of the JDK supported a graphical user interface through a package called the *Abstract Windowing Toolkit* (AWT). In newer versions Sun has introduced the *Swing* package, which includes and expands upon the AWT. Swing contains many more components than just those in the AWT, so you can build more sophisticated interfaces. More importantly, Swing implements the Lightweight User Interface Framework, which includes "pluggable look and feel." This new feature means that an end user who prefers the look of Sun's Motif interface can have that look, even though you, the developer, may prefer the basic Java interface. Over time, expect other "look and feel" combinations, such as Mac OS, Windows, and Solaris, to be built for Swing. (We'll introduce Swing in Chapter 12, "Building the User Interface with JFC Swing Components.")

Java 2D

Sun has extended the AWT package to include a set of tools for dealing with two-dimensional drawings and images. These extensions include provision for colorspaces (`java.awt.color`), text (`java.awt.font`), line art (`java.awt.geom`), and printing (`java.awt.print`). There are also about three dozen new objects in the packages `java.awt.*` and `java.awt.image.*`.

Accessibility

Many users who are visually impaired use screen readers to read HTML pages to them. Other people, who have limited vision, need to display text in large fonts in order to read the information comfortably. In the past Sun has been criticized because Java applets displayed only a graphical image, inaccessible to visually impaired users. Sun has addressed these concerns by adding specific provision for accessibility into the JDK. You'll use the new package `java.awt.accessibility` to ensure that your programs will work well with screen readers, screen magnifiers, and speech recognition systems—a group of hardware and software products collectively known as *assistive technology*.

Drag-and-Drop

Sun has committed itself to supporting drag-and-drop data transfer between Java and native applications as well as between Java applications and within a single Java application. JDK 1.2 is a first step in that direction. Currently drag-and-drop between a Java application and a native application requires support from the native operating system. Sun has not added this capability to the Swing package, since they are committed to making Swing 100% Pure Java.

Application Services

The term "application services" covers a range of capabilities that can be used by any member of the JFC. Sun has included seven new services for use by Java Foundation Classes:

- *Keyboard navigation.* Allows you to assign keystroke combinations to events that would typically be selected by mouseclicks (such as selecting a menu item or changing an item on a dialog box.)

- *Multithreaded event queue.* Makes it easier for multiple threads to share a single user interface.

- *Undo.* Allows you to reverse the effects of a previous user choice.

- *Bounded range model.* Allows you to manage controls that have a bounded range, such as scroll bars and progress meters.

Make sure your Java programs are accessible

The Web page at `http://java.sun.com/products/jfc/accessibility/doc/index.html` contains information about the utilities Sun developed to allow Java to work with assistive technology.

- *Custom cursors*. Gives you control over the appearance of the cursor and the location of the hotspot.
- *Debug graphics utility*. Lets you highlight each Swing component (in bright red) as it is being drawn, so that you can visually ensure that the component is being drawn correctly.
- *Repaint batching*. Increases the efficiency of screen repainting.
- *Target manager*. Lets you dynamically change the effect of various events such as mouseclicks.

JavaBeans Enhancements

JavaBeans is a specification that describes Java objects suitable for use in a visual development environment. If you drop a "bean" into a JavaBeans-aware development environment, you can define its behavior by filling in a dialog box or connecting it with lines to other beans. We'll talk about JavaBeans in Chapter 19, "Building Components with JavaBeans."

Interaction with Applet Semantics

In prior versions of the JDK there were some conflicts between applet and JavaBeans semantics. This problem made it difficult to use some beans in an applet. These conflicts are fixed in JDK 1.2.

Better Design-Time Support

JDK 1.2 beans are "smarter" than older beans—they can send more information back and forth to the builder environment, allowing you to give them more sophisticated behavior.

Beans Runtime Containment and Services Protocol

JDK 1.2 beans are better "citizens" than older beans when the program is running. They can get more information from their context, and can participate in an AWT presentation.

Collections

Sun is gradually improving the set of collection classes shipped with the JDK. Version 1.2 includes nine concrete classes, as well as a variety of algorithms and abstract classes.

When discussing collection classes it's useful to know a bit about data structures. Table 1.2 summarizes the key characteristics of three important kinds of collection.

TABLE 1.2 **Fundamental collections**

Name	Ordered?	Duplicates allowed?
Set	No	No
List	Yes	Yes
Map	No	Yes

These collections may be implemented in any of several data structures. A *hashtable* is a highly efficient structure that can look up most items in just one step. Large hashtables may require a significant amount of memory.

An *array* is an efficient structure, though it may be difficult to add or delete entries if you're also trying to preserve order.

A *tree* structure maintains order naturally. One of the most common kinds of tree—a balanced binary tree—is particularly efficient when you need fast lookup.

The nine concrete classes are:

- HashSet   A set backed by a hash table
- ArraySet   A set backed by a resizeable array
- ArrayList   A list implemented in a resizeable array
- LinkedList   A useful starting point if you want to build a deque or queue class
- Vector   A variant of the ArrayList
- HashMap   A map implemented in a hash table
- ArrayMap   A map backed by a resizeable array
- TreeMap   A map implemented by a balanced binary tree
- Hashtable   A variant of HashMap

Version Identification

As Java matures you'll find that your classes will need to know which version of the Java Runtime Environment, the Virtual Machine, and other classes are available. With JDK 1.2, you can get the version number of a package specification by writing:

```
String theVersion =
myObject.getPackage().getSpecificationVersion();
```

RMI Enhancements

As Java moves out onto the Internet and organizational intranets there will be many occasions for an application on one host to invoke a method of an object on a different host. Java permits this remote call through a mechanism called *Remote Method Invocation*, or RMI.

In JDK 1.2 Sun has added support for persistent references to remote objects. This support is called Remote Object Activation.

Many programmers have expressed an interest in communicating over the net by using the *Secure Sockets Layer* (SSL). In JDK 1.2, that's now possible by using custom socket types.

Serialization Enhancements

Often you'll need to "snapshot" the objects in your application and save them to the hard drive. For example, the user might choose **Save** in your application, and will expect to reopen your application in the same state as he or she left it.

The basis for writing objects to the hard drive is called *serialization*. JDK 1.2 includes a Persistent Fields API that allows you to specify the persistent fields of your classes independently of the rest of the class. The existing serialization mechanisms can then be used to write out the persistent fields or read them back in when you need to restore an object.

Reference Objects

JDK 1.2 allows you to build a special Reference object (defined in `java.lang.ref`) that contains information about a Java reference. One type of reference object is the "weak reference." With a weak reference you can keep track of information in memory, while granting the garbage collector permission to reclaim the referenced object. You might use this mechanism to implement a simple cache that releases objects when memory is low.

Audio Enhancements

The earliest releases of Java did not include much provision for sound—a serious shortcoming for a language so well-suited for multimedia. Sun quickly closed this gap. The latest version of the JDK offers the best sound support yet.

Java Sound

JDK 1.2 contains a new, higher-quality sound engine that plays MIDI files as well as traditional sounds (such as .au, .wav, and .aiff formats). The new sound engine is backward-compatible with the sound engine in JDK 1.1—no programming changes are required.

getNewAudioClip Method

Prior to JDK 1.2, one played audio clips through an applet context. This design presented a problem for application programmers who wanted to play audio clips, but were not running an applet.

The new `getNewAudioClip` method is an `Applet` class static method—associated with the class, rather than any particular instance of the class. This method allows application programmers as well as applet programmers to make a new audio clip based on an URL.

Performance Enhancements

When the subject of Java comes up, someone always points out that native code runs about 20 times faster than Java. While that figure may have been true at one time, Sun has been working hard to close the gap. The greatest successes come from the use of Just-in-Time (JIT) compilers, but they've also introduced improved performance for multi-threaded programs and even better memory management. This section describes the performance improvements associated with JDK 1.2.

Solaris Native Thread Support

One of the shortcomings of multitasking systems is the time that it takes to fork a process. Operating system vendors such as Sun have made a considerable investment in "lightweight processes" or threads at the operating system level.

In order to be platform-independent, Sun ensured that services offered by the first versions of the JVM were completely independent of the underlying operating system. Thus, threads are included in any version of Java, without regard to whether the underlying operating system supports threads.

When the underlying operating system *does* support threads, however, it makes sense for the JVM to take advantage of that fact. Since the native threads have been highly optimized, native threads will typically run much faster than the threads written in a platform-neutral JVM.

Since Sun Microsystems makes both Java and a family of UNIX workstations (with highly optimized threads) it makes sense that Sun would add native thread support to the version of the JVM that runs on their own Solaris operating system. (Solaris is a variant of UNIX.)

The fact that the JVM is using native threads does not mean that your Java code has to change at all. You still make, control, and destroy threads the same way you do on any platform. If the underlying platform is Solaris, however, your code will now run faster.

Memory Compression for Loaded Classes

Starting in JDK 1.2, constant strings are shared between classes, reducing the memory needs of all classes. Since Java strings are immutable, you don't need to worry about some other class changing your class's string.

You can compile to native code

If your application needs true native speed but you still want to work in Java, consider one of the new compilers that generate native code. Just remember that you'll lose many of the benefits of the JRE when you compile your Java as a native application.

Faster Memory Allocation and Garbage Collection

As programmers have started to take advantage of multithreading, resources that are shared among threads become the constraining factor in performance. In JDK 1.2, Sun has given each thread some independent memory allocation and garbage collection assets. The effect of this change is a marked improvement in performance for multithreaded programs.

Monitor Speedups

Some threads must be marked as synchronized so they don't conflict with other threads for resources. Inside the Java Runtime Environment there's a monitor function that makes sure that only one synchronized thread is running at once. Sun has improved the performance of the monitor, which leads to further speedups for multithreaded code.

SEE ALSO

➤ *Learn more about synchronized threads, page 467*

Native Library JNI Port

Way back when Apple chose the PowerPC as the successor to the Motorola 680X0, they made an amazing discovery. About 80 percent of a typical Macintosh application used just 20 percent of the application's code—and most of that was in Apple's own routines, a section called the Mac Toolbox. By porting the Toolbox to the PowerPC, they were able to improve the performance of older applications that had been written for the Motorola processor.

Sun has been using that same lesson to improve the performance of Java. Most of a application or applet's time is spent deep inside Sun's code, not out at the level that you and I write. Sun has rewritten their core libraries to use the Java Native Interface (JNI). Since your program is now running native code when it runs Sun's libraries, your program gets a performance boost.

JIT Compilers

The name "Just-In-Time" compiler is a bit misleading. To most professional programmers, a compiler is a program that runs on their machine—the binary output is distributed to the end users. The Java compiler is a compiler in this sense of the word. The JIT compilers, however, run on the end user's machine, just ahead of the Java interpreter.

The first time the JIT compiler sees a piece of code, it passes it through to the interpreter, but it also compiles it and saves the native code. If the program loops back through this same section and the JIT compiler sees this code again, it doesn't bother to run the interpreter—it just executes the native code.

Both Microsoft and Netscape have included JIT compilers in their Web browsers, giving end users a 13- to 15-fold performance improvement inside loops. Since most modern programs are loops within loops, the performance gain is substantial.

In JDK 1.2, Sun has included both a Solaris and a Win32 JIT compiler.

Extensions Framework

An *extension* is a group of Java packages (typically stored in a JAR file) that implement an API that extends the Java platform. The Extensions Framework allows your program to download and install extensions onto the Java platform. (Extensions come in a package named javax.)

JDK 1.2 includes one new extension, the Servlet Extension, described later in this section.

Java IDL

Sun already has one mechanism to allow objects on one machine to invoke methods on other machines—it's called Remote Method Invocation (RMI). When you're communicating from one Java class to another, RMI is efficient and easy to use. Sometimes, however, your Java program will need to communicate in a broader environment, which may include programs written in C++, SmallTalk, or COBOL. That's where the new Java IDL comes in.

In order to understand why Sun introduced the *Interface Definition Language* (IDL) for Java, you need to understand something about *Object Request Brokers* (ORBs). This section describes the distributed processing environment that makes ORBs and IDL necessary.

What Is an ORB?

Traditionally business applications were built either as a monolithic application (one-tiered) or as a database with a front-end (two-tiered). Modern business applications are often built with three or more tiers, such as a graphical user interface, a service module, and a database. Figure 1.9 illustrates these three models.

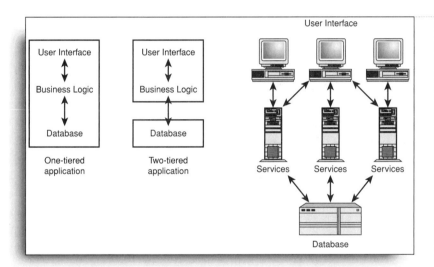

FIGURE 1.9
Multi-tiered applications are often distributed across many physical machines.

Suppose you wanted to build a distributed application. If you knew which host offered which service, you could use Java sockets to connect to other applications. If each client and each server were written in Java, you could even use Runtime Method Invocation.

But in a large, sophisticated distributed application, you might not know where the servers resided. In fact, a really sophisticated application might move servers around, as hosts are taken offline, or fail. The service should continue to be offered by some host on the network, and should be findable by every client application. It's also safe to assume that not every server is written in Java (yet).

An Object Request Broker is the unifying piece of software for a large, sophisticated distributed application. With an ORB, the clients don't have to know where each server is located. They call the ORB, and the ORB connects them to the service. Figure 1.10 illustrates how an ORB interacts with the rest of the network.

FIGURE 1.10

With an ORB on your network, clients can find distributed software anywhere on the net.

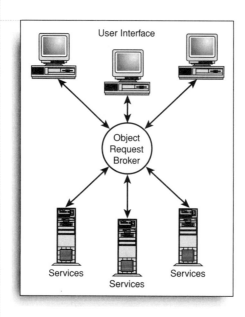

Internet clients and servers communicate with ORBs by using the Internet Inter-ORB Protocol, or IIOP, defined by the Object Management Group.

The software Sun calls the Java IDL is, in fact, an ORB written in Java.

What Is IDL?

In order for clients and servers to communicate about services, they need a common language. Since servers are written in a variety of languages, including C++ and Java, no single programming language is entirely satisfactory for describing the service interfaces. Instead, the Object Management Group has defined a new language—the Interface Definition Language (IDL)—to allow programmers to describe services.

With the introduction of Sun's `idltojava` compiler, Java now conforms to the Common Object Request Broker Architecture,

CORBA and the IIOP

If you plan to use an ORB, you should learn more about CORBA and the IIOP. You can get the complete CORBA/IIOP 2.1 specification from the Web, at `http://www.omg.org/corba/corbaiiop.htm`.

CORBA. (Other languages with an IDL mapping include C++, C, Smalltalk, COBOL, and Ada.)

Input Method Framework

The Java character type (char) supports Unicode. Unicode is a 16-bit encoding standard that supports the thousands of characters found in languages such as Chinese, Japanese, and Korean. There's only one problem—few keyboards support thousands of keys. People who wish to type in one of these ideographic languages use an *input method* to map keys on their keyboard to Unicode characters.

JDK 1.2 makes it easy for you to implement a variety of input methods to allow users to edit Chinese, Japanese, or Korean text.

JAR Enhancements

The JAR format is becoming increasingly important, especially with the new Extensions Framework described earlier in this section. For example, Sun has introduced policies and mechanisms for handling dependencies on extensions and other classes distributed as JAR files.

With JDK 1.2, Sun has enhanced the command-line tool used for managing JARs. It has also enhanced the API that allows Java programs to read and write JAR files.

JNI Enhancements

For all the power of Java, sometimes a programmer needs to get to platform-specific code. You can link C++ or other programs into your Java application by using the *Java Native Interface—JNI*.

In JDK 1.2 Sun added several enhancements suggested by their users and licensees. For example, under JDK 1.1, a native library loaded by one class became visible from all other classes. This practice led to namespace collisions and violated Java's type-safety rules. In JDK 1.2, the same native library cannot be loaded into more than one class loader.

A native library that wants to use the new JNI 1.2 services must export the function

```
jint JNI_OnLoad(JavaVM *vm, void *reserved)
```

When OnLoad() is called, the native library must return 0x00010002 to indicate that it wants version 1.2 services.

Reflection Enhancements

Most of the time, if you have a reference to an object, you already know about the object's methods and instance variables. In fact, in many cases, you'll have designed the object yourself.

But suppose you want to write a tool, such as a debugger, that works on classes written by other people. You may not have the source code, and your tool may not know anything about the class before it receives the reference to the object.

To deal with this class of programs, JDK 1.1 introduced *reflection*—the ability to examine an object and learn about its public interface.

Based on their experience with JDK 1.1, Sun designers have introduced numerous small enhancements in the reflection mechanism in JDK 1.2.

JDBC-ODBC Bridge Enhancements

Many programs need to access data that is stored in a relational database—the sort of database that is usually accessed by using the Structured Query Language (SQL, pronounced see-quel). Java gives you access to SQL through the Java Database Connectivity or JDBC package, java.sql.

Some vendors—notably, Microsoft—support the Open Database Connectivity standard, ODBC. The ODBC standard is complex, and is oriented toward C and C++ programmers. Rather than force you to learn ODBC, Sun allows you to access an ODBC-compliant database from the JDBC interface. In JDK 1.2 this mechanism is called the JDBC-ODBC bridge.

The latest version of the bridge uses the JNI API and assumes that the ODBC drivers can handle multithreaded access. Both of these changes improve performance. The new version also allows you to specify a character encoding on the connection. This change makes it easier to handle international characters.

Servlets

Recall from earlier in this section the new Extensions Framework. Sun has stated that they intend to offer a series of "standard extensions." The first of these extensions is the Java Servlet API. A servlet is a Java program intended to be run on a server (such as a Web server). Servlets occupy the same place that CGI programs do on many servers today. Because they are written in Java, however, servlets are platform-independent.

javadoc Doclets

Even the best programmers often allow the documentation of their classes to drift out of date. Most programmers, however, do a good job of keeping source comments current. `javadoc` is a documentation tool that builds package and class documentation based on source comments. Figure 1.11 shows the sort of documentation `javadoc` produces.

Internationalize your Java program

Java contains many provisions that ease internationalization of your program. Visit `http://java.sun.com/products/jdk/1.1/intl/html/intlspecTOC.doc.html` to learn more about Java internationalization.

FIGURE 1.11

You can use `javadoc` to produce package documentation in HTML.

By default, javadoc writes its documentation in HTML. Some programmers have expressed a desire to have documentation in other formats, such as Adobe's Portable Document Format, PDF. Other programmers are content with HTML, but would like a different "look and feel" than the one chosen by Sun.

Starting in version 1.2, programmers can use the Doclet API to design their own javadoc output.

JVM Debugger Interface

Save time writing your doclet

To get started fast in writing doclets, don't use the Doclet API directly. Make a copy of the standard doclet—the one that writes HTML—and modify it to suit your needs.

Starting in JDK 1.2, Sun offers a low-level debugging API called the JVM Debugger Interface, or JVMDI. Expect Sun to build high-level debugging APIs on top of the JVMDI in future releases. Then Sun (and, undoubtedly, third parties) will build debuggers by using these high-level interfaces.

A Tour of the Java World

Find out how others are using applets—for communication, navigation, and lightweight applications

Learn about Netscape LiveConnect—a fast and easy way for non-programmers to add sophisticated behavior to their Web pages with Java

See how expert programmers are using Java to build complete applications

Java Applet Examples

According to Wired's HotBot search engine, about 700,000 Web pages now include at least one Java applet. Some of those, of course, are new Java developers trying out scrolling text, Tumbling Duke, or even "Hello, World!". This section shows some of the more innovative uses of Java applets.

If you are just learning to program, use these sample applets as examples of what you might build later. For now, concentrate on the basics of learning algorithms and data structures. If you're an experienced programmer, you should be able to build applets similar to these by the time you finish this book.

As a programmer, it's easy—and misleading—to think of programs in terms of their complexity. In fact, some of the most useful programs have been based on relatively simple concepts. The original VisiCalc—first of the electronic spreadsheets—was conceptually simple, but revolutionary.

Applets are programs that run with the help of another program, such as a Web browser. Given the increasing impact of the Internet and the World Wide Web, applets may prove to be the most influential class of programs ever written.

One way to organize applets is to focus on their purpose. In general, you can use applets for four purposes:

- Display information that's on the server (including real-time information) to the end user.
- Send information from the end user to the server.
- Help the user navigate server information (which is then displayed through conventional protocols).
- As an application, allow an end user to interact with the local program without necessarily sending information back and forth to a server.

Displaying Personalized Information

One of the most important uses for applets is to display information—particularly dynamic information—that's available on the Web server.

Static information can be displayed by the Web browser itself or by browser plug-ins. Plug-ins can also be written to display dynamic information by using a streaming protocol. RealNetworks (`http://www.real.com/`), for example, distributes a plug-in called RealPlayer that can deliver both streaming audio and streaming video.

Applets offer a flexible, platform-independent way to deliver dynamic content on a Web page. For example, the My Yahoo! service of the popular Yahoo! Internet catalog allows users to enter a personal profile describing their news interests. With their profiles in place, users can open a news ticker applet that scrolls the headlines of stories that match their interest profile.

Figure 2.1 shows the personalized news ticker from My Yahoo! in action, scrolling the headlines across the screen. When you see a story you want to read, just double-click the headline.

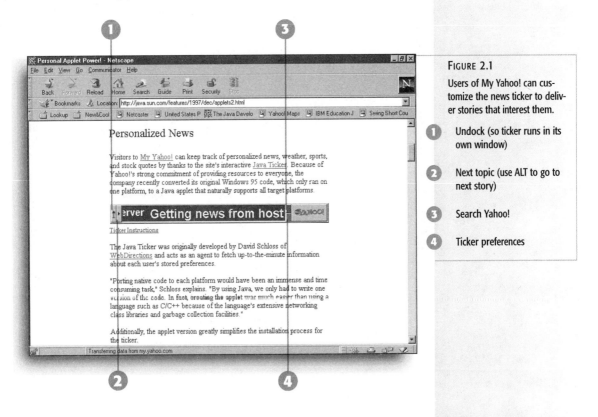

FIGURE 2.1

Users of My Yahoo! can customize the news ticker to deliver stories that interest them.

1. Undock (so ticker runs in its own window)

2. Next topic (use ALT to go to next story)

3. Search Yahoo!

4. Ticker preferences

Learn how to build sophisticated user interfaces in Chapter 11, "Bulding the User Interface with the AWT."

Displaying Real-Time Data

Java is particularly well-suited for displaying real-time data. The Texas Disaster Operations Center of the American Red Cross commissioned Paul Curtis and Terrapin Associates to build an applet that shows an animated track of a storm. Hurricane and tropical storm advisory data comes to the system from the National Weather Service by satellite. Figure 2.2 shows the applet in action, tracking Tropical Depression Paka as it moved across the Pacific in mid-December, 1997.

FIGURE 2.2

A Java applet can display data from a file or a real-time feed.

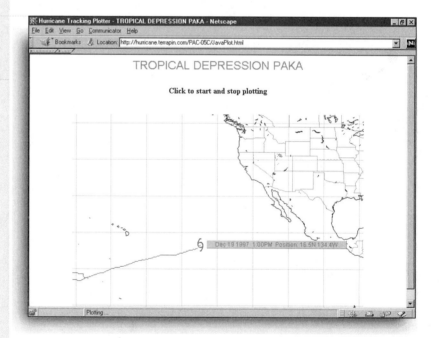

SEE ALSO

➤ *Learn how to read and write files, page 500*

Navigating Large Quantitites of Information

The National Library of Medicine's Visible Human project has obtained a complete anatomical record of the human body—14 gigabytes of high-resolution medical images—transverse CT, MRI, and cryosection images of the body taken at one millimeter intervals.

Figure 2.3 shows a Java applet that gives you access to the database of slices. When you move the cutting line in one view, the other two views update automatically. Once you're happy with your choice of images and resolution, click Load to download the image. Figure 2.4 shows a sample image.

What are all these medical imaging terms?

CT is Computed Tomography. MRI is Magnetic Resonance Imaging. Cryosections are photographs taken of slices of the frozen cadaver.

You can learn more about the Visible Human Project at `http://www.nlm.nih. gov/research/visi- ble/visible_human. html`.

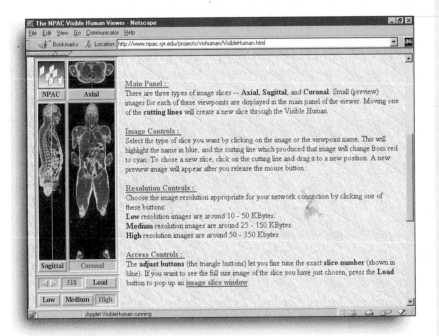

FIGURE 2.3

The cutting line on each of the three views of the Visible Human is a control in its own right.

From our point of view as programmers, one of the nicest features of this applet is the fact that the source code is available online. Visit `http://www.npac.syr.edu/projects/vishuman/ Source.html`. If you're just starting out in Java, don't expect the source code to mean too much just yet. Keep reading. (You might want to visit the source after you've read Chapter 11, "Building the User Interface with the AWT.")

FIGURE 2.4

Once you've selected a view
and a slice, you can download
the image and examine it in
detail.

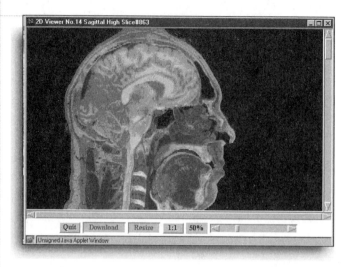

You can learn how to build even more sophisticated user interfaces by reading Chapter 12, "Building the User Interface with
JFC Swing Components."

Sending Information Back to the Server

Many mortgage brokers and lenders use the Uniform Residential
Loan Application (URLA). Heritage Bank and Trust Company
(http://www.hbtc.com/) in Lafayette, Indiana uses a Java applet
(shown in Figure 2.5) that implements the URLA.

Programmer Perry Smith elected to implement the application
as an 11-page "booklet." Users use the drop-down menu to
select any page, fill it out, and then move on to the next page.
When the application is complete, the user clicks the **Submit**
button to send the application back to the bank.

SEE ALSO

➤ *Learn how to send information over the network, page 516*

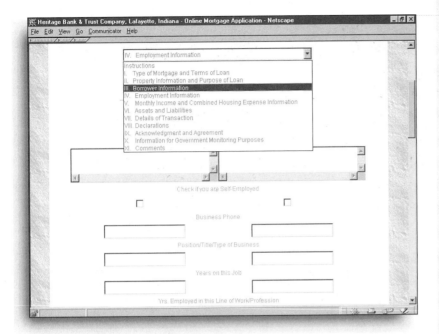

FIGURE 2.5

Heritage Bank allows users to apply for a mortgage online, by using a Java applet.

Navigating with Applets

Unlike static Web pages, Java applets can deliver real-time information (as shown by the storm tracker). You can even give the end user control over which information he or she receives (as illustrated by the Visible Human browser).

Another use of Java is to improve your control over information that is presented through the Web browser. Sun's XeoMenu and MerzCom's MerzScope both address this topic, with two very different solutions.

Not surprisingly, some of the most creative uses of Java come from Sun itself. Visit JavaSoft's home page (http://java.sun.com/) and follow the link to the "Java-enabled Menu" (http://java.sun.com:81/index.html). Figure 2.6 shows the page Sun had up in late December 1997; they change it every few days.

FIGURE 2.6

As you drag the mouse over menu items, the items change color, the text changes to italics, and a drop-down menu appears.

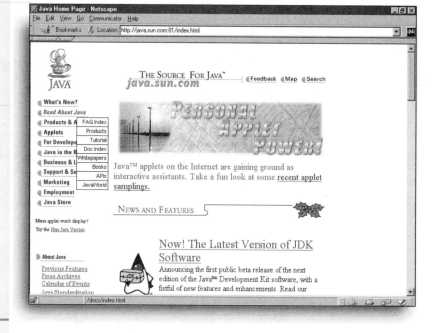

Use Java-enabled menus

The Java-enabled menu was written by Patrick Chan of Sun. He calls it XeoMenu. You can download the source from `http://java.sun.com:81/share/classes/menu/source/source.html`.

If you've ever struggled through a complex Web site, you know how important it is to keep the site visitor oriented. MerzCom offers a site map (called MerzScope) that runs as an applet. Visit `http://www.merzcom.com/try/maps.html` to see their offer. Figure 2.7 shows one of their maps in action.

FIGURE 2.7

In a MerzScope map, you can use the mouse to zoom in and out or pan across the site.

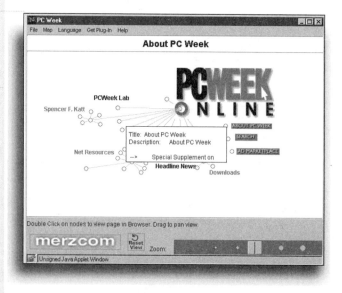

To learn about advanced user interfaces, see Chapter 14, "Advanced User Interface Design with the JFC."

Using Netscape LiveConnect

As you examined the Heritage Bank applet, you may have been thinking, "I don't need to use Java to send information back to the server, I can do that by using an HTML form." You're right, of course. You choose Java when you want more control over the look and feel of the form, or you want to use a program to validate fields before sending the information to the server. Running Java on the client machine will also lighten the load on the server.

Nevertheless, writing a Java applet does take more work than writing an HTML form. For every person who can write a Java applet, there are hundreds who can write JavaScript, and thousands who can write HTML. If you'd like the simplicity of an HTML form but need the programming power of an applet, consider taking advantage of a Netscape technology called LiveConnect.

Figure 2.8 shows an example of LiveConnect. In Danny Goodman's article, "The Java/JavaScript Connection," he shows a Java clock that is customizable from an HTML form. The JavaScript code includes onChange handlers that control the appearance of the clock applet (which is named clock2 in the JavaScript). For example, to change the foreground and background colors, the JavaScript programmer wrote an onChange handler that calls a JavaScript function:

```
function setColor(form) {
  var bg = form.backgroundColor.options(form.
backgroundColor.
➥selectedIndex).value
  var fg = form.foregroundColor.options(form.
foregroundColor.
➥selectedIndex).value

  // send data to applet
  document.clock2.setColor(bg, fg)
}
```

FIGURE 2.8

The appearance of this Java clock applet is controlled from an HTML form.

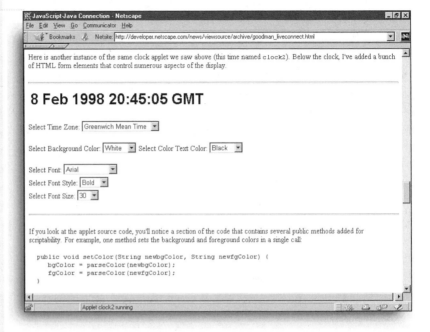

The applet includes a public method, setColor(), to receive the message from the JavaScript function:

```
public void setColor(String newbgColor, String newfgColor) {
  bgColor = parseColor(newbgColor);
  fgColor = parseColor(newfgColor);
}
```

LiveConnect is one example of a trend in software engineering called component technology. Instead of requiring programmers to develop an entire application, programmers concentrate on writing smaller functional pieces called components. Applets, plug-ins, and ActiveX controls are all components. Non-programmers assemble components into a finished solution.

Details on the customizable clock

You can read Goodman's article online at http://developer.netscape.com/news/viewsource/archive/goodman_liveconnect.html. His article includes a link to the Java source of the clock applet.

As a programmer, think of ways that an end user might want to use your applet as a component. Look for ways to give your applet some flexibility, perhaps through parameters, so non-programmers can assemble your applet into their Web-based application.

LiveConnect allows you to integrate Java applets with JavaScript and with Netscape Navigator plug-ins. Figure 2.9 illustrates the communications paths between Java, JavaScript, and the plug-in.

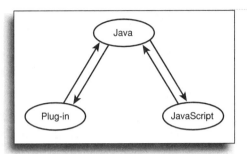

FIGURE 2.9
LiveConnect is Netscape's
approach to integrating Java,
JavaScript, and plug-ins.

Note that LiveConnect doesn't allow the plug-in to communicate directly with a script written in JavaScript. All communications go through Java. This design isn't a problem, however; Netscape makes it easy for plug-in programmers to write the small amount of Java necessary. The JavaScript programmer has the illusion that he or she is communicating directly with the plug-in.

If you're a programmer and you'd like to learn how to write platform-specific plug-ins, read *Netscape Plug-Ins Developers Kit* (Que, 1997). If you'd prefer an overview of the Netscape family of technology (which Netscape calls the Open Network Environment, or ONE) see *Developing for Netscape ONE* (Que, 1997). Chapter 14 of that book is titled "Principles of LiveConnect."

From inside your applet, you can use LiveConnect to read JavaScript data and HTML forms. You can also call JavaScript methods. From JavaScript, you can call Java methods in an applet that you've installed on your page. To learn more about how to build Java applets that interact with JavaScript, see Chapter 24, "Organizing and Reusing Your Code."

Java Application Examples

Unlike applets, Java applications are designed to run on their own, without the help of a Web browser. (They do need to have the Java interpreter, however.)

Where can I learn more about LiveConnect?

Encourage folks who use your applets to learn about JavaScript and LiveConnect. *Special Edition Using JavaScript,* 2nd Edition (Que, 1997) gives an in-depth description of that scripting language. *Special Edition Using Netscape LiveConnect* (Que, 1997) shows how to use LiveConnect to stitch plug-ins and JavaScript together by using Java.

This section introduces three Java applications that you can download from the Internet. While the source code for these applications is not available, they give you an idea of the breadth of capability built into Java.

- *Icon Presenter*. A lightweight Java application that may meet your intranet needs for presentation software.
- *The U.S. Postal Service's Postage Statement application*. A suite of 13 applications that help bulk mail customers fill out application forms.
- *The ParaChat server*. A Java chat server that runs on your machine, or theirs.

Icon Presents

You may have used Microsoft PowerPoint, Astound, or one of the other commercial presentation tools. Now there's a Java contender in the pack: Icon Presents from Icon Software and Web Design. Icon Presents is a new product, but it offers many of the basic features that made its competitors successful. With Icon Presents you can set up simple colored backgrounds (or use background images) and work with a variety of fonts. Icon Presents is easy to install and, at under 100K, it can be readily distributed around an intranet.

Figure 2.10 shows a slide being built in Icon Presents.

U.S. Postal Service's Postage Statement Application

Application and viewer available online

Download both Icon Presents and its companion viewer from the Icon Software and Web Design site: `http://www.ultranet.com/~dandage/iconpresents/`.

The U.S. Postal Service has half a million bulk mail customers, and handles nearly 100 billion pieces of bulk mail per year. Requests for bulk mailings come in on double-sided forms and must be checked for errors. Errors translate into lost time and money, both for the mailer and the Postal Service.

In 1996 the Postal Service hired Enterprise Productivity Systems, Inc. to build a set of 13 Java applications. These applications generate the various forms associated with bulk mailing. Before it prints the form, the application ensures that the form is filled out correctly. The Postal Service can complete their tasks more quickly since there are no errors on the forms.

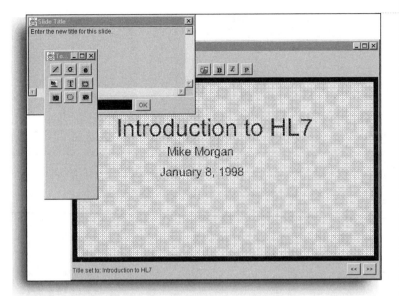

FIGURE 2.10

Icon Presents is just the beginning of applications written in
Java.

Figure 2.11 shows one of these applications in action: Postal Form PS3541NC, used by bulk mailers to apply to send periodicals at classroom rates. The buttons at the top of the window allow the user to move from one major section of the form to the next. The buttons at the bottom allow the user to save the contents of the form as file, open such a file, zoom in and out, and print the form. As you fill out the form, the Java application checks the contents of each field (as shown in Figure 2.12).

The installation script for these applications doesn't work perfectly on all platforms. If you have a problem running the application in the manner suggested by the installation script, try this step-by-step procedure.

Troubleshooting the postal form applications

1. Make sure you have the JDK or a Java interpreter installed on your machine. (There's one in the EPS/Hot Postal Statements/java/bin directory in the installation kit, but if you have the JDK, you don't need to use the downloaded copy.)

2. Change to the EPS/Hot Postal Statements directory.

3. Type java HotForm PostalForms.PS3541NC (or whichever form you want to run).

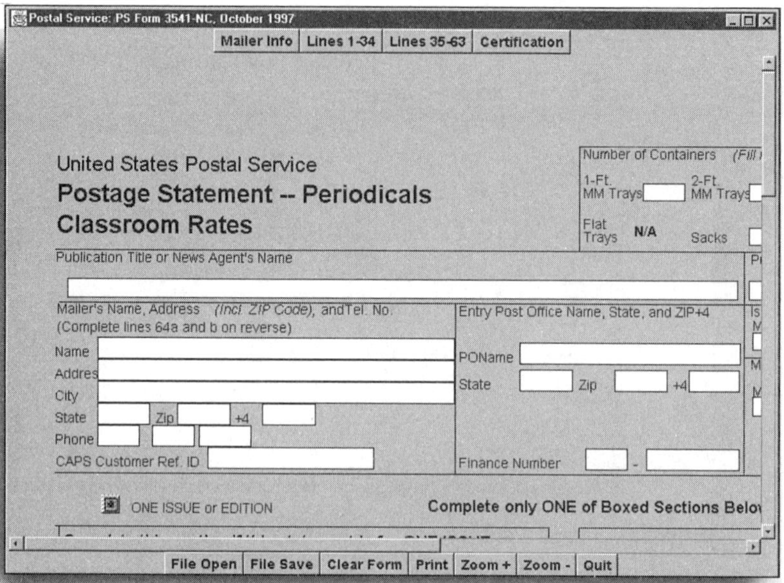

FIGURE 2.11

When a bulk mailer uses one
of these Java applications, the
Post Office can process the
form faster.

FIGURE 2.11

When a bulk mailer uses one
of these Java applications, the
Post Office can process the
form faster.

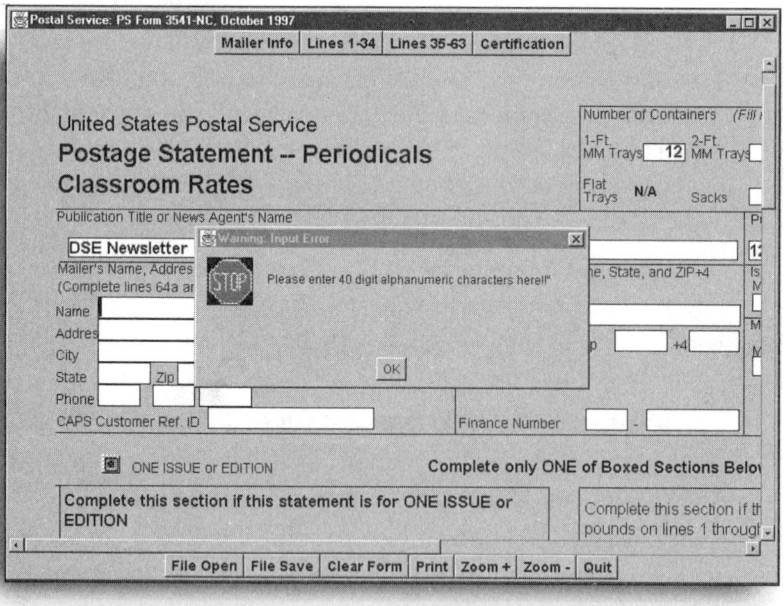

FIGURE 2.12

If you fill out a field incorrect-
ly, HotForm stops you and tells
you how to correct the error.

ParaChat Server

Regent University's Center for Leadership Studies
(http://www.regent.edu/acad/cls/) offers graduate degrees in
organizational leadership. Much of its instruction is done over
the Internet. One way for students to communicate with one
another is through a private chat room. The Center's chat facility (shown in Figure 2.13) is based on Paralogic's Java-based chat
server.

**Learn more about the USPS appli-
cations online**

Read the story for yourself in
the November '96 "Memo to
Mailers," online at http://
www.usps.gov/busi-
ness/mtm/mtm1196/
art7text.htm. You can
download the applications from
http://www.usps.gov
/formmgmt/webforms/.

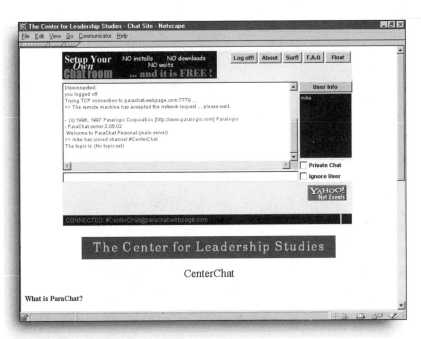

FIGURE 2.13
Unlike many chat servers,
Paralogic's ParaChat works
well behind firewalls.

Because of the poor reputation most chat rooms have, it was
important to Regent that the chat room be private (inside a
secured server), spamproof, and flameproof.

Paralogic (http://www.paralogic.com/) sells a sophisticated server—it will support more than 1,000 simultaneous connections—
or you can place a chat room on one of their machines.

Visit Parachat's home page

To get started fast in Java-based chat, visit the Parachat site operated by Paralogic at `http://www.parachat.com/`. For a full description of free or for-fee chat rooms on Paralogic's servers, visit `http://www.parachat.com/get-pchat.htm`. To learn more about the Java-based server, read `http://www.parachat.com/server.htm`.

For organizations just getting started with chat, it's easy to set up a chat room. Just add code for the ParaChat applet to your own page and take a few seconds to register your chat room. You can even set up a chat room for free—Paralogic covers the cost of those sites by placing discreet ads in those chat rooms.

If you only have a few dozen simultaneous users, consider ParaChat Professional, which gives you an advertisement-free customizable chat room for a few dollars per month. Users with heavier traffic and more rooms should consider setting up their own server. Sites with heavy traffic (more than 500 simultaneous users) will also want to look into MuxSock, Paralogic software that allows you to multiplex the Java sockets, extending the capability of the server to over 1,000 simultaneous connections on a single host. Users with heavier demands will probably want to add an additional server—Paralogic makes this step easy by building in load-leveling capability in the server.

Getting Started Fast

Download version 1.2 of the Java Development Kit—the essential toolkit for developing Java

Explore the components of the JDK, including the Java compiler, interpreter, and debugger

Build your first Java application—I'll take you step-by-step through the process of building a running *HelloWorld*

Transform your application into an applet—we'll turn *HelloWorld* into *HelloApplet*

Learn about the hidden methods of an applet and how they're used throughout its life

Obtaining the JDK

The first step in writing a Java program is to get a copy of the Java Development Kit (JDK) from Sun. While it's possible to write Java without the JDK, there's no good reason to avoid it. The JDK is free and runs on most common platforms. Other companies, such as IBM, supply Java development environments for a variety of computers. If Sun's JDK doesn't run on your computer, check with your hardware vendor to see if Java is available on your machine.

Minimum Requirements

Sun has targeted Java to run on any machine. They have focused their JDK development efforts on a smaller group. This section describes the minimum hardware and operating system requirements needed for the JDK.

Your Computer

While Java runs on nearly every computer, the JDK itself runs on fewer machines. Here's the list of hardware and operating system combinations supported by Sun.

- Microsoft Windows 95
- Microsoft Windows NT 4.0
- Sun Solaris 2.4, 2.5, 2.5.1, and 2.6 on SPARC
- Sun Solaris 2.5, 2.5.1, and 2.6 on x86

If you need to run the JDK but don't have Windows or Solaris, don't despair. Many hardware vendors have ported the entire JDK to their machines. See the comments on "Other JDKs," later in this section.

Disk Space

A typical copy of the JDK installer requires about 10MB. The installer will expand into a set of files about twice its size. Thus, you should budget around 30MB to get started. (You can delete the installer itself if you need to free up the space after you're done.)

You'll also want to allow another 30MB for the documentation. If you're tight on space, you can use the online version, but it's slower than a local copy.

Other JDKs

If you're not using a common operating system such as Sun's Solaris or Microsoft's Windows NT, don't worry. Even though there may not be a Sun JDK available for your computer, you may still be able to develop Java programs. Check with your computer vendor to see if they've ported the JDK to your operating system.

For example, IBM has released versions of the JDK for AIX (IBM's version of UNIX), OS/400 (which runs on the popular AS/400), and OS/390 (a mainframe operating system).

Downloading to Windows NT, Step-by-Step

This section describes the process of downloading Sun's JDK to your desktop computer. In this example I'll assume you use a Windows NT system—other operating systems work similarly.

Connecting to JavaSoft

The easiest way to find the current JDK is to start at http://java.sun.com/. Scroll down the page until you see the Spotlight section on the left margin. In that section you'll see a link for the Java Development Kit.

Downloading the JDK

Once you're on the download page, read the information about the JDK, then scroll down till you see the "Downloading the Java Development Kit" section. Note the version number; make sure you're getting the version you expect. Figure 3.1 shows the download section of a typical JDK release.

Run Java on other machines

Find out which operating systems support Java by using the Sun Web application at http://java.sun.com/cgi-bin/java-ports.cgi. Note that not all operating systems that support Java support the JDK.

Developing advanced Java

If you want to take advantage of the newest features in the JDK, you'll want to use the Sun JDK. If you're developing Java professionally and you want to be sure to have access to the latest features, get one of the machines that Sun supports with the JDK.

Getting pre-release versions of the JDK

If you want to be sure to have access to the latest versions of the JDK, consider downloading public betas. Learn more about beta software at http://java.sun.com/jdc/ by becoming a member of the Java Developer Connection (JDC). Membership is free.

FIGURE 3.1

Start your download by selecting your operating system.

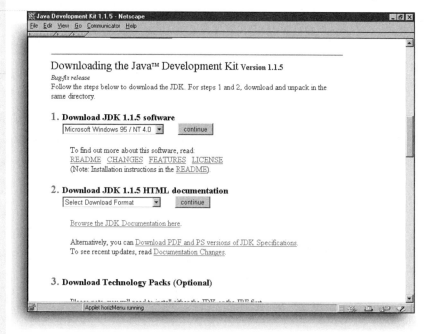

Read the README file

From the download page you'll find links to various text files, including a README file, a list of changes, and a list of features supported in this version of the JDK. Use the README file to get an overview of the download and installation process.

Caution: You cannot distribute the JDK

Note that the license agreement prohibits you from distributing the JDK. If you develop a Java applet, you don't need to send the end user anything—the browser contains a Java Runtime Environment (JRE). If you want to distribute a stand-alone application, you can download the JRE from Sun and bundle it with your application or instruct the user how to get the JRE directly.

You might want to print out the README file as some of the recommendations about setting environment variables can get tricky. If you don't get them right, you'll get errors when you try to use the JDK tools.

Below the download section for the JDK you'll see options for the documentation and other software. You can download either the documentation or the JDK first—in this example, we'll start with the JDK itself. When you're done, come back to this page and follow the same procedures to download the documentation.

Before leaving this page, scroll down to the end. Sun has put many useful links on this page, including links to Java documentation (beyond that supplied in the documentation kit). Consider bookmarking this page so you always have the latest information on Java.

Use the pull-down menu to select your operating system, and then click the **Continue** button. The license agreement for the JDK appears. Read the license agreement; if you want the JDK, you must accept the agreement.

After you navigate the license agreement, you finally arrive at the download page itself. Figure 3.2 shows this page. Note that you can download the JDK either from Sun's FTP server or via HTTP. If your network connection permits you to use FTP, do so; it's faster and more reliable. If you must, use HTTP.

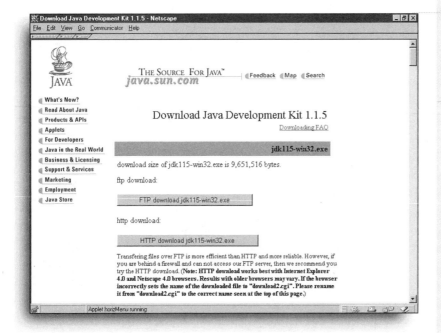

FIGURE 3.2

This version of the download page allows you to get the Windows 95/NT version of the JDK.

You can download the installation kit into any convenient directory; the installer will place the components into the proper directories.

Be sure to note the name of the file you're downloading—it's given at the top of the download page. Some network connections change the name of the downloaded file to match the name of the page from which it is downloaded. If your software makes this mistake, switch the name back to the one given by Sun before continuing the installation process.

Get the JDK on CD-ROM

If your network connection is slow or unreliable, consider getting the JDK via CD-ROM. Sun refers to this offer throughout the download process. If you take them up on the offer, they'll include additional Java resources on the CD-ROM.

Installing the JDK

The JDK installer for Windows 95/NT is an executable archive. Double-click this file to start the installation process. Follow the instructions to make the JDK directory.

When you finish installation, feel free to delete the installer programs for both the JDK and the documentation. You won't need them again unless you need to reinstall the software.

Setting Environment Variables

Java uses the CLASSPATH environment variable to tell it where to look for Java classes. As a developer you'll want to add new class libraries to the CLASSPATH variable.

If you've installed the JDK in the default location for your platform, the JDK tools will find the lib directory without searching CLASSPATH. You'll still need to set CLASSPATH if you install third-party programs.

To see if CLASSPATH is set on a Windows machine, type set at the command prompt. If you find that CLASSPATH is set, you can clear it by typing set CLASSPATH=. Of course, if you set CLASSPATH in a startup file such as Autoexec.bat, you'll want to remove that entry in order to permanently unset CLASSPATH.

On a Windows 95 machine you can edit the CLASSPATH entry in the Autoexec.bat file. On a Windows NT machine use the System Control panel and this step-by-step procedure.

1. From the **Start** menu, choose **Settings**, **Control Panel**, as shown in Figure 3.3.

2. In the resulting folder, locate the system **Control Panel** and double-click it.

3. In the **System Properties** dialog box, choose the **Environment** tab, shown in Figure 3.4.

4. Select the CLASSPATH variable in the upper window (marked System Variables). When you click the variable name, the variable and its current value appear in the edit fields at the bottom of the dialog box.

5. Add the path of your library directories to the value of CLASSPATH.

Be sure to download the documentation into the JDK directory

You should unpack both the documentation and the JDK into the same directory. The documentation installer will make a docs folder in the JDK directory. Sun's links are designed to look for the documentation in that folder.

Don't unzip `classes.zip`

As you explore your JDK and third-party products, you may run across zip files such as `lib/classes.zip`. Don't unzip these files—they are designed to be read directly by the Java runtime environment. In the newest JDK, these zip files are being replaced by Java Archives, or JAR files, that serve the same purpose but aren't likely to be confused with zip archives.

FIGURE 3.3

On a Windows NT machine, set
up your environment variables
through the System control
panel.

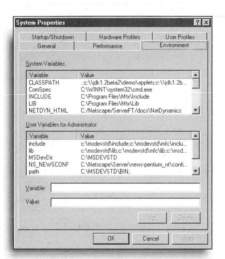

FIGURE 3.4

In the System Properties dialog
box, select the Environment tab
to change the CLASSPATH
variable.

When you're working in your development directory (described
in the next section) you'll find it useful to be able to refer to the
tools by name, rather than having to specify the full path. Thus,
you'd prefer to type `javac myClass.java` rather than typing
`C:/jdk1.2/bin/javac myClass.java`.

The solution is to set the PATH variable. Include the bin directory
of your JDK in the PATH, so that the operating system can find
the JDK tool.

Setting Up a Development Directory

You can place a development directory anywhere you like on your hard drive. (Remember to set the PATH variable so you don't have to type the full path to every JDK tool.) For example, you might store code for the Model 1000 project in `C:\Projects\Model1000\` on a Windows machine, or `\home\myname\projects\model1000\` under UNIX. If you're using a development environment, such as Symantec Café or Together/J, follow the instructions that came with your tools to set up a development directory.

As you gain experience in Java you'll undoubtedly develop several libraries of classes. (In Java these libraries are called packages.) You can add these libraries to your CLASSPATH variable or wrap your calls to Java tools in a batch file or shell script that sets its own version of CLASSPATH. For example, to compile all of the Java programs in the current directory on a Windows machine, you could type

```
javac -classpath .;C:\usr\local\classes\;
➥C:\projects\model1000\java\lib\classes.zip *.java
```

To avoid retyping this long line each time you need to compile, just put this line into a batch file. If you name the file, say, `compile.bat`, you now only need to type `compile` to invoke the `javac` compiler on all Java files. (If you're using UNIX, you can get the same effect by using a shell script.)

The JDK Essentials

When you download the JDK, you'll find a bewildering array of files and tools. This section gives you an overview of the JDK tools you'll use nearly every time you write a Java program. In the next section, "Other JDK Components," we'll take up the remaining JDK tools.

Examine the directory into which you installed the JDK; you'll find six folders.

- bin—the executable JDK tools themselves

- demo—a variety of applets, as well as sample code for Java Foundation Classes (JFC)

- docs—extensive documentation on Java

- include—C and C++ header files used to build the Java environment

- lib—libraries and archives (in .lib, .zip, and .jar format) used by the JDK

- src—the source for Sun's Java libraries. Use this source to learn how Sun's classes work.

You'll also see several text files at the top level of the JDK directory tree. You'll want to look at the README file. You'll also want to use your Web browser to examine index.html—that file is the starting point for the entire JDK. It includes links to the pages installed on your hard drive as well as information on Sun's Web server.

The Java Compiler

Quite possibly the most important tool in the JDK is javac, the Java compiler. This section describes what javac does and how you can test it.

What Is *javac*?

Recall (from "Write Once, Run Anywhere" in Chapter 1, "What Is Java, and Why Is It Important?") that the Java compiler—javac—translates Java source code to instructions for the *Java Virtual Machine* (JVM). Figure 3.5 illustrates how javac fits into the Java world.

> **Getting started even faster**
>
> If you can't wait to write some Java, skip this section for now and go right to "Building Your First Application," later in this chapter. Eventually you'll need to know something about each tool in the JDK, but if you prefer, you can start writing Java right away. I, too, am a programmer—I understand.

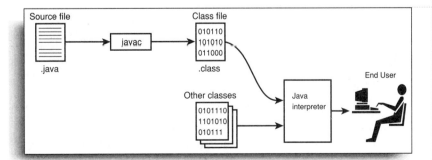

FIGURE 3.5

You'll use Java to compile your programs into .class files.

Testing Your Installation

To test your copy of `javac`, go to a command prompt. (On a UNIX system, go to a shell prompt.) Change to your development directory, and type `javac`.

You should get a usage message back telling you about the dozen or so options available. If you get a message complaining that the command or program doesn't exist, check your PATH variable and make sure it includes the bin subdirectory of your JDK directory. Thus, if you placed the JDK in a directory called jdk1.2, make sure your PATH variable includes jdk1.2/bin (or jdk1.2\bin in Windows).

The Java Interpreter

Once you've used the compiler to make a `.class` file, you'll want to run your program on the JVM. The JDK contains two stand-alone versions of the JVM, called `java` and `jre`. (There's also a JVM in appletviewer, a utility for running applets.)

What Is *java*?

For most of your work with the JDK, you'll want to run applications by using the Java intepreter named java. When you type `java MyClass`, the Java interpreter examines the class named `MyClass` for a method named `main()`. (Later in this chapter, in the section "Building Your First Application," we'll see that `main()` must be declared to be `public` and `static`, and we'll explore what those keywords mean.)

If the interpreter finds `main()`, it transfers control to that method and your application runs.

Sun provides several variants of `java`. One of the most useful is `javaw`, provided on Windows platforms so that your application has a Java console window into which to write its output.

What Is the *jre*?

As a developer, you'll want to learn and use many of the options available with the Java interpreter. Your end users don't need most of those options—you may prefer that they use the Java

Runtime Environment, or jre. Like java, there's a Windows version of jre. Unlike javaw, jrew does *not* display a console. This feature is useful when you want to make your Java application look like a traditional application.

Testing Your Installation

Both java and jre support a -help option. To test your installation and see a usage message, type java -help or jre -help. If your command interpreter complains that it cannot find the command, doublecheck your PATH variable. Both programs are in the bin subdirectory of your JDK directory.

Testing an Applet

As you begin to write Java applets, you'll want to test them quickly and efficiently. You could use your favorite Web browser, but you know how long that program takes to load. For a faster solution, use the JDK appletviewer.

What Is the Appletviewer?

The appletviewer is the world's weakest Web browser. It doesn't understand much HTML—in fact, about the only tag it does understand is <APPLET>. As you might expect, however, it excels in displaying applets.

Testing Your Installation

The JDK comes with several sample applets. To test appletviewer, we'll use appletviewer to open one of these applets. Change to the Tic-Tac-Toe applet subdirectory of the demo directory in your JDK. If your JDK is in C:\JDK1.2, type cd C:\jdk1.2\demo\applets\TicTacToe.

In this directory you'll see the source code for the applet (TicTacToe.java), the class file (TicTacToe.class), and an HTML file that loads the .class file (example1.html).

Type appletviewer example1.html. Within a few seconds you should see a window similar to the one shown in Figure 3.6. Go ahead and play a game. When you're done, click the close box to exit appletviewer.

FIGURE 3.6

Use the appletviewer to quickly test your new applets.

Debugging Your Java Code

If you're a UNIX user, you may be familiar with a debugger called dbx. It's a command-line oriented tool that allows you to examine the variables in a running program. Your JDK includes such a tool—it's called jdb. If you're more familiar with Windows-oriented environments, such as Microsoft Visual C++ or Borland C++, you may find jdb a bit primitive. Many of the IDEs offer better debuggers, but learning jdb is a good starting point for learning to debug Java programs.

What Is *jdb*?

In an ideal world, all of our programs would work correctly the first time. As a professional programmer, you know just how far from ideal the world is. If you don't have a debugger, you need to insert print statements into your code to examine the behavior while the program is running. This practice is tedious, since you must recompile the program, run it, examine the behavior, and (if necessary) insert still more print statements.

You can use jdb as an interpreter for your bytecodes. By running your program under jdb you'll be able to see each variable and examine its value.

Testing Your Installation

You can make sure your copy of jdb was correctly installed by typing jdb at a command prompt. You should get the message Initializing jdb, and then a right-angle-bracket prompt (>). To see the commands available to you, type help. To quit, type quit or exit.

SEE ALSO
➤ *To learn how to use* jdb, *see page 449*

Generating Documentation

Larry Wall, developer of the programming language Perl, claims that all great programmers share three virtues: laziness, impatience, and hubris. Wall is correct in his assessment of programmers—you'll note that nowhere does he claim we have virtues that make us great documenters.

In fact, most maintenance programmers will tell you that they don't bother reading documentation, since they know the original programmer either didn't write it or at least didn't update it. Professional programmers know there's only one place to look to understand how a program works: the source code. Yet our impatience makes us long for a better way—some way of learning how to use a class library, for example, without having to read the source.

Sun gives us a solution: javadoc. This section shows you how javadoc generates HTML pages documenting your programs without requiring you to do anything more than document the source code.

What Is *javadoc*?

To make a set of documentation for a Java package, you use javadoc. Even if you haven't taken any special pains to include good comments in your source code, you'll get some use from javadoc. It will generate one HTML page for every .java file, plus one for the package as a whole. It also produces a class hierarchy (tree.html) and an index (AllNames.html). For each .java file, javadoc records the name of the class and the full signature of each method. Figure 3.7 shows some javadoc output.

You can add information to the javadoc documentation by placing special comments in your source files. In general, you may use either the // or /*...*/ styles to include comments in your Java programs. To make a comment visible to javadoc, use the /**...*/ style. Listing 3.1 shows an example of good commenting style.

FIGURE 3.7

Use javadoc to maintain your package documentation.

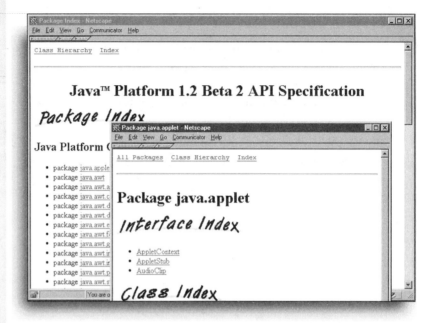

LISTING 3.1   *HelloWorld.java*—This simple application contains *javadoc* comments

```
1  /**
2   * Serves to test a Java environment.
3   * @author Mike Morgan
4   * @version 1.0
5   */
6  public class HelloWorld
7  {
8    public static void main(String[] args)
9    {
10     System.out.println("Hello, world!\n");
11   }
12 }
```

Note that the javadoc comment must appear immediately before the element it comments—in this case, the class as a whole. Note, too, that javadoc ignores leading asterisks (*) and spaces— they're there just to make the source code look nice. The lines with at signs (@) are labeled paragraphs. If you type `javadoc -author -version HelloWorld.java`, you'll get the output shown in Figure 3.8.

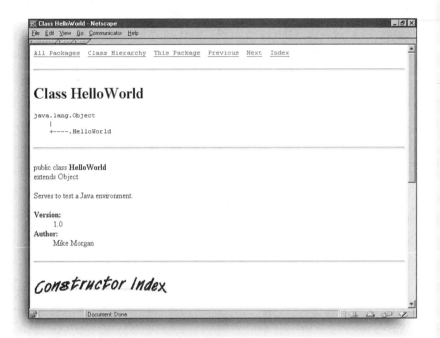

FIGURE 3.8
Produce HTML pages of documentation with `javadoc`.

Testing Your Installation

You can test `javadoc` with any class file. If you like, type in `HelloWorld.java` (or download it from this book's Web site). You can find the book's Web site opening `http://www.mcp.com/` in your browser. From there, click on the Downloads link. In the text box under Book Information enter the ISBN (0-7897-1627-5), and click search. Finally, select the directory titled ch03 and look for `HelloWorld.java` and run `javadoc` on this class.

Other JDK Components

Most of the work you'll do with the JDK will involve the components described in the previous section: `javac`, `java`, `jdb`, and `javadoc`. Occasionally you'll need to use some of the other tools available. This section describes two tools: `javah` and `javap`, and the interface to the API documentation.

Make a link to the images directory

In order to use Sun's graphics (such as constructor-index.gif) in your `javadoc` HTML output, you'll need to copy the images directory from your JDK's docs/api directory. If your operating system supports symbolic links, you can save a bit of disk space by placing a link in your development directory to /JDK1.2/docs/api/images. Be sure to change the "JDK1.2" if you've put your JDK in another directory.

Integrating with C and C++

Java is a powerful language, but there are times when you'll want to write platform-specific code in a language such as C or C++. You might need the performance boost that native code can give you, or you might need to access a library written in another C or C++. This section introduces the javah tool, which helps you integrate C or C++ with Java.

In order to provide a link between C/C++ and Java, Sun provides the Java Native Invocation (JNI) methods. To add native methods to your Java classes, you need to follow the following five-step process.

Add native methods to your Java classes

1. Write your Java program
2. Compile the Java
3. Write a .h file
4. Write the native method
5. Build a shared library

Declaring a Native Method

Suppose you wanted to rewrite the HelloWorld application (shown earlier in Listing 3.1) so that the actual work was done in C. You might write something like the code in Listing 3.2.

LISTING 3.2   *NativeHello.java*–This version of Hello World! depends on native code

```
1  public class NativeHello
2  {
3    public native void sayHello();
4    static
5    {
6      System.loadLibrary("hello");
7    }
8  }
```

The first method, sayHello(), is declared to be native, so we don't write any Java to implement it. The next section is a static code segment—when the Java interpreter instantiates this class, it will run this segment. This segment, in turn, loads the native library named hello.

Listing 3.3 shows the code you would use to instantiate a copy of the NativeHello class.

LISTING 3.3 *Main.java*—This class starts the process of loading the native code

```
1 public class Main
2 {
3   public static void main(String[] args)
4   {
5     new NativeHello().sayHello();
6   }
7 }
```

When the end user runs Main, the Java interpreter calls that class's main() method. That method makes a new copy of NativeHello, then calls the new object's sayHello() method. As we said earlier, the act of instantiating NativeHello loads the hello library; calling sayHello() runs the native code.

You can compile this Java just as you would a class without native methods. Compile both NativeHello.java and Main.java—you'll have to wait till you've written and compiled the native code to test your new classes.

What Is *javah*?

If you're familiar with C and C++, you know that those languages use .h files (often called header files) to declare classes. You may also know that C++ uses a technique known as "name mangling" to generate unique names for each method in each class. Java uses a similar mechanism to ensure that all methods have unique names. As a C or C++ programmer, you need to know how Java has named your method in order for your code to link to the Java correctly. You'll use the javah tool to generate your .h files from the .java files.

If you've written the NativeHello class above, invoke javah by typing javah NativeHello.java. javah will write NativeHello.h into your development directory. The signature of your sayHello() method is

Java_NativeHello_sayHello(JNIEnv*, jobject)

In general, native methods will be named Java_ followed by the package name, followed by an underscore (_), followed by the class name (and another underscore), followed by the method name. In this case we wrote NativeHello into the default package, so the package name (and its trailing underscore) are omitted.

The two parameters—JNIEnv* and jobject—are used to allow the Java environment and the native method to communicate. JNIEnv* is a pointer to the JNI environment; you can use it to access Java parameters. In a non-static method such as sayHello(), jobject refers to the instance that is calling the method; if the method is static, jobject refers to the class itself. In the case of sayHello() we don't use either parameter.

Writing a Native Method

Listing 3.4 shows a C program that implements Java_NativeHello_sayHello().

LISTING 3.4   *sayHello.c–This C program implements NativeHello.sayHello()*

```
1  #include <jni.h>
2  #include "NativeHello.h"
3  #include <stdio.h>
4
5  JNIEXPORT void JNICALL
6  Java_NativeHello_sayHello(JNIEnv* env, jobject obj)
7  {
8    printf("Hello, world!\n");
9    return;
10 }
```

You should always include jni.h since it has the declarations that link Java with the native code. You need to include the output of javah for the function prototype. In this example we've also included stdio.h since we want to use printf().

Use your C/C++ compiler to compile sayHello.c to sayHello.obj. For example, on Solaris you could write

```
cc -G -I/usr/local/java/include I/usr/local/java/
➥include/solaris sayHello.c -o libhello.so
```

to write a library named libhello.so. On a Windows 95 or Windows NT machine that has Microsoft Visual C++ you could write

```
cl -Ic:\java\include -Ic:\java\include\win32 -LD sayHello.
➥c -Fehello.dll
```

Adjust the include paths as necessary to match the configuration of your machine.

Under Windows, shared libraries are called Dynamic Link Libraries (DLLs), while on UNIX they're called shared object or .so files. In either case, be sure the name (hello) matches the name of the library given in the Java loadLibrary() call (as shown earlier in Listing 3.2).

Testing Your Installation

Now that you've got the two class files (Main.class and NativeHello.class) and the shared library, you need to put them where the Java interpreter can find them. Leave the class files in your development directory. On most operating systems, you can put the shared library wherever you like, as long as you set the library path environment variable to point to that directory. For example, suppose you decide to put your shared library in /usr/local/lib. On a Solaris system (in the C shell) type setenv LD_LIBRARY_PATH /usr/local/lib.

If you're on a Windows 95 or Windows NT machine, put your DLL into one of the directories your operating system searches for DLLs. Java's loadLibrary() method follows the operating system's path.

Installing native libraries on a Macintosh

If you have access to a Macintosh-compatible C/C++ compiler, you can run JNI-enabled code on PowerPC-based Macintoshes. (Sorry—it won't work on a 68K machine.) MacOS doesn't have a `LIBRARY_PATH` environment variable, so just put an alias to the shared library in System Folder:Extensions:JavaSoft Folder.

Now you can run the application from the Java interpreter by typing java `NativeHello`. You should see the traditional programmer's greeting, "Hello, World!".

Disassembling Java

Occasionally you may have a class file with no source or documentation. You can find out what the class file contains by running `javap`, the Java disassembler. By default, `javap` will report the class name and all public variables and methods. You can use command-line options to get private or protected members. You can even use the `-c` switch to get a look at the disassembled byte-codes of each method.

Accessing the API Documentation

When you downloaded the JDK, you also had the opportunity to download the API documentation. If you did so (and were careful to unpack it into the same directory you used for the JDK itself), the index.html page in the JDK directory contains a link to that documentation on your hard drive.

There's also a link to the online copy of the documentation. If you didn't download the documentation, or you want to check to see if there's newer information online, follow the link on that index page, or go directly to `http://java.sun.com/products/jdk/1.2/docs/`. (There's a last-modified date at the very bottom of the page, so you can see which version of the documentation you have.)

Building Your First Application

In order to build an application, you need to have the JDK installed. Once that's done, you'll follow a three-step process.

Build a Java application

1. Enter the code into a text file.

2. Compile all classes by using javac.

3. Run the application by using java.

This section walks you through these three steps, using the HelloWorld application in Listing 3.1 as an example. Recall from Listing 3.1 that the program has just three lines:

```
public class HelloWorld
{
  public static void main(String[] args)
  {
    System.out.println("Hello, world!\n");
  }
}
```

Writing the Code

If you're not using an IDE, you can enter the code with any convenient text editor. On a Windows system, NotePad or WordPad are available; on UNIX, you can use vi or emacs.

Note that Sun suggests several naming conventions when writing Java. The compiler doesn't care what you call your classes and methods, but if you follow the naming conventions, your code may be somewhat more maintainable. The major naming conventions are:

- Class names use mixed case, starting with a capital letter. For example, say `NativeHello` and `HelloWorld`, not `nativeHello` or `Helloworld`.

- Methods use mixed case, starting with a lowercase letter. Thus, write `sayHello()`, not `SayHello()` or `sayhello()`.

- Name data members by following the same convention as methods. Thus, you might want a member named `thePoint` rather than `ThePoint` or `thepoint`.

- Constants are generally written all in uppercase. For example, write `PI` rather than `pi`.

- Generally, accessor methods will have names that begin with `get` or `set`. Thus, to read the capacity of a truck you should look for a method named `getCapacity()`. To set the destination you would use `setDestination()`.

Caution: Be sure to save the file as plain text

If you use a word processor such as WordPad or Microsoft Word to write your program, be sure to save the file as plain text.

- If the data member is Boolean, it's often clearer to use is or has rather than get as a prefix. Thus, to see if a truck has a destination, call hasDestination(). To see if the truck is available, call isAvailable().

If you're familiar with these conventions you'll be able to read any Java code you might come across. In this book we'll often adopt additional conventions in order to further increase readability:

- We'll give classes names that start with an initial capital T, denoting type. We'll bend that rule when the class is also intended to be the starting class for an application or an applet, in order not to confuse end users. This convention helps us distinguish classes we've built from those provided in the Sun API.

- We'll start protected and private members (both methods and data) with an initial underscore (_).

- We'll denote constants with an initial lowercase k, so the tax rate on a truck might be kTaxRate. (This convention is contrary to the convention you'll find in the JDK, where constants are written all in uppercase.)

- We'll give local variables and parameters names that start with a or the.

- We'll avoid abbreviations, so you won't have to wonder if the method for accessing a truck's capacity was getCap(), getCpcty(), or getCapacity().

Here's a design convention: avoid using public data members. By forcing access to data members to go through accessor functions, we're free to change the internal representation without interfering with other classes that might use our data.

Step by Step Through the Code

In this section we walk through the code for the HelloWorld class so that you can see why each line is written the way it is. Even though there are just three lines of code, this tiny program illustrates many of the principles you'll use in writing any Java application.

- The class is declared to be `public`.
- The class contains a member named `main()`.
- `main()` is declared to be `public static` and to return `void`.

What's a *public* Class?

Recall from "Building on the Strengths of C++" in Chapter 1, "What is Java, and Why is it Important?" that Java provides several levels of access—`public`, `protected`, `private`, and a default level. Anyone who wants can access classes and members that are `public`. When you write an application, you need to declare the application's main class as `public` so that the Java environment can find it and run its `main()` method.

Why is *main()* Static?

Most methods and variables are associated with instances of a class. Each instance of class `Truck` can have its own `driver`, its own `destination`, and its own `capacity`. There are a few methods and variables that you might want to associate with the class as a whole. For example, you might want to define `Truck.sizeOfFleet` in such a way that every new truck increments `sizeOfFleet`. Which instance's `sizeOfFleet` member would you increment? The answer is, none of them—you would associate `sizeOfFleet` with the class as a whole.

Methods and variables that belong to the class are called *static*. The application's `main()` method belongs to the class (though it may call `new` to instantiate one or more objects).

Why is *main()* in a Class, Anyway?

In C++, you can place functions and data outside any class. Unlike C++, everything in Java is inside a class. Thus, in C++ it's common to define `main()` outside any class, and have `main()` bring objects into existence and pass control to them. In Java, you define one class as the starting point of your application. The end user calls the `main()` method of that class, and the work proceeds from there.

Which approach is best? Who's to say? The Java designers prefer their way, and we're not likely to change their mind. As long as you're working in Java, accept the fact that every piece of data and every method (including `main()`) belongs inside some class.

Passing Arguments

If you're familiar with MS-DOS or the UNIX shell, you've undoubtedly passed parameters from the command line. Who hasn't typed `dir myFile.txt` (in MS-DOS) or `ls -l myFile.text` (in UNIX)? When you write a Java application, you can pass arguments in on the command line. The Java environment places each argument into a `String`, and then passes the array of `Strings` to `main()`. Thus, when you define `main()`, you write

```
...main(String[] args)
```

In your program, you can then read and respond to the value in `args[0]`, `args[1]`, and so forth. You can count the number of arguments by looking at `args.length()`. We don't use any command-line arguments in our `HelloWorld` class, so we never read `args[]`.

Calling *System.out.println()*

One of the benefits of object-oriented programming is that we can be lazy. That is, we are encouraged to find someone else who has already written parts of our program and call their code. The engineers at Sun have already written plenty of code that we can use—it's packaged into libraries that start with names like `java`, `sun`, and `System`. We'll see how to include these packages in the next section, "Building Your First Applet." For now, we'll use the one built-in package, `java.lang`, and its `System` object. `System` contains a data member called `out`, which encapsulates the concept of "standard output" commonly found in MS-DOS and UNIX programs. `out` is an object of type `PrintStream` and supports a method named `println()`. `println()` takes one para-meter—the string to be printed on the standard output. Here's where the work of `main()` gets done—in the one line

`System.out.println("Hello, world!\n");`

Running the Application

Once you've entered `HelloWorld.java` or downloaded it from the Web site, you're ready to compile and run it. Make sure you've put the source code in a development directory. The compiler doesn't care, but you'll find it easier to organize your classes when you have one directory tree where you keep your Java source and class files.

Compiling the Application

Open a command prompt window. Make sure you're in your development directory, and then type `javac HelloWorld.java`. Note that the file name must match the name of the class exact-ly—including capitalization. Even on a Windows system, which is typically case-insensitive, you must type the file name the way the compiler expects to see it. There are four possible outcomes you'll see whenever you run `javac`:

- The command interpreter cannot find `javac`—check your PATH variable to make sure the bin subdirectory of your JDK folder is in the path.

- The compiler returns without comment—your code has compiled successfully.

- Your compiler emits one or more warnings—you should examine the warning to see if you've made a coding error.

- Your compiler emits one or more errors—you have made a coding error.

You must eliminate the causes for all compiler errors before you can run the application. Your goal should be to eliminate all warnings as well. While your program may run, warnings are an indication that you may have made a mistake. You should almost always be able to write the code in such a way as to eliminate the warnings.

Occasionally, you may get a warning that tells you that you are using a deprecated method. Rerun the compiler with the -deprecated switch to find out the exact problem. Deprecated methods are those that are still supported but are no longer recommended—they'll no longer be supported in some future release. When writing new code you should strive to eliminate all deprecated calls.

Once your code has compiled successfully, it's time to run your program.

Starting the Interpreter

Once again, make sure you're in a command interpreter window. Change to your development directory. Now type java HelloWorld. Note that you don't need the .class extension, since the Java interpreter knows that it runs class files.

If all goes well, you'll see "Hello, World!" in the command prompt window.

Troubleshooting

If all doesn't go well...the most common problem new Java programmers experience is an incorrect CLASSPATH variable. If either your compiler or interpreter complain about missing classes, make sure every class archive is listed in CLASSPATH. If your class files are "loose" files in a directory, list the directory. If they're archived into a .zip file or .jar file, you must name the archive in CLASSPATH. You shouldn't have much trouble with HelloWorld—it doesn't use any other classes except System.out—but applets and more sophisticated applications will draw classes from many packages.

Building Your First Applet

Once you've written a simple application, you may want to write an applet. Judging from the name, you might suspect that the applet is simpler than the application. That's not true. Applications may provide either a command-line interface (as `HelloWorld` does) or a graphical user interface (GUI). Applets invariably use a GUI. As anyone who's written "Hello, World" in Windows will tell you, GUI programs are many times more complex than command-line programs.

The good news is that Java is an object-oriented language, and the engineers at Sun have written a complete applet that you can use as a starting point. As we'll see in a moment, all you have to do is build a class that inherits from `java.applet.Applet`, then override any methods in `Applet` that don't meet your requirements.

Applets have a "life-cycle"

If you'd like to know more about how the browser calls the various methods of your applet, look at "Life Cycle of an Applet," later in this chapter.

Step by Step Through the Code

Listing 3.5 shows an applet version of `HelloWorld`. In this section we'll walk through this code to see why it works.

LISTING 3.5 *HelloApplet.java*—You can easily adapt an application to make an applet if you inherit from Sun's code

```
1  import java.applet.Applet;
2  import java.awt.Graphics;
3
4  public class HelloApplet extends Applet
5  {
6    public void paint(Graphics theGraphics)
7    {
8      theGraphics.drawString("Hello, World!", 0, 50);
9    }
10 }
```

Importing Packages

The first two lines of `HelloApplet.java` tell the compiler to use class definitions from two specific packages: `java.applet` and java.awt. (AWT stands for the Abstract Windowing Toolkit.) Specifically, these directives tell the compiler to use the Applet object from java.applet and the Graphics object from java.awt.

The import statement is simply a shorthand notation. We could have written

```
public class HelloApplet extends java.applet.Applet
```

and

```
public void paint (java.awt.Graphics theGraphics)
```

but most programmers prefer the aesthetics of import. If we planned to use many classes from java.applet or java.awt we could have written

```
import java.applet.*;
import java.awt.*;
```

to give the compiler permission to use any class from those packages. In practice, this asterisk notation is used frequently, though we lose the immediate ability to identify where a class is defined. If we didn't know Java well, we wouldn't know whether the Graphics class was part of java.applet or java.awt.

Extending *Applet*

The most powerful statement in HelloApplet is in the class definition HelloApplet extends Applet. With that one statement we've said that our little class, HelloApplet, inherits all of the methods and variables of Sun's much larger class, Applet. Applet already knows how to communicate with the Web browser. It knows how to communicate with the graphical interface inside the browser window. It even knows how to redraw its content (though that content is empty). What it doesn't know is how to do any work. By extending Applet we get a complete applet, ready to go. All we have to do is add content.

Using *Applet's paint()* Method

An applet draws into a graphical space provided by the Web browser. Whenever that space is covered (by another window) or disappears (because the user has minimized the window) it

Watch out for name conflicts

If two classes in different packages have the same name, you can run into problems if you use the asterisk (*) notation on both packages. To make sure you get the class you want, fully qualify it in your code or in the import statement.

becomes invalid. When it becomes visible again, the applet must repaint itself. In fact, internally, Applet calls a method called repaint(). That repaint() method, in turn, calls paint(). In order to draw something into the applet's graphical space, we need to do the work in paint().

Recall in the earlier section, "Building Your First Application," that we did our work in main(). In that program we wrote

```
System.out.println("Hello, World!\n");
```

to write "Hello, World!\n" to the command line. In an applet we need to draw rather than just output to standard out. The graphical space allocated for us by the browser is represented by a Graphics object, so we begin the paint() method by accepting that Graphics object (which we call theGraphics).

The Graphics class supports over three dozen public methods, including drawLine(), draw3DRect(), and fillArc(). Since we want to put a string into the graphic, the method we're interested in is drawString(). drawString() takes three parameters—the string we want to draw, and the x and y coordinates where we want to start drawing. We've chosen the coordinates 0 and 50 to start the string against the left margin, down a ways from the top.

Running the Applet

We compile HelloApplet in much the same way as we compiled HelloWorld. Recall from the previous section that if the compiler cannot find classes, you need to doublecheck CLASSPATH. Note that CLASSPATH does not include the current directory by default—you must specifically add that directory (represented by a period) to the CLASSPATH.

When we compiled the HelloWorld application, we were able to run it immediately by using the Java interpreter. An applet requires a browser environment, so we'll have to write some HTML to display the applet.

Writing the HTML

Listing 3.6 shows a simple Web page that includes the HelloApplet applet. This Web page will work with the appletviewer—you'll want to improve the HTML by adding a head, title, background color, and perhaps some text before you use it on your Web site.

LISTING 3.6   *helloApplet.html*—**You must write an *HTML* file in order to test an applet**

```
1   <HTML>
2   <BODY>
3   <APPLET CODE="HelloApplet.class" WIDTH="200" HEIGHT="200">
4   </APPLET>
5   </BODY>
6   </HTML>
```

Getting Started Quickly with a Simple *Applet* Tag

The <APPLET> tag shown in Listing 3.6 is about as simple as an <APPLET> tag can get. You must include the CODE attribute in order to tell the browser which class to load. You need to specify the height and width of the graphical space so the browser can allocate it. Other than that, everything in this tag is defaulted.

Note that you must close the applet tag with </APPLET>. Many new Java users forget the closing tag, leaving the appletviewer confused.

Using the Full *Applet* Tag

From time to time you may need to add other elements to the <APPLET> tag. Listing 3.7 shows a more complete example.

LISTING 3.7   *bigApplet.html*—**You can use more attributes, parameters, and even HTML in the *<APPLET>* tag**

```
1   <HTML>
2   <BODY>
3   <APPLET CODEBASE="http://myserver.mydomain.com/applets">
4   CODE="SomeApplet.class" WIDTH="200" HEIGHT="200"
```

```
 5  ALT="A simple applet" NAME="hello"
 6  ALIGN="Center" VSPACE="2" HSPACE="2">
 7  <PARAM NAME="Auto" VALUE="True">
 8  <PARAM NAME="Interface" VALUE="Full">
 9  Your browser doesn't understand Java. If you had a Java-enabled
    browser
10  you'd see something like this:<BR>
11  <IMG SRC="applet.gif" ALT="Image of Applet" HEIGHT="200" WIDTH=
    "200">
12  You can get a Java-aware browser from
13  <A HREF="http://home.netscape.com/">Netscape
    Communications</A>.
14  </APPLET>
15  </BODY>
16  </HTML>
```

In this version of the <APPLET> tag, we've specified a CODEBASE where the browser should look for the class file. (By default the browser asks for the applet from the same server and directory that provided the HTML page.) This version also includes some descriptive text about the applet (in ALT) and a NAME (for use by LiveConnect).

SEE ALSO

➤ *To learn about LiveConnect, see page 61*

The final set of attributes, ALIGN, VSPACE, and HSPACE, provide alignment and vertical and horizontal spacing.

Following the opening <APPLET> tag, you may place parameters (in <PARAM> tags). Give each parameter a name and a value; you'll be able to read the parameters in your code.

It's a good idea to make your applets customizable with parameters. Parameterized applets are more useful as components.

Before you close the <APPLET> tag you can include some HTML. This HTML will only be displayed if the browser did not understand the <APPLET> tag, so you should display a message telling the user what he or she is missing. In Listing 3.7, I show some HTML that tells the user about the problem, puts up a graphic showing what the applet looks like, and then offers a link to the Netscape site so that they can download Netscape Navigator.

Design Tip: Running your applet without parameters

Try to avoid having required parameters—if someone other than you uses your applet, they may not know how to use all the parameters. Your applet should behave in a reasonable manner with no parameters at all.

Running Your Applet with Appletviewer

Figure 3.9 shows our applet in action. It doesn't do much, but it works!

FIGURE 3.9

The fastest and easiest way to test an applet is with the appletviewer.

Seeing Your Applet in a Web Browser

Eventually you'll want your applet to appear on a Web page. Figure 3.10 shows `HelloApplet` viewed with Microsoft Internet Explorer. Figure 3.11 shows the same applet in Netscape Navigator.

FIGURE 3.10

Microsoft displays a gray rectangle to show the applet's reserved space.

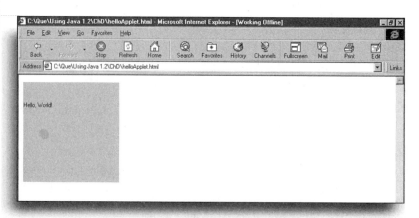

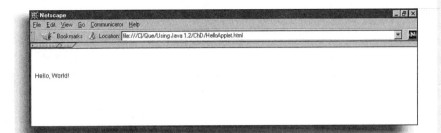

FIGURE 3.11

Netscape displays the applet against a transparent background.

Life Cycle of an Applet

We've seen Applet's paint() method. As you might guess, repainting the screen is only one part of an applet's life cycle. This section shows you the various stages of an applet's life and suggests various tasks you may want to undertake at each step. If you'd like to see these steps in action, compile LifeCycle.java, given in Listing 3.8. You can construct an HTML file based on the pattern given in HelloApplet.html—just change the name of the class file.

LISTING 3.8 *LifeCycle.java*—This applet demonstrates the stages in the life of an applet

```
1  import java.applet.Applet;
2  import java.awt.Graphics;
3
4  public class LifeCycle extends Applet
5  {
6     public LifeCycle()
7     {
8        System.out.println("Constructor running...\n");
9     }
10    public void init()
11    {
12       System.out.println("This is init \n");
13    }
14     public void start()
15    {
16       System.out.println("Applet started.\n");
17    }
```

continues…

LISTING 3.8 **Continued**

```
18    public void paint(Graphics theGraphics)
19    {
20      theGraphics.drawString("Hello, World!", 0, 50);
21      System.out.println("Applet just painted.\n");
22    }
23    public void stop()
24    {
25      System.out.println("Applet stopped.\n");
26    }
27    public void destroy()
28    {
29      System.out.println("Applet destroyed.\n");
30    }
31  }
```

If you run the LifeCycle applet from the appletviewer, you'll receive standard out messages in the command prompt window. If you're using a Web browser, you can open the Java console. For example, to open the Java console in Netscape Communicator 4.0, choose **Communicator, Java Console**. Figure 3.12 shows the console in action.

FIGURE 3.12

You can write to the Java console to help debug your applets.

Constructor

Every class has a constructor—you'll spot it because it has the same name as the class. You can put initialization code in the constructor. Restrict yourself to code that should only be run once during the life of the applet.

init( )

When the browser sees an <APPLET> tag it instructs the Java class loader to load the specified class. The Java environment in the browser makes an instance of the class (by calling its constructor). It then calls the instance's init( ) method. The init( ) method is the best place to put code that should only run once during your applet's lifetime. Experiment with the LifeCycle applet in different browsers to see the circumstances under which the constructor and init( ) are called.

start( ) and *stop( )*

Once your applet is loaded and initialized, the Java environment calls start( ). If the user leaves the page or minimizes it, the applet's stop( ) method is called. The start( ) method will be called again when the user returns to the page.

If your applet should take special action when the user enters or leaves the page, place the code for those actions in start( ) or stop( ).

paint( )

The Java environment calls paint( ) whenever it suspects that the applet's graphic space may have been obscured. As a result paint( ) gets called far more often than you might suspect. Experiment with the LifeCycle applet in various browsers to see when paint( ) gets called. Design your applets so that paint( ) is as efficient as possible—this method is where your program will spend much of its time.

Use Navigator's Java console as a debugging aid

You can type commands into Navigator's Java console. Enter a question mark (**?**) to see a list of commands. If you enter nine (**9**) you'll put the console in maximum debugging mode—it will show you all sorts of information about your running applet.

Caution: Browsers load applets inconsistently

Not all browsers load and unload applets in the same way. For best results, put once-only code into init( ) rather than the constructor.

destroy()

Put up Navigator's Java Console, open a page with the LifeCycle applet on it, and exit Navigator. If you watch the console closely, you'll see LiveCycle's "destroy" message just before the console itself disappears. In general, browsers will try to keep applets around (at least in their stopped state) as long as they can. When the browser's memory is full or the user exits the browser, the applet's resources are released. Just before the browser destroys the applet's memory, it calls destroy(). Use destroy() to release any resources your applet may have acquired.

If you're experienced in C++, you may be puzzled by Java's lack of a destructor. Java relies on garbage collection—you don't have to explicitly delete objects. Nevertheless, your C++ habits will stand you in good stead—most programmers prefer to release resources as soon as they know they're done with them. The code you put into destroy() should therefore resemble code you might write in a C++ destructor: look through your constructor and init() code, identify any resources (such as object references) you acquired, and release them. If your applet acquired other resources during its lifetime (such as nodes on a linked list) release them by setting the references to null.

Outside of applets, you get the same effect by writing a finalize() method. The garbage collector calls an object's finalize() method just before the object's memory is reclaimed. You can use finalize() to dispose of system resources or perform other cleanup.

PART

II

The Java Language

Understanding Java Data Types and Operators

Find out what numbers you can—and can't—store in Java's numeric classes

Learn how to build and populate collections of items—called arrays—in a single line of code

Find out how memory management in Java differs from the technique used in C++ and why Java's approach is better

Primitive Data Types

Java is an object-oriented language. As we saw in Chapter 3, "Getting Started Fast," every bit of code and every variable is kept inside a class, and classes are the templates for object instances. Almost everything in Java is an object. This section describes those few data types that separate "everything" from "almost everything."

The term "data types" refers to various ways of storing information in the computer. For example, if you had a medical application, you might need a type for the concept of "medication." The medication type—let's call it TMedication to follow the naming conventions we adopted in Chapter 3—might include data members such as:

- Manufacturer's name for this medication
- Manufacturer
- Generic name
- Strength (for example, 100 mg)
- Packaging (for example, caplet, syringe, eye drop)

Some of these members may be classes themselves. For example, there's probably a TManufacturer class that holds information about the manufacturer's name and address.

Some of the members are instances of classes that are built into Java. For example, Java supports a String class; we might use that class to store the names of the medication.

Eventually, though, all of our classes come down to *primitive types*—those data types that the Java compiler understands without having to be shown the internal structure. For example, a medication's strength might be represented by the TStrength class, but TStrength may contain a numeric strength and a String strength unit. Figure 4.1 illustrates how these primitive types are used by TStrength and TMedication.

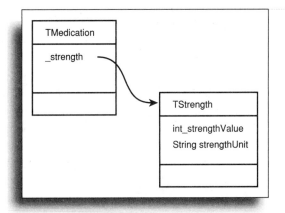

FIGURE **4.1**

All classes eventually are built out of primitive types.

This section describes the eight primitive types supported by the Java language.

- `byte`
- `short`
- `int`
- `long`
- `float`
- `double`
- `char`
- `boolean`

The first four types—`byte`, `short`, `int`, and `long`—are used to represent integers of various sizes. The next two, `float` and `double`, are used for floating point numbers. The `char` type is used for characters, and `boolean` is a simple true-false container.

SEE ALSO

➤ *To get a shorter overview of the primitive data types, see page 716*

Working with Integers

Integers are the foundation of computer arithmetic. Use integers to represent whole numbers—numbers that have no fractional part. (Later in this section we'll explore floating-point numbers, which are used to store numbers with fractional parts.)

Declaring an Integer Variable

To make an integer variable you do two things: first, decide on the maximum and minimum size you ever want that number to be. Second, declare the integer by giving it a name. Table 1.1 (in Chapter 1, "What Is Java and Why Is It Important?") listed the maximum and minimum sizes supported by Java's primitive types. A portion of that table appears in Table 4.1 for your reference.

TABLE 4.1   **Java integer types**

Type	Minimum Negative Value	Maximum Negative Value	Minimum Positive Value	Maximum Positive Value
byte	-128	-1	0	127
short	-32, 768	-1	0	32, 767
int	-2, 147, 483, 648	-1	0	2, 147, 483, 647
long	-9, 223, 372, 036, 854, 755, 808	-1	0	9, 223, 372, 036, 854, 775, 807

What happened to unsigned numbers?

If you've written C or C++, you're familiar with signed and unsigned integer types. You also know that these differences were often a source of error. That distinction is gone in Java—every Java integer type is signed.

For example, suppose you want to have a counter that runs from 1 to 100. That range fits nicely inside byte. Let's give it the name aCounter to follow the naming conventions introduced in the "Building Your First Application" section of Chapter 3. To bring this counter into existence, you write

```
byte aCounter;
```

New programmers often wonder, "If you're not sure how large or small a number might be, why not just declare everything long?" The answer is that the various integer types are actually storage sizes. A byte is eight bits—it can store 28 or 256 possible values. The Java designers split this range almost evenly—there are 128 possible negative values, 127 positive values, and zero, for a total of 256 values.

A short is two bytes, or 16 bits, an int is four bytes, and a long is eight bytes. While you can store a whopping 2^{64} or 1.8×10^{19} different values in a long, you'll use up memory eight times faster than if you used a byte.

If you're an experienced C or C++ programmer, you may be wondering why we didn't initialize aCounter. That's because Java, unlike C and C++, always initializes every primitive type. Integers are initialized to zero.

Checking for Overflow

In other languages (such as C and C++) the maximum number that can be stored in a particular type varies from one machine to the next. The designers of Java standardized on the sizes given in Table 4.1, making it easier for you to check for overflow and underflow.

Here's the sort of thing that can go wrong. Suppose you've written

```
byte myByte = 127;
myByte += 1;
System.out.println("The value of myByte is " + myByte +
".\n");
```

What value will be reported for myByte? If you guessed –128 you're right—127 is the maximum positive value for a byte, so adding one to it rolls it over to the minimum negative value. This phenomenon is known as integer overflow, and it occurs in virtually all programming languages. (The mirror image of overflow is underflow: –128 – 1 = 127.)

The best defense against overflow and underflow is to think about your code. Ask yourself, "What assumptions have I made about the input to this method? Could those assumptions ever be violated?" Be particularly careful about overflow in intermediate results. For example, suppose you wrote

```
short theFirstNumber = 1000;
short theSecondNumber = 1000;
short theProduct = (theFirstNumber * theSecondNumber) /
➡1000;
```

This code won't behave as you expect. The product of theFirstInt and theSecondInt is 1,000,000, but it overflows the short and produces 16,960. After integer arithmetic, the final value in theProduct is 16, not 1,000.

Arbitrarily large integers

JDK 1.1 added a new class—BigInteger—that can support integers of any size. The operations are more complex, so you trade speed for precision, but it's nice to know it's available if you need it.

Don't rely on Java's overflow detector

It's nice that Java looks out for you, but don't assume the compiler is as smart as you are—check your routines for possible overflow and underflow.

Java tries to detect opportunities for overflow. For example, it will recognize that `theFirstNumber * theSecondNumber` gives a result that may be greater than a `short`, and will require you to explicitly cast the resulting `integer` back to a `short` if you want to proceed.

Suppose that you received `theFirstNumber` and `theSecondNumber` as parameters, instead of setting them yourself. You might expect the programmer (or user) who calls your method to ensure "reasonable" values such as 100 and 100. Try to make your code bulletproof—perform a "reasonableness" check on the values passed to you, and throw an exception if you're not prepared to handle the numbers. You can learn more about exceptions, Java's method for handling errors, in Chapter 10, "Simplifying Code with Exceptions."

Checking for Integer Division

You'll note in the example just given that 16,960 divided by 1,000 gave 16, not 16.960. When you perform operations on two integers, the result is an integer. Since integers don't have a fractional part, the fraction (0.960) is discarded.

If you're not used to this behavior, watch out. It can lead to unexpected results. For example, 10 * (9/10) is 0, not 9. The result of integer 9 divided by integer 10 is zero, so 10 * 0 yields zero.

Watch Out for Divide-By-Zero Exceptions

If your program has the misfortune of dividing by zero, the program will throw an `ArithmeticException` at runtime, leaving the user to deal with the mess. The user will see something like this on the Java console or command prompt window.

```
java.lang.ArithmeticException: / by zero
    at Test.main (Test.java:19)
```

Either design your program so that divide-by-zero errors cannot occur, or catch `ArithmeticException` and deal with it in a responsible manner. (We'll deal with exceptions in depth in Chapter 10.)

Operators

Java supports eight kinds of operators for integer numbers.

- assignment operators
- comparison operators
- unary sign operators
- addition, subtraction, multiplication, and division operators
- increment and decrement operators
- bitwise shift operators
- the bitwise logical negation operator
- bitwise AND, OR, and XOR operators

The equality and comparison operators always produce a boolean result (`true` or `false`). The other binary operators return either an `int` or a `long` (never a `byte` or a `short`). If either of the two operands is a `long`, the result is a `long`. If the result of applying the operator would overflow an `int`, the result is converted to a `long`. Otherwise the operators return an `int`.

Assignment Operators

First, there are five assignment operators. These operators follow the pattern

```
LHS op RHS;
```

where *LHS* refers to a variable on the left side, *RHS* refers to an expression that returns a value on the right side, and *op* is one of the following operators.

- `=`   For simple assignment; places the value in the right side into the variable on the left side
- `+=`   Adds the right side to the variable on the left side and stores the result in the variable
- `-=`   Subtracts the right side from the variable on the left side and stores the result in the variable
- `*=`   Multiplies the variable on the left side by the value on the right side and stores the result in the variable
- `/=`   Divides the variable on the left side by the value on the right side and stores the result in the variable

Thus, anInteger = 5; places the value 5 into anInteger, and
aNumber +=3; adds 3 to aNumber.

Comparison Operators

You can test for equality by using ==, and for inequality with !=.
Thus, if you write

```
short aFive = 5;
short aTwo = 2;
if (aFive == aTwo)
  System.out.println("Five equals two!\n");
else
  System.out.println("Five is not equal to two.\n");
```

you'll get the correct result. You can test relative values with <,
<=, >, and >= (which stand for "less than," "less than or equal to,"
"greater than," and "greater than or equal to" respectively).

Unary Sign Operators

You can change the sign of a value by using the – operator.
Thus, if aVariable contains 5, -aVariable is –5.

Addition, Subtraction, Multiplication, and Division Operators

You can do simple arithmetic in Java about like you'd expect. If
you write 5 + 3 you'll get 8. If aVariable contains 5 and you
write aVariable + 3 you'll still get 8. Subtraction (-), multiplication (*), and division (/) work the same way.

Note that you can combine arithmetic and assignment into one
operator, as shown earlier in this section in the comments on
assignment operators.

Increment and Decrement Operators

You can add or subtract one to a variable by using special increment and decrement operators. For example, if aVariable contains 5, executing aVariable++ returns 6, and changes the
contents of aVariable to 6. The decrement operator (--) works
the same way.

You can apply increment and decrement operators either before a variable (called prefix) or after a variable (called postfix). If you use the operator in the prefix position, the value of the variable is changed before the operator returns the value. If you place the operator in the postfix position, the value of the variable is returned, and then the operator is applied (to increment or decrement the variable). Thus, if aVariable contains 5,

```
aVariable--
```

returns 5, but

```
--aVariable
```

returns 4. In either case aVariable ends up with 4 as its value.

Bitwise Shift Operators

You can view any integer as a pattern of bits. Thus, the byte 74 (which is 0x4A in hexadecimal) is

```
0100 1010
```

in binary. If you apply an arithmetic shift operator (>>) to this byte, you'll shift the pattern a specified number of places to the right (and the sign bit will be copied to the right). Thus,

```
byte aByte = 0x41;
int anInt = aByte >> 1;
```

places 0010 0100 or 0x20 into anotherByte. You can avoid copying the sign bit by using the logical right-shift operator, >>>. If you write

```
byte aByte = -0x41;
int anInt = aByte >> 1;
```

you'll get –0x21, but

```
byte aByte = -0x41;
int anInt = aByte >>> 1;
```

yields 0x7FFFFFDF since a zero has been shifted into the integer's sign bit.

Left-shifts (<<) work the same way. There is, of course, no difference between the arithmetic and the logical left-shift, since there's no sign bit on the right end.

Note that shifting an integer to the left has the effect of multi-plying it by two, and shifting it to the right divides it by two.

You can combine shift and assignment operators. Thus,

```
anotherByte >>>= 3;
```

shifts the contents of `anotherByte` three places to the right, extending the sign bit as needed. Writing

```
byte aByte = 0x41;
aByte >>>= 1;
```

has the same effect as writing the somewhat longer

```
byte aByte = 0x41;
aByte = aByte >> 1;
```

Often, your meaning will be clearer by combining the shift and the assignment operators, and the compiler may be able to gen-erate tighter code.

The Bitwise Logical Negation Operator

You can complement every bit in an integer by using the tilde (~) operator. Thus, ~74 is 1011 0101, which is 0xB5, or −75. Remember that Java integers use the highest bit as a sign bit, so 0100 1010 is a positive number, but 1011 0101 is a negative number.

Bitwise AND, OR, and XOR Operators

The single-ampersand (&) and single vertical bar (¦) form bitwise AND and OR operators respectively. The AND of two bits is 1 if both bits are 1; the OR is 1 if at least one bit is one. Thus

```
     0110  1001
&    1111  0000
     0110  0000
```

while

```
     0110  1001
¦    1111  0000
     1111  1001
```

The uparrow (^) provides the exclusive-OR or XOR operation. If two bits are XORed the result is 1 if and only if exactly one of the two bits was 1. Thus,

```
  0110 1001
^ 1111 0000
  1001 1001
```

You can combine an assignment operator with these bitwise operators. Thus,

```
aByte &= theMask;
```

places the result of the bitwise AND into aByte.

Floating Point Numbers

Floating point numbers are like piles of sand—whenever you move them you lose a little sand, and pick up a little dirt. The reason for this is that the computer stores the significant bits (called the *mantissa*) separately from the *exponent*. As you do arithmetic that changes the exponent, the significance of the bits in the mantissa changes. Bits that are insignificant in one step may show up as significant parts of the number later in the calculation.

Like integer types, the floating point types come in multiple sizes: float, which is stored in 32 bits, and double, which is stored in 64 bits. Table 4.2 shows the maximum and minimum sizes of these two types.

TABLE 4.2   **Java floating point types**

Type	Minimum Negative Value	Maximum Negative Value	Minimum Positive Value	Maximum Positive Value
float	-0.40282347 e+38	-1.40239846 e-45	1.40239846 e-45	3.40282347 e+38
double	-1.79769313 48623147e +308	-4.94065645 841246544e -324	4.94065645 841246544e -324	1.79769313 48623157e +308

Also like integers, floating point numbers are initialized to zero. Thus,

```
float myFloatingPointNumber;
```

produces a number with a defined value of zero.

Arbitrary-precision fixed-point numbers

Starting with JDK 1.1, the Java developers added a class for arbitrary-precison fixed-point numbers. It's called **BigDecimal**. Consider using this class in lieu of the primitive floating point types if you only need fixed-point precision.

Accumulating Errors

Unlike integers, operations on floating point numbers often produce unexpected results. Consider the code in Listing 4.1. You'd expect the result of adding 0.1 ten times to be equal to 1.0. Alas, remember the analogy of the piles of sand. After ten addition operations, some of the "dirt" in the mantissa has become significant—theSum is now 1.0000001.

LISTING 4.1   *FloatTest.java*–**This code doesn't produce the result you'd expect**

```
1  public class FloatTest
2  {
3    public static void main(String[] args)
4    {
5      float aOne = (float) 1.0;
6      float theSum = 0;
7      for (byte i=0; i<10; i++)
8        theSum = theSum + (float) 0.1;
9      if (aOne == theSum)
10       System.out.println("The numbers are the same: " + aOne +
         " and " + theSum + ".\n");
11     else
12       System.out.println("The numbers are different: " + aOne +
         " and " + theSum + ".\n");
13   }
14 }
```

If you must compare floating point numbers, you need to use the technique shown in Listing 4.2.

LISTING 4.2   *SafeFloatTest.java*–**This code takes pains to compare floating point numbers safely**

```
1  public class SafeFloatTest
2  {
3    final static float kDelta = (float) 0.00001;
```

```
4    public static boolean areEqual(float aFloat, float anotherFloat)
5    {
6      boolean theResult;
7      if (Math.abs(aFloat - anotherFloat) < kDelta)
8        theResult = true;
9      else
10       theResult = false;
11     return theResult;
12   }
13
14   public static void main(String[] args)
15   {
16     float aOne = (float) 1.0;
17     float theSum = 0;
18     for (byte i=0; i<10; i++)
19       theSum = theSum + (float) 0.1;
20     if (areEqual(theSum, aOne))
21       System.out.println("The numbers are the same: " + aOne +
         " and " + theSum + ".\n");
22     else
23       System.out.println("The numbers are different: " + aOne +
         " and " + theSum + ".\n");
24   }
25 }
```

Note that I wrote areEqual() with a single exit point—return theResult;. Most professional programmers prefer to write their routines with a single exit point—they're easier to debug that way. If I had written

```
if (Math.abs(aFloat - anotherFloat) < kDelta)
    return true;
  else
    return false;
```

I might have missed one of the returns later when I was maintaining this code. With a single return at the bottom, I'm sure to know where this method exits.

Often you need to use numbers that require only a few decimal places of precision. For example, dollars-and-cents calculations usually need only two decimal places. Consider storing these values in integers (for example, in whole cents). This technique allows you to avoid the problems of floating-point numbers and still maintain all the precision you need.

Where does abs() come from?

Note that abs() is a member of class java.lang.Math. Rather than use import, I elected to specify Math when I used abs() in areEqual().

Declaring Constants

Note that `SafeFloatTest` uses a Java idiom to declare a constant: by specifying that `kDelta` be `final static`, I've told the compiler that I don't intend to modify that value. If I were to attempt to modify `kDelta`, I would get a compile-time error (since `kDelta` is `final`). To make the constant available to all instances of the class (as well as to `main()`, which is `static`) I declare the constant to be `static`. You can use this idiom for any data type, not just `floats`.

All too frequently programmers insert specific numbers into a program. Then, when requirements change, they have to hunt down those numbers and change them. This procedure is time-consuming and error-prone—so much so that professional programmers deride the practice by calling these instances "magic numbers."

The solution is to declare constants (as `final static`). Use the constants wherever you would have used magic numbers. If you need to make a change, you only need to change the constant in one place.

Operators for Floating-Point Numbers

Floating-point numbers support five types of operators.

- assignment operators
- comparison operators
- unary sign operators
- addition, subtraction, multiplication, and division operators
- increment and decrement operators

The symbols for these operators are identical to the ones used for integers. The rules for combining types are similar to those used for integers. The result of a binary operation that involves at least one `double` is a `double`. In a binary operation with an integer the floating-point number retains its type. (Thus, a `float` plus a `short` is a `float`, and an `int` times a `double` is a `double`.) Binary operations that involve only `floats` return `float`.

Characters

If you're coming to Java from C or C++, the biggest change you may see in data types is in the char type. In C and C++, there is no byte type, and char is eight bits wide. Java has a perfectly good eight-bit type: byte. char is 16-bits wide (the same as a short) but is intended for use as a Unicode character.

Strictly speaking, char is an unsigned 16-bit type. The char type will support the same operators as integers, but if you find yourself using char for arithmetic there's probably a mistake in your design. Remember that mixing unsigned and signed quantities can lead to subtle defects in your code.

The default value for a char is \u0000, the Unicode version of zero.

SEE ALSO

➤ *To learn more about Unicode and the* char *type, see page 730*

Working with *booleans*

Most of us who've worked in C and C++ have made up our own Boolean type out of unsigned chars. In Java, we have a native Boolean type: boolean. By definition, a boolean occupies only a single bit of storage, and have a default value of false. You can apply ten operators to booleans.

- assignment (=)
- equality (==)
- inequality (!=)
- logical NOT (!) to reverse true to false and vice versa
- AND (either by & or by &&)
- OR (either by ¦ or by ¦¦)
- XOR (^)
- if-then-else (?:)

Recall from the discussion on integers that & and ¦ perform a bitwise AND and OR respectively. While the same operators work as logical AND and OR on booleans, it's easy to make a mistake and perform the bitwise operation when you want a logical operation. Avoid using the single-ampersand and single vertical bar forms of the `boolean` logical operators; use `&&` and `¦¦` exclusively when you're working with `boolean`s.

The `?:` is identical to the C and C++ conditional operator. For example,

```
(theCounter == 0) ? i++ : i—;
```

means the same thing as (but is more cryptic than)

```
if (theCounter == 0)
  i++;
else
  i—;
```

In nearly every case the longer form is clearer and compiles to the same code; you should usually choose the longer form.

In C and C++, it was possible to place executable statements inside the conditional portion of an `if` statement. For example, it was common to write

```
if (c=getc()) ...
```

In Java the expression inside the conditional must evaluate to a `boolean`. The old approach, relying on side effects, was of dubious value and led to cryptic code. I don't think we'll miss it.

More Complex Types

Primitive types have their uses, but for real work you'll want more complex types. For example, in C and C++ we used to cobble together strings out of `char` arrays. The characters in these "strings" had no idea that they were supposed to work together. It was common for programmers to accidently overflow the array and corrupt other variables.

Java gives us three ways to address these needs.

- Java arrays are indexed collections of similar items; they may contain primitive types, objects, or other arrays.

- The Java environment comes with a rich set of pre-built

classes, including a `String` class.

- You can build your own classes to implement special needs.

Understanding Arrays

Set up an array

1. Declare the array—specify what the array will contain, and give it a name.

2. Allocate memory—specify the capacity of the array.

3. Populate the array—place data in the "slots" of the array.

You can combine two or even all three of these steps into a single line of code.

Declaring the Array

Declaring an array is much like declaring a single-item variable. If you wanted a `short` variable named `theCounter` you would write

```
short theCounter;
```

If you want an array of `shorts` you could write

```
short theCounters[];
```

Allocating Memory

In general, you use `new` to allocate memory in Java. Thus, if you want an array of `shorts` named `theCounters` to have 100 elements, you can write

```
short theCounters[];
theCounters[] = new short[100];
```

You can combine these two statements into one:

```
short theCountes[] = new short[100];
```

You can also allocate memory implicitly; we'll see that technique when we discuss "Populating the Array," next.

Caution: Array Index Must be an
`int`

Array indexes must either be of type `int` or be able to be cast as an `int`, which means that the largest possible array has 2,147,483,647. In practice, most Java implementations will run out of memory long before you've allocated an array of that size.

Populating the Array

Once you have an array with some memory you can start setting elements. If you've already written

```
short theCounters[] = new short[100];
```

you can now write

```
theCounters[0] = 100;
theCounters[1] = 200;
```

and so forth.

You populate several elements at a time by surrounding them in curly braces. The statement

```
int aSetOfNumbers[1000] = {2, 4, 6, 8}
```

declares an array of `int`s, allocates memory for 1000 of them, and populates the first four elements (0 through 3). There are 997 unpopulated elements in this array.

For the ultimate in simplicity, you can declare an array, implicitly allocate memory, and populate its elements, all on one line.

```
float aSetOfFloats = {3.14159, 2.71828}
```

declares an array of `float`s, allocates enough memory for two elements, and populates those two elements.

Learning About Pre-Built Classes

One of the joys of using an object-oriented language is that you can reuse code that you or others have written. Sun has provided many classes for you to use as a starting point in your programs. In this section we'll look at the `String` class, as well as several classes written as "wrappers" for the primitive types.

String Class

Find the documentation on *String* class

1. Point your Web browser at the `index.html` page in your JDK folder and follow the link to the JDK documentation page. (Choose the link that says **local** if you've downloaded and installed the JDK documentation; otherwise follow the link to the JavaSoft site.)

2. Follow the link to **Java Platform API**, and then choose **Index**.

3. On the index page choose the letter **S**, and scroll all the way to the bottom of the page, where you'll see methods named `String()`. Your screen should resemble Figure 4.2. These are the `String()` constructors.

4. Next to each `String()` constructor you'll see a link to the **java.lang.String** class. Follow that link. You'll recognize this page (shown in Figure 4.3) as coming from `javadoc`.

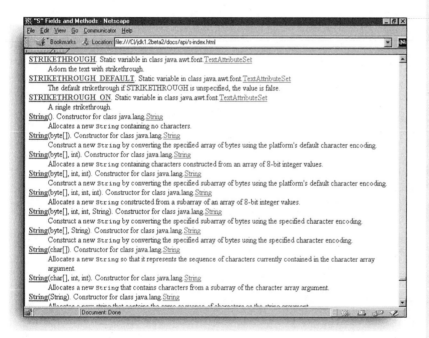

FIGURE 4.2
You can find any class in any package by searching for its constructors in the index.

Scroll down the page that describes the `String` class. You'll see a description of the class, followed by a list of the constructors available. Further on down the page you'll see a list of the methods available for this class. (See Figure 4.4.)

Based on the information you find in this documentation, you can now use `String`s in your programs. For example, Listing 4.3 shows a simple `String` and `Date` demonstration. This applet displays the current time (whenever `paint()` is called and compares it to the time the applet was started). This example introduces

the DateFormat class, a built-in class that converts Dates into formatted Strings. This applet has three sections: instance variable
declarations, init(), and paint().

FIGURE 4.3

Read about Sun's pre-built
classes in the JDK documentation.

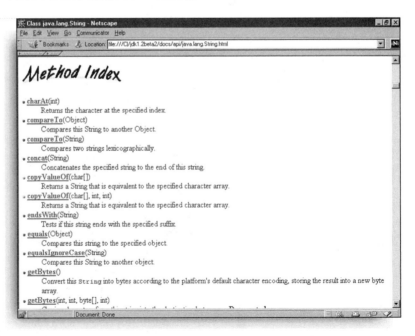

FIGURE 4.4

You need to know about a
class's methods in order to use
it in your program.

LISTING 4.3 *StringDemo.java*–Use built-in classes such as *String* to simplify your Java programs

```
1  import java.applet.Applet;
2  import java.awt.Graphics;
3  import java.util.Date;
4  import java.text.DateFormat;
5  import java.util.TimeZone;
6
7  public class StringDemo extends Applet
8  {
9    // declare the instance variables
10   private Date _startTime;
11   private DateFormat _formatter;
12   private String _startTimeString;
13
14   public void init()
15   {
16     _startTime = new Date();
17     _formatter = DateFormat.getTimeInstance(DateFormat.LONG);
18     _formatter.setTimeZone(TimeZone.getDefault());
19     _startTimeString = _formatter.format(_startTime);
20   }
21
22   public void paint(Graphics theGraphics)
23   {
24     Date theCurrentTime = new Date();
25     String theCurrentTimeString =
26                 _formatter.format(theCurrentTime);
27     String theMessage[] = {"This applet was started at " +
28                             _startTimeString + ".",
29                        "The time is now " +
30                        theCurrentTimeString + "."};
31     for (byte i=0; i<theMessage.length; i++)
32       theGraphics.drawString(theMessage[i], 0, 50+(15*i));
33   }
34 }
```

This class has three instance variables: a Date, a DateFormat, and a String. When init() runs, it makes a new Date—the default date and time is the current date and time. It then uses the DateFormat class's static "factory" method to make an instance of

DateFormat—this instance, named _formatter, is designed to display time only in the LONG format (which includes the seconds and the time zone). Then init() gets the default TimeZone of this computer and sets that TimeZone into _formatter. Finally init() uses _formatter to write the the formatted time string into _startTimeString.

Whenever paint() is called, it makes a new Date and uses the instance's DateFormat to format the current time. It uses string concatenation—the plus (+) operator—to build a two-line message (which is stored in an array). Finally, paint() steps through the array writing out the message.

Figure 4.5 shows the result of running StringDemo.

FIGURE 4.5

The StringDemo applet formats two Dates and displays them during paint().

Wrappers for Your Numbers

Recall that we opened the section "Primitive Data Types" with the words "Almost everything in Java is an object." It's that "almost" that sometimes causes problems—there are times when you wish your long, float, or boolean was a true object. Conveniently, the designers of Java anticipated your need, and have provided wrapper classes for the primitive types.

Recall from the section "Building Your First Application" in Chapter 3, that Java class names begin with a capital letter by convention. The wrapper classes for the primitive data types have the same name as the primitive type, but with the first letter capitalized. Thus, we could rewrite FloatTest (from Listing 4.1) as NewFloatTest (shown in Listing 4.4).

LISTING 4.4   *NewFloatTest.java*–The original *FloatTest* written with wrappers

```
 1  public class NewFloatTest
 2  {
 3    private final static Float _oneTenth = new Float(0.1);
 4    public static void main(String[] args)
 5    {
 6      Float aOne = new Float(1.0);
 7      Float theSum = new Float (0);
 8      for (byte i=0; i<10; i++)
 9        theSum = new Float(theSum.floatValue() + _oneTenth.
    floatValue());
10      if (aOne.equals(theSum))
11        System.out.println("The numbers are the same: " + aOne +
    " and " + theSum + ".\n");
12      else
13        System.out.println("The numbers are different: " + aOne
    + " and " + theSum + ".\n");
14    }
15  }
```

There are two advantages to using object wrappers instead of primitive types. First, when we pass an object to a method, the method is able to work on the object itself. (You may know this technique as *call by reference*. When you pass a primitive type Java uses *call by value*—the receiving method gets the value of the number, but cannot change it.

Second, you can derive your own classes from Java's built-in wrapper classes. If you have a unit that must be accurate to the nearest thousandths place, you can write a class that accepts a delta (similar to SafeFloatTest.java in Listing 4.2) of, say, 0.0001.

We're not taking advantage of either of these features in NewFloatTest.java—this program simply illustrates how to use Float instead of float.

Building Your Own Classes

In Chapter 7, "Object-Oriented Analysis: A New Way of Looking at Software," and Chapter 8, "Object-Oriented Design and Programming," we'll look at the process by which you develop your own classes. In this section we summarize that process, concentrating on the structure of a class.

- Identify the messages the class must be able to receive.
- Identify the information the class must remember.
- Decide where the class fits into the class hierarchy.
- Design and write methods that implement your required messages.

Methods

Suppose that we're designing an application for use by hospital nurses who are required to give medication doses to patients. Along the way, we decide to build a class called TPatient. What must we be able to "say" to TPatient? Here are two of the messages.

- Ask the patient object which medications are due at this time—this message returns a list of TMedications.
- Ask the patient to take a dose—this message returns a TDosingResult.

Suppose the nurse is making his or her medication rounds and comes to the bedside of patient Sarah Jones. She enters Ms. Jones's patient ID—possibly by scanning a barcode on the patient's wristband, or selecting the patient's name from a list on the screen. The application sends a message to the Ms. Jones's instance of TPatient.

```
TMedicationList theList = new TMedicationList;
theList = thePatient.getMedicationList(theCurrentTime);
```

The getMedicationList() method takes the current time as a parameter, and returns a list of all the medications that Ms. Jones should receive at this time. This list is displayed to the user—we'll address user interfaces starting in Chapter 11, "Building the User Interface with the AWT." Once the nurse has retrieved the medications from the medication cart, she offers them to the patient. Hopefully the patient takes all of her doses, but it's possible that there's a different outcome. For example:

- The nurse might accidentally drop the dose.

- The nurse may exercise his or her professional judgment and determine that the dose shouldn't be given.

- The patient might refuse one or more doses.

- The patient may vomit immediately after taking the dose.

As designers we'll record the fact that the nurse attempted to give the dose by sending

```
TDosingResult theDosingResult = new TDosingResult();
theDosingResult = thePatient.setDosingEvent(theMedication,
➥theCurrentTime);
```

The class `TDosingResult` is used to capture the range of possible outcomes of an attempted dosing event.

Data Members

What does an instance of `TPatient` need to know in order to respond to its messages? In order to respond to `getMedicationList()` it needs a list of medication orders. Figure 4.6 illustrates this design. Each order should contain a dosing schedule—for example, the physician may have ordered diphenhydramine 50 mg q4d, which means that the medication should be given four times a day. In most hospitals the dosing intervals are 8 a.m., 12 noon, 4 p.m., and 8 p.m., and the doses may be given up to an hour early or an hour late. Thus, if the program asks the patient for a list of medications due at 11 a.m., `TPatient`' `getMedicationList()` method would examine the collection of medication orders, selecting those medications due during the noon dosing interval. The medications from those orders would then be assembled into a `TMedicationList` and returned to the calling program.

Once the nurse has attempted to give the dose and has recorded the results by using the user interface, the system needs to communicate that information to the current `TPatient` object by using its `setDosingEvent()` method. This method, in turn, can store `TDosingEvents` in a collection such as a list. As designers, we need to go on to design `TDosingEvent`—we'll need to find out from nurses and pharmacists what information to capture. For the purposes of `TPatient`, it's enough to know that we need a collection of TDosingEvents. As we think about how this collection will be used, we can decide on exactly which collection type to choose. For example, if we want to be able to get to any specific dosing event quickly, we might choose an indexed structure such as a hashtable. If dosing events are typically accessed sequentially, we might use a linked list. In practice, we'll often want to write this information to a database. Java includes a database interface called JDBC (Java Database Connectivity) that allows you to read and write from commercial database managers.

FIGURE 4.6

In order to implement TPatient.getMedica-tionList() your design contains a list of TMedica-tionOrders.

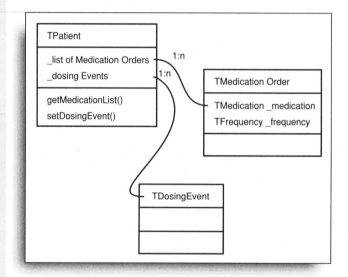

Placing a Class into the Hierarchy

Chances are that TPatient is not the only person in our system. We may want to collect information about other people in the hospital—our finished system may include TNurse, TPhysician, and TPharmacist. Likewise we may decide that certain patients have special medication requirements not covered by TPatient, so we could derive more specific classes from TPatient. Figure 4.7 illustrates a class hierarchy into which TPatient might fit.

In an object-oriented language such as Java, a class is said to inherit methods and data members from its parent. For example, if TPerson has a getID() method, TPatient has it too. If we're happy with TPerson's version of getID(), we don't have to write any new code—we can just use the inherited method. If we need to do something special in TPatient, we're still free to call the parent's method as part of our implementation.

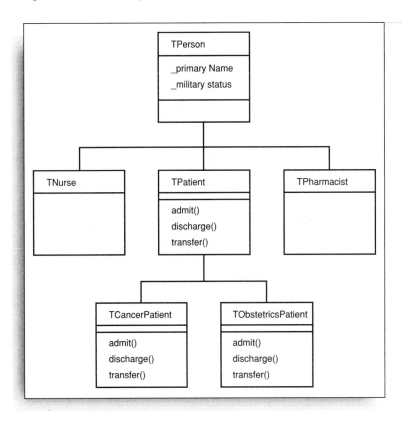

Designing and Writing Methods

In the course of writing methods we will identify data members and other methods that we need to use in our class. Many of these members will be for our use only—we wouldn't want others outside our class to know about them or be able to access them. For each data member or method we can include an access specifier.

Java supports three access specifiers.

- `public` Access is allowed from any object
- `protected` Access is allowed by any instance of the class, any descendant, and any other class in this package
- `private` Access is allowed only by instances of the class

If you don't specify an access specifier, access is allowed by any class in the package.

In the course of designing your classes, you may also identify messages that you want to send to the class as a whole. For example, a hospital administration class might want to ask TPatient, "How many patients are there?" You might meet that need by adding a static data member short _census. (Hospitals call the number of patients the census.) The TPatient constructor could then increment _census. A discharge method in TPatient would be responsible for decrementing _census. You could then give users of the TPatient class read-only access to the daily census through an access method, getCensus() which would simply return _census.

Restrict access to data members

In general, you should make your class's data members private, and provide public access functions (get... and set...) so users of your class can get to selected data members.

You don't have to provide external access to all of your data members—only the ones that other classes will really need.

Initializing an Instance

You may want to initialize the data members in your class constructor. You may also need to initialize data members that you inherit from the parent class. In Java code the parent class is called super. Thus, when a patient is admitted the system would make a new TPatient by calling a constructor such as this one.

```
TPatient(int theID, String theName, String theRoom)
{
    super._ID = theID;
    super._name = theName;
    _room = theRoom;
    ...
}
```

Understanding *this*

Just as super refers to the current class's parent class, this refers to the current object itself. You can use this to accomplish three goals.

- Code in which fields and methods are explicitly shown as belonging to this may be clearer. For example, writing

```
super.ID = theID;
super.name = theName;
this.room = theRoom;
```

makes it clear that you didn't just forget super in the third line.

- You can use this to disambiguate two variables (for example, a class variable and a local variable) of the same name. Of course, if you're following the naming conventions used in this book, you won't have any of these naming conflicts.

- You can now pass the current object to a method.

Memory Management

In many languages (including both C and C++) the programmer can allocate memory either on the *stack* or on the *heap*. (These two memory pools are described later in this section.) In those older languages, the programmer had to explicitly allocate and deallocate memory for each object. For example, a C++ programmer might write

```
TPatient* theCurrentPatient = new TPatient("12554J", "Jones,
➡Sarah");

. . .

delete theCurrentPatient;
```

In this bit of code, the programmer has allocated a chunk of memory big enough to hold one instance of the TPatient class. The program goes on to use that object; when it's done, the programmer must explicitly delete the object, freeing the memory. If the programmer forgets to call delete, the object will remain in memory forever. If the programmer makes this mistake too often, all of memory can be exhausted and the program will crash.

By just declaring the object, the C or C++ programmer gets space on the stack. For example,

```
TPatient theCurrentPatient;
```

reserves a chunk of memory big enough for one TPatient on the stack. In general, stack memory is deallocated automatically when the routine in which it was allocated is done. (C and C++ programmers say the variable goes "out of scope.")

The Java compiler insists on knowing the exact size and location of anything that it puts on the stack. In practice, this means that objects are allocated from the heap, while object references are kept on the stack.

Understanding the Stack

The stack is a memory pool that grows from one end of memory toward the other. When a programmer calls a function or method, the calling routine places the parameters on the stack and transfers control to the new routine. The new routine reads its parameters from the stack. It can also allocate new variables on the stack. When the called routine is done, the return value is placed on the stack. In Figure 4.8, the method is returning a floating point value. Finally, the system restores the stack pointer to the position it had before the function or method was called, releasing the memory on the stack. (Figure 4.8 illustrates this process.)

FIGURE 4.8

The stack pointer moves up when you pass parameters or allocate local variables on the stack.

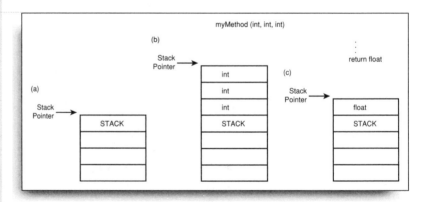

The Java interpreter uses the stack mainly for its own variables. Nearly everything you allocate will go on the heap.

Understanding the Heap

The heap occupies the opposite end of memory from the stack, as illustrated in Figure 4.9. Unlike the stack, the heap is allocated and deallocated in chunks that have nothing to do with function calls. In C++ and Java, you allocate an object on the heap by using the `new` operator. In C++, you deallocate the object by using `delete`. In Java, you never need to deallocate the object—that work is done by the garbage collector, described later in this section.

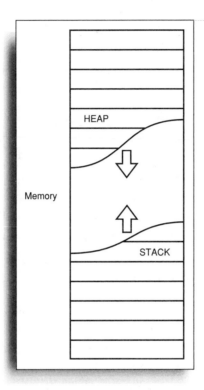

FIGURE **4.9**

If the stack and the heap ever collide, your program will crash or your variables will be corrupted.

Understanding Java Memory Management

If you know C or C++, you're used to thinking about pointer variables that reference the memory on the heap. In the example

```
TPatient* theCurrentPatient = new TPatient("12554J", "Jones,
➥Sarah");
```

`theCurrentPatient` is actually a pointer to the chunk of memory on the heap. Java works the same way, but you don't need the asterisk (*) since everything (except primitive types) is a pointer. The terminology changes, too—Java calls these variables references instead of pointers.

Thus, in Java, you can write

```
TPatient theCurrentPatient;
```

to get a reference to a TPatient. You can then allocate memory (on the heap) by writing

```
theCurrentPatient = new TPatient("12554J", "Jones, Sarah");
```

Of course, usually you'll decide to put the two lines together.

```
TPatient theCurrentPatient = new TPatient("12554J", "Jones,
Sarah");
```

Java's Garbage Collector

Since Java has no delete operator, you may be wondering why Java references don't leak memory. The answer is the Java has a *garbage collector*. Periodically the Java runtime software will go through memory looking for objects on the heap that no one references. It will then mark that memory as free, so that it rejoins the pool of available heap memory.

For the most part, garbage collectors are a blessing. Studies find that programmers often get confused about when to safely release memory. C and C++ programmers often deallocate the memory that a pointer is pointing to, and then use the pointer as though the memory were still available. This mistake leads to subtle defects—in a lightly-loaded development environment the freed memory often still contains the object, so the code runs successfully. When the software goes into production (with many more users or processes loading memory) the deallocated memory is swiftly used again. When a program attempts to read from deallocated memory it gets corrupt data. If it uses the invalid pointer to write to memory, the program corrupts other variables.

The problem with garbage collectors is that you cannot always predict when they will run. When the garbage collector is running, the system may be momentarily unavailable. In a *realtime system* in which fractions of a second matter, a garbage collector may run at an inopportune moment, critically changing the behavior of the system. The good news is that memory is inexpensive and most systems don't have such critical timing needs.

The better news is that you can help the garbage collector along by explicitly setting variables to null when you're done with them. Then force the garbage collector to run when you want it to run, rather than waiting for it to run when the system is low on memory.

Defining a Cleanup Routine

Experienced C++ programmers are used to writing destructor routines that deallocate components allocated in the constructor (or during the life of the object). For example, suppose that you have a C++ constructor like the following:

```
TPatient(char* thePatientID, char* thePatientName) :
TPerson(thePatientID, thePatientName)
{
  fMedicationList = new TMedicationList();
  fDoseEventList = new TDoseEventList();
  ...
}
```

In C++, when you deallocate this object in the destructor you must release the memory associated with fMedicationList and fDoseEventList.

```
~TPatient()
{
  delete fMedicationList;
  delete fDoseEventList;
}
```

The destructors for those two lists would, in turn, release all of the list nodes.

While you don't write destructors in Java, it's good practice to write a cleanup routine that does the same thing. For example, you could write

```
cleanup()
{
  _medicationList.cleanup();
  _medicationList = null;
  _doseEventList.cleanup();
  _doseEventList = null;
}
```

Cleaning Up in the *finalize()* Method

When the garbage collector runs, it gives your class one last chance to clean up, by calling your class's finalize() method. If you've defined finalize(), it will be called just before your object is deleted. If you haven't defined a cleanup routine, you should do any necessary cleanup here. If you have defined a cleanup routine, you can just check to see if it needs to be called, as shown in the following code fragment.

```
public class CleanableObject
{
  private boolean _dirty;
  CleanableObject()
  {
    ...
    _dirty = true;
  }
  public void cleanup()
  {
    ...
    _dirty = false;
  }
  protected void finalize()
  {
    if (_dirty)
      this.cleanup();
  }
}
```

In this example, dirty keeps track of whether the object needs to be cleaned up or not. When the object is first brought into existence (by a constructor) the _dirty bit is set. If cleanup() is called, the _dirty bit is cleared. When the garbage collector runs, it calls finalize(), which checks the status of _dirty and calls cleanup() if needed.

When you use exceptions, you get to list the error conditions your program handles (in a catch block). You can also specify a finally clause; just before your exception-handler exits, it runs the code in finally. It's good programming practice to close files and sockets in the finally clause. Use this opportunity to set any references you won't be needing again back to `null`. We'll look at exceptions in detail in Chapter 10.

SEE ALSO

➤ *To learn about sockets (part of Java's mechanism for communicating over the network), see page 516*

CHAPTER 5

Using Branches and Loops

Find out how to safely add branching statements such as *if* and *switch* to your code

See how to redirect the flow of control in your program by using a variety of jump statements

Learn how to get out of a loop safely when you need to recover from an error

Learn three ways to insert a loop—and find out when you should use each one

Branching Statements

If you take your finger and run it down your program's design, you'll inevitably come to a place where you determine that the flow of control should go one way under one set of circumstances and another way under a different set of circumstances. In Java, and most other languages, you'll usually implement this logic with an `if` or `if-else`. In some cases you may find it clearer to express what you want with a `switch` statement.

Often, once you've made your decision and the program logic has branched, you'll need to transfer control to someplace else in the program. Many years ago you might have used a `goto` statement to accomplish that goal; most professional programmers today avoid `goto` because it tends to make programs more difficult to read and debug. (When a professional programmer wants to insult code with convoluted control statements such as `goto`, he or she will frequently call it "spaghetti code.") Java doesn't even have the `goto` statement. You can accomplish the same object more safely using the Java statements `break`, `continue`, `return`, or `throw`.

if and *if-else* Statements

In Java you can write

```
if (some-boolean-conditions)
   ...
```

Unlike C and C++, where the condition may return an `int`, Java requires that the condition evaluate to a `boolean`. This change is not arbitrary—it prevents the programmer from making certain common mistakes. For example, in C or C++ you can write

```
if (myVariable = true)
   ...
```

While at first glance this code may appear to be correct, closer inspection of the condition reveals that this is an assignment statement, not a check for equality (which takes the double-equals operator, `==`). This program will cheerfully assign `true` to `myVariable`. Since the assignment succeeds, the branch is taken.

That's not what the programmer intended!

Like most languages, Java also supports `if-else`:

```
if (some-boolean-condition)
  ...
else
  ...
```

If you want to perform more than one statement in either the `if` or the `else` clause, you must use a compound statement—one surrounded by curly braces. Thus, you might write:

```
if (theCurrentPatient.hasPRNDoses())
{
  // determine if the patient needs a PRN dose
  ...
}
```

(PRN doses are doses given only if needed.)

Building Safe *if* Statements

Branches add paths to the code; they therefore increase complexity, decrease maintainability, and increase testing costs. You should be careful when you use `if` statements to avoid introducing a defect into the code. As you code, mentally keep track of the growing complexity of your code. McCabe's Cyclomatic Complexity Metric is one good measure of complexity. This metric measures the number of different paths the program might take as it passes through your code.

SEE ALSO

➤ *To learn how to measure code complexity and compute McCabe's Cyclomatic Complexity Metric, see page 662*

Often, as you design the product, you'll find that some set of circumstances comes about, say 80 percent of the time, and variants occur the remaining 20 percent of the time. Write the usual, or nominal, case first. Make sure the logic for the nominal case is clear. Then add the variant cases, being careful not to obscure the meaning of the code.

Mentally recompute McCabe's metric every time you add a branch. As the metric climbs past 5, begin to think of ways to break the method into simpler parts. Often you'll want to write a private or protected method and call it from inside the public method. Try to avoid having any single method in which the McCabe's metric is much greater than 10.

Testing Your *if* Statements

Often your if conditions will involve numeric comparison. Suppose you've written

```
if (theTestVariable > kLimit)
    . . .
```

Are you sure that test should be > and not >= or <? Walk through that code on your desk to make sure that the boundary case (theTestVariable == kLimit) is handled correctly. Test when theTestVariable is one greater than kLimit, and when it's one less. Once you're satisfied that your design is right, check the actual code, single-stepping the method by using the debugger. Finally, make sure these three test cases appear in the product test plan, so that any errors introduced later are caught.

SEE ALSO

➤ *For more about* jdb, *the Java debugger, see page 449*

➤ *To learn more about test plans, see page 438*

While you're testing the if condition, check the logic of both the if and the else clauses. Occasionally, programmers get them backwards or get so focused on the if clause that they miss an error on the else side of the statement.

Replace chains of if-else with one switch statement

Long chains of if-else statements are prone to error and are difficult to read and maintain. If you find yourself writing such chains, consider replacing them with one switch statement.

Choosing Between the *if* Statement and the Conditional Operator

Like C and C++, Java supports a conditional operator: :?. You can write

```
(theTestVariable > kLimit): doThis() ? doThat();
```

If the Boolean condition is true, this statement will call doThis(). Otherwise, doThat() will execute. This code is logically identical with this if statement

```
if (theTestVariable > kLimit)
    doThis();
else
    doThat();
```

Which one should you choose? The Java compiler will turn both forms into the same bytecodes, so there's no performance advantage to either style. In most cases the longer form (`if-else`) is clearer. I recommend that you always go with the form that makes your intent clearest.

The *switch* Statement

Suppose you want to transfer control to one of several paths, depending upon which set of circumstances exists. You could write

```java
if (test-condition-1)
{
  doThis();
  ...
}
else if (test-condition-2)
{
  doThat();
  ...
}
else if (test-condition-3)
{
  doSomethingElse();
  ...
}
```

but that code might be diffult to read and maintain. If you can design your code so that the test condition is represented by a single integer, you can write

```java
switch (theTestCondition)
{
  case 0:
    doThis();
    ...
    break;
  case 1:
    doThat();
    ...
    break;
  case 2:
```

```
        doSomethingElse();
        ...
        break;
    default:
        doTheDefaultThing();
}
```

When the flow of control reaches the switch statement, the test condition is evaluated. If the resulting integer matches one of the case statements inside the switch, control passes to the first statement in that case and continues until it hits a break statement. (The break statement transfers control back outside the switch.)

If none of the case statements match the integer test condition, control transfers to the default case.

Building Safe *switch* Statements

Using switch statements instead of nested if statements can improve the readability of your code, but there are plenty of opportunities to make a mistake. Here are some tips to increase the likelihood of your switch statements working correctly.

- Put the case statements in an order that make sense. Order the cases by likelihood—put the most common case first. If nothing else makes sense, use numeric order.

- Use symbolic constants instead of numbers, like the following:
```
switch (theUserResponse)
{
  case kFile:
    ...
    break;
  case kEdit:
    ...
    break;
  case kView:
    ...
    break;
  ...
  default:
    ...
}
```

- Remember that, from the perspective of McCabe's metric, switch statements add considerable complexity in just a few lines. Limit your case actions to straight-line code, even if you have to call a private or protected method to do it.

- Don't forget your break statements. If you do, control will fall through from one case to the next. If you intentionally allow this to happen, include a comment to that effect.

- Use the default case to handle legitimate defaults.

- If there is no legitimate default, throw an exception in the default case.

SEE ALSO
➤ *For more discussion about throwing exceptions, see page 245*

Testing Your *switch* Statements

You should plan at least one test case for each path identified by McCabe's metric. McCabe's Cyclomatic Complexity Metric adds 1 for every case in a switch statement, plus 1 for the default case.

Jump Statements

Java provides four ways for you to transfer control from one place in your program to another. Although these statements don't branch in and of themselves, you'll often want to use them in connection with a branching statement such as an if or switch, or a looping statement such as while or for. These four jump statements are:

- break
- continue
- return
- throw

Leaving a Loop with *break*

We've already seen one use of the break statement—it breaks you out of a case action in a switch statement. You can also use break to get out of a loop. (We'll talk about loops in the next section, "Iteration Statements.")

For example, you can write

```
for (int i=0; i<1000; i++)
{
  ...
  if (isFinished() == true)
    break;
}
```

This loop will run for 1000 iterations, unless isFinished() becomes true. If isFinished() returns true, control passes to the break statement and then out of the loop to the first executable statement after the closing brace of the loop.

It's possible to set up labels in your code and use break as a goto *label*. Most professional programmers avoid this practice—it contributes to errors and decreases your code's readability. If you're an experienced programmer and have decided that you really, really need a goto just this once, you can write

```
someLabel:
  ...
  break someLabel;
```

Please don't tell anybody where you learned this!

Skipping the Rest of a Loop with *continue*

Sometimes you'll be deep inside a loop and you'll write code that determines that it can skip the rest of this iteration. Just pass control to a continue statement. The program will bypass the rest of that iteration and go on with the next. For example, you might write

```
for (int i=0; i<1000; i++)
{
  ...
  if (isNotThereYet() == true)
    continue;
  ...
}
```

If isNotThereYet() returns false, control continues to the rest of the loop. If isNotThereYet() is true, control passes to continue and then back to the top of the loop. The continue statement allows you to bypass everything inside the loop that appears after the continue itself, but the loop keeps running with the next iteration.

Like break, continue can take a label. If you use a labeled continue, control will pass to the statement associated with that label. Again, this practice is permitted by the compiler, but is avoided by most programmers.

Exiting a Method with *return*

Inside a method, constructor, or static initializer you can call return. Control will return to the place that called the method, constructor, or static initializer.

If you're writing a method that has a non-void return type, you must give the method something to return. For example, you can write

```
public boolean hasPRN()
{
  boolean theResult;
  ...
    theResult = false;
  ...
      theResult = true;
  return theResult;
}
```

In the course of executing hasPRN(), theResult (which is initially false) will be explicitly set to either true or false. At the end of the method, return returns theResult.

Managing Exceptional Conditions with *throw*

In many programming languages you're obliged to check for errors after every function call. Your code ends up looking like the following:

```
int theStatusCode = doSomething();
if (theStatusCode != 0)
  handleErrorFromDoSomething();
else
{
```

Have only one return **per method, and put it at the end**

It's certainly possible to sprinkle return statements throughout your method, but doing so will make your code more difficult to debug. For best results, define a local variable to hold the result, set the result in the method, and return that result at the end. That way, if you decide you want to execute some statement (such as a debug statement) just before the method exits, you don't have to hunt around for all of the return statements—you know there's only one, and it's at the end of the method.

```
    theStatusCode = doSomethingElse();
    if (theStatusCode != 0)
      handleErrorFrom DoSomethingElse();
    else
      ...
}
```

This code fragment is complex and error-prone. This style of coding forces the programmer to think about errors (many of which may be rare) while he or she should be thinking about the nominal path through the code. In practice many programmers write the nominal case first, ignoring errors, like the following:

```
doSomething();
doSomethingElse();
```

They promise themselves that they'll go in and add error-handling code before they ship the product, but in the press to get the product out the door, sometimes they don't put enough error-checking in, and they ship a defect.

Modern programming languages such as Java allow you to handle errors as exceptions. You can write

```
try
{
  doSomething();
  doSomethingElse();
}
catch (OneKindOfException theException)
{
  doSomethingAboutThisException();
  ...
}
catch (AnotherKindOfException theException)
{
  doSomethingAboutThisDifferentException();
  ...
}
catch (Exception theException)
{
  handleThisGeneralException();
  ...
}
```

Exceptions are objects, and they form a hierarchy like objects from other classes. Thus, when you're still working out your program logic you may choose to write

```
try
{
  doSomething();
  doSomethingElse();
}
catch (Exception theException)
{
  System.out.println("Exception: " + theException + ".\n");
}
```

As you finish this product, you'll want to add more `catch` clauses to handle more exceptions. But if you forget one, you can be sure the general `Exception` handler will at least print out the error.

The way to set one of these `catch` clauses in motion is to `throw` an exception. The general syntax is

```
void someMethod() throws SomeException
{
  ...
  if (someErrorCondition)
    throw new SomeException;
}
```

where `SomeException` is a throwable exception you've defined elsewhere.

Note that it's also possible to rethrow an exception if you can't handle it at one level or if you want to make sure an external logger gets a chance to hear of the exception. For example, you might write

```
public static void main()
{
  try
  {
    TPatient theCurrentPatient = new TPatient(...);
    theCurrentPatient.admit();
    ...
  }
```

```
    catch (Exception theException)
    {
       System.out.println("Exception: " + theException +
➥".\n");
    }
}
```

and in TPatient

```
public void admin() throws AWTException()
{
  try
  {
    // set up a user interface based on the Abstract
➥Windowing Toolkit (AWT)

     ...

  }
  catch (AWTException theException)
  {
    // handle the AWTException

     ...

    throw theException;
  }
}
```

SEE ALSO

➤ *To learn more about* try, throw, catch, *and exceptions, see page 245*

Iteration Statements

Some of the most powerful statements in any programming language are those that allow you to iterate, or loop. Often you'll want to use a data structure, such as an array, and will perform some operation on every element in the structure. You might also work your way through the structure until some condition becomes true, and then use break to exit the loop.

Java supports three iteration statements: while, do-while, and for. Here are three rules of thumb for deciding which statement to use.

- If you need to have the program loop zero or more times, use while.

- If you want to be sure the loop always executes at least once, use do-while.

- If the control rules for your loop are more complex, use for. In practice, for is usually used when you know how many times you want to loop.

Building "Zero-Or-More" Loops with the *while* Statement

Java's while statement has the form

```
while (someBooleanExpression)
    ...
```

In practice, you'll usually use a compound statement (one or more statements surrounded by curly braces) as the body of a while. Then control passes to the while statement; the program checks to see if the Boolean expression is true. If it is, the program executes the body of the while and then passes control back to the top to test the condition again.

You'll exit from the loop when any one of three conditions occurs.

- The loop's condition becomes false
- Your program encounters a break statement inside the loop
- Your program throws an exception that is caught outside the loop

While it's possible to execute a return out of the middle of a loop, it's considered to be poor practice. If you find that you're done processing, execute a break and transfer control out of the loop and then execute return.

Building "One-Or-More" Loops with the *do-while* Statement

The do-while loop stands the while loop on its head. The syntax is

```
do
{
  ...
} while (someBooleanExpression);
```

Caution: Beware the infinite loop

If you're not careful, you may accidentally write a while loop that never exits. Be sure that something in the body of the loop eventually changes the while's condition to false, or the program may lock up your computer.

Unlike the while, the body of the do-while is guaranteed to be executed at least once. This style is useful when the loop's condition depends upon something you do inside the loop. For example, you might write a program like the one in Listing 5.1.

LISTING 5.1   *ReaderDemo.java—*The heart of this program is a *do while* loop

```java
1  import java.io.File;
2  import java.io.FileReader;
3  import java.io.IOException;
4  import java.io.FileNotFoundException;
5
6  public class ReaderDemo
7  {
8    private static final String _fileName = "demo.txt";
9    public static void main(String[] args)
10   {
11     try
12     {
13       File theFile = new File(_fileName);
14       System.out.println("Reading from file " + theFile + ".");
15       if (theFile.canRead())
16       {
17         FileReader theFileReader = new FileReader(theFile);
18         int theChar;
19         if (theFileReader.ready())
20         do
21         {
22           theChar = theFileReader.read();
23           if (theChar != -1)
24             System.out.print((char)theChar);
25         } while (theFileReader.ready() && theChar != -1);
26       }
27       else
28         System.out.println("Cannot read file: " + _fileName +
     ".");
29     }
30     catch (FileNotFoundException theException)
31     {
32       System.out.println("Caught exception " + theException +
     ".");
```

```
33        }
34        catch (IOException theException)
35        {
36            System.out.println("Caught exception " + theException +
      ".");
37        }
38    }
39 }
```

This program will attempt to read the file at least once. After that it will check to make sure the last read did not return –1 (which indicates that the end of the file has been reached). If the result of the read() is not –1, the loop continues.

Building General Loops Using the *for* Statement

The workhorse of the looping family is the for loop. The syntax is

```
for (initial-condition; continuing-condition;
➥iteration-action)
   ...
```

Like while and do-while, it's customary to use a compound statement rather than a single line as the body of a for loop.

Here's a common for loop.

```
for (short i=0; i<kLimit; i++)
{
   ...
}
```

In this loop a counter variable, i, is declared and defined to be zero in the initial condition. Upon entering the loop for the first time, i is zero. This loop will continue as long as the continuing condition (i<kLimit) is true. After each loop, the interation-action (i++) will occur. Listing 5.2 shows a simple example with two for loops, as well as some if statements. The Fibonacci series is a mathematical series in which every term is the sum of the two terms preceding it. The first two terms of the series are both one.

LISTING 5.2   *Fibonacci.java—*The heart of this class is a listing of the **Fibonacci series**

```java
1  import java.lang.Integer;
2  import java.lang.Short;
3
4  public class Fibonacci
5  {
6    private static final short kLimit = 46;
7    private static int _fibonacciArray[];
8    public static void setSeries(int theMaxFibonacci)
9    {
10       if (theMaxFibonacci < 2)
11          theMaxFibonacci = 2;
12       _fibonacciArray = new int[theMaxFibonacci];
13       _fibonacciArray[0] = 1;
14       _fibonacciArray[1] = 1;
15
16       // the array is now seeded; start in slot 2
17       for (int i=2; i<_fibonacciArray.length; i++)
18          _fibonacciArray[i] = _fibonacciArray[i-1] + _
   fibonacciArray[i-2];
19    }
20    public static void showSeries(short theLineWidth)
21    {
22       for (int i=0; i<_fibonacciArray.length - 1; i +=
   theLineWidth)
23       {
24          for (int j=0; (j<theLineWidth) &&
25                        (i+j < _fibonacciArray.length - 1);
26                        j++)
27          {
28            System.out.print(_fibonacciArray[i+j] + ":");
29            if (j == theLineWidth - 1)
30               System.out.print("\n");
31          }
32       }
33       System.out.println(_fibonacciArray[_fibonacciArray.length
   - 1]);
34    }
35    public static void main(String[] args)
36    {
37       Integer theMaxFibonacci = new Integer(1000);
38       Short theLineWidth = new Short((short)10);
```

```
39      boolean isOKSoFar = true;
40      switch (args.length)
41      {
42        case 0:
43          // this case is OK; we'll use the defaults
44          break;
45        case 2:
46          try
47          {
48              theLineWidth = Short.valueOf(args[1]);
49          }
50          catch (NumberFormatException theException)
51          {
52              System.out.println("numbersPerLine does not appear to
    be a number.");
53              isOKSoFar = false;
54          }
55
56          // drop through to next case
57        case 1:
58          try
59          {
60              theMaxFibonacci = Integer.valueOf(args[0]);
61          }
62          catch (NumberFormatException theException)
63          {
64              System.out.println("seriesLength does not appear to
    be a number.");
65              isOKSoFar = false;
66          }
67          if (theMaxFibonacci.intValue() > kLimit)
68          {
69              System.out.println("Usage: maximum seriesLength is "
    + kLimit + ".");
70              isOKSoFar = false;
71          }
72          break;
73        default:
74          System.out.println("Usage: Fibonacci seriesLength
    numbersPerLine");
75          isOKSoFar = false;
76      }
77      if (isOKSoFar)
```

continues…

LISTING 5.2   **Continued**

```
78      {
79          setSeries(theMaxFibonacci.intValue());
80          showSeries(theLineWidth.shortValue());
81      }
82  }
83 }
```

Sometimes you need to write code that "runs forever"—an intentional infinite loop. Many programmers will simply choose to write

```
while (true)
{
    ...
}
```

That's a good solution—it's clear, readable, and works. You may also see an idiom for such a loop in programs written by old C and C++ users.

```
for (;;)
    ...
```

By removing the initial condition, the continuing condition, and iteration action, this programmer literally told the program that we don't have any special starting conditions—we can initialize variables prior to the loop if we need to—and we certainly don't have any condition that must be satisfied to keep the loop running.

PART

III

Thinking in Objects

Methods: Adding Code to Your Objects

Find out how to interpret the signature of a method

Learn how to choose an appropriate access specifier

See how to write methods that apply to the whole class

Understand how to use abstract methods in an abstract base class

Use the JDK documentation as a starting point for code reuse

Understanding Methods and Data

Object-oriented programs are not necessarily faster or easier to write than procedural programs, so why has the software industry gotten so excited about objects? Most experts agree that, while writing an object-oriented program isn't any faster line-for-line, it simplifies code reuse and decreases the number of lines of code you'll write during a project.

SEE ALSO

➤ *To learn more about code reuse, see page 666*

In order to assess a class to determine its reusability, you need to know how to read a method. You should also pay attention to data. I'll assume here that the original designer followed the practice of making the data `private` (or, at least, `protected`), so as a user of the class, you'll be working through access methods. This section describes how to read a method, emphasizing the method's *signature*. (The signature is the combination of the method's name, parameters, and keywords such as the return type and access specifier.)

Defining Access

The section "Building on the Strengths of C++" in Appendix B, "Java for C++ Programmers," states that Java allows you to specify four levels of access to a method. These levels are

- `public`   Any object may call this method
- `protected`   Access is allowed by any instance of the class, any descendant, and any other class in this package
- `private`   Access is allowed only by instances of the class
- `default`   If no access specifier is used, any object in the package may access the method

Think of your classes as tiny specialized servers. Your `public` methods define the service offered by the class. As you implement the `public` methods, you may find that the method becomes too complex, or you see an opportunity to share code between two methods. Break out common code in a `protected` or `private` method.

How do you decide whether to use private or protected on these "methods of convenience"? Since you'll usually want to make your classes reusable, ask yourself if a derived class would want to use the method. If the answer is yes, make the method protected. If the method is so specific that you cannot envision even a derived class needing to call it, make it private.

I try to avoid using the default access level—access from any other class in the package. This access level sometimes makes sense when you're building a package of tightly integrated classes. If the method is truly useful to outside classes, I make it public. If access to the method should be limited, I make it protected or private, and let other classes work strictly through the public interface.

Here's an example. Suppose we're building the class TPatient, and we want a public method getMedicationsDue() that returns a list of medications that are due now. This public method will need to access our internal data structure that stores information about open medication orders. The data structure itself should be private so that we can flexibly change the implementation. Some of the access methods, such as getScheduledOrders(), should be public. We can imagine a physician or pharmacist needing to review all of the orders for a patient, not just those that are due now. Other access methods, such as cleanOutDrawer(), should be protected. We don't want an outside class (except possibly a derived class) to be able to tell the database that all of the medications have been removed from a drawer (because the patient has been discharged or transferred). That method should be called only by the TPatient class itself (as part of the discharge() or transfer() method).

Reading the Method Interface

As you design your classes you'll find yourself asking "What messages do I want to send this class?" and "What answer do I expect?" The message becomes the name of the method, and the answer is often sent in the method's return type. Details of the message should be sent as *parameters*, also known as *arguments*.

Why does the compiler say "No method matching … found"?

If you attempt to access a method that is not accessible from your class, the compiler will complain with a misleading error message:

No method matching *theMethodName* found in class *className*.

private and protected methods are hidden so well that the compiler cannot even see that they're there. If you get this message, check your access specifiers and try again.

Understanding Return Types

Once you've decided who should be allowed to call your method, you need to think about what the method returns. You can have your method return a primitive type, such as an int, or an object, such as TPatient.

Many professional programmers recommend that you avoid using primitive types in your interfaces—either as return types or as parameters. If you define your interfaces strictly in terms of objects, you'll have flexibility later to modify the internal representation to meet new needs or take advantage of a performance enhancement. Your interface specification should reflect the abstract service offered by your class, not the specific implementation you've chosen.

Many programmers, whose habits go back to C++, frown on allowing methods to return objects that they themselves brought into existence. In languages without a garbage collector, that practice often leads to memory leaks. Even in Java, it's not a bad idea to be careful about memory management. Some applications are quite sensitive to performance and cannot tolerate the time it takes to run the garbage collector.

If you don't want to return anything from a method, declare it to have return type void.

Passing Arguments to a Method

If you want a method to return an object, consider making the object outside the method, and then passing it to the method. This design approach is consistent with the idea that your class offers a service. Let those who desire your service come to you— don't design your classes so that you have to go out and hunt down resources or make them yourself.

If you intend to return an object, just have the caller pass a reference to the object to you as a parameter. You can then call methods on that object to effect your changes. When you exit, the calling routine gets back the modified object, since all objects are passed in Java using call-by-reference.

When you're writing a derived class, make sure your methods take the same range of arguments as the base class. For example, suppose class TPerson handles both military and civilian persons. If you're implementing TPatient in a military hospital, don't assume in your implementation that each person has a military status. Doing so would limit the usefulness of your derived class and could lead to subtle defects during maintenance. Either implement the full interface or make a derived class that specifically checks for your limitations (such as TMilitaryPatient).

Using Methods in a Medical Application

Suppose you're designing a pharmacy class, TPharmacy, and you want to capture the fact that the pharmacy distributes medications to the wards. You could choose to have the pharmacy call the THospital class and ask for a list of wards. But we live in a day when everyone in medicine is sensitive to costs. What happens if the administrator of the local nursing home decides to outsource her pharmacy needs to your hospital? The THospital class doesn't know about the nursing home's wards, so you'll have to change your design.

A better design is to have the wards find the pharmacy. You might choose to make a sendMedications() method on TPharmacy that tells the pharmacy to send medications to the ward. sendMedications() would then take a reference to a ward as a parameter. When the medications are sent to the ward, TPharmacy has the reference in hand and can notify the ward that the medications are being delivered.

In this design, any ward that needs to use the pharmacy's services is free to do so—whether the ward is in the hospital or at a nursing home.

Building Basic Access Methods

Access methods are the simplest methods to write—so simple, in fact, that you may be tempted to write too many of them. Before writing a method that allows your class's client to read or even change an instance variable, ask yourself why the client would need to call this function. If you cannot think of any reason, leave the function out, or make it private.

Call-by-reference or call-by-value

Actually, all parameters in Java are passed by value. The variables we think of as objects, however, are really references to objects, so when you pass an object reference, you're effectively passing the object by using call-by-reference.

What if you have no parameters?

In Java, like C++, just provide the parentheses. For example, you can write

```
double
➥aRandomNumber =
➥java.lang.Math.
➥random();
```

Consider declaring your get access functions final. A final method cannot be overridden in a derived class. By declaring get methods final, you may get a slight performance boost. By *not* declaring set methods final, you allow users of your class to respond to changing requirements by overriding your set method.

Understanding Static Methods

Occasionally you'll need to send a message to the class itself, rather than to an instance of the class. For example, suppose you have a class TDose that represents the individual dose of medicine. Each TDose instance has a location—the dose may be in the pharmacy storeroom, it may be in the pharmacy (where it is waiting to be sent to a ward), or it may be on the ward. If you want to know where a dose is, you can ask it where it is by calling its getLocation() method.

A dose also knows what kind of drug it is, what its strength and packaging are, who its manufacturer is, and what its lot number is. You can provide get access methods for each of these pieces of information.

Suppose that a manufacturer issues a recall notice for all instances of a particular drug with lot number 261X54. You could write your program to go through every storage location in the pharmacy storeroom, every box in the pharmacy, and every drawer on the ward, looking for doses that match the recall notice. A better way is to ask the class, TDose, to give you a list of where all matching instances are. You might write

```
theRecallList = TDose.getListOfMatches(medicationIdentifier,
➡manufacturerIdentifier, lotIdentifier);
```

In order to associate a method (or, for that matter, a data member) with a class rather than each instance, you use the keyword static. Thus, in your class definition, you'd write

```
public class TDose
{
   static public TDoseList getListOfMatches(TMedication
➡theMedication, TManufacturer theManufacturer, TLot theLot)
   {
```

```
        ...
    }
        ...
}
```

What Are Abstract Methods?

Many programmers prefer to make base classes abstract. Their rule is that they never derive a concrete class from a concrete class. An abstract class is one that is intentionally incomplete—you can't make an instance of it, because one or more of its methods has been "left blank." You declare a method to be abstract by using the `abstract` keyword:

```
abstract TStatus getStatus();
```

Since this method is `abstract`, the class that declares it cannot be instantiated—it is an abstract base class. To use this base class, you need to derive a concrete class from it; in the concrete class you then write an implementation for `getStatus()`.

Other Method Keywords

In addition to `static`, `abstract`, and `final` there are two other keywords you may sometimes use. If you intend to implement the method using native code such as C or C++, declare the method to be `native`. For a step-by-step procedure for building native methods, see Chapter 23, "Making and Using Java Archives."

If you begin to use multiple threads in your program, you face the danger that two or more methods might try to access the same data at the same time, leading to data corruption. To prevent this problem from occurring, you can declare a method to be `synchronized`. In a given object, only one `synchronized` method can be running at a time. The first `synchronized` method gets a "lock" on the object. Other `synchronized` methods must wait until the lock is released.

SEE ALSO
➤ *To learn more about synchronization, see page 467*

Abstract classes and interfaces

Abstract classes are one way of providing abstraction. Another way is to use a Java interface. In general, use abstract classes when the concept you're modeling is best described by a noun (such as "person"). Use interfaces when the concept you're modeling is best described by an adjective (such as "controllable"). To learn more about interfaces, see Chapter 9, "Increasing Program Sophistication by Using Interfaces."

Methods in the JDK

Now that you know something about how methods are declared, take some time to explore the documentation that came with the JDK. Point your browser to the index.html page in your JDK directory. From there, follow the JDK Documentation link (either to your local directory or to the JavaSoft Web site) and read the javadoc-generated documentation at the Java Platform API link.

paint()

Recall from the section of Chapter 3, "Getting Started Fast," titled "Building Your First Applet," that class Applet has a special method named paint(). When the applet's graphical space needs to be redrawn, paint() gets called. Whatever code you've put into the method in your derived class gets run.

Take a look at the documentation on Applet. You won't find paint() listed in the class. Instead, read up the hierarchy. java.applet.Applet is derived from java.awt.panel, which in turn is derived from java.awt.Container. Container, in turn, is a java.awt.Component. The paint() method is defined in Component and is overridden by Container.

Use the JDK documentation to become familiar with the capabilities of the various classes. We'll talk about specific methods, particularly of user interface classes such as the AWT, in later chapters. (For example, Chapter 11, "Building the User Interface with the AWT," begins a four chapter section on the user interface.)

main()

If you declare a static void method for your class and name it main(), the Java runtime will find that method when you attempt to invoke your class as an application. Your main() method should accept an array of Strings (String[]) as its parameter—the runtime environment will pass any command-line parameters through that array.

SEE ALSO

➤ *To learn how to write a* main() *method, see page 86*

Object-Oriented Analysis: A New Way of Looking at Software

Learn how to improve your software by following well-defined processes

See how the analysis process can increase your customers' satisfaction

Use the industry-standard Unified Modeling Language (UML) to document your analyses and designs

Use cases to document the interaction of your system with users and external systems

Prepare class diagrams to capture the structure and relationships between your classes

Write interaction diagrams to document your system's dynamic behavior

Case-Based Analysis

Way back in the 1970s, the field of computer programming underwent a revolution of sorts. As programs grew larger and more sophisticated, programmers found it increasingly difficult to finish on time or to ensure that the program was correct. Several expert programmers introduced the concept of performing certain steps before coding—these steps include analysis and design. Using these methods, programs were organized into discrete modules. Modules communicated with each other through well-defined mechanisms such as parameters.

In the late 1980s, programmers became frustrated with their existing methods of analysis, design, and programming—applications were more complex than the methods could support. A new set of methods was developed. The new methodology is *object-oriented*. The object-oriented methods are based on the concept that software modules should reflect real-world entities. Each module—called a *class*—contains its own data and code and has a well-defined interface for use by other classes. The data in an object is stored in variables. Each code routine in the object is called a *method*.

This chapter begins the two-chapter introduction to the processes of software analysis and design. Many software engineers divide software development into four distinct phases or activities:

- Analysis—Identifying the user's requirements
- Design—Developing a software solution to the user's needs
- Implementation—Building the software solution
- Test—Verifying that the finished software meets the requirements

Some developers prefer to apply these activities one after the other, as phases. Figure 7.1 illustrates this approach, known as the waterfall model. Others begin with the riskiest work first (in order to reduce overall risk) and spiral out until the software is done, as illustrated in Figure 7.2.

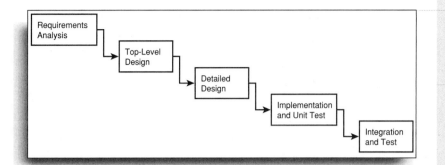

FIGURE 7.1

Some designers carry out the
development activities one
after the other.

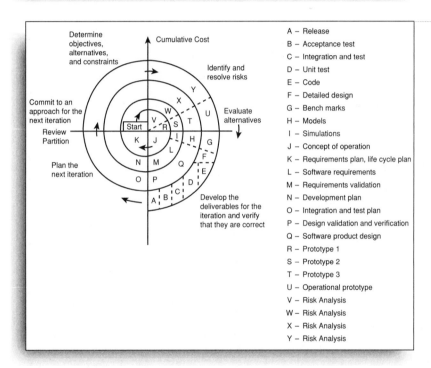

FIGURE 7.2

In the spiral model of development, you concentrate on
building the riskiest portions of
the system first.

For our purposes, the order in which you carry out these four
activities is less important than the fact that you don't miss a
step. It's not necessary that you complete all of the analysis
before you begin design, or all of the design before you begin to
code, but if you attempt to design software without understanding the user's needs and requirements, or if you start coding

without a design, your software isn't likely to be useful to the end user. In the spiral model, you start by performing analysis on the part of the system that is associated with the most risk—typically schedule and cost risk. You design that part, code it, and ensure that it meets the user's requirements. After that, you perform more analysis on the next-riskiest part of the system. This way, once you pass a certain point, you have a version of the system that is shippable while you continue to add new features in response to user needs.

Why Use Processes?

Watts Humphrey and the researchers at the Software Engineering Institute (SEI) at Carnegie-Mellon University have found that most successful software developers use a series of well-defined processes. They have arranged various levels of competence in development processes into a Capability Maturity Model, or CMM. Figure 7.3 illustrates the CMM.

FIGURE 7.3

Most development organizations remain stuck at Level 1 of the Capability Maturity Model.

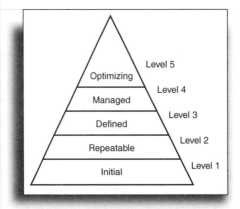

Level 5
Optimizing
Level 4
Managed
Level 3
Defined
Level 2
Repeatable
Level 1
Initial

Level 1 doesn't mean "bad"

An organization at Level 1 doesn't necessarily write bad software. Performance at Level 1 depends mostly on the skilled team and manager, making it difficult to guarantee repeatability.

Most software development organizations are at Level 1 of the CMM—they have little concept of process. Each individual analyst, designer, or programmer does his or her work as he or she sees fit. With a different mix of people on each project, the organization finds it difficult to consistently deliver on-time, on-budget, quality software.

In a Level 2 organization, someone has identified and standardized the major processes, including management processes. There's a company way of doing analysis, design, and so forth. Basic management controls are in place to make sure these standards are followed.

By Level 3 these standards have been documented and are the subject of periodic review. They've been integrated into a coherent mechanism for producing software. Staff and managers are trained in these standard processes. A Software Engineering Process Group (SEPG) is in place and is responsible for maintaining the process standards.

The hallmark of a Level 4 organization is that the output of each process is measured. If the standard says that a programmer should be able to develop 15 lines of debugged code per day, each programmer's productivity is measured. If a programmer is working above or below the standard, someone takes note. A person who is exceeding the standard may have found a way to improve the process. A person whose output is below the goal may not be using the standard process or may have encountered problems not addressed in the standard. The goal is not necessarily to maximize productivity or quality (though that's certainly nice). The goal is the same as it was since Level 2: to use standardized processes to ensure repeatability, so that the company can set and meet realistic deadlines and budgets. By measuring the output of each process (in terms that are meaningful for both quality and productivity), the organization can reduce the variance of its processes. Again, the goal is not (yet) to maximize— that takes place in Level 5. The goal of Level 4 is only to measure and to reduce variance.

In the rare organization that reaches Level 5, the measured output of each process is used to improve the processes themselves. In a large organization there's a certain amount of inertia involved in changing a process—often the SEPG will recommend that a modified process be used on just one project, as a test. If the modified process proves to be superior to the company's standard process, the modified process becomes the new standard.

Learn more about the CMM

For more information about software processes and the Capability Maturity Model, visit the Software Engineering Institute's Web site at `http://www.sei.cmu.edu` `/`. One of the foundation papers, "Capability Maturity Model for Software, Version 1.1," is available as a PDF file at `http://www.sei.` `cmu.edu/products/pub-` `lications/93.reports/9` `3.tr.024.html`. For a detailed description of key practices at each level, see `http://www.sei.` `cmu.edu/products/pub-` `lications/93.reports/9` `3.tr.025.html`.

The boundary between analysis and design may be fuzzy

In object-oriented analysis and design, you're often thinking about the solution at the same time you record requirements. You often build prototypes to clarify your understanding of requirements or revisit certain requirements during design.

Since the original CMM work was done for software development, SEI has enhanced the model and has developed additional versions of the CMM. See `http://www.sei.cmu.edu/technology/` `process.html` for an overview of SEI's work in this area. See `http://www.sei.cmu.edu/technology/psp/` to learn more about the Personal Software Process (PSP), a related effort that describes how individual programmers can increase their quality and productivity. PSP's figures show that, over the course of learning the PSP, programmers reduced their defect rate from an average of over 116 defects per thousand lines of code to just under 49 defects per thousand lines of code. On average, this same group of programmers increased its productivity (in lines of code per hour) by nearly 21 percent.

This chapter describes one approach to the process of analysis. Chapter 8, "Object-Oriented Design and Programming," takes up the process of design and implementation. We'll take up the testing process in Chapter 16, "Testing and Debugging Java Code."

Using the Unified Modeling Language During Analysis

Many developers have thought about different notations for analysis. Something like an industry standard has emerged over time, representing the best work of developers like Grady Booch, Jim Rumbaugh, and Ivar Jacobson. This standard is called the Unified Modeling Language, or UML. It was developed by Booch, Rumbaugh, and Jacobson (of Rational Software) with input from Microsoft, Hewlett-Packard, Unisys, IBM, and other major software developers. In November 1997, UML was accepted as an adopted technology by the Object Management Group (`http://www.omg.org/library/schedule/` `Technology_Adoptions.htm#tbl_UML_Specification`).

A model is a representation of your *application domain*—the business area in which your software will work. For example, this chapter draws examples from the domain of a patient ward in a hospital. During analysis you build a model of the relevant parts of the problem domain; during design you use the model as a context for your solution. Models contain the following in the UML:

- **use cases**   Sequences of transactions performed by the system in response to triggering events initiated by an actor.

- **actors**   Stereotypes of a class that interact with the software under development. Typical actors are human users and other software systems.

- **classes**   A description of the common structure and behavior of a set of objects. Attributes and operations capture static structure and behavior; you use state diagrams to document dynamic behavior.

- **class packages**   Clusters of logically related classes. In UML, a package has a specification module and an implementation module. The implementation module is often known as the body of the package. (If you're familiar with C++, think of the specification module as the header file and the body as the .cpp file; in Java, both the specification module and the body are contained in the same file—the .java file.)

- **objects**   Entities with state, behavior, and identity. Objects with similar structure and behavior are defined in a common class.

- **operations**   Operations are services provided by a class or objects of a class. Operations can have a return type that defines the class's response to the request for service.

- **components**   Software modules (defined during the design process). Components include main programs, packages, subprograms, and tasks.

Learning the UML

Rational Software maintains an online UML resource center at http://www.rational. com/uml/index.shtml. The full specification is available online at http:// www.omg.org/library /schedule/Technology _Adoptions.htm#tbl_ UML_ Specification.

The Unified Modeling Language is not a programming language

UML is a visual modeling language. You can use it to develop object-oriented models that can be implemented in many different languages, including C++, Smalltalk, Ada, and, of course, Java.

- component packages   Clusters of logically related components. Like class packages, component packages consist of a specification module and an implementation module (often called a body).

- processor nodes   Hardware components capable of executing programs.

- device nodes   Hardware components with no computing power (such as modems and terminals).

By using UML notation you can prepare diagrams that show each of these elements as well as the relationships between them. A complete UML model includes six types of diagrams:

- class diagrams   Show the existence of classes and how they are related to one another (see Figure 7.4).

- use case diagrams   Used to specify or characterize the functionality and behavior of a whole application interacting with one or more external actors (see Figure 7.5).

- interaction diagrams   Sequence diagrams and collaboration diagrams; sequence diagrams emphasize the execution of an interaction over time. Collaboration diagrams emphasize the sequence of messages that implement an operation or transaction (see Figure 7.6).

- component diagrams   Used to show relationships between component packages and components (see Figure 7.7).

- state diagrams   Also known as a state transition diagram. These diagrams show the state space of a given class, the events that cause the transition from one state to another, and the actions that result from a state change (see Figure 7.8).

- deployment diagram   A single diagram showing how processes are assigned to processors. This diagram also includes devices and connections (see Figure 7.9).

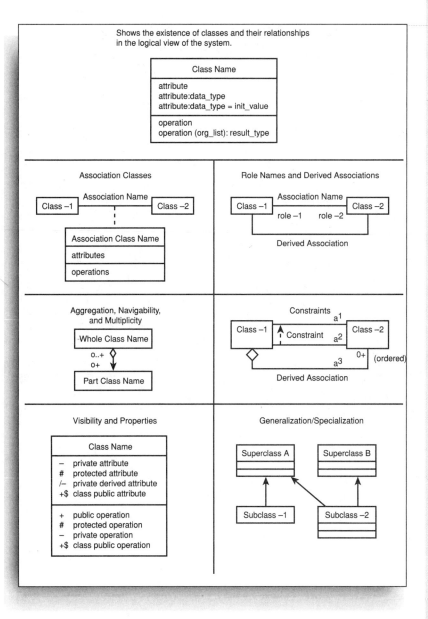

FIGURE 7.4

Class diagrams are used throughout analysis and design.

FIGURE **7.5**

Use cases capture the major points at which users interact with your software.

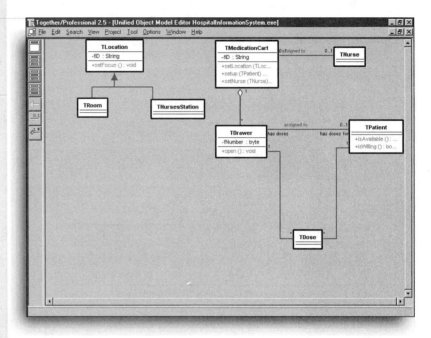

FIGURE **7.6**

Sequence diagrams capture your classes' dynamic behavior, while collaboration diagrams record static interaction.

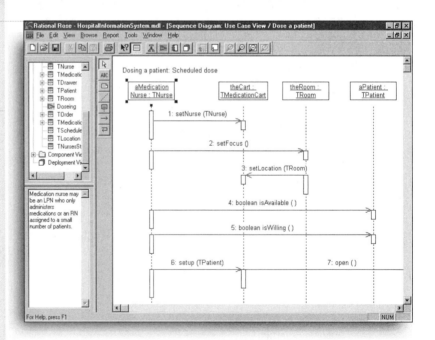

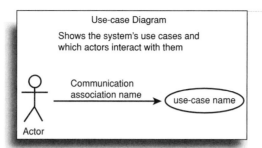

FIGURE 7.7

Use component diagrams during architectural design to help map classes onto larger components.

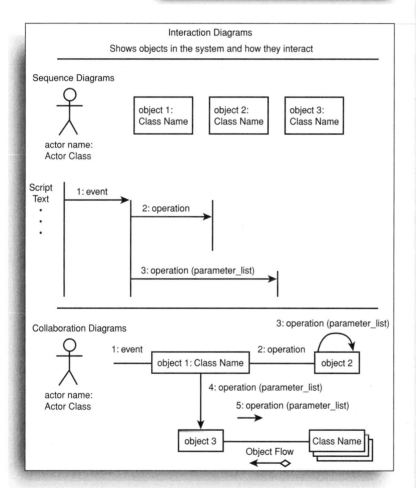

FIGURE 7.8

Use state diagrams to capture the details of your classes' dynamic behavior.

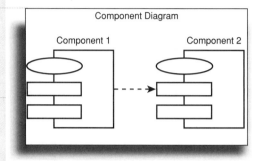

These diagrams, in turn, are organized into four views:

- Use case view   Showing how the system appears to the users (including external systems)
- Logical view   Capturing all information about the classes and the entities they represent
- Component view   Showing how the solution maps onto software modules
- Deployment view   Showing how the processes are mapped onto the hardware

Remember that these are different views of the same system. Each view emphasizes a different aspect of the system, but the same entity typically appears in more than one view.

During analysis, you're most concerned about the use case and logical views. During design you begin to build a component view and, eventually, a deployment view.

Applying Use Cases to Analysis

One of the best ways to get started in analysis is to let the user talk about his or her vision of the software. During the process, they inevitably talk about their business processes—it's up to you as the analyst to define your software's scope, so you know which business processes flow through the software and which ones go around the software.

UML and process

UML is designed to be process-neutral—that is, you can use UML notation with any of the popular analyses and design processes. The UML authors note, however, the value of a "use-case driven, architecture-centric, iterative, and incremental process."

After the user has described the business processes to be automated, you should draw the user into a series of "what if" discussions. Listen for places in which you may need to include flexibility in your design; in a fast-changing environment, some processes will inevitably change. Make sure your software is able to change as well.

Based on this discussion with the user, you should be able to identify one or more *use cases*. A use case is a sequence of transactions performed by the system in response to some triggering event initiated by an actor. A use case should represent a significant portion of a user's task. The use case may contain several different scenarios to capture various interactions between the actor and the use case.

Follow this step-by-step procedure for a first cut model of the software.

Moving from business processes to class design

1. Review your notes of the business processes to be automated; highlight all nouns that you find.

2. Use each noun that is in the scope of your software as the basis for a class of objects. Pay particular attention to nouns that describe people who interact with our software—we'll call these people *actors*.

3. Identify anything an object of the class must remember and make it an instance variable. If there's something the class as a whole must remember, make it a class variable (implemented in Java as a `static` variable).

4. Look at the verbs used in your notes and identify which nouns (or classes) they apply to. Use these verbs as the basis for operations. (In Java you'll use methods to implement operations.) If the class as a whole should respond to the request, make it a class operation (implemented in Java as a `static` method).

5. Look for places where you can say that one class is a kind of another class. (This relationship is often known as the is-a or a-kind-of relationship.) Arrange these classes into a generalization/specialization hierarchy.

Improve reuse by broadening your scope

The broader you can make the scope of your system (within reason) the more reusable your software will be.

6. Look for places where an object of one class is an object's component in another class. This relationship is known as aggregation. Document these relationships on the class diagram.

7. Make sure that for each class you've provided a way for objects to be instantiated (built), as well as a way for them to be destroyed.

8. Make sure you've provided a way for each attribute to be initialized, set, and read.

Many software tools are available to help you build graphical models based on UML. These tools are generally called *Computer-Aided Software Engineering* (CASE) tools. They serve the software developer in much the same way as computer-aided design (CAD) tools serve the architect. You may want to look into the following:

- Together/J, from Object International, Inc. (http://www.oisoft.com/TogetherJ/index.html)

- Rational Rose, from Rational Software (http://www. rational.com/products/rose/)

- ObjectTeam, from Cayenne Software (http://www. cayennesoft.com/objectteam/)

- ClassDesigner, from Cayenne Software (http://www. cayennesoft.com/classdesigner/)

Figures 7.4–7.9 illustrate the major types of notation used in UML drawings. You can get a printable version of all of the notation used in UML from http://www.rational.com/uml/ qr/uml_poster.html.

The Dose Administration Use Case Example

I'll illustrate the process of UML analysis by building a model of the process in which a nurse in a hospital ward administers doses to patients. We start the process by talking to users—nurses—about how they do this job. They tell us that there are three major types of doses they give:

- Scheduled doses—Given at fixed times (8 a.m., noon, 4 p.m., and 8 p.m., for example)
- PRN doses—Given as required (subject to the physician's order)
- Controlled substances—May be scheduled or PRN, but require special safeguards

The next three sections show how we build a model of these different kinds of dosing. In these descriptions, I've set each noun in **bold** and each verb in *italics* the first time that they appear. (These descriptions are somewhat simplified from real hospital practice.)

The Scheduled Dose Scenario

Here's what the nurses told us about how they give scheduled doses:

First, most **doses** are *given* on a standard **interval**, typically 8 a.m., noon, 4 p.m., and 8 p.m. Sometimes a **physician** will *order* a dose to be given off-interval (for example, 10 a.m.). A dose is considered on-time if it is given within one hour of the ordered time.

When the beginning of the dosing interval arrives, the **nurse** *gets* a **medication cart** from the **nurses' station**. The **medication cart** *contains* a **drawer** for each **patient**. Each drawer *contains* the doses for one patient.

The nurse *takes* the medication cart to the first **patient room**. He or she *checks* to make sure the patient is there. (Sometimes the patient is in the bathroom or away from the **ward** in X-ray or physical therapy.) If the patient is there, the nurse checks to be sure the patient is willing to take his or her medication. If the patient *refuses* all doses, the nurse makes a **note** in the **Medication Administration Record** (MAR). If the patient is willing to *take* at least one dose, the nurse *sets up* the doses. The nurse *follows* any special instructions (crush and give with applesauce, for example) on the **order**.

The nurse then *offers* the doses to the patient. The patient may *refuse* one or more doses at this point. Several other **complications** may occur that prevent the nurse from dosing the patient:

- The nurse drops the **pill** or otherwise *wastes* the dose.
- The patient *expels* (vomits) the dose.
- The nurse may *determine* that the dose should not be administered.

If the dose is given as ordered, the nurse *records* that fact in the MAR. If the dose is not given as ordered but an attempt can be made later, the nurse sets a **reminder**. If the dose is not given at all, the nurse *sets* a reminder to *make* a **progress note** in the **patient's record** and *enters* the **reason** that the dose was not given into the MAR.

After the doses are given, the nurse *moves on* to the next **bed** and the next patient.

Once the nurse has attempted to dose all of the patients on the ward, the nurse *reviews* the list of reminders. If there are reminders that tell the nurse to dose a patient, they *have priority* over reminders to prepare progress notes. Figure 7.10 shows a sequence diagram of this use case prepared using Rational Rose, a UML-capable tool.

FIGURE 7.10

Save time during analysis by using a UML-capable visual editor.

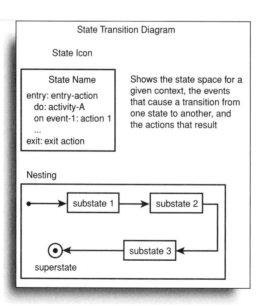

Off-interval doses are *handled* like reminders. When the nurse has *finished* all of the available work, he or she *returns* the medication cart to the nurse's station. When there is a need to dose another patient (an off-interval dose or a patient returning to the ward, for example), the nurse *removes* the medications from the patient's drawer and carries them to the room (rather than moving the entire medication cart).

The PRN Dose Scenario

If a patient *requests* a PRN dose, the nurse check's the patient record to see what **PRN orders** are available. If an appropriate order *is available* and *can be dosed* now, the nurse goes to the **PRN cabinet** and retrieves the dose. Dosing now proceeds as it does for a scheduled dose.

Once the nurse has administered a PRN dose, the nurse sets a reminder to *check* the patient and prepare a progress note showing the effect of the PRN.

The Controlled Substance Scenario

The physician may occasionally write an order for a narcotic or other **controlled substance** to be given as a scheduled dose. More frequently, such medications are ordered PRN. When the order is for a controlled substance, the nurse goes to the **narcotics cabinet** to obtain the medication.

If the nurse wastes the narcotics dose, he or she must find an **authorized witness**—typically the supervising nurse—to *witness* the destruction of the dose.

Classes and Objects

Classes encapsulate information about some real-world entity (such as a nurse, a patient, or a medication). Your goal should be to specify operations for each class that relates directly to the role of the class in your application domain. Similarly, each class should include attributes that are needed by those operations. In Java, you'll implement operations as methods and attributes as data members.

We can build a list of classes based on nouns identified in the dosing administration scenarios. In this list we've used the class names based on the naming conventions identified in Chapter 3, "Getting Started Fast." For example, dose becomes TDose and nurse becomes TNurse. Figure 7.11 shows a class diagram showing some of these classes. This class diagram was built in Together/Professional, a member of the same family as Together/J.

FIGURE 7.11

CASE tools save time when you're building complex software.

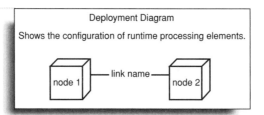

Identifying Attributes

As you interview users and read through your notes, capture information on the class diagram. For example, as you learn how the nurse uses the medication cart, you may decide that TMedicationCart should remember which nurse is currently using it. Add a TNurse attribute to TMedicationCart to record this information.

In general, you should hide the implementation details of your classes by keeping data members private. At most, you should expose the implementation to subclasses (by using the protected access specifier). Three rules of thumb to help you decide whether you should keep a data member private or expose it (as protected or public) follow this paragraph. In general, you should keep data members private. If you're tempted to make data protected or public and can answer all three of these questions with No, then you may be justified in exposing your data.

- Does deriving a new class require design changes in the base class?

- Can an operation on the derived class change the behavior of the base class?

- Is the effort required to inherit from the class out of proportion to the size of the class?

Choosing Public Methods

In your early class diagrams you may want to simply add `get` and `set` methods for attributes, which are usually `private`. Strive to make these methods relevant to the application domain. For example, you may decide that `getNurse()` is a relevant method for `TMedicationCart` (since you can use it in reports), but that `setNurse()` should be replaced with `logon()` and `logoff()`. Thus, the nurse may log on to the medication cart at the beginning of the interval and log off when the dosing is complete.

Some public methods will be obvious from the verbs in your notes. To identify other possible methods, build a sequence diagram or collaboration diagram for each major use case. For example, the sequence diagram in Figure 7.10 shows that the nurse logs on to the medication cart and then goes into a patient's room. I opted to add the method `setCurrentLocation()` to class `TRoom` to allow me to record the fact that the nurse is working in that room. This mechanism allows me to record the location of the nurse and the cart; if someone else needs to find the cart, they'll be able to call `TMedicationCart`'s `getLocation()` method.

I later moved `setCurrentLocation()` to `TLocation`, the parent class of `TRoom`. You will see why when you examine the class hierarchy in the next section.

In general, make sure the names for your operations are meaningful and well-defined in the application domain. If the end user would recognize and feel comfortable with `get` and `set` names, feel free to use them. In many cases the end user has his or her own terms for these operations or includes the get or set methods in his or her own (higher level) operations. In those cases you should choose the higher-level, more meaningful name.

Access specifiers in UML

When you're reading a UML diagram, you can tell at a glance which access specifier applies to which member. Private members are prefaced by a dash (–), protected members with a pound sign (#), and public members with a plus sign (+).

Tip: Keep your interaction diagrams up-to-date

As you review your diagrams with users, make sure your interaction diagrams accurately capture the way users work through their tasks. You'll use this work flow as the basis for the design of your user interface.

Always include get and set methods for JavaBeans

If you're writing a class that will be used as a JavaBean—Java's approach to component software—you should include **get** and **set** methods for each attribute. We'll list the design guidelines for JavaBeans in Chapter 20, "Designing Good Beans."

If you get stuck looking for alternatives to get and set names, ask yourself why the object is retrieving the internal value. What is its activity or responsibility? What is the class trying to achieve by setting the value of this internal state? Questions such as these help bridge the gap between the implementation and the application domain.

Defining Static Members

Sometimes you have an attribute or method that applies to the class itself, rather than to a specific instance. For example, hospitals are interested in the total number of patients currently registered—they refer to this number as the daily census. We could write the following:

```
public class TPatient
{
  static int fCensus = 0;
  static int getCensus()
  {
    return fCensus;
  }
  void admit()
  {
    ...
    fCensus++;
  }
  void discharge()
  {
    ...
    fCensus--;
  }
}
```

In this design we have a class variable fCensus, which records the daily census. fCensus is incremented when a patient is admitted. fCensus is decremented when a patient is discharged. Any object can call getCensus() to get the value of fCensus.

Building a Class Hierarchy

Much of the power of object-oriented design comes from the fact that we can build a generalization-specialization hierarchy based on is-a relationships between classes. We can also build aggregation hierarchies based on has-a relationships. For example, Figure 7.11 records the fact that TRoom is a kind of TLocation. (The same can be said for TNursesStation.) Any public or protected method or attribute in TLocation is a member of both TRoom and TNursesStation. This abstraction allows us to record the fact that a nurse has moved the cart into a patient's room by calling setFocus() on the room, even though the method is actually defined in TLocation. When the nurse is done dosing the patients, he or she can return the physical cart to the nurses' station and record in the software that the nurses' station now has the focus for that cart.

The is-a Relationship

When one class is a specialization of another, we say that an is-a relationship exists between them. Thus, TNurse is-a TEmployee, and TRoom is-a TLocation. Nurses have all of the characteristics of employees, but the reverse is not true.

is-a in UML

The is-a relationship in UML is shown by drawing an arrow from the more specific to the more general class.

In Java, we implement the is-a relationship with inheritance. When we say the following, we're saying that an is-a relationship exists between MyApplet and Applet and that TEmployee is the more general class.

```
public class MyApplet extends Applet
```

In Java, all classes are ultimately derived from a built-in class called Object. The first declaration has the same effect as if you had written the second declaration:

```
public class TMedicationCart

public class TMedicationCart extends Object
```

If you want to allow some method to handle any object, pass Object to that method as a parameter.

In general, you can take advantage of generalization-specialization hierarchies by passing parameters at the highest level possible. For example, suppose we define both TControlledSubstance and TMedication as kinds of TAbstractMedication. Any method that can handle TAbstractMedication can handle instances of either TMedication or TControlledSubstance. Suppose that a prescriber has written one order for diphenhydramine (a non-controlled medication) and another for the narcotic morphine. If, during dosing, the nurse were to drop both doses and declare them wasted, each dose would tell the nurse what do based on its own nature. The dose of diphenhydramine would tell the nurse to destroy the dose and offer to order another from the pharmacy. The dose of morphine, being a controlled substance, would tell the nurse that he or she needs a witness. Once an authorized witness has confirmed that the dose has been properly destroyed, the system would tell the nurse to get a replacement dose from the ward's narcotics cabinet. That instances of derived classes can stand in for instances of base classes is called *polymorphism*.

During analysis, take care that your relationships reflect the true semantics of the application domain and not some implementation convenience. For example, there might be some utility in writing the following during analysis:

```
public class TNurse extends TEmployee
```

During design, we may decide that the aspects of TNurse that interest us (authorization to approve wasting a controlled substances, for example) are precisely those attributes and operations that distinguish a nurse from other employees. If we have no interest in the nurse's base pay, social security number, or years of service, we may decide to implement TNurse as a top-level class (derived only from TObject) and avoid the overhead of TEmployee.

If you're careful to get the semantics right, the Java compiler will provide powerful safeguards, conveniences, and efficiencies in the resulting classes.

If you're trained in formal mathematics, you may find the Liskov substitution principle useful:

If, for every object o[sub]1 of type S there is an object o[sub]2 of type T such that for all programs P defined in terms of T, the behavior of P is unchanged when o[sub]1 is substituted for o[sub]2, then S is a subtype of T.

Thus, if you've written a program for TLocation and its behavior is unchanged when you substitute an instance of TRoom for an instance of TLocation, then TRoom is a subtype of TLocation.

If you find this sort of principle useful, by all means use it. If you prefer to take an intuitive approach to identifying is-a relationships, feel free to do so.

Note, too, that you can override one or more of the base class's operations in the derived class. For example, the operation getReplacementDose() on class TAbstractMedication might include a call to the pharmacy. If the medication is in the subclass TControlledSubstance, the nurse may be sent to the on-ward narcotics cabinet instead of the pharmacy.

Here are some rules of thumb for deciding whether to override a base class operation in a derived class:

- If, intuitively, the base class is a generalization of the derived class and the override restricts the boundaries of the base class, go ahead and override. For example, we might derive TNursesAide from TNurse and limit nurses' aides from certain dosing functions.
- If the semantics of the base class and the derived class are compatible, an override may be acceptable. The base class's method should assume no less than its derived class counterpart; the return value of the base class should assume no more. For example, if TNursesAide's giveDose() method assumes that the dose will never be for a controlled substance, then the base class TNurse must make the same assumption in its version of giveDose().
- If the base class really doesn't support the semantics of the derived class's methods, but you want to put the method into the base class for convenience, consider using a Java interface in the derived class's specification instead of overriding the base class methods.

Be careful not to confuse is-like-a relationships with is-a relationships. For example, you may conclude upon review that a nurses' aide is not a nurse—a nurses' aid is like a nurse. You might then find (or invent) an abstract class that can serve as the basis for both classes. Thus, both TNurse and TNursesAide might be derived from TAbstractCaregiver.

The has-a Relationship

The has-a relationship implies containment. Sometimes you see authors use is-part-of or uses for implementation for the same concept.

Use the has-a relationship to specify aggregation. For example, the medication cart contains several drawers—one for each patient. Thus, there is a one-to-many has-a relationship between the cart and the drawers, and a one-to-one relationship (though not a has-a relationship) between drawers and patients. These relationships are shown in Figure 7.12.

FIGURE 7.12

Use the UML aggregation symbol (the line with a diamond) to model a has-a relationship.

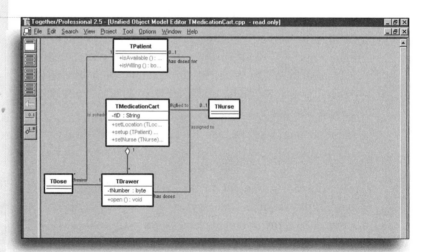

Other Relationships

When you specify a relationship between two classes in UML, you give the relationship a name. You can also define roles for both ends of the relationship link. For example, the link between TDrawer and TDose is marked with an asterisk at the TDose end, indicating that there can be zero or more doses in a drawer. (If at least one dose is required, the link would be marked 1..*.) The link between TDose and TPatient is similar—a patient may have zero or more doses, but a dose is always for exactly one patient.

The relationship between TPatient and TDrawer is simple—they're always one-to-one.

The uses-a Relationship

Be careful to distinguish has-a relationships from uses-a relationships. For example, TDrawer has-a TDoses in it, but the doses are not part of the drawer. TDrawer, on the other hand, is a component of TMedicationCart—drawers don't exist apart from the cart.

The makes-a Relationship

In object-oriented designs we'll usually make (instantiate) all of our objects in main(), and then let them interact. Occasionally we'll need to have one object make a new instance of another class. For example, in a hospital system, we'll have an ADT module (Admissions, Discharges, and Transfers). When a patient is admitted, we'll instantiate a new TPatient and assign that patient to a TBed in a TRoom.

When you define a makes-a relationship, be certain you know which class is responsible for destroying the newly made object. Even though Java takes care of garbage collection on its own, you should still have a defined life-cycle for each object. For example, if a TPatient is instantiated in the admission process, he or she may be deleted in the discharge process.

Consistency Checks

Most CASE tools produce reports that tell you about inconsistencies between your diagrams. Here's a simple check you should always perform for yourself:

- Make sure you know how objects of every class come into existence.
- Make sure you know how to modify the attributes on every class.
- Make sure you know how to delete any object.

Use inner classes to implement has-a relationships

If you have a component class that will never be accessed apart from its container, implement the component class as an inner class inside the container class's definition. The component will have access to the container's private members, but no one outside the container class will be able to get to the component. In addition, the inner class will have access to all of the outer classes data members—even private ones.

Many designers refer to this checklist as AMD for Add, Modify, and Delete.

For example, our finished hospital information system needs to have utility functions to allow us to add and delete instances of TRoom and TNursesStation. We won't run these functions often—perhaps just once in any given hospital—but if we forget them, we'll be embarrassed to find that we can't install the system.

Object-Oriented Design and Programming

Learn to use the Unified Modeling Language (UML) to design Java programs

Use architectural design to get a big picture of your application

Learn about common design patterns that can shorten your design time

Find out which methods require detailed design

Use Java coding idioms to implement your design

Design Methodologies

In its simplest form, analysis is the process of identifying a software project's requirements. Once you and your customer have agreed on what the software must do, it's time to start designing.

Recall from Chapter 7, "Object-Oriented Analysis: A New Way of Looking at Software," that the Object Management Group has formally adopted the Unified Modeling Language (UML) as a technology standard. While there are several good notations available, I recommend you use UML. As an emerging standard, most software tools (and a growing number of software engineers) are using this notation.

In addition to the notation, you need a design methodology—a set of processes by which you develop a solution that satisfies your project's requirements.

This section reviews the portions of the UML notation that are relevant to design. Then I'll walk through a typical set of design processes that are grouped into three major activities:

UML and process

UML is designed to be process-neutral; you can use UML notation with any of the popular analyses and design processes. The UML authors note, however, the value of a "use-case driven, architecture-centric, iterative, and incremental process."

- `architectural design`   A top-level assignment of software components (such as objects) to hardware components (such as processors). The completed design typically shows a set of subsystems including the user interface and any external communications.

- `design by pattern`   A middle level of design, in which classes, objects, and their underlying components are arranged according to one or more predefined design patterns whenever possible.

- `detailed design`   The process of choosing a design for each class's data and methods.

Whether you use a waterfall process (as shown in the preceding chapter's Figure 7.1) or a spiral model (shown in Figure 7.2), you should plan on including all three design activities in any project. In this chapter I'll assume that you're using the spiral model—in my examples I'll concentrate on the elements with the greatest risk first.

UML Design Notation

Whatever design process you use, you should plan to document the work product in UML. This section describes the UML diagrams that are most useful during the design activities.

Recall (from Chapter 7) that during analysis you capture both the static and the dynamic behavior of the desired system. The static description of the application is shown in a class diagram; the dynamic description is shown on an interaction diagram. There are two kinds of interaction diagrams: sequence and collaboration.

You usually want to capture the static and dynamic descriptions at about the same time. As you add a class to the class diagram, you may want to go to the collaboration diagrams and show how they are used. As you add a message to a sequence diagram, you need to also add it to the class diagram. In any system much larger than a toy, you'll find the chore of keeping these diagrams consistent burdensome. I recommend you choose one of the Computer-Aided Software Engineering (CASE) tools such as Together/J (from Object International), Rational Rose (from Rational Software), Select Enterprise (from Select Software), or ClassDesigner or ObjectTeam (from Cayenne Software). The examples in this chapter were designed with Rational Rose.

SEE ALSO

➤ See the list of CASE tools (including vendor URLs), page 170

The Deployment Diagram

Sometimes you'll write an application that runs on only a single computer, such as a PC. Often, however, your application will span several machines. For example, you might have an application whose user interface runs on a PC or Macintosh, with business logic running on a Windows NT server and a database running on a UNIX machine. In an embedded system for, say, satellite communications, you might have one processor dedicated to the user interface, while another is responsible for keeping the antenna pointed at the satellite.

Most operating systems support the concept of a *process*—a single, executable entity. In a good design each process is focused on a single functional area—it is said to be *functionally cohesive*. Here are some typical processes you might find in your application:

- Database interface
- I/O driver for a single device
- Data capture
- Data display

Some processes will be *transient*—or activated to perform some function—and then will become inactive. Other processes are *persistent*—they remain active for the life of the application. If you're coming to Java from a UNIX background, you can equate persistent processes with UNIX daemons. If most of your experience has been in Windows NT, think of persistent processes as system services. These concepts, typically part of the operating system, can be implemented portably in Java.

There may be more than one *thread* of execution within a process. Each thread represents a concurrent execution path. In fact, most modern operating systems (such as UNIX and Windows NT) allow you to split a process into more than one thread by means of a single call to the operating system. Java supports the concept of a thread at the language level. Turn to Chapter 17, "Concurrent Programming with Threads," to learn more about this topic.

To emphasize the concurrent nature of some processes, UML refers to a single-threaded process as a *task*. Much of the work of architectural design consists of grouping classes (and their methods) into tasks and assigning those tasks to processors.

In UML you use a deployment diagram to reflect the variety of processors available to you, as well as to show which task is assigned to which processor. Figure 8.1 shows an early version of a deployment diagram, after the processors and other devices have been identified and some of the processes have been allocated. Shaded nodes are processors; unshaded nodes are devices. Process names such as AllocateMedicationForPatient are shown under each processor. When tasks are shown on a deployment diagram, they are shown as parallelograms inside the processor nodes.

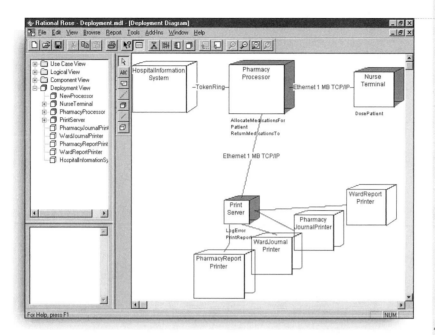

FIGURE 8.1

When you begin architectural design, use this diagram to allocate processes to processors.

Updating the Class Diagrams and Interaction Diagrams

Most designers would prefer that the class diagrams and interaction diagrams stabilize at the end of analysis. When using an interactive process model such as the spiral model, however, it's sometimes difficult to figure out just when analysis is complete. As a practical matter, you should review the documents you produced during analysis and any changes that have become necessary during design.

Here's a list of refinements you may want to apply to your class and interaction diagrams during design:

- For each association relationship between two classes, identify which class will provide a service to the other. (This identification is called dependency in UML.)
- For each association, make sure you've got the *cardinality* correct (one-to-one, many-to-one, one-to-many, or many-to-many). You (or your CASE tool) will use the cardinality as one factor in determining how you implement the association.

Consider modeling processors and processes explicitly

In a complex application with many processors and processes, consider using a class diagram to capture the relationship between these two kinds of entities. You may have more than one kind of processor (a Sun SPARC and an 80188, for example) and more than one kind of process (persistent versus transient, for example). Model the relationship between processes and processors with the association is allocated to.

Remember, it's write once, run anywhere!

Although you need to know how your code is divided across processors, be careful not to use this knowledge to get lazy and write platform-specific code. You get your greatest benefit from Java if you insist on platform-independent code.

- Consider adding an explicit association class for more complex associations.

- Add any access methods (`get` and `set`) that may be necessary for your private or protected data members.

- Look for places in your inheritance hierarchy where one concrete class is derived from another. If the base class will never have instances, make it an abstract class. If the base class will have instances, consider defining an abstract class than can serve as the base class for both concrete classes.

- During analysis you may have prototyped a user interface (at least on paper). If you haven't done so already, add classes for the components of the user interface to your class and interface diagrams.

- Add controller classes that define the collaboration between application domain classes and the user-interface classes. (These controller classes are based on the Facade design pattern described later in this section.)

- Add collection classes to reflect one-to many, many-to-one, and many-to-many relationships.

Choose association names wisely

Make sure you give meaningful names to associations. In many CASE tools, the tool adds a data member to the client class that references the server class.

Architectural Design

During architectural design you should work to address four issues about your software solution:

- Identify (or design) the characteristics of the underlying hardware.

- Map class methods to processes and processors, defining a set of tasks.

- Design the concurrency model for the tasks.

- Design the global error-handling policies, showing how each task recovers from faults.

Whether you address these issues one after the other or iteratively is up to you. Here's a step-by-step procedure that represents one possible path through architectural design.

Allocating methods to tasks

1. Begin by assuming that all objects execute concurrently, each object in its own thread. In most applications this assumption will lead to far too many tasks—we'll reduce that number in a moment.

2. Examine the interaction diagrams to identify which classes need to collaborate. For each collaboration, determine whether to implement the collaboration as a *task rendezvous* or simple procedure calls.

3. For each set of classes that can collaborate through simple procedure calls in a single thread, collapse their threads into one (single-threaded) task.

4. Define the task rendezvous for each pair of collaborating tasks.

5. Allocate each task to a processor. If the hardware design is not frozen, add processors or increase the processor capability as necessary to accommodate all tasks.

6. Iterate through Steps 1–5 until each processor can handle all of the tasks allocated to it with just half of its capacity (to leave room for growth).

7. Identify the faults that are possible in each thread and design a mechanism for recovering from each fault (or notifying a human operator if recovery is not possible).

Later in this chapter we'll talk about design patterns. Patterns are called *frameworks* at the architectural level. A framework is a reusable design expressed as a set of abstract classes and a particular pattern of collaboration. You can learn more about frameworks online, at Dr. Ralph Johnson's frameworks home page: `http://st-www.cs.uiuc.edu/users/johnson/frameworks.html`. You'll also want to visit the Taligent home page on IBM's site: `http://www.software.ibm.com/ad/taligent`. IBM is a big supporter of Java; many of the resources at this page are Java-related.

Allocating Classes to Threads

One good strategy for identifying threads is to start by identifying *events*. Look at your interaction diagrams—particularly your

---

Consider using the Architecture Tradeoff Analysis method

Most software needs to be maintainable. It may also need to be survivable, secure, interoperable, extensible, reliable, available, or meet specific performance objectives. You can make intelligent tradeoffs between these families of requirements by using the Architecture Tradeoff Analysis (ATA) method, described at `http://www.sei.cmu.edu/technology/product_line_systems/ata_method.html`.

sequence diagrams—to identify events. The leftmost entity on the sequence diagram (the one that starts a sequence) is nearly always an event.

The relationship between events and threads may be one-to-one or many-to-one; a thread may handle a single event or a group of related events. You should be suspicious of designs in which a single event initiates action in more than one thread. Such a design may indicate that you haven't partitioned your classes correctly.

In complex systems with more than a few dozen events, you should partition events into groups and allocate the groups to threads. That way you won't end up with dozens of threads competing for processing time. Sometimes a natural grouping is present. In the medical dose administration application, there is only one nurse using the terminal at a time, so all of the user-interface events on that terminal could be allocated to a single group and then to a single thread.

Computation-intensive work can be allocated to its own task. For example, if part of dose administration requires a complex (and time-consuming) database query, you might consider starting a separate thread for that query, and delivering that information to the user (perhaps in a separate window) when the result becomes available.

One common event group consists of alarm events. Consider an embedded system, such as a satellite tracking system, which moves an antenna to stay centered on a moving satellite. You might need to generate an alarm if the antenna doesn't respond to a move command, or if the system is in danger of losing the signal. You might also want to generate an alarm if the system cannot communicate with other hardware components (such as a control interface). For this kind of a system, consider a separate alarm thread that checks for any of these alarm conditions and reports its results to the user interface (and perhaps to a remote-control interface).

The process of allocating classes to tasks is an iterative one. Identify which event (or event group) is associated with each task; sometimes a class may have more than one event. Place all of the classes related to an event or event group into one thread. As you proceed, you may see a need to split a thread into two more threads, or you may discover opportunities to collapse several threads into one sequential process.

Dealing with Shared Classes

As you work, you will sometimes find a class that belongs in more than one process. That's not a problem—that simply tells you that that concept is used in more than one part of the application. Sometimes, however, you'll find that a single instance of the class needs to be shared between two or more processes. Classes in which instances are shared in this way are called *shared classes*. For example, in the dose distribution application you may find that an instance of class TDose comes into existence in the AllocateMedicationForPatient process in the pharmacy, but then is needed on the nurse's workstation when the dose is administered to the patient. You can implement shared classes in one of three ways in Java:

- Rethink your design; perhaps the class is shared only because it represents two more concepts, which can be separated into their own classes.

- If the instances are on a single Java virtual machine, use synchronized methods to ensure that only one thread has access to the instance at a time.

- If the instances are in processes that reside on different virtual machines (for example, on different processors), use a RemoteObject (defined in the java.rmi.server.RemoteObject package).

SEE ALSO
➤ *Learn more about class synchronization, page 467*

Designing Task Rendezvous

Once you've combined events into event groups and allocated those groups to tasks, it's time to determine how threads communicate with one another. The point at which two threads meet to exchange information or synchronized control is known as a rendezvous.

Rendezvous may be an associative class

The rendezvous itself has attributes and behavior. Consider modeling your more sophisticated rendezvous as associative classes.

Caution: Don't use a spin-wait when a blocking wait will do

Some designers implement a waiting rendezvous by simply spinning in place, constantly checking to see if the other task is ready to communicate. This design needlessly wastes CPU resources. Use a blocking wait and let the runtime environment notify you when the other task is ready.

Use an interaction diagram to capture interprocess communications

If your application has many processes, use a UML interaction diagram (particularly a sequence diagram) to model the communications between processes.

Often one task will be ready to rendezvous before the other. As part of your design you should decide what the task should do in this situation. For example, you might:

- Wait indefinitely (a *waiting rendezvous*).
- Start a timer, and time out if the other task is not ready when the timer expires (a *timed rendezvous*).
- Return immediately (a *balking rendezvous*).
- Raise an exception and treat the communications failure as an error (a *protected rendezvous*).

Identifying Failure Modes and Criticality Effects

Software is increasingly being used in critical applications in which property may be damaged or people may be hurt if the application fails. If your application is critical, consider performing a Failure Modes and Criticality Effects Analysis, or FMCEA (often pronounced for-mee-ka). You may identify three sources of failure:

- Hardware failure
- Failure in other software
- Failure in your software

For example, if you're writing a satellite tracking application, it's important that the motors on the antenna respond to your movement commands. Ask yourself how this hardware component could fail. What would happen to the application in that case? How can you detect the failure? How could you recover?

A hardware engineer can tell you how hardware components fail and which failure modes are most common. For example, a motor can jam or the control wires leading to it may break. If the motor fails, your application will not be able to aim the antenna at the moving satellite, interrupting communications. Within your application, you can detect the failure by monitoring a position sensor. If you call for the motor to move and the position sensor doesn't report movement, then either the motor or the position sensor has failed.

Although we usually think of failure in hardware, software can break as well. Suppose we are using a commercial product such as a database manager. A fault in the database manager could corrupt the database, causing us to get incorrect information when we execute a query.

Some failure modes are rare, but have catastrophic effects. Other failure modes lead to minor problems, but are so common that they become a nuisance. In either of these cases, you should ensure that your software can detect the failure; then design a mechanism for recovering from the failure.

Building Diagnostics to Detect Failure

Here's a step-by-step procedure for designing diagnostics for your software:

Designing diagnostics

1. Prepare a block diagram showing every hardware and software component that your software communicates with.

2. Identify the failure modes for each component and the criticality effects for each failure mode.

3. If the failure mode is common or the criticality is severe, add software (and hardware if necessary) to ensure that the component is independently observable and controllable.

4. Use each component's observability and controllability as the basis for software that determines whether the failure has occurred. This software is your *diagnostic*.

5. Schedule the diagnostic to run regularly and to report failures to a human operator.

The frequency with which you run your diagnostic depends on the nature of your application. Often you'll want to have several levels of diagnostic—a non-intrusive diagnostic might be scheduled to run continually, whenever the system is idle. A more intensive diagnostic might be run whenever a failure is detected, in order to identify the failing component. Here's one hierarchy of diagnostics you may find useful:

- Level 1—A comprehensive diagnostic in which the output of each component is observed or measured by a human operator, rather than relying upon the observation made by the software. The system must typically be taken offline. The complete diagnostic may require several hours.

- Level 2—Similar to Level 1, but operators are only required to observe components with a critical failure mode. The system may be taken offline, but the diagnostic should be able to be completed in about half the time required by a Level-1 diagnostic.

- Level 3—Similar to Levels 1 and 2, but with even fewer components checked by physical observation or measurement. The goal is to verify the correct operation of key components in ten minutes or less. The system may be placed offline while the diagnostic is run.

- Level 4—An automated self-test that can be run whenever a problem is suspected, or as part of periodic maintenance. The goal is that the system be offline for no more than 30 seconds.

- Level 5—A regular self-test that is run regularly during normal operation. A Level-5 diagnostic must not interfere with normal system operation.

Recovering from Faults

Mission-critical systems are often designed with redundant hardware components. For example, many database managers are designed for warm failover. If your client application is unable to contact the primary database host, it should attempt to contact the secondary host, and then notify a human operator that a failover has occurred.

In Java you can detect failures of all sorts by using *exceptions*. Exceptions are special objects (descended from the Throwable class) that report conditions that a reasonable application might want to catch. I recommend that you begin thinking about the variety of hardware and software failures that may occur in your

Consider building predictive diagnostics

Once you have ensured observability and controllability of all components, you may want to add predictive diagnostics. For example, a pneumatic system with a slow leak may continue to perform within specifications, but at a somewhat slower speed. If your software is monitoring the response of a mechanical component and notices that the mechanical system is running slower than usual, you may be able to bring the problem to the operator's attention and recommend that they run a diagnostic looking for air leaks.

application while you're still doing architectural design, and design an exception hierarchy to match those faults.

Once you've identified the exceptions that your classes can throw, start working on a policy for handling each exception. If you have redundant hardware, your strategy for some exceptions might be failover to the other hardware and report the problem to a human operator. Some exceptions (such as a divide-by-zero exception) represent a programming error. You might want to catch those and bring them out to the console, so that you can fix them during testing.

Sometimes a fault cannot be fixed within the system and will require human intervention. Part of your system design should include a series of logs in which you capture detailed information about each failure, and an alarm mechanism to let a human operator know that something bad has happened. For example, if the communications link between the pharmacy computer and the nurse's workstation goes down, both computers should alert their operator to the problem, so that someone can begin to isolate and repair the fault.

Arranging Classes into Packages

In Java, *packages* take the place occupied by libraries in other languages. One of the principal uses of packages is to support code reuse. As you work through your architectural design, think about how you might reuse this software in the future and group classes into reusable chunks.

Often you'll decide that the entire application belongs in a single package. That's fine—just insert a `package` statement at the top of each class file. The following line in a class file assigns this class to the package named `com.mcp.usingjava12.pharmacy`:

```
package com.mcp.usingjava12.pharmacy;
```

If you're using a CASE tool to generate your Java, go to the component diagram and identify the source-code components. Then assign each component to a package. Your CASE tool will add the `package` statement to each class file for you. We'll talk more about packages in Chapter 15, "Understanding Packages."

How do I choose a package name?

In order to keep package names unique, Sun recommends that you form your package name based on your Internet domain, only in reverse. Note, too, that the package name implies a directory structure. The files in `com.mcp.usingjava12.pharmacy` belong in the directory named `com/mcp/usingjava12/pharmacy`.

Design by Pattern

Within the software industry numerous *design patterns* have emerged. A design pattern is a standard way of arranging software components (typically classes) to accomplish an objective. A typical pattern will give you a standard way of arranging several classes (typically 2 to 12) to accomplish a particular objective.

Many of these patterns can be implemented in any language. Others rely on features found in object-oriented languages such as C++, but can be easily implemented in Java. The classic book that identifies patterns is *Design Patterns: Elements of Reusable Software* (Addison-Wesley, 1995) by Gamma, Helm, Johnson, and Vlissides (often known as the Gang of Four, or GoF). As a professional software developer, you should make it a point to become familiar with the major patterns. When you recognize a standard pattern in your architectural diagrams, you may be able to implement it with existing code, or at least with an existing design. By using patterns, you reduce the time required to develop your application and will increase the reliability of your software.

Many of the best patterns are expressed in the following form:

```
IF      you find yourself in CONTEXT
        for example, EXAMPLES,
        with PROBLEM,
        entailing FORCES
THEN    for some REASONS
        apply DESIGN FORM AND/OR RULE
        to construct SOLUTION
        leading to NEW CONTEXT and OTHER PATTERNS
```

Keywords like CONTEXT and EXAMPLES are expanded in the pattern. In this context the term FORCES refers to broad requirements, such as the architectural abilities.

As you can see, once you've mastered a number of patterns, you can spot patterns (and, hence, solutions) quickly based on your architecture diagrams.

This section describes some of the major patterns identified in the industry. These patterns are often grouped into three categories:

- Creational patterns
- Structural patterns
- Behavioral patterns

The Java Abstract Windowing Toolkit (AWT) was explicitly written to follow the design patterns. The Composite pattern (one of the GoF's structural patterns) is at the heart of the AWT. The `Component` class is called `Component` and the `Composite` class is called `Container`.

The AWT uses the Strategy pattern (a behavioral pattern) to lay out the parts of a window. Each `Container` can have its own `LayoutManager`.

Since Java is designed to be platform-independent, the designers of AWT were careful not to tie the AWT to native GUI objects (called widgets). Instead, they used the structural pattern called Bridge: When you work with an AWT graphical `Component`, that `Component` communicates with a native peer object. As a Java programmer, you can't get to the native object, but you can control it through the AWT `Component`.

Peer objects are instantiated by using the Abstract Factory creational pattern. The Toolkit brings a new `ComponentPeer` into existence when you add a `Component` to a `Container`.

Understanding Creational Patterns

Creational patterns are used to bring new objects into existence. Sometimes you can use more than one creational pattern in the same design. For example, you might use Abstract Factory to store a set of Prototypes to use as the basis for generating new objects. The Builder pattern can use any of the other creational patterns to do its work.

Here are the five creational patterns identified by the Gang of Four:

- Abstract Factory—Provides an interface for creating families of related or dependent objects without specifying their concrete classes.

Learn about patterns on the Web

You can find many patterns online, at `http://hillside.net/patterns/patterns.html`. There's a Frequently Asked Questions list at `http://g.oswego.edu/dl/pd-FAQ/pd-FAQ.html`. For detailed information about the 23 patterns in the GoF book (as well as many other excellent patterns), visit the Portland Pattern Repository at `http://c2.com/cgi/wiki?DesignPatterns`, or see `http://rampages.onramp.net/~huston/patterns.htm`.

■ Builder—Separates the construction of a complex object from its representation, so that the same construction process can create different representations.

■ Factory Method—Defines an interface for creating an object, but lets subclasses decide which class to instantiate. Factory Method lets a class defer instantiation to its subclasses.

■ Prototype—Specifies the kinds of objects to create using a prototypical instance and creates new objects by copying this prototype. (Some authors refer to this pattern as Exemplar to avoid confusion with the concept of a software prototype.)

■ Singleton—Ensures that a class has only one instance and provides a global point of access to it.

Using Structural Patterns

Structural patterns have to do with how objects fit together. For example, if you're reusing a class from another project and it doesn't have the interface you want, use the Adapter pattern to modify the interface. If you're developing a new class but want its implementation to vary without having to rewrite its client classes, use the Bridge pattern.

The Gang of Four identified seven structural patterns:

■ Adapter—Converts the interface of a class into another interface that clients expect. The Adapter pattern lets classes work together even though they may have incompatible interfaces.

■ Bridge—Decouples an abstraction from its implementation, so that the two can vary independently.

■ Composite—Composes objects into a tree structure to represent part-whole hierarchies. Often useful when your class diagrams show an aggregation hierarchy.

■ Decorator—Attaches additional responsibility to an object dynamically. May be used as a dynamic alternative to subclassing.

Start with Factory Method and migrate to another creational method

When you're getting started on an application, consider building new objects using the Factory Method pattern. It's less complicated and more customizable than the other creational patterns. Once you've built a prototype and know where you need flexibility (and where you don't), you can move the design toward Abstract Factory, Prototype, or Builder as necessary.

- Facade—Provides a unified interface to a set of interfaces in a subsystem. The Facade pattern is intended to make the subsystem easier to use.

- Flyweight—Supports large numbers of fine-grained objects efficiently.

- Proxy—Provides a surrogate or placeholder for another object in order to control access to it.

Working with Behavioral Patterns

Behavioral patterns are concerned with the assignment of responsibilities to and between objects. There are 11 behavioral patterns in the GoF book:

- Chain of Responsibility—Decouples the sender of a request from its receiver by giving more than one object a chance to handle the request. Each receiving object passes the request along the chain until one of them handles the request.

- Command—Encapsulates a request as an object. By using the Command pattern, you can parameterize clients based on the kind of requests they receive. You can also queue requests in a collection class, log them, and support undoable operations.

- Interpreter—Embeds an interpreter for a language in the application. Useful for supporting runtime queries or validating user input.

- Iterator—Provides a way to access the elements of an aggregate object sequentially without exposing the object's underlying representation. You'll often choose the Iterator pattern when you are traversing a Composite structure.

- Mediator—Defines an object that encapsulates how a set of objects interact.

- Memento—Captures and externalizes an object's internal state so the object can be restored to this state later.

- Observer—Defines a one-to-many dependency between objects so that when one object changes state, all of its dependents are notified and updated automatically.

See this example of the Decorator pattern in Java

Jonathan Chashper has provided a nice example of the Decorator pattern used with Java exceptions at `http://www.geocities.com/CollegePark/Library/4275/decorator.html`. He explains his approach and gives two examples with Java source code.

Prototype works well with Composite and Decorator

If you find yourself making heavy use of the Composite and Decorator patterns, consider using Prototype as your creational pattern. They tend to work well together.

- State—Allows an object to alter its behavior when its internal state changes. To the outside world the object appears to change its class.

- Strategy—Defines a family of algorithms, encapsulates each one, and makes them interchangeable. By using the Strategy pattern you can change the algorithm independently of the clients that use it.

- Template Method—Defines the skeleton of an algorithm in a base class, but defers some steps to the subclasses.

- Visitor—Represents an operation to be performed on the elements of an object structure. The Visitor pattern lets you define a new operation without changing the classes of the elements on which it operates.

Detailed Design

Until now, most of our design work has been language-independent. While we've assumed that we were working in an object-oriented environment, we could implement our design in C++ or Smalltalk, just as well as in Java. Now it's time to focus on the Java-specific design steps.

Prepare a Compilable Specification

If your CASE tool can generate Java, generate the Java files and examine them. Chances are good that the Java captures the static relationships shown on your class diagrams. The methods are stubs. For example, Rational Rose generates the following Java for the `wasGivenSuccessfully(TPatient thePatient)` method:

```
public boolean wasGivenSuccessfully(TPatient thePatient) {
}
```

You need to fill in the blanks before you can successfully compile this Java. For example, I added the following lines to the `wasGivenSuccessfully()` method, so the compiler didn't complain about the lack of a `return` statement:

```
boolean theDummyResult = true;
return theDummyResult;
```

Learn more about the Observer pattern

The Observer pattern is one of the more popular in software engineering. Learn more about it at `http://www.kinetica.com/ootips/observer-pattern.html`.

Another repository of behavioral patterns

Many of the best patterns were first discovered in Smalltalk, an older, object-oriented language. You can see some of the behavioral patterns identified by users of that language at `http://www.mk.dmu.ac.uk/~gperkins/Smalltalk/`.

Consider generating Java from your CASE tool

Most CASE tools can generate at least some Java-based on your class diagrams. Examine the capabilities of your CASE tool; make sure you understand the ramifications of your design decisions on names and attributes.

I recommend that as soon as you've filled in these return statements that you immediately compile the Java code generated by your CASE tool. If you have any compile errors, go back and fix your static design. Once the Java generated from your model compiles, place those files under configuration control.

Once you've finished identifying and describing all of the classes, you're ready for the final step of detailed design (in which you design each method).

Designing the Methods

Since you've already decomposed your application into classes and methods, the average size of a method is likely to be low—20 lines is a good target. Short methods are easy to design; you can use any of several methods to sketch out their behavior:

- UML action diagram

- Conventional flowchart

- Nassi-Schneiderman flowchart

- Formal Program Design Language, or PDL (often called pseudocode)

- Informal PDL (often called structured English)

The mechanism is inherently a state machine in some cases, so you might choose a state diagram or state table to represent the logic of the method.

In most cases I prefer pseudocode. I place the pseudocode directly into the source file, as comments, and then leave those comments in place as documentation for the method.

Writing the Pseudocode

Not all methods require detailed design documentation. Your methods will fall into one of these seven categories:

- constructors   Called to make a new instance of your class

- clean-up or finalize   Called when you're done with an instance

- copy   Called to copy the contents of one instance to another

Does your CASE tool support reverse engineering?

Many CASE tools can build UML diagrams from Java source code. If your CASE tool allows you to do this, then you can make changes in your source code as you work on your methods and reverse-engineer that code to keep your diagrams up-to-date.

How big should a method be?

Many experts strive to keep each method down to about 20 lines; about half a page or one screenful. The advantage of this approach is that each method can be seen and understood at a glance, which reduces maintenance time.

You can shorten your methods and reduce code complexity by introducing *private methods*—methods that can be accessed by your class, but are unavailable to other classes.

- set   Called to assign a value to a data member
- get   Called to retrieve a value from a data member
- I/O   Called to communicate with an external device
- domain-specific   A method specific to your application

I recommend that you write pseudocode (or otherwise document the logic) for copy methods and domain-specific methods. I also recommend that you document any method that throws an exception.

To learn more about integrating Java with database management systems, see Chapter 21, "Using the Java Database Connectivity Package."

Java Programming Idioms

Programmers have found that in nearly all programming languages there's more than one way to accomplish a particular task. In some cases programmers have decided that there's one best way, or at least one usual way. These common approaches are called programming idioms, and you'll see them come up again and again when you read other programmers' code.

Java is a young language, so not too many Java-specific idioms have been developed yet. However, Java's syntax is so similar to C++ that most C++ idioms work well in Java. This section lists some of the common idioms that work well in Java.

Idioms are closely related to tips, which are widely available on the Web and in print. The magazine *JavaWorld* is a good starting point for tips. Visit http://www.javaworld.com/javaworld/ javatips/#nuts for the current list, and http://www.javaworld. com/javaworld/javatips/jw-javatips.index.html for a complete index.

Map Relationships to Code

During analysis you identified a variety of relationships between classes. You should get in the habit of recognizing certain

---

RDBMS or ODBMS

If you're using a relational database management system (RDBMS) such as Oracle or Sybase, your detailed design should include the schema of the database. If you're using an object-oriented database management system (ODBMS) such as ObjectStore, you can avoid this step. Simply use your CASE tool to mark objects as persistent. If you use Rational Rose as your CASE tool and ObjectStore as your database manager, download Blueprint (free at http://www.odi.com/ content/products/ blueprint/blueprint. html) and let it write all the code ObjectStore needs to integrate the database with your Java.

Idioms in print

For a good selection of C++ idioms (many of which are appropriate for Java) see James Coplien's *Advanced C++: Programming Styles and Idioms* (Addison-Wesley, 1992).

standard relationships and translating them into a Java design. The standard relationships (with examples) are as follows:

- is-a   A parakeet IS-A bird
- has-a   A parakeet HAS-A wing
- uses-a   A parakeet USES-A perch
- creates-a   A parakeet CREATES-AN egg

Coding the is-a Relation

The is-a relationship holds between classes and says that one class is a specialization of another. On UML class diagrams use the generalization arrow to point from the specialized class back to the more general class.

The most common way to represent an is-a relation is by sub-classing. We could say the following:

```
public class Parakeet extends Bird {
. . .
}
```

Any `public` characteristic of `Bird` is also a characteristic of `Parakeet`.

Coding the has-a Relation

The has-a relationship is also called the is part of or uses for implementation relationship. On UML class diagrams use the aggregate symbol to denote has-a.

Suppose that your class diagram shows that class A has-a class B. If class B is an independent concept that may be used by other classes, implement it in its own class file and put a reference to an instance of B into A. Thus, if your design needs to capture the fact that birds, bugs, and bats all have wings, you might write the following:

```
public class Bird {
  private Wing leftWing;
  private Wing rightWing;
  . . .
}
```

Idioms on the Web

For another view of Java idioms, visit `http://c2.com/cgi/wiki?JavaIdioms`. Many of these recommendations are more like design patterns than idioms; the distinction is a fine one. Be sure to read the comments that have been posted on each idiom—some of these idioms are controversial.

On the other hand, if you are building a class A that totally encapsulates the concept of class B, implement class B as an *inner class* of class A. An inner class is a class definition included within another class definition. Thus, if you're planning to write a program about birds and nobody will ever need to get to a `Wing` except the `Bird` that owns it, you could write the following:

```
public class Bird {
  class Wing {

    . . .

  }
  private Wing leftWing;
  private Wing rightWing;

  . . .

}
```

The advantage of this approach is that the concept of a wing is now totally encapsulated by class `Bird`. No other class can refer to a `Wing`. By making the code reflect your view of the real world, you're less likely to make an error and use a `Wing` inappropriately.

Coding the uses-a Relation

As your classes go about their business (which is implemented in methods), they will have occasion to use instances of other classes. For example, to bring your parakeet to a rest, you might write the following:

```
Perch aPerch = new Perch();
theParakeet.land(aPerch);
```

In order to land, the parakeet much have a perch; the relationship between `Parakeet` and `Perch` is a uses-a relationship. Implement uses-a relationships by passing the used class as a parameter to the using class's method.

You also have a uses-a relationship when a method in one class uses the services of another class. For example, you might write the following:

```
public class Parakeet {

  . . .

  public boolean isSick(Veterinarian theVet)
  {
```

```
    return theVet.check(this);
  }
}
```

Coding the creates-a Relation

Most of the time relationships are between one class and another (for example, is-a), or between one instance and another (such as uses-a). The creates-a relationship is unusual in this regard: It is a relationship between an instance and a class. For example, when your parakeet is in the family way, you may write the following:

```
Egg layEgg() {
  Egg theEgg = new Egg();
  return theEgg;
}
```

Class Parakeet here calls upon class Egg to make a new instance. Whatever object is using this instance of Parakeet now has an instance of Egg as well.

Implement Callbacks with Interfaces

Java interfaces resemble abstract classes in which every method is abstract. They are used in Java to implement classes that would otherwise belong to more than one inheritance hierarchy. I describe interfaces in Chapter 9, "Increasing Program Sophistication by Using Interfaces."

Sometimes you need to implement a uses-a relationship in which the used object can communicate with the using object. If you know about this need when you design both classes and you're willing to strongly couple the two classes, you can simply code a reference to the used object into the using object's class. More commonly, you don't want a high degree of coupling, so you use a *callback* method. A callback method allows an object of one class to tell an object of another class where to find it. In C++ you can pass a function pointer as a method paramter. When the using instance wants to communicate with the used object, it simply invokes that function. Java doesn't allow you to pass function pointers, but you can accomplish the same thing by using interfaces.

One common naming convention is to name callback methods add.... You can easily implement callbacks by using an interface that encapsulates the add... behavior. An example follows.

Suppose we want to make a new dose for a patient and have the nurse administer the dose. We can pass the software object to the nurse, but something may happen to the physical object—when the nurse is ready to dose, the pill may not be in the patient's drawer. In that case we want the dose to tell the pharmacy that it needs another copy of itself sent up to the ward. Here's the interface:

```
public interface Replaceable
{
   // in an interface we only declare the method, we don't
➥define it
   public void needsReplacement();
}
```

Now we make sure that TDose is replaceable:

```
public class TDose implements Replaceable
{
   public void needsReplacement()
   {
     // send up a replacement dose
     . . .
   }
   . . .
}
```

Class TNurse expects to get a Replaceable instance when the nurse attempts to access the physical dose:

```
public class TNurse
{
   private Replaceable fEvent;
   public setCurrentDose(Replaceable theEvent)
   {
     fEvent = theEvent;
   }
   public void notifyAboutMissingDose()
   {
       fEvent.needsReplacement();
```

```
  }
    . . .
}
```

When the nurse realizes that the physical dose is missing and notes this fact through her user interface, class TNurse calls notifyAboutMissingDose. The only thing we have exposed to TNurse about the dose is that it is replaceable. Our instance of TDose knows what kind of dose it is and takes action to tell the pharmacy to send up another physical copy of itself. TDose can also initiate any logging or auditing steps required. For example, if the medication is a controlled substance, extra steps are required to record the fact that a narcotic is missing.

Implement Schema Evolution through Prototypes

If your application includes a database, you'll need to define the layout of the data for your database manager. These layouts are called *schema*. After your application is fielded, you'll commonly need to add attributes to the objects that you're storing in the database. Most commercial database managers allow you to do this through a mechanism called *schema evolution*. That mechanism takes care of the database, but how do you modify the instances that are already in memory without stopping the system? In our hospital application, must we stop the entire hospital from dosing patients in order to make a minor change to some class?

We can solve this problem by using the Prototype (also known as Exemplar) design pattern. An Exemplar object is a static object that's always available. Here's an example:

```
public class TDose
{
  public TDose (Exemplar theExemplar) {
    /* null */
  }
  public TDose make() {
    return new TDose();
  }
  public TDose make(TMedication theMedication, TPatient
➥thePatient) {
```

```
        return new TDose(theMediation, thePatient);
    }
    public boolean isDue() {
        . . .
    }
    public boolean wasGivenSuccessfully() {
        . . .
    }
    protected TDose() {
        fMedication = NULL;
        fPatient = NULL;
    }
    protected TDose(TMedication theMedication, TPatient
    thePatient) {
        fMedication = theMedication;
        fPatient = thePatient;
    }
    private TMedication fMedication;
    private TPatient fPatient;
}
```

This example looks like a typical Java class, except that I've made all of the constructors except one `protected` (for use by derived classes). I've replaced those constructors with a new method: `make()`. The remaining public constructor takes an `Exemplar` as its parameter. Here's the declaration of `Exemplar`:

```
class Exemplar {
    public Exemplar() { /* null */ }
}
```

Now we can make a `TDose` Exemplar:

```
TDose dose = new TDose(Exemplar());
```

The `make()` methods do the work of a constructor, but they are simply methods on an instance of the class. Instead of writing the first line of code shown here, you write the second.

```
TDose jonesIbuprofen = new TDose(ibuprofen800mgCaplet,
➥MrsJones);

TDose jonesIbuprofen = dose->make(ibuprofen800mgCaplet,
➥MrsJones);
```

What's the advantage of the Exemplar-based method? Suppose that after the system is up and running, the hospital's pharmacist wants to split the concept of dose into two new concepts: TGeneralDose and TControlledSubstanceDose, where a TControlledSubstanceDose is a dose of a narcotic. If we were using constructors, we would have to change all our calls to the TDose constructor to either TGeneralDose() or TControlledSubstanceDose(), depending upon the nature of the medication in the dose. With the Exemplar-based approach, we simply rewrite make():

```
public TDose make(TMedication theMedication, TPatient
➥thePatient) {
    TDose theResult;
    if (TMedication.isControlledSubstance())
       theResult = new TControlledSubstanceDose
➥(theMedication, thePatient);
    else
       theResult = new TGeneralDose(theMedication,
➥thePatient);
    return theResult;
}
```

A further advantage of this approach is that the thousands of existing doses can continue in the system, unchanged, until they are given to patients. All new doses will be made using the new version of make().

If old instances of an object will not disappear quickly in your application, consider writing a new method that converts an existing object to the proper kind of new object. The logic is likely to be similar to the new make(). The following is an example:

```
public TDose cutover(TDose theOldDose) {
    TDose theResult;
    if (theOldDose.fMedication.isControlledSubstance())
       theResult = new TControlledSubstanceDose(theOldDose);
    else
       theResult = new TGeneralDose(theOldDose);
    return theResult;
}
```

You'll also need to write constructors that copy all of the data members of a TDose to the corresponding data members of TControlledSubstancesDose() and TGeneralDose(). Once you have

Use the Exemplar object as a "mother hen"

You can use the Exemplar object to keep track of all instances that it makes. By doing this, you can easily run cutover() on all existing instances. You can also implement logging or audit functions that iterate over the collection maintained by the Exemplar.

Compile-time type checking versus runtime flexibility

One of Java's strengths is compile-time type checking. You are giving up some of that protection to gain flexibility by using Exemplars. Use this idiom when the benefits of runtime flexibility outweigh the benefits of compile-time type checking. This idiom is particularly appropriate when you are designing first-of-a-kind systems in which objects may have to be changed after many of them have been instantiated.

these new methods, you can write a utility that iterates over each collection of TDoses and converting them, in place, to the appropriate new class. When you're done you can change TDose so that it's abstract, making it so that no one can ever make an instance of TDose again.

Beyond the Basics

Increasing Program Sophistication by Using Interfaces

Learn why multiple inheritance is not available in Java, and why you should like it that way

Discover how you can use interfaces to capture abstract behavior

Understand the options available to you in the interface declaration

Learn to use interfaces as types

See how to make a reference directly to an interface

Understanding Multiple Inheritance

In Chapter 7, "Object-Oriented Analysis: A New Way of Looking at Software," and Chapter 8, "Object-Oriented Design and Programming," you learned to look at the world as a set of classes. Classes could be related by a variety of associations, including HAS-A (composition), USES-A, and CREATES-A. One of the most useful associations is IS-A, in which one class is said to be a specialization of another.

You can usually stay comfortably within a single inheritance hierarchy. Figure 9.1, for example, illustrates a typical inheritance hierarchy for part of the animal kingdom.

FIGURE 9.1

Use UML class diagrams to capture inheritance hierarchies.

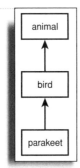

Sometimes you find a class that logically belongs to two (or occasionally more) inheritance hierarchies. For example, class TParakeet is certainly a bird, but in a retail application it is a product. Figure 9.2 shows how you might represent this situation in UML.

FIGURE 9.2

You can show multiple inheritance on a UML class diagram.

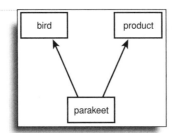

Some languages, such as C++, allow you to directly implement multiple inheritance. While this technique is powerful, it is a nightmare for compiler designers and can lead to subtle defects in the code. When Sun designed Java, it elected to leave multiple inheritance out.

Of course, sometimes you really need multiple inheritance. What, as a Java programmer, are you to do?

Interfaces as an Alternative to Multiple Inheritance

The solution is *interfaces*. An interface behaves as though it were an abstract class in which every method was abstract. Unlike an abstract class, however, you can add an interface to a class that is already part of a different inheritance hierarchy. An interface lists a set of methods that a class implementing the interface must support. The implementation is in the class, not the interface.

Here's an example based on Figure 9.2. Start by identifying the behavior you expect from anything that is a product shown in Listing 9.1.

LISTING 9.1 *Product.java*–**An interface file resembles a class file with no method bodies**

```
1  public interface Product()
2  {
3      // set the price of the product
4      public void setPrice(float thePrice);
5
6      // sell one instance of the product
7      public void sell();
8
9      // buy a quantity of the product at a specified wholesale price
10     public void buy(short theQuantity, float theWholesalePrice);
11  }
```

Now, in Listing 9.2, declare that a parakeet is a product:

Interfaces are equivalent to protocols

Some object-oriented languages allow you to specify a set of agreed-upon behaviors for a class. They call these agreements "protocols." Protocols in those languages are equivalent to interfaces in Java.

Filenames must match interface names

Just as public classes must be defined in a file that matches the class name, so must public interfaces appear in a file that bears their name.

LISTING 9.2 *TParakeet.java*–**Implement the interface's method bodies in the class file**

```java
public class TParakeet extends TBird implements Product
{
  private final float kDailyFoodPrice = 0.60;
  static short fPrice;
  static float fAccount;
  short fInventory;

  public void setPrice(float thePrice)
  {
    fPrice = thePrice;
  }

  public void sell()
  {
    // remove one bird from inventory, and add its sale price
    // to the account
    fInventory--;
    fAccount += fPrice;
  }
  public void buy(short theQuantity, float theWholesalePrice)
  {
    // add the new birds to the inventory; pay for them
    // out of the parakeet account
    fAccount -= theQuantity * theWholeSalePrice;
    fInventory += theQuantity;
  }
  public void feed()
  {
    // every day, feed the birds. Pay for the food out of the
    // parakeet account
    fAccount -= fInventory * kDailyFoodPrice;

    // now do for the bird whatever the base class (TBird)
  says
    super.feed();
  }
}
```

Now you can setPrice(), buy(), and sell() parakeets as required by the Product interface. You can also feed all the birds in the inventory, which decrements the class's account balance by the price of the food. The method feed() calls the base class's feed() method, so anything that is true of birds in general happens when your parakeets are fed. Instances of class TParakeet function both as a TBird and as a Product.

Interfaces are more flexible than abstract classes

You can use interfaces to give a defined set of behavior to classes that are otherwise unrelated.

Interfaces as Abstract Behavior

Here's a more elaborate example from a medical application. Suppose the nurse attempts to give a dose, but finds that the patient is out of the room, perhaps to X-ray or physical therapy. She wants to be reminded to check the patient's room again in a few minutes. In the meantime she wants to go on dosing other patients. Start by writing an interface that captures this new behavior.

```
public interfae Remindable
{
  public void beReminded();
  public static final long kMinute = 60000; // in millisec-
onds
}
```

You might add the following code to class TNurse:

```
public class TNurse implements Remindable
{
  private TReminder fReminder;
  TNurse()
  {
    fReminder = new TReminder();
  }
  public void giveDose()
  {
    . . .
    // if patient is not available, set a reminder
    if (!fReminder.remindMe(this, 15*kMinute))
      // oops; can't set reminder!
  }
  public void beReminded()
```

Why are so many interfaces given adjective names?

In many cases you'll use an interface when no true class generalization relationship exists. For example, there's nothing about **TNurse** that makes it a specialization of **Remindable**—that's simply a characteristic of a nurse. The English language uses adjectives to name characteristics, and you can follow this pattern when naming many interfaces.

```
    {
        // tell nurse to attempt to dose the patient; if
patient is not
        // available, optionally set another reminder
        giveDose();
    }
    . . .
}
```

You then implement a class TReminder that includes a method remindMe():

```
public synchronized boolean remindMe(TNurse theNurse, long
time)
{
    boolean theResult = true;
    int index = findNextSlot();
    if (index == NOROOM)
    {
        theResult = false;
    }
    else
    {
        waiting[index] = theNurse;
        waitFor[index] = time;
        new WaitThread(index).start();
    }
    return theResult;
}
```

SEE ALSO

➤ *Learn about threads, page 454*

➤ *For more on the* synchronized *keyword, page 467*

Declaring Your Intentions

Like classes, an interface consists of a declaration and a body. This section describes the requirements for both parts of the interface and gives you recommendations for designing your interfaces.

The Interface Declaration

You must include both an interface declaration and an interface body in an interface file. The minimum declaration has the keyword `interface` and the name of the interface. For example, you can write the following:

```
interface Product
```

You'll often want to declare the interface publicly accessible, as in the following:

```
public interface Product
```

You can also declare *superinterfaces*, which function like base classes for interfaces. For example, if your application runs in a retail pet store, you might want to develop a small interface hierarchy, like the one illustrated in Figure 9.3. You could then write lines like the two following:

```
public interface TLiveProduct extends TAbstractProduct;

public interface TGeneralProduct extends TAbstractProduct;
```

Choosing good names

Some developers like to give interfaces special names, perhaps starting them with the letter **i**. I recommend against this practice. If your interface might ever become a full-fledged class, give it a name that follows your naming convention for classes; that way you won't have to rewrite any code when you make the change.

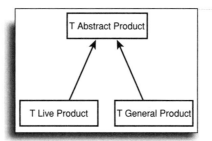

FIGURE 9.3
Interfaces can extend other interfaces.

Any class that implements `TLiveProduct` must implement both the methods of `TLiveProduct` and the methods of `TAbstractProduct`.

If you're writing an interface that extends more than one interface, separate the elements on the list of superinterfaces with commas.

Remember that the interface hierarchy and the class hierarchy are completely separate. A class can extend a class, an interface can extend an interface, and a class can implement an interface. No other relationships are allowed.

Making interfaces public

Your interface will be accessible from any class if you include the keyword **public**. If you forget this keyword your interface will not be accessible outside the package in which you declare the interface. If you leave off the **package** statement, your interface is part of the anonymous package.

The Interface Body

The interface body can contain method declarations such as the following:

```
public void beReminded();
```

It can contain constant declarations such as the following:

```
public static final long kMinute = 60000;
```

Declaring Methods

Choose your interface methods well

Once you've defined an interface and made it available to other developers, you can't easily extend it. If you add a method to the interface, every class that implements that interface has to add the same method. If you must extend an interface, derive a new interface from the old one.

What's an Exception?

Most programmers have learned to put error-handling code in their programs to prevent disaster. In Java you can wrap your code in a `try{...}` block and then `catch{...}` errors (called `Exceptions`) in special pieces of code called `Exception` handlers. You must declare any `Exceptions` that aren't caught in your method in an `Exception` list that appears after the parameter list in the method declaration.

The method declarations are identical to those you've already seen in class definitions, except for the fact that the method body is omitted and replaced with a semicolon. You must include a return value and any parameters (including their types). You may include an access specifier (such as `public`), but the method will always be publicly accessible regardless of your access specifier. If the method throws an `Exception`, you must list them here.

SEE ALSO

> *You take up the subject of* Exception*s in the section titled "Error-Handling with Try and Throw" on page 245*

Declaring Constants

Since all data members are implicitly constant, you must initialize them when you declare them.

Constants declared in the interface body are available as constant members of classes that implement the interface. That's why you could write the following in TNurse:

```
fReminder.remindMe(this, 15*kMinute)
```

Since interface constants are implicitly public, you can use the constant from any class that has access to the interface. If you've declared the interface `public`, any class can read all of the constants—a feature you may find handy. Thus, any class, and not just one that implements Remindable, can use Remindable.kMinute to get the number of milliseconds in a minute.

Implementing an Interface

When you tell the compiler that a class implements a particular interface, you are asking the compiler to tell you if you forget and break the contract. Suppose you wrote the following and forgot to include buy():

```
public class TParakeet extends TBird implements Product
{
  . . .
  public void setPrice(float thePrice)
  {
    . . .
  }

  public void sell()
  {
    . . .
  }
  public void feed()
  {
    . . .
  }
}
```

You'd get a message similar to this one:

```
class TParakeet must be declared abstract. It does not
➥define
void buy(short, float) from interface Product.
public class TParakeet implements Product
                ^
```

Couldn't get much clearer than that, could you?

Passing Interfaces as Types

Now that you have an interface, you can use it as a type just as you would a class. Since the interface represents just a portion of the implementing class' full functionality, you can use interfaces to expose a limited portion of the functionality of the class. You did this in Chapter 8's example, when you wrote the following in TNurse.:

```
public setCurrentDose(Replaceable theEvent)
```

Interface constants are implicitly public, static, and final

An interface cannot have variable data members. Any data members you declare are interpreted as constants, and are set as public, static, and final. It's not a bad idea to explicitly declare these members as public, static, and final to remind yourself (and other programmers) of this fact (though Sun recommends against this style).

Avoid using most modifiers

You are not permitted to declare an interface data member transient, volatile, or synchronized, nor can you declare any member private or protected. While it's not illegal to declare the member (or the methods) abstract, it's redundant—Sun recommends against it. You can add the native keyword in the class file if you want to implement the interface's method by using native code.

Method signatures must match

Your implementing class must use exactly the same signature (the name plus the number and type of arguments) as the interface body. You don't have to use the same argument names, but you should—it makes your code more readable.

The only thing `setCurrentDose` knows about its parameter is that it's replaceable; it doesn't know that it's a dose, and it doesn't know any other dose characteristics.

Assume you have a nurse named Smith and a patient named Jones, and that the patient has an available dose of ibuprophren.

```
NurseSmith.setCurrentDose(jonesIbuprophen);
```

The compiler is perfectly happy with this code, but if you want to make it clear to other programmers that `setCurrentDose()` only knows about the `Replaceable` aspects of the dose, you could add an explicit cast:

```
NurseSmith.setCurrentDose((Replaceable) jonesIbuprophen);
```

You can see the benefits of this approach more clearly in Listing 9.3. An annotated version of the class and interface hierarchies is shown in Figure 9.4.

FIGURE 9.4

The concrete classes in this example depend both on abstract classes and on interfaces.

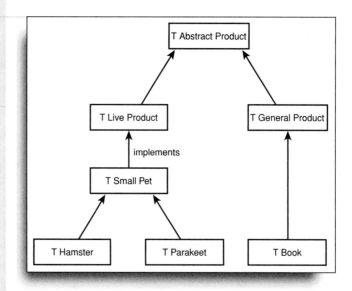

LISTING 9.3   *TStore.java*–**This class implements a retail pet store**

```
1  interface TAbstractProduct
2  {
3     public short getPrice();
4     public String getPrintableType();
5  }
6  interface TLiveProduct extends TAbstractProduct
7  {
8     public String food();
9  }
10 interface TGeneralProduct extends TAbstractProduct
11 {
12    public short itemsPerCase();
13 }
14 abstract class TSmallPet implements TLiveProduct
15 {
16    float fPrice;
17    TSmallPet(float thePrice)
18    {
19       fPrice = thePrice;
20    }
21    public short getPrice()
22    {
23       return fPrice;
24    }
25 }
26 class THamster extends TSmallPet
27 {
28    THamster(float thePrice)
29    {
30       super(thePrice);
31    }
32    public String getFood()
33    {
34       return "seeds";
35    }
36    public String getPrintableType()
37    {
38       return "golden hamster";
39    }
40 }
```

continues...

LISTING 9.3 Continued

```
41  class TParakeet extends TSmallPet
42  {
43    TParakeet(float thePrice)
44    {
45      super(thePrice);
46    }
47    public String getFood()
48    {
49      return "seeds and cuttlestone";
50    }
51    public String getPrintableType()
52    {
53      return "parakeet";
54    }
55  }
56  class TBook implements TGeneralProduct
57  {
58    private static final short kItemsPerCase = 144;
59    float fPrice;
60    String fTitle;
61    TBook(float thePrice, String theTitle)
62    {
63      fPrice = thePrice;
64    }
65    public float getPrice()
66    {
67      return fPrice;
68    }
69    public String getPrintableType()
70    {
71      return "Book entitled " + fTitle;
72    }
73    public short itemsPerCase()
74    {
75      return kItemsPerCase;
76    }
77  }
78  public class TStore
79  {
80    static THamster theHamster;
81    static TParakeet theParakeet;
```

```
82    static TBook theBook;
83    public static void init()
84    {
85      theHamster = new THamster(4.95);
86      theParakeet = new TParakeet(17.99);
87      theBook = new TBook(14.95, "Understanding your Gerbil");
88    }
89    public static void main(String argv[])
90    {
91      init();
92      getInfo(theHamster);
93      getInfo(theParakeet);
94      getInfo(theBook);
95    }
96    public static void getInfo(TAbstractProduct theItem)
97    {
98      System.out.println("This product is a " +
      theItem.getPrintableType() + ".");
99       System.out.println("The price is " + theItem.getPrice() +
      " each.");
100
101    }
102  }
```

Each product in this program—the hamster, the parakeet, and the book—implements an interface that is derived from TAbstractProduct. Since TAbstractProduct supports getPrice() and getPrintableType(), you can write getInfo() in TStore, knowing that those two methods are available in any TAbstractProduct. Since getInfo() doesn't know any more about the product than the fact that it is a TAbstractProduct, none of the other methods on the products are available to it. By limiting the functionality of getInfo(), you've made a big step toward ensuring product correctness.

By the way, the output of running TStore's main method is about what you'd expect:

```
This product is a golden hamster.
The price is 4.95 each.
```

```
This product is a parakeet.
The price is 17.99 each.


This product is a Book entitled "Understanding your Gerbil".
The price is 14.95 each.
```

SEE ALSO

➤ *The* TNurse *interface example, page 214*

Making a Reference to an Interface

Suppose that I need to make a collection of products in my pet store. Until I actually make the products, I don't know whether they're hamsters, parakeets, books, or something else. It's perfectly legal to make a reference to an interface, as long as I assign the reference to an instance of a class that implements that interface before I use it. Thus, I can write the following:

```
public class TStore {
  private TLiveProduct critter;
  public static void main(String argv[])
  {
    critter = new TParakeet(17.99);
  }
}
```

Listing 9.4 shows a more useful application for this technique. (This program relies on the interfaces and product classes shown in Listing 9.3. The class and interface inheritance hierarchies are the same as those shown in Figure 9.4.) In this version of the store, I declare that the store has an inventory that is stored in a collection called theInventory. The only thing revealed about this collection is that I can iterate over it by using a ListIterator. (ListIterator is an interface that was added to the JDK API in version 1.2.)

In init() you make a new LinkedList (to actually store the items) and assign the LinkedList's listIterator() as the store's inventory ListIterator. Then you use the iterator to add some items to the inventory.

Finally, you've modified main() so that it simply uses the iterator to step through the underlying collection. You could make your inventory as large or as small as you like—this version of main() works for all of them.

Iterators versus `for` loops

If you're coming to Java from Smalltalk, my use of an iterator here will seem quite natural. If most of your experience has been in C or C++, however, you may wonder why I didn't use an array and a `for` loop. The answer is that Java collections allow for dynamic resizing, and are usually easier to code than arrays with `for` loops.

LISTING 9.4   *TBigStore.java*–Pass interface-based objects through a *collection* class

```
1  public class TBigStore
2  {
3    static java.util.ListIterator theInventory;
4    public static void init()
5    {
6      java.util.LinkedList theInventoryCollection =
7                             new java.util.LinkedList();
8      theInventory = theInventoryCollection.listIterator();
9
10     // add some items to the inventory
11     theInventory.add(new THamster((float)4.95));
12     theInventory.add(new TParakeet((float)17.99));
13     theInventory.add(new TBook((float)14.95,
14                          "Understanding your Gerbil"));
15   }
16
17   public static void main(String argv[])
18   {
19     init();
20
21     // interate over inventory, getting info on each item
22     while (theInventory.hasNext())
23       getInfo((TAbstractProduct) theInventory.next());
24   }
25
26   public static void getInfo(TAbstractProduct theItem)
27   {
28     System.out.println("This product is a " +
29   theItem.getPrintableType() + ".");
29     System.out.println("The price is " + theItem.getPrice() +
     " each.");
30     System.out.println();
31
32   }
33 }
```

Be sure to cast elements coming out of collections

The elements of a `LinkedList` (and other `Collections`) are `Objects`. You need to cast these elements back to the proper type, as you did in the line in Listing 9.4's `main()`:

```
getInfo((
➥TAbstractProduct)
➥theInventory.next()
➥);
```

Simplifying Code with

Exceptions

Learn why the old status-code based way of handling errors is prone to leave defects in your code

See how you can wrap your code in a *try* block to catch error conditions

Learn how to transfer control from deep in your code to an exception-handling routine

Explore the JDK *Exception* hierarchy to see what exceptions are already defined for you

Find out how to extend the *Exception* hierarchy to make your own exception classes

Learn how to recover from an exception and retry the failing operation

Error-Trapping: What's Wrong with the Old Way?

We, as an industry, systematically mislead programming students. If you're a student in a traditional computer science program, you're being misled right now. If you've had a few months of experience as a programmer since you graduated from such a program, you know what I'm talking about.

When you teach people to program, you inevitably bow to the constraints of an academic calendar and give them assignments that they can complete in a few days—sometimes in just a few hours. In order to give them a meaningful learning experience, you usually allow them to skip one of the most important parts of a program: error checking. In consequence, many of our new "professional programmers" come to the job unprepared for the volume of code they must write to trap errors that occur at runtime.

Some authors, including Frederick Brooks, the author of the classic *The Mythical Man Month* (Addison-Wesley, 1975), have estimated that it takes three times longer to write a software product than it does a software program. A program is defined as a piece of code that is used by itself by the person who developed it (or informally by a few others). A product is intended to be used by people other than the original developer. As such, it must be extensively tested, and all runtime errors must be handled at runtime.

An Example of a Program

Here's an example written in pseudocode. Suppose you want a program to open a text file that you have on the hard drive and display its contents to the screen. You might write a program like this:

```
Get the command-line parameter that names the file
Open the file for reading, getting a file handle
```

```
While (there's data in the file)
{
  read a line from the file
  write the line to the screen
}
close the file
```

If you've studied programming at the college level, you probably wrote programs like this one around your sophomore year. What's wrong with this program? Nothing, as long as you don't expect too much of it. If you, the programmer, are also the user, it should do just fine. Look at what can go wrong:

- The user fails to specify a command-line parameter.
- The user gives a filename, but no such file exists.
- The *system file table* (a data structure in the operating system) has overflowed, meaning there are too many files open systemwide.
- Your process has exceeded the number of open files allowed by the operating system.
- The file exists, but you can't get read access.
- You can read the file, but discover that the data is binary, not text.
- You can read the file, but discover that it's empty.
- An I/O error occurs on the device while reading the file.

You can probably think of even more things that can go wrong, but you get the idea. See if you can convert this program into a product.

Making a Program Bulletproof with Error Traps

When you're reading and writing disk files, you're usually talking to the operating system. (Java insulates you from the operating system, but the principle is the same.) Rewrite the program and add some protection from the runtime errors named:

```
Get the command-line parameter that names the file
  Check to make sure the parameter is not empty
```

```
    If the parameter is empty, tell the user about the
    ➥problem and exit


Open the file for reading, getting a file handle
  If the file table has overflowed,
    {
       wait an arbitrary number of milliseconds
       retry an arbitrary number of times
         if we still cannot get access, tell the user the
         system is too busy and exit
    }
  If our process has too many files open, tell the user
    about the problem and exit
  If the file does not exist, tell the user about the
  ➥problem and exit
  If we can't get permission to read, tell the user
  ➥about the problem
    and exit


read a line from the file (to see if there's data
➥present)
 if the data is not text, tell the user about the
 ➥problem and exit
 if an I/O error occurs, tell the user about the
 ➥problem and exit
if (there's no data in the file)
  tell the user the file is empty, and exit


While (there's data in the file)
{
  write the line to the screen
  read a line from the file
    if the data is not text, tell the user about the
    ➥problem and exit
    if an I/O error occurs, tell the user about the
    ➥problem and exit
}
close the file
```

The 6-line program has become a 22-line behemoth. It's easy to see that the second version will take at least three times longer to code than the first. What's less apparent is that the second version is more likely to contain a logic error. You've had to keep two kinds of issues before you while writing it: the logic itself (represented in the first version) and the error-handling code (represented by the additional lines in the second version).

Making Your Program Bulletproof with Exception-Handling

There's a better way and the designers of Java adopted it. It's called *exception handling*. An *exception* is an event that occurs during the execution of a program and disrupts the normal flow of instructions. Implicit in that definition is the notion that there *is* a normal flow of instructions. The first version of your file-reading program shows such a normal flow. Here's how to use exceptions:

Adding exception-handling to your program

1. Wrap the normal flow of instructions in a `try` block.

2. Note which errors can occur during the normal flow of instructions and make sure each one throws an exception.

3. Catch and handle all exceptions in `catch` blocks.

Error-Handling with *try* and *throw*

Here's how your file-reading program might look if you use exception-handling:

```
try
{
  Get the command-line parameter that names the file
    Check to make sure the parameter is not empty
    If the parameter is empty, throw "parameter empty"
    ➡exception

  try {
    Open the file for reading, getting a file handle
  } catch (file-table-overflowed exception) {
```

If you must use status codes, wrap them in exceptions

If you're calling a native library or other code that returns status codes for errors, wrap the calls in Java methods that throw an exception based on an abnormal status code.

One `try` block or many?

If you prefer, you can wrap each statement that might throw an exception in its own `try` block. I prefer to use a single `try` block for the entire method—I think it's easier to read. Some programmers prefer to switch back and forth, using the style that makes the most sense at the time.

```
        wait an arbitrary number of milliseconds
        retry an arbitrary number of times
        if we still cannot get access, tell the user the
        system is too busy and exit
    }

    read a line from the file (to see if there's data present)

    While (there's data in the file)
    {
      write the line to the screen
      read a line from the file
    }
    close the file
} catch (any other exception) {
    tell the user the name of the exception and exit
}
```

This version of the program has three advantages:

- It's physically shorter than the version built with traditional error-checking code: 13 lines instead of 22.

- It's easier to read—The program logic isn't interrupted by error-checking code.

- It will probably be easier to debug—Exceptions contain a stack trace that you can examine if you choose.

This section describes how to build the try block, how to throw exceptions, and how to propagate exceptions outside your method. The remainder of this chapter talks about the Exception itself (an implementation of the interface Throwable) and ways of catching and handling exceptions.

SEE ALSO
➤ *Learn about interfaces, page 230*

Building the *try* Block

Begin by building the try portion of your file-reading program in Java. You need a stub catch clause to catch the generic Exception. Listing 10.1 shows this program.

Every try requires a catch or a finally

If you choose to wrap any of your code in a **try** block, you must include at least one **catch** or **finally** block (described in this chapter's "Catching an Exception").

LISTING 10.1 *FileReader1.java*–This version of FileReader doesn't catch any specific exceptions

```
1  public class FileReader1 {
2    public static void main(String args[])
3    {
4      try
5      {
6        // Get the command-line parameter that names the file
7        // Check to make sure the parameter is not empty
8        // If the parameter is empty, throw "parameter empty"
           exception
9        if (args.length == 0)
10         throw (new Exception("Usage: FileReader1 filename"));
11
12       // Open the file for reading, getting a file handle
13       java.io.BufferedReader theStream =
14         new java.io.BufferedReader (
15           new java.io.FileReader(args[0]));
16
17       // Read a line from the file (to see if there's data
           present)
18       // While (there's data in the file)
19       String theInputString = new String();
20       while ((theInputString = theStream.readLine()) != null)
21       {
22         // Write the line to the screen
23         System.out.println(theInputString);
24       }
25       // Close the file
26       theStream.close();
27     }
28     catch (Exception e) {
29       System.err.println(e.getMessage());
30       e.printStackTrace();
31     }
32   }
33 }
```

What happened to the `file-table-overflowed` exception?

Java handles operating system-native exceptions (like file-table overflow) itself, so you don't need it in this program.

How to construct an `Exception`

Every `Exception` object defined by Sun has two constructors—a default constructor and one that takes a `String`. You should strive to use the one with the `String`, in order to pass as much specific information about the problem as possible.

This program works by wrapping a JDK `FileReader` in a JDK `BufferedReader`, and then calling the `FileReader.readLine()` method. Check out the `BufferedReader` page in your JDK documentation. You see that it's simply a buffer designed to surround otherwise inefficient readers (such as FileReader). Search for the word throws on this page—you see each exception that BufferedReader's methods can throw. You call the constructor, readLine(), and close(). The only exception that can be thrown by those methods is IOException.

Likewise, examine FileReader. You call one of its constructors—the one that takes a String as a parameter. That constructor can throw FileNotFoundException.

Of course, you also throw a general exception yourself, with the usage message inside.

All of these exceptions are handled by a single, general-purpose catch block:

```
catch (Exception e) {
    System.err.println(e.getMessage());
    e.printStackTrace();
}
```

This catch block catches any Exception (including, of course, the three that you've named). When one of those exceptions occurs, your program prints out the message associated with the exception, and then prints a stack trace to show you exactly where the error occurred.

Compile this program and run it. Enter the following code (with an appropriate CLASSPATH):

```
java FileReader1
```

You get this code:

```
Usage: FileReader1 filename
java.lang.Exception: Usage: FileReader1 filename
        at FileReader1.main(FileReader1.java:10)
```

This stacktrace information is handy when you're troubleshooting your code—it tells you that the exception was thrown from line 10 of your main routine. You may or may not decide to keep the call to printStackTrace() in your production code—that's up to you.

Now call the program in the expected fashion: Give it the name of a text file as its parameter. (Here I used the name of the source file, since it's a handy example of text.)

```
java FileReader1 FileReader1.java
```

Now the program behaves as expected—you should see a dump of your program's source code. If you use `FileReader1.class` as the parameter you get a dump of the binary contents of the class file. That's less than useful when dumped to the screen, but is correct program behavior.

Finally, ask the program to read a file that doesn't exist:

```
java FileReader1 quux.txt
```

You get another exception:

```
C:\Que\USINGJ~1.2\ch10>java -classpath .;
➥C:\jdk1.2beta2\lib\classes.zip FileReader1 quux.txt
quux.txt
java.io.FileNotFoundException: quux.txt
    at java.io.FileInputStream.<init>(FileInputStream.java:58)
    at java.io.FileReader.<init>(FileReader1.java:37)
    at FileReader1.main(FileReader1.java:15)
```

This chapter's "What, Exactly, Are You Throwing?" talks about exceptions themselves. Likewise, "Catching an Exception" elaborates on the `catch` block. For now, examine this business of try-ing and throwing.

Throwing Method *Exceptions*

In Listing 10.1 you put all the work into `main()`. In this case that means that `main()` only had seven executable lines—you're counting semicolons. In most cases, however, you want to keep most of the work down in the class's other methods and let `main` do its work through those methods. Look at a more practical class that uses exceptions in its methods. This class, `TMedication`, captures basic information about a medication in a pharmacy. It reads a list of medications from a disk file and stores them in a Java `Vector` named `fFormulary`. (In a pharmacy, the formulary is the list of available medications.)

LISTING 10.2   *TMedication.java*–This class captures the concept of a
medication line item

```
1  public class TMedication
2  {
3     // The formulary file should have three fields:
4     // Drug name, strength, and package (e.g., oral, IV, otic)
5     protected static final short kNumberOfFields = 3;
6
7     // turn debug statements on or off
8     private static final boolean kDebug = false;
9
10    String fDrugName;
11    Short fStrength;
12    String fPackage;
13
14    protected static java.util.Vector fFormulary;
15
16    TMedication(String theDrugName, Short theStrength, String
       thePackage)
17    {
18      fDrugName = theDrugName;
19      fStrength = theStrength;
20      fPackage = thePackage;
21    }
22
23    protected static void init()
24    {
25      fFormulary = new java.util.Vector();
26    }
27
28    public static void main(String args[])
29    {
30      try {
31        // Get the command-line parameter that names the meds
           file
32        // Check to make sure the parameter is not empty
33        // If the parameter is empty, throw "parameter empty"
           exception
34        if (args.length == 0)
35          throw (new Exception("Usage: TMedication filename"));
36
37        // make an empty collection to hold the formulary
38        init();
39
```

```
40        // load the forumulary from the disk file
41        System.out.println("Loading medications from " + args[0]
          + ".");
42        load (args[0]);
43        System.out.println();
44
45        // show the info a few medications
46        System.out.println("Here is all of the Ibuprofen:");
47        show ("Ibuprofen");
48        System.out.println();
49        System.out.println("Here is all of the Dramamine:");
50        show ("Dramamine");
51        System.out.println();
52        System.out.println("Here is all of the Tylenol:");
53        show ("Tylenol");
54        System.out.println();
55
56        // dump the entire formulary
57        System.out.println(
58          "Here is a list of all medications in the
            formulary:");
59        show();
60      }
61    catch (Exception e) {
62      System.err.println(e.getMessage());
63      e.printStackTrace();
64    }
65  }
66  protected static void load(String theFileName) throws
    Exception
67  {
68    try {
69      // belt and suspenders—make sure the file name is
         nonempty
70      if (theFileName.length() == 0)
71        throw (new Exception("Error: File name is empty"));
72
73      // Open the file for reading, getting a buffered reader
74      java.io.BufferedReader theStream =
75        new java.io.BufferedReader (
76          new java.io.FileReader(theFileName));
77
78      // Read a line from the file (to see if there's data
         present)
```

continues…

LISTING 10.2   Continued

```
79        // While (there's data in the file)
80        String theInputString = new String();
81        while ((theInputString = theStream.readLine()) != null)
82        {
83            // Write the line to the screen as a double-check
84            System.out.println(theInputString);
85
86            // and write it into the formulary
87            java.util.StringTokenizer theTokenizer =
88               new java.util.StringTokenizer(theInputString);
89            if (theTokenizer.countTokens() != kNumberOfFields)
90               throw(new Exception("Illegal input in formular
                     file"));
91
92            // the first token should be the medication name
93            String theDrugName = theTokenizer.nextToken();
94            Short theStrength =
                 Short.valueOf(theTokenizer.nextToken());
95            String thePackage = theTokenizer.nextToken();
96            TMedication theMedication =
97               new TMedication(theDrugName, theStrength,
                     thePackage);
98
99            if (kDebug)
100            {
101               System.out.println("DN: " + theDrugName);
102               System.out.println("S: " + theStrength.toString());
103               System.out.println("P: " + thePackage);
104            }
105
106            // store the entire object
107            fFormulary.add(theMedication);
108
109            // abandon theTokenizer and theMedication; GC will
                 clean
110            // them up later
111        }
112        // Close the file
113        theStream.close();
114    }
115    // a FileNotFound Exception is a kind of IOException
116    // be sure to catch it first if you want special
117    // handling
```

```
118        catch (java.io.FileNotFoundException e) {
119          System.err.println(e.getMessage());
120          e.printStackTrace();
121        }
122        catch (java.io.IOException e) {
123          System.err.println(e.getMessage());
124          e.printStackTrace();
125        }
126     }
127
128     protected static void show(String theKey)
129     {
130         // we allow multiple values per key; get them all
131         java.util.Iterator theIterator = fFormulary.iterator();
132         short theCount = 0;
133         while (theIterator.hasNext())
134         {
135           TMedication nextMedication = (TMedication)
                 theIterator.next();
136           if (nextMedication.fDrugName.equals(theKey))
137           {
138             System.out.println(nextMedication.toString());
139             theCount++;
140           }
141         }
142       if (theCount == 0)
143         System.out.println("Formulary does not contain " +
               theKey);
144     }
145
146     protected static void show()
147     {
148       // show all entries in the formulary
149       java.util.Iterator theIterator = fFormulary.iterator();
150       while (theIterator.hasNext())
151         System.out.println(theIterator.next().toString());
152     }
153
154     public String toString()
155     {
156       return fDrugName + " " + fStrength.toString() + "mg " +
             fPackage;
157     }
158 }
```

Go through one piece at a time. In particular, examine each method to see what exceptions it can throw and which exceptions it catches. Any exceptions that are thrown in a method and not caught there must be declared as part of the method's signature.

Class Declarations

You declare two constants at the top of the file, kNumberOfFields and kDebug; three instance variables, fDrugName, fStrength, and fPackage; and a class variable, fFormulary. fFormulary is a Java Vector, a collection that behaves like an array, but can resize itself dynamically.

The Class Constructor

The TMedication class constructor is nearly trivial. It takes the three parameters that are needed for the instance variables and builds an instance.

Setting Up the Class with *init()*

The init() method is a static method that builds the fFormulary Vector. It is called once, from main(). A quick check of the JDK documentation reveals that the Vector constructor doesn't throw any exceptions.

Integrating the Class with *main()*

The main() method is, of course, the integration point for the class. The functionality of the application resides in other methods, but all of it is visible from main().

main() explicitly throws an instance of Exception for improper usage; this Exception is caught at the bottom of main().

The Exception constructor itself doesn't throw any exceptions. As you've already seen, init() doesn't throw any exceptions, either.

The next "paragraph" of main() calls load(), which you examine in a moment. It then calls show() three times with a String parameter, and once with no parameters. Looking at load()'s signature, you see that it can throw an Exception, which you catch in main(). Neither version of show() throws any Exceptions.

Become familiar with Java collections

One hallmark of a professional programmer is the appropriate use of data structures. Take the time to become familiar with java.util.Abstract Collection, java.util. Dictionary, java.util.AbstractMap, as well as all of their derived classes. You should also learn how java.util.Enumeration, java.util.Iterator, and their kin work.

Reading the Disk File with *load()*

In theory, it should be impossible for main() to call load() with a null parameter. Unfortunately, too often the words "in theory" are code words for "not really." Someday you might change your code in main(), or someone else might use load() in a way you don't expect. You practice defensive programming—if a null file-name slips through, you catch it and throw an Exception. You don't catch this exception in load(); instead, you declare it in the method's signature, and leave it up to the calling routine to either catch the Exception or throw it to the next highest level. (Any exceptions that are not caught by the time they leave main() cause the program to exit.)

Some of the other method calls in load() do throw exceptions. The FileReader constructor can throw a FileNotFoundException, and the BufferedReader.readLine() method can throw a more general IOException. You catch both exceptions in load, so you don't burden the calling routine.

Note that you don't exit in load()'s catch block; you report the exception to the user, but go on in main() to attempt to show() the data. Depending upon your design, you can always call exit() to end the application.

The load() method uses a StringTokenizer to take apart the line from the file. StringTokenizer.nextToken() can throw NoSuchElementException. You don't catch NoSuchElementException, nor do you declare it in the method signature; yet the compiler didn't complain. What happened to the rule that you must either catch or declare every Exception? Is there a compiler bug?

No, but there is a rather controversial exception. If you examine the documentation page for java.util.NoSuchElementException, you see that it belongs to the RuntimeException class. The Java designers determined that some exceptions (such as ArithmeticException, ArrayStoreException, and IndexOutOfBoundsException) may occur in so many places in your program that the burden of requiring programmers to catch or declare them all would be excessive. The designers grouped all such exceptions under the RuntimeException class, and allow

Exit from an exception handler with a non-zero status

By convention, a status code of zero indicates successful completion. If you're exiting from an exception handler, use a non-zero status code such as exit(1).

**Derive your exceptions from
`Exception`, not
`RuntimeException`**

When you build your own
`Exceptions` (described later in
this chapter in "What, Exactly, Are
You Throwing?"), you should derive
them from `Exception` rather
than `RuntimeException`.
That way, you are forced to either
`catch` your exceptions or declare
them. Either way, the signature of
your methods will be more complete, which is nearly always to your
advantage when you're trying to
remove defects from your code.

**Catch more specific exceptions
before more general ones**

Note the comment at the bottom of
`load()`. Exceptions form a hierarchy; `FileNotFound
Exception` is a kind of
`IOException`. If you reverse
the order of the two `catch` clauses, the program won't be able to
find the
`FileNotFoundException`
handler.

**Consider handling your
`RuntimeExceptions`**

The fact that the compiler doesn't
require you to `catch` or declare
your `RuntimeExceptions`
doesn't mean that you shouldn't do
so. If you know you might throw
the `Exception`, go ahead and
handle it in the usual manner—users
of your code will appreciate knowing your class' full public interface.
Just remember that
`RuntimeExceptions` usually
represent programming errors—if
you're throwing them, there's a
problem with your code.

them to be thrown at runtime without an explicit `catch` or declaration.

Like the `NoSuchElementException`, the `NumberFormatException` that
can be thrown by the `Short` constructor is a `RuntimeException`.
This exception, in particular, is a good candidate to be caught,
since it opens a potential hole that could allow corrupt data into
the formulary. You don't catch it in this version, so bad input
throws an exception that propagates out to `main()` and termi-
nates the program.

Finally, `load()` calls `close()` on the `BufferedReader`. This method
can throw an `IOException`, which you're already catching.

Two Versions of *show()*

The first version of `show()` lists all of the medications whose
name match the parameter. `show()` uses an `Iterator`, whose
`next()` method can throw a `NoSuchElementException`. The
`NoSuchElementException` is a kind of `RuntimeException`, however,
so it need not be caught or declared.

The second version of `show()` is a simplification of the first—it
simply lists all elements of the formulary by using an `Iterator`. It
can throw the same (runtime) `Exceptions` as the first version of
`show()`.

Implementing *toString()*

Most classes should have some form of `toString()`—either
inherited from a base class or implemented on their own. Your
`TMedication` class has its own `toString()`, which puts together a
printable string based on the three instance variables.

Neither the `String` concatenation nor the call to
`Short.toString()` throws any exceptions, so you have nothing in
this method to `catch` or declare.

Testing *TMedication*

Once you've built `TMedication.class`, you can run it with any of
five test cases:

- No file named on the command line

- A file named that does not represent any real file

- A file named that doesn't contain numbers in the second column

- A file named that doesn't contain three columns of data

- A properly formatted formulary file

Build TMedication and satisfy yourself that the Exceptions work correctly in the first two cases. The following file tests the third case:

```
Ibuprofen 800 caplet
Dramamine BAD caplet
Ibuprofen 200 capsule
```

If you test with this file, you should get a message similar to this one:

```
C:\Que\USINGJ~1.2\ch10>java -classpath .;
➥C:\jdk1.2beta2\lib\classes.zip TMedication form2.txt
Loading medications from form2.txt.
Ibuprofen 800 caplet
Dramamine BAD caplet
BAD
java.lang.NumberFormatException: BAD
    at java.lang.Integer.parseInt(Integer.java:720)
    at java.lang.Short.parseShort(Short.java:89)
    at java.lang.Short.valueOf(Short.java:108)
    at java.lang.Short.valueOf(Short.java:122)
    at TMedication.load(TMedication.java:94)
    at TMedication.main(TMedication.java:42)
```

The following file tests the next case:

```
Ibuprofen 800 caplet
Dramamine caplet
Ibuprofen 200 capsule
```

If you test with this file, you should get a message similar to this one:

```
C:\Que\USINGJ~1.2\ch10>java -classpath .;
➥C:\jdk1.2beta2\lib\classes.zip TMedication form3.txt
```

Strive for completeness in test cases

Use McCabe's cyclomatic complexity measure (described in "Organizing Your Code" in Chapter 24, "Organizing and Reusing Your Code," to compute the number of independent paths through each method. Build at least one test case for each path.

```
Loading medications from form3.txt.
Ibuprofen 800 caplet
Dramamine caplet
Illegal input in formulary file
java.lang.Exception: Illegal input in formulary file
  at TMedication.load(TMedication.java:90)
  at TMedication.main(TMedication.java:42)
```

This data tests the final case (the one with a properly formatted formulary file):

```
Ibuprofen 800 caplet
Dramamine 100 caplet
Ibuprofen 200 capsule
```

This well-behaved output is received:

```
C:\Que\USINGJ~1.2\ch10>java -classpath .;
➥C:\jdk1.2beta2\lib\classes.zip TMedication
➥formulary.txt
Loading medications from formulary.txt.
Ibuprofen 800 caplet
Dramamine 100 caplet
Ibuprofen 200 capsule

Here is all of the Ibuprofen:
Ibuprofen 800mg caplet
Ibuprofen 200mg capsule

Here is all of the Dramamine:
Dramamine 100mg caplet

Here is all of the Tylenol:
Formulary does not contain Tylenol

Here is a list of all medications in the formulary:
Ibuprofen 800mg caplet
Dramamine 100mg caplet
Ibuprofen 200mg capsule
```

What, Exactly, Are You Throwing?

The previous section alludes to the fact that exceptions form a hierarchy and that you can extend that hierarchy yourself to make your own Exception classes. Now it's time to be more specific.

Go to the JDK class hierarchy page (docs/api/tree.html in your JDK directory) and look for for java.lang.Exception. You should see a page similar to that shown in Figure 10.1. Note that Exception is a kind of Throwable. You see dozens of derived classes by scrolling down through Exception. Pay particular attention to java.lang.RuntimeException—remember that these are the exceptions the compiler won't warn you about if you forget to include them in a catch clause or method declaration. Figure 10.2 illustrates this same hierarchy in a way that shows you the big picture.

FIGURE 10.1

Throwable includes Exceptions (which you should catch, unless they're RuntimeExceptions) and Errors (which you should not catch).

FIGURE 10.2

Class Throwable includes both Error and Exception.

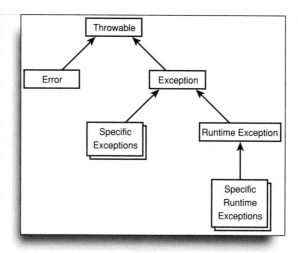

Understanding *Throwable*

Throwable is the parent class of both Exception and Error. Not surprisingly, only Throwables can be thrown by a throw statement. Unexpected conditions detected by the Java Virtual Machine (JVM) are usually thrown as Errors. You shouldn't try to catch these—they indicate a serious problem at the JVM level, and the JVM may be unable to continue. As you saw in the previous section, you should either catch Exceptions or declare them in your method declaration. The compiler won't require you to catch or declare Errors. It won't require you to catch or declare RuntimeExceptions, either (though you should do so as often as possible).

Exploring the JDK *Exception* Hierarchy

In general, you should catch the most specific Exception you can. When you're writing prototype code and are trying to get the logic right, it's okay to just say something like the following at the bottom of main():

```
catch (Exception e) {
    System.err.println(e.getMessage());
    e.printStackTrace();
}
```

As your product moves toward production, however, take the time to go through every method (and every API call inside each method) and identify both the `RuntimeExceptions` and the other `Exceptions` that can be thrown. Replace the `catch (Exception e)` block with a series of more specific `catches`, remembering to `catch` the most specific `Exception` first.

Defining Your Own Exceptions

The inheritance hierarchy under `Exception` is huge. In many cases you find that Sun has already defined an `Exception` class that describes the condition you want to `throw`. In other cases, you need to throw an exception of your own.

Here's a procedure that helps you decide whether you need to define your own exception:

Writing your own exception class

   1. Review the Java class hierarchy (at `docs/api/tree.html` in your JDK directory), looking for an existing `Exception` class that meets your needs.

   2. If no existing JDK `Exception` class meets your needs, devise a naming convention or package name that distinguishes your `Exception` from those of other developers.

   3. Group related `Exceptions` into your own hierarchy, derived from the most specific `Exception` class that's appropriate in the JDK `Exception` hierarchy.

   Write two constructors for your new `Exception` class—one that takes no arguments and one that takes a `String`.

   5. Add any other constructors, data members, and methods you think appropriate for your new `Exception` class.

If you want to throw your own exceptions, don't just throw a general `Exception` (as we did in Listing 10.2). Instead, define your own specific `Exception` and `catch` it.

Sometimes you find a specific derived class of `Exception` and subclass it. At other times your `Exception` won't resemble any of the existing derived classes, so you derive a new class directly from `Exception`.

Follow a naming convention

You may want to adopt a naming convention so your `Exception` classes don't interfere with names that might be chosen by Sun in the future. If you follow the convention of starting all class names with a T, you should have little problem. You should also place user-defined exceptions in your own package. Make sure all of your exceptions end with the word `Exception`.

Add your own exception for use by TMedication to comply with this book's naming recommendation:

Put user-defined exceptions in a package

Avoid the temptation to leave your user-defined exceptions in the anonymous package. Every class you write for production code should go into a named package. Package-naming conventions are discussed in further detail in Chapter 15, "Understanding Packages."

LISTING 10.3   *TUsageException.java*–User-defined exception avoids a general *Exception* being thrown out

```
1  // Package names imply a directory path. The class file for
2  // this file should be in com/mcp/que/usingJava12.
3  package com.mcp.que.usingJava12;
4  public class TUsageException extends Exception
5  {
6     public TUsageException()
7     {
8     }
9     public TUsageException(String s)
10    {
11       super(s);
12    }
13 }
```

While you could add other data members and even methods to your new class, they're not necessary. TUsageException is a perfectly good example of a user-defined exception, small as it is. To round out TMedication, replace both throw (new Exception . . .) lines with throw (new COM.mcp.que.usingJava12. TUsageException . . .). Of course, if you prefer, you can simply import COM.mcp.que.usingJava12.* and name the exception directly.

Now if you run TMedication without specifying a formulary file, you get the following message:

```
Usage: TMedication filename
```

This is the stacktrace:

```
com.mcp.que.usingJava12.TUsageException: Usage: TMedication
   ↪filename
        at TMedication.main(TMedication.java:35)
```

Having removed all references to Exception from the program, you should be confident that you've either caught or declared all (non-runtime) Exceptions at a fairly specific level.

SEE ALSO

➤ *To learn how to define your own packages, see "Writing Your Own Packages" on page 413*

Catching an Exception

As you saw in the previous examples, every `try` block must be followed by one or more `catch` blocks (or a `finally` block, which is described later in this section). You must put the first `catch` block immediately after the closing brace of the `try`—there can be no intervening code.

This section shows you the choices you have in the `catch` code— you can handle the exception or pass it on to the next level of code. You can also pass control to a `finally` block to effect cleanup.

Catching

The general form of the `catch` block is as follows:

```
catch (aThrowable variableName) {
  Java statements
}
```

Remember that the `Throwable` is nearly always an `Exception`. If your program throws an `Error`, you should let the program die.

Use the `variableName` to get access to the internals of the `Exception`. You can write detailed information about the `Exception` to your program's standard error output by writing the following:

```
catch (FileNotFoundException e) {
  System.err.println("Caught FileNotFoundException: " +
  ➥e.getMessage());
}
```

In general, you can take one of six actions when you catch an exception:

- Fix the problem and call the method again.
- Try to work around the problem and continue.
- Take an alternate path through the rest of the method.
- Rethrow the `Exception` to let a higher level of software handle the problem.

Consider using
`getLocalizedMessage()`

If there's a possibility that your code may be used someday by non-English-speaking users, replace your calls to `getMessage()` with `getLocalizedMessage ()`. That way they'll be able to see the message in their own language.

- Throw a different Exception to let a higher level of software handle the problem.
- Exit.

In practice, you'll nearly always choose to exit without attempting to recover.

To *exit()*, or Not to *exit()*

While it's certainly possible to attempt to resume after an Exception has been thrown, there's no clean mechanism for going back and retrying the operation that threw the Exception in the first place. In most cases you'll decide that the problem cannot be repaired and end up calling exit() at the end of your Exception handler.

If you want to try to fix the problem and resume, you can use code like this:

```
short theErrorCounter = 0;
while (someCondition)
{
  try {
    // code to set the condition
  }
  catch (someException e) {
    if (theErrorCounter < kErrorLimit)
      // attempt to repair the fault
    else
      throw ;
  }
}
```

If you use this mechanism, be sure to use a counter or some other mechanism to decide when enough is enough, so you don't get hung in an infinite loop.

Performing a Postmortem

During development you may want to write a general Exception handler that can perform a postmortem on the dead code. If you prefer, you can write a user-defined Exception that includes an instance of an `Object` as a data member. Then pass `this` to your `Exception` constructor.

You can query the `Object` for its class by using `Object.getClass()` in the general `Exception` handler. Look at the documentation page on `Class` to see the range of methods available to you. As a minimum, you might want to call `getName()` or `toString()`. Depending upon which class threw the error, you could then call a more sophisticated printout of the class's internal state. This information, plus the stacktrace that comes in every `Exception`, will help you spot the problem quickly.

Passing *Exceptions* On

When the runtime system detects an `Exception`, it begins searching down the call stack, looking for an appropriate `Exception` handler. The runtime system transfers control to the first appropriate handler it finds. In this case "appropriate" means that the handler either matches the `Exception` class, or the handler matches one of the classes above the `Exception` class in the inheritance hierarchy.

Suppose your program includes the following code:

```
public void someMethod() throws MalformedURLException {
  . . .
}
public void someOtherMethod() throws EOFException {
  . . .
}
public void yetAnotherMethod() throws EOFException {
  . . .
  try {
    someMethod();
    someOtherMethod();
} catch (MalformedURLException) {
  . . .
}
public static void main(String args[]) {
  . . .
```

```
try {
  yetAnotherMethod();
} catch (IOException) {
  . . .
}
}
```

If someMethod() throws MalformedURLException (which is a kind of IOException) the catch() block in yetAnotherMethod() will catch it, since MalformedURLException matches MalformedURLException. If someOtherMethod() throws EOFException (which is also a kind of IOException) the catch() block in yetAnotherMethod() won't match, and Exception propagates out to main(); main() catches it in the IOException handler, since an EOFException is a kind of IOException.

Tracing the Call Stack

Here's an example. Suppose a program has the call stack illustrated in Figure 10.3. The method main() called a method assign(), which is called isControlled(). The method isControlled() throws a FileNotFoundException. If isControlled catches FileNotFoundException or one of its ancestors (IOException or Exception), control remains within isControlled. In this case, isControlled does not have such a handler and it declares that it can throw FileNotFoundException, so the runtime continues searching. It next checks assign(), where it finds a handler for IOException. Since IOException matches an ancestor of FileNotFoundException, control passes to this catch block in assign.

FIGURE 10.3
This program is three levels deep in methods.

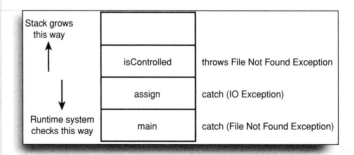

isControlled	throws File Not Found Exception
assign	catch (IO Exception)
main	catch (File Not Found Exception)

Stack grows this way ↑

Runtime system checks this way ↓

In fact, there is a `FileNotFoundException` handler in `main()`, but the runtime will not find it since it stopped checking when it found the match in `assign()`.

Rethrowing an *Exception*

You can rethrow the `Exception` if your `Exception` handler cannot either repair the problem, or determine that the program must exit. It is passed back to the runtime system, which continues to search up the call stack. If the `Exception` is not handled by the time it leaves `main()`, the program exits.

You can also throw a different exception than the one you originally caught. You might do this if you are able to learn more about the problem (and so can throw a more specific `Exception`), or if you encounter a problem within your `Exception` handler.

If you choose to rethrow the original `Exception`, the stacktrace in the `Exception` still points to the place from which the `Exception` was originally thrown. You can put a new stacktrace into the `Exception` by calling `fillInStackTrace()` before you rethrow the `Exception`:

```
throw e.fillInStackTrace();
```

Cleaning Up with *Finally*

There's still one problem with the `TMedication` example. You opened a `BufferedReader` named `theStream` inside `load()`. If, in the course of reading the file, you encounter a misformatted line, you throw an `Exception` that takes you right out of `load`, and you never have a chance to `close theStream`.

Even if you choose to have the `Exception` handled outside `load()` (by no means the best design), you should include a `finally` clause after the `catch` clauses. The runtime system always executes the statements within the `finally` block regardless of what happens within the `try` block. Move the code to close the `BufferedReader` to a `finally` block:

```
catch (java.io.IOException e) {
  System.err.println(e.getMessage());
  e.printStackTrace();
```

Strive to catch specific exceptions

In this example, if `isControlled()` had a `catch` block for `Exception`, the `FileNotFoundException` and any other `Exception` would have stopped there. This fact explains why you should always use the most specific `Exception` possible, consistent with program readability.

If you use `fillInStackTrace()`, be sure to catch `Throwable`

If you choose to use `fillInStackTrace()`, you must `catch` (or declare) `Throwable` rather than `Exception` in one of the higher layers of software. `fillInStackTrace()` returns a `Throwable`, not an `Exception`. This practice is an exception to the rule that you should only catch `Exception` and its descendents.

Why doesn't C++ have `finally`?

If you're coming to Java from C++, you may be wondering why the C++ exception-handling mechanism doesn't have `finally`. C++ has destructors–you can put your cleanup code in there. Remember that the code in the `finally` block is always called at the end of the method, whether an exception was thrown or not.

```
}
finally {
  theStream.close();
}
```

Using *finally* in Constructors

Often you'll want to allocate resources inside a constructor and release them if the constructor fails. For example, if you're constructing `TDose` you may need to connect to a database to get information about the associated `TMedication` and `TPatient`:

```
public class TDose
{
  // private network connection to database
  // keep this connection alive for the life of the
  ➥object
  TDose()
  {
    try {
      // connect to the database
    }
    finally {
      // close and abandon the database connection--
      ➥WRONG!!
    }
  }
}
```

This program won't work correctly; the database connection will be closed and abandoned every time the constructor is called, not just when the database connection fails. Here's the proper design:

```
public class TDose
{
  // private network connection to database
  // keep this connection alive for the life of the
  ➥object
  TDose()
  {
    try {
      // connect to the database
    }
    catch (DatabaseException e) {
      // close and abandon the database connection HERE!!
```

```
        System.err.println("Unable to connect to the dat
        ➥base");
        throw e;
      }
    }
  }
```

The Mysterious Lost *Exception*

If you throw an Exception that should be passed outside the method and then throw another exception inside the method's finally block, the Java runtime loses the first Exception. This behavior may be a problem for your application. Listing 10.4 shows how this problem occurs:

LISTING 10.4   *TLostExceptionDemo.java*—Be careful that this problem doesn't happen to you

```
1  // quickly implement some trivial user-defined exceptions
2  class TImportantException extends Exception {}
3  class TUnimportantException extends Exception {}
4
5  public class TLostExceptionDemo {
6    protected void doImportantStuff() throws TImportantException {
7      throw new TImportantException();
8    }
9
10   protected void doUnimportantStuff() throws TUnimportantException
     {
11     throw new TUnimportantException();
12   }
13
14   public static void main (String args[]) throws
15     TImportantException, TUnimportantException
16   {
17     TLostExceptionDemo theDemo = new TLostExceptionDemo();
18     try {
19       theDemo.doImportantStuff();
20     } finally {
21         theDemo.doUnimportantStuff();
22     }
23   }
24 }
```

The output of this program is as follows:

```
C:\Que\USINGJ~1.2\ch10\userdefinedexception>java -classpath .;
➥C:\jdk1.2beta2\lib\classes.zip TLostExceptionDemo
TUnimportantException
  atTLostExceptionDemo.doUnimportantStuff(TLostExceptionDemo.
java:11)
  at TLostExceptionDemo.main(TLostExceptionDemo.java:21)
```

What's happening here? When doImportantStuff() is called, it throws TImportantException. Since that exception isn't caught inside main(), control is about to leave main(). On the way out, main()'s finally block is called. A new exception is thrown inside the finally block. It doesn't get caught, either. Now control passes outside main() (and, in this case, back to the runtime system), but the only exception visible is the TUnimportantException thrown in finally.

You can ensure that this problem doesn't occur by catching all Exceptions inside the method (before finally can run) or by being careful that nothing you do in finally can throw an Exception.

V

Building a User Interface

Building the User Interface with the AWT

Learn how to put buttons, labels, and pop-up menus into a window

See how to capture events such as mouseclicks and key-presses

Use a layout manager to control the appearance of your user interface

See how to define your own layout manager in case the standard managers don't meet your requirements

Write applets that have smooth, flicker-free animation

AWT Basics

If you've written a program for Microsoft Windows or the Macintosh in a language such as C++, you appreciate how much work is involved in opening a window and drawing into it. The introductory Windows programming example in *Visual C++ 5 Developer's Guide* (Sams, 1997) is over 100 lines, not including the module definition file! The same program written using Microsoft Foundation Classes (a programming framework similar to the Java Abstract Windowing Toolkit, or AWT) takes about 30 lines.

The original AWT in version 1.0 of the JDK did its work by instantiating *peer objects* from the native operating system. For example, suppose you asked Java to put a button on the screen and then ran your application on a Windows machine. The Java runtime would handle your request by asking Windows to make a new button. After that, your Java object and the corresponding Windows object would communicate about mouseclicks and other events in order for the button to behave as you expected.

Starting in JDK 1.1, Sun made substantial changes to the user-interface components. Figure 11.1 illustrates the current state of affairs. The original AWT from JDK 1.0 is gone; in its place is the AWT that was introduced in JDK 1.1. Java user-interface classes that do their work through peer objects are still available; they're now called *heavyweight components*. As you might guess, there are also *lightweight components* that don't tie you to the native operating system's peer objects. Instead, they support *pluggable look and feel*—a topic we'll take up in the next chapter.

FIGURE 11.1

A revised version of the AWT is still available in the Java Foundation Classes.

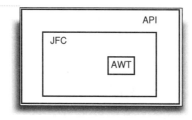

As a platform-neutral language, Java makes many of the details of graphical user interface (GUI) programming invisible—but they don't go away. As we saw in Chapter 3, "Getting Started Fast," you can build a simple applet with a GUI interface in just 10 lines of code. (See Listing 3.5, HelloApplet.java.) It takes just a few more lines to add a main() routine and a standalone Frame, allowing the applet to double as an application. (Listing 11.1 shows such a program.)

LISTING 11.1   *HelloApplication.java*–If you're going to write an applet, consider adding the code to make it a standalone application

```
1  import java.applet.*;
2  import java.awt.*;
3  import java.awt.event.*;
4
5  public class HelloApplication extends Applet {
6    public static void main(String[] args) {
7      HelloApplicationFrame theApplication =
8        new HelloApplicationFrame("Hello Application");
9      theApplication.setSize(200,200);
10     theApplication.show();
11   }
12
13   public void paint(Graphics theGraphics) {
14     theGraphics.drawString("Hello, World!", 0, 50);
15   }
16 }
17
18 class HelloApplicationFrame extends Frame {
19   private HelloApplication fApplet;
20
21   public HelloApplicationFrame(String name) {
22     super(name);
23     addWindowListener(new HelloWindowAdapter());
24     fApplet = new HelloApplication();
25     fApplet.init();
26     fApplet.start();
27     add(fApplet);
28   }
29   class HelloWindowAdapter extends WindowAdapter {
```

continues…

LISTING 11.1   **Continued**

```
30    public void windowClosing(WindowEvent e) {
31        fApplet.stop();
32        fApplet.destroy();
33        System.exit(0);
34    }
35 }
```

Take some time to understand how this program works in this first section; then we'll use it as the foundation for building more sophisticated user interfaces with the AWT.

Take a few minutes now to compile HelloApplication.java. Play with it as both an application and as an applet, to satisfy yourself that it works well in either environment. (You need an HTML file to use HelloApplication as an applet. The one in Listing 11.2 works well.) Figure 11.2 shows this program in action.

LISTING 11.2   *HelloApplication.html*–**You need an HTML file with an <APPLET> tag in order to view *HelloApplication* as an applet**

```
1  <HTML>
2  <BODY>
3  <APPLET CODE="HelloApplication.class"
4  WIDTH="200" HEIGHT="200">
5  </APPLET>
6  </BODY>
7  </HTML>
```

SEE ALSO

➤ *For more information on pluggable look and feel, page 310*

Understanding Components and Containers

As you learned in Chapter 3, you can write a one-line main() method and get a command-line application started. In order to build a GUI program, however, someone needs to provide a place in which to draw. (In GUI programs all elements of the interface are drawn—even text.) If you're writing an applet, the browser is responsible for that detail. If you're want your program to function as an application, you have to do that work yourself.

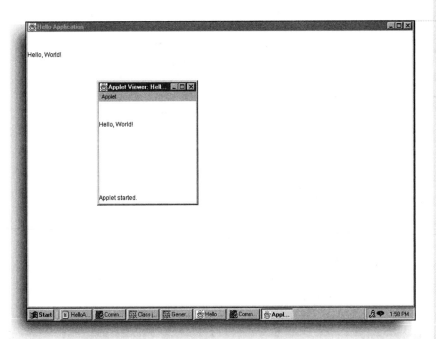

FIGURE 11.2

HelloApplication can be run as an applet or an application.

The place in which to draw is called a *container*, and is derived from the Java java.awt.Container class. The elements of the user interface itself are called *components*, and they all derive from java.awt.Component. Some of the components supplied with the AWT include the following:

- java.awt.Button
- java.awt.Canvas
- java.awt.Checkbox
- java.awt.Choice
- java.awt.Container
- java.awt.Label
- java.awt.List
- java.awt.ScrollBar
- java.awt.TextComponent
- java.awt.Composite

Most of these components provide familiar functionality. A `Button`, for example, works like you expect buttons to work in any GUI. The classes `Canvas` and `Composite` allow you to use drawing primitives to build a custom GUI component. What's most significant about this list is that it includes `java.awt.Container`. That fact means that you can build a new drawable area and add it to an existing `Container`. The AWT supplies a variety of `Container` subclasses, including `Panel`, `ScrollPane`, and `Window`.

`Window`, in turn, has two subclasses in the AWT: `Dialog` and `Frame`. (Each of those classes has further subclasses, but we're not concerned about those just now.) To add a GUI to an application, you must supply a top-level `Frame` into which the application can add `Component`s. That's what we're doing in line 18 of Listing 11.1:

```
class HelloApplicationFrame extends Frame
```

Introducing the JDK 1.1 Delegation Event Model

What happens to HelloApplicationFrame in the applet?

You invoke `main()` if you run `HelloApplication` as an application, which starts by making a new `HelloApplicationFrame` and then transfers control to it. If you load `HelloApplication` as an applet, the browser and the Java runtime work together to make a new frame inside the browser window. Then the Java runtime calls the applet's `init()`, `start()`, and `paint()` methods.

Much of the work of writing a user interface has to do with communication. If the operating system detects a key being pressed or a mouse button coming up, it must notify the right application. The application, in turn, must find out which components are interested in that activity and send them a message. Starting with JDK 1.1, Sun introduced a new way of communicating information about events: the *delegation event model*. The model was different prior to JDK 1.1. Don't worry about how the user interface worked in JDK 1.0—it's gone for good. Do be aware that the mechanism did change; if you have occasion to read old code or you have old books on Java, don't copy the way they do things. Its use is discouraged in JDK 1.1 or later, since it doesn't support some of the newest features (such as Java's component model, JavaBeans, which is taken up in Chapter 19, "Building Components with JavaBeans").

How does the delegation event model work? Every element of communication between the GUI and the program is defined as an *event*. Application classes register their interest in particular events from particular components by asking the component to

add their *listener* to a list. When the event occurs, the event
source notifies all registered listeners.

There are two different kinds of events: low-level and semantic.
All of them are derived from `java.awt.AWTEvent`. A low-level
event is concerned with the physical aspects of the user interface—mouse clicks, key presses, and the like. Semantic events
are based on low-level events. For example, to choose a menu
item, a user may click the menu bar and then click a menu item.
To click means to press the mouse button down and then up
again. This series of low-level events (mouse-down on the menu
bar, mouse-up on the menu bar, mouse-down on the menu item,
and mouse-up on the menu item) are all combined into one
semantic event.

You can see the list of low-level events derived from `AWTEvent` by
examining the class hierarchy in your JDK documentation. Low-
level events are subclasses of `ComponentEvent`:

- `ContainerEvent` Sent whenever components are added or
  removed
- `FocusEvent` Alerts your program that the component has
  gained or lost user focus (as evidenced by user activity such
  as mouseclicks or keypresses)
- `InputEvent` Includes subclasses `KeyEvent` and `MouseEvent`
- `WindowEvent` Notifies your program that the user has used
  one of the operating system-level window controls, such as
  the minimize control or the close control

In addition to these events, `ComponentEvent` includes a special
type of event that is not used with the delegation event model:
`PaintEvent`. A `PaintEvent` signals that the operating system wants
to redraw a portion of the user interface. A component must
override `paint()` or `update()` to make sure it handles the
`PaintEvent` correctly.

Look at line 23 of Listing 11.1:

```
addWindowListener(new HelloWindowAdapter());
```

This line is part of `HelloApplicationFrame`'s constructor. As the
new `Frame` is being built, this program tells the `Frame` that it is

---

One listener or many?

All standard AWT components
allow you to register as many
listeners as you like. The API
supports a unicast interface that
only allows a single listener. If
you attempt to add more than
one listener to a component
that's based on the unicast
model, you'll get a
`TooManyListeners`
exception.

**Should I override `paint()` or
`update()`?**

Examine the JDK documentation for `Component`. You find
that `update()` clears a component, sets the foreground
color, and then calls
`paint()`. Unless you have a
reason to change the way the
entire component is redrawn,
just override `paint()`.

Should I implement a listener or derive an adapter?

Listeners are interfaces. If you make your application class a listener you'll need to implement every method in the event. If you derive your own adapter class from the event adapter, you only need to override the methods you really want to handle. In Listing 11.3 we use listeners when the event has only a single method, and an `adapter` for `WindowEvent` because it has many methods.

interested in certain events. Rather than notify it directly, however, the constructor tells it to send the notifications to an *adapter*—a convenience class that handles only one kind of event. Our adapter is called `HelloWindowAdapter`; it's an instance of `WindowAdapter`, which is interested in `WindowEvents`. When the frame sends a `WindowEvent`, `HelloWindowAdapter` looks to see if the message is `windowClosing`. If it isn't, `HelloWindowAdapter` ignores it, but if it is, the program starts the process of shutting down.

Since `HelloApplication` is written as both an applet and an application, it begins its shutdown by calling the methods a browser calls when it wants to shut down an applet—`stop()` and `destroy()`. Finally it calls `exit()`, ending the application and allowing the `Frame` to close.

Class `AWTEvent` also includes these semantic events:

- `ActionEvent`   Notifies your program about component-specific actions such as button-clicks
- `AdjustmentEvent`   Tells you that a scrollbar has been adjusted
- `ItemEvent`   Notifies your program when the user interacts with a choice, a list, or a check box
- `TextEvent`   Tells you when the user changes text in a `TextArea` or `TextField` component

Is a mouseclick a low-level event or a semantic event?

Many user actions, mouseclicks for example, send events at both the low level and the semantic level. If you move your mouse onto a `Button` and click the mouse button, you'll get a series of `MouseEvents`: one for when the mouse enters the component, one for the button-press, one for the button-release, and one for the click itself. You'll also get a single `ActionEvent` from the `Button` saying that it was clicked.

Drawing and Adding—Constructing the User Interface

In Listing 11.1 we implemented the applet's `paint` method by calling `drawString()` on the `Graphics` object. The `drawString()` method is one of the drawing primitives that has been available in Java from its earliest days. `Graphics`'s drawing methods also include the following:

- `draw3DRect()`
- `drawBytes()`
- `drawImage()`
- `drawOval()`
- `drawPolyline()`
- `drawRoundRect()`

- `drawArc()`
- `drawChars()`
- `drawLine()`
- `drawPolygon()`
- `drawRect()`

The methods also include a whole range of fill..., get..., and set... methods. Much of the time, however, you're less interested in the image that appears on the screen than your are in the controls (which are implemented as Components). You call the Container's add() method to add controls to your Container. See this line from Listing 11.1:

```
add(fApplet);
```

Listing 11.3 shows a more elaborate version of Listing 11.1. In this program you see more AWT components at work: a Button, a TextField, a Checkbox, a Choice, and several Labels.

Making radio buttons

You may have noticed that the AWT doesn't include radio buttons (a group of buttons designed so that, at most, one selection is active). To make radio buttons, just build a CheckboxGroup. It's in the JDK documentation.

LISTING 11.3 *HelloPlus.java*–This version of the application/applet has some working AWT components

```java
1  import java.applet.*;
2  import java.awt.*;
3  import java.awt.event.*;
4
5  public class HelloPlus extends Applet {
6    private Button fButton;
7    private TextField fTextField;
8    private Label fLabelForTextField;
9    private Checkbox fCheckbox;
10   private OKDialog fDialog;
11   private Label fLabelForChoice;
12
13   public static void main(String[] args) {
14     HelloApplicationFrame theApplication =
15       new HelloApplicationFrame("Hello Application");
16     theApplication.setSize(200,200);
17     theApplication.show();
18   }
19
20   public void init() {
21     add (new Label("Hello, World!"));
22
23     fTextField = new TextField("TextField");
24     add(fTextField);
25     fLabelForTextField = new Label("Your text is TextField");
```

continues…

LISTING 11.3   Continued

```
26      add(fLabelForTextField);
27
28      setBackground(java.awt.Color.red);
29      fButton = new Button("White");
30      fButton.setBackground(java.awt.Color.white);
31      add(fButton);
32
33      fCheckbox = new Checkbox("Checkbox");
34      add(fCheckbox);
35      fDialog = OKDialog.makeDialog("You clicked the checkbox!");
36      Choice theChoice = new Choice();
37      theChoice.addItem("Choice Item 1");
38      theChoice.addItem("Choice Item 2");
39      theChoice.addItem("Choice Item 3");
40      add(theChoice);
41      fLabelForChoice = new Label("You haven't chosen anything");
42      add(fLabelForChoice);
43
44      fButton.addActionListener(new ActionListener(){
45        public void actionPerformed(ActionEvent e) {
46          if (fButton.getLabel() == "White") {
47            setBackground(java.awt.Color.white);
48            fButton.setLabel("Red");
49          }
50          else {
51            setBackground(java.awt.Color.red);
52            fButton.setLabel("White");
53          }
54          Component theComponents[] = getComponents();
55          try {
56            if (theComponents.length == 0)
57              throw (new AWTException("Cannot find the
                       components"));
58          } catch (AWTException theException) {
59            System.err.println("Exception: " +
       theException.getMessage());
60            theException.printStackTrace();
61            System.exit(1);
62          }
63          for (short theIndex = 0;
```

```
64              theIndex < theComponents.length; theIndex++)
65              getComponent(theIndex).setBackground
                ➡(getBackground());
66          if (fButton.getLabel() == "White")
67            fButton.setBackground(java.awt.Color.white);
68          else
69            fButton.setBackground(java.awt.Color.red);
70        }
71      });
72
73      fTextField.addActionListener(new ActionListener() {
74        public void actionPerformed(ActionEvent e) {
75            fLabelForTextField.setText("Your text is " +
76                                    fTextField.getText());
77        }
78      });
79
80      fCheckbox.addItemListener(new ItemListener(){
81        public void itemStateChanged(ItemEvent e) {
82          if (fCheckbox.getState())  // the box is checked
83            fDialog.show();
84          else
85            fDialog.setVisible(false);
86        }
87      });
88
89      theChoice.addItemListener(new ItemListener() {
90        public void itemStateChanged(ItemEvent e) {
91          try {
92            Object theSelectedItem[] =
93              e.getItemSelectable().getSelectedObjects();
94            if (theSelectedItem.length != 1)
95              throw(
96                new AWTException(
97                  "Number of selected items in choice is " +
98                                    theSelectedItem.length));
99            fLabelForChoice.setText("Your choice is " +
100               theSelectedItem[0]);
101         } catch (AWTException theException) {
102         System.err.println("Exception: " +
                theException.getMessage());
103         theException.printStackTrace();
```

continues...

LISTING 11.3   Continued

```
104            System.exit(1);
105          } // end catch
106        } // end method
107      }); // end addItemListener
108    } // end init
109
110  } // end HelloPlus
111
112  class HelloApplicationFrame extends Frame {
113    private HelloPlus fApplet;
114
115    public HelloApplicationFrame(String name) {
116      super(name);
117      addWindowListener(new HelloWindowAdapter());
118      fApplet = new HelloPlus();
119      fApplet.init();
120      fApplet.start();
121      add(fApplet);
122    }
123
124    // We're still within HelloApplicationFrame;
125    // these adapters are inner classes
126    class HelloWindowAdapter extends WindowAdapter {
127      public void windowClosing(WindowEvent e) {
128        fApplet.stop();
129        fApplet.destroy();
130        System.exit(0);
131      }
132    } // end inner class HelloWindowAdapter
133  /*
134    class Hello???Adapter extends ???Adapter {
135      public void ??????(???Event e) {
136        ???
137      }
138    } // end inner class Hello???Adapter
139  */
140  } // end HelloApplicationFrame
141
142  class OKDialog extends Dialog {
143    private Button fOKButton;
```

```
144    static private Frame fFrame;
145
146    private OKDialog(Frame theParent, String theMessage) {
147      super(theParent, true); // call Dialog's modal constructor
148      fOKButton = new Button("OK");
149      add(fOKButton, BorderLayout.CENTER );
150      Label theMessageLabel = new Label(theMessage);
151      add (theMessageLabel, BorderLayout.NORTH );
152      pack();
153
154      fOKButton.addActionListener(new ActionListener(){
155        public void actionPerformed(ActionEvent e) {
156          setVisible( false );
157        }
158      }
159      );
160
161    } // end constructor
162
163    static public OKDialog makeDialog(String theMessage) {
164      if (fFrame == null)
165        fFrame = new Frame();
166      OKDialog theResult = new OKDialog(fFrame, theMessage);
167      fFrame.setSize(theResult.getSize().width,
168                     theResult.getSize().height);
169      return theResult;
170    }
171 } // end OKDialog class
```

Take a minute to compile HelloPlus.java and run it as an application or an applet. Your screen should resemble Figure 11.3. Then come back here and we'll walk through the code.

FIGURE 11.3
By default, HelloPlus fills a 200×200 pixel panel.

The first difference you'll notice between HelloPlus and HelloApplication is that we've added several data members to the class: fButton, fTextField, and so forth. You'll often need to refer back to user-interface components during the life of the program—it's convenient to have all of the components available as members. (If you don't want to carry these references around in the class, you don't have to. theChoice is an example of a user-interface component that is not referenced as an instance variable.)

The biggest area of change is in init(). We've used init() to build the user interface; the components are added to the applet when we're running as an applet, and to the application frame when we're running as an application.

Understanding *fTextField* and *fLabelForTextField*

We start init() by adding our ubiquitous Hello, World! label. Then we instantiate a new TextField and add it to the interface. We follow this with a new Label, likewise added to the interface. Now look at these listing lines:

```
fTextField.addActionListener(new ActionListener() {
        public void actionPerformed(ActionEvent e) {
            fLabelForTextField.setText("Your text is " +
                                        fTextField.getText());
        }
    });
```

Here's a construct we haven't seen before. Since we added a TextField we're able to get a semantic event—the ActionEvent—which has only one method. That method was actionPerformed(). While the action differs from one component to the next, the method for listening to these events is the same. We don't need an adapter, since there's only one method in the event. Instead, we declare a new ActionListener and define it right here inside addActionListener(). In this case, the body of the method is quite simple:

```
fLabelForTextField.setText("Your text is " +
                            fTextField.getText());
```

When you change the text in the text field and press **Enter**, the Java runtime sends an `ActionEvent` to your listening program, which changes the text in `fLabelForTextField`.

Understanding *fButton*

This version of the program starts with a red background on the frame and a white button labeled `White`. When you click the button it sends an `ActionEvent` to the listening program. The definition of the listener starts at line 44:

```
fButton.addActionListener(new ActionListener(){
      public void actionPerformed(ActionEvent e) {
        if (fButton.getLabel() == "White") {
          setBackground(java.awt.Color.white);
          fButton.setLabel("Red");
        }
        else {
          setBackground(java.awt.Color.red);
          fButton.setLabel("White");
        }
        Component theComponents[] = getComponents();
        try {
          if (theComponents.length == 0)
            throw (new AWTException("Cannot find the
              ➥components"));
        } catch (AWTException theException) {
          System.err.println("Exception: " +
          ➥theException.getMessage());
          theException.printStackTrace();
          System.exit(1);
        }
        for (short theIndex = 0;
             theIndex < theComponents.length; theIndex++)
        getComponent(theIndex).setBackground
        ➥(getBackground());
        if (fButton.getLabel() == "White")
          fButton.setBackground(java.awt.Color.white);
        else
         fButton.setBackground(java.awt.Color.red);
      }
    });
```

How do I add more adapters?

The components in `HelloPlus.java` don't need adapters, since their events only have one method. If you want to receive events with more than one method, consider using adapters. I've left an adapter template in Listing 11.3, commented out, with question marks where the name of the event, the name of the method, and the body of the method should be.

We handle the button-click in three steps:

1. Change the Container's background and the label of the button to reflect the Container's new state.

2. Step through each Component in the Container, setting its background to match the background of the Container.

3. Since Step 2 changed the background of the button, change it back to match the button's label.

Understanding *fCheckbox* and *fDialog*

The Checkbox, fCheckbox, is added the same way the other components we've seen have been added, but then we do something different—we make a new Dialog. Our plan is to have a modal dialog box come up whenever the end user checks the Checkbox, and we have to go through a couple of extra steps to make this work.

If you examine the documentation for class Dialog you see that all of its constructors need an owner; a Frame or another Dialog that serves as the parent of the new Dialog in the Window hierarchy. If you're writing a pure application, you can use the application's Frame as the owner of the Dialog. In this case we can be called as either an applet or an application. An Applet is a Panel, not a Frame, so we have to start our own Frame to serve as the parent.

At the bottom of the HelloPlus.java listing you see a definition of class OKDialog. After the constructor, which is private, you'll see a factory method: makeDialog().

```
static public OKDialog makeDialog(String theMessage) {
    if (fFrame == null)
      fFrame = new Frame();
    OKDialog theResult = new OKDialog(fFrame, theMessage);
    fFrame.setSize(theResult.getSize().width,
                        theResult.getSize().height);
    return theResult;
  }
} // end OKDialog class
```

Why does fCheckbox **get an** ItemListener?

Unlike **Button** and **TextField**, a **Checkbox** doesn't send an **ActionEvent**. Instead, it sends an **ItemEvent**. The principle is the same as the **ActionEvent**, however—we just instantiate a new **ItemListener**.

The class OKDialog has a static Frame member fFrame. When makeDialog() is first called it instantiates a new Frame and assigns it to fFrame. Next, makeDialog() instantiates a new OKDialog, using fFrame as the parent. It scales the Frame to the same size as the OKDialog and returns a reference to the OKDialog for use by the calling class.

The OKDialog constructor instantiates a button and a label and adds them to the dialog; it then calls pack() to shrink the dialog window to a size that contains just the components. The listener attached to the dialog's button simply makes the dialog window invisible.

Understanding *theChoice*

In Java, a Choice is a pop-up list that displays one item at a time. We add a Choice (called theChoice; it's a local variable, not an instance variable) and a matching Label. Then we add an ItemListener. When we get an itemStateChanged() event, we use getItemSelectable() to get a reference back to theChoice, and then call getSelectedObjects() to get an array of selected items. If theChoice is working correctly, we should only be able to get back a single item. (We throw an exception if that condition doesn't hold.) Finally, we modify fLabelForChoice to reflect the user's choice.

SEE ALSO

➤ *Learn more about exceptions, page 245*

Working with Layouts

Compile HelloPlus and run it as an applet or an application. Resize the window and notice what happens to the components. Figure 11.4 shows a maximized window in which the components have room to spread out; in Figure 11.5 the window is tall and narrow—the components appear one above the other.

> **Why do we have compass directions in add()?**
>
> You may have noticed that the calls to **add()** in OKDialog() include strings. For example, we add the message label by saying
>
> add(theMessageLabel, BorderLayout.NORTH);
>
> These strings are part of the BorderLayout, which is described in the next section.

FIGURE 11.4

When the components have enough room, they're laid out one beside the other.

FIGURE 11.5

When the windows is narrow, the components flow one above the next.

You don't have to worry about the precise location of every component, or whether the user is working on a 640X480 screen or a Macintosh with a 9-inch monitor. That's because every Java window has an associated LayoutManager. If you don't specify the manager, Java supplies one for you. This section walks you through the standard layouts:

- FlowLayout   The components are added left to right, top to bottom. This layout is the default layout for Panel.

- GridLayout   Similar to FlowLayout, but each component gets a cell of equal size.

- BorderLayout   Divides the container into five areas: North, South, East, West, and Center. This layout is the default layout for Windows (except special-purpose Windows like FileDialog).

- CardLayout   Used to display one component at a time, like a stack of index cards.

- GridBagLayout   A flexible (and complicated) layout used when none of the other layout managers will do.

Using *FlowLayout*

Figures 11.4 and 11.5 showed how HelloPlus.java looks when you use the default layout for Panel, FlowLayout. (Recall that an Applet is a kind of Panel.) If you're happy with this design—all the components laid out left to right, top to bottom, with each component taking up whatever amount of space it requires—you don't have to do anything. Just call add() to place each component into the Container.

Does every Container have a layout manager?

By default, Java supplies a layout manager for every new Container. It's possible to turn it off (by calling setLayout(null)) and use absolute positioning to lay out your components. That's a poor idea, though. Your application won't display correctly on different-sized monitors.

If you're working in a `Window` where the default layout is `BorderLayout`, you'll need to change the layout manager if you want a `FlowLayout`. Just write the following before you `add()` any components:

```
setLayout(new FlowLayout());
```

Using *GridLayout*

Figure 11.6 shows how `HelloPlus` looks in a `GridLayout`. A `GridLayout` is similar to a `FlowLayout`, but each component gets the same size cell as all of the others. The cell size is determined by the size of the largest component. To apply a `GridLayout` to `HelloPlus`, just add this line to the top of `init()`:

```
setLayout(new GridLayout(rows, columns));
```

rows gives the number of rows and *columns* gives the number of columns. If you set either value to 0, Java will use as many dimensions as necessary to display all of the components in the layout.

Using *BorderLayout*

`BorderLayout` is particularly appropriate when you have one large component and several smaller ones, since you can place the large component in the center position. Figure 11.7 illustrates the general design of `BorderLayout`, while Figure 11.8 shows `HelloPlus.java` in this layout.

You need to make three changes in order to modify `HelloPlus.java` to use a `BorderLayout`:

- Set the layout to `BorderLayout` in `init()`.
- Assemble some of the components into groups on `Panels`.
- Change `add()` so that it passes the location `String`.

Different layouts require different versions of `add()`

If you've already been using the `BorderLayout()` and are now switching to a `FlowLayout`, be sure to remove the `String` parameter in `add()`.

Fine-tune your layouts

Each of the layout managers allows you to make small changes to the layout. For example, `FlowLayout` supports `setAlignment()`, `setHgap()`, and `setVgap()`, to set the alignment, the horizontal gap, and the vertical gap, respectively. You can also set these values in the constructor.

Java is forgiving

If you specify both the number of rows and the number of columns and then add more components than the product of those two numbers, the layout manager will behave as though you had specified a 0 for the number of columns. I don't recommend that you rely upon this feature. It's not documented, so the behavior could change at some point.

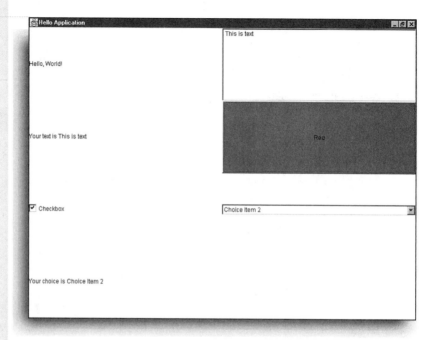

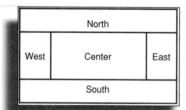

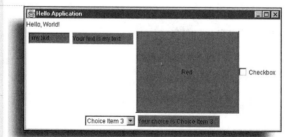

Here's a code snippet that shows these changes **in bold**:

```java
public void init() {
    setLayout(new BorderLayout());

    add (new Label("Hello, World!"), BorderLayout.NORTH);

    Panel theWestPanel = new Panel();
    fTextField = new TextField("TextField");
    theWestPanel.add(fTextField);
    fLabelForTextField = new Label("Your text is
    ➥TextField");
    theWestPanel.add(fLabelForTextField);
    add(theWestPanel, BorderLayout.WEST);

    setBackground(java.awt.Color.red);
    fButton = new Button("White");
    fButton.setBackground(java.awt.Color.white);
    add(fButton, BorderLayout.CENTER);

    fCheckbox = new Checkbox("Checkbox");
    add(fCheckbox, BorderLayout.EAST);
    fDialog = OKDialog.makeDialog("You clicked the
    ➥checkbox!");

    Panel theSouthPanel = new Panel();

    Choice theChoice = new Choice();
    theChoice.addItem("Choice Item 1");
    theChoice.addItem("Choice Item 2");
    theChoice.addItem("Choice Item 3");
    theSouthPanel.add(theChoice);
    fLabelForChoice = new Label("You haven't chosen an
    ➥thing");
    theSouthPanel.add(fLabelForChoice);
    add(theSouthPanel, BorderLayout.SOUTH);
```

Using *CardLayout*

Figure 11.9 shows how HelloPlus.java looks when you switch to CardLayout. Like BorderLayout, you need to do more than just

---

I changed layouts and now my components aren't visible

You must use the two-parameter version of add() when you add components to a BorderLayout. Double-check the Constraint, too—the only valid Constraints are BorderLayout.NORTH, SOUTH, EAST, WEST, and CENTER. If you leave off the Constraint or mistype it, you may not see your component.

call setLayout(). CardLayout shows one component at a time; you call next() and previous() to move from one card to another. In my design, I used a BorderLayout for the application and put the contents into a CardLayout in a Panel in the SOUTH position. I put two buttons into a Panel in the NORTH position; from those buttons I issued calls to next() and previous(). Here are the code changes from HelloPlus:

```
public void init() {

    setLayout(new BorderLayout());
    Panel theControls = new Panel();
    Button thePreviousButton = new Button("Previous");
    theControls.add(thePreviousButton);
    Button theNextButton = new Button("Next");
    theControls.add(theNextButton);

    add(theControls, BorderLayout.NORTH);

    fContents = new Panel();
    fContents.setLayout(new CardLayout());

    fContents.add (new Label("Hello, World!"), "Hello");

    Panel theTextPanel = new Panel();
    fTextField = new TextField("TextField");
    theTextPanel.add(fTextField);
    fLabelForTextField = new Label("Your text is
    ➥TextField");
    theTextPanel.add(fLabelForTextField);
    fContents.add(theTextPanel, "Text");

    setBackground(java.awt.Color.red);
    fButton = new Button("White");
    fButton.setBackground(java.awt.Color.white);
    fContents.add(fButton, "Button");

    fCheckbox = new Checkbox("Checkbox");
    fContents.add(fCheckbox, "Checkbox");
    fDialog = OKDialog.makeDialog("You clicked the
    ➥checkbox!");
```

```
Panel theChoicePanel = new Panel();
Choice theChoice = new Choice();
theChoice.addItem("Choice Item 1");
theChoice.addItem("Choice Item 2");
theChoice.addItem("Choice Item 3");
theChoicePanel.add(theChoice);
fLabelForChoice = new Label("You haven't chosen an
➥thing");
theChoicePanel.add(fLabelForChoice);
fContents.add(theChoicePanel, "Choice");


add(" fContents, BorderLayout.SOUTH);


theNextButton.addActionListener(new ActionListener() {
  public void actionPerformed(ActionEvent e) {
    CardLayout theLayout = (CardLayout)
    ➥fContents.getLayout();
    theLayout.next(fContents);
}});


thePreviousButton.addActionListener(new ActionListener() {
  public void actionPerformed(ActionEvent e) {
    CardLayout theLayout = (CardLayout)
    ➥fContents.getLayout();
    theLayout.previous(fContents);
}});
```

Moving to a new card

In addition to next() and previous(), the CardLayout supports first(), last(), and show(). The latter allows you to display a card by name.

FIGURE 11.9
You can use CardLayout to simulate a deck of index cards, with one card showing at a time.

Using *GridBagLayout*

Although you can control such factors as alignment and horizontal and vertical gap in the other layout managers, the GridBagLayout gives you the ultimate in flexibility. At its simplest,

GridBagLayout works like a grid, except that it puts each component in a cell of its preferred size. You specify constraints—called GridBagConstraints—that further control how the layout will appear.

Figure 11.10 shows HelloPlus.java laid out using a GridBagLayout. Here's the code that produced this layout:

```
public void init() {
    GridBagLayout theGridBag = new GridBagLayout();
    setLayout(theGridBag);
    GridBagConstraints theConstraints =
      new GridBagConstraints();

    // have all components expand to their largest size
    theConstraints.fill = GridBagConstraints.BOTH;

    // set the first label to span a row
    theConstraints.gridwidth = GridBagConstraints.REMAINDER;
    theConstraints.weightx = 1.0;

    Label theHello = new Label("Hello, World!",
    ➥java.awt.Label.CENTER);
    theGridBag.setConstraints(theHello, theConstraints);
    add(theHello);

    // the text field and its label are a row
    theConstraints.gridwidth = GridBagConstraints.RELATIVE;
    theConstraints.weightx = 1.0;
    fTextField = new TextField("TextField");
    theGridBag.setConstraints(fTextField, theConstraints);
    add(fTextField);
    fLabelForTextField = new Label("Your text is
    ➥TextField");
    theConstraints.gridwidth = GridBagConstraints.REMAINDER;
    theConstraints.weightx = 0.0;
    theGridBag.setConstraints(fLabelForTextField,
    ➥theConstraints);
    add(fLabelForTextField);
```

```
// make the button double-height
setBackground(java.awt.Color.red);
theConstraints.gridwidth = 1;
theConstraints.gridheight = 2;
theConstraints.weightx = 0.0;
theConstraints.weighty = 1.0;
fButton = new Button("White");
theGridBag.setConstraints(fButton, theConstraints);
fButton.setBackground(java.awt.Color.white);
add(fButton);

// let the checkbox end its own row
theConstraints.gridwidth = GridBagConstraints.REMAINDER;
theConstraints.gridheight = 1;
fCheckbox = new Checkbox("Checkbox");
theConstraints.weightx = theConstraints.weighty = 0.0;
theGridBag.setConstraints(fCheckbox, theConstraints);
add(fCheckbox);
fDialog = OKDialog.makeDialog("You clicked the
➥checkbox!");

// and the choice and corresponding label span
➥another row
Choice theChoice = new Choice();
theChoice.addItem("Choice Item 1");
theChoice.addItem("Choice Item 2");
theChoice.addItem("Choice Item 3");
theConstraints.gridwidth = GridBagConstraints.RELATIVE;
theConstraints.weightx = 1.0;
theGridBag.setConstraints(theChoice, theConstraints);
add(theChoice);
fLabelForChoice = new Label("You haven't chosen
➥anything");
theConstraints.gridwidth = GridBagConstraints.REMAINDER;
theConstraints.weightx = 0.0;
theGridBag.setConstraints(fLabelForChoice,
➥theConstraints);
add(fLabelForChoice);
```

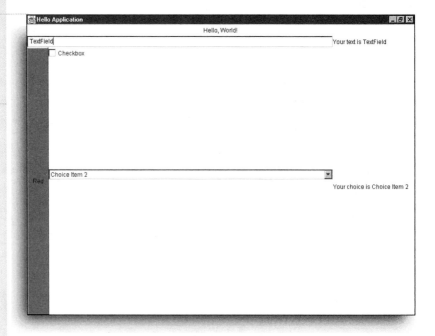

As you can see, most of the changes have to do with manipulating the data members of the GridBagConstraint as we move from row to row and cell to cell. Here are the major data members:

- fill   Specifies whether and how the component can grow when extra space becomes available. Use NONE to specify that the component cannot grow, BOTH to specify that the component can grow in both dimensions, and HORIZONTAL or VERTICAL to specify that the component can grow in only one dimension.

- gridwidth   Specifies the number of cells in a row; use RELATIVE for the next-to-last cell and REMAINDER for the last cell.

- gridheight   Specifies the number of cells in a column; use RELATIVE for the next-to-last cell and REMAINDER for the last cell.

- weightx   Specifies how to distribute extra horizontal space. A cell with weightx=0 receives no extra space. If all the weights are 0, the extra space is placed at the left and right edges.

- weighty   Plays an analogous role to weightx in distributing extra vertical space.

Other data members are available; see the documentation in the JDK if you need still more control over a GridBagLayout.

Making Your Own Custom Layout

If you find that none of the standard layouts meet your requirements, consider making your own implementation of LayoutManager2. (LayoutManager, a simpler class, doesn't support a constraints Object.) You will have to supply eight methods:

- public void addLayoutComponent(String name, Component comp)   Called by the Container; you only need to fill in the body if your layout manager wants to know the names of the components.

- public void removeLayoutComponent(Component comp)   Used by layout managers that know the names of their components; other layout managers can find the component by using Container.getComponents().

- public float getLayoutAlignmentX(Container target)   Specifies how the component would like to be aligned relative to other components. The component will be aligned at the origin if you return 0, the component will be aligned as far as possible away from the origin if you return 1; 0.5 will center the component. (There's a getLayoutAlignmentY() method that works the same way in the y axis.)

- public void invalidateLayout(Container target)   Instructs the layout manager to discard any cached information.

- `public Dimension preferredLayoutSize(Container parent)` Returns the ideal size of the parent `Container` based on the preferred sizes of the components and the `insets()` of the `Container`.

- `public Dimension maximumLayoutSize(Container target)` Returns the maximum size of this `Component`.

- `public Dimension minimumLayoutSize(Container parent)` Returns the minimum size of the parent `Container`, based on the minimum sizes of the components and the `insets()` of the `Container`.

- `public void layoutContainer(Container parent)` Invokes each `Component`'s `resize()`, `move()`, and `reshape()` methods to implement the layout strategy.

Consider implementing `toString()` as well

While not required, it's customary to implement a `toString()` method in your custom layout manager, for the convenience of your class users.

Improving Animation

As you develop your user interfaces—particularly user interfaces for applets—you may find a need for animation. If you explore the graphics primitives in the AWT you discover `drawImage()`; it's the graphical analog of `drawString()` that we've been using for a while. It may occur to you to put up an animation using a technique similar to that shown in Listing 11.4.

LISTING 11.4 *Animation1.java*–**This applet loads and displays a series of images in rapid succession**

```
1  import java.awt.*;
2  import java.applet.Applet;
3
4  public class Animation1 extends Applet implements Runnable {
5      int fFrame = -1;
6      int fDelay;
7      Thread fThread;
8      Image[] fEarth;
9
10     public void init() {
11         fEarth = new Image[30];
12         String theString;
13         int theFramesPerSecond = 10;
```

```
14
15          //load in the images
16          for (int i=1; i<=30; i++)
17          {
18          System.err.println("Starting load from " +
19              getCodeBase() +
20              " of ./Earth" + i +".gif");
21              fEarth[i-1] = getImage (getCodeBase(),
22                                      "./Earth"+i+".gif");
23          }
24
25          //How many milliseconds between frames?
26          theString = getParameter("fps");
27          try {
28            if (theString != null) {
29                theFramesPerSecond = Integer.parseInt(theString );
30            }
31          } catch (NumberFormatException e) {}
32          fDelay = (theFramesPerSecond > 0) ?
33                  (1000 / theFramesPerSecond) : 100;
34      }
35
36      public void start() {
37          // start a new thread for the animation
38          if (fThread == null) {
39              fThread = new Thread(this);
40          }
41          fThread.start();
42      }
43
44      public void stop() {
45          // stop the animation thread
46          fThread = null;
47      }
48
49      public void run() {
50          // run at a low priority; animation is second-place to
            content
51          Thread.currentThread().setPriority(Thread.MIN_PRIORITY);
52          long theStartTime = System.currentTimeMillis();
53
54          //Here comes the show.
```

continues...

LISTING 11.4   **Continued**

```
55        while (Thread.currentThread() == fThread) {
56
57          //Advance the frame.
58          fFrame++;
59
60          //Display it.
61          repaint();
62
63          //Delay depending on how far we are behind.
64          try {
65              theStartTime += fDelay;
66              Thread.sleep(Math.max(0,
67                                      theStartTime-
68                          System.currentTimeMillis()));
69          } catch (InterruptedException e) {
70                  break;
71          }
72      }
73    }
74
75    //Draw the current frame
76    public void paint(Graphics g) {
77      g.drawImage(fEarth[fFrame % 30], 0, 0, this);
78    }
79 }
```

Figure 11.11 shows a screen shot of this applet in action.

FIGURE 11.11

The Earth spins in three versions of the animation applet.

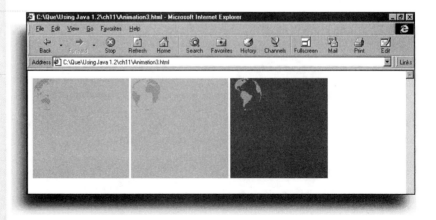

We're going to use this applet as the basis for building a smooth, flicker-free animation applet. Let's examine this first attempt in detail.

You'll notice that this applet implements an interface called Runnable. Runnable allows the applet to start a new thread of control, so the animation can proceed independently of the user interface.

Our list of instances variables includes a reference to the animation thread (fThread) and a reference to the array of images. We're using thirty frames of the revolving Earth, so we call this array fEarth.

In init() we loop from 1 to 30, loading the images of Earth. (They're stored in files named Earth1.gif through Earth30.gif.)

Next, we look for an applet <PARAM> called fps (frames per second). If we find it, we attempt to parse it into a number. If we don't find it or if we can't read it, we use 10 frames per second as the basis for calculating the delay between calls to paint().

When the browser first shows the applet it calls init() followed by start(). The browser will call stop() if the user iconifies the browser window or moves to a different page. We handle start() by checking to see if the animation thread has already been set up. If it hasn't, we instantiate it. In either case, we start() the thread and destroy it in stop().

The required method of Runnable is run(). The Java runtime environment calls this method whenever there is time to run our thread. Our version of run() starts by setting the animation thread's priority to a low value, since any user interaction should take precedence over the animation. Then we simply step through the frames, repaint on each loop, and delay as necessary to match the desired frame rate.

Finally, the work is done in paint() itself (as it is in most graphics-intensive applets). We simply draw the current frame onto the screen.

SEE ALSO
➤ *For more information on threads, see page 454*
➤ *For more information on interfaces, see page 230*

Using the *MediaTracker* for Smoother Animation

As you experiment with this code you'll discover that it sometimes jerks a bit. This happens when the image doesn't load fast enough to support the animation, particularly when someone is loading this applet over the Internet.

There's a simple fix to this problem that requires just six lines of code. You add an instance of the MediaTracker class to your applet. The MediaTracker knows which images are already loaded into memory and can prevent you from using an image that has not been fully loaded. Here's a step-by-step procedure for adding a MediaTracker to any animation project.

Adding a *MediaTracker*

1. Add a MediaTracker as an instance variable:
   ```
   MediaTracker fTracker;
   ```

2. In init(), instantiate a new MediaTracker:
   ```
   fTracker = new MediaTracker( this );
   ```

3. As each image is loaded, place it under the control of the MediaTracker:
   ```
   fTracker.addImage ( fEarth[i], 0 );
   ```

   The second parameter to this method, 0, is an ID number that will be used to refer to this set of images.

4. Before the while loop in run(), call waitForID():
   ```
   try {
      fTracker.waitForID( 0 );
   } catch (InterruptedException e) {
      return;
   }
   ```

5. Before using the images in paint(), double-check that they're loaded:
   ```
   if (fTracker.checkID( 0 ))
   ```

Decreasing Flicker through Double-Buffering

You may have also noticed an annoying flicker in your animation program. This flicker occurs because there's a delay between the start of paint() and the time the image is actually loaded from the disk. You can eliminate the flicker by preloading the image into memory—a technique called *double-buffering*. Like the MediaTracker technique, double-buffering requires just a few lines of code. Here's a step-by-step procedure for adding double-buffering:

Adding double-buffering to an animation

1. Add an off-screen buffer and its graphics context to the list of instance variables:
```
Image fOffScreenImage;
Graphics fOffScreenGraphics;
```

2. In init(), instantiate the off-screen buffer and paint it blue:
```
fOffScreenImage = createImage( getSize().width,
➡getSize().height);
fOffScreenGraphics = fOffScreenImage.getGraphics();
fOffScreenGraphics.setColor(Color.blue);
fOffScreenGraphics.fillRect(0, 0, getSize().width,
➡getSize().height);
```

3. Override update(), which is responsible for clearing the background and calling paint():
```
public void update( Graphics g ) {
  fOffScreenGraphics.setColor(Color.blue);
  fOffScreenGraphics.clearRect(0, 0, getSize().width,
➡getSize().height);
  fOffScreenGraphics.fillRect(0, 0, getSize().width,
➡getSize().height);
  paint(g);
}
```

4. Modify paint() so that it updates the off-screen image and draws the on-screen image from the off-screen image:
```
fOffScreenGraphics.drawImage(fEarth[i], 0, 0, this);
g.drawImage(fOffScreenImage, 0, 0, this);
```

Listing 11.5 shows the revised animation applet, with double-buffering and a MediaTracker. You can use an HTML file to put the two applets up side-by-side, as a before-and-after demonstration. For smoothest performance, though, put Animation2 on a Web page without Animation1, so its thread doesn't compete with Animation1's thread.

Don't try this with AppletViewer

AppletViewer's performance with animation is sometimes poor. Use a Web browser such as Netscape Navigator (part of Netscape Communicator) to view these applets.

LISTING 11.5 **_Animation2.java_**–This version of the Animation applet is noticeably smoother and is flicker-free

```
1 import java.awt.*;
2 import java.applet.Applet;
3
4 public class Animation3 extends Applet implements Runnable {
5     int fFrame = -1;
6     int fDelay;
7     Thread fThread;
8     Image[] fEarth;
9     MediaTracker fTracker;
10    Image fOffScreenImage;
11    Graphics fOffScreenGraphics;
12
13    public void init() {
14      fEarth = new Image[30];
15      String theString;
16      int theFramesPerSecond = 10;
17      fTracker = new MediaTracker( this );
18      fOffScreenImage = createImage(getSize().width,
19                                        getSize().height);
20      fOffScreenGraphics = fOffScreenImage.getGraphics();
21
22      // fill the offsceen buffer with blue
23      fOffScreenGraphics.setColor(Color.blue);
24      fOffScreenGraphics.fillRect(0, 0,
25                      getSize().width, getSize().height);
26
27      //load in the images
28      for (int i=1; i<=30; i++)
29      {
30         fEarth[i-1] = getImage (getCodeBase(),
31                                  "./Earth"+i+".gif");
32         fTracker.addImage(fEarth[i-1], 0);
33      }
34
35      //How many milliseconds between frames?
36      theString = getParameter("fps");
37      try {
38        if (theString != null) {
39            theFramesPerSecond = Integer.parseInt(theString );
40          }
```

```
41        } catch (NumberFormatException e) {}
42        fDelay = (theFramesPerSecond > 0) ?
43                  (1000 / theFramesPerSecond) : 100;
44    }
45
46    public void start() {
47        // start a new thread for the animation
48        if (fThread == null) {
49            fThread = new Thread(this);
50        }
51        fThread.start();
52    }
53
54    public void stop() {
55        // stop the animation thread
56        fThread = null;
57    }
58
59    public void run() {
60        // run at a low priority; animation is second-place to
          content
61        Thread.currentThread().setPriority(Thread.MIN_PRIORITY);
62        long theStartTime = System.currentTimeMillis();
63
64        //Here comes the show.
65        try {
66         fTracker.waitForID(0);
67        } catch (InterruptedException e) {
68          System.err.println("Interrupted Exception: " +
            e.getMessage());
69          e.printStackTrace();
70          return;
71        }
72        while (Thread.currentThread() == fThread) {
73
74          //Advance the frame.
75          fFrame++;
76
77          //Display it.
78          repaint();
79
80          //Delay depending on how far we are behind.
```

continues…

LISTING 11.5   **Continued**

```
81              try {
82                      theStartTime += fDelay;
83                      Thread.sleep(Math.max(0,
84                                      theStartTime-
85                              System.currentTimeMillis()));
86              } catch (InterruptedException e) {
87                      break;
88              }
89          }
90      }
91
92      public void update( Graphics g) {
93
94          // fill the offsceen buffer with blue
95          fOffScreenGraphics.setColor(Color.blue);
96          fOffScreenGraphics.clearRect(0, 0,
97                          getSize().width, getSize().height);
98          fOffScreenGraphics.fillRect(0, 0,
99                          getSize().width, getSize().height);
100         paint(g);
101     }
102
103     //Draw the current frame
104     public void paint(Graphics g) {
105       if (fTracker.checkID( 0 )) {
106         fOffScreenGraphics.drawImage(fEarth[fFrame % 30], 0, 0,
          this);
107         g.drawImage(fOffScreenImage, 0, 0, this);
108       }
109     }
110 }
```

Building the User Interface with JFC Swing Components

Learn why Swing may well be the most important addition to JDK 1.2

Tour the Swing component library

See the new layout managers available with Swing components

Learn how Swing events differ from those provided by the AWT

The Swing Architecture

When Java was introduced, the only available graphical user interface (GUI) was the Abstract Windowing Toolkit (AWT). Recall from Chapter 11, "Building the User Interface with the AWT," that AWT components are considered heavyweight in that each Java component has a peer object from the native GUI.

Sun also offers lightweight components, which don't have a peer object. Instead, they offer a pluggable look and feel. If the end user is running on a Windows 95 machine but prefers the look and feel of Sun's Motif interface, he or she can select that interface in the running application. When Sun developed these lightweight components, it did so as part of a project called "Swing." Because of that, the lightweight user-interface components are usually called *Swing components*.

Swing components are one part of the Java Foundation Classes (JFC). Figure 12.1 illustrates the relationship of the AWT and the Swing components to the JFC.

Is Swing part of the AWT?

The Swing components come in the `java.awt.swing` package, but most developers reserve the term AWT component for the heavyweight components and refer to the components in `java.awt.swing` simply as *Swing components*.

FIGURE 12.1

The Swing components are the JFC's lightweight user-interface components.

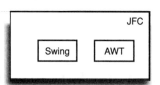

Understanding the JFC

While the JFC was released about the same time JDK 1.1 was released, Sun didn't make a big deal about it. Most of Sun's description of the new JFC has centered on Swing; because of that, many people have the idea that Swing is all there is to the JFC and that the JFC was released as part of JDK 1.2. The link is so strong that Sun unofficially calls JFC 1.1 "Swing 1.0."

The JFC includes:

- The lightweight user-interface components (codenamed Swing)
- The delegation event model

- Printing capability
- Clipboard data transfer
- Better integration with system colors
- Mouseless operation
- Drag-and-drop operation
- Better assistive technology support for people with disabilities
- Improved 2D graphics operations

SEE ALSO

➤ *Learn more about the delegation event model, see page 274*

➤ *Learn more about pluggable look and feel, see page 362*

➤ *Learn more about drag and drop, see page 385*

➤ *Learn more about assistive technologies, see page 387*

➤ *Learn more about 2D graphics, see page 391*

A Short Tour of Swing

Sun supplies Swing in 14 packages:

- `java.awt.swing` Components, adapters, default component models, and interfaces.
- `java.awt.swing.basic` The user-interface classes (known as *delegates*) for the Windows look and feel.
- `java.awt.swing.beaninfo` Support classes for use when Swing components are used as JavaBeans (described in Chapter 19, "Building Components with JavaBeans").
- `java.awt.swing.border` The `Border` interface and classes, which define specific border rendering styles.
- `java.awt.swing.event` Swing-specific event types and listeners.
- `java.awt.swing.jlf` The user-interface classes for the Metal look and feel.
- `java.awt.swing.motif` The user-interface classes for the Motif look and feel.

JFC is not the only class library in town

Before JFC was developed, Netscape developed a set of classes called the Internet Foundation Classes, or IFC. Microsoft has also developed the Application Foundation Classes, or AFC. Netscape has announced that the JFC supersedes the IFC, leaving Microsoft and Sun to battle it out.

- `java.awt.swing.multi` The multiplexing user-interface classes that allow you to create components from different factory classes.

- `java.awt.swing.plaf` Used by developers who want to write their own pluggable look and feel (PLAF).

- `java.awt.swing.table` The Swing `Table` class and its kin.

- `java.awt.swing.target` The support classes for `Action` target management.

- `java.awt.swing.text` Support for the Swing document framework.

- `java.awt.swing.undo` Support classes for implementing undo and redo.

- `java.awt.accessibility` Support for working with assistive technology to make Java programs accessible for people with disabilities.

My Swing packages have different names

There is a version of Swing that works with older JDKs (prior to 1.2) in which the package names all start with `com.sun.java`. If you're using the final version of JDK 1.2, you should use the `java.awt` versions of the Swing packages.

Can your browser run Swing components?

Swing is an emerging technology—not all Java-compatible browsers understand Swing, but most can be configured to run Swing applets. To test your browser (and to get any necessary instructions on reconfiguring your browser) visit `http://java.sun.com/products/jfc/swingdoc-current/applets.html`.

Tip: Run SwingSet first

Before you begin developing with Swing components, make sure you can run an existing Swing-based application. Sun includes SwingSet in the JFC. Make sure it loads and runs without errors.

Installing the Swing Kit

The JFC is developed separately from the JDK. Even if you're sure that you have the latest version of the JDK, there may be a newer release of the JFC. Visit `http://java.sun.com/products/jfc/` to see what's new with the JFC.

Download the latest version of the JFC and extract it into any convenient directory. The top-level directory from the installation kit is referred to as your *Swing directory*, also known as `SWING_HOME`. Look at the README.txt file in the Swing directory and follow any instructions that apply for setting up the environment on your platform.

SwingSet is an excellent overview of the Swing components. You find it in `SWING_HOME/examples/SwingSet`. Follow the instructions in the README.txt file in that directory to run the application.

Component APIs

You can choose buttons, labels, lists, and a few other user-interface components with the AWT. With the Swing components, Sun provides a richer interface more akin to the full range available in Microsoft Foundation Classes or the Macintosh Toolbox. There are over twice as many Swing components as there are AWT components. The Swing components include the following:

- Labels
- Bordered panes
- Progress bars
- ToolTips
- Buttons
- Radio buttons
- Check boxes
- Tool bars

- Sliders
- Combo boxes
- Menus
- Trees
- Scroll bars
- List boxes
- Tabbed panes
- Tables

All of these components are lightweight—instead of building a peer component from the native operating system, they look for a library of pluggable look and feel classes. Three such libraries come with Swing 1.0:

- `SWING_HOME/windows.jar` A look and feel strongly resembling Windows 95/Windows NT 4.0

- `SWING_HOME/motif.jar` A look and feel based on Sun's own Motif interface

- `SWING_HOME/metal.jar` A platform-independent look and feel, called the Java look and feel in earlier releases

Most of Sun's demo applets allow you to change look and feel from a control at runtime. Figure 12.2 shows Simple, one of the examples, in the default look and feel (called Metal).

FIGURE 12.2

Assume that users will switch from one look and feel to another.

Compare Figure 12.2 with Figure 12.3. Figure 12.2 shows Simple with the Metal look and feel. By choosing the **Windows** radio button, you can switch Simple to the Windows look and feel, shown in Figure 12.3. Similarly, you can use the Motif look and feel, which is shown in Figure 12.4.

FIGURE 12.3

Compare the Windows look and feel to Metal and Motif.

FIGURE 12.4

The Motif look and feel is based on an interface Sun designed to its UNIX operating system.

Using the *TPanelTester* Application

Become familiar with all three pluggable look and feel styles

Pluggable look-and-feel (PLAF) is here to stay. Use SwingSet to explore all three PLAFs, as well as others that will surely become available in the future. Remember that the decision about which look and feel to use is left to the user. Strive to make sure your design looks good in all available PLAFs.

The examples in this chapter are based on subclasses of JPanel. In order to run the various panels, you need an application to display the panel. Listing 12.1 shows the generic panel tester.

LISTING 12.1 *TPanelTester.java*–**Change the name in this panel tester to match the panel under test**

```
1  import java.awt.swing.*;
2
3  public class TPanelTester extends JFrame {
4      public TPanelTester() {
5          super("Panel Tester");
6
7          // change TLabelPanel to match the name of the panel
    under test
```

```
8          JPanel thePanelUnderTest = new TLabelPanel();
9          setContentPane(thePanelUnderTest);
10     }
11
12     public static void main(String[] args) {
13          JFrame theFrame = new TPanelTester();
14     theFrame.addWindowListener(new java.awt.event.WindowAdapter() {
15          public void windowClosing(java.awt.event.WindowEvent e)
16             {System.exit(0);}
17     });
18          theFrame.pack();
19          theFrame.setVisible(true);
20     }
21 }
```

Using *JPanel*

You first looked at Panels in Chapter 11. A JPanel is a light-weight version of Panel; it is used in most of this section's examples.

Working with Icons

In Chapter 11 you learned that subclasses of java.awt.Container can contain java.awt.Components and that Containers themselves are Components. It is this hierarchy that allows you to add Panels to Frames, for example. All of the Swing components are derived from JComponent, which is a java.awt.Container. This means that every JComponent can contain other components, either AWT or Swing. One consequence of this fact is that you can add a graphical icon to a JButton, a JLabel, or another Swing component. Swing provides Icon as an interface; to implement it you must provide a paintIcon() method, a getIconWidth() method, and a getIconHeight() method. The paintIcon() method is as follows:

```
paintIcon(Component c, Graphics g, int x, int y);
```

x and y specify the drawing origin; the drawing itself happens in Graphics g. You can use the Component to get a property such as the foreground or background color—in practice, it's usually ignored.

Should I import java.awt.swing.*?

There's no performance impact if you import an entire package (including java.awt.swing). I usually won't import a few references to a package—I'll include a reference to it whenever I use it or import only the classes that I need. Choose the approach that makes your code most readable.

Doublebuffering is built into JPanel

Recall from Chapter 11's "Improving Animation" that you can reduce flicker with doublebuffering. Doublebuffering is built into JPanel; check the documentation for the setDoubleBuffered() method.

Swing supports one Icon class for you—ImageIcon—which is used for displaying Images. Listing 12.2 an example of an Icon.

LISTING 12.2 *TBigBlackDot.java*—**You can add this *Icon* to Swing buttons and labels**

```
1  public class TBigBlackDot implements java.awt.swing.Icon {
2    public void paintIcon(java.awt.Component c,
3                          java.awt.Graphics g, int x, int y) {
4      g.setColor(java.awt.Color.black);
5      g.fillOval(x, y, getIconWidth(), getIconHeight());
6    }
7    public int getIconWidth() {
8      return 100;
9    }
10   public int getIconHeight() {
11     return 100;
12   }
13 }
```

Adding an Instance of *JLabel*

A label allows you to place static text on the screen. You took our first look at Label in Chapter 11. The Swing JLabel improves upon java.awt.Label by allowing you to add an Icon and giving you better control over the position of the text. Listing 12.3 shows a JLabel in action on a JPanel.

LISTING 12.3 *TLabelPanel.java*—**This panel contains a label with a *BigBlackDot* icon**

```
1  public class TLabelPanel extends java.awt.swing.JPanel {
2    public TLabelPanel() {
3      java.awt.swing.JLabel theLabel =
4        new java.awt.swing.JLabel("Example of BigBlackDot");
5
6      // we don't have to settle for plain vanilla text
7      java.awt.Font theBigBoldFont =
```

```
8        new java.awt.Font("Serif",
9                           java.awt.Font.BOLD,
10                          32);
11    theLabel.setFont(theBigBoldFont);
12
13    // now add an icon
14    java.awt.swing.Icon aDot = new TBigBlackDot();
15    theLabel.setIcon(aDot);
16    theLabel.setPreferredSize(new
17      java.awt.Dimension(600, 150));
18
19    // place the text to the right of the icon
20    theLabel.setHorizontalAlignment(java.awt.swing.JLabel.RIGHT);
21
22    // and add the whole thing to the panel
23    add(theLabel);
24  }
25 }
```

Figure 12.5 shows an instance of TLabelPanel.

FIGURE 12.5
You can add icons to a
JLabel and control the text's
position and appearance.

Using *JButton*

JButton behaves much like Button; you add it to a JPanel and listen for its Action with an ActionListener.

Just as with JLabel, you can add an Icon to JButton by calling the
setIcon() method.

Be sure to set your JButton's
background color

By default, a new JButton
has the same background color
as the container, and it won't
stand out. Always include a line
like the following to make the
button highly visible:

```
theButton.setBack-
➥ground(SystemColor.
➥control);
```

Adding an Instance of *JCheckBox*

You know you can implement check boxes with
`java.awt.Checkbox`. You implemented radio buttons by placing
the `Checkbox` into a `CheckboxGroup`. The concept of a radio button
in Swing is handled explicitly—Swing has its own `JRadioButton`
class with an associated `ButtonGroup`. You use `JCheckBox` just to
implement check boxes.

Using *JRadioButton*

To make a group of radio buttons, make instances of
`JRadioButton` and add them to a `ButtonGroup`. Listing 12.4 shows
an example of some radio buttons.

**Take advantage of
AbstractButton**

Several Swing components, including **JButton**, are derived from
AbstractButton. Review the
documentation for
AbstractButton—you find
methods that allow you to enable
and disable the button, methods
that allow you to control the internal
alignment, and ways to associate an
accelerator key with the button.

**Make up your own Icons for
JCheckBox**

JCheckBox has its own icons to
signify the selected and unselected
states. If you prefer, you can make
your own Icons and use them in
setIcon() and
setSelectedIcon().

LISTING 12.4 *TDoseNotGivenPanel.java*–**This panel contains a group of
radio buttons**

```
1  public class TDoseNotGivenPanel extends java.awt.swing.JPanel {
2    public TDoseNotGivenPanel() {
3
4      // make room for a label and four buttons
5      setLayout(new java.awt.GridLayout(5, 1));
6
7      java.awt.swing.ButtonGroup aReason =
8        new java.awt.swing.ButtonGroup();
9      java.awt.swing.JLabel theLabel =
10       new java.awt.swing.JLabel("Dose not given because");
11     theLabel.setFont(new java.awt.Font("SansSerif",
12                                         java.awt.Font.BOLD, 14));
13     add(theLabel);
14
15     java.awt.swing.JRadioButton thePatientNotAvailableButton =
16       new java.awt.swing.JRadioButton("Patient not available");
17     thePatientNotAvailableButton.setHorizontalAlignment(
18       java.awt.swing.AbstractButton.LEFT);
19     thePatientNotAvailableButton.setKeyAccelerator('A');
20     thePatientNotAvailableButton.setSelected(true); //default
21     add(thePatientNotAvailableButton);
22     aReason.add(thePatientNotAvailableButton);
```

```
23
24    java.awt.swing.JRadioButton thePatientOffWardButton =
25      new java.awt.swing.JRadioButton("Patient off ward");
26    thePatientOffWardButton.setHorizontalAlignment(
27      java.awt.swing.AbstractButton.LEFT);
28    thePatientNotAvailableButton.setKeyAccelerator('O');
29    add (thePatientOffWardButton);
30    aReason.add(thePatientOffWardButton);
31
32    java.awt.swing.JRadioButton thePatientRefusedButton =
33      new java.awt.swing.JRadioButton("Patient refused dose");
34    thePatientRefusedButton.setHorizontalAlignment(
35      java.awt.swing.AbstractButton.LEFT);
36    thePatientNotAvailableButton.setKeyAccelerator('R');
37    add (thePatientRefusedButton);
38    aReason.add(thePatientRefusedButton);
39
40    java.awt.swing.JRadioButton thePatientExpelledDoseButton =
41      new java.awt.swing.JRadioButton("Patient expelled dose");
42    thePatientExpelledDoseButton.setHorizontalAlignment(
43      java.awt.swing.AbstractButton.LEFT);
44    thePatientNotAvailableButton.setKeyAccelerator('X');
45    add (thePatientExpelledDoseButton);
46    aReason.add(thePatientExpelledDoseButton);
47  }
48 }
```

Figure 12.6 shows the JPanel that results from the code in
Listing 12.4.

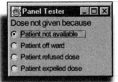

FIGURE 12.6

Use a ButtonGroup to
implement a set of radio
buttons.

Remembering State with *JToggleButton*

JToggleButton is the parent class of both JCheckBox and JRadioButton, but it's a concrete class that you can use in your design. A JToggleButton is indistinguishable from a JButton when unselected. When someone clicks JToggleButton, it goes to its selected state and stays there. (By default, it looks like a pushbutton that's locked in the down state.)

Managing Text

Swing's JTextComponent gives you more than you'd expect from a simple field or text area. Its methods include the following:

- copy()
- cut()
- paste()
- getSelectedText()
- getSelectionStart()
- getSelectionEnd()
- getText()
- setText()
- setEditable()
- setCaretPosition()

Figure 12.7 illustrates the inheritance hierarchy that derives from JTextComponent.

JTextField and JTextArea resemble their AWT counterparts, but JTextPane is something new. It implements a complete text editor; you can format text and embed images. Words wrap where you expect them to, based on their current font, size, and style. TProgressNotePanel, a class used in the pharmacy application, is shown in Listing 12.5. Figure 12.8 shows the TProgressNotePanel itself.

Protect your passwords

When a user enters a password or other sensitive information, the information should not become visible on the screen. Use JPasswordField instead of JTextField to ensure privacy. Use setEchoChar() if you want to override the default echo character: ('*');.

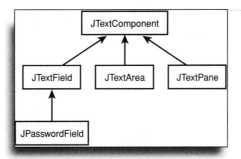

FIGURE 12.7

Each member of the
`JTextComponent` family
supports the methods of a simple text editor.

LISTING 12.5 *TProgressNotePanel.java*–**Progress notes that report
significant events in the care of patients**

```
1  public class TProgressNotePanel extends java.awt.swing.JPanel
2  {
3    public TProgressNotePanel() {
4      setLayout(new java.awt.BorderLayout());
5      setPreferredSize(new java.awt.Dimension(400,400));
6      java.awt.swing.JTextPane theText =
7  new java.awt.swing.JTextPane();
8
9      java.awt.swing.text.MutableAttributeSet theAttributes =
10        new java.awt.swing.text.SimpleAttributeSet();
11     java.awt.swing.text.StyleConstants.setFontFamily(
12 theAttributes,
13                                           "Serif");
14     java.awt.swing.text.StyleConstants.setFontSize(
15 theAttributes, 18);
16     java.awt.swing.text.StyleConstants.setBold(theAttributes,
17 true);
18     theText.setCharacterAttributes(theAttributes, false);
19
20     add(theText, java.awt.BorderLayout.CENTER);
21   }
22 }
```

FIGURE 12.8

You can get a full text editor in just nine lines of code.

Giving Feedback with *JProgressBar*

Chapter 17, "Concurrent Programming with Threads," talks about starting more than one independent thread of control. Sometimes you want a thread running in the background while the user goes on with his or her work. You can put up a progress bar to report the progress in that thread, and if you like, allow the user to control that thread. Listing 12.6 and Figure 12.9 show one way to use a JProgressBar.

LISTING 12.6 *TBackgroundPanel.java*–You can use a *JProgressBar* to report a thread's progress

```
1  import java.awt.swing.*;
2  public class TBackgroundPanel extends JPanel {
3      private Thread fThread;
4      private Object fLock;
5      private boolean fNeedsToStop = false;
6      private JProgressBar fProgressBar;
7      private JButton fStartButton;
8      private JButton fStopButton;
9
10     public TBackgroundPanel() {
```

```
11      fLock = new Object();
12      setLayout(new java.awt.BorderLayout());
13      add(new JLabel("Status"), java.awt.BorderLayout.NORTH);
14      fProgressBar = new JProgressBar();
15      add(fProgressBar, java.awt.BorderLayout.CENTER);
16      JPanel theButtons = new JPanel();
17
18      fStartButton = new JButton("Start");
19      fStartButton.setBackground(java.awt.SystemColor.control);
20      theButtons.add(fStartButton);
21      fStartButton.addActionListener(new
22  java.awt.event.ActionListener() {
23        public void actionPerformed(
24    java.awt.event.ActionEvent e) {
25          startTheThread();
26      }
27      });
28      fStopButton = new JButton("Stop");
29      fStopButton.setBackground(java.awt.SystemColor.control);
30      theButtons.add(fStopButton);
31      fStopButton.addActionListener(new
32  java.awt.event.ActionListener() {
33        public void actionPerformed(
34  java.awt.event.ActionEvent e) {
35          stopTheThread();
36      }
37      });
38      add(theButtons, java.awt.BorderLayout.SOUTH);
39    }
40
41    public void startTheThread() {
42      if (fThread == null)
43        fThread = new TBackgroundThread();
44      if (!fThread.isAlive())
45      {
46        fNeedsToStop = false;
47        fThread.start();
48      }
49    }
50
51    public void stopTheThread() {
52      synchronized(fLock) {
```

continues…

LISTING 12.6 Continued

```
53        fNeedsToStop = true;
54        fLock.notify();
55      }
56    }
57
58    //inner class, so it has access to private members of panel
59    class TBackgroundThread extends Thread {
60      public void run() {
61        // run at a low priority; after all, we _
62        // are_ a background thread
63        Thread.currentThread().setPriority(
64 Thread.MIN_PRIORITY);
65        int theMinimum = 0;
66        int theMaximum = 100;
67        fProgressBar.setValue(theMinimum);
68        fProgressBar.setMinimum(theMinimum);
69        fProgressBar.setMaximum(theMaximum);
70        for (int i=0; i<theMaximum; i++) {
71          fProgressBar.setValue(i);
72
73          // do the real work of the background thread
74          // here
75
76          synchronized(fLock) {
77            if (fNeedsToStop)
78              break;
79            try {
80              fLock.wait(100);
81            } catch (InterruptedException e) {
82              // ignore the exception
83            }
84          }
85        }
86        // clue the garbage collector that we're done
87 with the thread
88        fThread = null;
89      }
90    }
91 }
92
93 }
```

TBackgroundPanel is a generic JPanel that can be used to display and control a background thread. The class has six instance variables:

- Thread fThread The background thread itself. See Chapter 17 to learn more about threads.

- Object fLock A simple object used to synchronize the foreground and background threads.

- boolean fNeedsToStop A bit of shared data that tells the background thread that the foreground thread wants it to stop.

- JProgressBar fProgressBar The Swing progress bar.

- JButton fStartButton and JButton fStopButton The controls to start and stop the background thread.

The TBackgroundPanel constructor builds the user interface, including the pair of buttons that communicate with the background thread. The listeners are designed to start and stop the thread by calling TBackgroundPanel's methods startTheThread() and stopTheThread(). TBackgroundThread is an inner class, so it has access to all of the instance variables of TBackgroundPanel. Like most threads it has only one method: run().

When the user clicks fStartButton, startTheThread() instantiates a new TBackgroundThread and tells it to start(). When the thread starts, its run() method immediately sets the priority to the minimum value—the user interface has a higher priority, so the application feels responsive to the user. The TBackgroundThread sits in a tight loop doing whatever work it does. That work has been left as a comment in this version. You could download a file, query a database, or anything else that takes so much time that you don't want the user to have to wait.

Use fLock to synchronize the foreground and background threads

The boolean variable fNeedsToStop is shared between the two threads. If you're not careful, it's possible both threads could be using the variable at once. You use the Object fLock as a *semaphore* to prevent this, so that only one thread can work with fNeedsToStop at a time.

How do I attach functions to the buttons on the toolbar?

You can add JButtons and other components to your toolbar; use an ActionListener to handle mouseclicks, just as you would with any other button.

As it runs, TBackgroundThread continually reports its status to fProgressBar. It then checks the state of fNeedsToStop. fNeedsToStop is true if the user has clicked fStopButton, and run() breaks out of its loop.

Adding Toolbars and ToolTips

It's easy to add toolbars and ToolTips to your Swing components. If you have a JButton named fButton, just write the following to add a ToolTip to the button. You can use this technique on any JComponent.

```
fButton.setToolTipText("This is the tooltip");
```

A JToolBar is simply another JComponent. You can write code like the following to build a toolbar:

```
JToolBar theToolBar = new JToolBar();
JButton aButton = new JButton("One");
theToolBar.add(aButton);
JButton anotherButton = new JButton("Two");
theToolBar.add(anotherButton);
```

SEE ALSO

➤ *Learn more about event listeners, page 274*

The Long-Awaited Tabbed Pane

The Windows32 user interface (implemented in Windows 95 and Windows NT 4.0) included a tabbed pane, which is commonly used throughout Windows applications. Unfortunately, the AWT interface did not include a tabbed pane—early Java programmers cobbled one together by using the CardLayout.

You get your own JTabbedPane with Swing. You can add one to a BorderLayout with just a few lines of code, as shown in Listing 12.7.

LISTING 12.7 *TTabbedPanel.java*–Add tabs to a *JTabbedPanel*

```
1  import java.awt.swing.*;
2  public class TTabbedPanel extends JPanel {
3  {
```

```
 4    private JTabbedPane fTabbedPane;
 5    public TTabbedPanel() {
 6      setLayout (new java.awt.BorderLayout());
 7      fTabbedPane = new JTabbedPane();
 8      fTabbedPane.addTab("One", null, makePane("One"));
 9      fTabbedPane.addTab("Two", null, makePane("Two"));
10      fTabbedPane.addTab("Three", null, makePane("Three"));
11      fTabbedPane.setSelectedIndex(0);
12      add (fTabbedPane, java.awt.BorderLayout.CENTER);
13    }
14    protected void makePane(String theString) {
15      // customize makePane to display the exact info you want
16      // on each panel
17      JPanel thePanel = new JPanel();
18      thePanel.setBackground(SystemColor.control);
19      thePanel.add(new JLabel(theString));
20      return thePanel;
21    }
22  }
```

Other Swing Components

Swing is a huge component library; in addition to the components described here, there are JSliders, JComboBoxes, JLists, and many other widgets. A JSlider resembles a JScrollBar, but with it you can add major and minor tick marks and display a Border around the slider. A JComboBox resembles the AWT's Choice component but has more capability. (For example, you can use a JComboBox to supply a list of default choices, and then allow the user to enter his or her own value if none of the defaults are appropriate.) Use JList just as you would use List in the AWT. You can listen for ListSelectionEvents just as you do other events—just add a ListSelectionListener.

> **JList doesn't support scrolling**
>
> Unlike its AWT counterpart, JList doesn't support scrolling directly. That's not a problem, though—just add it to a ScrollPane or JScrollPane to restore that capability.

Writing Swing Applets

Swing introduces a new class—JApplet—that is derived from Applet. Many of the new methods you find in JApplet have to do with accessibility for people with disabilities. The other new capability has to do with something called JRootPane.

JRootPane allows you to place contents into one of several layers. In order from front (closest to user) to back (farthest from user) the layers are as follows:

1. glassPane A JComponent that fills the entire viewable area of the JRootPane. By default, the glassPane is not visible.

2. layeredPane A subclass of JComponent designed to hold dialog boxes, menu pop-ups, and other components that should appear to be floating between the user and the content.

3. menubar An optional component; if present, it appears anchored to the top of the JRootPane.

4. contentPane The JComponent where most of the contents will be drawn.

SEE ALSO

➤ *Learn more about adding accessibility to your programs, page 387*

Using the *contentPane*

To add components to a JApplet, you should usually add them to the contentPane. You don't write the first line of code:

```
theApplet.add(theComponent);
```

You write, as you would in AWT, this line of code:

```
theApplet.getContentPane().add(theComponent);
```

Working with the *JLayeredPane*

By placing most of your components in the contentPane (which is farthest away from the user), you make it possible to add special components such as menu pop-ups or dialog boxes in a layer closer to the user (such as the layeredPane).

Adding Menus to *JApplets*

If you've worked with the AWT, you know that you cannot easily add menus to an applet. AWT menus need to be attached to a Frame, but an Applet is a Panel. You can set a JMenuBar on the JRootPane with JApplet. It is positioned along the upper edge of the JApplet's JRootPane.

Using the contentPane's default layout manager

By default, the **contentPane** has a **BorderLayout** layout manager.

A JLayeredPane has several layers

If you plan to use the layeredPane, be sure to read the JDK documentation on java.awt.swing.JLayeredPane. This class supports six distinct layers. From back to front, those include the FRAME_CONTENT_LAYER, the DEFAULT_LAYER, the PALETTE_LAYER, the MODAL_LAYER, the POPUP_LAYER, and the DRAG_LAYER. In addition, you can make up layers of your own.

Drawing On the *glassPane*

The glassPane is closest to the user. If you need to draw something that should appear in front of all components, including dialog boxes, menu pop-ups, and other components on the layeredPane, add it to the glassPane.

Using Swing-Specific Layouts

In addition to the AWT layouts that you used in the previous section, Swing comes with five layouts of its own:

- ScrollPaneLayout Built into the ScrollPane component.

- ViewportLayout Built into the Viewport component.

- BoxLayout Built into the Box component, but available as an option in other components.

- OverlayLayout A layout manager in which every component is added on top of every previous component.

- SpringLayout A layout manager in which space is allocated based on a set of constraints associated with each component.

Taking Advantage of *ScrollPaneLayout* in *JScrollPanes*

You'll never need to instantiate a ScrollPaneLayout. Instead, make a new JScrollPane. You get the nine areas associated with the ScrollPaneLayout automatically:

- JViewport In the center; use it for your contents.

- JScrollBar Two; one for horizontal scrolling, the other for vertical.

- JViewPort Two; one for row headers, the other for column headers.

- Component Four; one for each corner.

Each JViewport has its own layout manager, the ViewportLayout.

Working with *ViewportLayout*

Like the ScrollPaneLayout, you don't need to make your own ViewportLayout. You get it automatically with every Viewport. Just add a component to the Viewport—the ViewportLayout will position it based on the properties of your Viewport.

Using *Box* and *BoxLayout*

You can use Box to get BoxLayout automatically

If you plan to use **BoxLayout**, subclass **Box** rather than **JPanel**. **BoxLayout** is the default layout manager for **Box** and provides several methods that give you detailed control over the layout.

The BoxLayout resembles the AWT FlowLayout, except that with it you can specify the axes—either x or y. Unlike GridLayout, each component can occupy a different sized cell. Write the following to use the BoxLayout in the y-axis:

```
setLayout(new BoxLayout(this, BoxLayout.Y_AXIS));
```

Figure 12.10 illustrates a BoxLayout in the y-axis.

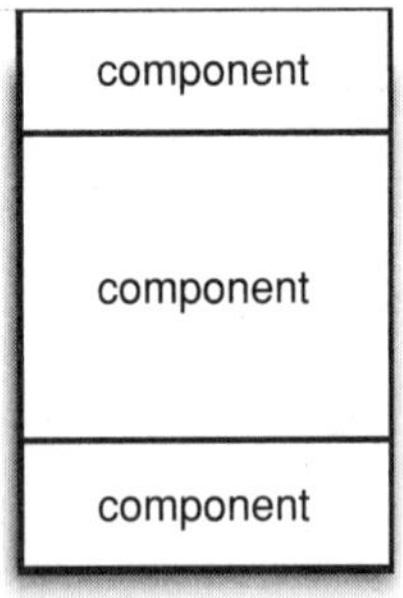

FIGURE 12.10

This BoxLayout is set up for the y-axis and has three components.

Building Advanced Designs with *OverlayLayout* and *SpringLayout*

Use createSpring() to make spring constraints

Sun recommends that you use createSpring() to combine the integer constants into a spring. createSpring() returns an Integer that can be passed directly to add().

The OverlayLayout positions each component over the top of the others. The size of the complete layout is the size of the largest component.

The SpringLayout changes the space allocated to each component as components are added and removed. Use the class constants to specify how you want the component cells to change. For example, you might write the following:

```
mySpringLayout.add(myComponent,
                    new Integer(
➥SpringLayout.RIGHT_MARGIN_CAN_CHANGE ¦

➥SpringLayout.TOP_MARGIN_CAN_CHANGE));
```

Swing Listeners and Events

Recall from the first section of this chapter, "The Swing Architecture," that one of the distinctive features of the JFC is the delegation event model. While the AWT components can still use the now-deprecated JDK 1.0 model for communicating about actions, Swing components only use the delegation event model. In fact, Swing takes the delegation event model to new heights, based upon the Model-View-Controller (MVC) design pattern.

SEE ALSO

➤ *Learn more about MVC, page 336*

Many Swing events rely on the MVC pattern

Many Swing events, such as those that refer to the "model," assume that you're using the MVC pattern. See the information in Chapter 13, "Designing for a JFC Interface," before attempting to build a listener for these events.

Understanding Swing Events

Chapter 11 introduced the delegation event model and talked about low-level and semantic events. Swing has its own event package for Swing-specific events. Use the java.awt.swing.event package for the event listeners and the events themselves; the event sources are the Swing components. Here's a list of the Swing event classes—DocumentEvent is an interface—and their meanings:

- AncestorEvent Ancestor added, moved, or removed.
- CaretEvent The text caret has changed.
- ChangeEvent A component has had a state change.
- DocumentEvent A document has had a state change.
- HyperlinkEvent Something has happened with respect to a hypertext link.
- InternalFrameEvent An AWTEvent that adds support for JInternalFrame objects.

- `ListDataEvent` Contents of a list have changed, or an interval has been added or removed.

- `ListSelectionEvent` The selection on a list has changed.

- `MenuEvent` A menu item has been selected (posted) or deselected (cancelled).

- `PopupMenuEvent` Something has changed on a `JPopupMenu`.

- `TableColumnModelEvent` The model for a table column has changed.

- `TableModelEvent` The model for a table has changed.

- `TreeExpansionEvent` A tree node has been expanded or collapsed.

- `TreeModelEvent` A tree model has changed.

- `TreeSelectionEvent` The selection in a tree has changed status.

- `UndoableEditEvent` An undoable operation has occured.

Using Swing Event Listeners

What is an ancestor?

In Windows jargon, an *ancestor* is a member of the path of containers that goes back to the root window. Assume you put a `JPanel` into a `Frame`, put a `JLabel` on the `JPanel`, and finally put an `Icon` in the `JLabel`. The `JLabel`, the `JPanel`, and the `Frame` are all ancestors of the `Icon`.

Like their AWT counterparts, Swing event listeners are interfaces. Unlike AWT, Sun hasn't yet implemented adapter classes, so you need to override every listener method in order to implement a listener. For example, you might write the following to implement an `AncestorListener` (which has three methods):

```
public class myAncestorListener implements AncestorListener
➡{
  public void ancestorAdded(AncestorEvent e) {
    // ignore this one
  }
  public void ancestorRemoved(AncestorEvent e) {
    // don't care about this one either
  }
  public void ancestorMoved(AncestorEvent e) {
    // do something in this case
    Here is code to handle the case of a moving ancestor
  }
}
```

Understanding Swing Event Sources

Swing events originate in the Swing components. Here's a list showing which events come from which sources. Remember the component hierarchy—an event sent by a JComponent is sent by every class that derives from JComponent.

- ActionEvent

  AbstractButton

  DefaultButtonModel

  JDirectoryPane

  JTextField

  Timer

- AdjustmentEvent

  JScrollBar

  Spinner

- AncestorEvent—JComponent

- CellEditorEvent—DefaultCellEditor

- ChangeEvent

  AbstractButton

  DefaultBoundedRangeModel

  DefaultButtonModel

  DefaultCaret

  DefaultSingleSelectionModel

  FontChooser.Patch

  JProgressBar

  JSlider

  JTabbedPane

  JViewport

  StandardDialog

  StyleContext

- DocumentEvent—AbstractDocument

- `ItemEvent`

    `AbstractButton`

    `DefaultButtonModel`

    `JComboBox`

- `ListDataEvent—AbstractListModel`

- `ListSelectionEvent`

    `DefaultListSelectionModel`

    `JList`

- `MenuEvent—JMenu`

- `PropertyChangeEvent`

    `AbstractAction`

    `DefaultTreeSelectionModel`

    `DirectoryModel`

    `JComponent`

    `TableColumn`

- `TableColumnModelEvent—DefaultTableColumnModel`

- `TableModelEvent—AbstractTableModel`

- `TreeExpansionEvent—DefaultTreeModel`

- `TreeSelectionEvent`

    `DefaultTreeSelectionModel`

    `JTree`

- `VetoableChangeEvent—JComponent`

- `WindowEvent—JPopupMenu`

Of course, you still have access to events sent by AWT components:

- `ComponentEvent` From `Component`

- `FocusEvent` From `Component`

- `KeyEvent` From `Component`

- `MouseEvent` From `Component`

- `MouseMotionEvent` From `Component`

- `ContainerEvent` From `Container`

- `WindowEvent` From `Window`

Designing for
a JFC Interface

See how the Model-View-Controller design pattern
simplifies software maintenance

Learn how to switch from one look and feel to another
at runtime

Use *DebugGraphics* to lower your testing costs

Working with the Model-View-Controller Design Pattern

In Chapter 11, "Building the User Interface with the AWT," we introduced the concept of an event. We said that, in general, user interface components are sources for events (such as mouseclicks) and listeners that you implement in your classes receive events.

In Chapter 12, "Building the User Interface with JFC Swing Components," you learned that many of the Swing components are based on a design pattern called Model-View-Controller, or MVC. You'll notice that the panels you implemented in Chapter 12 didn't have any logic behind them—they were pure user interface. That's because most of the mechanisms for listening to Swing events are based on MVC. Now turn your attention to MVC.

The concept of MVC is simple:

- Store internal state in a set of classes called the *model*
- Display data from the model in a *view*
- Change data in the model in a *controller*

Figure 13.1 illustrates an example of an MVC-based design for a weather-reporting station. The model consists of the temperature, barometric pressure, wind speed, and so on. There may be several views of the data—a snapshot of the current conditions, a line graph showing the conditions over the past 24 hours, and a line graph showing the conditions over the past 7 days. In this case the controller isn't part of the user interface at all—it's implemented by the interface between the computer program and the weather instruments.

Here's another example. Figure 13.2 illustrates a design in which physicians are constantly entering new medication orders and discontinuing others. The model contains a list of all of the current orders for each patient. The controller is implemented in the interface with the prescribing physician. This system could support many views: a list of current medication orders, a list of medications due within the next hour, or a list of possible adverse drug reactions, based on the patient's current list of medication orders.

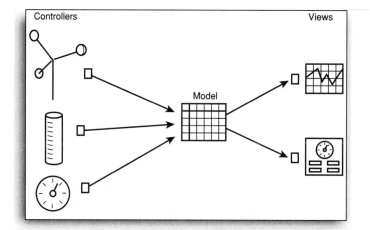

FIGURE 13.1
This simple weather station has several controllers, several views, and one model.

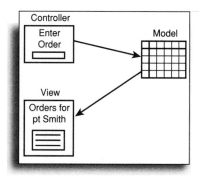

FIGURE 13.2
In this case both the controller and the view are on the same computer.

The remainder of this chapter elaborates on this concept.

SEE ALSO

➤ *Learn more about the delegation event model, page 274*

➤ *For more information on design patterns, page 196*

Understanding the Model

When I talked about class design in Chapter 7, "Object-Oriented Analysis: A New Way of Looking at Software," you observed that the state of a class is stored in its instance variables (and, to some extent, its class variables). You learned that these variables are usually made private; if the outside world needs to access them they do so through get... and set... methods, or through higher-level methods.

Now you're working at the design pattern level, and are concerned with groups of interrelated classes rather than the internals of one class. Many of the principles are the same:

- Identify data that should be preserved, and place it in the model.
- Define ways that the user will change the model; make sure the model classes support all of the methods necessary to implement these ways. (These methods will be the interface between the model and the controller.)
- Define ways the user will view the data in the model; make sure the model classes support all of the methods necessary to implement these ways. (These methods will be the interface between the model and the view.)

Saving and Restoring Model Data with *Serializable*

Data in the model may be stored in memory, in a disk file, or in a database. That's no problem when the data members are primitive types, but how do you save an object reference? Object references are implemented by pointers to memory, and an object that resides at one place in memory may be located someplace quite different when you load it back in from the hard drive. The solution is to serialize the objects—to write them out in such a way that new instances can be created when the object is restored to memory. (This latter is process is called deserialization.) It is common for the model's classes to implement `Serializable`, an interface that notifies the compiler that the data members (including objects) can to be serialized and deserialized.

Figure 13.3 illustrates a class that has implemented `Serializable`. `MySerializedClass` extends `MyNonSerializedClass`, and includes references to an instance of `AnotherSerializedClass` and `YetAnotherSerializedClass`, as well as its own primitive data members.

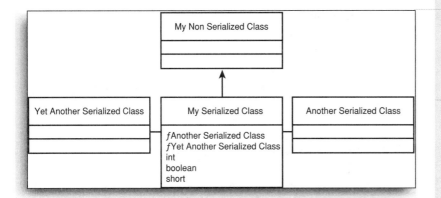

FIGURE 13.3
A serializable class may optionally save some of the data
members of its non-serializable
superclass.

When an instance of MySerializedClass is serialized, all of its
primitive data members are serialized. Then the serialization
method (writeObject()) is called on each of the object references
in MySerializedClass. If the designer of MySerializedClass needs
some of the public or protected data members of the (nonserial-
izable) superclass, he or she must override writeObject() and
explicitly write those data members.

When an instance of MySerializedClass is restored (deserialized)
the runtime environment will recursively call readObject() to
restore each of the classes that MySerializedClass references. It
will call the no-argument constructor of the superclass. If the
class designer has overridden readObject() in order to restore
protected and private members of the superclass, super's no-
argument constructor will still be called first.

Listing 13.1 shows an example of a Serializable class. If we had
chosen not to implement writeObject() and readObject(), the
runtime would have called defaultWriteObject() and
defaultReadObject() for us.

**Make sure all of your object refer-
ences are Serializable**

If your **Serializable** class
includes references to objects
that are not **Serializable**,
you'll get an exception
(**NotSerializableExce
ption**) when you attempt to
save that object.

LISTING 13.1 *TDose.java*–This class implements its own serialization methods

```
1   public class TDose implements java.io.Serializable
2   {
3       String fLotID;
4       java.util.Date fExpirationDate;
```

continues…

LISTING 13.1 Continued

```
 5
 6    public TDose() {
 7      fLotID = "";
 8      fExpirationDate = new java.util.Date();
 9    }
10
11    private void writeObject( java.io.ObjectOutputStream out )
12      throws java.io.IOException {
13      out.defaultWriteObject();
14      out.writeObject( fLotID );
15      out.writeObject( fExpirationDate );
16    }
17
18    private void readObject( java.io.ObjectInputStream in )
19      throws java.io.IOException,
             java.lang.ClassNotFoundException
20    {
21      in.defaultReadObject();
22      fLotID = (String)in.readObject();
23      fExpirationDate = (java.util.Date)in.readObject();
24    }
25  }
```

Use the methods in `DataInput` and `DataOutput`

If you choose to implement `Externalizable`, you should become familiar with the `DataInput` and `DataOutput` classes. These classes include methods to read and write primitive types. For example, you'll get `readByte()` and `readBoolean()` in `DataInput`, and `writeByte()` and `writeBoolean()` in `DataOutput`.

Sometimes your class contains object references or primitive data that should not be serialized. Simply declare those members `transient`, and the serialization routines will skip over them.

You can implement `writeObject()` and `readObject()` in order to be sure your class knows when it is being serialized or deserialized. If you have `transient` data you should be sure to reconstruct it from the non-transient members in `readObject()`.

If you want even more control over the serialization process, have your class implement `Externalizable`. You'll need to override `writeExternal()` and `readExternal()`, but now you'll actually be writing the routines the runtime uses to read and write your data to and from the external stream. (You might want this degree of control, for example, if your data is sensitive and must be encrypted before being serialized.)

Like `transient` data, `static` data is not serialized or deserialized by the default methods. If you need to serialize `static` data with your instances, you'll need to override `writeObject()` and `readObject()`.

Evolving Your Model Data with *serialVersionUID*

Suppose you're designing your hospital pharmacy system, and have designed the `TMedication` class that describes each medication. You've entered hundreds of instances of `TMedication`. They're `Serializable`, and they've been written to a disk file so you can restore them whenever you like. `TMedication`'s class diagram is shown in Figure 13.4.

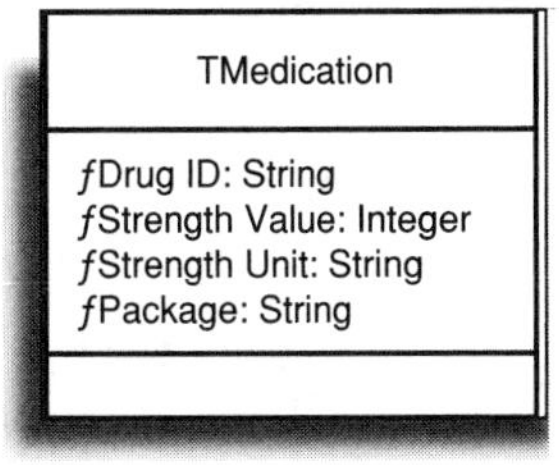

FIGURE 13.4
There are hundreds of instances of `TMedication` stored on the hard drive.

> **Component implements Serializable**
>
> `java.awt.Component` implements `Serializable`, so anything you store in a `Component` or one of its subclasses will be serialized unless you mark it `transient` or `static`.

Now the pharmacist decides you should also include the drug manufacturer's name in `TMedication`. You can certainly add the data member—the new verson of `TMedication` looks like this:

```
public class TMedication implements Serializable {
   private String fDrugID;
   private Integer fStrengthValue;
   private String fStrengthUnit;
   private String fPackage;
   private String fManufacturer;
   . . .
}
```

But what happens after you compile this new version of the class? The next time you try to restore an instance of `TMedication` from the hard drive you find that the stored version doesn't include `fManufacturer`, and the deserialization fails.

> **Java will resist deserializing obsolete data**
>
> In fact, in Java, the runtime environment will not deserialize an instance that doesn't match the current version of the class. This means that the deserialization routine won't become confused, but it also means that you may lose the use of your serialized data unless you take control of the versioning mechanism.

Java computes a serialVersionUID by default

If you don't supply a `serialVersionUID` member for your **Serializable** classes, Java computes one for you based on your data, methods, extensions, and interfaces. It is this ID Java uses when it is determining whether or not it can deserialize an instance.

The solution is to add a special member to your class:

```
static final long serialVersionUID = aUniqueID;
```

While `static` data usually isn't written to the output stream during serialization, this member is an exception. If you've defined `serialVersionUID` it will be written out along with the instance variables. When the instance is deserialized, the runtime system will first compare the `serialVersionUID` on the input stream with the `serialVersionUID` of the current class. If they don't match, the instance is not loaded from the input stream.

If there's any possibility that you might want to change your class after you've serialized instances, and you want to be able to restore those instances, you should follow this procedure:

Implementing version IDs

1. Explicitly add a `serialVersionUID` to your `Serializable` class.

2. Add a `static` minor version ID to your class, and write it out in `writeObject()`.

3. In your `readObject()` method, read back the minor version ID and use it to `switch` to a method that reads back just the members associated with that minor version.

4. In `readObject()` set any unused members to an appropriate value (such as zero or "Not on file") so the restored class is able to function as a member of the current `serialVersionUID` version.

If you use `serialVersionUID`, you should make sure the ID number is unique. The best way to ensure this is to use a program supplied by Sun called serialver. You can type

```
serialver className
```

at the command line to get a unique ID for the class, or you can type

```
serialver -show
```

to get the GUI version of the program. Figure 13.5 shows the GUI version being used to get the version number of the Swing component `JButton`.

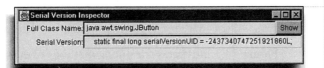

FIGURE 13.5

Copy the contents of the Serial Version field into your program for a unique ID.

Using Models in the User Interface

In addition to using MVC in your application, you can use the MVC pattern right in the user interface. In fact, that's what much of Swing's event-handling is all about. Consider a Swing JCheckBox. If you knew nothing at all about how Sun implemented it, you might guess that it's based on the MVC pattern. A checkbox has a state—it's either checked or unchecked. The state is stored in a model. You can click the checkbox to change the model—that's a controller. When the model changes state, the icon used to represent the checkbox changes—that's a view.

Now look at how Sun actually build JCheckBox. Figure 13.6 illustrates the inheritance hierarchy of JCheckBox. You shouldn't be surprised to find that JCheckBox includes a ButtonModel (derived from AbstractButton) and a ComponentUI (derived from JComponent).

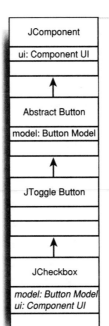

FIGURE 13.6

JCheckBox is derived from AbstractButton, which has a ButtonModel member, and JComponent, which has a ComponentUI member.

Concentrate for a moment on ButtonModel—we'll talk about ComponentUI in a moment, when we discuss delegates.

Figure 13.7 illustrates the public methods of ButtonModel. As you can see from these methods, a button has a surprisingly complex internal state. You can get and set Boolean parameters that determine whether or not the button is enabled, whether or not it has been pressed, and whether or not it is selected. You can get and set an accelerator key. Finally, the button is able to send three different kinds of Event—ActionEvent, ChangeEvent, and ItemEvent—so you can add or remove listeners for each of these Events.

FIGURE 13.7

ButtonModel stores the internal state of an AbstractButton.

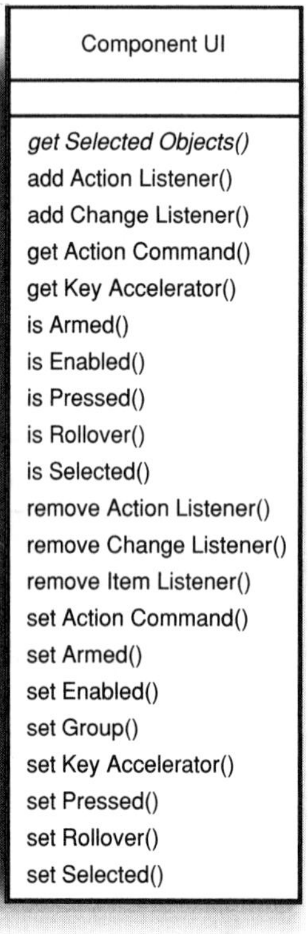

Component UI
get *Selected Objects()*
add Action Listener()
add Change Listener()
get Action Command()
get Key Accelerator()
is Armed()
is Enabled()
is Pressed()
is Rollover()
is Selected()
remove Action Listener()
remove Change Listener()
remove Item Listener()
set Action Command()
set Armed()
set Enabled()
set Group()
set Key Accelerator()
set Pressed()
set Rollover()
set Selected()

Note that nothing in the model has anything to do with appearance of the button or the way it responds to mouseclicks or keypresses directly. At the model level you can tell the button it is

Working with the Model-View-Controller Design Pattern

enabled or disabled, and it will remember what you tell it. Only later—in the view—will the appearance of the button onscreen change. Similarly, you can assign an accelerator key, but it is up to the user interface (through the associated controller class) to determine how and when to respond to that keypress.

`ButtonModel` isn't really a class—it's an interface. When you make a new `JCheckBox` the `model` reference points to an instance of `java.awt.swing.DefaultButtonModel`. `DefaultButtonModel` implements `ButtonModel`, and adds some methods of its own. For example, you can call `fireActionPerformed()` to programmatically send an `ActionEvent`.

Working with Delegates

In principle, the view and the controller are separate entities. As you saw in Figure 13.1 earlier, they could even be running on different machines. For most desktop applications, however, the view and the controller are closely related. For example, you might give an end user visibility into the state of the files on the hard drive by using a `JTree` class. You might then want to allow the user to rearrange the contents of the hard drive (possibly moving files from one location to another) through the same interface, even though changing the data in the model is a controller responsibility.

This close coupling between the view and the controller is so common that the two of them are often considered to be a single unit—a "delegate." Figure 13.8 illustrates the relationship between `JButton`'s model and its delegate.

When you say

```
JButton myButton = new JButton("My Button");
```

in Java, you get a new instance of the `JButton` class, which has a `model` member and a `ui` member. I've already talked about `model`; it will reference a `DefaultButtonModel`. `ui` will reference a `ButtonUI`, which is derived from `ComponentUI`. Figure 13.9 shows the public methods of these two classes.

FIGURE 13.8

A JButton uses a model and a delegate to deliver its behavior.

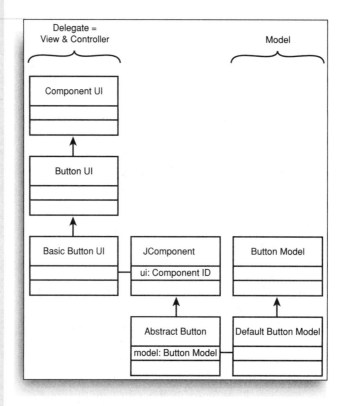

FIGURE 13.9

ButtonUI adds only one new method to ComponentUI.

Note that ButtonUI and ComponentUI are both rather general. In order to build a real delegate someone has to build a more concrete class. Fortunately, that someone probably isn't you or me. Sun has taken the lead in providing classes that extend these delegate classes—that's what pluggable look and feel is all about.

Take a look at the class hierarchy in the JDK documentation; scroll down to java.swt.swing.plaf.ButtonUI. You'll see that Sun has provided a BasicButtonUI subclass, as well as other subclasses, such as MenuItemUI, that are derived from ButtonUI purely for convenience. Figure 13.10 illustrates the relationship between ButtonUI, BasicButtonUI, and other look-and-feel classes.

In Swing 1.0 your widgets will be in the Java look-and-feel, known variously as the cross-platform look and feel or JLF.

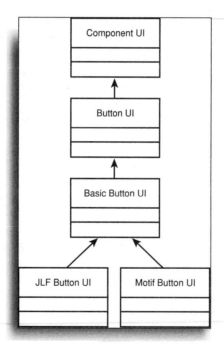

FIGURE 13.10

BasicButtonUI implements the Windows 95 look and feel, and serves as the base class for other look-and-feel classes.

A Simple Swing Application with *JButton*

If you already have some experience with the AWT and the delegation event model, you may find it easiest to get started with Swing by pretending that the Swing components are AWT components. Here's a program that does just that.

Listing 13.2 shows a JButton and a couple of JTextFields in action. You can run this panel by using the TPanelTester application class shown in Listing 12.1 of Chapter 12.

LISTING 13.2 *TLoginPanel.java*–**This demo shows how to hook up a *JButton***

```
1    import java.awt.*;
2    import java.awt.event.*;
3    import java.awt.swing.*;
4
5    public class TLoginPanel extends JPanel
6    {
7      JLabel fStatusLabel;
8      JTextField fUserName;
9      JTextField fPassword;
10     JButton fLoginButton;
11
12     public TLoginPanel() {
13       fStatusLabel = new JLabel("Please log in");
14       add(fStatusLabel);
15       fLoginButton = new JButton("Login");
16       add(fLoginButton);
17       fUserName = new JTextField(10); //10 visible columns
18       add(fUserName);
19       fPassword = new JPasswordField(10);
20       add(fPassword);
21
22       // now listen for the JButton's action
23       fLoginButton.addActionListener(new ActionListener() {
24         public void actionPerformed(ActionEvent e) {
25           if (isValid(fUserName.getText(), fPassword.getText()))
26             fStatusLabel.setText("Welcome!");
27           else
28             fStatusLabel.setText("Sorry!");
29
30           // either way, clear the fields so the user can
31           // try again
32 fUserName.setText("");
33           fPassword.setText("");
34         }
35       });
```

```
36    }
37    protected boolean isValid(String theUserName,
38       String thePassword) {
39  boolean theResult = false;
40       // stub for now; in real life, go to the database
41       if (theUserName.equals("Mike.Morgan") &&
42           thePassword.equals("fizzbin"))
43         theResult = true;
44       return theResult;
45    }
46  }
```

Figure 13.11 shows this application in action.

A More Complex Example with a *JTextField* and a *JTextArea*

Listing 13.3 shows a more complete example that will be used as the basis for the example in the next section. Figure 13.12 shows the resulting application.

LISTING 13.3 *TAddMedicationOrdersApp.java*–This simple application can serve as a template for many swing applications

```
1   import java.awt.*;
2   import java.awt.event.*;
3   import java.awt.swing.*;
4
5   public class TAddMedicationOrdersApp extends JFrame {
6     static final int kWidth - 350;
7     static final int kHeight = 180;
8     JTextField fMedicationOrder;
```

continues…

LISTING 13.3 Continued

```
9    JTextArea fMedicationOrderList;
10   ScrollPane fMedicationOrderListPane;
11
12   public TAddMedicationOrdersApp(String theLabel) {
13
14     // set up the overall appearance
15     super(theLabel);
16     setLayout(new FlowLayout());
17     setBackground(Color.lightGray);
18
19     // place the entry panel on the left
20     JPanel theEntryPanel = new JPanel();
21     theEntryPanel.setBorder(
         BorderFactory.createEtchedBorder());
22     theEntryPanel.setLayout(new BorderLayout());
23     JLabel theInstructions =
24       new JLabel("Type order and press <ENTER>");
25     theEntryPanel.add(theInstructions, BorderLayout.NORTH);
26
27     fMedicationOrder = new JTextField();
28     theEntryPanel.add(fMedicationOrder, BorderLayout.SOUTH);
29
30     theEntryPanel.add(Box.createVerticalStrut(6));
         // bottom margin
31
32     // place a view of the list on the right
33     JPanel theListPanel = new JPanel();
34     theListPanel.setBorder(BorderFactory.createEtchedBorder());
35
36     // make these elements appear one above the other
37     theListPanel.setLayout(new
38       BoxLayout(theListPanel, BoxLayout.Y_AXIS));
39     JLabel theTitle = new JLabel("Current orders");
40     theListPanel.add(theTitle);
41     theListPanel.add(Box.createVerticalStrut(10));
42
43     // make an empty text area with 6 rows and 20 columns
44     fMedicationOrderList = new JTextArea("", 6, 20);
45     fMedicationOrderList.setEditable(false); // read only
46     fMedicationOrderListPane =
```

```
47          new ScrollPane (java.awt.ScrollPane.SCROLLBARS_ALWAYS);
48        fMedicationOrderListPane.add(fMedicationOrderList);
49        theListPanel.add(fMedicationOrderListPane);
50        theListPanel.add(Box.createVerticalStrut(6));
51
52        // now hook up the listener
53        fMedicationOrder.addActionListener( new ActionListener() {
54          public void actionPerformed(ActionEvent e) {
55
56            // perform any validation on the order here
57            fMedicationOrderList.append(
               fMedicationOrder.getText());
58            fMedicationOrderList.append("\n");
               // force to new line
59
60            // Validate turns on the scrollbar if necessary
61            fMedicationOrderListPane.validate();
62
63            // clear the text field
64            fMedicationOrder.setText("");
65          }
66        });
67
68        // add the two panels to the frame,
           with a strut for cosmetics
69        Container aContainer = getContentPane();
70        aContainer.setLayout (new FlowLayout());
71        aContainer.add(theEntryPanel);
72        aContainer.add(Box.createHorizontalStrut(30));
73        aContainer.add(theListPanel);
74      }
75
76      // have a main routine so this class can be
         run as an application
77      public static void main(String args[]) {
78        TAddMedicationOrdersApp theFrame =
79          new TAddMedicationOrdersApp("Add Medication Order");
80
81        theFrame.addWindowListener(new WindowAdapter() {
82          public void windowClosing(WindowEvent e) {
83            System.exit(0);
```

continues…

LISTING 13.3 **Continued**

```
84        }
85    });
86
87    theFrame.setSize(kWidth, kHeight);
88    theFrame.setVisible(true);
89  }
90 }
```

FIGURE 13.12

TAddMedicationOrders App has the beginnings of a model, though here the data is stored in the JTextArea.

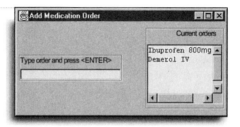

Use struts to improve your layouts

Most interface designs benefit from some open space in the layout. Use Box's horizontal and vertical struts to add space between components, as shown in Listing 13.3, lines 41, 50, and 72.

This program copies data from the JTextField directly to the JTextArea. The weakness of this program is that there's little opportunity to put another view on the data. Suppose, for example, that you wanted to determine whether there were any adverse drug interactions for the medications that have been ordered. This task is complicated by the fact that the interaction report depends not only on the medication being ordered now, but on medication orders that are already active for the patient. For now, assume you have a class TInteraction that reports possible interactions given a list of medications.

Here are three ways of implementing this design by using the simple form of the delegation event model. After you look at these three alternatives you'll look at an MVC-based approach.

- You could add another listener to fMedicationOrder to send the medication order to the TInteraction. Figure 13.13 illustrates this design. TInteraction will also need to access fMedicationOrderList so it can get the complete list of orders for this patient.

The problem with this approach is that it doesn't work. The AWT event model doesn't guarantee any particular order in which Event messages are delivered. The TInteraction class might get the ActionEvent from fMedicationOrder before fMedicationOrderList gets it. When the TInteraction class reads fMedicationOrderList, there's no way to know if fMedicationOrderList has already been updated.

- You could attach a listener to fMedicationOrderList, as shown in Figure 13.14. When it updates it could send a message on to the TInteraction class. This design can probably be made to work, but it isn't very maintainable. Now fMedicationOrderList is being used explicitly as a model, as well as being a view. If you ever want to change the design so the medication list isn't displayed, you may have to change the entire design.

- As a third option, you could leave the one listener in place on fMedicationOrder, but tell it to update the fMedicationOrderList and then get the updated list and send it on to fInteraction. Figure 13.15 illustrates this approach. Once again, this design can be made to work—in fact, it may be the best of these three approaches—but you've still tied fInteraction to fMedicationOrderList. You can't change fMedicationOrderList at some point in the future without wondering if you've broken fInteraction.

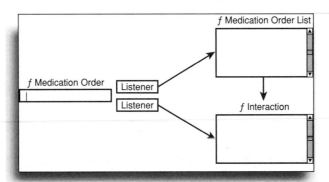

FIGURE 13.13

There's no guarantee whether fMedicationOrderList or fInteraction will get the event first.

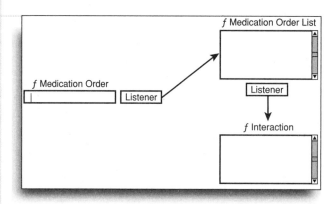

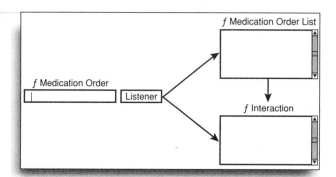

Instead of trying to force an improved design onto the design
from Listing 13.3, you would be better off starting with a new
design—an MVC-based design. Figure 13.16 illustrates such a
design.

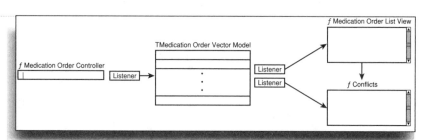

You use a Vector as a model—Vector is one of the container
classes available in the JDK. Since each patient only has a few
medications, there's little penalty in just iterating over the container to examine all of the medications for possible interactions.

fMedicationOrder is largely unchanged, but we'll change its name to fMedicationOrderController to reflect its new role. Likewise we'll rename fMedicationOrderList to fMedicationOrderListView. We have a new JLabel, too—fMedicationInterationWarningView.

Listings 13.4 through 13.6 show the finished implementation of this design. TMedicationOrderListView is designed to work through an adapter; the adapter calls changed when it has new information from the model. In this case, you simply rebuild the entire view from the model. If the list were longer, or you wanted to be more efficient, you could just send updates to tell the view how to change itself.

LISTING 13.4 *TMedicationOrderListView.java*–**This design, based on the MVC pattern, is far more maintainable than the one in** *TAddMedicationOrdersApp1.java*

```
1  import java.util.*;
2  import java.awt.swing.*;
3  public class TMedicationOrderListView extends JTextArea {
4    public TMedicationOrderListView (int theNumberOfRows) {
5      super("", theNumberOfRows, 10);
6      setEditable(false); // readonly
7    }
8    /**
9      Adapter calls changed to notify view of change in model
10    */
11   public void changed (Vector theVector) {
12     setText("");
13     Enumeration theEnumerator = theVector.elements();
14     while (theEnumerator.hasMoreElements()) {
15       String theMedicationOrder =
16         (String) theEnumerator.nextElement();
17       append(theMedicationOrder + "\n");
18     }
19
20     // force everybody to refresh; makes scrollbar visible
21     // if it's needed
22     getWindowAncestor().validate();
23   }
24  }
```

LISTING 13.5 *TMedicationOrderVectorModel.java*—**The new model is the biggest change between the two versions of this program**

```
1    import java.util.*;
2    import java.awt.swing.*;
3    import java.awt.swing.event.*;
4    public class TMedicationOrderVectorModel {
5      protected Vector fData = new Vector();
6      protected EventListenerList fChangeListeners =
7        new EventListenerList();
8
9      public TMedicationOrderVectorModel() {
10     }
11
12     public void addElement(String theOrder) {
13       fData.addElement(new String(theOrder));
14       fireChange();
15     }
16
17     public Vector getData() {
18       return fData;
19     }
20
21     public void addChangeListener(ChangeListener aListener) {
22       fChangeListeners.add( ChangeListener.class, aListener);
23
24       // alert the new listener about our current state
25       aListener.stateChanged(new ChangeEvent(this));
26     }
27
28     public void removeChangeListener(ChangeListener aListener) {
29       fChangeListeners.remove (ChangeListener.class, aListener);
30     }
31
32     protected void fireChange() {
33       ChangeEvent aChangeEvent = new ChangeEvent(this);
34       Object[] theListeners =
35         fChangeListeners.getListenerList();
36
37       // start at the end of the list. Remember that the list has
38       // pairs; a class and an instance
39       for (int i=theListeners.length-2; i>=0; i-= 2) {
40         if (theListeners[i] == ChangeListener.class) {
```

```
41          ChangeListener aChangeListener =
42              (ChangeListener) theListeners[i+1];
43          aChangeListener.stateChanged(aChangeEvent);
44       }
45     }
46   }
47 }
```

Now that you have a (list) view and a model, it's time to put it together with the controller and wrap the whole thing up in a frame. Listing 13.6 shows the completed solution.

LISTING 13.6 *TAddMedicationOrderApp2.java*–**This model is based on the MVC Pattern, and is more maintainable than the one in Listing 13.3**

```
1   import java.util.*;
2   import java.awt.swing.*;
3   import java.awt.swing.event.*;
4   import java.awt.event.*;
5   import java.awt.*;
6
7   public class TAddMedicationOrderApp2 extends JFrame {
8     public static int kWidth = 300;
9     public static int kHeight = 250;
10
11    TMedicationOrderListView fMedicationOrderListView =
12            new TMedicationOrderListView(5);
13    TextArea fConflicts = new TextArea ("", 3, 20);
14    TMedicationOrderVectorModel fModel = new
      TMedicationOrderVectorModel();
15    TextField fController = new TextField(10);
16
17    // adapter to map from model to ListView
18    private static class
      TMedicationOrderVectorToListViewAdapter
19      implements ChangeListener {
20        TMedicationOrderVectorModel fModel;
21        TMedicationOrderListView fView;
22
23      public TMedicationOrderVectorToListViewAdapter (
```

continues…

LISTING 13.6 Continued

```
24          TMedicationOrderVectorModel theModel,
25        TMedicationOrderListView theView) {
26        fModel = theModel;
27        fView = theView;
28      }
29
30      public void stateChanged(ChangeEvent e) {
31        fView.changed(fModel.getData());
32      }
33    } //close TMedicationOrderVectorToListViewAdapter
34
35    private static class
36      TMedicationOrderVectorToInteractionViewAdapter implements
37        ChangeListener {
38          TMedicationOrderVectorModel fModel;
39          TextArea fView;
40
41      public TMedicationOrderVectorToInteractionViewAdapter(
42        TMedicationOrderVectorModel theModel,
43        TextArea theView) {
44        fModel = theModel;
45        fView = theView;
46      }
47
48      public void stateChanged(ChangeEvent theChangeEvent) {
49          // determine if there is a drug interaction
50          // here is a stub
51          fView.setText("");
52          Vector theData = fModel.getData();
53          Enumeration theEnumerator = theData.elements();
54          while (theEnumerator.hasMoreElements()) {
55            String anOrder =
                (String) theEnumerator.nextElement();
56            if (anOrder.equals("Drug A")) {
57              Enumeration anotherEnumerator =
                  theData.elements();
58              while (anotherEnumerator.hasMoreElements()) {
59                String anotherOrder =
60                  (String) anotherEnumerator.nextElement();
61                if (anotherOrder.equals("Drug B")) {
62                  fView.append("A/B Contraindicated\n");
```

```
63                    }
64                    if (anotherOrder.equals("Drug D")) {
65                        fView.append("A/D Contraindicated\n");
66                        break;
67                    }
68                  } //end inner while
69                } //end 'if drug A'
70                // look for adverse interactions with other drugs
71                // as required
72              } //end outer while
73              if (fView.getText().equals(""))
74                fView.setText("No contraindications\n");
75          }
76      } //TMedicationOrderVectorToInteractionViewAdapter
77
78      private static class
79        TMedicationOrderFieldToMedicationOrderVectorAdapter
80          implements ActionListener {
81        TMedicationOrderVectorModel fModel;
82        TextField fController;
83
84        public
85          TMedicationOrderFieldToMedicationOrderVectorAdapter (
86            TextField theController, TMedicationOrderVectorModel
87            theModel) {
86            fModel = theModel;
87            fController = theController;
88        }
89
90        public void actionPerformed(ActionEvent e) {
91          String theMedicationOrder = fController.getText();
92          theMedicationOrder = theMedicationOrder.substring(0,
93                                    theMedicationOrder.length());
94
95          fController.setText("");
96          fModel.addElement(theMedicationOrder);
97        }
98      }
        //close MedicationOrderFieldToMedicationOrderVectorAdapter
99
100     public TAddMedicationOrderApp2( String theLabel ) {
```

continues…

LISTING 13.6 Continued

```
101        super(theLabel);
102        fConflicts.setEditable(false); // readonly
103        setLayout( new FlowLayout());
104        setBackground(Color.lightGray);
105        JPanel theControlPanel = new JPanel();
106        theControlPanel.setLayout(new
107          BoxLayout(theControlPanel, BoxLayout.Y_AXIS));
108        JLabel theControlTitle = new JLabel("Control");
109        theControlTitle.setHorizontalTextPosition(
           JLabel.CENTER);
110        theControlPanel.add(theControlTitle);
111        theControlPanel.add(Box.createVerticalStrut(10));
112        theControlPanel.add(fController);
113        Container aContainer = getContentPane();
114        aContainer.setLayout(new FlowLayout());
115      aContainer.add(theControlPanel);
116      aContainer.add(Box.createHorizontalStrut(30));
117        JPanel theViewPanel = new JPanel();
118        theViewPanel.setBorder(
119          BorderFactory.createEtchedBorder());
120        theViewPanel.setLayout(
121          new BoxLayout(theViewPanel, BoxLayout.Y_AXIS));
122        JLabel theTitle = new JLabel("Views");
123        theViewPanel.add(theTitle);
124        theTitle.setHorizontalAlignment(JLabel.CENTER);
125        theViewPanel.add(Box.createVerticalStrut(10));
126        ScrollPane theScrollPane = new
127          ScrollPane(java.awt.ScrollPane.SCROLLBARS_ALWAYS);
128        theScrollPane.add(fMedicationOrderListView);
129        theViewPanel.add(theScrollPane);
130        theViewPanel.add(Box.createVerticalStrut(10));
131        theViewPanel.add(fConflicts);
132      aContainer.add(theViewPanel);
133
134        TMedicationOrderFieldToMedicationOrderVectorAdapter
135          theControllerToModelAdapter = new
136            TMedicationOrderFieldToMedicationOrderVectorAdapter(
137                                          fController, fModel);
```

```
138      fController.addActionListener(
         theControllerToModelAdapter);
139
140        TMedicationOrderVectorToInteractionViewAdapter
141           theModelToInteractionViewAdapter = new
142             TMedicationOrderVectorToInteractionViewAdapter(
143                                                 fModel,
             fConflicts);
144        fModel.addChangeListener(
          theModelToInteractionViewAdapter);
145
146        TMedicationOrderVectorToListViewAdapter
147           theModelToListViewAdapter = new
148             TMedicationOrderVectorToListViewAdapter( fModel,
149                                       fMedicationOrderListView);
150        fModel.addChangeListener(
          theModelToListViewAdapter);
151      }
152
153      public static void main(String args[]) {
154        TAddMedicationOrderApp2 theFrame = new
155          TAddMedicationOrderApp2("Medication Order Entry");
156
157        theFrame.addWindowListener(new WindowAdapter() {
158          public void windowClosing(WindowEvent e) {
159             System.exit(0);
160          }
161        });
162
163      theFrame.setSize(kWidth, kHeight);
164      theFrame.setVisible(true);
165     }
166 }
```

Notice that you can mix AWT and Swing components in a single application. Figure 13.17 shows the finished application in the Windows 95 look and feel.

Mix AWT and Swing with care

Some users have reported problems painting containers that mix AWT and Swing. For best results use Swing containers such as **JFrame** and **JPanel**, or stick with either pure Swing or pure AWT.

FIGURE 13.17

This user interface combines AWT and Swing components in an MVC design pattern.

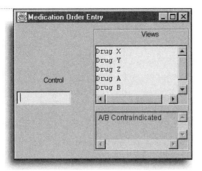

Switching the User Interface at Runtime

With the heavyweight AWT components every GUI component had its peer object. On a Windows machine AWT Buttons look like Windows buttons because they are Windows buttons. There's no way to switch an AWT Button from Windows to, say, Motif, because AWT relies upon the underlying operating system to actually draw the button image and handle user interaction.

More to the point, AWT doesn't use MVC. Figure 13.18 contrasts the way user interaction is handled in AWT and Swing.

Recall that in the MVC pattern the model holds the internal state while the view and the controller implement the user interaction. (When the view and controller are combined they're known as a delegate.) By separating the user interaction portion of the component from its internal state Sun made it possible to change look and feel at runtime. All you have to do is set a new look and feel for the application, and then notify each component to change to a new delegate.

Using the Look-and-Feel API

Sun's designers have assigned the responsibility for managing your program's look and feel to java.awt.swing.UIManager. If you plan for your program to run on more than one look and feel, you should become familiar with this class. If you plan to allow the user to switch looks and feels at runtime, you need to know many of the details of UIManager. Here are a few of the methods you'll find useful.

- static AbstractLookAndFeel[] getAuxiliaryLookAndFeels()
  Returns a list of looks and feels available on this machine

- static AbstractLookAndFeel getLookAndFeel() Returns a reference to the current look and feel

- static void setLookAndFeel(AbstractLookAndFeel theLookAndFeel) Sets the default look and feel to the one specified by the parameter, or throws UnsupportedLookAndFeelException

- static void setLookAndFeel(String className) Sets the default look and feel to the one specified by the parameter, or throws ClassNotFoundException, InstantiationException, IllegalAccessException, or UnsupportedLookAndFeelException

If you're planning to develop your own look and feel, or if you'd just like to learn more about how this new mechanism works, explore AbstractLookAndFeel—you'll subclass this class if you plan to write your own look and feel. You should also examine BasicLookAndFeel and its derived class, MotifLookAndFeel, to see how Sun implemented these looks and feels. Note that, in code, the letters UI (for User Interface) are synonymous with "look and feel delegate." Thus, WindowsButtonUI.paint() paints the button icon associated with a button in the Windows 95 look and feel.

> **You can mix looks and feels in a single component**
>
> If you have a component that needs a combination of looks and feels, consider switching that component to java.awt.swing.plaf .multi.MultiLookAnd Feel. That class will allow you to build a Vector of UIs for a single component, and may save you the work of writing your own look and feel.

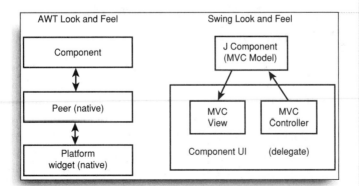

FIGURE 13.18
Swing components work through delegates, which implement MVC.

Making the Switch at Runtime

You can provide menu items, buttons, or other controls to allow the user to switch from one look and feel to another at runtime. Suppose you've provided a control that offers the Motif look and feel in the panel class `TheCurrentPanel`. Simply add the following code to the listener for that control.

```
try {
  UIManager.setLookAndFeel(
➥ "java.awt.swing.plaf.motif.MotifLookAndFeel");
  SwingUtilities.updateComponentTreeUI
(TheCurrentPanel.this);
  TheCurrentPanel.this.validate();
} catch (ClassNotFoundException e) {
  System.err.println( "Your machine does not appear to
➥ support the Motif look and feel.");
} catch (IllegalAccessException e) {
  System.err.println( "Your machine does not appear to
➥ support the Motif look and feel.");
} catch (UnsupportedLookAndFeelException e) {
  System.err.println( "Your machine does not appear to sup-
port the Motif look and feel.");
} catch (InstantiationException e) {
  System.err.println( "Could not switch to Motif
➥ Look and Feel.");
}
```

Debugging the Interface with *DebugGraphics*

What is regression testing?

A regression test is a test to make sure that everything that was working in the last version is still working in the current version. You should run a regression test as part of each software build or maintenance release.

As user interfaces moved from the old command-line-oriented world of MS-DOS and the UNIX shell to the new graphical user interfaces, testing costs went up. With a command-line interface you could load a text file with test commands and pipe them to the program. Then you could capture the output to a log file and compare it with a known good run. Often you'd write code all day and then run a *regression test* overnight to make sure you didn't break something.

Activating and Deactivating *DebugGraphics*

GUIs can be harder to debug, because the program's action is dependent upon events triggered by user interaction rather than simple typed commands. The latest version of the JFC supports DebugGraphics options as part of JComponent. You activate DebugGraphics by calling

```
setDebugGraphics(anOption);
```

on any JComponent. The option will apply to the component and all of its children.

There are four options:

- DebugGraphics.LOG_OPTION A text message is printed about every graphics operation.
- DebugGraphics.FLASH_OPTION The object will flash several times.
- DebugGraphics.BUFFERED_OPTION The Java runtime will make an external window that displays the operations on the component's offscreen buffer.
- DebugGraphics.NONE_OPTION Turns off DebugGraphics.

You can OR any of the three activating options together to combine effects. (It makes no sense to OR the NONE_OPTION with any of the others.) You can also pass a zero to setDebugGraphicsOptions(); it has no effect.

To get the current state of DebugGraphics call getDebugGraphicsOptions(); it returns an int.

Adding Debug to a *JComponent*

Here's an example of how you might use DebugGraphics in a typical JComponent. If you wanted to add DebugGraphics to the fPassword in TLoginPanel (shown in Listing 13.2) you could write
```
fPassword.setDebugGraphicsOptions(DebugGraphics.LOG_OPTION);
```
to the constructor.

Advanced User Interface Design with the JFC

Learn to use the newest features of JDK 1.2 and the Swing JFC

Cut, copy, and paste objects from one model to another

Add drag-and-drop capability to your Java programs

Ensure that your programs are accessible to people with disabilities

Use the improved 2D graphics interface

Working with *Transferable* Objects

Many applets and applications rely on the built-in cut, copy, and paste operations available in Java's text components. If you're using a Model-View-Controller pattern, however, you may need a richer version of cut, copy, and paste. For example, instead of copying or cutting the text itself you may need to transfer an object represented by the text. In the example developed in this chapter you'll transfer a String as a stand-in for a more sophisticated object.

Figure 14.1 illustrates a simplified design in which two text components simply serve as views into two different models. You could use a String-based transfer capability to copy or cut the text, but that wouldn't change the models.

FIGURE 14.1

This design has two models, and a List to allow the user to view each one.

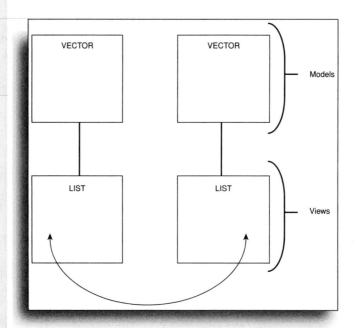

This section shows how to implement data transfer operations such as cut, copy, and paste within a single Java program. The Java interface Transferable specifies the minimum required methods that a transferable object must support.

You can use many of these same techniques to exchange data between one Java program and another, or even between a native application and a Java program. You can also build on this foundation to implement drag-and-drop capabilities. Sun is extending the JFC so that drag-and-drop will work between Java programs and native applications, as well as from one Java program to another.

SEE ALSO

➤ *Learn more about interfaces, page 230*

Understanding *DataFlavor*

One of the things that makes data transfer (whether by cut, copy, and paste or by drag-and-drop) an interesting problem is the fact that different models deal with the data in different ways. In the design shown in Figure 14.1, suppose that the Vector in each model contains instances of TMedication. What should happen if the user copies a TMedication into a TextField? Ideally your program would be smart enough to transfer a String representation of the underlying TMedication. What should happen if the user pastes a TMedication into a native application, such as the Windows Notepad? Again, your application should know how to convert its data into plain text so it can paste the text.

The solution to this problem of multiple data representations is called DataFlavors. A DataFlavor is an object whose internal structure is invisible to the outside world—in object-oriented parlance the object is said to be *opaque*.

In the example from Figure 14.1, you might choose to transfer a TMedication as a String, as text, or as a complete TMedication itself. Depending on your application, you might also choose to allow it to be transferred as a TDose or other application-specific class.

> **Cutting and pasting complex objects**
>
> While it's common to allow complex objects to be pasted as a **String** or as text, the reverse is not true. In most applications you needn't feel obligated to allow a user to copy an arbitrary string and paste it into your model as an object.

Implementing *Transferable*

In order to transfer an object from one model to another, you must make sure the class of objects implements Transferable. Transferable has three methods:

- getDataTransfer(DataFlavor)

What is
MimeTypeParseException?

Starting in JDK 1.2 Sun makes it easier to transfer data to and from the native operating system (by using the Multipurpose Internet Mail Extension, or MIME). In order to support this mechanism they added `MimeTypeParseExtension`. If you're trying to maintain compatibility with a JDK 1.1.x platform, don't use `MimeTypeParseException`.

- getTransferDataFlavors()
- isDataFlavorSupported(DataFlavor)

Listing 14.1 shows an implementation of TMedication as a Transferable class.

LISTING 14.1 *TMedication.java*—**This version of** *TMedication* **implements the required** *Transferable* **methods**

```
1  import java.awt.datatransfer.*;
2  import java.io.IOException;
3  import java.util.mime.MimeTypeParseException;
4
5  public class TMedication implements Transferable
6  {
7      private String fName;
8      private TStrength fStrength;
9      private String fPackage;
10
11     public TMedication()
12     {
13         fName = new String("");
14         fStrength = new TStrength();
15         fPackage = new String("");
16     }
17
18     public TMedication(String theName, int theStrength,
           String theStrengthUnits, String thePackage)
19     {
20         fName = new String(theName);
21         fStrength = new TStrength(theStrength,
             theStrengthUnits);
22         fPackage = new String(thePackage);
23     }
24
25     public String toString()
26     {
27         return fName + " " + fStrength.toString() + " " +
             fPackage;
28     }
29
30     public DataFlavor[] getTransferDataFlavors()
31     {
32         DataFlavor[] theDataFlavors;
```

```
33          theDataFlavors = new DataFlavor[2];
34          try {
35            theDataFlavors[0] = new DataFlavor(
              Class.forName("TMedication"), "TMedication");
36            theDataFlavors[1] = new DataFlavor(
              Class.forName("String"), "String");
37          } catch (ClassNotFoundException e) {
38              System.err.println("Exception: " + e.getMessage());
39              System.exit(1);
40          } catch (MimeTypeParseException e) {
41              System.err.println("Exception: " + e.getMessage());
42              System.exit(1);
43          }
44          return theDataFlavors;
45      }
46
47      public boolean isDataFlavorSupported(DataFlavor theFlavor)
48      {
49          boolean theResult = false;
50          try {
51            if (theFlavor.equals(new DataFlavor(
              Class.forName("TMedication"), "TMedication")) ||
52                theFlavor.equals(new DataFlavor(
                  Class.forName("String"), "String")))
53                theResult = true;
54          } catch (ClassNotFoundException e) {
55              System.err.println("Exception: " + e.getMessage());
56              System.exit(1);
57          } catch (MimeTypeParseException e) {
58              System.err.println("Exception: " + e.getMessage());
59              System.exit(1);
60          }
61          return theResult;
62      }
63
64      public Object getTransferData(DataFlavor theFlavor)
65        throws UnsupportedFlavorException, IOException
66      {
67          Object theResult = null;
68          try {
69          if (theFlavor.equals(new DataFlavor(
            Class.forName("TMedication"), "TMedication")))
70            theResult = this;
```

continues…

LISTING 14.1 Continued

```
71          else
72            theResult = this.toString();
73          } catch (ClassNotFoundException e) {
74              System.err.println("Exception: " + e.getMessage());
75              System.exit(1);
76          } catch (MimeTypeParseException e) {
77              System.err.println("Exception: " + e.getMessage());
78              System.exit(1);
79          }
80          return theResult;
81      }
82
83      class TStrength
84      {
85          private Integer fStrengthQuantity;
86          private String fStrengthUnits;
87
88          public TStrength()
89          {
90              fStrengthQuantity = new Integer(0);
91              fStrengthUnits = new String("");
92          }
93
94          public TStrength(int theStrengthQuantity,
            String theStrengthUnits)
95          {
96              fStrengthQuantity = new Integer(theStrengthQuantity);
97              fStrengthUnits = new String(theStrengthUnits);
98          }
99
100         public String toString()
101         {
102             return fStrengthQuantity.toString() +
                fStrengthUnits;
103         }
104     }
105 }
```

SEE ALSO

➤ *Learn more about throwing exceptions, page 245*

TMedication: A Class Walkthrough

TMedication is an example of a moderately complex class. It has three data members—fName, fStrength, and fPackage. fName and fPackage are implemented as Strings, but fStrength is implemented by using an inner class—TStrength. TStrength, in turn, includes an Integer for the numeric portion of the strength, and a String for the units. Figure 14.2 illustrates the design of TStrength.

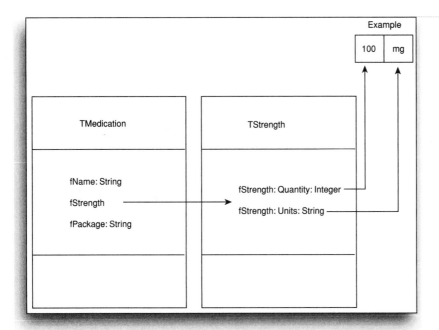

FIGURE 14.2

TStrength is an inner class of TMedication that encapsulates the concept of a medication's strength.

TMedication has two constructors. The more interesting of the two takes a name, a numeric strength, a String for the strength units (such as milligrams or milliliters), and a package name (such as tablets or caplets). It then uses these parameters to build a new instance of TMedication.

Since we plan to offer a String DataFlavor we also include the method toString() in both TMedication and TStrength. You'll frequently want to include a String conversion method such as toString(), even when the class is not Transferable—toString() makes it easier to debug your classes by allowing you to write or save String representations of your objects.

What's an Integer?

Class Integer encapsulates a primitive int. By wrapping your ints in Integers you get the benefits of objects as data members, at the cost of some additional overhead.

Building the *DataFlavors* Array in *getTransferDataFlavors()*

When you paste an object from the clipboard to a destination, or when you drag an object from a DragSource to a DragTarget, the runtime environment negotiates with the target container to see which DataFlavor it should transfer. In getTransferDataFlavors() we tell the runtime environment which DataFlavors we support, listed in order of preference. Usually you'll prefer to transfer the richest DataFlavor that both the source and the target mutually support. For example, when we're transferring a TMedication, we'd prefer to transfer the object itself if the target can handle it. Failing that, we're content to transfer a String. We therefore need two DataFlavors: TMedication and String.

Our implementation of getTransferDataFlavors() builds an array of DataFlavors and populates it with two new DataFlavors—one based on TMedication and the other based on String. To make a new DataFlavor write

```
new DataFlavor(Class.forName("TMedication"), "TMedication");
```

The first parameter to the constructor is a Class object, which is used to tell the DataFlavor what class it represents. The second parameter is a human-readable String, useful when you need to identify the DataFlavor.

By using this form of the constructor our new DataFlavor has a representationClass of TMedication and a mimeType of "application/x-java-serialized-object." If you need more control over the MIME type, examine the documentation for DataFlavor—there are several other constructors that give you different ways of setting the MIME type.

Since we're building these DataFlavors from inside the TMedication class, we'd be quite surprised if we got a ClassNotFoundException. Likewise, String is built into Java, and should always be present. In this case either a ClassNotFoundException or a MimeTypeParseException would represent a serious internal error, so we print a message and quit.

Using reflection

Reflection is Java's mechanism for allowing your program to examine classes and objects at runtime. The Class class is part of the reflection API that was introduced in JDK 1.1. We'll use reflection extensively when we work with JavaBeans, beginning in Chapter 19, "Building Components with JavaBeans."

Cross-platform transfers rely upon MIME types

As Java moves into the mainstream the ability to cut and paste or drag-and-drop between Java programs and native applications becomes increasingly important. Your Transferable objects should offer a rich variety of MIME types in order to participate in these transfers.

Implementing *isDataFlavorSupported()*

The second method required by Transferable is isDataFlavorSupported(). During the negotiation between the runtime environment and the transfer target, the runtime will ask your Transferable instance whether it supports certain DataFlavors. You already provided a list of supported flavors in getTransferDataFlavors()—now all you have to do is answer true when you're asked if you support one of those flavors.

Our implementation of isDataFlavorSupported() simply compares the parameter with each of the two DataFlavors we support. If they match, we reply true. We handle exceptions in the same way we did in getTransferDataFlavors().

Applying *getDataTransfer()* to *TMedication*

Once the negotiation with the transfer target is complete, the runtime environment will ask us for a specific DataFlavor by calling getDataTransfer. We simply return a representation of this that is based on the requested DataFlavor.

If the target accepts TMedication, we return this itself. Otherwise we return a String representation of this (by calling toString()). Exceptions are handled in the same way they were in the other two methods.

A Framework for Cut, Copy, and Paste

Now that we've made a Transferable class, we're ready to hook up the transfer mechanisms. Listing 14.2 shows TDemoFrame, a simple application that demonstrates the two models shown in Figure 14.1.

LISTING 14.2 *TDemoFrame.java*–This application shows how to implement cut, copy, and paste

```
1  import java.awt.*;
2  import java.util.Vector;
3  import java.util.Enumeration;
```

continues…

LISTING 14.2 Continued

```
4
5  public class TDemoFrame extends Frame implements
6  java.awt.datatransfer.ClipboardOwner
7  {
8      private Vector fMedicationModel1;
9      private Vector fMedicationModel2;
10     private java.awt.datatransfer.Clipboard fClipboard;
11     private java.awt.List fList1;
12     private java.awt.List fList2;
13
14     private java.awt.MenuBar mainMenuBar;
15     private java.awt.Menu menu1;
16     private java.awt.MenuItem miNew;
17     private java.awt.MenuItem miOpen;
18     private java.awt.MenuItem miSave;
19     private java.awt.MenuItem miSaveAs;
20     private java.awt.MenuItem miExit;
21     private java.awt.Menu menu2;
22     private java.awt.MenuItem miCut;
23     private java.awt.MenuItem miCopy;
24     private java.awt.MenuItem miPaste;
25     private java.awt.Menu menu3;
26
27     public TDemoFrame()
28     {
29         // build a static model with some medications in it
30         fMedicationModel1 = new Vector();
31         fMedicationModel1.addElement(new Tmedication(
             "Ibuprophen", 800, "mg", "tablet"));
32         fMedicationModel1.addElement(new Tmedication(
             "Tylenol", 100, "mg", "caplet"));
33         fMedicationModel1.addElement(new Tmedication(
             "Dramamine", 25, "ml", "liquid"));
34
35         // make an empty model for the right-hand side
36         fMedicationModel2 = new Vector();
37
38         // make a new, empty clipboard
39         fClipboard =
             new java.awt.datatransfer.Clipboard("Demo");
40
```

```
41          setLayout(new BorderLayout());
42          setSize(495, 305);
43
44          fList1 = new java.awt.List();
45          for (Enumeration e=fMedicationModel1.elements();
            e.hasMoreElements();)
46                  fList1.add(e.nextElement().toString());
47          fList1.setBounds(36, 48, 204, 124);
48          add(fList1, BorderLayout.WEST);
49
50          fList2 = new java.awt.List();
51          fList2.setBounds(252, 48, 213, 119);
52          add(fList2, BorderLayout.WEST);
53
54          setTitle("A Basic Cut and Paste Application");
55
56          mainMenuBar = new java.awt.MenuBar();
57          menu1 = new java.awt.Menu("File");
58          miNew = new java.awt.MenuItem("New");
59          menu1.add(miNew);
60          miOpen = new java.awt.MenuItem("Open...");
61          menu1.add(miOpen);
62          miSave = new java.awt.MenuItem("Save");
63          menu1.add(miSave);
64          miSaveAs = new java.awt.MenuItem("Save As...");
65          menu1.add(miSaveAs);
66          menu1.addSeparator();
67          miExit = new java.awt.MenuItem("Exit");
68          menu1.add(miExit);
69          mainMenuBar.add(menu1);
70          menu2 = new java.awt.Menu("Edit");
71          miCut = new java.awt.MenuItem("Cut");
72          menu2.add(miCut);
73          miCopy = new java.awt.MenuItem("Copy");
74          menu2.add(miCopy);
75          miPaste = new java.awt.MenuItem("Paste");
76          menu2.add(miPaste);
77          mainMenuBar.add(menu2);
78          menu3 = new java.awt.Menu("Help");
79          mainMenuBar.setHelpMenu(menu3);
80          mainMenuBar.add(menu3);
81          setMenuBar(mainMenuBar);
```

continues…

LISTING 14.2 Continued

```
82
83          TDemoWindow aDemoWindow = new TDemoWindow();
84          this.addWindowListener(aDemoWindow);
85          TDemoAction lDemoAction = new TDemoAction();
86          miOpen.addActionListener(lDemoAction);
87          miExit.addActionListener(lDemoAction);
88          miCut.addActionListener(lDemoAction);
89          miCopy.addActionListener(lDemoAction);
90          miPaste.addActionListener(lDemoAction);
91
92          setLayout(new BorderLayout(0,0));
93          setVisible(false);
94          setTitle("");
95      }
96
97      public TDemoFrame(String title)
98      {
99          this();
100         setTitle(title);
101     }
102
103      public synchronized void show()
104     {
105         super.show();
106     }
107
108     static public void main(String args[])
109     {
110         (new TDemoFrame()).show();
111     }
112
113     class TDemoWindow extends java.awt.event.WindowAdapter
114     {
115         public void windowClosing(
            ↪java.awt.event.WindowEvent event)
116         {
117             Object object = event.getSource();
118             if (object == TDemoFrame.this)
119                 TDemoFrame_WindowClosing(event);
120         }
121     }
```

```
122
123      void TDemoFrame_WindowClosing(
         java.awt.event.WindowEvent event)
124      {
125          setVisible(false); // hide the Frame
126          dispose();         // free the system resources
127          System.exit(0);    // close the application
128      }
129
130      class TDemoAction implements java.awt.event.ActionListener
131      {
132           public void actionPerformed(
             java.awt.event.ActionEvent event)
133          {
134              Object object = event.getSource();
135              if (object == miExit)
136                  miExit_Action(event);
137              else if (object == miCut)
138                  miCut_Action(event);
139              else if (object == miCopy)
140                  miCopy_Action(event);
141              else if (object == miPaste)
142                  miPaste_Action(event);
143          }
144      }
145
146      private void miExit_Action(
         java.awt.event.ActionEvent event)
147      {
148          System.exit(0);
149      }
150
151      private void miCut_Action(
         java.awt.event.ActionEvent event)
152      {
153        // find out which item has been selected
154        int theItem = fList1.getSelectedIndex();
155
156        if (theItem >= 0)
157        {
158          // copy it to the clipboard
159          fClipboard.setContents(
           (TMedication)fMedicationModel1.elementAt(theItem), this);
```

continues…

LISTING 14.2 Continued

```
160
161            // and remove it
162            fMedicationModel1.removeElementAt(theItem);
163            fList1.remove(theItem);
164        }
165    }
166
167    private void miCopy_Action(
       java.awt.event.ActionEvent event)
168    {
169       // find out which item has been selected
170       int theItem = fList1.getSelectedIndex();
171
172       if (theItem >= 0)
173          // and copy it to the clipboard
174          fClipboard.setContents(
          (TMedication)fMedicationModel1.elementAt(theItem), this);
175    }
176
177    private void miPaste_Action(
       java.awt.event.ActionEvent event)
178    {
179        TMedication theMedication =
          (TMedication) fClipboard.getContents(this);
180        if (theMedication != null)
181        {
182           fMedicationModel2.addElement(
             (Object)theMedication);
183           fList2.add(theMedication.toString());
184        }
185    }
186
187    public void lostOwnership(
       java.awt.datatransfer.Clipboard theClipboard,
188                          java.awt.datatransfer.Transferable
                            theContents)
189    {
190        System.err.println("Just lost ownership of
          clipboard");
191    }
192 }
```

Figure 14.3 shows the finished application before any items have been transferred. Figure 14.4 shows the result of cutting all of the items from the left-most List and pasting them into the right-most List.

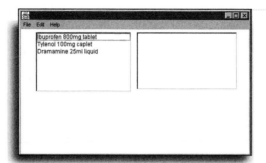

FIGURE 14.3
When you first start the application there are three medications in fList1.

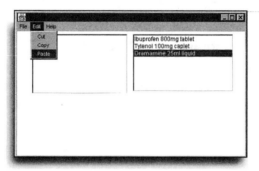

FIGURE 14.4
You can select and cut each item in fList1 and paste it into fList2.

Cut, copy, and paste do their work by moving data through an object called the clipboard, an instance of class Clipboard. Note that TDemoFrame implements java.awt.datatransfer. ClipboardOwner. You must implement this interface if your class will provide data to a clipboard. The one required method is lostOwnership().

Building the Models

In any program that relies on the Model-View-Controller design pattern, you'll have a *model* that holds the data, a *view* that shows the data to the user, and a *controller* that allows the user to interact with the model. In Java it's common to combine the view and the controller into a single construct called a *delegate*.

Model-View-Controller is useful for cross-platform drag-and-drop

You should get in the habit of using the Model-View-Controller (MVC) pattern for all Transferable objects. Starting in JDK 1.2 Sun supports drag-and-drop between Java programs and native applications; you can help your programs participate in these exchanges by using the MVC pattern.

Our first task in the TDemoFrame constructor is to build a model that contains some TMedications. To implement the model I chose a Vector—one of the new container classes that are part of JDK 1.2. Unlike an array, a Vector is resizable—we can add or remove empty "slots" as the program runs, ensuring that we won't overflow as we might with an array.

We populate the first model (fMedicationModel1) by calling the TMedication constructor. The second model (fMedicationModel2) is initially empty.

Next we make a new instance of Clipboard. The String parameter is used to set a name on this instance of Clipboard. Since we have only one Clipboard in this program, we don't take advantage of the Clipboard name.

SEE ALSO
➤ *Learn more about the Model-View-Controller design pattern, page 336*

Building the Delegates

Delegates encapsulate the user interface

Recall that, in the Model-View-Controller pattern, the user interface is defined by the View and the Controller. In most Java programs you'll find it convenient to combine the View and Controller into a single user interface element, often called the delegate.

After we make the models we can begin to lay out the user interface. We specify a layout manager—in this case, BorderLayout()—and a frame size. Then we build fList1, which serves as the delegate for the first model.

To populate fList1 we make an *Enumeration* of the fMedicationModel1 Vector. An Enumeration of a collection allows us to access the elements of the collection in an orderly fashion, even when the collection itself is unordered. Thus, we can succinctly copy the string representation of each TMedication in the Vector into the List:

```
for (Enumeration e=fMedicationModel1.elements();
    e.hasMoreElements();)
        fList1.add(e.nextElement().toString());
```

The second model is initially empty, so we just place its List in the Frame with no text in it.

Adding a Menu

By convention, cut, copy, and paste are menu items. There's no technical reason we couldn't associate these functions with Buttons or some other control, but users might become confused. In the next section of the constructor we make a new MenuBar (called mainMenuBar) and add several Menus and MenuItems. Except for miCut, miCopy, miPaste, and miExit, these MenuItems are not hooked up.

Hooking Up the Listeners

This application includes a WindowListener and an ActionListener. The WindowListener, of course, listens for the windowClosing message in the WindowEvent—we've seen that code in nearly every GUI application we've written.

Since this application is so simple, I elected to send all ActionEvents to the same listener, named lDemoAction. In a more complex application you might prefer to have a dedicated listener for each event source.

Since TDemoFrame is used as the basis for an application, it must have the required main() method. In this case main() makes a new instance of TDemoFrame and calls its show() method, which makes the new Frame visible.

Class TActionDemo is our ActionListener, and implements the one required method: actionPerformed. It checks the Event to find out which MenuItem initiated the ActionEvent, and dispatches the appropriate method. For example,

```
... if (object == miCopy)
     miCopy_Action(event);
```

tells the program to call miCopy_Action() when the MenuItem associated with "copy" is chosen.

An Implementation of *Copy*

When the user chooses Copy from the Menu our program calls miCopyAction(), which has just two steps:

1. Figure out what the user wants to copy.

2. Copy it to the clipboard.

Design so as to minimize surprises

Many experts in user interface design recommend the "principle of least surprise." They strive to build interfaces that the user will find intuitive, or at least similar to other user interfaces they've used in the past. As you build Java applications, learn what your users expect, and test your interface frequently to make sure your users don't consider parts of the interface "surprising."

I chose a List as the delegate (rather than, say, a TextArea) because List supports the getSelectedIndex() method. I can find out which line the user selected by writing

```
int theItem = fList1.getSelectedIndex();
```

Now I can take advantage of the fact that, once set up, the model and the list stay in one-to-one correspondence. When the user selects the second line of the List (which has index 1) the corresponding entry in the Vector has index 1. To copy the TMedication to the Clipboard we simply write:

```
fClipboard.setContents((TMedication)fMedicationModel1.
                                    elementAt(theItem),
                                    this);
```

If the user chooses Copy from the Menu but hasn't selected anything in the list, getSelectedIndex() returns a –1. We guard our method by including

```
if (theItem > 0)
```

before we attempt to copy anything to the Clipboard.

An Implementation of *Cut*

The method miCut_Action() strongly resembles miCopy_Action(). We do everything we did for Copy, but then we remove the instance from the model and the list.

An Implementation of *Paste*

Following a successful cut or copy operation, we can paste. In a more general application we would want to check to see what was selected before we pasted. In this simple demo I've locked the transfer target to the second model and its associated list.

The miPaste_Action() method has three steps:

1. Check the Clipboard to be sure we have something to paste.
2. Add the pasted item to the model.
3. Add a String representation of the pasted item to the List.

Once again, I've chosen to allow the method to update the List directly, rather than updating the model and having the model

---

Caution: Transferables are not typesafe

When you pass items to and from a Clipboard or, for that matter, in and out of a collection such as a Vector, they are implicitly stored as Objects. You must be sure to cast these Objects back to their original type when you retrieve them.

Should the controller update the view?

Notice that we allow miCopy_Action() to remove the String from the List at the same time that it removes the TMedication from the Vector. If you're an MVC purist you'd allow miCopy_Action() to change the model, and then have the model update the List. For a simple application like this one I choose not to be a purist.

update the list. Whether you choose this simple approach or go to the extra work of keeping a pure MVC design is up to you, and depends largely on the overall complexity of your model and view.

We retrieve the `TMedication` from the `Clipboard` by calling

`(TMedication) fClipboard.getContents(this);`

Notice that we must cast the contents of the `Clipboard` back to `TMedication`—when it comes out of the `Clipboard` the object knows only that it is `Transferable`.

We guard against the possibility that the user chose to paste when the clipboard was empty by writing

`if (theMedication != null)`

Then we update the model and the `List`:

```
fMedicationModel2.addElement((Object)theMedication);
fList2.add(theMedication.toString());
```

The New Drag-and-Drop Package

Starting in JDK 1.2 Java supports drag-and-drop. The basic mechanism strongly resembles cut and paste, but now you need a listener to tell you that a drag-and-drop operation is in progress. When you start a drag the cursor should change to a distinctive icon or image; you'll probably want to use one symbol for a move operation and another for a copy. As the cursor passes over places that do not accept a drop, the icon should change to reflect that fact. When you arrive at a drop target, the icon should reflect the fact that a drop would now work.

The new `java.awt.dnd` package includes three interfaces and twelve classes:

- `DragSourceListener` This interface is implemented by components that originate drag and drop operations in order to give feedback to the user.

- `DragTargetListener` A callback interface used by the `DropTarget` class.

What else can I do with drag-and-drop?

In addition to simple copies and moves, some platforms support an operation called "link" that sets up a relationship between two entities. The JDK allows you to specify that a drag is establishing a link, but because the nature of a link varies so widely from one platform to the next, Sun discourages you from using this kind of control.

- `FlavorMap` Use this interface to map between platform-specific data types and MIME type strings.

- `DnDConstants` This class defines the verb constants for drag-and-drop operations, such as `ACTION_COPY` and `ACTION_MOVE`.

- `DragSource` The class that originates a drag-and-drop operation.

- `DragSourceContext` The integrating class of the drag-and-drop operation. This class manages event notifications to the `DragSourceListener` and provides the `Transferable` object for the data transfer.

- `DragSourceDragEvent` The `Event` class (derived from `DragSourceEvent`) that is sent from the `DragSourceContextPeer` through the `DragSourceContext` to the `DragSourceListener`.

- `DragSourceDropEvent` This `Event` resembles `DragSourceDragEvent`, but it is used to tell the `DragSourceListener` when the operation completes.

- `DragSourceEvent` The base class for `DragSourceDragEvent` and `DragSourceDropEvent`.

- `DropTarget` Any `Component` that accepts drop operations should have an associated `DropTarget`.

- `DropTargetContext` When a drag-and-drop operation is in progress and the cursor passes over a `Component` that has an associated `DropTarget`, the runtime system instantiates a new `DropTargetContext`. The `Component` can use this instance to provide user feedback and to actually complete the data transfer.

- `DropTargetContext.TransferableProxy` This class is an inner class used by `DropTargetContext`.

- `DropTargetDragEvent` The `DropTargetListener` receives `dragEnter()`, `dragOver()`, and `dragScroll()` messages through this class.

- `DropTargetDropEvent` The `DropTargetListener` receives the `drop()` message through this class.

- `DropTargetEvent` The base class for `DropTargetDragEvent` and `DropTagetDropEvent`.

Ensuring Accessibility

At one time computers, especially computers with GUI interfaces, were considered to be beyond the reach of people with disabilities. If you couldn't control the mouse or see the screen you were "out of luck." Today's generation of *assistive technologies* have made that attitude a thing of the past.

The principal assistive technology for GUIs is the *screen reader*— a hardware-software combination that translates written text into the spoken word. (Some models of screen reader translate the text into Braille.) People who have limited vision but are not blind often benefit from a *screen magnifier*—an application that allows the entire GUI to be magnified—often up to 16 times. The quality of the user's experience with a screen magnifier depends largely upon the GUI's ability to smooth fonts and highlight text.

You should also design your Java programs so that the user doesn't need to move the mouse—make sure there's a keyboard method that corresponds with every mouse gesture. Some people must use non-keyboard methods of input. If you use Sun's latest accessibility technology your programs should work with most of these alternative input devices just as well as they work with a mouse and keyboard.

To make a user interface component accessible the component needs to implement the `Accessible` interface. When an assistive technology wants to know if a `Component` is accessible, it will use the `instanceOf` operator to determine whether or not the `Component` implements `Accessible`.

The list of methods associated with `Accessible` is long. Fortunately, most of the Swing components already implement `Accessible`, so if you're careful to build your user interface with Swing components your program is already a long way towards being accessible. You may want to modify some of the `Accessible` methods when you subclass a Swing component.

Learn to design for accessiblity

Learn more about accessibility, especially Web page accessibility, at `http://www.trace.wisc.edu/world/web/index.html`. You can also use the application at `http://www.cast.org/bobby/` to check your HTML against a list of rules designed to maximize accessibility.

Everyone appreciates keyboard shortcuts

It's not only the disabled who'll thank you for keyboard shortcuts. Most of us appreciate the option of using the keyboard, particularly if you're on a laptop or one of the new handheld PCs.

Ensure cultural and international accessiblity, as well

You can make sure your accessible user interface works in a variety of cultural and language environments. Examine the documentation for `java.awt.accessibility.AccessibleResourceBundle` and `java.awt.accessibility.AccessibleEnumeration` to see how to get the localized strings for the `accessibility` package.

Here are the methods required by `Accessible`. Many of these methods are not specific to `java.awt.accessibility`. For example, `setBounds` is implemented in `java.awt.Component`, so it's available in many classes in the AWT, as well as in the Swing components. If a particular method doesn't make sense for your `Component`, you can accept the default behavior inherited from a base class such as `Component` or provide a null method.

- `addAccessibleSelection()` Extends the `Component`'s selection to include the specified item.

- `addFocusListener()` Adds a listener to receive `FocusEvents` from this `Component`. *Focus* is the user's attention, usually as indicated by a mouseclick or keypress.

- `clearAccessibleSelection()` Clears the `Component`'s selection, so that nothing is selected.

- `contains()` Returns `true` if the specified `Point` is physically within the bounds of the `Component`.

- `doAccessibleAction()` Performs a specified action.

- `getAccessibleActionCount()` Returns a count of the number of available actions, the first being the default action.

- `getAccessibleActionDescription()` Returns a `String` description of the specified action.

- `getAccessibleAt()` Returns the `Accessible` child located at the specified `Point`.

- `getAccessibleChild()` Returns a specified `Accessible` child.

- `getAccessibleChildrenCount()` Returns the number of `Accessible` children in this `Component`.

- `getAccessibleDescription()` Returns a `String` describing the `Component`.

- `getAccessibleName()` Returns a `String` giving the name of this `Component`.

- `getAccessibleParent()` Returns a reference to the parent of this `Component`, or `null` if the `Component` does not have an `Accessible` parent.

- `getAccessibleRole()` Returns an instance of the `AccessibleRole` class that describes the role of this `Component`. Typical roles include `PUSH_BUTTON`, `TABLE`, or `LIST_ITEM`.

- getAccessibleSelection() Returns an Accessible object based on the current selected item.

- getAccessibleSelectionCount() Returns the number of items currently selected.

- getAccessibleStateSet() Returns an AccessibleStateSet object, which consists of a number of AccessibleState constants. Typical states include ACTIVE, FOCUSED, and SELECTABLE.

- getAccessibleText() Returns an AccessibleText object. The AccessibleText class supports the concepts of CHARACTER, WORD, and SENTENCE in order to support screen readers and similar assistive technologies.

- getAccessibleValue() Returns the value of this Component as a Number.

- getBackground() Returns the background color of the Component.

- getBounds() Returns the bounding Rectangle for the Component if it is on the screen.

- getCursor() Returns the Cursor associated with this Component.

- getFont() Returns the Font associated with this Component, if any.

- getFontMetrics() If the Component has an associated Font, returns the FontMetrics of that Font.

- getForeground() Returns the foreground color of the Component.

- getLocale() Returns the Component's Locale if it has been set, otherwise returns the Locale of the Component's parent.

- getLocation() Returns the Component's coordinate location on the screen relative to the location of its parent.

- getLocationOnScreen() Returns the location of the Component in screen coordinates.

- getMaximumAccessibleValue() Returns the maximum value of this Component as a Number.

- getMinimumAccessibleValue() Returns the minimum value of this Component as a Number.

- getNextAccessibleSibling() Returns the next sibling of this Component, if a preferred sibling exists. You could use this method to set up a default order for tabbing through the Components.

- getPreviousAccessibleSibling() Returns the previous sibling of this Component, if a preferred sibling exists.

- getSize() Returns the height and width of the Component in a Dimension object.

- isEnabled() Reports back whether the Component is enabled or not.

- isFocusTraversable() Reports back whether the Component can accept focus or not.

- isShowing() Returns true if the Component is present on the screen, even if it is obscured by another Component.

- isVisible() Returns true if the Component intends to be visible, even if it is not showing because one of its ancestors is not visible.

- removeAccessibleSelection() Removes the specified item from the object's selection.

- removeFocusListener() Detaches the specified FocusListener from this Component.

- selectAllAccessibleSelections() Selects every selectable item in the Component. The Component must support multiple selections in order for this method to work.

- setAccessibleDescription() Provides a String description for use by getAccessibleDescription().

- setAccessibleName() Provides a String name for use by getAccessibleName().

- setAccessibleValue() Sets the value of this Component as a Number.

- setBackground() Sets the background color of the Component.

- setBounds() Specifies the bounding Rectangle for the Component.

- setCursor() Specifies the Cursor for this Component.

- setEnabled() Enables or disables the Component, depending upon the parameter.

- `setFont()` Sets a `Font` for this `Component`.

- `setForeground()` Sets the foreground color of the `Component`.

- `setLocale()` Sets the `Locale` for this `Component`, for use in localizing the user interface.

- `setLocation()` Sets the location of the `Component` relative to its parent.

- `setSize()` Sets the height and width of the `Component`.

- `setVisible()` Shows or hides the `Component`, depending upon the paramenter.

SEE ALSO
➤ *Learn more about interfaces, page 230*
➤ *Learn more about Swing components, page 310*

Using the 2D API

JDK 1.1 included a nice graphics class, called `java.awt.Graphics`. To graphics professionals, however, `Graphics` left some features to be desired. More mature GUI platforms, such as Windows 95 and the Macintosh, support features that are just not present in JDK 1.1's `Graphics`.

Now, in JDK 1.2, all of that has changed. Sun has provided a much richer two-dimensional graphics class, called `java.awt.Graphics2D`. This section describes the major improvements available in `Graphics2D`. Listing 14.3 shows a demonstration program, `PathsFill.java`, that shows how to display shapes by using `Graphics2D`. The `PathsFill` class is a type of `Canvas`, so `Graphics2D` is able to draw on it by casting the `Graphics` parameter to `paint()` as a `Graphics2D`. The class also contains a `main()` method, allowing us to run it from the command line. Compile `PathsFill.java` by typing

```
javac PathsFill.java
```

and run it by typing

```
java PathsFill
```

at the command line. You should see a spiral of shapes in a variety of colors.

Making an `Object` Accessible

If you want to make an `Object` available to assistive technologies and the `Object` isn't derived from `Component`, derive it from `AbstractAccessible`. This class contains default implementations of the `Accessible`-required methods.

`Graphics2D` is abstract

`Graphics2D` is an abstract class—you must either subclass it yourself, or rely on Sun's subclasses in order to actually draw anything.

Learn more about 2D graphics online

If you're a member of Sun's Java Developer Connection you can read the technical article "New 2D Graphics Features" by Monica Pawlan. It's available at `http://developer.java.sun.com/developer/technicalArticles/monicap/2DGraphics/Intro/simple2D.html`. The extended example in this section, Listing 14.3, is drawn from Pawlan's article.

LISTING 14.3 *PathsFill.java*–This program, from Monica Pawlan's article on the JDC site, demonstrates the major capabilities of 2D graphics

```java
import java.awt.*;
import java.awt.event.*;
import java.awt.geom.*;

public class PathsFill extends Canvas {

    public PathsFill() {
    setBackground(Color.cyan);
    }

    public void paint(Graphics g) {
    int n = 0;
        Dimension theSize = getSize();

        Graphics2D g2;
        g2 = (Graphics2D) g;
       g2.setRenderingHints(Graphics2D.ANTIALIASING,
        Graphics2D.ANTIALIAS_ON);

        GeneralPath p = new GeneralPath(1);
        p.moveTo( theSize.width/6, theSize.height/6);
        p.lineTo(theSize.width*5/6, theSize.height/6);
        p.lineTo(theSize.width*5/6, theSize.height*5/6);
        p.lineTo( theSize.width/6, theSize.height*5/6);
        p.closePath();

        g2.setColor(Color.blue);
        g2.draw(p);

        AffineTransform at = new AffineTransform();
    at.scale(.5, .5);
    at.translate(theSize.width/2, theSize.height/2);
    g2.setTransform(at);
        g2.setColor(Color.red);
        g2.fill(p);

        Color colorArray[] = new Color[10];
        colorArray[0] = Color.blue;
        colorArray[1] = Color.green;
        colorArray[2] = Color.magenta;
```

```
40          colorArray[3] = Color.lightGray;
41          colorArray[4] = Color.pink;
42          colorArray[5] = Color.white;
43          colorArray[6] = Color.yellow;
44          colorArray[7] = Color.black;
45          colorArray[8] = Color.gray;
46          colorArray[9] = Color.orange;
47
48          for(n = 0;   n < 10; n++){
49              at.scale(.9, .9);
50          at.rotate(15, theSize.width/2, theSize.height/2);
51          g2.setTransform(at);
52                  g2.setColor(colorArray[n]);
53                  g2.fill(p);
54          }
55
56      }
57
58      public static void main(String s[]) {
59        WindowListener l = new WindowAdapter() {
60          public void windowClosing(WindowEvent e) {System.exit(0);}
61        public void windowClosed(WindowEvent e)
          {System.exit(0);}
62        };
63        Frame f = new Frame("Simple 2D Demo ...");
64        f.addWindowListener(l);
65        f.add("Center", new PathsFill());
66            f.pack();
67        f.setSize(new Dimension(500,500));
68        f.show();
69      }
70 }
```

Understanding Coordinate Spaces

One of the reasons that graphics display is an interesting problem is that not all graphics devices have the same coordinate system or resolution. This problem is compounded for Java, which
has staked its reputation on being the "Write Once, Run
Anywhere" language. In order to live up to this name, Sun needed a way for designers to produce graphics that look good
regardless of the device's characteristics.

In some cases you may want to write a program that allows a user to draw, and then play back that file of captured points. If the playback device has different characteristics than the one on which the original drawing was captured, there's a potential for error.

Sun solved this problem by introducing a *user coordinate space*, also known in some of Sun's documentation as *user space*.

Using Transforms

In order to actually display a Graphics2D object on a device you must transform the object from user space to a specific *device space*. While you may apply a transform at any time, you'll start with a default transform that is selected for you based on the target of your Graphics2D object.

All transforms from user space to device space share three characteristics:

- The origin is in the upper left-hand corner of the target space (such as a screen or printed page).
- Increasing numbers in the X dimension move to the right.
- Increasing numbers in the Y dimension move down.

If you specify a screen or an image buffer as the target for your drawing, you'll get the identity transform. If your target is a printer or other high-resolution device, you'll get a default transform of 72 user-space coordinates per device inch.

Understanding Rendering

Rendering is the mechanism by which the graphics object is made to appear on the output device. With Graphics2D-based objects, rendering proceeds in four conceptual steps. (Because of optimization, Sun does not guarantee that each step will be performed each time an image is rendered—they only guarantee that the finished graphic will appear as though it has gone through all four rendering steps.)

Do you really need to know how rendering works?

You can use the Graphics2D class without understanding how the class places your shape, text, or image on the screen. If you're building sophisticated graphics that may be rendered on different devices (such as monitors and printers) you need to know the basics of both coordinate spaces and color spaces. If you like, skip this section while you're learning to use Graphics2D, and then return here when you're ready to build a sophisticated graphic.

The four steps are:

1. Determine where to render.
2. Constrain the current rendering operation to the current `Clip`.
3. Determine what colors to render.
4. Apply the colors to the destination drawing space.

By understanding how the `Graphics2D` class processes each step you'll be better able to produce high-quality graphics.

Determining Where to Render a Shape

The first step in rendering is to determine the area of the screen, printed page, or other output device that is affected by the rendering operation. `Graphics2D` objects can be either shapes, text, or images. If the object is a shape, the "where to render" question is answered by computing the outline of the shape. If the object is text, `Graphics2D` computes the outline of the text by using information about the font. In the case of an image, the class simply computes a bounding box into which the image is rendered. This section provides details on how each of these three kinds of objects is rendered.

In Listing 14.3, for example, you see the lines:

```
Graphics2D g2;
g2 = (Graphics2D) g;
```

where g is the `Graphics` object passed in as the parameter of `paint()`. Next, the program constructs a new shape inside a `GeneralPath`:

```
GeneralPath p = new GeneralPath(1);
p.moveTo( theSize.width/6, theSize.height/6);
p.lineTo(theSize.width*5/6, theSize.height/6);
p.lineTo(theSize.width*5/6, theSize.height*5/6);
p.lineTo( theSize.width/6, theSize.height*5/6);
p.closePath();
```

Finally, the author uses the new shape:

```
g2.draw(p);
...
g2.fill(p);
...
for (n=0; n < 10; n++) {
  at.scale(.9, .9);
  at.rotate(15, theSize.width/2, theSize.height/2);
  g2.setTransform(at);
  ...
  g2.fill(p);
}
```

where at is an AffineTransform, described in a moment.

When the object is a shape, as it is in this case, the Graphics2D class will determine where to render it by following a four-step procedure to compute the outline of the shape:

1. Compute a Stroke to fill based on the Shape.

2. Transform the Shape from user space into device space.

3. Call Shape.getPathIterator() to extract the outline of the Shape. (The outline is an instance of class PathIterator, which may contain curved segments.)

4. If the Graphic2D object cannot handle the curved segments in the PathIterator, it calls an alternative version of Shape.getPathIterator() that accepts a flatness parameter. This alternative version only returns straight line segments.

The Shape's outline will be rendered by using an implementation of the java.awt.Stroke interface. To make an ellipse, you might write

```
draw(Ellipse2D.Float(10.0, 10.0, 150.0, 100.0));
```

but the Graphics2D class will implement that call as

```
BasicStroke theStroke = new BasicStroke();
theStroke.createStrokedShape(new Ellipse2D.Float(10.0, 10.0,
➥150.0, 100.0);
```

BasicStroke is a class that implements Stroke. Figure 14.5 illustrates the concept of a mitre limit, the part of BasicStroke that determines whether two lines are joined when they pass close to each other.

How does BasicStroke work?

The default constructor specifies a line width of 1.0, a CAP_SQUARE style at the ends of lines, a JOIN_MITRE style where lines come together, a *mitre limit* of 10.0, and no dashing. (A mitre limit is the limit at which to trim the mitre join where two lines come together.)

`Ellipse2D` is an abstract `Shape`; `Ellipse2D.Float` is a concrete class that accepts floating point coordinates.

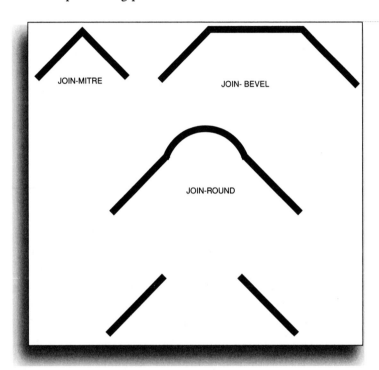

FIGURE 14.5
Class `BasicStroke` supports three different ways to join lines—JOIN_MITRE is the default.

To transform the `Shape` into device space, `Graphics2D` calls the currently defined transform. Transforms are instances of class `AffineTransform`, which supports the following types of transform:

- `GENERAL_ROTATION` Rotation through an arbitrary angle
- `GENERAL_SCALE` Scale by arbitrary factors in X and Y
- `GENERAL_TRANSFORM` Arbitrary conversion of the input coordinates
- `IDENTITY` The output is identical to the input
- `QUADRANT_ROTATION` Rotation through a multiple of 90 degrees
- `TRANSLATION` The graphic is moved in the X and Y dimensions
- `UNIFORM_SCALE` The graphic is scaled uniformly in both dimensions

In Listing 14.3 you see the lines that set up and use an `AffineTransform`:

```
AffineTransform at = new AffineTransform();
at.scale(.5, .5);
at.translate(theSize.width/2, theSize.height/2);
g2.setTransform(at);
```

and later

```
for(n = 0;   n < 10; n++){
  at.scale(.9, .9);
  at.rotate(15, theSize.width/2, theSize.height/2);
  g2.setTransform(at);

  . . .

}
```

Determining Where to Render Text

If the `Graphics2D` represents text rather than a shape it is rendered by using *glyphs*—integer codes used by `Fonts` to represent text graphically. If the text is in a `String`, the `String` is sent to the current `Font` which is asked to compute a `java.awt.font.GlyphSet` based on the `Font`'s default layout.

If the text is in a `StyledString`, the `StyledString` itself computes the `GlyphSet` based on its own font attributes.

If the text is already a `GlyphSet`, this step is skipped.

Once `Graphics2D` has a `GlyphSet` it asks the current `Font` to convert the glyphs to shapes. It then starts the process of rendering the shapes, as described earlier in this section.

Determining Where to Render an Image

If the `Graphics2D` is an image (as indicated by a call to the `drawImage()` method, the class computes a bounding rectangle for the image in a local coordinate system called *image space*. If the programmer has specified a transform, that transform is used to convert the bounding rectangle from image space coordinates to user space coordinates. If the programmer doesn't supply a transform, an identity transform is used.

The bounding rectangle—now in user coordinate space—is transformed again, into device space.

Constraining the Graphic with *Clip*

Graphics2D inherits getClip() and setClip() methods from its base class, Graphics. You can use setClip() to limit the rendering to a specified rectangle. You specify the clipRect in user space—Graphics2D transforms it into device space by using the current transform.

After Graphics2D has computed the rendering region (for either a graphic, text, or an image) it applies the clipRect to define the region that will actually be rendered.

Determining the Colors

If the Graphics2D object is an Image the class samples the colors in the Image based on the current transform. (If you specify an Image transform, that transform is also applied during color-sampling.)

For text and graphic instances of Graphics2D the class looks at the current Paint implementation. You set the Paint instance by calling Graphics2D.setPaint(). Paint itself is an interface; Sun has provided GradientPaint and TexturePaint to allow you to implement special effects.

Instead of a Paint-based object you can set a Color. PathsFill, in Listing 14.3, uses this approach. You'll notice lines like

```
g2.setColor(Color.blue);
```

and

```
g2.setColor(Color.red);
```

The Graphics2D color model is based on a proposed standard Red-Green-Blue (RGB) color space called *sRGB*.

Whether you've provided a Paint object or a Color object, Graphics2D uses it to obtain a PaintContext—a specific mapping of colors and textures into device space—and is now ready to apply the colors.

When should you use
`setClip()`?

Suppose you had a complex graphic, or an animation, in which performance was important. You could improve performance by limiting the rendering area by using setClip().

Learn about sRGB online

The sRGB color space model is under review by the World Wide Web Consortium. Read about it at http://www.w3.org/pub/WWW/Graphics/Color/sRGB.html.

See a representative
`Composite`

Sun provides one example of a
`Composite`-based class:
`AlphaComposite`. This class
implements a set of blending and
transparency rules based on T.
Porter and T. Duff's paper,
"Compositing Digital Images," SIG-
GRAPH 84, 253-259. Read the API
documentation on
`AlphaComposite` to see the
essence of these rules.

Applying the Colors

`Graphics2D` objects are drawn on a `java.awt.Composite` object.
The `Composite` interface contains pre-defined rules to combine
the source with colors that have already been drawn.

SEE ALSO

➤ *Learn more about* `Composite`, *page 274*

Dealing with Compatibility Issues

Not only does Sun have to deal with a range of device compatibility, they also have had to ensure that changes in JDK 1.2 don't
break the `Graphics` API of JDK 1.1. To help your `Graphics2D`
objects deal with the range of rendering environments they may
encounter, use `Graphics2D.setRenderingHints()`. This method
accepts hints that you may want to add to improve the performance and appearance of your graphics.

For example, suppose you know that an image contains a number of diagonal lines that would benefit from antialiasing. You
might specify `ANTIALIASING_ON`—at runtime, the environment and
the device driver would negotiate whether or not to actually
make the antialiasing pass. If you've specified `RENDER_SPEED` the
device driver may ignore the `ANTIALIASING_ON` directive entirely,
while for `RENDER_QUALITY` the driver may use the best antialiasing
algorithm at its disposal, even though that algorithm may
require extra time.

The hint list includes

- `ANTIALIASING ON` and `ANTIALIASING_OFF` Controls whether or
  not an extra step is applied to smooth jagged edges

- `RENDER_SPEED` and `RENDER_QUALITY` Controls whether the rendering algorithm should optimize for performance or
  appearance

Notice the line in Listing 14.3 that sets these hints:

```
g2.setRenderingHints(Graphics2D.ANTIALIASING,
➥Graphics2D.ANTIALIAS_ON);
```

Completing the Project

Understanding
Packages

Understand how the compiler searches the directories on your hard drive to find a class

See what classes are already available to you in the built-in and JDK-external packages

Find out how to import classes for reuse

See how to make your own reusable packages

Learn how to name and organize your source files and directories in order to build a manageable collection of packages

Understand *javadoc*, Sun's tool for building and maintaining package documentation

What Is a Package?

Throughout this book, we've seen and used classes that have been stored in packages—`java.awt.Button`, `java.awt.swing.JButton`, and so forth. In this chapter we'll look a bit more closely at this concept of a package. We'll see how the Java runtime environment finds packages. We'll talk about how you can write your own package, and we'll talk about how to document your package.

A *package* is simply a collection of related classes. Take a look at the class hierarchy that came with your JDK to see a good example of how to organize classes into packages. (Use your Web browser to examine this class hierarchy—if you downloaded the documentation when you downloaded your copy of the JDK, it's at `/docs/api/tree.html` in your JDK directory.) Figure 15.1 shows the class hierarchy, displayed in Netscape Communicator.

FIGURE 15.1

Use your Web browser to read the documentation about Sun's packages.

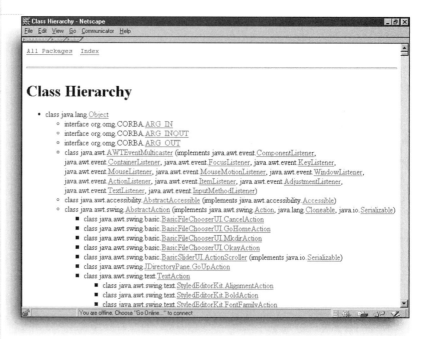

How Does the Compiler Find an Object?   PART **VI**

CHAPTER **15**   405

How Does the Compiler Find an Object?

Suppose you write the following line in a Java program.

```
TQuux myQuux = new TQuux();
```

How does the Java compiler find the class TQuux?

First, the compiler checks to see if this class is part of the built-in package named java.lang. You don't have to import java.lang.* or specify it in your code—the compiler will always look for classes there.

If the compiler can't find TQuux in java.lang, it looks at the import statements you've written into this class. Suppose your class includes the line

```
import com.mcp.que.usingjava12.chapter15.TQuux;
```

The compiler now knows which TQuux you mean—it goes and looks for the package com.mcp.que.usingjava12.chapter15. If it finds that package, it looks inside it for class TQuux.

If you haven't specified a TQuux class in an import statement, the compiler looks at your other import statements—the ones that tell the compiler to use every public class in a package. Suppose you wrote

```
import java.awt.*;
import java.applet.*;
import com.mcp.que.usingjava12.chapter14.*;
import com.mcp.que.usingjava12.chapter15.*;
```

These import statements tell the compiler that you'll be using classes from each of these four packages, but they don't tell the compiler which specific classes you plan to use. When you name a class (such as TQuux), the compiler searches all of these libraries looking for a public class named TQuux. If it finds exactly one such class, it uses it. If it finds no matching class, or if it finds more than one class named TQuux, it reports an error and asks you to give it more information on where to find TQuux.

If you're only using one or two classes out of a package you may decide to specify the package right in the code without using an import statement. This approach can have the benefit of increasing readability, because the reader doesn't have to guess which

Is this information only for the compiler?

Although I refer to the compiler in this section, the Java runtime environment uses a similar mechanism to find class files. Usually you'll want to bundle your runtime class files into archives to ensure that installation is correct. We'll talk more about Java archives in Chapter 23, "Making and Using Java Archives."

Won't using the asterisk form of import bloat my software?

Unlike C and C++ #include directives, import doesn't link any class you don't actually use. Whether you use the asterisk form or the class-name form of import has to do with readablity, not code size (though some compilers take a bit longer to run when you use the asterisk form of the import statement heavily).

The asterisk form of import isn't a wildcard

The asterisk in an import tells the compiler to look at every public class named in that package. It's not like the wildcard can be used in your command interpreter. You can't write

java.awt.B*;

to get all of the classes whose names start with *B*.

package contains that class, but it can make the lines unwieldy (and hence, more difficult to read). At any rate, be aware that you always have the option of writing

```
com.mcp.que.usingjava12.chapter15.TQuux myQuux =
    new com.mcp.que.usingjava12.chapter15.TQuux();
```

if you prefer.

Setting *CLASSPATH*

Whether you've used a built-in class, an import statement with a class name, an import statement with an asterisk, or a fully qualified name in your code, the compiler now knows in which package(s) to search for the class. But where will it look for the package? That answer is determined by the environment variable named CLASSPATH.

When you first obtained and installed your copy of the JDK, you were told how to set CLASSPATH. CLASSPATH contains the list of places where you store class libraries. You should follow the specific instructions Sun provides with your version of the JDK. In general, on a Windows machine you set CLASSPATH by using the System control panel—choose **Start**, select **Settings**, choose **Control Panel**, double-click the System control panel, and then choose the Environment tab. Figure 15.2 shows the current CLASSPATH on my machine.

FIGURE 15.2

In a Windows environment, set environment variables like CLASSPATH by using the System control panel.

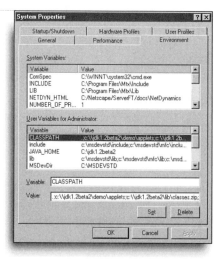

If you're a UNIX user, you can set environment variables in your startup file. The name of your startup file depends on which command interpreter (called a *shell*) you're using:

- If you use the Bourne shell, put

  ```
  CLASSPATH=value; export CLASSPATH
  ```

  into your `.profile` file in your home directory. (Make sure you don't put any spaces on either side of the equals sign.)

- If you're a C shell user, put

  ```
  setenv CLASSPATH value
  ```

  into the `.login` file in your home directory.

- The Korn shell looks at the ENV environment variable and uses its value as a filename. In that file you can specify the value of CLASSPATH. Use the same syntax you use with the Bourne shell. (If you don't set the ENV variable, you can place your environment variable definitions in the `.profile` file.)

SEE ALSO

➤ *Learn more about* CLASSPATH, *page 68*

Using *CLASSPATH* to Find Packages

The Java compiler uses each directory named in the CLASSPATH variable as the root in its search for packages. Suppose you're running on a Windows machine and your CLASSPATH variable contains

```
.;C:\JDK1.2\lib
```

Now suppose that your code includes the lines

```
com.mcp.que.usingjava12.chapter15.TQuux myQuux =
  new com.mcp.que.usingjava12.chapter15.TQuux();
```

The compiler will start by looking in your current director ('.') for a directory named com. If it finds it, it will look inside that directory for one named mcp. Inside there it expects to find que, which should contain usingjava12, which should contain chapter15. Inside that chapter15 directory it looks for the class TQuux in one of the class files.

Which shell am I running?

Your UNIX system administrator specifies your shell as part of your account information. You can tell which shell you're running by using the **ps** command. Look in the output for a process such as **sh** (for Bourne shell), **csh** (for C shell), or **ksh** for Korn shell.

Where's CLASSPATH on a Macintosh?

The Macintosh doesn't have environment variables. Instead, the Macintosh version of the JDK is smart enough to find the default classes and will look in the current directory for other classes. Use the Preferences dialog box in the Java compiler to specify other directories to the search path.

If that search fails, it retries the same path, starting from `C:\JDK1.2\lib`. If *that* search fails, the compiler gives up and issues the dreaded `java.lang.NoClassDefFoundError`, since it has no place else to turn.

Suppose that instead of fully specifying the package name in your code you had written

```
import java.awt.*;
import java.awt.swing.*;
import com.mcp.usingjava12.chapter14.*;
import com.mcp.usingjava12.chapter15.*;

   . . .

TQuux myQuux = new TQuux();
```

The compiler would have searched your CLASSPATH directories in the same way as before, but it would have looked for a directory named `java` and a subdirectory named `awt`. There it would have looked for the `TQuux` class. Not finding it, it would have started the search again, looking in the `java\awt\swing` directory. Then it would have searched for `com\mcp\usingjava12\chapter14`, and tried to find `TQuux` in there. Finally it would have searched `com\mcp\usingjava12\chapter15`.

The compiler tries to optimize much of this searching, but if you get the impression that you can speed up some compiles by keeping a short CLASSPATH, you're right. A typical CLASSPATH on a developer's machine might include just four directories to search:

- The java/lib directory (or its equivalent on your machine)
- A class directory in your development environment
- A browser-specific directory
- The current directory, named dot ('.').

Putting Packages Inside Archives

Prior to JDK 1.1, Java developers either shipped their class files in special archives based on the PKZip format (called zip files) or as individual class files, "loose" in the package's directory. Both of those methods still work, but now Sun has given us a better way—Java ARchives, or JAR files.

In addition to specifying directories in your CLASSPATH variable, you can specify an entire archive (either a JAR file or a zip file). We'll talk more about JAR files in Chapter 23, "Making and Using Java Archives."

SEE ALSO

➤ *Learn more about naming JAR files in* CLASSPATH, *page 654*

Exploring the Built-in Package

You can use any class in the package named java.lang without specifying the package name in your code or in an import statement. That package contains four interfaces, 27 classes, 20 errors, and 24 exceptions. The interfaces are

- Cloneable   Indicates that a class can make a field-for-field copy of itself.

- Comparable   Indicates that a class has a natural ordering, such as the alphabetical ordering of Strings or the numerical ordering of int.

- Runnable   Used to set up separate threads.

- Runtime.MemoryAdvice   A new interface in JDK 1.2, used to tell the program when memory is running low.

We've already used many of the common classes in java.lang, such as Integer, String, System, Thread, and Throwable. Take some time to explore JDK documentation of the remaining classes, exceptions, and errors. Some of them have very specific uses, such as the Compiler class (which supports Java-to-native-code compilers). Others, such as Boolean, Byte, Character, Double, and Float, are wrapper classes for Java primitives.

SEE ALSO

➤ *Learn more about wrapper classes, page 120*

Understanding Reflection

Reflection is the process of examining classes and objects at run-time. For example, if you have an Object and you want to know what public methods it supports, you can write

```
Class aClass = myObject.getClass();
Method[] theMethods = aClass.getDeclaredMethods();
for (int i=0; i<theMethods.length; i++)
  System.out.println(theMethods[i].getName());
```

Reflection is useful when writing development environments, where you may need to examine an object at runtime. You'll see examples of objects being examined at runtime when we look at JavaBeans in Chapter 19, "Building Components with JavaBeans."

You'll find classes such as `Constructor`, `Field`, `Method`, and `Modifier` in the `java.lang.reflect` package.

Using *References*

As you continue in your development as a Java programmer, you may want to learn about the `Reference` class, a new feature in JDK 1.2. The `Reference` class is to a Java reference as the `Class` class is to Java classes. That is, you can use `Reference` objects to reflect upon a reference at runtime in much the same way as we've used `Class` objects to reflect upon objects at runtime. To learn more about the `Reference` class and its descendents, see the documentation on `java.lang.ref`.

Using Classes from External Packages

Except for `java.lang`, you'll have to specify the package name either in the code or in an `import` statement in order to use classes from other packages. You can use other packages from the JDK, third-party packages, or packages you write yourself.

Exploring the Java Platform Core Packages

We've already been using plenty of Sun's Java packages, such as `java.awt`, `java.awt.swing`, and `java.util`. In all, Java has 12 top-level packages (with plenty of subpackages):

- `java.applet`   Java's `Applet` class.

- `java.awt`   All of the GUI components, including Swing. The heavyweight components of the AWT are described in Chapter 11, "Building the User Interface with the AWT." The lightweight components, known as the Swing components, are described in Chapter 12, "Building the User Interface with JFC Swing Components."

- `java.beans`   the JavaBean classes, described in Chapter 19 and Chapter 20, "Designing Good Beans."

- `java.io`   Java's general communications facilities, described in Chapter 18, "Communicating in Java: Streams and Sockets."

- `java.lang`   Java's built-in classes.

- `java.math`   Contains `BigDecimal` and `BigInteger`, introduced in Chapter 4, "Understanding Java Data Types and Operators."

- `java.net`   Java's network communications facilities, described in Chapter 18.

- `java.rmi`   The basis for Java's Remote Method Invocation mechanism.

- `java.security`   Implements Java's security mechanism.

- `java.sql`   The basis for the Java Database Connectivity Package, described in Chapter 21, "Using the Java Database Connectivity Package."

- `java.text`   A set of classes that deal with the details of text management.

- `java.util`   Utility classes, including JDK 1.2's new collection classes.

SEE ALSO
➤ *Learn more about* `java.io` *streams, page 500*

➤ *Learn more about* `java.net` *sockets, page 516*

Understanding the *org.omg* Packages

In addition to the `java` packages we just explored, the Java Platform Core Packages include `org.omg.CORBA` (and six subpackages) and `org.omg.CosNaming` (which has one subpackage). The org.omg packages were produced by the Object Management Group (OMG), an industry association that focuses on object-oriented technology. CORBA stands for Common Object Request Broker Architecture, a technology that supports distributed applications. JDK 1.2 contains complete support for CORBA, and even includes a simple Object Request Broker (ORB) written in Java. You can learn more about CORBA online at http://www.omg.org/. That Web site also includes a list of Java/CORBA Web demos. Visit http://corbanet.dstc.edu.au/ for one such example.

The org.omg.CosNaming package facilitates the mapping from OMG's language-neutral Interface Definition Language, IDL, to Java. With this package you can write code like

```
org.omg.CORBA.Object anObjectReference =
  orb.resolve_initial_references("NameService");
org.omb.CosNaming.NamingContext aNamingContext =
org.omg.CosNaming.NamingContextHelper.narrow(anObject
➡References);
```

This code asks the Object Request Broker for its NameService reference, and then narrows that service down to the object of type NamingContext.

SEE ALSO

➤ *Learn more about Object Request Brokers, page 522*

Using Third-Party Packages

As you continue working with Java, you'll want to use classes from other vendors. For example, if you choose to use Visual Café—an Integrated Development Environment from Symantec—you'll have access to symantec.itools.lang and symantec.itools.net. Third-party libraries nearly always come with installation instructions, including information about how to change your CLASSPATH variable, but problems with CLASSPATH continue to rank as the subject of the most frequently asked questions about Java. Now that you know how the compiler searches for packages, you can debug your CLASSPATH variable yourself if you need to.

Writing Your Own Packages

Up until now, most of the code we've written has gone into the default package—the one you get if you don't include a `package` statement in your class. While this practice is fine when you're developing simple programs for your own use, as a professional programmer who releases code for use by others, you need to organize your classes into named packages. You'll get three benefits by putting your classes into packages:

- It will help you organize your hard drive (and your thinking) into functional "chunks."
- It will reduce the problem of name collisions.
- You can "hide" classes from outside users.

Organizing Your Hard Drive

Psychologists have found that most people can only keep track of five to nine items at a time. They've found that people who are experts in some subject and seem to have thousands of facts at their fingertips, don't have a superior memory. Instead, they have a superior way of "organizing" their knowledge. They see their subject as being organized into five to nine "conceptual chunks," each of which is organized into five to nine chunks, and so forth.

Bill Joy, co-founder of Sun Microsystems, says it this way: "Java feels like C when programming in the small, and like Smalltalk when you're programming in the large." By "programming in the small," he means when you're coding individual lines and expressions—the sort of work we talked about in Chapter 6, "Methods: Adding Code to Your Objects." "Programming in the large" has to do with design tasks—we talked about those in Chapter 8, "Object-Oriented Design and Programming."

As an expert in the software you write, you should strive to organize your projects in much the same way as experts organize their knowledge: in conceptual chunks. During your design activities, you should think about architectural issues—which piece of software talks to which, and how does the entire system hang together. In Java, that's the time to be thinking about packages. For a small system, one package may be all you need, but for many projects, you'll want to break your system up into several conceptually different pieces, placing each piece in a subpackage.

Here are three tips for building packages that will help you (and the users of your software) understand how your software works.

- Put each class (except for inner classes) in a file by itself.
- Build a root directory that will hold all of your packages.
- When a project has more than five to nine outer classes, split it into subprojects. Strive to keep the fan-out at each level within the five- to nine-chunk limit.

Figure 15.3 illustrates this sort of project design.

FIGURE 15.3

Organize your projects into packages and subpackages, obeying the five- to nine-chunk limit.

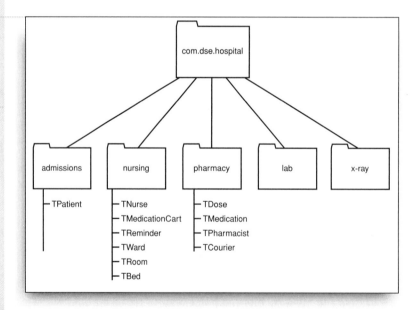

The JDK itself is huge compared to any project you and I are likely to write, yet it has only the 12 top-level packages listed earlier in the chapter. Strive to emulate Sun and limit the number of packages or subpackages that you place at any given level.

Choosing a Unique Name

Recall from our discussion about CLASSPATH earlier in this chapter that the compiler (and, for that matter, the runtime environment) expects to see only one class of a given name. Suppose you wrote

```
import nursing.*;
import pharmacy.*;
. . .
TDose theDose = new TDose();
```

If exactly one of those two packages has a class named TDose, all is well. If both packages include TDose, the compiler doesn't know which one you plan to use, so it complains about the conflict and doesn't compile your program. To fix this problem you'll need to fully qualify your classes:

```
pharmacy.TDose theDose = new pharmacy.TDose();
```

If the class ends up being used on a machine that already has a pharmacy package, you've got a potential for disaster. Suppose that after your package is installed the user's CLASSPATH contains

```
.;C:\java\lib;C:\theirPharmacy\lib;C:\ourPharmacy\lib
```

and that both C:\theirPharmacy\lib and C:\ourPharamcy\lib contain a directory named Pharmacy. Although your program worked well on your development machine, it will fail to install correctly on the user's machine. You could resort to wrapper scripts that set a local copy of CLASSPATH, but there's another way to decrease the likelihood of naming conflicts.

Sun recommends that everyone use their fully qualified domain name reversed, as the basis for their package names. Thus, if your organization's domain name is baz.com, all of your packages would begin with

```
com.baz
```

If everyone follows this recommendation, the only possible conflict you might have is with other developers in your own organization. You can make package names as specific as you like. If you work in the medication division of the Baz Corporation, and your project is in the Pharmacy Software department, and you name your project "San Diego," your package name could be

```
com.baz.medical.pharmacy.sandiego
```

Within that package you could easily have several subpackages, each of which could contain additional subpackages. Any common code you share with other pharmacy applications could be in

```
com.baz.medical.pharmacy
```

Any code you share across your entire company could be in

```
com.baz
```

and so forth.

Using Access Specifiers

Recall that from our very first applications we were writing

```
public class classname
```

We said then that public made the class accessible by anyone. If we left that access specifier off, the class was accessible only by classes inside the package. This means that we can have the sort of design illustrated in Figure 15.4.

FIGURE 15.4

Use access specifiers and inner classes to keep your package interfaces clean.

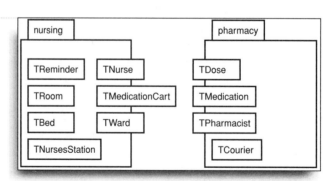

During your architectural design you'll identify some classes that must be used throughout the system. TPatient and TMedication are examples of such classes in the pharmacy application. Other classes, such as TNursesStation, are not needed outside of their package—they're used to implement the functionality of the public classes in their package. Leave the `public` access specifier off those classes. They'll default to being accessible only by other classes within the package. From the point of view of other packages, these hidden packages don't even exist.

Adding a Class to a Package

While the relationship between package names and the directories named in CLASSPATH variable isn't complicated, there are many variations. For example, the six lines of Table 15.1 could each be used to name the same directory of class files. Since you, as the programmer, are in control of the `package` statements in your code, but the end user is responsible for setting the CLASS-PATH directory, I recommend you keep your CLASSPATH variable as simple as possible, and hide the complexity in the package name.

TABLE 15.1   Combinations of *CLASSPATH* directories and package names

CLASSPATH **Directory**	**Package**
C:\pharmacy\lib	com.mcp.que.usingjava12.chapter15
C:\pharmacy\lib\com	mcp.que.usingjava12.chapter15
C:\pharmacy\lib\com\mcp	que.usingjava12.chapter15
C:\pharmacy\lib\com\mcp\que	usingjava12.chapter15
C:\pharmacy\lib\com\mcp\que\usingjava12	chapter15
C:\pharmacy\lib\com\mcp\que\usingjava12\chapter15	(None)

Once you've designed your CLASSPATH variable and set your package name, you need only add a `package` statement to the top of each source file. For example, to add a class to the

`com.mcp.que.usingjava12.chapter15`, write

`package com.mcp.que.usingjava12.chapter15;`

The `package` statement must go right at the top of your source file. You can put comments ahead of it, but make sure it appears before any `import` statements or any `class` definitions.

Inner classes are always hidden

The Java compiler requires that any `public` class be in a file whose name matches the class name. You can't make an inner class public because it must be inside the class definition of its outer class; therefore, all inner classes are implicitly hidden.

Be careful to install your class files in the correct directory

Don't wait until you're working on a large project to start using package names. The first few times you work with packages, you won't get the directory structure right, and you'll get compile-time errors. Climb that learning curve on small projects so you don't have to climb it on the large ones.

Should the domain name be capitalized?

At one time it was popular to build a package name with the top-level domain capitalized. For example, you would have written

`COM.mcp.que.using-java12.chapter15`

Those days are gone—every part of the package name should be in lowercase.

javadoc as "literate programming"

javadoc supports what Donald
Knuth, Professor Emeritus of "The
Art of Computer Programming" at
Stanford, calls "literate programming." Simply put, literate programming is a style of programming in
which you mix comments into the
source code and rely on an intelligent parser to pull them out and
make them useful. For Knuth's own
design of literate programming, see
*The CWEB System of Structured
Documentation*, by Donald Knuth
and Silvio Levy (Addison-Wesley,
1994).

Customize javadoc's output
with doclets

Starting with JDK 1.2, javadoc
supports doclets—pieces of code
that customize the tool's output.
javadoc comes with a default
doclet, or you can write your
own—in Java, of course. Learn more
in docs/tooldocs/
javadoc/overview.html
in your JDK directory.

What can you do with a
doclet?

You could write doclets to parse
javadoc comments into Adobe's
Portable Document Format (PDF)
files, Adobe Postscript, Rich Text
Format (RTF) or even a different
style of HTML. See /docs/
tooldocs/javadoc/index
.html in your JDK directory to
learn how to write your own
doclet.

Building *javadoc* Documentation

If you're just building Java programs for your own amusement,
then, of course, the level of documentation is up to you. As a
professional programmer, however, your work is subject to being
maintained or even reused by other programmers. The quality
of your packages will therefore be measured largely by the quality of your documentation. Fortunately, Sun has provided a high-
quality tool in the tradition of "literate programming"—javadoc.

In Chapter 3, "Getting Started Fast," we initially talked about
javadoc—the documentation toolkit distributed with the JDK.
Sun used javadoc to produce the HTML pages that make up
their JDK documentation—in fact, javadoc is ideally suited for
developing documentation for every class in a package.

At least one study found that 50 percent of the development
effort of a typical system comes after its initial release. (See
Software Maintenance Management, by B. P. Lientz and E. B.
Swanson, Addison-Wesley, 1980.) If these results are anything
close to correct, the quality of your documentation is crucial for
your program's success.

SEE ALSO

➤ *Get an overview of* javadoc, *page 74*

Figure 15.5 illustrates how javadoc fits into Java documentation
strategy. As input, you should provide either a set packages or a
set of .java source files. The tool will parse the packages and
classes it encounters, and will generate a set of documentation
that covers the public and protected classes, interfaces, constructors, methods, and fields. The default doclet produces its output
in HTML—the JDK's platform API documentation is an example of its output.

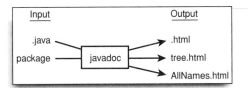

Input		Output
.java		.html
package	javadoc	tree.html
		AllNames.html

FIGURE 15.5

By default *javadoc* produces one *.html* file for every *.java* file, one for each package, plus a class hierarchy and an index of all members.

Using *javadoc*

By default javadoc produces lists of classes and members in the package. You can make this information more useful by including special javadoc comments in the source code. A regular comment begins with // (which comments out a single line) or /*…*/ (which comments out a block). A javadoc comment begins with /**…*/—the block comment can contain special tags that are read by the current doclet.

Sun suggests the following template for javadoc comments:

```
/**
 * A concise but complete summary of the entity, terminated
 * by the first period that has whitespace after it (or by
 * the first tagged paragraph.
 * One or more optional tagged paragraphs
 */
The documented entity (typically, a class, method, or data
member).
```

The "concise but complete summary" terminated by a period is often called the "summary sentence."

The default doclet copies the summary sentence to the top of the HTML file that describes that entity. The following are valid entities:

- class
- interface
- Any constructor
- Any method
- Any data member

Check your platform documentation

The Solaris version of javadoc has a slightly different user interface than the Windows version. Both versions are covered in the JDK documentation. The Solaris version is described in the JDK directory at /docs/tooldocs/solaris/javadoc.htm1, while the Windows version's documentation is at /docs/tooldocs/win32/javadoc.html.

There's more about javadoc online

For the latest info on javadoc, visit the tool's home page—http://java.sun.com/products/jdk/javadoc/.

Include HTML tags in your javadoc comments

If you're using a doclet that writes HTML (such as the default doclet) you can include HTML tags right in your comments. They'll be passed through to the browser and translated there.

Pay no attention to the extra asterisks

The only asterisks `javadoc` cares about are the ones that define the beginning and end of the comment: `/**`...`*/`. It will silently ignore asterisks and whitespace in the comment—you can use them to improve the appearance of the comments in your source files.

Keep similar tags together

If you have more than one of the same kind of tag, keep them together so that `javadoc` knows where the list is. Thus, if a document has three authors, you should have a block of three `@author` tags.

`javadoc` ignores `javadoc` comments that do not immediately precede the declaration of a valid `javadoc` entity. Thus, you could write

```
/**
 * The medication nurse responsible for dosing
 * the patients.
 */
public class TNurse extends TEmployee
```

Tagged Paragraphs

In addition to summary sentences, you can add specific fields into each `javadoc` comment. These fields can be retrieved selectively by using command line parameters with the default `doclet`, as shown later in this section.

A tagged paragraph must start with an at-sign ('@'). Immediately following the at-sign you should put a keyword, followed by the tag's parameters. For example, to document a class you could write:

```
/**
 * The medication nurse responsible for dosing
 * the patients.
 * @author Mike Morgan
 * @version 1.2
 * @see TEmployee
 */
public class TNurse extends TEmployee
```

Class and Interface Tags

If you're tagging a class or interface, you may use any combination of these tags:

- `@author` *name-text*   Name one author of the document. Multiple `@author` tags are allowed. For example, I might write

  `@author Mike Morgan`

- @version *version-text*   Name the version of software. The @version tag is optional; if you use it, only one @version tag is allowed.

  @version 1.2

- @see *classname*   Generates a "See also" hyperlink to the named class. Whitespace in the classname is significant. Multiple @see tags are allowed. You might write

  @see TEmployee

- @see *classname#member*   Generates a "See also" hyperlink to the named member of the named class. Whitespace in the classname is significant. You may specify parameters for a method; make sure the parameters are separated by a single blank space. Multiple @see tags are allowed. To refer to the factory method at the facility level, you could write

  @see TFacility#createEmployee()

- @since *since-text*   Adds a comment to the documentation that this interface has been supported "Since since-text." By convention the since-text refers to a software release number. Thus, you might write

  @since 1.0

- @deprecated *deprecation-text*   Adds a deprecation comment to the documentation. By convention, the *deprecation-text* describes a non-deprecated alternative to the old deprecated member, or the phrase "No replacement." To make deprecation as painless as possible, provide specific guidance:

  @deprecated Use allDone() instead

Constructor and Method Tags

If you're tagging a class or interface, you may use any combination of the following tags:

- @param *parameter-name description*   Adds a (potentially multiline) comment to the parameters section of the documentation. For example, to document the TNurse constructor, you might write:

Integrate your javadoc **comments with your version control system**

If you're using a version control system such as the Revision Control System (RCS) or the Source Code Control System (SCCS) that supports embedded version numbers, place the version control system's code on the @version line and let the version control system update it whenever you do a new get.

```
@param theName String description giving the name of the
➥new employee in free Unicode text in a String; the
➥maximum size is 60 characters.
```

- `@return` *description*   Adds a Returns section with a description of the return value. You could write

```
@return Boolean showing whether or not the dose was
➥given correctly.
```

- `@exception` *fully-qualified-class-name description*   Adds a Throws section with a hyperlink to the exception. To throw a custom exception you could write

```
@exception MissingMedicationException The nurse cannot
➥find the medication but the pharmacy says they put
➥it in the drawer. This exception leads to the nurse
➥getting a replacement dose.
```

- `@see` *classname*   Generates a "See also" hyperlink to the named class. Whitespace in the classname is significant. Multiple `@see` tags are allowed, as shown here:

```
@see TMedication
@see TDose
```

- `@see` *classname#member*   Generates a "See also" hyperlink to the named member of the named class. Whitespace in the classname is significant. You may specify parameters for a method; make sure the parameters are separated by a single blank character. Multiple `@see` tags are allowed. You could write

```
@see TMedication#disposeOfControlledSubstance(
➥theWitness )
```

- `@since` *since-text*   Adds a comment to the documentation that this interface has been supported "Since `since-text`." By convention the `since-text` refers to a software release number. This tag is identical to the one shown under the class tags in the previous section.

- `@deprecated` *deprecation-text*   Adds a deprecation comment to the documentation. By convention, the *deprecation-text* describes a non-deprecated alternative to the old deprecated member, or the phrase "No replace-ment." This tag is identical to the one shown under the class tags in the previous section.

Data Member Tags

You can tag data members with any combination of @see, @since, and @deprecated tags, all described in the previous sections.

The *javadoc* Command Line

To generate javadoc documentation you can type

```
javadoc [options] packagename
```

or

```
javadoc [options] sourcename.java
```

where either the *packagename* or the *sourcename* may contain wildcards. The brackets around [*options*] indicates that the options are, optional. The following are the command-line options:

- -doclet *filename* Specifies the class file for the doclet. If not supplied, the default (HTML) doclet is used.

- -sourcepath *path-to-packages* Specifies the directory of the top-most parent package you wish to document. If not supplied, the current directory is used.

- -sourcepath *path-to-sourcefiles* Specifies the directory that contains the source files you wish to document. If not supplied, the current directory is used.

- -classpath *path* Specifies the directories for the class files of the javadoc tool itself. It may also be used to specify the path to source files, though Sun recommends the use of -sourcepath instead.

- -public Shows only the public classes and members.

- -protected Shows the public and protected classes and members. (-protected is the default.)

- -package Shows only the package, protected, and public classes and members.

- `-private`   Shows all classes and members.

- `-lflag`   Passes the *flag* to the Java runtime system when it runs `javadoc`.

- `-encoding` *name*   Specifies the source file encoding name. If not supplied the platform's default converter is used.

Using the Default *doclet*

Passing a file full of parameters

If you prefer, you can call `javadoc` with an at-sign parameter. This parameter is interpreted as a filename. The file itself contains additional parameters, one per line.

If you use the standard or default `doclet`—that is, if you don't specify a `-doclet` option on the command line—you get ten more options available to you. (Other `doclets` may have different options; see the documentation for whichever `doclet` you plan to use.)

The following are the options supported by the default `doclet`:

- `-linkall`   Generates hyperlinks to all named classes, even if they aren't included in the current `javadoc` run.

- `-doencoding` *name*   Specifies the output HTML file encoding name.

- `-version`   Includes the @version tags.

- `-author`   Includes the @author tags.

- `-noindex`   Supresses the package index.

- `-notree`   Supresses the class/interface hierarchy.

- `-d` *directory*   Specifies a destination directory for the HTML files.

- `-nodeprecated`   Supresses paragraphs tagged with the @deprecated tag.

- `-breakindex`   breaks up the index file into 26 files, one for each letter of the alphabet. See Figure 15.6 for an example.

- `-footer` *text*   Places the specified text at the bottom of each HTML page, just before the `</BODY>` tag. If *text* contains spaces, you must enclose it in single or double quotes.

FIGURE 15.6

Use the -breakindex
option when you have a large
number of members in a single
index file.

Building a Custom Doclet

To customize the output of javadoc you can write your own
doclet (in Java, of course). Your doclet must have a method
public static boolean start(), and can use the classes and
methods in the Doclet API. Then specify your doclet by using
the -doclet option on the javadoc command line. Listing 15.1
shows a simple doclet; this doclet lists the classes in your
package.

LISTING 15.1   *ListClass.java*–**This simple doclet simply lists the classes in
your package**

```
 1  import sun.tools.javadoc.*;
 2  public class ListClass {
 3    public static boolean start(Root theRoot) {
 4      ClassDoc[] theClasses = theRoot.classes();
 5      for (int i=0; i<theClasses.length; i++) {
 6        System.out.println(theClasses[i]);
 7      }
 8      return true;
 9    }
10  }
```

This package imports `sun.tools.javadoc.*`—the package that contains the Doclet API. (See the documentation that came with your JDK for more details on the classes and methods available in that package.)

The required `start()` method takes one parameter—an instance of class `Root`. `Root` tells your doclet about the user's command-line choices, and in particular, about the package or source file on which the doclet is working. `Root`'s `classes()` method retrieves an instance of `ClassDoc` for every class on which `javadoc` is working, and `println()` prints the name of the class. There's more information stored in a `ClassDoc`; be sure to check your JDK documentation.

Compile this doclet by typing

```
javac ListClass.java
```

and then run it by typing

```
javadoc -doclet ListClass myPackage
```

When you're ready to develop your own doclet, use Sun's standard doclet as your starting point. It's in the `docs/tooldocs/javadoc/source` directory in your JDK directory. The `start()` method is in the `Standard` class. From there you can follow how the standard doclet does its work. For example, it generates HTML from `HtmlWriter` and the derived `HtmlDocWriter` classes.

Save time by subclassing the standard doclet's classes

Unless your needs are special, you don't have to write a doclet from scratch. Subclass the classes of the standard doclet and override just those methods you need to change. For example, to use your own custom horizontal rule, override

```
public void hr()
```

in `HtmlWriter`.

Testing and Debugging Java Code

Learn why you'll get better, more reliable software if you combine reviews with testing

Learn how to conduct unit tests of your methods and classes

Develop a procedure for finding and fixing defects in your programs

See why Software Configuration Management is critical to successful development

Discover how to integrate large programs in Java

Learn to use *jdb*, the symbolic debugger that comes with your JDK

The same principles apply to hobbyists

If you're a hobbyist, write shareware, or otherwise don't have a well-defined "customer," adapt these same objectives to your situation. For example, if you are the only user of your programs, your need for user-friendliness may be lower than that of a corporate programmer, but you may still want to ensure correctness and adaptability.

Understanding Software Quality

As a programmer, you're under pressure to make your software satisfy your customer's needs and desires. Unfortunately, sometimes their goals and yours come into conflict. Sometimes their goals are even in conflict with each other. For example, Figure 16.1 shows a system with three primary objectives: high security, high performance, and user-friendliness. For a given runtime environment the developer can design a system to function anywhere within the triangle, but he or she cannot put the system at all three corners at once.

FIGURE 16.1

Much of design is a series of tradeoffs between competing objectives.

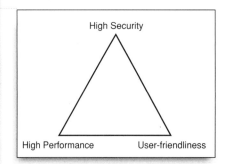

Many developers identify two types of software development objectives: external and internal.

External objectives are those aspects of the system the customer can see. Such a list may include the following:

- Correctness—The degree to which the software satisfies its specification and design.
- Usability—Often called the user-friendliness of a system.
- Efficiency—The degree to which the system conserves system resources such as memory and processor time.
- Reliability—The likelihood that the system will deliver its results consistently and without failure.
- Integrity—A measure of the system's ability to protect its data from unauthorized access or corruption. Security is one aspect of integrity.

- Adaptability—A measure of the system's ability to be used, without modification, in a different environment or for a different purpose.

- Accuracy—The degree to which the system is free from quantitative error.

- Robustness—A measure of how well the system performs even when the input is incorrect or the environment (such as the processor or network) is overloaded.

As a programmer, you're interested not only in the external characteristics of the software, but also in the internal characteristics—those aspects that are only seen by programmers. These characteristics include the following:

- Maintainability—The ease with which you can modify the software to make it more useful for its original purpose.

- Flexibility—The extent to which you can modify the system to operate in a different application.

- Portability—The degree to which you can modify the system to operate in a different environment.

- Reusability—A measure of the ease with which you can use parts of the software in other systems.

- Readability—A measure of how easy it is to read and understand the source code on a line-by-line basis.

- Testability—The extent to which the software can be tested (both at the unit and the system level).

- Understandability—A measure of how easy it is for a programmer to understand the program, not only on a line-by-line basis but also as a whole.

These two types of objectives are closely related, in much the same way as your overall health (an external characteristic) is related to your cholesterol level and blood pressure (internal characteristic). If you tell your doctor you'd like to be healthy (an external goal), he or she may measure your internal characteristics and set a series of internal goals and plans (such as lowering your cholesterol by changing your diet, or lowering your blood pressure with medication).

What do you measure?

Does your organization notice and reward programmers who deliver their code on time, even if the code contains defects? Are careful programmers who deliver high-quality code penalized if they deliver it behind schedule? Your organization may be sending an inadvertent message that quality is not important.

I'm a hobbyist—who can help me review my software?

If you're working on your own, you can still benefit from software reviews. Consider using the Internet to find other programmers in a similar situation, and put together teams of code readers and design reviewers. Use the comp.lang.java.* newsgroups or some of the newsgroups available through the Java Developer Connection as a starting point to find reviewers.

This chapter focuses on improving the quality of the system, by whatever standard you and your customer define quality. Most systems will benefit from improved code readability, but when building a high-performance system, you may decide to sacrifice some readability in order to optimize an algorithm. Which objectives you choose are up to you—how to get you to those objectives, in Java, is the subject of this chapter.

Many organizations focus on getting the program ready on time. Toward the end of the development cycle they begin to test; when the software passes the test they ship the product. Unfortunately even extensive tests often leave half the defects in the product undiscovered. For best results you should use a combination of software review and testing. The following is a procedure that can help you deliver high-quality software.

Developing high-quality software

1. Conduct a series of reviews even before the code is written (during analysis and design), and fix any defects these reviews reveal.

2. As you implement the code, conduct a series of code reviews, and fix any defects these reviews reveal.

3. As methods and classes are completed, subject them to unit test.

4. When your testing reveals defects, debug the program to locate the cause of the defect.

5. Design and implement a change to fix the defect.

6. Once a class passes its unit tests, place it under configuration management, ensuring that changes will only be made under controlled conditions. (See the section "Placing Your Code Under Configuration Management," later in this chapter.)

7. As your classes are completed, integrate them into a finished product.

The next several sections describe each of these steps.

Using Software Reviews

Table 16.1 shows the results of attempting to improve software quality by using ten different methods. (This data was originally reported by Capers Jones in *Programming Productivity*, McGraw-Hill, 1986.) The significant point of this table is that no single method was capable of removing more than around 60 percent of the defects, but the combination of methods allowed programmers to remove nearly all defects. Even more interesting is that testing—often the only element of a quality assurance plan—removed fewer than half of the defects in the code.

Does your code have a defect or a bug?

I use the term "fault" to refer to a failure or anomaly that is detected at runtime (during testing, or by a user). When the fault is reported and found to be valid it is called a "defect." I try to avoid using the term "bug"—the image it conjures up is not consistent with the seriousness of a software defect.

TABLE 16.1 **Defect-Detection rates**

Removal Step	Lowest Rate	Modal Rate	Highest Rate
Personal checking of design documents	15%	35%	70%
Informal group design reviews	30%	40%	60%
Formal design inspections	35%	55%	75%
Formal code inspections	30%	60%	70%
Modeling or prototyping	35%	65%	80%
Personal desk-checking of code	20%	40%	60%
Unit testing (single routines)	10%	25%	50%
Function testing (related routines)	20%	35%	55%
Integration testing (complete system)	25%	45%	60%
Field testing (live data)	35%	50%	65%
Cumulative effect of complete series	**93%**	**99%**	**99%**

As Table 16.1 shows, reviews are more effective than tests. They also discover a different kind of defect than testing does. In order to build an effective software quality assurance plan, you need to include design and code reviews along with your test activities. Reviews include code inspections, walkthroughs, and reading. This section describes the various methods of conducting a review.

Measure yourself

As you review and test your software, measure how many defects you find and remove during each step. Decide for yourself whether design reviews, code inspections, unit testing, or other defect removal techniques are cost-effective.

Should managers come to the review?

As the term is used here, a *review* is a technical process designed to assess or improve the quality of the software. This is a different meeting than the one used by management to assess the schedule and budget. In order to allow the engineers to concentrate on their work instead of trying to "look good," managers should decline any invitations to sit in on the reviews.

Talk to the walls

Much of the benefit of review comes from having to describe your program in a way that other people will understand. If you're stuck for a reviewer, consider talking through your code with your dog, a plant, or even the walls—many times the activity of explaining how something works will reveal a defect.

Most forms of review are conducted by someone other than the software's author. We all have blind spots in our thinking, and often another programmer can spot an error within seconds that we've read right over.

Conducting Analysis and Design Reviews

Chapter 7, "Object-Oriented Analysis: A New Way of Looking at Software," described the Unified Modeling Language (UML). You should prepare for a review during the analysis and design activities by preparing documentation in UML notation. During the analysis review you should review the use cases and requirements documents. During the preliminary design review you should concentrate on class diagrams and interaction diagrams—especially sequence diagrams. When you get to the detailed design review you should have both public and private methods identified and designed, and all of the data members identified.

Set specific goals for each review. Typical goals for a detailed design review include the following:

- *Make the design more understandable.* The design resembles the code that will eventually be produced, but in a condensed form. For example, you may use a state diagram that the reviewer can comprehend at a glance, instead of a series of `switch` statements.

- *Save implementation time.* By reviewing the design, you save the time you would have spent implementing an incorrect piece of the design. You also increase the quality of the finished code, since the implementation is likely to be cleaner.

- *Avoid missing design defects.* Be careful not to review too much at once, or your reviewers may miss defects. Look at design documents for design defects, and source code for implementation defects.

- *Spot possible design improvements.* During review you may uncover a more efficient algorithm, a more flexible design, or a better way to meet the customer's requirements.

In order to make sure your designs are reviewable, you must make sure the purpose and function of each package, class, and method are clear. Even when you're reviewing your own code you'll appreciate having clear design objectives.

Conduct a design review in a systematic manner. Watts Humphrey, developer of the Personal Software Process, suggests a six-step process for use during design reviews (*A Discipline for Software Engineering*, 1995, Addison-Wesley).

- Check to make sure the design includes all required elements.

- Verify the overall program structure and flow.

- Check the program's logic for correctness. Start with the nominal case for all loops and recursive methods.

- Check the program's logic for robustness—make sure that every branch, loop, or recursive method behaves correctly even in the face of bad input or a heavily loaded environment.

- Check the method calls to ensure that all of the parameters and their types are correct. Check the limits and error conditions for every call.

- Check all special variables, parameters, datatypes, and files.

Conducting a Code Inspection

A code inspection is a formal review based on a set of checklists. The original work on code inspections was done by Michael Fagan at IBM—you can read his paper, "Design and Code Inspections to Reduce Errors in Program Development," in *IBM Systems Journal* 15, no. 3, pages 182–211. Code inspections are the single best technique for removing defects from your product—some users report removing 60 to 90 percent of all defects during this single step.

A code inspection is characterized by the following:

- Checklists that focus the reviewers on areas that have been problems in the past. (Table 16.2, coming up later in this section, shows a simple checklist suitable for reviewing Java code.)

Use javadoc to prepare detailed design documentation

After the high-level design review, begin preparing for the detailed design review. Many documentation tools can prepare Java package, class, and method declarations directly from your UML diagrams. Add javadoc comments to this generated code and use the javadoc output as the basis for the detailed design review.

Do you trust the compiler?

Some programmers skip some steps in the design review and wait for the compiler to tell them about any problems. While this process may seem to save time, it often allows defects to slip through and surface as faults much later in the development process.

You can inspect designs, too

Don't limit yourself to code inspections. You can experiment with formal design inspections as well.

- An emphasis on defect detection, not correction.
- A preparation period, so that the meeting itself can focus on reporting the defects, not discovering them.
- Distinct roles assigned to the participants.
- A trained moderator who keeps the process moving.
- Data that is collected during each inspection and used to tune the overall inspection process.

A code inspection moves through nine steps:

- Planning—To start the inspection process the author gives the design documents or the code to a moderator. The moderator selects reviewers, schedules the inspection meeting, and distributes the documents and a checklist.
- Overview—If the reviewers are new to the project, the author may provide a one-hour overview to introduce terminology or general requirements.
- Preparation—Each reviewer spends about 90 minutes going over the design documents or code, looking for errors. Depending on the code and the reviewers, they may be able to read around 1000 lines of code in that time.
- Inspection meeting—Someone, often the author, reads through the code with the reviewers. The reviewers point out places that they found the material unclear, overly complex, or just plain wrong. The meeting should last no more than two hours. Depending upon the code and the reviewers, you may get through perhaps 200 to 1000 lines of code in that time.
- Third-hour meeting—An optional time for interested reviewers to work with the program's author to identify corrections to the defects that have been discovered.
- Inspection report—Within a day of the meeting the moderator produces a report listing each defect found, including its severity and type. The moderator should also note the amount of time spent in preparation and the meeting, so that management can track the cost-effectiveness of inspections.

- Rework—The author addresses each defect reported.

- Follow-up—If the number of defects was high—for example, if more than five percent of the design or code will have to be changed—the moderator should schedule a re-inspection of the material. Otherwise the moderator may decide to review the rework with the author privately.

- Refining the process—Over time, management and the moderators should use the data produced by inspections to refine the checklists, set the optimum amount of material to be reviewed, and to assess the effectiveness of the process.

You should have at least five people—you may have many more—participate in the inspection:

- Moderator—A specially trained person charged with setting the pace. The inspection shouldn't go too fast and run past a defect someone has discovered, but it can't go too slowly or it becomes ineffective. The moderator should make sure the reviewers don't get bogged down in fixing defects—the purpose of the inspection meeting is to report defects the reviewers think they've found.

- Author—The programmer who wrote the code should be in attendance, but usually doesn't present, and certainly doesn't run the meeting. The author may provide an overview, but the code should speak for itself.

- Reviewers—Typically at least two people who have an interest in the design or code. At a design review the reviewer might be the programmer who will implement the code. The architect who prepared the design may also serve as a reviewer.

- Scribe—Someone to record the defects that are recorded, and to note any action items the moderator assigns.

After you've conducted a few inspections you'll have plenty of material on which to base your checklists. Table 16.2 shows a simple checklist suitable for reviewing Java code; use this version only until you have enough data to write your own. Prepare a separate checklist for each method or class; make sure all the elements are checked off, and that all the defects have been corrected, before you move on to your next activity.

Don't confuse inspections with performance appraisals

Be careful that your organization's management doesn't attempt to use inspections as a basis for performance appraisals. In the inspections you need to encourage brutal honesty. Performance appraisals should be based on the quality of the finished product.

TABLE 16.2 **A code inspection checklist for Java**

Item to check	Guidance
Completeness	Verify that the code covers all of the design.
imports	Verify that all imports are correct.
Initialization	Check variable and paramter initialization.
	■ At program initiation
	■ At the start of every loop
	■ At each method entry
Calls	Check method call parameters to be sure they match.
Names	Check name spelling and use.
	■ Does it follow project naming conventions?
	■ Does it follow JavaBean design patterns (if required) (see Chapter 19, "Building Components with JavaBeans")
Output format	Check that line stepping and spacing are correct.
{} pairs	Ensure that {} are proper and matched.
Logic operators	Verify the proper use of ==, =, ¦¦, and so on.
	Check every logic function for proper parentheses.
switch statements	Ensure that every case clause has a break.
Line-by-line check	Check every line of code for
	■ Correct statement syntax
	■ Proper punctuation
Standards	Ensure that code conforms to project coding standards.
I/O	Verify that all streams and sockets are
	■ Properly declared
	■ Opened
	■ Closed

Where do your moderators get trained?

Remember that inspection moderators should receive formal training. Learn about a training simulator developed by the Advanced Learning Technologies project in Scott Stevens' paper, "Intelligent Interactive Video Simulation of a Code Inspection" in *Communications of the ACM* 32, no. 7 (July, 1989), pages 832-43. You can also contact the Software Engineering Institute at Carnegie Mellon University in Pittsburgh for information about its training materials.

Using a Code Walkthrough

We've said that inspections are the most effective way to remove defects from your code. Why, then, would you even consider another method, such as a code walkthrough?

Remember that inspections are formal processes; it may take a while to get your moderators and reviewers trained in these processes. In the meantime, you would like to begin getting some benefits from reviews.

You may also have times when a code author would like a less formal review of a smaller piece of code, and doesn't want to incur the time and expense associated with an inspection. The inspection may well come later, but the programmer wants the benefit of a review right away. In these cases, consider conducting a walkthrough.

Unlike an inspection, the walkthrough is hosted and moderated by the program's author. Also unlike an inspection, the purpose is to actually improve the code, not just to detect defects. Conduct your walkthroughs by following this three-step process.

Conduct a code walkthrough

1. The programmer selects one or more reviewers and distributes the code.

2. All reviewers read the code, looking for errors.

3. Reviewers come to a meeting (designed to last no more than one hour) in which they report the results of their review to the program's author.

While code reviews are somewhat less effective than inspections, they can provide a quick check before the inspection, or can help an organization transition into inspections.

Using Code Readers

While inspections require a fair amount of advance planning, an author may call for a code reading at any time. Here are the steps to follow for a code reading.

Should you compile code before you review it?

Many people prefer to compile their code before the review. I do not. While the compiler can certainly catch many things that the reviewers will never find, running the code through the compiler can make reviewers lazy.

Conduct a code reading

1. The programmer selects two reviewers and distributes the code—typically around 4,000 source lines.

2. All reviewers read the code looking for errors, at a typical rate of about 1,000 lines per day. The programmer encourages a friendly competition between the reviewers.

3. Reviewers may come to a meeting (which lasts no more than 2 hours) to describe the defects they found. At the author's option, the reviewers may skip this meeting and send comments directly to the author.

Testing Your Methods and Classes

Which code should you build first?

If you've adopted the spiral model of development described in Chapter 7, you should build and test your riskiest classes and methods first. If you need the services of other classes that haven't been built yet, write stubs for those methods. If you need a calling routine, write a test harness in **main()** that calls each of your methods, gives it a series of test cases (perhaps from a file), and checks the results (perhaps against a file of known good results).

Once you've completed your code reviews it's time to compile your classes and begin to conduct unit tests. I recommend you provide a main() routine for every class—even the ones that are not applications—and use main() to call a class self-test. You can start testing a class as soon as the main() routine and one method are complete. Test each method separately, and then begin integrating them into a single class. (Integration is described later in this chapter.)

As you build your methods you'll identify certain assumptions that you're making about your code and its environment. Consider adding an assert() method to your software to tell you when these assumptions are violated. You can write

```
package assert;
public class Assert
{
  static public void assert(boolean theAssertion, String
➡theMessage)
  {
    if (!theAssertion)
    {
      System.err.println("Assertion failed: " + theMessage);
      System.exit(1);
    }
  }
}
```

Now you can write code like

```
public myMethod(int[] anArray) // array cannot be longer
                               than 4
{
  assert.Assert.assert(anArray.length < 5, "Warning: the
length of anArray is > 4);
  . . .
}
```

This section describes four steps you can follow to ensure that each method and class is thoroughly tested:

- Start building your test plan during design; make sure the test plan covers all of the functional requirements.
- Use structured basis testing to generate the initial test cases.
- Use data-flow test analysis to generate still more test cases.
- Add other test cases as indicated.

Applying Structured Basis Testing

Structured basis testing is simply a way of identifying the total number of paths in a piece of software. It strongly resembles McCabe's Cyclomatic Complexity Metric, described in Chapter 24, "Organizing and Reusing Your Code." To compute the number of paths through a module, start with 1, add 1 for every path through a conditional (including those inside branching statements such as a `for` loop), and add 1 for every `case` in a `switch` statement (including 1 for the `default` case, even if it is missing).

Don't let the number of paths creep too high

The number of paths is only the starting point in generating test cases. If the number of paths through a method is greater than eight or so, it's time to consider redesigning that method.

Analyzing a Method's Data Flow

By some estimates, up to half of all programs are data declarations and initializations rather than program logic. Clearly we need to pay attention to our data, whereas basis path tests concentrate on logic flow alone.

Figure 16.2 illustrates three milestones in the life of a variable: defined, used, and killed. The usual pattern is that the variable is defined, used (one or more times), and killed—in that order.

Variables also live within some scope. For example, a local variable is defined inside a method, just after the method is entered, and is killed when the method is exited. Other patterns of use should at least raise a question, and may represent a defect.

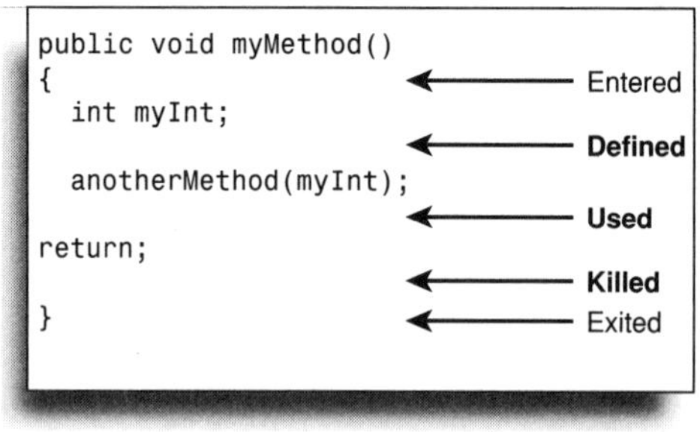

FIGURE 16.2

Typically a local variable is defined once after the method is entered, used one or more times, and then killed after the method is exited.

```
public void myMethod()
{
  int myInt;

  anotherMethod(myInt);

return;

}
```

Entered

Defined

Used

Killed

Exited

The compiler may catch some data-flow problems

Many compilers will at least warn you that a variable has been used before it was defined, or that it was declared but never used. Look hard at these warnings—they may be telling you about an error.

As you're examining the data flow of your variables, determine whether additional test cases are needed. For example, suppose your method contained the following code:

```
if (someBoolean)
   x=a;
else
   x=b;

if (someOtherBoolean)
   y=x+1;
else
   y=x-1;
```

A simple basis path analysis tells you to handle three cases: a straight-line case and one additional case for each conditional. In fact, you'd be better served by four test cases, as shown in Figure 16.3, which shows the cases that arise by following each path through the code.

Using Equivalence Partitioning

Every test case costs someone time and money. As you generate test cases with basis paths and data-flow analysis, be on the look-out for two or more cases that flush out the same errors. Retain whichever case covers more input data, and drop the others. This process is known as *equivalence partitioning*.

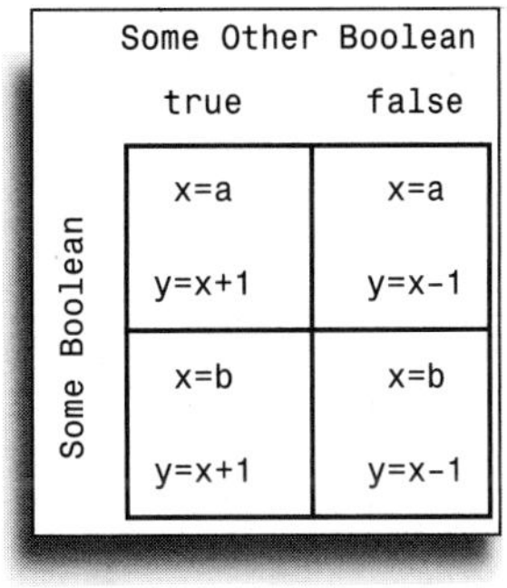

FIGURE 16.3

There are four test cases, not three, indicated by the code in this example.

Trust Your Experience

As you gain experience with Java you'll learn what kinds of mistakes you, personally, tend to make. You should keep a record of your mistakes—particularly those that have come out during reviews or previous testing. Use that personal checklist as a starting point for your own one-person code review. As you're building the test plan, place special emphasis on routines that contain code you know to be a bit suspicious, overly complex, or just those places where you are less than completely comfortable.

Boundary Analysis

As you go through a method, look at its loops. Are you completely sure that you don't have an off-by-one error somewhere? Generate test cases that stress these loop limits. If your program contains the line

```
if (theValue > kLimit)
```

you should add at least three test cases (unless they're already present in the test plan):

- Case 1 `theValue = kLimit - 1`
- Case 2 `theValue = kLimit;`
- Case 3 `theValue = kLimit + 1`

Ensure that the program works as you expect in all three cases.

Debugging

Harlan Mills, inventor of the powerful "cleanroom" technique of building software, says, "Programs do not acquire bugs as people acquire germs, by hanging around other buggy programs. Programmers must insert them." (Quoted in Steven McConnell's *Code Complete*, Microsoft Press, 1993, p. 590.)

Mills is right. If you want to quit debugging your code, quit putting bugs into it. That's easier said than done, of course. Until we all stop writing buggy code, we'll have to keep finding the bugs and taking them out.

This section recommends some steps to take after you've identified a problem in your code through testing.

Putting Your Program in "Debug Mode"

In the "old days" with C++, we would often use the C preprocessor to write code like the following:

```
#define DEBUG
#ifdef DEBUG
  println("DEBUG: The value in step %d is %d\n", i,
➥theValue);
#endif
```

If you still have a C preprocessor, you can write the same thing with Java (it doesn't have to be a C or C++ program). You can write the whole thing in Java, however, by writing

```
static final boolean fDebug = true;
if (fDebug)
  System.err.println("DEBUG: The value in step " + i +
    " is " + theValue);
```

If you're careful to declare the debug boolean to be static and final, the compiler will not even put the debug code into the class file when the boolean is false.

It *is* possible to write perfect code!

While many developers report error rates of 10 to 50 errors per thousand lines of code, Harlan Mills reports that organizations using his "cleanroom development" technique are enjoying error rates more like 3 defects per 1000 lines of code. One project—the space-shuttle software—has achieved a record of zero defects in 500,000 lines of code.

Put your asserts inside the debug statement

For some applications you want to be sure the end user never sees an assert fire. That problem is easy to solve—just put your assert() calls inside the debug conditional statements, and set the debug boolean to false.

Interpreting Compiler Messages

Depending upon which compiler you use, you may be able to set optional "warning levels." I recommend that you set the compiler to ring every bell it can whenever it finds the least thing suspicious in your code. Then, don't "fix" the problem by ignoring the warning or changing the warning level—fix the code, even if you don't consider the warning to be a defect.

Often one of the first indications you get that there's a problem is when the compiler raises an error message or a warning. Here are some rules of thumb for interpreting these messages.

- Take the line number of the first reported error or warning with a small grain of salt. Most compilers get this one right, most of the time.

- Take the first error or warning message seriously; usually the compiler knows what it's talking about.

- Pay some attention to the second message and its associated line number. It may tell you about a real problem, or it may be that the compiler has become confused by the first error. If you fix the first error you'll often discover that the others solve themselves.

- Consider using two compatible compilers—one that is fast (such as the compiler that comes with Visual Café from Symantec) and one that gives great, informative error messages (such as javac from Sun). Switch between compilers to gain insight, and to rule out the occasional compiler defect.

Look for compilers with different heritages

Some reviewers have noted that Visual Café and javac are "bug for bug compatible with each other" because Symantec relies upon Sun's code base. If you suspect that a problem may be due to a compiler defect, consider switching to an independently developed compiler such as those in IBM's VisualAge for Java or Borland's JBuilder.

Using a Debugging Process

Some programmers report that they spend about half of their time debugging their code. What they often mean is that they spend that time on a combination of tasks, including the following:

- Testing their code to find the defects
- Isolating the source of each defect

- Applying a fix to the defect
- Testing the fix
- Fixing the fix (which usually isn't right the first time)

We've already talked about how to test your methods and classes. Here is a process that will take you through isolating a defect. In just a moment I'll give you a similar process for fixing the defect.

Systematic fault isolation

1. Characterize the problem—Determine the conditions under which the failure occurs, and the exact nature of the failure. Don't rush this step; if the problem is intermittent, stay here until you can make the problem stable.

2. Form a hypothesis—Based on your characterization, make an educated guess as to the cause of the problem.

3. Design an experiment to prove or disprove your hypothesis—Your experiment may involve using a symbolic debugger such as `jdb` (described in the last section of this chapter), adding `println()` statements, or using a different set of input data.

4. Run the experiment—Prove or disprove your hypothesis.

5. Repeat steps 1 through 4 until you're confident that you know what the cause of the problem is.

If your development environment doesn't include a language-sensitive editor, consider switching—they're quite valuable. A really good language-sensitive editor will help you indent your code, revealing errors like this one:

```
if (a < b)
  int temp = a;
  a = b;
  b = temp;
```

Java is less prone to intermittent faults than C or C++

In languages such as C or C++, an intermittent fault is usually a sign of either an uninitialized variable or a dangling pointer. Java initializes variables automatically, and doesn't have user-accessible pointers, so you're far less likely to see an intermittent fault. Intermittent faults in Java are usually due to race conditions or are GUI-related.

Start with `asserts` and `println`s, and then move to the debugger

I find that if I start using the debugger too soon, I waste time isolating the fault. I recommend you sprinkle `asserts` and `println`s liberally throughout your code (wrapping them in `if (fDebug). . .` statements), and then use the symbolic debugger once you've narrowed the problem down to a single method.

Do you see the error? The indentation tricks you into thinking that the all three assignment statements are part of the `if` statement. In fact, what the programmer meant to say was:

```
if (a < b)
{
  int temp = a;
  a = b;
  b = temp;
}
```

If you're trying to fault-isolate between two or more methods, and one of those methods has had a lot of other defects, suspect that the method is the faulty one. Defects are not evenly distributed. If you've got a module where your work was sloppy, chances are there's another defect there.

If you're trying to fault-isolate between two or more methods, and one of those methods is complex (for example, it has a McCabe's Cyclomatic Complexity Metric of eight or higher) suspect that the method is the faulty one. The more complex a method, the more chances there are to hide a defect.

Sometimes while you're testing you'll uncover a defect and will be "almost sure" you know what's causing it. Often you'll be right, but if you're not you can waste a lot of time trying to track down the defect by "quick-and-dirty" means. I recommend you set a time limit on quick-and-dirty debugging. When you spot the problem, look at your watch. If you're still hacking after, say, ten minutes, give it up and go to the process described at the beginning of this section.

SEE ALSO
➤ *To learn more about McCabe's Cyclomatic Complexity Measure, page 662*

Fixing Defects

If you've spent any time debugging you know that some defects are difficult to isolate but easy to fix; others are just the opposite. These facts might suggest why so many of us spend so much time debugging. Some studies suggest that as many as as 50 percent of the fixes we apply are wrong when we first put them in.

Fault isolation tip: Defects follow a pattern

If you've seen a similar problem before, suspect that you're seeing it again. We're all creatures of habit—if you have a certain way you write code that leads to this sort of defect, look for that kind of a problem first.

Did you use a language-sensitive editor?

If you're prone to syntax errors, or often forget to close a block comment (/* . . ./* . . . */) look at the code in one of those language-sensitive editors that color all of the keywords one color, the variables another, and the comments in some other color. You may suddenly get insight into the nature of the problem.

Don't forget to talk to the walls

Earlier I recommended that you conduct design and code reviews with the walls, if necessary, in order to force yourself to articulate every element of a program. You'll find that technique especially helpful when you're fault-isolating. When you hit a particularly knotty problem, tell the walls why this problem is "impossible" and "can't be happening"; you'll be surprised how insightful those walls can be.

When you're fault-isolating you may see several defects, and you may find more than one change you'd like to make. I recommend you resist this temptation. Work on one problem at a time. Apply one code change at a time. Get it right, and then move on to the next problem.

The following procedure will help you save time fixing defects.

Fixing a problem

1. *Design a fix*. If the design is extensive consider using a design review to ensure that the fix doesn't introduce a new defect.

2. *Pull a backup*. Be certain that you have a copy of the files you will change, either in your configuration management system or safe on a hard drive.

3. *Implement your fix*. If the code change is significant, consider using a code review to ensure that the fix doesn't introduce a new defect.

4. *Test the fix*. Run the same scenarios that caused the failure before. Make sure they run successfully now.

5. *Regression-test*. Rerun tests on the entire product to be certain that your change didn't cause something else to break. Take a look at JavaSpec from SunTest (`http://www.sun.com/suntest/`); you may decide that this testing system meets your needs.

Once you've fixed an error and satisfied yourself that everything is working, make a new copy of the file, just in case. Then start looking for other places in the code where similar defects may be hiding. For example, I was once notorious for leaving the `break` statement out of the `case` clause in a `switch` statement. It's nearly always the wrong thing to do, but often you can leave out a `break` without introducing an obvious fault. Whenever I traced a problem to a missing `break` I forced myself to take the time to search through the code looking at `case` clauses; sure enough, I'd made the same mistake in other places, but those defects hadn't shown up in testing.

Automate your regression tests

The only practical way to run a regression test is to automate it. Write a script that calls `main()` on each integrated class. Capture the output to a file. Compare that output to a known good run and log any differences.

Automate your GUI tests

When you start integrating your GUI classes you may decide that it's not enough to test from `main()`— you need to test from the user interface. Java presents a special challenge here, since the location of controls may move as the layout manager resizes the screen. Take a look at SunTest's JavaStar (`http://www.suntest.com/`) or Segue's Silk (`http://www.segue.com/`) to see if one of these tools meets your needs.

When should you optimize code?

Recall from the beginning of this chapter that the objectives of software development are not always compatible. Sometimes you have to choose between readable code and fast code. Follow the recommendations given in Chapter 22, "Improving Your Java Program's Performance," before you scramble your good, clear code to get a small performance gain.

Placing Your Code Under Configuration Management

Once all of the code in a class passes unit test, I recommend that you place the class under configuration management. (Some organizations call this mechanism Software Configuration Management, or SCM. Others refer to it simply as "change control.")

If you're working by yourself on a small project, your configuration management system may be as simple as a regular backup and a series of numbered versions. If you're working as part of a group, you should use an automated system that prevents two people from checking out the same code at the same time. In the UNIX world, the Source Code Control System (SCCS) and the Revision Control System (RCS) are both popular, and are often included with your UNIX development environment.

Do you need more than SCCS or RCS?

SCCS and RCS, which are freely available, allow you to place text files under configuration management. If you need to check in binary files, such as images, you may want to use a commercial configuration management package such as PVCS. See `http://www.intersolv.com/pvcs/` for specifics on that package.

Does your IDE work with a particular SCM system?

If you're using an Integrated Development Environment (IDE), check with the vendor to see if it has any special arrangements with an SCM vendor. For example, Symantec (maker of Visual Café) has included Versions, an intuitive version control solution from StarBase. Learn more at `http://www.starbase.com/sym.htm`

Integrating Your Application or Applet

Integration is the process of pulling the various classes and methods you've written into a running program. If your design is sound, and all of your methods work as designed, integration can go quickly. Of course, that's a big "if."

I recommend the following process for integrating object-oriented programs such as Java applets or applications.

Integrating a program

1. Design and code each method. Include `asserts` and `println` statements that help demonstrate the program's correct behavior.

2. In each class, build a `main()` routine that tests each method.

3. Arrange your classes and methods in a rough hierarchy; the class at the top is your `Applet` class, or, in an application, the one whose `main()` routine defines the application. The classes at the bottom of the hierarchy are those that are called by others, but do not, themselves, call any other classes.

4. Implement the riskiest classes first, and begin integrating them into the riskiest features. If you need a high-level class that hasn't been written yet, build a test harness—a driver method that allows you to exercise other methods. If you need a low-level class that hasn't been written yet, write a stub that returns a fixed value. Use this stub as a placeholder until the actual method gets written.

5. Once you have one method working with its class's `main()` method, add one more method to the growing program. Continue iterating through steps 4 and 5, implementing features and groups of related features, roughly in order from those with the greatest risk to those with the least.

6. As you work, conduct a daily "smoke-test." Toward the end of each day, have a team get a read-only copy of every module in the configuration management repository, compile it, and run the regression test against the growing program. If anyone's code fails to compile, or if the system fails its regression test, deal with those issues first thing in the morning before moving on to new tasks.

Pass a smoke-test every day

By requiring that you pass the smoke-test every day, you ensure that the product could ship at a moment's notice. It might not have all of the features that it will eventually have, but those that are there work, and they represent the riskiest of the feature set.

Using Incremental Integration

By adding one new method or class at a time—a mechanism called incremental integration—you get the following four benefits:

- *Errors are easier to locate*. If the code worked yesterday, and today it doesn't, you can track the problem immediately to the one method you just added.

- *Morale is better*. Every day you see a version of the running software. Even if all of the features aren't working, many are, and more become available every day.

- *Testing is more complete*. The riskiest classes are subjected to regression testing many times, while the less-risky classes are integrated.

- *The development schedule is shorter*. You can be designing the less-risky parts of the software while you're integrating other classes, allowing you to overlap certain activities and shorten the overall schedule.

Stress Test All of Your Code

Stress testing is the process by which you ensure the robustness of your program. Your test cases should include input data that violates your assumptions about data range or type. If a field should always be filled in, leave it empty. If a field should only take a numeric value, fill it with your mother's maiden name. Find someone who ignores all of your implicit assumptions, and breaks them.

As the program integration proceeds, conduct stress testing regularly. Make it part of your regression testing so that it runs during every build.

Load Test Your Server Applications

When you design server applications, estimate the maximum number of client connections you'll ever have to support. During testing, load the server with twice that number of connections and measure the response time. Make sure that, as part of your regular testing, you determine what will happen when large numbers of users connect.

Debugging an Application from the Command Line

Your JDK comes with a simple command-line-based symbolic debugger called jdb. This program is not state-of-the-art, but it's free, and will see you through simple debugging sessions quite well.

Starting *jdb*

The most common way to start the jdb debugger is to invoke it with a class name:

```
jdb myPackage.myClass
```

or with parameters

```
jdb -classpath %DEVELOPMENT_DIRECTORY%\classes
➥myPackage.myClass
```

Using a commercial debugger

If you're developing Java as anything other than a hobby, you should be using an IDE. All IDEs have some kind of symbolic debugger; check their documentation to learn how to use it.

Look for great things from the Java Virtual Machine Debugger API

jdb uses the Java Virtual Machine Debugger API, new in JDK 1.2. This interface is primarily of interest to people who write debuggers. Look for the commercial IDE vendors to integrate with the Debugger API as JDK 1.2 moves into the mainstream, giving commercial debuggers access to the JVM's memory management and thread execution routines, stack frames, local variables, and more. Read `docs/guide/jvmdi/jvmdi.html` in your JDK directory for a description of the interface.

When you start the debugger in this way it launches a new copy of the JVM, loads the specified class, and stops the interpreter just before `main()` is called.

For a complete list of `jdb` commands, start the debugger and type `help` or `?`. You can get more detailed information on some of the major commands in your JDK documentation directory, at `docs/tooldocs/win32/jdb.html` (or its counterpart in the `solaris` directory).

Working with Threads

If you'd like to work with the threads in an existing copy of the JVM you'll need to attach to the Java interpreter. To make a JVM attachable you must start the Java interpreter with the `-debug` option and give that copy of the JVM a session password.

To attach the `jdb` to a JVM you write

```
jdb -host hostname -password password
```

Whether you've started a new JVM or attached an existing one, use the `threads` command to list the current threads. Each thread has a hexademinal object ID; threads in the current group have a name of the form `t.index`.

Dumping the Stack

The JVM uses a stack to keep track of each method call. If, in your program, method A() calls method B() which calls method C(), your stack will resemble Figure 16.4. If you encounter a problem, you might find it useful to know that the interpreter was running method C() when the problem occurred. You can find this information by dumping the stack. (You'll also see information in each stack frame about how the method came to call the next method and which values existed in the class when the stack was dumped.)

In order to see stack-related information you must set the `-g` switch when you compile the class.

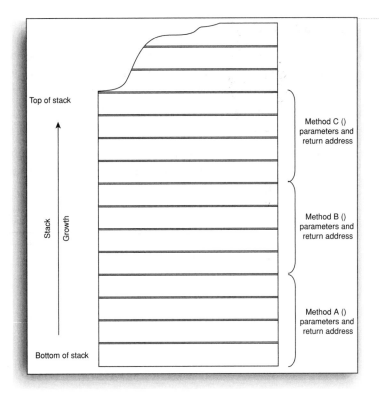

FIGURE 16.4
The Java Virtual Machine allocates stack frames as methods are called.

Top of stack

Stack Growth

Method C ()
parameters and
return address

Method B ()
parameters and
return address

Method A ()
parameters and
return address

Bottom of stack

After you've started the debugger, you can issue commands from the debugger's command line. The command to dump the stack is dump. Specify a class to dump by name or by hexadecimal ID. You can limit the dump by naming the instance variable you want to see. For example,

```
dump TDose.fPhysician
```

You can also print specific objects and their members. If you type

```
print TDose.fPhysician.fName
```

you'll invoke the toString() method of the specified object.

Use the up and down commands to change the current stack frame. Use the where command to dump the stack of a thread. (where all dumps the stack of all threads, where t@*index* dumps the stack of the specified thread, and where dumps the stack of the current thread.)

Setting Breakpoints

When you start the `jdb` with a new JVM it loads the specified class and stops just before executing `main()`. In order to control the application's behavior you should set breakpoints at key places in the code. Set a breakpoint by typing

```
stop at Object:line
```

where `Object` is the name of a class and `line` is the line number at which you want to stop. You can clear the breakpoint with the `clear` command.

Concurrent Programming with Threads

See how threads can improve your users' perception of performance

Learn how to make a new thread by subclassing `Thread` or by implementing `Runnable`

Find out about collisions—the biggest risk of using threads

See what a difference the JVM makes to the relative performance of threads

Using Threads

Back in Chapter 11, "Building the User Interface with the AWT," we saw the following line in Listing 11.5:

```
public class Animation1 extends Applet implements Runnable {
```

We said then that the Runnable interface allows the applet to start a new thread of control, so the animation can proceed independent of the user interface. Now it's time to explain the concept of a *thread* in more detail.

What Are Threads?

In order to explain threads we need to back up and explain processes. In a modern operating system (such as UNIX or Windows NT) the computer may have a single processor but will be doing many things at once. These operating systems are said to be *multiprocessing* since there are many separate activities going on at once, all sharing one processor. Figure 17.1 shows some of the dozens of processes that may be running on my computer at any given time.

Get a list of processes on your UNIX or NT machine

The process list in Figure 17.1 is from the Windows NT Task Manager. You can get a similar list on a UNIX machine by typing ps -ef at the command prompt if your UNIX is derived from System V; use ps -aux if your UNIX is rooted in BSD.

FIGURE 17.1

To get this list of processes in Windows NT, press **Ctrl+Alt+Delete**, choose **Task Manager**, and select the **Processes** tab.

① Monitor overall processor load here

② Monitor demand for virtual memory here

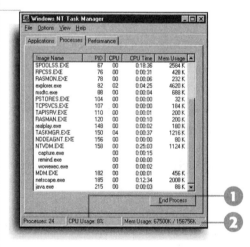

Operating systems give processes a great deal of protection from one another. A program running in one process cannot see or change data in another program unless both programs cooperate by using mechanisms collectively known as IPC (for *InterProcess*

Communication). This high degree of isolation is usually good news—it means that one misbehaving program can't take down the entire computer. (This high degree of isolation is the reason that General Protection Faults, or GPFs, are almost unheard of in Windows NT compared to Windows 95 or Windows 3.1.)

The downside of processes is that they are computationally expensive to start. In order for one process to split into two— operating systems generally call this *forking* or *spawning*—the operating system makes a complete copy of the process's memory, and then takes one execution path for one copy and another execution path for the other. (In Windows 95 and NT the operating system loads a new application from the hard drive into the new process's address space.) All of this copying and loading takes time—if you need a small, highly responsive program you may not want to fork many new processes.

In the late 1980s operating system vendors began offering threads—they were often called "lightweight processes." Like a process, a thread is a separate execution path. Unlike processes, there is no built-in protection between one process and another. The advantage of threads, of course, is that you can start them very quickly.

As far as your Java programs are concerned, every Java Virtual Machine has its own process. You may have noticed in Figure 17.1 that I've started a copy of the Java interpreter—java.exe appears on the very last line of the process list. Within a single Java program I can have as many threads running as I like.

> **How many threads can your computer support?**
>
> Although the starting of a thread is "lightweight" when compared to a process, there is still (in most computers) only one processor to go around. If you load up your program with too many threads, performance will suffer. Keep an eye on your overall system, as shown in Figure 17.2–if the CPU or memory usage regularly goes above 50 percent, consider adding resources or removing some of the load.

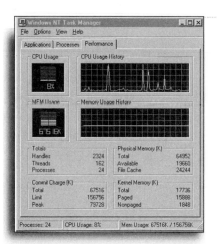

FIGURE 17.2

Use your operating system's tools to assess the impact your threads have on performance.

The easiest way to make a new thread in Java is to subclass Thread and make an instance of it. The constructor allows you to specify a name (in a String), a ThreadGroup, and a target. A ThreadGroup represents a group of threads (or other ThreadGroups) that share information among themselves. The target is an implementation of the Runnable interface, such as another Thread. If the target is not null, the JVM starts this thread by calling the target's run() method. (If the target is null, the JVM calls the new Thread's run() method to start it.)

Thread supports the following methods:

- activeCount() Returns the current number of active threads in this threadgroup.

- checkAccess() Checks with the current SecurityManager to determine if the current thread has permission to modify this thread.

- countStackFrames() Counts the depth of the stack, as measured in stack frames.

- currentThread() Returns a reference to the currently executing thread.

- destroy() Causes the thread to immediately exit, with no opportunity for cleanup.

- dumpStack() Prints a stack trace of the currently executing thread.

- enumerate() Prepares an array of threads consisting of a copy of every active thread in this ThreadGroup and its subgroups.

- getClassLoader() Returns the context ClassLoader for this Thread.

- getName() Returns the thread's name.

- getPriority() Returns the thread's priority. By default, every thread has the priority of the thread that started it. A thread can change its priority by calling setPriority().

- getThreadGroup() Returns a reference to this thread's ThreadGroup.

- `interrupt()` Interrupts the specified thread.

- `interrupted()` Tests to see if the current thread has been interrupted. `interrupted()` is a static method; compare it with `isInterrupted()`.

- `isAlive()` Returns `true` if the specified thread is still alive. A thread becomes alive when its `start()` method is called, and remains alive until it dies.

- `isDaemon()` Returns `true` if the specified thread is a daemon `Thread`. A thread is a daemon if it is designed to run in the background independent of any user interface. When all user interface threads have exited and the only threads running are daemons, the JVM exits.

- `isInterrupted()` Returns `true` if this `Thread` has been interrupted; compare it with `interrupted()`, which is static.

- `join()` Merges two threads by waiting for another thread to die. You can optionally limit the wait to a specified period of time.

- `run()` Begins to execute the thread's target `Runnable` object, if any.

- `setClassLoader()` Specifies a context `ClassLoader` for the thread.

- `setDaemon()` Marks the thread either as a daemon thread or as a user thread, depending upon the parameter.

- `setName()` Changes the name of the thread.

- `setPriority()` Checks to make sure the thread has permission to modify its own priority. If it does, it sets the priority as requested. Note that in no case will `setPriority()` set the priority to a value greater than that permitted for the thread's `ThreadGroup`. Priority is typically expressed through symbolic constants `MAX_PRIORITY`, `MIN_PRIORITY`, and `NORM_PRIORITY`.

- `sleep()` Causes the current thread to yield the processor and temporarily stop running for the specified time.

- `start()` Calls for this thread to begin execution—the JVM calls the `Thread`'s `run()` method.

**Whatever happened to stop(),
suspend(), and resume()?**

If you've worked with older versions
of Java you may know about the
Thread methods stop(),
suspend(), and resume().
While they're still present in the API,
they're now deprecated. Sun determined that they tended to lead to
deadlocks, it no longer recommends
their use.

**Look ahead to "The Great Thread
Race."**

The example given later in this
chapter, titled "The Great Thread
Race," shows how different versions
of the JVM implement scheduling
differently, even on the same platform.

- toString() Returns a String representation of the Thread
  with its name, priority, and ThreadGroup.

- yield() Causes the current Thread to yield the processor;
  the scheduler will allow other Threads to run.

SEE ALSO

➤ *Learn more about using threads for animation, page 300*

Competing for the Processor

As soon as a thread begins to run, it competes for the processor
with other threads that are running on the same Java Virtual
Machine. Sun offers two kinds of JVM on Windows NT and
Solaris machines, which differ in the kind of thread they offer.
Threads that rely upon the native operating system's thread
mechanisms are called *native threads*. Threads that are implemented entirely within the JVM are called *green threads*.

Operating system vendors such as Sun and Microsoft have
invested heavily in making sure their thread models offer great
performance. If you accept the native thread model you'll get a
performance boost, but you aren't guaranteed to get the same
behavior on all platforms. You may get consistent behavior by
choosing only JVMs that run green threads, but performance
will be less spectacular, and you could still have scheduling problems if you run native methods.

Making a *new Thread()*

The fastest and easiest way to build a multithreaded program is
to make a new Thread(). You can simply write the following:

```
Thread myThread = new Thread();
```

Sun offers seven different constructors for Thread. The most
elaborate of the seven accepts three parameters—other versions
allow you to leave off one or more of these parameters. The
three parameters are as follows:

- Threadgroup Used to place the new thread into a tree of other threads. If you leave it off or set it to null, the new thread is part of the current ThreadGroup. In order to place the new Thread into a ThreadGroup, the current thread must have permission—the checkAccess() method of the specified Threadgroup must not return a SecurityException.

- Runnable Used to set a target for the new thread to run. If you leave it off or set it to null the new thread starts by calling the current thread's run() method. If the new thread has a non-null target then the target's run() method is called when the new Thread is started.

- String Used to name the new thread.

Every thread has a priority—an integer value somewhere between java.lang.Thread.MIN_PRIORITY and java.lang.Thread.MAX_PRIORITY. The new thread is always made with the same priority as the currently running thread. Use setPriority() to adjust the priority (though you cannot set the priority to be higher than the maximum priority allowed by the thread's ThreadGroup).

There are also two kinds of threads in Java. Most threads are user threads—they have a user interface and exist in order to service that interface. Some threads run only in the background. They're called *daemon* threads. You can specify that a thread is a daemon thread by calling setDaemon().

Listing 17.1 shows a simple example of a new thread.

> **Make sure you have permission to change priority**
>
> You must also have permission (as determined by the current SecurityManager's checkAccess() method) in order to change the priority.

LISTING 17.1 *TNewThreadDemo1.java*—This simple program makes two new threads in the current group

```
1  public class TNewThreadDemo1 implements Runnable
2  {
3    public static void main(String argv[])
4    {
5      TNewThreadDemo1 aNewThreadDemo = new TNewThreadDemo1();
6
```

continues…

LISTING 17.1 Continued

```
7       Thread aNewThread = new Thread(aNewThreadDemo,
        "A New Thread");
8       aNewThread.start();
9       System.out.println("This line is the end of main.");
10      }
11
12      public void run()
13      {
14        while (true)
15        System.out.println("Current thread is " +
          Thread.currentThread().toString());
16        }
17  }
```

Examining *main()*

Let's walk through main() first:

```
public static void main(String argv[])
{
  TNewThreadDemo1 aNewThreadDemo = new TNewThreadDemo1();

  Thread aNewThread = new Thread(aNewThreadDemo,
➡"A New Thread");
  aNewThread.start();
  System.out.println("This line is the end of main.");
}
```

Since I want to work with some non-static variables (and main()
is a static method), I make a new instance—aNewThreadDemo1. I
construct a new thread for that instance. Since I used the two-
argument version of the thread constructor (specifying a
Runnable target and a name), Java will make the new thread in
the current ThreadGroup. Next, I start the new thread. When
aNewThread is started, Java calls the run() method from
TNewThreadDemo1.

Figure 17.3 illustrates the two threads that result from this program. The first thread is the user thread associated with main().
The JVM started it when I first ran the program. In response to
the statement

```
aNewThread = new Thread(aNewThreadDemo, "A New Thread");
```

**What are static methods and
variables?**

In object-oriented programming,
the keyword **static** means that
an entity is associated with the class
as a whole, and not with any particular instance. Static variables are
often called "class variables" and
non-static variables are called
"instance variables." A static method
such as **main()** cannot directly
read or write instance variables
since static methods don't have an
instance of the class.

**Don't forget to start() your
Threads**

Many debugging problems can be
traced to simple causes. If your new
thread doesn't seem to be running,
perhaps it isn't. Check to be sure
you called start().

Java made a new `Thread`, but that `Thread` wasn't active. Since I specified that `aNewThreadDemo` was to be used as the `Runnable` target, Java will use `TNewThreadDemo1`'s `run()` method when the new thread is `started`. (That's the reason that I declared `TNewThreadDemo1` to implement `Runnable`—the `Runnable` interface requires just one method: `run()`. I could also have extended `Thread`, since `TNewThreadDemo1` has no other base class.)

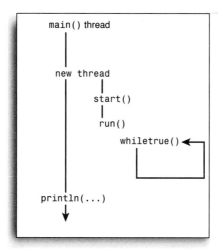

FIGURE **17.3**

When you make a new thread() and start it, there are two copies of your program running.

Following the call to `start()` in line 8, control in the new thread—`aNewThread`—passes to the `run()` method. Control in the old `Thread`—the one started by `main()`—continues on to the end of `main()`. Line 9 causes `main()` to output a line to standard output. Then the program waits for the remaining `Thread` to quit. As we'll see next, that will never happen with this program.

Handling Interruptions

When you split your process into threads you share control with those other threads. There's always a possibility that one of those threads could get into trouble and hang. For example, you might start a thread to download a large file from the network. If the network connection stops transmitting, the thread might become non-responsive. If your user thread is waiting for the I/O thread to complete, you need to have a way to abandon the I/O thread.

What are blocking and non-blocking calls?

You'll often see methods described as "blocking" or "non-blocking." A blocking method or function call is one that waits for some response, while a non-blocking call returns immediately. You should always put blocking calls into their own thread, and handle an interruption as described in this section.

The Java API gives you such a way—you call the thread's `interrupt()` method. For example, suppose you've written an `Applet` that starts a long, I/O intensive thread in `init()`. The user becomes tired of waiting for the I/O to complete and moves on to another page. The browser causes your `Applet`'s `stop()` method to be called. In `stop()` you might write:

```
public void stop()
{
  Thread theNowDeadThread = theOldIOThread;
  theOldIOThread = null;
  theNowDeadThread.interrupt();
}
```

Inside the I/O thread's `run()` method you can catch the `InterruptedException`. You must either deal with the interruption or pass it on. If you're in a method in which you can reassert the `Exception`, you may do so. If you're inside `run()` itself (or any other method that cannot throw `InterruptedException`) you can write the following when you catch `InterruptedException`:

```
Thread.currentThread().interrupt();
```

Most of the time, your thread should die when `interrupted`

If someone interrupts your thread, it usually means something has gone wrong. Depending upon your application, often the best that your thread can do is to print out any diagnostic messages, clean up any open I/O, and exit.

In most applications the thread will reraise the `InterruptedException` so that it can be handled by a higher level. (I say "in most applications" because sometimes you're hung on the I/O itself. Not all of Java's I/O routines handle `InterruptedException` correctly yet. If you're in an I/O intensive thread and you get an `InterruptedException`, consider taking that `Exception` as a cue to shut down your I/O and quit.)

Examining *run()*

Here, from Listing 17.1, is `run()`;

```
public void run()
{
  while (true)
  System.out.println("Current thread is " +
➡Thread.currentThread().toString());

}
```

In run() we go into an infinite loop, printing out the toString() information about the current thread. Since main's thread has continued processing inside main(), we expect to see only one thread using run(). In fact, we can see the name that we set up: A New Thread.

Of course, infinite loops are usually to be avoided. Listing 17.2 shows an improvement over the first version—we've replaced the infinite loop with a counter that runs from 0 to 1000, and added a sleep() period to the run() method.

sleep() is static

The sleep() method is a static method on class thread, so you can use sleep() to add a delay even when you're not working with threads. If you write the following, your program will pause for about one second:

```
Thread.sleep(1000);
```

LISTING 17.2 *TNewThreadDemo2.java*—This version includes *sleep()* in the *run()* method

```
1    public class TNewThreadDemo2 implements Runnable
2    {
3      static final short kLimit = 1000;
4      private short fLimit = 0;
5      public static void main(String argv[])
6      {
7        TNewThreadDemo2 aNewThreadDemo =
8          new TNewThreadDemo2();
9        Thread aNewThread = new Thread(aNewThreadDemo,
         "A New Thread");
10       aNewThread.start();
11     }
12     public void run()
13     {
14       while (fLimit++ < kLimit)
15       {
16         System.out.println("Current thread is " +
           Thread.currentThread().toString());
17         try
18         {
19           Thread.currentThread().sleep(10);
20         } catch (InterruptedException e) {
21         System.err.println("Child thread interrupted
           while sleeping.");
```

continues…

LISTING 17.2 **Continued**

```
22          System.exit(1);
23            }
24         }
25      }
26    }
```

In our new `while` loop we increment `fLimit`, constantly testing it against the constant `kLimit`. If `fLimit` is below `kLimit` we print out a simple message. (Here's where we could do other work, as well.)

Then we `try` to `sleep`. In order to compile we have to `catch` `InterruptedException`, because someone could `interrupt` us while we `sleep`. We continue in this way until `fLimit` has reached `kLimit`. At that point control drops through to the end of `run()`, and `aNewThread` is dead.

Extending *Thread*

In addition to calling `new Thread()` you can also make a class that is a subclass of `Thread`. In this case you'll have access to all of the methods of `Thread` listed earlier in this chapter, and can override any that you wish. (You'll nearly always override `run`, for example.)

Extending `Thread` is often a bit cleaner than trying to run a new `Thread` in the original program. Listings 17.3 and 17.4 show a more readable version of Listing 17.2.

It's important to `sleep`

Most threads should get some `sleep` during each loop. If you never `sleep`, the JVM may starve other threads, including the threads responsible for the user interface. This leads the user to conclude that the application or applet has frozen.

LISTING 17.3 *TNewThread.java*–**This class encapsulates the new thread's work**

```
1    class TNewThread extends Thread
2    {
3      static final short kLimit = 1000;
4      private short fLimit = 0;
5
6      public TNewThread(String aName)
7      {
8        super(aName);
9      }
```

```
10
11      public void run()
12      {
13          while (fLimit++ < kLimit)
14          {
15              System.out.println("Current thread is " +
                Thread.currentThread().toString());
16              try
17              {
18                  Thread.currentThread().sleep(10);
19              } catch (InterruptedException e) {
20                  System.err.println("Child thread interrupted
                    while sleeping.");
21                  System.exit(1);
22              }
23          }
24      }
25  }
```

LISTING 17.4 *TNewThreadDemo3.java*–The remaining class is now only a driver; it no longer needs to implement *Runnable*

```
1   public class TNewThreadDemo3
2   {
3       public static void main(String argv[])
4       {
5           TNewThread aNewThread = new TNewThread("A New Thread");
6           aNewThread.start();
7       }
8   }
```

Implementing *Runnable*

In Listing 17.3 we made TNewThread a subclass of thread. If we had wanted TNewThread to have some other base class (such as Applet) we couldn't have subclassed thread. We can get almost the same effect, however, by implementing Runnable. Listings 17.5 and 17.6 show a version of the demo program designed to implement Runnable rather than extending thread.

Getting to Thread's methods
from inside a Runnable class

By implementing **Runnable** we
can't override methods found in
Thread. We can always call them,
however, by calling them on
Thread.currentThread()
inside run().

LISTING 17.5 *TNewRunnable.java*–**This class now implements *Runnable***

```
1    class TNewRunnable implements Runnable
2    {
3      static final short kLimit = 1000;
4      private short fLimit = 0;
5
6      public void run()
7      {
8        while (fLimit++ < kLimit)
9        {
10          System.out.println("Current thread is " +
            Thread.currentThread().toString());
11          try
12          {
13            Thread.currentThread().sleep(10);
14          } catch (InterruptedException e) {
15            System.err.println("Child thread interrupted while
            sleeping.");
16            System.exit(1);
17          }
18        }
19      }
20    }
```

LISTING 17.6 *TNewThreadDemo4.java*–**This version doesn't give the new
object a name; we could add that to the class if we wanted**

```
1    public class TNewThreadDemo4
2    {
3      public static void main(String argv[])
4      {
5        TNewRunnable aNewRunnable = new TNewRunnable();
6        aNewRunnable.run();
7      }
8    }
```

In this version of the demo program we've changed line 6 of
TNewThreadDemo4 from start() to run(), because Runnables don't
have a start() method. We also removed the constructor in
TNewRunnable, because that class doesn't have a base class.

Writing Synchronized Classes

Remember that one of the major differences between threads and processes is that processes are protected from each other by the operating system. (Technically we say that different processes live in different address spaces.) Using threads, which have no such protection, allows us to get code up and running quickly, but there is a negative effect—one thread can access and even change data that another thread is sure "belongs to" it. The solution is to "synchronize" the threads.

When Threads Collide—Understanding the Need for Synchronization

The code in Listing 17.7 is designed to have two Threads fight over one object—in this case, a TextArea. This example is designed to simulate a (highly simplified) nuclear reactor. One Thread gradually pulls the control rods out—the other gradually slides them in. As long as both Threads get about the same amount of processor time, the rods will stay in one position. If they're pushed in too far, the reactor shuts down and millions of people go without electricity. If the rods are pulled too far out, the reactor overheats and goes into meltdown.

Think multithreaded

Experienced thread pogrammers encourage newcomers to "Think multithreaded." What they mean is to think about which data could be changed by more than one thread, and take steps to protect that data. The basic mechanism for protecting data in one thread from another is to synchronize the two threads.

LISTING 17.7 *TCollision.java*—This program is designed to have a data collision

```
1    import java.awt.*;
2    import java.applet.*;
3
4    public class TCollisionApplet extends Applet
5    {
6        java.awt.Panel fButtonPanel;
7        java.awt.Button fStartButton;
8        java.awt.Panel fMainPanel;
9        java.awt.TextArea fTextArea;
10       static final boolean kIn = true;
11       static final boolean kOut = false;
12
13       void started(java.awt.event.ActionEvent e)
14       {
```

continues...

LISTING 17.7 **Continued**

```
15          // the inThread moves the control rod in
16          // too far, and the power grid shuts down
17          TRodThread inThread = new TRodThread(kIn, fTextArea);
18          inThread.setPriority(Thread.NORM_PRIORITY);
19          inThread.start();
20
21          // the outThread moves the control rods out
22          // too far, and we go into meltdown
23          TRodThread outThread = new TRodThread(kOut, fTextArea);
24          outThread.setPriority(Thread.NORM_PRIORITY);
25          outThread.start();
26
27          fStartButton.setEnabled(false);
28      }
29
30      public void init()
31      {
32          super.init();
33          fButtonPanel = new java.awt.Panel();
34          fButtonPanel.setBounds(0, 240,426,21);
35          add(fButtonPanel);
36
37          fStartButton = new java.awt.Button("Start");
38          fButtonPanel.add(fStartButton);
39
40          fMainPanel = new java.awt.Panel();
41          add(fMainPanel);
42
43          fTextArea = new java.awt.TextArea();
44          fMainPanel.add(fTextArea);
45
46          // register listener
47          fStartButton.addActionListener(new
48            java.awt.event.ActionListener() {
49            public void
50              actionPerformed(java.awt.event.ActionEvent e) {
51              started;
52            }
53          });
```

```
54        }
55    }
56
57    class TRodThread extends Thread
58    {
59      static short fPosition = 10;
60      boolean fDirection;
61      static TextArea fTextArea;
62      short fUseCount = 0;
63
64      TRodThread(boolean theDirection, TextArea theTextArea)
65      {
66        if (fTextArea == null)
67          fTextArea = theTextArea;
68
69        fDirection = theDirection;
70      }
71      public void run()
72      {
73        String theDirectionString = fDirection ? "In" : "Out";
74        while (fPosition > 0 && fPosition < 20 && fUseCount < 1000)
75        {
76          if (fDirection)
77            fPosition++;
78          else
79            fPosition--;
80          fUseCount++;
81
82          // comment the next two lines of code out for a completely
83          // unexpected effect.
84          fTextArea.setText(String.valueOf(fUseCount) + " : " +
85            String.valueOf(fPosition) + "\n");
86        }
87        fTextArea.appendText("Final position = " +
88          String.valueOf(fPosition) + "\n");
89
90        fTextArea.appendText("Moved " + theDirectionString + " " +
91          String.valueOf(fUseCount) + " times.\n");
92      }
93    }
```

Analyzing *TCollisionApplet*

TCollisionApplet follows a familiar pattern. (Refer to Chapter 11 if you're not familiar with the Abstract Windowing Toolkit.) We start by defining a method (started) for handling a click on fStartButton. When the button is clicked, we'll make two new TRodThreads, one moving in, the other moving out. We set them both to the same priority, and start them within instants of each other. Then we disable the button to let the process run unimpeded.

To set up the Applet we add the button and a TextArea; then connect the listener to fStartButton.

Analyzing *TRodThread*

The interesting parts of this program are in TRodThread. Here's the run() method of that class, from Listing 17.7:

```
public void run()
{
String theDirectionString = fDirection ? "In" : "Out";
        while (fPosition > 0 && fPosition < 20 &&
➡fUseCount < 1000)
    {
      if (fDirection)
        fPosition++;
      else
        fPosition--;
    fUseCount++;

    // comment the next two lines of code out for a
    // completely unexpected effect.
    fTextArea.setText(String.valueOf(fUseCount) + " : "
    ➡+
        String.valueOf(fPosition) + "\n");
    }
    fTextArea.appendText("Final position = " +
      String.valueOf(fPosition) + "\n");

    fTextArea.appendText("Moved " + theDirectionString + "
    ➡" +
      String.valueOf(fUseCount) + " times.\n");
    }
```

When the TRodThread's run() method is called, it defines a String for use by the user interface, and then it begins to move the control rod in its assigned direction. (Recall that there are two threads—one moving the rod in, the other moving it out.)

After 1,000 trips through the loop, the applet exits and reports its results. (It also exits early if the rod moves too far in or out.)

Initially, we'll put a line in to write the current fUseCount and fPosition to fTextArea, in order to help us test out the code. Figure 17.4 shows the results.

Be sure to parameterize real code

In this simple example I've used "magic numbers" such as 0 and 20. For production code you'd want to place these numbers in named constants such as **kInnerTravelLimit**, or in a JavaBeans property.

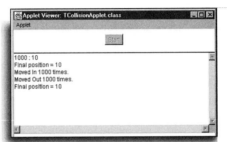

FIGURE 17.4

The program has run through 1,000 iterations and the control rod is stable.

As we continue to test, however, we notice that from time to time the results displayed in fTextArea are scrambled. Figure 17.5 shows one such occurrence. What has happened is that both Threads have been told to write their results to the same fTextArea. When they both start writing at once, the results look something like Figure 17.5.

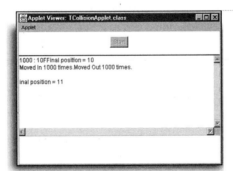

FIGURE 17.5

Sometimes the two threads try to write to the TextArea at the same time.

Protecting Critical Sections of Code

Beware of static data in a Runnable class

The static keyword on fTextArea in TRodThread is a warning sign; remember that static variables are shared among all the instances of a class. If the class is **Runnable** then multiple threads may read or write the common variable.

Threads can collide whenever two or more threads have free access to the same data. In this case there are two instances of TRodThread: inThread and outThread. Both instances are allowed to write to the same fTextArea.

The solution is to ensure that only one TRodThread has access to fTextArea at a time. Java includes a keyword—synchronized—that restricts access to a single thread.

We can rewrite the last lines of run() so that they read as follows:

```
synchronized(fTextArea)
{
   fTextArea.appendText("Final position = " +
       String.valueOf(fPosition) + "\n");

   fTextArea.appendText("Moved " + theDirectionString + " " +
       String.valueOf(fUseCount) + " times.\n");
}
```

Keep your critical sections short

Code protected in this way is called a *critical section*. The shorter your critical sections, the higher performance you'll get from your code.

Now when one TRodThread enters this critical section it "seizes" fTextArea. If the other Thread attempts to enter this section of code, it blocks at the synchronized statement until the first Thread exits the block.

Protecting Entire Methods

As you work your way through your Threads looking for critical sections, you need to ask yourself two questions—how big is the critical section and what is the shared resource. Place the curly braces of the synchronized statement around the critical section, and place the name of the shared resource object inside the parentheses of the synchronized statement.

If you find that the critical section is equivalent to an entire method, and the shared resource is the entire object, you can simply synchronize the method. For example, you might write the following:

```
synchronized void myMethod()
{
```

```
    . . .
}
```

This code is entirely equivalent to this:

```
void myMethod()
{
  synchronized (this)
  {
  ...
  }
}
```

Rendezvousing with *wait()* and *notify()*

Remember that in Chapter 8, "Object-Oriented Design and Programming," we talked task rendezvous. Two tasks (threads in Java parlance) rendezvous to synchronize their behavior or exchange information. We've just looked at the `synchronize()` statement, which offers one form of rendezvous. You can get more fine-grained control by using two `Object` methods: `wait()` and `notify()`. When you write the following your thread will block until someone calls `notify()` on that `Object`:

```
myObject.wait();
```

Here, in more detail, is what happens:

1. Your thread gains ownership of the `Object`'s monitor. We'll look at how you do that in just a moment.

2. You call `wait()` on the specified `Object`.

3. As a result of calling `wait()` you give up ownership of the `Object`'s monitor and block at the `wait()` statement.

4. Some time later some other thread gains ownership of that `Object`'s monitor and calls `notify()`.

5. The Java runtime environment notifies one thread that is waiting for that `Object`. If yours is that thread, you unblock.

6. As soon as you're able to regain ownership of the monitor, your thread's execution proceeds.

If you don't have ownership of the `Object`'s monitor before you

Remember that `Threads` need to sleep

Once you're satisfied with the behavior of `TRodThread`, go ahead and take out the diagnostic `println()`. When you do, you'll get a surprising result—one thread has completely starved the other. You'll need to add a call to `sleep()` or `yield()` to `run()` in order to make the threads give up time to each other again.

Use notifyAll() if you want to unblock everyone waiting on an Object

Object supports another method–**notifyAll()**–that sends out enough notifications to unblock all of the **Threads** waiting on a given object.

You're not limited to blocking rendezvous

If you want you can ensure that your thread is not left waiting forever. Call the one-argument or two-argument version of **wait()**–they both allow you to specify a timeout.

call **wait()** or **notify()**, you'll get an **IllegalMonitorStateException**. In order to gain ownership of an **Object**'s monitor, you must do one of three things:

- Call a synchronized instance method of that **Object**.
- Execute the body of a **synchronized** statement that synchronizes that **Object**.
- Execute a synchronized static method (but only if the **Object** is of type **Class**).

What About Deadlock?

The longer you work with concurrent systems the more bizarre occurrences you'll see. Many of these mishaps occur because of a phenomenon known as deadlock, which is usually illustrated by something called the Dining Philosophers Problem.

Suppose a group of philosophers has a dinner table set as shown in Figure 17.6. There is one chopstick between each plate. If two adjacent philosophers attempt to eat at the same time, they collide on the shared chopstick and neither is able to eat.

Philosophers have only two states—eating and thinking. Suppose that the table is empty. A philosopher moves into position A, seizes the two chopsticks on either size of his plate, and begins to dine. Sometime later a second philosopher arrives and takes position C. She has two chopsticks, so she can eat. While the first two philosophers are still at the table, a third philosopher moves into position B. This person will have to wait until the first two philosophers are through eating before he will have chopsticks available.

What happens if a philosopher moves into position E, and a moment later another philosopher sits down at position F? The philosopher at position E can eat, but the one at position F needs to wait for the philosopher at position E to finish. The waiting philosopher at F seizes the *one* chopstick available and holds onto it.

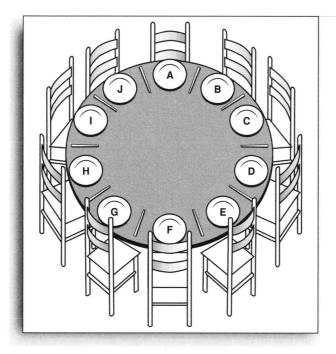

FIGURE 17.6

In a computer system, the philosophers represent tasks and the chopsticks represent resources.

Now another diner joins the table at position D. He, too, is unable to eat, because the chopstick between D and E is in use by the philosopher at position E. As soon as the diner at C leaves, the diner at position D seizes the chopstick he shared with her.

As time goes on you may eventually get to the point where every position at the table is filled, and each philosopher holds one chopstick. Unless someone is willing to give up his or her chopstick, no one can eat. The table is said to be *deadlocked*.

Deadlock is an important problem in computer science. If you design complex concurrent systems in which deadlock is a real possibility, you should review the computer science literature on the subject and become familiar with known ways of preventing, detecting, and breaking a deadlock. For most simple systems with just a few threads, you don't need to be too concerned about deadlock.

Deadlock is also known as "the deadly embrace"

Sometimes you'll find deadlock referred to in computer science literature as "the deadly embrace." It's the same phenomenon, but with a more colorful name.

The Great Thread Race—A Multithreading Example

In Chapter 25 of *Special Edition Using Java* (Que, 1996) Joseph Weber shows a program he calls "The Great Thread Race." That program was written back when JDK 1.0 was current—it relied upon now-deprecated methods such as stop(). This section shows an enhanced version of the Great Thread Race, updated to take advantage of JDK 1.2.

The Great Thread Race illustrates the fact that, in JDK 1.2 as in JDK 1.0, the behavior of the JVM scheduler varies widely. The Thread Race starts two or more threads—the racers. Each racer places a colored oval on the screen and begins to advance it to the right. In our version we give each racer a different priority, with priorities increasing as you move down the screen.

Figure 17.7 shows the behavior you'd expect to see. Thread 0, at the top of the screen, is running at MIN_PRIORITY. Thread 4, at the bottom, is running at MIN_PRIORITY + 4. Each thread in the middle—Threads 1, 2, and 3—is running at MIN_PRIORITY plus its thread number. Since a higher priority means the scheduler should allocate more processing time to a thread, we're not surprised to see that Thread 4 has pulled away from the others and is winning the race. However, it's a bit surprising that Thread 3 isn't doing better than Thread 2, and that Threads 1 and 0 are tied. This behavior is a characteristic of the JVM—in this case the Windows NT JVM from JDK 1.2.

FIGURE 17.7

This version of the Great Thread Race is running on the JDK 1.2 Virtual Machine.

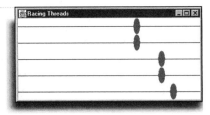

Figure 17.8 shows the same program running as a applet in AppletViewer. In this case the difference between the threads is not nearly as dramatic. Threads 0 and 1 are tied, as are Threads 2, 3, and 4. Once again, this kind of variation is typical when you change from one JVM to another—you should avoid writing code that depends heavily upon differing priorities.

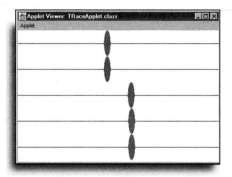

FIGURE 17.8

This version of the Great Thread Race is running on the JDK 1.2 AppletViewer.

The biggest surprises come from the two commercial Web browsers. Figures 17.9 and 17.10 show the same applet running under Netscape Navigator 4 and Microsoft Internet Explorer 4, respectively. In both cases there is no significant difference in the performance of any of the threads. What's even more interesting is that each of these four races was run on the same machine—a Windows NT Workstation—so the differences are caused entirely by differences in the JVMs, not in the underlying operating system.

Our version of the race is implemented as a program that will run as an applet or an application. It listens to MouseEvents, so you can pause all of the threads with a mousePress. The racers are in their own Runnable class—TRacer—but their threads are set up in the calling class, TRaceApplet.

Use threads, but don't rely on priorities

You'll have a better user interface if you use threads, and will make better use of the processor. You can even set thread priority in order to give the JVM some relative guidance. Just don't write a program that depends upon a particular behavior in response to those priorities.

FIGURE 17.9

When run in Navigator 4.04, thread priority seems to have no effect.

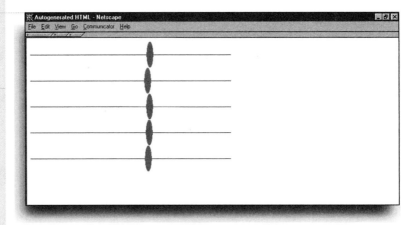

FIGURE 17.10

Microsoft's browser gives only a slight advantage to the high-priority thread.

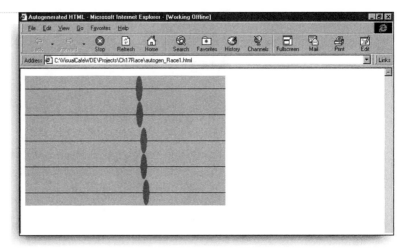

Walking Through *TRaceApplet*

Listing 17.8 shows TRaceApplet. Note that, despite the name, this program has a main() method and can be run as an application.

LISTING 17.8 *TRaceApplet*–This program sets up the user interface and starts the race

```
1   import java.applet.Applet;
2   import java.awt.Graphics;
3   import java.awt.GridLayout;
4
```

```
5    public class TRaceApplet extends Applet implements Runnable,
     TSuspendable
6    {
7      private TRacer fRacers[];
8      static private short fRacerCount = 0;
9      private Thread fThreads[];
10     static private Thread fMonitorThread;
11     static private boolean fInApplet = true;
12     private boolean fThreadSuspended = false;
13     static private java.awt.Frame fFrame = null;
14     private TWindowAdapter fWindowAdapter = null;
15
16     public void init()
17     {
18       if (fInApplet)
19       {
20        String theParameter = getParameter("NUMBER");
21         if (theParameter == null)
22           fRacerCount = 0;
23         else
24           fRacerCount = Short.parseShort(theParameter);
25       }
26       if (fRacerCount <= 0)
27         fRacerCount = 2;
28       if (fRacerCount > Thread.MAX_PRIORITY -
       Thread.MIN_PRIORITY + 1)
29           fRacerCount = (short)(Thread.MAX_PRIORITY -
       Thread.MIN_PRIORITY + 1);
30
31           if (!fInApplet)
32         fWindowAdapter = new TWindowAdapter();
33
34       // have one column, with one row per Racer
35       setLayout(new GridLayout(fRacerCount, 1));
36
37       // initialize the fRacers and fThreads arrays
38       fRacers = new TRacer[fRacerCount];
39       fThreads = new Thread[fRacerCount];
40
41       for (short i=0; i<fRacerCount; i++)
42       {
43         fRacers[i] = new TRacer("Racer# " + i, this);
```

continues…

LISTING 17.8 Continued

```
44
45         // scale the image so that all of the racers will fit
46         fRacers[i].setSize(getSize().width,
         getSize().height/fRacerCount);
47         add(fRacers[i]);
48       }
49     }
50
51    public void start()
52    {
53      // set up our own "monitor" thread
54      fMonitorThread = new Thread(null, this,
      "Monitor Thread");
55      fMonitorThread.start();
56    }
57
58    public void stop()
59    {
60      fMonitorThread = null;
61    }
62
63    public void run()
64    {
65      if (fMonitorThread == Thread.currentThread())
66      {
67        TMouseAdapter aMouseAdapter = new TMouseAdapter();
68        for (short i=0; i<fRacerCount;i++)
69        {
70          // this version of the Thread constructor specifies a
            // Runnable target
71          fThreads[i] = new Thread(fRacers[i]);
72
73          // should guarantee that the high-number thread wins
74          fThreads[i].setPriority(Thread.MIN_PRIORITY+i);
75          fThreads[i].start();
76          fRacers[i].addMouseListener(aMouseAdapter);
77        }
78        synchronized (fMonitorThread)
79        {
80          fMonitorThread.notify();
```

```
81          }
82        }
83
84        // now the world knows that all the racers are running
85        while (fMonitorThread == Thread.currentThread())
86        try
87        {
88          fMonitorThread.sleep(100);
89          synchronized(fMonitorThread)
90          {
91            while (fThreadSuspended)
92            {
93              fMonitorThread.wait();
94            }
95            synchronized(this)
96            {
97              notifyAll();
98            }
99          }
100       } catch (InterruptedException e)
101       {
102         System.err.println("The monitor thread was interrupted
            while sleeping.");
103         System.exit(1);
104       }
105     }
106
107     public String[][] getParameterInfo()
108     {
109      short theMaximumNumberOfThreads =
         (short)(Thread.MAX_PRIORITY - Thread.MIN_PRIORITY + 1);
110      String theParameterInfo[][] =
111      {
112        {"NUMBER",     "1-"+theMaximumNumberOfThreads,
          "number of racers"},
113      };
114      return theParameterInfo;
115     }
116
117     public String getAppletInfo()
118     {
119       String theAppletInfo = "Author: Michael L. Morgan\nDate:
```

continues…

LISTING 17.8 **Continued**

```
         19 March 98\nInspired by the Great Thread Race
         (Special Edition Using Java, Que, 1996, p. 551)";
120        return theAppletInfo;
121      }
122
123      public boolean isSuspended()
124      {
125        return fThreadSuspended;
126      }
127
128      public static void main(String argv[])
129      {
130        fInApplet = false;
131
132        //look for the number of racers on the command line
133        if (argv.length>0)
134        try {
135          fRacerCount = Short.parseShort(argv[0]);
136        } catch (NumberFormatException e)
137        {
138          fRacerCount = 5;
139        }
140
141        fFrame = new java.awt.Frame("Racing Threads");
142
143        TRaceApplet theRace = new TRaceApplet();
144        fFrame.setSize(400,200);
145        fFrame.add(theRace, java.awt.BorderLayout.CENTER);
146        fFrame.show();
147        theRace.init();
148
149        // be sure to wait until after init() to hook up listener
150        fFrame.addWindowListener(theRace.fWindowAdapter);
151        fFrame.pack();
152        theRace.start();
153
154        // don't pass here till all racers are started
155        synchronized (fMonitorThread)
156        {
157          try {
158            fMonitorThread.wait();
```

```
159        } catch (InterruptedException e)
160        {
161          System.err.println("Main thread interrupted while
           waiting for racers to start.");
162          System.exit(1);
163        }
164      }
165      System.out.println("And they're off!");
166
167      // wait till all the racers are finished
168      for (short i=0; i<fRacerCount; i++)
169      try
170      {
171        theRace.fThreads[i].join();
172      } catch (InterruptedException e)
173      {
174          System.err.println("The monitor thread was interrupted
           while waiting for the other threads to exit.");
175      }
176      System.exit(0);
177    }
178
179  class TWindowAdapter extends java.awt.event.WindowAdapter
180  {
181    public void windowClosing(java.awt.event.WindowEvent
         anEvent)
182    {
183      fFrame.setVisible(false);
184      fFrame.dispose();
185      System.exit(0);
186    }
187  }
188  class TMouseAdapter extends java.awt.event.MouseAdapter
189  {
190    public synchronized void mousePressed(
         java.awt.event.MouseEvent anEvent)
191    {
192      anEvent.consume();
193      fThreadSuspended = !fThreadSuspended;
194      if (!fThreadSuspended)
195        synchronized (fMonitorThread)
196        {
```

continues…

LISTING 17.8 Continued

```
197              fMonitorThread.notifyAll();
198          }
199      }
200    }
201  }
```

Let's begin by looking at how TRaceApplet runs when it's called as an Applet. In the declaration it implements both Runnable and TSuspendable. We'll see how TSuspendable's one method—isSuspended()—is implemented in just a moment.

This class has four class variables and four instance variables. The class variables are as follows:

- fRacerCount The number of racers, loaded from a <PARAM> tag or a command-line parameter.
- fMonitorThread A thread that starts all the racer threads.
- fInApplet A Boolean that tells us whether we were started as an applet or an application.
- fFrame The Frame, for use by the application version.

Each instance has these four variables:

- fRacers[] An array of TRacer objects.
- fThreads[] The threads for the TRacers.
- fThreadSuspended A Boolean to keep track of the mousePress.
- fWindowAdapter A custom WindowListener to handle the windowClosing message.

Understanding *init()*

Recall from Chapter 3, "Getting Started Fast," that an applet's init() method is called when it is first loaded into the Web browser. Here's the init() method of TRaceApplet (from Listing 17.8):

```
public void init()
{
  if (fInApplet)
    {
```

```
    String theParameter = getParameter("NUMBER");
    if (theParameter == null)
      fRacerCount = 0;
        else
      fRacerCount = Short.parseShort(theParameter);
  }
  if (fRacerCount <= 0)
    fRacerCount = 2;
  if (fRacerCount > Thread.MAX_PRIORITY -
➥Thread.MIN_PRIORITY + 1)
    fRacerCount = (short)(Thread.MAX_PRIORITY -
➥Thread.MIN_PRIORITY + 1);

  if (!fInApplet)
    fWindowAdapter = new TWindowAdapter();

  // have one column, with one row per Racer
  setLayout(new GridLayout(fRacerCount, 1));

  // initialize the fRacers and fThreads arrays
  fRacers = new TRacer[fRacerCount];
  fThreads = new Thread[fRacerCount];

  for (short i=0; i<fRacerCount; i++)
  {
    fRacers[i] = new TRacer("Racer# " + i, this);

    // scale the image so that all of the racers will fit
    fRacers[i].setSize(getSize().width,
➥getSize().height/fRacerCount);
    add(fRacers[i]);
  }
}
```

We initialized fInApplet to be true—we reset it to false in
main()—so the program knows that it's being run as an applet.
In its capacity as an applet it looks for the HTML <PARAM> tag
named NUMBER. If the program finds the tag, it uses it to get the
number of racers.

Listing 17.9 shows an HTML file that takes advantage of this
feature.

Let your applets run as applications

Whenever possible, I recommend that you include code
such as main() (shown in
TRaceApplet) in your
own Applets. That way you
can run your program as an
applet or as an application.
You'll want to run as an application when you regression test,
and perhaps if you later reuse
the code.

LISTING 17.9 *autogen_Race1.html*—**This HTML was originally written by Visual Café from Symantec**

```
 1  <HTML>
 2  <HEAD>
 3  <TITLE>Autogenerated HTML</TITLE>
 4  </HEAD>
 5  <BODY>
 6  <APPLET CODE="TRaceApplet.class" WIDTH=430 HEIGHT=270>
 7  <PARAM NAME="NUMBER" VALUE="5">
 8  </APPLET>
 9  </BODY>
10  </HTML>
```

If no readable <PARAM NAME="NUMBER"> tag is found, the program defaults to two racers. The following lines serve to limit the number of racers to the maximum number of discrete priority levels available, since the whole point of this program is to demonstrate the effect of priorities (or lack thereof):

```
if (fRacerCount > Thread.MAX_PRIORITY -
➡Thread.MIN_PRIORITY + 1)
      fRacerCount = (short)(Thread.MAX_PRIORITY -
➡Thread.MIN_PRIORITY + 1);
```

If we're not in an applet, the code in lines 31 and 32 serve to hook up the WindowListener, so that we'll handle windowClosing messages correctly.

Next we set up our layout and our arrays, and begin the process of building the user interface. We'll look at the TRacer constructor when we walk through the TRacer class. A TRacer is a java.awt.Canvas that implements Runnable, so we can resize it and add it to the current layout.

SEE ALSO

➢ *Learn more about* init(), start(), *and* stop(), *page 101*

Understanding *start()*

As we saw earlier in the chapter, threads can wait for Objects until they're notified that the Object has changed. Here's start() for TRacerApplet:

```
public void start()
{
  // set up our own "monitor" thread
  fMonitorThread = new Thread(null, this, "Monitor Thread");
  fMonitorThread.start();
}
```

We use fMonitorThread to start all of the TRacer threads, and then use it as the mechanism by which we rendezvous with those threads in order to implement the suspend and resume feature.

We instantiate fMonitorThread in start() via the three-parameter version of the thread constructor. We've set Threadgroup to null, so fMonitorThread is part of the same Threadgroup as TRaceApplet. We set the target to this, so fMonitorThread.start() will transfer control to TRaceApplet's version of run(). Finally, we give the Thread a name: Monitor Thread. The next line calls the new thread's start() method, and transfers control to run().

Understanding *stop()*

Earlier versions of the JDK included a Thread.stop() method that simply stopped the specified thread. Sun has determined that calling stop() without giving it an opportunity to clean up is a bad idea—it can leave some objects in an inconsistent state—so it has deprecated stop(). We can get a similar effect safely by simply setting fMonitorThread to null. We'll see how to use this technique when we look at run(), next.

Using *run()* to Centralize Control

As we've seen TRaceApplet is primarily responsible for setting up the user interface. It then transfers control to a new thread—fMonitorThread—in start(). Now control in the new thread passes to run()—from here, we actually start and monitor the race. Here's run():

```
public void run()
{
  if (fMonitorThread == Thread.currentThread())
  {
    TMouseAdapter aMouseAdapter = new TMouseAdapter();
```

> **Follow the design principle of "least surprise"**
>
> While its good to allow the HTML author who uses your applet to modify its behavior through <PARAM> tags, make sure your program works correctly for the HTML author who uses no <PARAM> tags. Then document the parameters you support externally in your applet's documentation, and internally through getParameterInfo() and getAppletInfo(), described later in this section.

```
for (short i=0; i<fRacerCount;i++)
{
  // this version of the Thread constructor specifies
➥a Runnable target
    fThreads[i] = new Thread(fRacers[i]);

    // should guarantee that the high-number thread wins
➥fThreads[i].setPriority(Thread.MIN_PRIORITY+i);
    fThreads[i].start();
    fRacers[i].addMouseListener(aMouseAdapter);
  }
  synchronized (fMonitorThread)
  {
    fMonitorThread.notify();
  }
}


// now the world knows that all the racers are running
while (fMonitorThread == Thread.currentThread())
try
{
  fMonitorThread.sleep(100);
  synchronized(fMonitorThread)
  {
    while (fThreadSuspended)
    {
      fMonitorThread.wait();
    }
    synchronized(this)
    {
      notifyAll();
    }
  }
} catch (InterruptedException e)
{
  System.err.println("The monitor thread was inter
➥rupted while sleeping.");
  System.exit(1);
}
}
```

In run() we first verify that we've got the correct thread. While we don't strictly need this line for this program, this double-check could save a maintenance programmer some grief when she implements more threads in TRaceApplet later. Next we set up a MouseListener to detect mousePressed, since we want to pause and resume the race on mousePressed.

Since the layout manager is full of TRacer objects, it's the TRacers and not the Applet that get MouseEvents. We build one MouseListener (aMouseAdapter) and attach it to each TRacer.

We also use the occasion of the for loop to make each new racer's thread, to assign the thread's priority, and to start the thread. Look at the line that constructs the Thread:

```
fThreads[i] = new Thread(fRacers[i]);
```

This single-parameter version of the thread constructor takes a Runnable target—the instance of TRacer. This design means that start will transfer control to TRacer's version of run(), and not our own.

As we'll see in a moment, we don't want to join() with these TRacer threads and wait for them to die until we know for certain that they've started. We're using fMonitorThread itself as the notification object, so we take ownership of fMonitorThread and send the notification out.

Now that all of the racers are running and the main thread is waiting for all of the threads to die, what should fMonitorThread do? The short answer is "sleep()," mostly, but fMonitorThread is also responsible for sending out suspend and resume notices to the racers. Once again we synchronize on fMonitorThread—then we say

```
while (fThreadSuspended)
{
  fMonitorThread.wait();
}
```

We'll see how fThreadSuspended can be set and unset in a moment, when we look at TMouseAdapter. For now it's enough to know that if someone wants us to suspend, we wait for fMonitorThread to be notified.

Set the Thread to null instead of calling stop()

Instead of calling Thread.stop(), Sun recommends that you set a stopping thread to null. I wrote the following in TRaceApplet:

```
public void stop()

{

  fMonitorThread =
null;

}
```

Since fMonitorThread will no longer match Thread.currentThread () in run(), the thread stops running and becomes a candidate for the garbage collector.

Leave "hooks" for features you might want to add later

This design allows us the flexibility of using more than one MouseListener later if we decide that we want to take a different action for each TRacer. For example, in some future design, we might use mousePressed to suspend just *one* racer, or to change that racer's priority on the run. We ensure that we have that flexibility by giving each TRacer its own MouseListener.

Consider including getParameterInfo() and getAppletInfo() in all of your applets

Your applets will be more useful if the user can customize them. Consider making as many features as possible configurable by the user, and set reasonable defaults for the HTML author who doesn't use any <PARAM> tags. Then document the general approach in getAppletInfo() and provide specifics for each parameter in getParameterInfo().

If fThreadSuspended is reset to false, we drop out of the while loop, synchronize on TRaceApplet, and send out a notice to all of the children. We'll look at how the children knew to suspend when we walk through TRacer.

Improving the User Interface with *getParameterInfo()* and *getAppletInfo()*

As professional programmers we're often writing components that will be reused by others. We'll see one Java approach to component software in Chapter 19, "Building Components with JavaBeans," but it's important not to forget that to HTML authors Applets are components. By adding getParameterInfo() and getAppletInfo() we make it easier for HTML authors to use our Applets correctly. Figure 17.11 shows the applet and parameter information as displayed by AppletViewer.

FIGURE 17.11

Choose **Info** from the **Applet** menu in AppletViewer to see the applet and parameter information.

Using *isSuspended()* as a Rendezvous Mechanism

isSuspended()is the smallest method in the program, but it might be one of the most important. This method, required by our TSuspendable interface, allows the racers to see whether or not TRaceApplet is suspended. We'll see how this mechanism works when we look at TRacer in a moment.

Running as an Application: Understanding *main()*

If the program is being run as an application then control initially passes to main(). There are three principal differences between the application version of this program and the applet version (though the same code can be both at different times). Table 17.1 summarizes these differences.

TABLE 17.1 *TRaceApplet* **may be run as an applet or as an application**

Difference	Applet	Application
Source of parameters	<PARAM> tag	Command line
Container	Browser window	Frame
Behavior upon exit	Finished race remains visible in browser window	Window is closed

After we initialize fRacerCount we set up a frame and the applet in a way that's become familiar. The next nine lines of main() complete the setup of the user interface, including the hookup of the WindowListener.

Note that it's possible to start() the applet and then call join() before the racers have even started. We synchronized on fMonitorThread and wait for that Object to notify us that it's OK to proceed into the joins. Since we know that run() sends one notification after all of the racers are started, we only wait for a single notification—not one from each racer.

As we saw in Figures 17.7 through 17.10 there's no guarantee which thread will win the race, so we join() with each of them. We won't exit until every racer is in.

SEE ALSO

➤ *Learn more about adding a* main() *method to an applet, page 438*

Using Adapters to Listen for *Events*

Inner class TWindowAdapter is now familiar to us—we saw this approach first in Chapter 11. TMouseAdapter is based on a similar design—when we get a mousePressed message, we remove the Event (since we're about to handle it). Then we invert fThreadSuspended. If it were true, it becomes false, and vice versa. This way, each mousePress has the effect of alternately stopping and starting the race.

Even a simple Applet can have a sophisticated user interface

To make your applets seem friendlier to the user, think about ways the user might interact with the applet. What should happen if the user clicks on some part of your applet? Once you've decided how to handle mouseclicks and other actions, add methods like isSuspended() to implement that behavior.

Once again, don't make assumptions about thread priority

As we saw in Figure 17.7 through Figure 17.10, there's no guarantee which thread will win the race. Take care when you write your programs that you don't implicitly assume that one thread will always finish ahead of the others. Be prepared to wait until the last thread is done—whichever thread that may be.

There are lots of Threads watching for fThreadSuspended to change, and fMonitorThread is the Object responsible for dispatching the notification. We take ownership of fMonitorThread and send the notification to all of the waiting Threads.

SEE ALSO

➤ *Learn more about adapters in "AWT Basics," page 274*

Walking Through *TRacer*

Compared to TRaceApplet, TRacer is relatively simple. It puts up a user interface (a line with a colored oval), advances the oval from left to right as it runs, and suspends and restarts upon command. Listing 17.10 shows this code.

LISTING 17.10 *TRacer.java–TRacer* **is a** *Runnable Canvas* **and is responsible for its own user interface**

```
 1  import java.awt.Graphics;
 2  import java.awt.Color;
 3
 4  public class TRacer extends java.awt.Canvas implements
    Runnable
 5  {
 6    private short fPosition = 0;
 7    private String fName;
 8    static private final short kNumberOfSteps = 1000;
 9    TSuspendable fAncestor;
10
11    public TRacer(String theName, TSuspendable theAncestor)
12    {
13      fName = new String(theName);
14      fAncestor = theAncestor;
15    }
16
17    public TRacer(String theName)
18    {
19      fName = new String(theName);
20      fAncestor = null;
21    }
```

```
22
23    public synchronized void paint(Graphics g)
24    {
25      g.setColor(Color.black);
26      g.drawLine(0,getSize().height/2, getSize().width,
      getSize().height/2);
27      g.setColor(Color.red);
28      g.fillOval(fPosition*getSize().width/kNumberOfSteps, 0,
      15, getSize().height);
29    }
30
31    public void run()
32    {
33      while (fPosition < kNumberOfSteps)
34      {
35        fPosition++;
36        repaint();
37        try
38        {
39          Thread.currentThread().sleep(10);
40          if (fAncestor != null)
41          {
42            synchronized (fAncestor)
43            {
44              if (fAncestor.isSuspended())
45                fAncestor.wait();
46            }
47          }
48        } catch (InterruptedException e)
49        {
50          System.err.println("Thread " + fName + " interrupted.");
51          System.exit(1);
52        }
53      }
54      System.out.println("Thread " + fName + " has finished
      the race.");
55    }
56
57    public static void main(String argv[])
58    {
59    java.awt.Frame theFrame = new java.awt.Frame("One Racer");
```

continues…

LISTING 17.10 **Continued**

```
60    TRacer aRacer = new TRacer("Test");
61    theFrame.setSize(400,200);
62    theFrame.add(aRacer, java.awt.BorderLayout.CENTER);
63    theFrame.show();
64    aRacer.paint(theFrame.getGraphics());
65    theFrame.pack();
66    aRacer.run();
67    System.exit(0);
68  }
69  }
```

TRacer has three instance variables and one constant. The constant, kNumberOfSteps, determines how long the racer's course is. The instance variables are as follows:

- fPosition The racer's position along its course.

- fName The racer's name.

- fAncestor A reference to the Container that manages the race—in this case, TRaceApplet. Note that we don't require this ancestor to be an applet; it can be any container that implements our TSuspendable interface (shown in Listing 17.11).

LISTING 17.11 *TSuspendable.java*—Use this interface to ensure that the ancestor is suspendable

```
1    public interface TSuspendable
2    {
3      public boolean isSuspended();
4    }
```

SEE ALSO
➤ *Learn more about using an interface as a type, page 233*

Understanding *TRacer*'s Constructors

Our implementation of TRacer includes two constructors:

```
public TRacer(String theName, TSuspendable theAncestor)
{
```

```
  fName = new String(theName);
  fAncestor = theAncestor;
}


public TRacer(String theName)
{
  fName = new String(theName);
  fAncestor = null;
 }
```

One constructor provided for TRacer takes a String name and a TSuspendable ancestor. The other takes only the name and sets the fAncestor to null. This second version is used by the test interface in main().

SEE ALSO

➤ *Learn more about adding* main() *to your classes, page 438*

*paint*ing the User Interface

Each time TRacer is repainted the colored oval must be drawn in the correct location. As we'll see in a moment, run() is responsible for advancing fPosition from zero to the maximum value at kNumberOfSteps. paint() actually redraws the racers. Here's paint() again, from Listing 17.10:

```
public synchronized void paint(Graphics g)
{
  g.setColor(Color.black);
  g.drawLine(0,getSize().height/2, getSize().width,
➥getSize().height/2);
  g.setColor(Color.red);
  g.fillOval(fPosition*getSize().width/kNumberOfSteps,
➥0, 15, getSize().height);
}
```

What does TRacer's paint() do?

TRacer's paint() method is responsible for drawing the line (for the racing lane) and scaling the oval's position based on the width and height of the canvas and the value of kNumberOfSteps.

Running the *TRacer*

When fMonitorThread back in TRaceApplet starts a new thread and transfers control to TRacer, TRacer's run() method is called. Since TRacer is a dedicated Runnable class, I don't bother checking to make sure we've got the right thread—I go right into running the race:

```
public void run()
{
  while (fPosition < kNumberOfSteps)
  {
    fPosition++;
    repaint();
    try
    {
      Thread.currentThread().sleep(10);
      if (fAncestor != null)
      {
        synchronized (fAncestor)
        {
          if (fAncestor.isSuspended())
            fAncestor.wait();
        }
      }
    } catch (InterruptedException e)
    {
        System.err.println("Thread " + fName +
  ➥" interrupted.");
        System.exit(1);
    }
  }
  System.out.println("Thread " + fName + " has
➥finished the race.");
}
```

The TRacer thread has three main responsibilities:

1. Increment the position (fPosition++).

2. Ask that the canvas be repainted (repaint()).

3. sleep for a while.

In addition, run() checks with fAncestor to see if it's been suspended. (That's why we care whether fAncestor is a TSuspendable.) If the ancestor has been suspended, each TRacer waits for its common ancestor to resume. When we look at main() in a moment, we'll see that our simple test interface doesn't bother with suspend and resume. We check to make sure fAncestor is not null, since the main() calls the single-parameter version of TRacer's constructor.

When the racer has finished the course, we print out a short message and exit. Remember that these Threads are actually in the fThreads array back in TRaceApplet, and the main() routine of TRaceApplet is waiting for all of the racers to finish and die. Once we exit run() the corresponding join() back in TRaceApplet will unblock. When all of the racers are done, TRaceApplet can exit.

Using *main()* as a Test Interface

As we saw in Chapter 16, "Testing and Debugging Java Code," its often convenient to give our classes a main() routine even if we don't plan to use them as an application in their own right. That's what this main() method is all about:

```
public static void main(String argv[])
{
  java.awt.Frame theFrame = new java.awt.Frame("One Racer");
  TRacer aRacer = new TRacer("Test");
  theFrame.setSize(400,200);
  theFrame.add(aRacer, java.awt.BorderLayout.CENTER);
  theFrame.show();
  aRacer.paint(theFrame.getGraphics());
  theFrame.pack();
 aRacer.run();
  System.exit(0);
}
```

We build a Frame and add one TRacer to it. Then we explicitly call run(). When the race is over, we call exit(). This simple technique allows us to exercise our TRacer class without relying upon the more complex TRaceApplet.

Practice defensive programming

In older languages such as C and C++ you would crash the program if you dereferenced a null pointer. In Java you won't crash, but you will get an exception that usually represents a programming error. Even if you're sure that a reference can "never" be null, assume that someone else will later reuse your code and make a mistake—check for null references and handle the error.

Communicating in Java: Streams and Sockets

Learn how to add basic I/O to your program

Find out how to work with byte-oriented streams

Learn how to bridge from byte streams to character streams

See how to implement simple network communication with the *URL* class

Learn how to use the *Socket* and *ServerSocket* interface when fine-grained control of the *Socket* is required

Write a simple client and server to serve as the basis for your own programs

Basic Communications with Streams

So far in this book, our applets and applications have resembled the design shown in Figure 18.1. We have a user interface and lots of self-contained data. Now we're going to add input and output (I/O), leading to the design shown in Figure 18.2.

FIGURE 18.1

Without I/O, your program is a closed box.

FIGURE 18.2

I/O gives your Java program access to your hard drive, the Web, and the rest of the Internet.

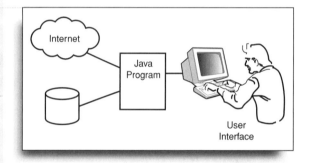

Applets are subject to security restrictions

Everything in this chapter applies both to applications and to applets. With applets, however, you must have special permission to read or write the hard drive, or to communicate anywhere on the network except the host from which the applet was loaded.

We'll begin this discussion by talking about generalized communications mechanisms called *streams* and *readers*. We'll use these facilities to read and write files on our hard drive. In the next section, "Connecting to the Internet: The URL Class," we'll look at a simple way to connect your program to existing Internet services. Finally, in "Low-Level Networking with the Socket Class," we'll explore how we can implement our own protocols and write our own special client and server.

A *stream* is a path of communication between a source of information and a destination. For our purposes, our Java program is at one end of the stream. If we're the source, the stream is an output stream. If we're the destination, we call the stream an input stream.

Readers and *writers* are analogous to streams, except for the fact that streams are based on bytes, and readers and writers are based on chars. In older languages such as C and C++, this distinction is not important. In Java, however, a char is a 16-bit entity designed to hold Unicode characters.

Writing Data with Output Streams

Figure 18.3 shows the OutputStream class hierarchy. Because all of the members of the OutputStream family are derived from one abstract class, we can learn many of the capabilities of the family by learning about any one class. In this section we'll start by exploring OutputStream itself, and then we'll look at its derived classes.

See java.io package for details

The stream, reader, and writer classes are all part of the java.io package. You can find complete documentation on each class, interface, and method in /docs/api/ Package-java-io. html in your JDK directory. You'll also need to import java.io.* or specify java.io as part of the class name in your code.

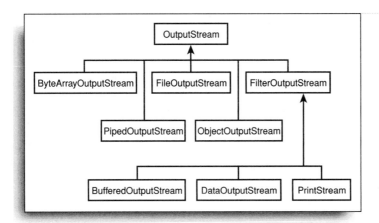

FIGURE 18.3
OutputStream itself is abstract, but has plenty of concrete-derived classes.

Exploring *OutputStream*

The most fundamental operation in OutputStream is write(). You can write an array of bytes, a "slice" of an array, or a single byte at a time. Here's an example:

```
OutputStream anOutputStream = someOutputStream;
byte[] someData = a buffer-full of data;

// write the first 100 bytes
anOutputStream.write(someData,0,100);

// write a single byte
```

```
anOutputStream.write((int)someData[0]);

// write out all of the data
anOutputStream.write(someData);
```

Note that nearly every method on every class in java.io can throw some form of IOException. To write your best code, wrap your I/O calls in try and catch statements.

Because ObjectStream is abstract, it can be connected to almost any kind of output device, from a network socket to a printer to a file. Depending upon the device, the data may be stored in a buffer before it is sent out. You can force the data to be copied from the buffer to the output device by calling flush().

When you're done with an OutputStream, you should call close(). This method explicitly releases all of the resources associated with the stream. If you don't call close(), the garbage collector may eventually reclaim the resources associated with a stream, but they are too scarce and too valuable for you to leave them for the garbage collector.

Using *ByteArrayOutputStream*

One place you can send your array of bytes is into your computer's local memory. The concrete stream that performs that task is ByteArrayOutputStream.

```
OutputStream anOutputStream = new ByteArrayOutputStream();
byte[] someData;

// fill someData with some data
someData = new byte[1024];
for (int i=0; i<1024; i++)
    someData[i] = i % 255;

// now write the data to the ByteArrayOutputStream
anOutputStream.write(someData);
```

ByteArrayOutputStream has two constructors. The no-argument version allocates a buffer with a 32-byte capacity. This capacity will grow if necessary, but asking for a few bytes at a time may fragment the available memory on some systems. If you know

Remember, ObjectStream is abstract

Because ObjectStream is abstract, I can't show you a constructor in this example. We'll see more tangible code when we look at the concrete classes coming up.

flush() has its limits

You can only flush() data that is stored in a buffer that's on your computer. If your data has been sent to an external buffer such as a printer buffer, flush() has no further effect.

Place I/O in its own thread

OutputStream.write() is a blocking call—the thread that calls it will be forced to sit and wait until the output is completed. (Similarly, InputStream.read() blocks are waiting for input.) You should put these calls into their own threads to avoid having your user interface "hang."

you're going to need, say, 1024 bytes, use the one-parameter version of the constructor:

```
OutputStream anOutputStream = new
ByteArrayOutputStream(1024);
```

In addition to the methods it inherits from OutputStream, ByteArrayOutputStream supports methods to read it into a new byte array, convert it to a string, or write the entire contents of the stream to a different stream.

Making a New File with *FileOutputStream*

One of the most useful things you can do with data is send it to the hard drive. Here's a code snippet that does just that:

```
OutputStream anOutputStream =
  new FileOutputStream("some/path/and/filename.dat");
byte[] someData;

// fill someData with some data
someData = new byte[1024];
for (int i=0; i<1024; i++)
  someData[i] = i % 255;

// now write the data to the ByteArrayOutputStream
anOutputStream.write(someData);
```

Adding Sophistication with *FilterOutputStream*

Some of the most powerful OutputStreams are subclasses of the FilterOutputStream class. These streams all have in common a constructor that takes another OutputStream as its parameter. In this way, they add functionality to a "lower-level" stream such as a FileOutputStream.

The three FilterOutputStream subclasses are

- BufferedOutputStream—An efficient version of OutputStream that writes bytes to an internal buffer that can be flushed to the underlying stream.

- DataOutputStream—A convenience class that gives you methods to write the Java primitive data types, such as writeShort(), writeChar(), and writeLong().

How useful is ByteArrayOutputStream?

You may be wondering how useful it can be to write data from a byte array into a byte array. You can use a ByteArrayOutputStream as a building block for more complex entities, including inter-process communications, or as a stand-in for other streams, such as network stream, during testing.

More constructors available

In addition to passing a platform-specific filename in a string, you can construct a new FileOutputStream from a File or FileDescriptor object. You can also append to an existing file by using FileOutputStream (*String*, true).

Treat FilterOutputStream as though it were abstract

FilterOutputStream is coded as concrete, but it adds no functionality to the stream you build on it. Don't bother to instantiate a FilterOutputStream object—only use its subclasses.

- `PrintStream`—A convenience class that offers two methods—`print()` and `println()`—that print the primitive data types onto the underlying stream.

Now we have enough classes and methods to write a simple but complete program. The program in Listing 18.1 implements the example we've been building throughout this section.

System.out and
System.err are
PrintStreams

You should recognize `print()`
and `println()`. We've been
using them throughout this book on
the built-in PrintStreams
known as `System.out` and
`System.err`.

LISTING 18.1 *TOutputDemo.java*—**This program writes to standard out**

```
1  import java.io.*;
2  public class TOutputDemo
3  {
4    public static void main(String argv[])
5    {
6      DataOutputStream theOutputStream;
7      try {
8        theOutputStream =
9          new DataOutputStream(new FileOutputStream("output.dat"));
10       int[] theData = new int[1024];
11       for (int i=0; i<1024; i++)
12         theData[i] = i;
13       for (int i=0; i<1024; i++)
14         theOutputStream.write(theData[i]);
15     } catch (IOException e) {
16       System.err.println("Exception: " + e.getMessage());
17       System.exit(1);
18     }
19   }
20 }
```

Implementing Interthread Communications with *PipedOutputStream*

Recall from Chapter 17, "Concurrent Programming with Threads," that threads differ from processes in that there is little built-in protection from other threads. You may want to design your multithreaded programs in such a way that you isolate each thread in its own class and then carefully identify places where threads need to communicate.

To allow one thread to write data to another, make an instance of `PipedOutputStream`, passing it a `PipedInputStream` as a parameter:

```
PipedInputStream theInputStream = new PipedInputStream();
PipedOutputStream theOutputStream =
  new PipedOutputStream( theInputStream );
```

Now, when you make a new thread, have one thread write to `theOutputStream`. The other thread will be able to read the contents from `theInputStream`.

SEE ALSO
➤ *Learn more about threads, page 454*

Writing Objects with the *ObjectOutputStream*

`ObjectOutputStream` works like one of the `FilterOutputStreams` in that you construct it by passing it an `OutputStream`. It supports primitive data type output methods such as `writeBoolean()` and `writeInt()`, just as `DataOutputStream` does, but it also supports `writeObject()`. By using `writeObject()`, you can output any Java object (because all objects are ultimately derived from `Object`). Thus, you can write

```
try {
  ObjectOutputStream theOutputStream =
    new ObjectOutputStream(new
    ➥FileOutputStream("objects.dat");
  theOutputStream.writeObject("This String is an Object.");
  theOutputStream.writeObject(new Date());
  theOutputStream.flush();
  theOutputStream.close();
} catch (IOException e) {
  System.err.println("Exception: " + e.getMessage());
}
```

Reading Data with Input Streams

Figure 18.4 shows the `InputStream` class hierarchy. Like `OutputStream`, all of the classes of `InputStream` are derived from one abstract class—in this case, `InputStream`. We'll look first at `InputStream` itself and then at the derived classes.

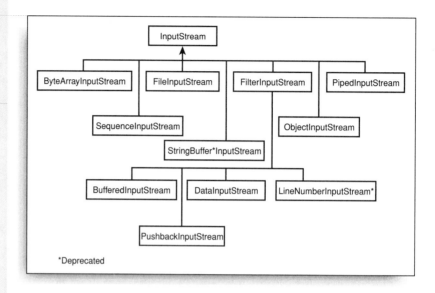

Examining *InputStream* Itself

The most important method in InputStream, of course, is read().
This method transfers bytes from the stream to an array. You can
write:

```
InputStream anInputStream = someInputStream;
byte[] someData = new byte[1024];
anInputStream.read(someData);
```

The method read() attempts to transfer a full buffer—in this
case 1024 bytes—from the InputStream to the array. The read()
method itself returns the number of characters actually transferred. (You can also call a zero-argument form of read(), which
attempts to transfer one byte.)

Just as with write() on OutputStream, there's a three-argument
version of read() that attempts to fill a slice of your buffer. If
you write

```
anInputStream.read(someData, 10, 100);
```

the InputStream will read data into someData, starting at index 10
and continuing for 100 bytes or until it runs out of data.

Detecting End-of-File

If you attempt to read past the end
of the file, read() returns a –1. It
also throws an EOFException.
Your code will be cleaner if you
catch the EOFException
instead of relying upon the status
code.

In addition to `read()`, `InputStream` supports six other methods:

- `available()`—Returns the number of characters that are available for reading before the `read()` blocks

- `close()`—Releases the resources associated with the stream

- `mark()`—Marks the current position in the stream

- `markSupported()`—Returns `true` if `mark()` and `reset()` have been implemented on this stream

- `reset()`—Repositions the stream back to the last mark

- `skip()`—Discards a specified number of characters from the stream

When you call `mark()`, the stream "remembers" all of the characters that you read until you call `reset()`. Then it repositions the stream so that subsequent `read()`s resume from the marked position. You can see that `mark()` and `reset()` require the stream to implement a memory—you specify the maximum size of that memory as a parameter to `mark()`.

The Subclasses of *InputStream*

The subclasses of `InputStream` are analogous to those of `OutputStream`. `ByteArrayInputStream` reads a `byte` array from memory; `FileInputStream` opens a file (specified by a `File`, `FileDescriptor`, or `String`). `FileInputStream` also supports the method `getFD()`, which returns the `FileDescriptor` of the open file.

`FilterInputStream` supports two subclasses analogous to those supported by `FilterOutputStream`: `BufferedInputStream` and `DataInputStream`. There is no input equivalent to `PrintStream`, although you can read input on the JDK 1.2 character-oriented streams described later in this section.

The `InputStream` family also supports a `PipedInputStream` (which communicates with the `PipedOutputStream` across thread boundaries) and an `ObjectInputStream` that can read Java `Objects` that have been written by `ObjectOutputStream`.

In addition to these classes, `InputStream` supports two stream types (plus two deprecated stream types) that have no `OutputStream` equivalent:

Pay attention to hardware considerations

For many applications, a stream is a stream; you can connect any source to any stream and the program will work. For high performance applications, however, you should take time to learn any hardware-specific optimizations that are possible. For example, if you're reading a disk file from a hard drive that buffers 4,096 bytes at a time, you may get a performance improvement from reading in multiples of 4,096.

Call `markSupported()` before using `mark()`

Most subclasses of `InputStream` don't fully support `mark()` and `reset()`. Before you call `mark()` and `reset()`, first call `markSupported()` to see if this stream supports those methods.

For best performance, use the most specific stream class possible

As Java matures, you can expect Sun to heavily optimize I/O classes such as the subclasses of `InputStream`. Use the most specific subclass that makes sense for your application in order to take advantage of that optimization. For example, if you know you're reading from the filesystem, use `FileInputStream` to take advantage of any buffering Sun has provided in that class to match the operating system's buffer sizes.

- `SequenceInputStream`—Builds one stream from a series of input streams. Constructors can accept either two `InputStreams` or an `Enumeration` of `InputStreams`

- `PushbackInputStream`—Allows you to "unread" a byte, a portion of the buffer, or the entire buffer

- `LineNumberInputStream`—Now deprecated

- `StringBufferInputStream`—Now deprecated

Using *ObjectOutputStream* and *ObjectInputStream*

Now that you've seen both `ObjectInputStream` and `ObjectOutputStream`, you can put them together to read and write your own objects. Suppose you have a class `TMedication`, illustrated in Figure 18.5.

FIGURE 18.5

`TMedication` contains a `String`, a `TStrength`, and another `String`.

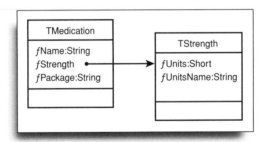

To write `TMedication` to an `ObjectOutputStream`, you could write

```
private void writeObject(ObjectOutputStream theOutputStream)
  throws IOException
{
  theOutputStream.writeObject(fName);
  theOutputStream.writeObject(fStrength);
  theOutputStream.writeObject(fPackage);
}
```

You could read the object back in by writing

```
private void readObject(ObjectInputStream theInputStream)
  throws IOException
{
  fName = theInputStream.readObject();
  fStrength = theInputStream.readObject();
  fPackage = theInputStream.readObject();
}
```

Of course, you'd also have to maintain a writeOut() and readIn() method for class TStrength. All of this could get tedious if you change the design of your classes often.

A better solution is to write your class's I/O methods like this:

```
private void writeObject(ObjectOutputStream theOutputStream)
  throws IOException
{
  theOutputStream.defaultWriteObject();
}
```

and

```
private void readObject(ObjectInputStream theInputStream)
  throws IOException
{
  fName = theInputStream.defaultReadObject();
}
```

These two methods search your Object for non-static, non-transient data members and write them out to the stream.

Character I/O with Readers and Writers

In addition to the hierarchies defined by OutputStream and InputStream, the JDK supports character streams that contain Unicode characters. Figures 18.6 and 18.7 illustrate the hierarchies for Writer (which is the character-oriented counterpart to OutputStream) and Reader (which is analogous to InputStream).

Design your classes for maintainability

By some estimates, organizations spend seven dollars on software maintenance for every dollar they spend in software acquisition. You can help reduce your organization's maintenance budget by avoiding unnecessary dependencies. This example shows how to eliminate one maintenance task: updating writeObject() and readObject() whenever the class design changes.

defaultReadObject() and defaultWriteObject() must be called from the proper methods

defaultReadObject() and defaultWriteObject() can only be called from your class's readObject() and writeObject(), respectively.

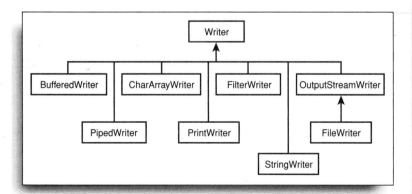

FIGURE 18.6

If you need to output characters, use a Writer rather than an OutputStream.

FIGURE 18.7

Readers work exclusively with 16-bit chars, designed for Unicode.

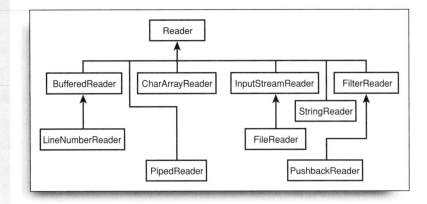

For the most part, readers and writers support methods that have the same name and function as their InputStream and OutputStream counterparts. Thus, Reader supports read(), close(), mark(), reset(), markSupported(), and skip(). Instead of available() it has ready(), which returns true if the next read() is guaranteed not to block. Similarly, Writer supports write(), close(), and flush().

Sometimes you'll need a bridge between the stream world—which reads and writes bytes—and character streams, which read and write chars. You can read input from a stream by filtering the stream through an InputStreamReader. Similarly, you can write chars to a stream in a specified character encoding by using OutputStreamWriter as a filter.

Unlike its InputStream counterpart, LineNumberReader is not deprecated. As this class reads, it watches for end-of-line patterns (\r, \r\n, and \n) and increments a counter. You can read the counter by calling getLineNumber() and set it by calling setLineNumber(). You can also read a line directly through this class by calling readLine().

SEE ALSO

➤ *Learn more about locking and synchronization, page 467*

Use readers and writers to support internationalization

If you'll eventually need to adapt your program for the global market, you should read and write Unicode, rather than ASCII, in your character I/O. Use readers and writers for this purpose rather than byte-oriented streams.

Why are there so many end-of-line patterns?

UNIX machines use a linefeed (\n) to mark the end of a text line, while Macintoshes use a carriage return (\r). Windows machines use both (\r\n). Because Java is platform-independent, it recognizes all three patterns.

Improving I/O with Related Classes

You can perform most I/O by using the stream, reader, and writer classes, but you might appreciate some of the other classes available in java.io. This section describes three such classes:

- A platform-neutral abstraction of a disk file, called File
- A RandomAccessFile
- A utility class that breaks a character stream into tokens based on whitespace, called StreamTokenizer

Using the *File* Class

When we looked at the constructors for FileInputStream and FileOutputStream, you may have noticed that I used a String as the input parameter. That String is platform-specific. If your Java program is running on a UNIX machine, the elements of the path are separated by forward slashes (/). On a Windows machine, you may need to use backslashes (\). The Macintosh uses colons (:) for the same purpose. You may also be subject to limitations on the number of characters in a file or directory name.

You can abstract away the platform-specific portions of file I/O by using the File class. Once you've constructed a File (which still requires some platform-specific information), the rest of your work is with a File object, which is platform-neutral.

Reading and Writing a *RandomAccessFile*

You may have noticed that streams (including character-based streams) support either input or output, but never both. For some applications, you need to access a file for both read and write at the same time. At those times, use RandomAccessFile. A RandomAccessFile resembles a combination of a DataInputFile and a DataOutputFile, with additional methods such as seek() thrown in to help you navigate through the file efficiently.

Reading a Stream with *StreamTokenizer*

When you're reading a character stream, you'll often need to break the input into words. *Words* are defined as blocks of characters separated by some kind of whitespace. Java has just the

---

Readers and writers are synchronized

Both readers and writers are synchronized, locking on an internal lock object. If you prefer, you can specify your own lock object in the constructor. Locking and synchronization are explained more fully in Chapter 17, "Concurrent Programming with Threads."

Be sure to test your program with large random access files

The RandomAccessFile stream tends to be used with files that are too large to be loaded into physical memory. For many applications, that means that the associated disk files are many megabytes in size. During your functional testing you may want to use a small, manageable file, but you should include some testing with very large files—at least twice the maximum size you think an end user might ever actually use.

thing—a `StreamTokenizer` that takes a reader as its constructor parameter. (There's an older form of `StreamTokenizer` that can be built from an `InputStream`, but that form is deprecated in JDK 1.2.) `StreamTokenizer` offers a number of useful methods, including

- `commentChar()`—Allows you to set single-line comments
- `eolsSignificant()`—Specifies whether an end-of-line pattern counts as "whitespace"
- `lineno()`—Returns the current line number
- `lowerCaseMode()`—Allows you to set the instance to force all tokens into lowercase
- `ordinaryChar()`—Allows you to specify which characters are to be considered "ordinary." An ordinary character is processed as a single-character token without regard to whether it is a string delimiter, comment character, or word character
- `parseNumbers()`—Specifies whether or not the tokenizer should attempt to recognize numbers and convert them to their numeric form
- `pushBack()`—Causes the next call to `nextToken()` to push the last token back onto the stream
- `quoteChar()`—Specifies which character is used to delimit strings
- `resetSyntax()`—Resets the instance to use the default syntax table, in which all characters are "ordinary"
- `slashSlashComments()`—Specifies whether the instance should or should not ignore lines with C++-style comments
- `slashStarComments()`—Specifies whether the instance should or should not ignore blocks with C-style comments
- `toString()`—Returns a `String` representation of the current token
- `whitespaceChars()`—Specifies which characters are whitespace
- `wordChars()`—Specifies which characters are word characters

Once you've got your `StreamTokenizer` set up, all you need to do is make repeated calls to `nextToken()` to get a series of tokens from the character stream.

Connecting to the Internet: The *URL* Class

Back in Chapter 3, "Getting Started Fast," I showed you how to write a tiny Java program—HelloWorld.java—with only one executable statement. The fact is, people have been writing tiny programs that write information to the screen ever since there were computer screens. One of the features that makes Java exciting is that you can connect to the Internet with a program that's not much more complex than HelloWorld.java.

SEE ALSO
➤ *HelloWorld.java in Listing 3.1, page 74*

Using *showDocument()* to Change Web Pages

Listing 18.2 shows HelloNet.java, a simple applet that connects you to a new Web page.

LISTING 18.2 *HelloNet.java*–This simple applet connects to three URLs

```
1  import java.awt.*;
2  import java.net.*;
3  import java.applet.Applet;
4  import java.awt.event.*;
5
6  public class HelloNet extends Applet
7  {
8    public void init()
9    {
10     setLayout(new GridLayout(3,1));
11     Button theBookSiteButton = new Button("Using Java 1.2");
12     theBookSiteButton.addActionListener(new ActionListener(){
13       public void actionPerformed(ActionEvent e) {
14         linkTo("http://www.mcp.com/info/0-7897/07897-1627-5/");
```

continues...

Use `StreamTokenizer` as the basis for text-processing utilities

You'll find examples of useful text-processing utilities in almost any book or Web site that describes perl or the UNIX utilities **sed** and AWK. You can duplicate the functionality of these utilities in Java (and often get a performance increase) by using a `StreamTokenizer` to take the input stream apart.

Internet connectivity is built into Java

For years Sun has been telling us that "the network is the computer," and their design of Java reflects that philosophy. Java is the only major language that allows you to connect your program to the Internet in just one line of code, as shown in Line 39 of Listing 18.2:

```
URL theURL = new
URL(theURLString);
```

LISTING 18.2 Continued

```
15        }
16      });
17      add(theBookSiteButton);
18
19      Button theMCPButton = new Button("Macmillan Computer
        Publishing");
20      theMCPButton.addActionListener(new ActionListener(){
21        public void actionPerformed(ActionEvent e) {
22          linkTo("http://www.mcp.com/");
23        }
24      });
25      add(theMCPButton);
26
27      Button theJavaSoftButton = new Button("JavaSoft");
28      theJavaSoftButton.addActionListener(new ActionListener(){
29        public void actionPerformed(ActionEvent e) {
30          linkTo("http://java.sun.com/");
31        }
32      });
33      add(theJavaSoftButton);
34    }
35
36    public void linkTo(String theURLString)
37    {
38      try {
39        URL theURL = new URL(theURLString);
40        getAppletContext().showDocument(theURL, "_top");
41      } catch (MalformedURLException e) {
42        System.err.println("Bad URL: " + theURLString);
43      }
44    }
45  }
```

Most of this applet is familiar to you by now. (If you're new to the Abstract Windowing Toolkit, take a look at Chapter 11, "Building the User Interface with the AWT.") This applet has three buttons, each with a Web destination name. When you click on a button, it fires the linkTo() method. This code is where the new Web-specific information appears.

First, we make a new URL object from the String. If the URL constructor cannot make sense out of theURLString, it throws MalformedURLException. Given a valid URL, linkTo() now transfers control to the browser's AppletContext and asks it to show the specified URL in the browser's topmost window.

This code has only three executable lines per button, plus three executable lines in linkTo(). Of course, it takes advantage of the fact that it's running inside a Web browser. The browser supplies the AppletContext, and it's the browser that actually fetches the document specified by the URL.

Calling Back the Server with *openStream()*

From within either an applet or an application, you can open a connection to a URL and read back the contents. The basic mechanism is a URL method called openStream():

```
 1: try {
 2:    DataInputStream theData =
 3:       new BufferedReader(new
 4:          InputStreamReader(theURL.openStream()));
 5:    String aLine;
 6:    while ((aLine = theData.readLine()) != null) {
 7:       System.out.println(aLine);
 8:    }
 9: } catch (IOException e) {
10:    System.err.println("IOException: " + e.getMessage());
11: } finally {
12:    theData.close();
13: }
```

The first line uses openStream() to retrieve the InputStream. URL.openStream() is really shorthand for

```
theURL.openConnection().getInputStream();
```

but most programmers will appreciate the shorter version.

Also on the first line, we wrap the InputStream first in an InputStreamReader (in order to bridge between the byte-oriented world of streams and the char-oriented world of readers). Then we wrap the InputStreamReader in a BufferedReader for efficiency—we'd prefer to read the stream a buffer at a time, rather than a byte at a time!

Why did I add "_top" to showDocument()?

If your Applet is buried down inside an HTML frame, the showDocument (String) page will also appear inside that frame. In this case, I knew that all three of these URLs should appear on a page by themselves, not in their own frame. I forced that behavior by adding "_top."

Finally, we call `theData.readLine()` successively, bringing in lines of data from the server. For this simple code snippet, we just send the data back out to standard out.

If anything goes wrong, we'll throw an `IOException` somewhere in there and catch it on the way out.

Low-Level Networking with the *Socket* Class

If you need finer-grained control than you can get with the `URL` class, you should switch to the `Socket` class. If you've done network programming before, you know that TCP/IP (the low-level protocol of the Internet) is based on connections established between sockets on two machines, typically called the *client* and the *server*.

When you write a server, you write a program that opens a socket (typically on a *well-known port number*) and waits for some client to connect. The client calls in from some unused port number (called an *ephemeral port*). As soon as the client and the server connect, it's common for the server to propose that the conversation continue on a different port. This design frees up the well-known port number to handle a new connection. Table 18.1 shows some common well-known port numbers. These services are offered both on TCP ports and on UDP ports. The RFC column refers to the Internet Request for Comments document, where you'll find the specification for the service.

Remember the `Applet` security restrictions

If you compile the `URL.openStream()` code into an applet and attempt to fetch data from some Web server, it probably won't work. Most browsers include a `SecurityManager`, which reports a `SecurityException` as soon as you attempt to contact a host other than the one you were downloaded from. To make this code work in an applet, either restrict yourself to connecting only to the applet's home server, or negotiate higher rights with the browser's `SecurityManager`.

Connection-oriented or connectionless ports?

Many Internet applications are based on the Transmission Control Protocol/Internet Protocol or TCP/IP. TCP/IP is connection-oriented—a connection is made, communication occurs, and then the connection is torn down, just like a phone call. The alternative—the User Datagram Protocol, or UDP—is connectionless, more like a telegram.

Where to get RFCs

You can download any RFCs that you'd like to read from `ftp://ds.internic.net/rfc/`. Check the login message you get when you connect—there are FTP sites on each continent. There may be one closer to you than `ds.internic.net`.

TABLE 18.1   **Common Internet services and their port numbers**

Service name	TCP port	UDP port	RFC	Description
echo	7	7	862	Server returns whatever the client sends
discard	9	9	863	Server discards whatever the client sends
daytime	13	13	867	Server returns the time and date in a human-readable format

Service name	TCP port	UDP port	RFC	Description
chargen	19		864	TCP server sends a continual stream of characters until the client terminates the connection
chargen		19	864	UDP server sends a datagram containing a random number of characters each time the client sends a datagram
time	37	37	868	Server returns the time as a 32-bit binary number—the number of seconds since midnight on January 1, 1900, UTC

Java provides two kinds of sockets: client sockets implemented in the Socket class, and server sockets implemented in the ServerSocket class.

Understanding the Client *Socket* Class

To connect to a host, your client program should include a line like

```
Socket theConnection = new Socket(hostname, portNumber);
```

(Remember the security restrictions that apply to applets.)

The Socket constructor throws an IOException if it has a problem. Otherwise, you can presume that the Socket is open and ready for communication:

```
BufferedReader theReader = new BufferedReader(
  new InputStreamReader(theConnection.getInputStream()));
BufferedWriter theWriter = new BufferedWriter(
  new OutputStreamWriter(theConnection.getOutputStream()));
```

Now you can read and write theReader and theWriter in the usual fashion. When you're done with theConnection, call

```
theConnection.close();
```

This step will also close all of the streams, readers, and writers you have associated with this Socket.

What does a port number tell you?

TCP/IP port numbers are managed by the Internet Assigned Numbers Authority (IANA). IANA has specified that well-known port numbers are always between 1 and 1023. For example, a Telnet server listens on TCP port 23, and the Trivial File Transfer Protocol (TFTP) server listens on UDP port 69. Most TCP/IP implementations allocate ephemeral port numbers between 1024 and 5000, but that design isn't specified by IANA.

Understanding *ServerSockets*

If you choose to write a server, you'll need to write a
ServerSocket. Such a socket binds a specified port. For example,
to bind port 8000, you write

```
ServerSocket theServerConnection = new ServerSocket(8000);
```

This code tells the underlying operating system that you intend
to offer a service on port 8000. (You aren't listening to that port
quite yet.) If the runtime environment is able to bind to the
specified port, it does so and sets the allowable backlog to a
default of 50. (This means that once you have 50 pending
requests to connect, all subsequent requests are refused. You can
specify a different backlog value in the ServerSocket connector.)
If the runtime environment cannot bind to the port (which happens if the port is already allocated to another service), you'll get
an IOException.

Once you've bound the port, you can attach the port and start
listening for connections by calling accept():

```
Socket aSocket = theServerConnection.accept();
```

Once the connection is made, accept() unblocks and returns a
Socket. You can open streams, readers, and writers on the Socket
just as you did from the client program.

Using Client and Server Sockets

Listing 18.3 shows a server framework. Our simple server sets up
the ServerSocket, then implements four steps:

1. Wait for a client to connect.

2. Accept the client connection.

3. Send a message to the client.

4. Tear down the connection.

LISTING 18.3   *TServer.java*—**Use this framework as the basis for your
own server**

```
1  import java.net.*;
2  import java.io.*;
3
```

```
4  public class TServer extends Thread {
5    private static final int kPortNumber = 8013;
6    private ServerSocket fServerSocket;
7
8    public TServer() {
9      super("TServer");
10     try {
11       fServerSocket = new ServerSocket(kPortNumber);
12       System.out.println("TServer up and running...");
13     } catch (IOException e) {
14       System.err.println("Exception: couldn't make server
           socket.");
15       System.exit(1);
16     }
17   }
18
19   public void run() {
20     Socket theClientSocket;
21
22     while (true) {
23
24       // wait for a client to connect
25       if (fServerSocket == null)
26         return;
27       try {
28         theClientSocket = fServerSocket.accept();
29
30         // accept the client connection
31
32         // send a message to the client
33         PrintWriter theWriter = new PrintWriter(new
34           OutputStreamWriter(theClientSocket.getOutputStream()));
35         theWriter.println(new java.util.Date().toString());
36         theWriter.flush();
37
38         // tear down the connection
39         theWriter.close();
40         theClientSocket.close();
41       } catch (IOException e) {
42         System.err.println("Exception: " + e.getMessage());
43         System.exit(1);
44       }
```

continues…

LISTING 18.3   Continued

```
45      }
46    }
47
48    public static void main(String[] args) {
49      TServer theServer = new TServer();
50      theServer.start();
51    }
52 }
```

Listing 18.4 shows a client designed to work with the server from Listing 18.3. This server has four steps:

1. Connect to the server.
2. Wait for a message.
3. Display the message to the user.
4. Tear down the connection.

LISTING 18.4   *TClient.java*–This class will help you design your client program

```
1  import java.net.*;
2  import java.io.*;
3
4  public class TClient {
5    private static final int kPortNumber = 8013;
6    public static void main(String args[]) {
7      Socket theSocket;
8      BufferedReader theReader;
9      String theAddress = "";
10
11     // check the command line for a host address
12     if (args.length != 1) {
13       System.out.println("Usage: java TClient <address>");
14       System.exit(1);
15     }
16     else
17        theAddress = args[0];
18
19     // connect to the server
20     try {
```

```
21      theSocket = new Socket(theAddress, kPortNumber);
22      theReader =
23        new BufferedReader(new
24            InputStreamReader(theSocket.getInputStream()));
25
26      // wait for a message
27      StringBuffer theStringBuffer = new StringBuffer(128);
28      String theLine;
29      int c;
30      while ((theLine = theReader.readLine()) != null) {
31
32        // show the message to the user
33        System.out.println("Server: " + theLine);
34        break;
35      }
36
37      // Tear down the connection
38      theReader.close();
39      theSocket.close();
40    } catch (IOException e) {
41      System.err.println("Exception: " + e.getMessage());
42    }
43   }
44 }
```

To test this code, first start the server:

```
java TServer
```

Now run the client. Note that `"localhost"` is a common name for a TCP/IP machine to use for itself—this invocation specifies that the server is running on the same machine as the client. We could also have used 127.0.0.1, the local loopback address.

```
java TClient "localhost"
Server: someDateandTime
```

To fault-isolate between the client and the server, use your computer's Telnet client to access the server by port number. Figure 18.8 shows this step. If you're able to connect and the server works as you expect, you have a problem with your client. Otherwise, you have a problem with the server.

FIGURE 18.8

Use your platform's Telnet client to attempt to connect to your new server's well-known port.

High-Level Networking with Object Request Brokers

If you're building a simple application for use by people with some computer skills, the client-server model is certainly adequate. But in many organizations, there may be dozens or even hundreds of servers and thousands of users running many different clients. The average user doesn't understand the client-server model, and arguably shouldn't have to.

There is a trend in programming to build finer-grained servers, making highly distributed applications. For example, one way to design the pharmacy application that we've been developing throughout this book is shown in Figure 18.9. In this design, nearly every class looks like a tiny server. Some of these classes are responsible for various aspects of the user interface, others implement business logic, and still others store the data and retrieve it from hard drives on machines around the network. In general, this design is called an *n-tier architecture*.

For example, if we built our medical application as a one-tier system, we'd put the database, application logic, and user interface on a single machine. Everyone would have to go to that machine to use the system. In a two-tier system, we would have a common database server, accessible from the network. Every client machine would have the user interface and the application

One-tier, three-tier, and n-tier architectures

A one-tier program has the user interface, the logic, and the data store all in one application on one computer. More modern applications are three-tier with a database server, a user interface client, and some "middleware" to stitch the two together. In the newest generation, n-tier, the distinctions between client and server are blurred and the servers offer very small, focused services.

logic. A three-tier system would split the user interface from the application logic—we might put the logic on a Web server in a servlet or CGI program and use a Web browser and HTML pages to implement the user interface (with some Java applets on the Web pages). In a three-tier system, the user interface is often called a "thin" client to remind us that it has no application logic in it.

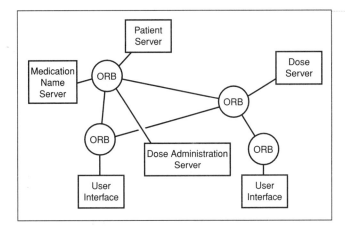

FIGURE 18.9
Many modern applications are highly distributed across many clients and servers.

In an n-tier architecture, every major class in the application logic could be a server, potentially running on a different machine. There might be one server to tell us where a patient is located, by ward and bed. Another server might tell us how to translate a medication stock number to a drug name, strength, and package. Still another server might tell us the medication orders that are active for a given patient. In an n-tier architecture, we still have a common database and a thin user-interface client.

With a growing number of server applications accessed by an array of clients, the network is faced with two problems:

- How can a client application find a server that offers the services it needs?

- What happens if a server's host or part of the network fails?

A number of companies, who collectively comprise the Object Management Group or OMG, have come up with an answer to these questions. They call the solution an ORB, for Object Request Broker. The defining specification for ORBs is CORBA, or Common Object Request Broker Architecture.

CORBA is based on the Object Management Architecture, which in turn has four ingredients:

- An ORB—Serves as the "software bus" for all distributed objects
- CORBAServices—Define system-level services on the ORB. Such services include security, naming, and transactions
- CORBAFacilities—Application-level services, such as compound documents
- Business objects—Real-world objects from the application domain

Communicating with an ORB

The original version of the Object Management Architecture came out in 1990. CORBA 2.0 was finalized in 1994. Why, then, is CORBA only now emerging into the marketplace? Part of that answer has to do with Java. Even though you can write code in C++, Ada, or even COBOL and have it communicate with an ORB, Java's high degree of object-orientation makes it a somewhat better "fit" with CORBA than some of those older languages. As an example of why that's so, Listing 18.5 shows a tiny interface defined in IDL, the Interface Definition Language defined by CORBA.

OMG doesn't include Microsoft

The Object Management Group doesn't include Microsoft, who have elected to go their own way. Their proprietary solution to this problem is called the Component Object Model, or COM, and is considered by many to be inferior to CORBA.

LISTING 18.5   *tiny.IDL*—It's difficult to imagine a class with a simpler interface than this one

```
1  Module TheModule
2  {
3    interface TheInterface
4    {
5      long TheVariable;
6    };
7  };
```

IDL is designed to be language-neutral, although much of it strongly resembles C++ (and, therefore, Java). The code in Listing 18.5 defines an interface to a service that offers only one capability: access to a `long` called `TheVariable`. Listing 18.6 shows the corresponding Java.

LISTING 18.6 *tiny.java*–**Generating Java directly from IDL by using idl2java**

```
1  package TheModule
2
3  public interface TheInterface
4  {
5     public int TheVariable;
6  }
```

You can write IDL files and pass them to the ORB to tell the ORB about the services your classes offer. If a client asks the ORB for a particular service, the ORB can tell the client how to get in touch with the proper class. If one of the machines offering that service goes down or drops off the network, the ORB can detect this problem and begin referring clients to other machines that offer the same service.

As we've learned, we should avoid exposing data outside of our class. Listing 18.7 shows another tiny IDL file, this one with a method instead of a field.

LISTING 18.7 *tiny2.IDL*–**Avoid making data members a public part of your interface**

```
1  Module TheModule
2  {
3     interface TheInterface
4     {
5        void TheFunction(in long TheParameter);
6     };
7  };
```

The `in` in this IDL code refers to the fact that `TheParameter` carries information to `TheFunction`, but not away from it.

> **How do you translate IDL into Java?**
>
> You can use an IDL-to-Java translator to write the Java that corresponds to IDL. Sun provides one such translator: the idl2java program. Others are available from the various ORB vendors.

Why does IDL include `in` and `out` keywords?

Some languages, such as Ada, make a distinction between parameters passed *to* a function and parameters passed *from* the function. For example, one might pass a parameter to a function by using *call-by-value*, but pass the parameter from the function by using *call-by-reference*. (In call-by-reference a pointer or "reference" to the parameter is passed, so that the actual parameter can be modified, while in call-by-value only the value of the parameter is passed.)

Try out an ORB online

You can see demos of Java/CORBA applets online. Visit `http://www.omg.org/` for a listing of Web-based demos, or visit one of my favorites: `http://corbanet.dstc.edu.au/`.

Obtaining an ORB

If you'd like to use the techniques described in this section (or if you'd just like to try them out), you'll need an ORB. Several companies offer ORBs that work well with Java:

- Visigenic—Their VisiBroker for Java is embedded into Netscape Navigator 4.0 and Enterprise Server 3.0 and higher. The ORB has also been licensed by Oracle and Novell. Although not all ORBs support CORBAServices yet, VisiBroker supports three, called "events," "naming," and "trader." For more information, visit `http://www.visigenic.com/`.

- Iona Technology—Their OrbixWeb (designed for Java) runs on over 15 operating systems, including Windows 95/NT, many flavors of UNIX, and several real-time operating systems such as pSOS and QNX. OrbixWeb supports several CORBAServices, including naming, transaction, and events. Learn more at Iona's Web site: `http://www.iona.com/`.

- Sun Microsystems—Their ORB, Joe, runs on Solaris and requires server code to be written in C++. Most Java developers will find VisiBroker or OrbixWeb to be a better match to their needs.

Both Visigenic and Iona offer free trial versions of their ORB at their Web sites.

Building a CORBA Application in Java

Here's an eight-step process for building a Java application that communicates via an ORB:

Building a Java CORBA application

1. Install the local ORB, setting up the PATH and other environment variables in accordance with the ORB vendor's instructions.

2. Write a specification for each communicating class in IDL.

3. Compile the IDL to produce stub client Java code and a server skeleton.

4. Write the client application code, based on the client stub.

5. Write the server object code, based on the server skeleton.

6. Compile the client and server code.

7. Start the Java server program.

8. Run the client application.

Building an IDL Interface

Listing 18.8 shows the IDL for a medication name server that returns the human-readable name of a medication in response to a request based on the drug's stock number.

Go further with CORBA and ORB technology

You can learn more about CORBA and ORB technology in "Teach Yourself CORBA in 14 Days" (Sams, 1998).

LISTING 18.8 **MedicationName.IDL–This server interface returns a medication name based on a drug's stock number**

```
1  Module Pharmacy
2  {
3    interface MedicationName
4    {
5      string GetMedicationName(in string StockNumber);
6    };
7  };
```

This IDL is platform- and ORB-independent as well as being language-neutral. You can use this IDL if you intend to implement on a Windows NT machine in C++ with an Iona ORB, or on a Solaris machine in Java with a Visigenics ORB. To compile this IDL into Java, run

```
idl2java MedicationName.IDL
```

Depending upon which vendor's idl2java program you use, you'll get back several files: a client stub, a server skeleton, and several helper classes. Listing 18.9 shows the MedicationName.java file generated by VisiBroker's translator.

LISTING 18.9 **MedicationName.java–This file is intended to be used as the defining file for the Java MedicationName class**

```
1  package Pharmacy;
2  /**
3  <p>
```

continues…

LISTING 18.9 Continued

```
 4  <ul>
 5  <li> <b>Java Class</b> Pharmacy.MedicationName
 6  <li> <b>Source File</b> Pharmacy/MedicationName.java
 7  <li> <b>IDL Soruce File</b> ::Pharmacy::MedicationName
 8  <li> <bLRepository Identifier</b> IDL:Pharmacy/MedicationName:1.0
 9  </ul>
10  <b>IDL definition:</b>
11  <pre>
12     interface MedicationName {
13       string GetMedicationName(
14         in string StockNumber
15       );
16     };
17  </pre>
18  </p>
19  */
20  public interface MedicationName extends org.omg.CORBA.Object {
21    /**
22    <p>
23    Operation: <b>::Pharmacy::MedicationName::GetMedicationName</b>.
24    <pre>
25      string GetCapital(
26          in string StockNumber
27      );
28    </pre>
29    </p>
30    */
31    public java.lang.String GetMedicationName(
32      java.lang.String State
33    );
34  }
```

Building the Server

The idl2java translator uses the IDL file as the basis for both a client stub and a server skeleton. Listing 18.10 shows a finished version of the server, which registers a `MedicationNameQuery` object with the server ORB. Listing 18.11 shows the finished implementation of `MedicationNameQuery`.

LISTING 18.10 **Server.java–This server registers a *MedicationNameQuery* with the local ORB**

```
1  public class Server {
2    public static void main(String[] args) {
3      try {
4        // Initialize the ORB.
5        org.omg.CORBA.ORB orb = org.omg.CORBA.ORB.init();
6
7        // Initialize the Basic Object Adapter
8        org.omg.CORBA.BOA boa = orb.BOA_init();
9
10       // Make the MedicationNameQuery
11       MedicationNameQuery serverQuery = new
         MedicationNameQuery("MedicationNameQuery");
12
13       // Export the new object
14       boa.obj_is_ready(serverQuery);
15       System.out.println(serverQuery + " is ready.");
16
17       // Wait for incoming requests
18       boa.impl_is_ready();
19     } catch (org.omg.CORBA.SystemException e) {
20       System.err.println:
21     }
22   }
23 }
```

LISTING 18.11 **MedicationNameQuery.java–This query object is responsible for actually answering the question**

```
1  import java.util.*;
2
3  class MedicationNameQuery extends Query._sk_Capital {
4
5    // provide a sample database for demo
6    String[][] MedicationNames =
7      {{"01234", "12345", "23456"},
8       {"Ibuprofen", "Dramamine", "Tylenol"}};
9
10   MedicationNameQuery(java.lang.String name) {
11     Super(name);
```

continues...

LISTING 18.11   Continued

```
12    }
13
14    public java.lang.String GetMedicationName(java.lang.String
      StockNumber)
15    {
16      String tempString, Name;
17      Name = "not in the database";
18      for (int i=0; i<10; i++)
19      {
20        tempString = MedicationNames[0][i];
21        if (tempString.equals(StockNumber))
22        {
23          Name = MedicationNames[1][i];
24          break;
25        }
26      }
27      return Name;
28    }
29 }
```

Building the Client

In order to use the ORB to look up a medication name, you
need some client software. The id12java translator provides you
with a client stub—Visigenics calls it st_MedicationName.java—
but you'll have to fill in the methods. Listing 18.12 shows a finished version of the client.

**LISTING 18.12   Client.java–This class is based on the *st_MedicationName.java*
file, which was written by idl2java**

```
1 public class Client {
2
3    public static void main(String args[]) {
4    try {
5      // Initialize the ORB
6      org.omb.CORBA.ORB orb = org.omb.CORBA.ORB.init();
7      // Locate a MedicationName object.
8      Pharmacy.MedicationName medQuery =
        Pharmacy.MedicationNameHelper.bind(orb, "MedicationNameQuery");
9
```

```
10    if (args.length < 1)
11    {
12      System.out.println("Usage: Client <Stock Number>");
13    }
14    else
15    {
16      String stockNumber = args[0];
17      // Query to determine the medication name
18      String theName = medQuery.GetMedicationName(stockNumber);
19      System.out.println("The medication name is " + theName
        + ".");
20    }
21  }
22  catch (org.omg.CORBA.SystemException e) {
23    System.err.println;
24  }
25 }
```

Running the Application

Make sure you've compiled all of the Java—not only the files you've written, but the helper classes written by idl2java. Then start the ORB. (If you're using VisiBroker, just type osagent at the command prompt.) The VisiBroker ORB runtime is known as SmartAgent because of its fault-tolerant capabilities; it will start running in response to your command.

Now start the Server application. Again, if you're using VisiBroker, type

```
vbj Server
```

to run the Server under the VisiBroker Java interpreter.

Finally, run the client and give it a stock name:

```
vbj Client 12345
```

When you started the server, you used the Basic Object Adapter to register your MedicationNameQuery class with the ORB.

Your query now goes from your client software to the MedicationNameHelper class. That name passes your query to the ORB, which looks up the MedicationNameQuery object. It finds out where the Server is running and passes the query to the

MedicationNameQuery registered by that program. The MedicationNameQuery runs and returns a String. If all has gone well, you should see this response:

The medication name is Dramamine.

Communications Between ORBs

The installation described here assumes that both the client and the server share an ORB on the same machine. In the real world, that assumption breaks down—the whole reason for using an ORB is that you want to be able to place servers anywhere and have the ORB keep track of them. Each vendor has their own mechanism for having ORBs find servers; ORBs communicate with each other by using the Internet InterORB Protocol, or IIOP.

Do I Have to Use CORBA?

Can I place a CORBA client in an applet?

You can place a CORBA client in an applet as long as you remember the security restriction: an applet is only allowed to communicate with the host from which it was downloaded. Run a proxy program–Visigenic calls theirs Gatekeeper–on your Web host. When the applet contacts the proxy, it will forward the request to the ORB.

What if my company's already using DCOM?

Microsoft offers a DCOM-to-CORBA bridge that allows DCOM client ORBs to communicate with CORBA server ORBs. If you want to run servers written in Java, offer them on a CORBA ORB–end users who already have a DCOM ORB on their client will be able to reach your server through the bridge.

Many developers consider CORBA to be the best option for distributed applications in an enterprise environment (where you have a mix of operating systems, computers, and languages). Under certain conditions, however, you may want to examine two alternatives.

The first of these alternatives is Java's Remote Method Invocation (RMI) mechanism. RMI is a "Java-only" solution—you can invoke methods on other objects around the network, but only if everything is written in Java.

The other alternative is Microsoft's proprietary mechanism, the Distributed Component Object Model (DCOM). Microsoft ships a DCOM-based ORB (not a CORBA ORB) with their Web browser. You can even use Microsoft's Visual J++ to build a DCOM server and client in Java. Java DCOM applications, however, work only with Microsoft Internet Explorer on a 32-bit Windows platform. That's the restriction many organizations balk at.

Building Components with JavaBeans

Learn how to use Beans by playing with the BeanBox

Connect two Beans together with an event listener without writing a line of code

Learn the five criteria Sun has set in order for a class to be a Bean

Customize your Bean's appearance in a visual development tool

Package your Beans in a JAR for use in a visual development environment

Understanding Component-Based Software

End users will use IDEs to use your Beans

There are currently over a dozen commercially successful visual development environments for Java—they're generally called Integrated Development Environments (IDEs) or Rapid Application Development (RAD) tools. In Appendix E, "Building Java Applets in an IDE," we'll take a tour of one such IDE–Visual Café for Java, from Symantec.

Once, all code was hammered out a line at a time. Now tools such as Visual Basic allow end users to assemble applications from prebuilt components. In general, the technology that allows vendors to build visual programming environments is called *component-based software engineering*. Instead of building software the old way, where the programmer writes the whole application, we can build components that sophisticated users can use to assemble the finished program.

The Java technology that allows you to build components is called JavaBeans. When using this technology, you write a small functional component, a Bean, which usually has a graphical interface. (There's a related technology, called Enterprise JavaBeans, that focuses on components that encapsulate business logic and data rather than the graphical user interface.)

In the next section of this chapter, "Java Beans Fundamentals," and in the next chapter, "Designing Good Beans," we'll look at how you write Beans. For now, we're going to explore what it's like to be a user of JavaBeans.

A software *component* is a piece of software that is isolated into a discrete, reusable element—often a single object in an object-oriented language. When you drew the buttons and the Juggler onto the BeanBox window, you were adding three components—JavaBeans—to the application.

Comparing JavaBeans and ActiveX/COM

JavaBeans is by no means the only component technology available. In the PC world, Microsoft has offered VBX and OCX controls for years. These technologies have evolved into Active/X controls, popular on Web pages. Of course, these Microsoft technologies run best in Microsoft Windows—in most cases, they run *only* in Windows. The growing popularity of the Internet has led to interest in platform-independent components. Sun has addressed this need by introducing JavaBeans.

JavaBeans technology offers four advantages:

- JavaBeans are compact. Even the smallest Active/X control comes in a large file. In general, Beans are downloaded as part of applets and may be downloaded again whenever the browser cannot find the applet in its cache. Active/X controls are installed—the first time you download an Active/X control, it takes up residence on your hard drive.

- JavaBeans are portable. If you build an applet out of Beans that use 100% pure Java, you should be able to run those Beans on any machine with a JVM.

- JavaBeans supports introspection and activation framework mechanisms. Introspection allows a program to learn about the components at runtime. The Java Activation Framework allows a Bean to learn about the container into which it has been placed. These mechanisms compare favorably with the complex registration mechanisms used by other component architectures.

- JavaBeans were designed to work well in a graphical Rapid Application Development (RAD) environment. Commercial development tools such as Visual Café for Java are even more capable than the BeanBox.

Understanding Introspection

In order to use a component in a graphical environment, the component must allow another program, such as a visual editor, to examine it and read out its list of data members and methods. When you selected a button in the BeanBox example, you could see and change the value of the `label` data member in the PropertySheet window. When you dragged the end of the line onto the Juggler and clicked the mouse, the BeanBox was able to display a list of methods from the Juggler. JavaBeans accomplishes these tasks through the introspection API. The low-level

Working with JavaBeans in an ActiveX environment

You can use your JavaBeans as ActiveX controls by wrapping them in the ActiveX bridge. See `http://splash.java-soft.com/beans/soft-ware/bridge` for details. Sun also provides support for going the other way and converting ActiveX controls into JavaBeans.

elements of the introspection API are designed for use by tool-builders. Through the low-level API, a programmer can gain access to nearly all of a class's internals.

The design tool uses the high-level introspection API to determine which parts of a Bean are user-accessible. You'll use this API indirectly in a later section when you change the value of two button labels and connect the buttons to the Juggler.

Examining a Single Bean

In order to qualify as a Bean, a Java class must meet five requirements:

- Be instantiable. You can't make an interface or an abstract class into a Bean.

- Have a default constructor. If your class is named TMyBean, you must supply a no-parameter constructor (TMyBean()).

- Be persistent. It must implement either the Serializable interface or the Externalizable interface, which allows it to be copied out to a stream as a series of bytes.

- Follow JavaBeans design patterns. Sun has written some simple rules you should follow regarding naming and design conventions.

- Use the delegation event model. If it uses events, it must process or generate these events by using the model that was introduced in JDK 1.1 rather than the old model left over from JDK 1.0.

The JavaBeans design patterns are summarized in a set of five rules:

- For simple properties, your program should provide getProperty() and setProperty() methods. The get method must return the same type that the set method accepts. If the property is read-only, omit the set method; if the property is write-only, omit get.

Usually, you'll use Serializeable

If you use Externalizable, you have complete control over how your class is written to the stream. Most of the time you won't want that degree of control—you'll be content to just have the bytes written out and read back in.

There's an alternative to following the design patterns

You may ignore the design patterns entirely as long as you specify the interface you chose in the BeanInfo file, described later in this chapter.

- If the property is `boolean`, you can replace the `get` method with an equivalent `is` method. Thus, instead of writing

```
boolean getDoable()
setDoable(boolean theValue)
```

you can write

```
boolean isDoable()
setDoable(boolean theValue)
```

- You can add an indexed property—one that is represented by an array—by using the usual `get` and `set` convention (as passing a reference to the entire array), or by writing special indexed versions of `get` and `set`. Thus, if you have a property called `TRainbow` represented by an array of `Colors`, you can write

```
Color getRainbow(int theColorNumber)
setRainbow(int theColorNumber, Color theColor)
```

as well as the usual

```
Color[] getRainbow()
setRainbow(Color[] theColors)
```

- If you're adding an event, use the pattern

```
public void addEventListenerType(EventListenerType
theEvent)
public void removeEventListenerType(EventListenerType
theEvent)
```

where *EventListenerType* extends `java.util.EventListener`.

- All public methods are available for use by visual tools and other users.

JavaBeans Fundamentals

When you write most classes, you are responsible for both the logic and the appearance of the class. When you're writing components, you share that responsibility with the person who uses your classes. When you write a JavaBean, you define how the

---

Not everyone understands indexed properties yet

Not all IDEs, including the BeanBox, understand indexed properties. Double-check any IDEs that you expect users to use to see if they're ready for indexed properties.

Use a modified pattern for unicast events

If you must throw a unicast event, be sure to add the `throws TooMany-ListenersException` clause to the method declaration.

Read the design patterns online

The complete text of the JavaBeans design rules is given in the JavaBeans specification at `http://www.java-soft.com/beans/spec.html`.

Bean behaves. You also get to set its initial appearance through the default constructor. The Bean's user, however, is able to specify the location and appearance of the Bean. Be sure to keep this difference in mind as you define your Bean classes.

Understanding Properties

The design rules listed earlier in this chapter introduced the three types of properties:

- Simple properties, which are gettable and settable.
- Boolean properties, in which is... replaces get....
- Indexed properties, in which the property is stored in an array and get... and set... are overloaded with versions that get or set a single array element.

Using Events to Manage Properties

Not only can your Beans send and receive events, they can also be involved in sophisticated collaborations with other JavaBeans. You can use events to build what are called *bound properties*, which generate events whenever they are changed. Suppose you're building an application that captures a customer order. As the customer adds items to the order, the container that represents the order fires events to a Total object, which keeps track of the total amount spent, the freight, the taxes, and other information the customer may want to know.

You can also build *constrained properties*. If you make a property vetoable, listeners can cancel the change. Here's an example: I once built an application that allowed workers in a warehouse to assemble loads of material and put them away in storage. Each stock item had a storage class, and there were rules for how the storage classes could be combined. For example, if the first item the worker put on a load was dog food, he or she couldn't also put, say, ice cream on the same load. The system was smart enough to determine that dog food goes in general storage and ice cream goes in the freezer.

You could implement this logic in a JavaBean. Figure 19.1 illustrates a design in which a `TLoadBean` has bound property items. When someone calls `setItems()` the first time, the method uses the zone of the first item to set the zone of the load. After that, whenever someone calls `setItems()` and changes the items list, the change is sent to the load's zone. The zone has the right to veto the change if it sees items on the list that it cannot handle (such as general storage rejecting the ice cream).

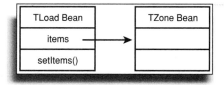

FIGURE 19.1
Use constrained properties when one object needs the authority to veto a change in another object.

SEE ALSO
➤ *Learn more about bound and constrained properties, page 565*
➤ *Learn more about Enterprise JavaBeans, page 572*

Customizing the PropertySheet

When you're writing the code for Beans, remember that the end user is only one of your audiences. You're also working for the user, who is often working with a visual development tool. If your Bean uses simple properties such as a `java.awt.Color`, you may be satisfied with the default PropertySheet. If you implement sophisticated properties, however, you may want to use the JavaBeans customization facilities. You can use three classes and interfaces to customize the appearance of your Bean in a visual development environment:

- `Customizer` Use the `java.beans.Customizer` interface to provide your own GUI implementation of the property sheet.

- `PropertyEditorSupport` Extend this class to implement a custom editor for a specific property.

- `BeanInfo` Add a class derived from `SimpleBeanInfo` to customize how the Bean appears in the builder.

Open the source files for `ExplicitButton` in your editor. They're in `demo/sunw/demo/buttons` on your BDK directory. We'll use

Store business logic in an Enterprise JavaBean

Not all Beans have a graphical representation. You can build invisible JavaBeans that encapsulate your organization's business logic. We'll talk about these Beans, called Enterprise JavaBeans, in Chapter 20, "Designing Good Beans."

that class, written by Sun, to show how to customize the property sheet.

Look first at `ExplicitButton.java`. You'll see that this class is a subclass of `OurButton`. The only difference between `ExplicitButton` and `OurButton` is the customization.

Implementing *Customizer*

Listing 19.1 shows the code for `ExplicitButtonCustomizer`. This class is a `Panel` that allows a visual builder to explicitly change the properties of an `ExplicitButton`. Sun has added a text field and label to the `Panel`. The customizer listens for a `KeyReleased` event and then changes the label in the target button.

Add an `ExplicitButton` to the BeanBox and open the PropertySheet to see this custom PropertySheet in action (see Figure 19.2).

LISTING 19.1   *ExplicitButtonCustomizer.java*—**You'll find this code in demo/sunw/demo/buttons on your BDK directory**

```
1  package sunw.demo.buttons;
2
3  import java.awt.*;
4  import java.awt.event.*;
5  import java.beans.*;
6
7  public class ExplicitButtonCustomizer extends Panel implements
   Customizer, KeyListener {
8
9      public ExplicitButtonCustomizer() {
10     setLayout(null);
11     }
12
13     public void setObject(Object obj) {
14     target = (ExplicitButton) obj;
15
16     Label t1 = new Label("Caption:", Label.RIGHT);
17     add(t1);
18     t1.setBounds(10, 5, 60, 30);
19
20     labelField = new TextField(target.getLabel(), 20);
```

```
21    add(labelField);
22    labelField.setBounds(80, 5, 100, 30);
23
24    labelField.addKeyListener(this);
25    }
26
27    public Dimension getPreferredSize() {
28    return new Dimension(200, 40);
29    }
30
31    /**
32     * @deprecated provided for backward compatibility with
      old layout managers.
33     */
34    public Dimension preferredSize() {
35    return getPreferredSize();
36    }
37
38    public void keyTyped(KeyEvent e) {
39    }
40
41    public void keyPressed(KeyEvent e) {
42    }
43
44    public void keyReleased(KeyEvent e) {
45    String txt = labelField.getText();
46    target.setLabel(txt);
47    support.firePropertyChange("", null, null);
48    }
49
50    //---------------------------------------------------------
      ------------
51
52    public void addPropertyChangeListener(PropertyChange
53    Listener l) {support.addPropertyChangeListener(l);
54    }
55
56    public void removePropertyChangeListener(PropertyChange
57    Listener l) {support.removePropertyChangeListener(l);
58    }
59
```

continues...

LISTING 19.1 **Continued**

```
60      private PropertyChangeSupport support = new
        PropertyChangeSupport(this);
61
62      //------------------------------------------------------------
        ------------
63
64      private ExplicitButton target;
65      private TextField labelField;
66  }
```

FIGURE 19.2

The `ExplicitButton`
class has its own custom
PropertySheet.

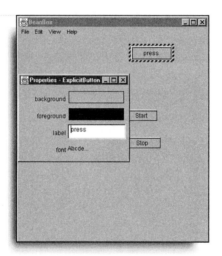

Extending *PropertyEditorSupport*

If the simple PropertySheet property editors don't meet your
needs, add your own editor by extending `PropertyEditorSupport`.
Listing 19.2 shows the code Sun wrote to add a custom property
editor to the otherwise-standard PropertySheet. Sun has specified a list of six molecule names that the user may choose and
has provided a `getJavaInitializationString()` method to set up
the default value. Figure 19.3 shows this editor at work.

LISTING 19.2 *MoleculeNameEditor.java–*Sun uses the *Molecule* class to
demonstrate a custom property editor

```
1  package sunw.demo.molecule;
2
3  /**
```

```
4    * Special case property editor for molecule names.
5    */
6
7   public class MoleculeNameEditor
8   extends java.beans.PropertyEditorSupport {
9
10      public String[] getTags() {
11      String result[] = {
12              "HyaluronicAcid",
13              "benzene",
14              "buckminsterfullerine",
15              "cyclohexane",
16              "ethane",
17              "water"};
18      return result;
19      }
20
21      public String getJavaInitializationString() {
22      return (String)getValue();
23      }
24
25  }
```

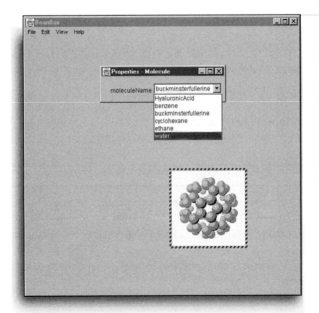

FIGURE 19.3
Use a subclass of
PropertyEditorSupport
to give your user a custom
property editor.

Extending *BeanInfo*

Whether you're writing your own complete property sheet or just giving the user a single editor, you use the BeanInfo class to tie together all of the information a visual development tool might need about your Bean. Listing 19.3 shows the BeanInfo class Sun built for ExplicitButton. In this class, Sun's designers accomplished six things:

- Line 12—Tells the visual tool the names of all of the properties.
- Line 36—Tells the visual tool which property should be the default when a new PropertySheet is opened.
- Line 42—Tells the development tool which events the class supports and how they are named.
- Line 64—Tells the development tool where to find the custom PropertySheet.
- Line 70—Tells the development tool to display a small icon in the toolbox (or its equivalent).
- Lines 84 and 85—Defines constants for the BeanInfo class to tell the tool which class and customizer this BeanInfo class applies to.

LISTING 19.3 *ExplicitButtonBeanInfo.java*—Use a class derived from *SimpleBeanInfo* to pass information to the visual development environment

```
1   package sunw.demo.buttons;
2
3   import java.beans.*;
4
5   /**
6    * BeanInfo for an ExplicitButton.
7    *
8    * @see sunw.demo.buttons.ExplicitButton
9    */
10  public class ExplicitButtonBeanInfo extends SimpleBeanInfo {
11
12      public PropertyDescriptor[] getPropertyDescriptors() {
13          try {
14              PropertyDescriptor background =
15                  new PropertyDescriptor("background",
                    beanClass);
```

```
16          PropertyDescriptor foreground =
17                  new PropertyDescriptor("foreground", beanClass);
18          PropertyDescriptor font =
19                  new PropertyDescriptor("font", beanClass);
20            PropertyDescriptor label =
21                  new PropertyDescriptor("label", beanClass);
22
23            background.setBound(true);
24            foreground.setBound(true);
25            font.setBound(true);
26            label.setBound(true);
27
28            PropertyDescriptor rv[] = {background, foreground,
            font, label};
29            return rv;
30        } catch (IntrospectionException e) {
31            throw new Error(e.toString());
32        }
33    }
34
35
36    public int getDefaultPropertyIndex() {
37    // the index for the "label" property
38        return 3;
39    }
40
41
42    public EventSetDescriptor[] getEventSetDescriptors() {
43        try {
44            EventSetDescriptor push = new
            EventSetDescriptor(beanClass,
45                "actionPerformed",
46                java.awt.event.ActionListener.class,
47                "actionPerformed");
48
49            EventSetDescriptor changed = new
            EventSetDescriptor(beanClass,
50                "propertyChange",
51                java.beans.PropertyChangeListener.class,
52                "propertyChange");
53
54            push.setDisplayName("button push");
```

continues…

ExplicitButtonBeanInfo is a complex class

ExplicitButtonBeanInfo class is an example of a complex BeanInfo class. The designer has demonstrated all of the major customization features. For a simpler example of **BeanInfo**, see MoleculeBeanInfo in the BDK.

Don't forget to mention extra classes in the manifest

If you use customization files or resources, be sure to include them in the JAR and list them in the manifest file (with Java-Beans set to false).

LISTING 19.3   Continued

```
55              changed.setDisplayName("bound property change");
56
57              EventSetDescriptor[] rv = { push, changed};
58              return rv;
59          } catch (IntrospectionException e) {
60              throw new Error(e.toString());
61          }
62      }
63
64      public BeanDescriptor getBeanDescriptor() {
65      BeanDescriptor back =
        new BeanDescriptor(beanClass, customizerClass);
66          back.setValue("hidden-state", Boolean.TRUE);
67          return back;
68      }
69
70      public java.awt.Image getIcon(int iconKind) {
71        if (iconKind == BeanInfo.ICON_MONO_16x16 ||
72              iconKind == BeanInfo.ICON_COLOR_16x16 ) {
73              java.awt.Image img =
                    ➥loadImage("ExplicitButtonIcon16.gif");
74      return img;
75      }
76      if (iconKind == BeanInfo.ICON_MONO_32x32 ||
77              iconKind == BeanInfo.ICON_COLOR_32x32 ) {
78              java.awt.Image img =
                    loadImage("ExplicitButtonIcon32.gif");
79      return img;
80      }
81      return null;
82      }
83
84      private final static Class beanClass =
        ExplicitButton.class;
85      private final static Class customizerClass =
        ExplicitButtonCustomizer.class;
86      }
```

Managing Persistence

You already know that, at a minimum, your Bean must implement Serializable. You can use this opportunity to provide powerful persistence features. For example, you can declare your class to have a version, so that incompatible .ser files are not loaded into the class. See Chapter 13, "Designing for a JFC Interface," to learn how to add the static SerialVersionUID to your class.

SEE ALSO

➤ *Learn more about serialization, page 338*

Packaging Your Bean

Once you've written your Bean, you must store it in a Java Archive, or JAR file. All of the IDEs, including the BeanBox test environment, expect your Beans to come in a JAR. Each IDE has a different way of installing the Beans from a JAR into that environment. Check the IDE documentation to find out how to use Beans in your environment.

SEE ALSO

➤ *Learn more about storing Beans in a JAR file, page 654*

Instant Java–Building Java Applications Visually

To get started as a Bean developer, you need the Beans Development Kit (BDK). You can download it for free from http://java.sun.com/beans/. The BDK includes extensive documentation and examples of well-written Beans.

When you use Beans, you'll usually be working in a commercial IDE such as Visual Café for Java, Borland's JBuilder, or IBM's Visual Age for Java. When you test your Beans, however, you may want to use the BeanBox, which is a very simple container designed by Sun and distributed as part of the BDK.

Use the documentation supplied with the BDK

To see examples of well-written Beans, install your BDK and then point your Web browser to beans/doc/examples.html in the BDK directory. When you start the BeanBox you'll see a toolbox of samples; these samples are provided in the demo/sunw/demo/ directory in the BDK directory.

On Windows computers, choose the BDK from the Programs menu

If you're installing the BDK on a Windows computer, you'll see the BeanBox on the Programs menu. Just choose Start.

Follow the instructions on Sun's Web site to install the BDK. The latest versions are packaged using ZeroG's InstallAnywhere. All you have to do is double-click on the package.

About the BeanBox

Figure 19.4 shows the BeanBox. If you examine the run batch file, you'll see that it simply sets the CLASSPATH variable and then calls upon the Java interpreter to start one specific class. Note that the BeanBox itself is a Java application—you must have the JDK properly installed in order for it to run. The BeanBox has three windows:

- ToolBox—Lists the components (called JavaBeans) that the application knows about.
- BeanBox—The Java applet or application that you are building with JavaBeans.
- PropertySheet—A list of the data members of the Bean that is currently selected.

FIGURE 19.4
The BeanBox is a convenient container for testing new JavaBeans.

Dropping Buttons into the BeanBox

To explore the capabilities of the BeanBox, begin by selecting the Bean named OurButton from the ToolBox. Now click in the BeanBox window and draw the shape that you want the button to be. (OurButton is derived from `java.awt.Canvas`, not from `java.awt.Button`, so you can draw it any shape you like.)

Make sure the new button is selected—you'll see the property list change in the PropertySheet window to display the properties of the OurButton Bean. The default value for each property is displayed. Change the value of Label from Press to Start.

Repeat the process for a second button, but name this one Stop. When you're done, your screen should resemble Figure 19.5.

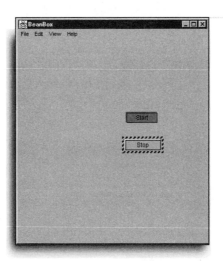

FIGURE **19.5**

Add buttons to the BeanBox by selecting them in the ToolBox and then drawing them in the BeanBox.

Creating Start and Stop Events

Draw a Juggler into the BeanBox just as you did with the two buttons. In this step, we're going to connect an event listener in the Juggler to listen for mouse clicks on the buttons.

In general, you add events to objects in the BeanBox by using the following procedure:

Shop for an IDE that allows you to connect events

The ability to connect events to methods is one of the most powerful capabilities of JavaBeans, but not all Integrated Development Environments (IDEs) support it. When you're ready to purchase an IDE, look for this important feature. Not all IDEs implement it in the same way as the BeanBox does—some of them will support it through a wizard.

Adding events to objects in the BeanBox

1. Select the object that will send the event.

2. Choose Edit, Events, and then choose the triggering event from the hierarchical menu. You'll see a line appear from the sending object.

3. Place your cursor inside the receiving object and click.

4. Choose the method in the receiving object that should be invoked to handle the event.

Start by selecting the Start button, because that's the object we'll use to send the event. Now choose Edit, Events, action, `actionPerformed` from the menu. You'll see a line stretching from the Start button to your cursor. Place your cursor anywhere inside the Juggler and click. This action tells the Juggler that you want it to listen for the `actionPerformed` event in the button.

When you click the mouse button to connect the line to the Juggler, you'll see a list of Juggler's methods. You want the Juggler's animation to start when you click on the Start button and stop when you click on the Stop button. Choose the `startJuggling` method from the list (as shown in Figure 19.6).

How does the BeanBox decide which methods to offer?

When you connect an event to an object, the BeanBox will list those methods that either take no argument or take a single argument whose type matches the event. In this example, that argument must be of type `actionPerformed`.

FIGURE 19.6

You can hook up the delegation event model without writing a line of code.

Click OK. The BeanBox will generate an adapter class for the Juggler. (This step may take a few seconds.) The BeanBox is actually writing the same sort of code that you learned to write in Chapter 11, "Building the User Interface with the AWT."

Repeat the process by connecting the Stop button to the animation's `stopJuggling` method.

Now choose View, Disable Design Mode, and click the Start button. You'll see the Duke juggle his beans.

SEE ALSO

➤ *Learn more about events, page 274*

Building and Using a "Hello" Bean

In this section we'll build a simple Bean, install it into the BeanBox, and add it to a container.

Writing the "Hello" Bean

Listing 19.4 shows a simple Bean. This Bean is derived from the AWT class `Canvas`, so we can draw on it or resize it.

LISTING 19.4   *HelloBean.java*–**We'll use this simple Bean to demonstrate how to build and install a new Bean**

```
1  package com.mcp.que.usingjava12.chapter19.hello;
2
3  import java.awt.*;
4  import java.io.Serializable;
5
6  public class HelloBean extends Canvas implements Serializable
7  {
8    public HelloBean()
9    {
10     setSize(60, 40);
11     setBackground(Color.white);
12   }
13 }
```

Make a new directory under the `beans/demo` directory: `beans/demo/mcp/que/usingjava12/chapter19/hello`. The directory where you place the class file must match the name of the package. We'll simplify that step by developing in the package directory.

Remember the five requirements a class must satisfy in order to serve as a Bean. We need to check to see if HelloBean meets these requirements:

- Is instantiable. HelloBean is not an interface or an abstract class, so it can be instantiated.

- Has a default constructor. We built HelloBean() for precisely this purpose.

- Is persistent. HelloBean implements Serializable, so it's persistent.

- Follows the JavaBeans naming patterns. We don't declare any new properties, methods, or events in this class. A quick review of the API documentation shows that Canvas (like other API components) follows the naming conventions.

- Uses the delegation event model. All of the AWT and Swing components satisfy this requirement. Because we inherit from Canvas, their event model is our event model.

SEE ALSO

➤ *Learn more about package directory requirements, page 404*

Putting the Bean in a JAR

What is make?

make is a programmer's tool that builds (or rebuilds) target files based on a file of dependencies. Targets are only rebuilt if some of the files they depend upon are newer than the existing target file. For UNIX systems, Sun provides gnumake in the BDK, and for Windows systems they provide nmake.

In Chapter 23, "Making and Using Java Archives," we'll talk about how to build a JAR file. For now, we're happy to use a modification of the makefile Sun provides.

Listing 19.5 shows the makefile that's designed to be used with gnumake on a UNIX system.

LISTING 19.5   *hello.gmk*—Use this version of the makefile if you use a UNIX machine and plan to run *gnumake*

```
1  CLASSFILES=
   com/mcp/que/usingjava12/chapter19/hello/HelloBean.class

2

3  JARFILE= ../jars/HelloBean.jar

4

5  all: $(JARFILE)

6

7  # The first target is the new JAR file
```

```
 8  # We'll make secondary targets as necessary
 9  #(JARFILE): #(CLASSFILES) $(DATAFILES)
10      echo "Name:
    com/mcp/que/usingjava12/chapter19/hello/HelloBean.class" \
11        >> manifest.tmp
12      echo "Java-Bean: true" >> manifest.tmp
13      jar cfm $(JARFILE) manifest.tmp
14      @/bin/rm manifest.tmp
15
16  # Compile the Java source into a class file
17  %.class: %.java
18      export CLASSPATH; CLASSPATH=. ; \
19      javac $<
20
21  # make clean
22  clean:
23      /bin/rm -f com/mcp/que/usingjava12/chapter19/hello/*.class
24      /bin/rm $(JARFILE)
```

This program declares variables named CLASSFILES and JARFILE, which will be used later in the makefile. The first target is named all. The make utility will select this target if you write

```
make all
```

or if you just write

```
make
```

If you attempt to make the named target (all, which leads to JARFILE), the make utility examines the date and time stamps of the dependence files and determines that only one (CLASSFILES) even exists. Because the JAR file doesn't exist yet, make makes the JAR file by following these rules:

- Write the name of the class file to a temporary file named manifest.tmp.

- Append the Java Beans line to manifest.tmp.

- Invoke Sun's jar utility to build the JAR file. The cfm switches say to create a new JAR file using the first file, $(JARFILE), as the name of the JAR file, and the second, manifest.tmp, as the name of the manifest file that names each file in the JAR.

Invoke make depending upon your platform

If you're using UNIX, Sun recommends that you invoke the GNU make utility, **gnumake**. On Windows, use **nmake**.

Lines 17 through 19 provide a rule by which files ending in .java can be converted into files ending in .class. Because the utility is trying to make HelloBean.class, it looks for (and finds) HelloBean.java and invokes javac.

The final target, clean, is useful when you want to remove unneeded files so you can start over.

Listing 19.6 shows the same file, but written for nmake, a Windows make utility.

LISTING 19.6   *hello.mk*–Use this version of a makefile on a Windows computer with *nmake*

```
 1  CLASSFILES= com\mcp\que\usingjava12\chapter19\hello\HelloBean.class\
 2
 3  JARFILE= ..\jars\HelloBean.jar
 4
 5  all: $(JARFILE)
 6
 7  # The first target is the new JAR file
 8  # We'll make secondary targets as necessary
 9  #(JARFILE): #(CLASSFILES) $(DATAFILES)
10      jar cfm $(JARFILE) << manifest.tmp
        com\mcp\que\usingjava12\chapter19\hello\*.class
11  Name: com/mcp/que/usingjava12/chapter19/HelloBean.class" \
12  Java-Bean: true
13  <<
14
15  .SUFFIXES: .java .class
16
17  {com\mcp\que\usingjava12\chapter19\hello}.java{com\mcp\que\
    usingjava12\chapter19\hello}.class
18  # Compile the Java source into a class file
19      set CLASSPATH=.
20      javac $<
21
22  # make clean
23  clean:
24      -del com\mcp\que\usingjava12\chapter19\hello\*.class
25      -del $(JARFILE)
```

From the UNIX command line, type

```
gnumake hello.gmk
```

Under Windows, type

```
nmake -f hello.mk
```

The make utility will compile your program, build a manifest file, and add the manifest file and class file to the JAR file that it makes in the beans/jars directory.

Adding the Bean to the ToolBox

You can permanently install a Bean into the BeanBox by placing the JAR file into the beans/jars directory, or you can use the LoadJar menu item on the File menu to load a JAR file from anywhere. (Beans loaded using LoadJar will disappear from the ToolBox the next time the BeanBox is restarted.)

Working with *HelloBean* in the BeanBox

Now select HelloBean in the ToolBox, draw such a Bean in the BeanBox, and leave the Bean selected. You'll see the Bean's properties in the PropertySheet. Recall from Listing 19.4 that we didn't put any properties or methods into HelloBean. What you see is all inherited from Canvas. You can change these properties by using the editors associated with the PropertySheet. You can also use Canvas's events by choosing Events from the Edit menu.

Play with the properties and events. Convince yourself that this new Bean works just as well as the demo Beans provided by Sun. Experiment with the Bean's source file, adding methods and events. Rerun make and use LoadJar to place the updated Bean in the BeanBox.

For example, you could add a data member named fColor to HelloBean, and write a getColor() and setColor() method. Then you'd be able to see and change color from the PropertySheet. To do something with the color, you can override paint() (from Canvas):

The JAR file captures the package path

Once you've written the JAR file, you no longer have to worry about the package path. The JAR file itself stores the path to com.mcp.que. usingjava12.hello, so you can put the JAR file wherever you need to in order for your IDE to read it.

```
public void paint(Graphics g)
{
  g.setColor(fColor);
  g.fillRect(20, 5, 20, 30);
}
```

Don't forget to initialize properties in the constructor

Be sure to set **fColor** to a default color in the constructor.

You'll probably want to call `repaint()` from your `setColor()` method so that setting the color from the PropertySheet has an immediate visible effect.

Working with the Bean in a Program

Sometimes you may want to write a Bean, set its properties in a visual environment, and then save it to a file and use it in a program. By convention, save the Bean to a file with a `.ser` suffix. In your program, don't use `new()`. Not only will you not load the serialized Bean, but you won't give the Bean's ClassLoader a chance to run. Instead, write

```
MyBean aBean = (MyBean) Beans.instantiate(null,
➥"MySerializedBean");
```

The first parameter to instantiate is the ClassLoader; null gives you the default ClassLoader. The second parameter is the name of the `.ser` file from which to load the Bean.

If you want to work with your Beans in a program, just remember to use the `instantiate` method. You can set properties and hook up event listeners in the usual fashion.

Designing Good Beans

Learn the reasons behind each of Sun's rules for Beans

See how to use a *BeanInfo* class to provide detailed information to the tool user

Build sophisticated properties that propagate outside the Bean or allow other Beans to veto changes

Find out about the latest changes in JavaBeans—a new set of features collectively known as "Glasgow"

Write Beans for your server by using the Enterprise JavaBeans model

Allow Beans to interact using the InfoBus, a communications system developed by Lotus and Sun

Making a Class into a Bean

As we said in Chapter 19, "Building Components with JavaBeans," a class must follow five rules in order to qualify as a Bean:

- Be instantiable—You can't make an interface or an abstract class into a Bean.

- Have a default constructor—If your class is named TMyBean, you must supply a no-parameter constructor TMyBean().

- Be persistent—It must implement either the Serializable interface or the Externalizable interface, which allow it to be copied out to a stream as a series of bytes.

- Follow JavaBeans design patterns—Sun has written some simple rules you should follow regarding naming and design conventions.

- Use the delegation event model—If your Bean uses events, it must process or generate those events by using the model that was introduced in JDK 1.1 rather than by using the old model left over from JDK 1.0.

This section takes a look at the life cycle of a Bean, so you can understand why each of these requirements is necessary.

Supporting a Zero-Argument Constructor

Not only must a Bean be instantiable, but it must support a default constructor. Recall from Chapter 19 that you don't make a new Bean by calling new()—you use Beans.instantiate(). Beans.instantiate() takes two parameters—the ClassLoader you want to use, and the filename of the saved Bean. Internally, Beans.instantiate() calls the default constructor for the Bean class to make a new, default Bean. Then it restores the properties by reloading the Bean from the .ser file.

If you make your Bean class abstract, or you fail to provide a default constructor, Beans.instantiate() will be unable to load your Bean.

If you forget to follow one of these rules, you won't get any error messages

If you forget to follow one of the five rules for writing Beans, the JVM won't crash and the compiler may not complain, but your Java program may behave strangely. It's up to you to ensure that your classes are "good beans."

Set the ClassLoader to null

You won't usually want to use a specific ClassLoader. You can get the default ClassLoader in Beans.instantiate() by setting the ClassLoader parameter to null.

Supporting Persistence

You can meet the persistence requirement by having your class implement either Serializable or Externalizable. Unless you need to control *how* your Bean is written to and read from the stream, stick with Serializable—it's much simpler.

When you declare a class to be Serializable you must ensure that each data member is either Serializable itself or is declared transient. All of the primitive types—such as byte, char, and int—are Serializable. So are many of Sun's classes, such as String.

Make sure references to other objects are transient

If your Bean class has relationships with other objects, declare those data members to be transient. That way those other objects won't be saved or restored. If your class is an aggregate made up of other objects you must save, make sure those other objects come from Serializable classes.

Defining Useful Methods and Properties

Unless you specify differently in the BeanInfo class, all of your public methods will be exposed to the Bean's user in the development environment. Properties are exposed in accordance with the design rules given in Chapter 19.

You can also specify that a property is *bound*—that is, that the value of that property should be propagated outside of the Bean to any class that cares to listen for changes. For example, you might want to add a slider to your program. If the value of the slider is bound, whenever the value of the slider changes, any interested object will be informed of its new value. You'll learn how to implement a bound property later in this chapter in the section "Using Advanced Event Models."

You might also want to use a bound property to manage the locale in an internationalizable program. If the user changes the locale from the U.S. to, say, France, you might want that change to propagate to the other Beans in the program, so that each one can modify its interface in accordance with the rules of the new locale.

If you want other Beans to have even more control over your Bean's properties than you get from bound properties, specify that a property be *constrained*. When you constrain a property, the Bean invites other Beans to sign on as vetoing agents. When your Bean wants to change a constrained property, it first gives

Follow the JavaBeans design rules

Unless you use the BeanInfo class to specify differently, Bean containers will expect your Bean to follow the naming conventions such as get...(), set...(), and is...(). Unless you've got a good reason to use different conventions, you can save yourself work by writing your code Sun's way.

Remember to use the delegation event model introduced in JDK 1.1

If your code uses the old event model left over from JDK 1.0, it won't work in a Bean container. While the old model is still available, it is deprecated—use the new model for your Beans.

Constrained properties should also be bound

In general, if you've specified that a property be constrained so listeners can veto changes, you should also make the property bound so listeners are notified when the change is actually made.

any class that is listening for a VetoableChange a chance to stop, or veto, the change. If none of the listening classes throws a PropertyVetoException, the change proceeds.

We'll talk more about constrained properties in the section "Using Advanced Event Models" later in this chapter.

Tailoring Events

Recall from Chapter 19 that you were able to connect the Start button to the Juggler without writing any code. When the user clicked the Start button, the Juggler's startJuggling() method was called. Similarly, when a user clicked the Stop button, Juggler's stopJuggling() method was called.

Let's look a bit more closely at how these Beans were hooked up.

Take a look at the source code for OurButton. It's in demo/sunw/demo/buttons/OurButton.java in your BDK directory. Notice the method addActionListener():

```
public synchronized void addActionListener(ActionListener l)
{
    pushListeners.addElement(l);
    }
```

When you selected the Start button and chose **Edit**, **Events**, **Action**, **ActionPerformed** from the menu, the BeanBox looked through the methods for an addActionListener() method (by using introspection). When it found this method, it allowed you to connect an ActionListener to this class.

Recall that the BeanBox allowed you to draw a line from the Start button to the Juggler. When you clicked the Juggler, you got a list of its methods. Examine the Juggler class's source code, which is in demo/sunw/demo/juggler/Juggler.java in your BDK directory. When you try to connect a line that represents an ActionEvent to this class, the BeanBox looks through the class (again, by using introspection) for methods that take an ActionEvent as their parameter and handle actionPerformed. It finds two: startJuggling() and stopJuggling():

```
public void startJuggling(ActionEvent x) {
    startJuggling();
```

```
}
```

and

```
public void stopJuggling(ActionEvent x) {
   stopJuggling();
}
```

These methods simply call their zero-argument counterparts.

Next, BeanBox adds any methods that take zero arguments. Most of the methods in Juggler fit this description, so you see a long list in the BeanBox.

Providing *BeanInfo*

You're not required to implement a BeanInfo class in order to use a class as a Bean, but it's a good idea to add one. By adding a BeanInfo class, your Bean can tell the PropertySheet more about how the user can interact with your Bean in the visual tool. The following is a procedure for writing your BeanInfo class.

Writing a BeanInfo class

1. Review every method, property, and event and decide whether or not you want to expose this feature to the tool-user.

2. If you decide to expose the feature, decide whether it should be available to all users, or whether it should be marked as "hidden" or "expert." A hidden feature is intended to be used only by the tool. An expert feature is made available in "expert" mode—the tool-builder specifies how a tool-user gets into expert mode.

3. For each exposed property, add the property to the getPropertyDescriptors() method with code similar to these lines from Sun's MoleculeBeanInfo class:

```
try {
    PropertyDescriptor pd = new
    PropertyDescriptor("moleculeName", Molecule.class);
        pd.setPropertyEditorClass(MoleculeNameEditor.
        ➥class);
        PropertyDescriptor result[] = { pd };
```

Implement BeanInfo or extend SimpleBeanInfo

Note that **BeanInfo** is an interface. If you choose to build your **BeanInfo** class by implementing **BeanInfo** itself, you must provide every method in the interface. A simpler approach is to extend **SimpleBeanInfo**, a class Sun provides that contains "noop" (pronounced "no-op," meaning "no operation" or do-nothing) methods and a convenient **loadImage()** method.

Remember to look at derived features, too

As you review your Bean for features, be sure to look at the Bean's base class, and include any methods, properties, and events you find there in your review.

How to set "expert" and "hidden"

PropertyDescriptor, **EventSetDescriptor**, and **MethodDescriptor** are all derived from **FeatureDescriptor**. **FeatureDescriptor** includes methods **setExpert()** and **setHidden()** that you can use to set these attributes.

```
        return result;
    } catch (Exception ex) {
        System.err.println("MoleculeBeanInfo:unexpected
        ➥exception: " + ex);
        return null;
    }
```

4. Follow a similar procedure with `getEventSetDescriptions()` and `getMethodDescriptors()` to specifically add those features to the Bean's interface. Note that you can also set defaults for each of these features; build tools can use the defaults to simplify the user interface for the builder.

5. If you want to associate an icon with your Bean, override the `BeanInfo` class's `getIcon()` method. You may specify any of four icon styles:

   - 16×16 color
   - 32×32 color
   - 16×16 mono
   - 32×32 mono

   If you only plan to use a single icon, Sun recommends that you provide the 16×16 color.

6. Review the `BeanInfo` documentation and decide whether you want to provide any other information about your Bean. You can override `getBeanDescriptor()` to specify a customizer. For example, `ExplicitButtonBeanInfo.java` (in `demo/sunw/demo/buttons` in the BDK directory) contains this method:

```
public BeanDescriptor getBeanDescriptor() {
    BeanDescriptor back = new BeanDescriptor(beanClass,
        ➥ customizerClass);
    back.setValue("hidden-state", Boolean.TRUE);
    return back;
}
```

Remember to set the GIF background to transparent

Your icons will be more attractive in most visual tools if you use your graphics editor to set the background color to transparent. Visit `http://www.yahoo.com/ Arts/Design_Arts/ Graphic_Design/Web_ Page_Design/Web_Page_ Design_and_Layout/ Graphics//Transparent_ Images/` to learn more about transparent GIFs.

Don't forget to include your icons

If you override `getIcon()`, don't forget to include the GIF files in your JAR file.

Using Advanced Event Models

The ability to connect events in a visual tool is a convenience. You can allow the tool-user to build even more sophistication into a program by providing bound and constrained properties. Recall from the previous section that bound properties are propagated outside of the Bean to other Beans that are listening for the PropertyChange event. Constrained properties send a VetoableChange event; if one of the listening Beans doesn't approve the change, it throws PropertyVetoException back to the changing Bean. That Bean is expected to abandon the attempt to change that property.

Writing Bound Properties

The following is the procedure for making a property into a bound property.

Making a bound property

1. Declare an instance variable (in this example, called fChanges):
   ```
   private PropertyChangeSupport fChanges =
       new PropertyChangeSupport(this);
   ```

2. Write a method addPropertyChangeListener():
   ```
   public void addPropertyChangeListener
   ➥(PropertyChangeListener l) {
       fChanges.addPropertyChangeListener(l);
   ```

3. Write a similar method removePropertyChangeListener().

4. In the property's set method, call fChanges.firePropertyChange(). The parameters are the name of the property (as a String), the old value, and the new value.

5. As a courtesy to tool-users, call setBound() on the PropertyDescriptor in your BeanInfo class.

To see a finished example of a Bean with a bound property, visit OurButton.html in your BDK doc directory. This file contains a color-annotated version of OurButton's source code. The instance variables, including the line

```
private PropertyChangeSupport changes =
  new PropertyChangeSupport(this);
```

are at the bottom of the page. The `addPropertyChangeListener()` method contains a single line:

```
changes.addPropertyChangeListener(l);
```

The `removePropertyChangeListener()` method is similar.

You'll see calls to `firePropertyChange()` in `setDebug()`, `setLargeFont()`, `setFontSize()`, `setLabel()`, `setFont()`, `setForeground()`, and `setBackground()`. For example, here's the implementation of `setBackground()`:

```
public void setBackground(Color c) {
  Color old = getBackground();
  super.setBackground;
  changes.firePropertyChange("background", old, c);
}
```

Writing Constrained Properties

You can set a property to be constrained by following a procedure similar to that just given for bound properties.

Making a constrained property

1. Declare an instance variable (in this example, called `fVetos`):
   ```
   private VetoableChangeSupport fVetos =
     new VetoableChangeSupport(this);
   ```

2. Write a method `addVetoableChangeListener()`:
   ```
   public void addVetoableChangeListener
   ➡(VetoableChangeListener l) {
     fVetos.addVetoableChangeListener(l);
   ```

3. Write a similar method `removeVetoableChangeListener()`.

4. In the property's set method, either add a `catch` clause for `PropertyVetoException` or specify that the method `throws PropertyVetoException`.

5. In the property's set method, call `fVetos.fireVetoableChange()`. The parameters are the name of the property (as a `String`), the old value, and the new value.

Use ChangeReporter to watch bound properties

Your BDK contains an example Bean named **ChangeReporter** that you can use to display changes to bound properties. Connect the **PropertyChangeEvent** from a Bean such as **OurButton** to the `reportChange()` method of a **ChangeReporter** bean. When you change any bound property in the **OurButton**, you'll see a message in the **ChangeReporter**.

6. If a VetoableChangeListener vetos the change, your method will get a PropertyVetoException. If control passes to the next statement after fireVetoableChange(), you may assume that none of the listeners vetoed the change. Go ahead and change the property.

7. As a courtesy to tool-users, call setConstrained() on the PropertyDescriptor in your BeanInfo class.

Open JellyBean.html in your BDK's doc directory to see an example of a constrained property in action. The lines in green are used to implement the constrained property, PriceInCents.

Just as we saw in OurButton, you fire change events in the set...() method. Adapted from JellyBean, here's setPriceInCents():

```
public void setPriceInCents(int newPriceInCents)
  throws PropertyVetoException {
  int oldPriceInCents = ourPriceInCents;

  // First tell the vetoers about the change. If anyone
  // objects, we don't catch the exception but just let it
  // pass on to our caller.
  vetos.fireVetoableChange("priceInCents",
                           new Integer(oldPriceInCents),
                           old Integer (newPriceInCents));

  // No one vetoed, so go ahead and make the change.
  ourPriceInCents = newPriceInCents;
  changes.firePropertyChange("priceInCents",
                           new Integer(oldPriceInCents),
                           old Integer (newPriceInCents));

}
```

This class also contains an instance variable vetos, analogous to changes, and an addVetoableChangeListener() and a removeVetoableChangeListener(), analogous to the add... and removePropertyChangeListener() methods shown from OurButton earlier.

How to make sure constrained properties are also bound

Many listeners will listen for both VetoableChange events (which implement constrained properties) and PropertyChange events (which implement bound properties). If you implement VetoableChanges, you should usually implement PropertyChange events as well.

JellyBean also has a bound property

The example Bean JellyBean also has a bound (but unconstrained) property, Color. The lines that implement Color are shown in brown in JellyBean.html.

Understanding Glasgow Beans

"Glasgow" is Sun's code name for the next generation of JavaBean technology. Although Glasgow's schedule isn't perfectly synchronized with the rollout of JDK 1.2, the two products are being released at about the same time. This section describes the three major features of Glasgow:

- *The Extensible Runtime Containment and Services Protocol.* This protocol allows a Bean to examine its environment (for example, a Web browser, a word processor, or even another Bean) to discover the attributes or services that may be available to it.

- *The Drag-and-Drop Subsystem.* Drag-and-drop from a native application to a Java application requires a high degree of integration with the native operating system. Sun is standardizing the way Java applications will work with user gestures made in the native environment.

- *The JavaBeans Activation Framework.* When a JavaBean is introduced to a new environment, it may encounter data it doesn't recognize. The Java Activation Framework allows the Bean to examine data, determine its capabilities, and instantiate a new JavaBean to encapsulate that data.

The JavaBeans Runtime Containment and Service Protocol

Sun has proposed the addition of a new class—BeanContext—to model the environment of a JavaBean. BeanContext would also support events such as the BeanContextMembershipEvent and the BeanContextEvent. The BeanContextMembershipEvent is fired when a Bean is either added or deleted from an environment. The BeanContextEvent is the abstract root of a hierarchy of events that occur in a BeanContext.

In order to become aware of its environment, a Bean must first implement java.beans.BeanContextChild. A BeanContextChild includes methods that allow the enclosing environment to set the BeanContext.

The upshot of these changes is that you can now add a Bean to an environment (such as a Web browser) and have the Bean determine its context; from the context it can look up the services that are available. Other Beans could monitor (and even veto) `BeanContextMembershipEvent` so they have knowledge of (or even control of) which context is set.

Glasgow also defines a `Visibility` interface that allows a Bean to discover whether a GUI display is appropriate. A Bean running on a Macintosh or a Windows computer might display its GUI; the same class running on the server, a mainframe, or other environment where a GUI is not appropriate will call a non-GUI design environment.

Integrating with Native Drag-and-Drop

Java's distinctive feature, of course, is its platform independence, but drag-and-drop between Java and native applications necessarily introduces a platform-specific component. Starting in JDK, 1.2, Java supports drag-and-drop between Java programs and

- OLE (for Windows 95 and Windows NT)
- CDE/Motif (for UNIX)
- Mac OS

as well as with other Java applications.

To see how drag-and-drop works, take a look at the cut and paste example in Chapter 14, "Advanced User Interface Design with the JFC." Figure 20.1 shows the user interface of that application. Drag-and-drop strongly resembles cut and paste. You use the following elements to implement drag-and-drop:

- A `DragSource` The place from which the data is transferred
- The source `Component` The GUI item associated with the `DragSource`
- One or more `DropTargets` The destination for the data
- The destination `Components` The GUI items associated with the `DropTargets`
- `Transferable` data The data that should be associated with the drag

Veto `BeanContextMembership Event` if the Bean isn't ready to leave

If another Bean is not in a state to be removed, just veto its `BeanContextMember-shipEvent`. A Bean might also veto being added to a context if it is unable to function in that context.

Learn more about the Runtime Containment and Service Protocol online

The Runtime Containment and Service Protocol was described at JavaOne 98 in the session, "Advanced Topics in JavaBeans Components." You can view this session or listen to the audio at `http://java.sun.com/ javaone/javaone98/se ssions/T306/`.

FIGURE 20.1

In this cut-and-paste example the program moves `Transferable` data from the `TextField` to the `List` through the `Clipboard`.

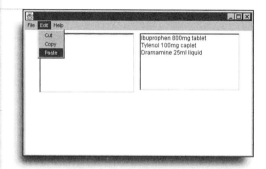

Don't depend upon the iconic representation

Not all platforms support an iconic representation of the object being dragged. Don't make any of your features depend upon this icon being present.

Consider implementing `DragAutoScrolling Support`

If your `DropTarget Component` is large, the exact location of the user's destination may not be visible. You can ensure that the `Component` will automatically scroll by implementing the `DragAutoScrolling Support` interface, and calling `autoScrollContent()` repeatedly while the gesture intersects the boundary of the `DropTarget Component`.

Avoid transferring groups of objects

Some platforms permit you to select a group of objects and transfer them. This action is implemented by placing all of the objects in a `Transferable Container` and transferring the container. There's no consistency between platforms on this behavior, however, so you're wise to avoid it.

The exact nature of the gesture used to initiate the drag is platform-dependent. When the user drags, it's customary to change the cursor to a distinctive shape that may include an icon representing the `Transferable` data. As the cursor passes over `DropTargets`, the runtime environment sends out notices to the `DragSource` and the `DropTarget`. The `DragSource` receives a "Drag Over" notice; the `DropTarget` receives a "Drag Under" notice. Typically, your `DragSource` should respond by changing the cursor to show that a drop is permitted here. The `DropTarget`'s `Component` may respond by highlighting in some way to show the user where the data would go.

When the user "drops" the data onto a `DropTarget`, one of three actions may occur, depending upon the gesture. The program may

- Move the `Transferable` data from the `DragSource` to the `DropTarget`, updating the `Components` in the process.

- Copy the `Transferable` data from the `DragSource` to the `DropTarget`, updating the `DropTarget`'s component.

- Link the `DropTarget` to the data in the `DragSource`, making a "reference," possibly updating either or both `Components`.

When the user drops, the `DragSource` and the `DropTarget` negotiate the exact flavor of data to be transferred. For example, a given data item may have representation as an object, a Unicode `String`, or ASCII text. See Chapter 14 for a full discussion of data flavors.

SEE ALSO

➤ *Learn more about data transfer, page 368*

Using the Java Activation Framework

It's not unusual for a JavaBean to encounter data without knowing much about that data. For example, a user might want to use a Bean on a Web page in much the same way as users today use browser plug-ins: have the Bean open an arbitrary piece of data and display it (or allow the user to interact with it). In order to support this sort of feature, Sun needed to give Beans the capability to examine data at runtime. Sun's solution, the Java Activation Framework (JAF), is implemented as a standard extension. Sun has written a reference implementation of the JAF, available at `http://java.sun.com/beans/glasgow/jaf.html`. The JAF provides the following four services:

- It discovers the type of an arbitrary piece of data.

- It encapsulates access to data.

- It discovers the operations available on a particular type of data.

- It instantiates the software component that corresponds to the desired operation on a particular piece of data.

Figure 20.2 illustrates the architecture of the JAF. As shown, the JAF has five major components:

- `DataSource` Contains a `String` giving the MIME type of the data and a stream carrying the data itself. Sun provides two implementations: a `FileDataSource` for information coming from a file, and a `URLDataSource` for data originating on the network.

- `DataHandler` Serves as the go-between for JAF clients with the rest of the JAF.

- `DataContentHandler` Converts an `InputStream` into a data object, and vice versa. The `DataContentHandler` implements `Transferable`, so you can use `DataFlavors` to get the type of data that you prefer.

- `CommandMap` Gives the client a set of operations that are defined on the data, based on the data's MIME type. The `CommandMap` can also return a Bean designed to manipulate the data. For example, you might have one Bean designed to view your data, another designed to print it, and yet another (heavier) Bean that allows the user to edit the object.

- `CommandObject` This object implements the operations selected by the JAF client.

FIGURE 20.2

JAF clients interact with the
`DataSource` and the
`DataHandler`.

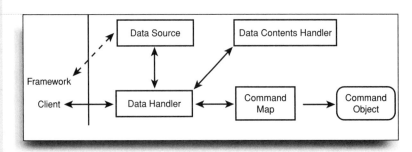

Building Enterprise JavaBeans

Middleware is closely related to CORBA

If you're using the Common Object Request Broker Architecture (CORBA) to design your application, you can break your classes down into three categories: user interface (usually a GUI), database (usually relational, through JDBC), and middleware. You can use off-the-shelf products as your database, and off-the-shelf Beans as the basis for your user interface. Now, with Enterprise JavaBeans, you can get code reusability for the rest of your application.

So far all of the Beans you've seen have included a visible GUI component that's part of the user interface. Sun is now extending the JavaBeans model to include invisible Beans that you might use to implement what's often called *middleware*. Middleware is the software that implements business logic—it sits between the user interface and the database.

Suppose you wanted to implement an order entry system for telemarketers. You could design their screens with the conventional Beans you've seen in this chapter and in Chapter 19. You could connect to the database that knows about your products and inventory levels by using the Java Database Connectivity Package, JDBC, described in Chapter 21, "Using the Java Database Connectivity Package." But where would you put the logic that describes how an order is placed? Where, for example, would the credit approval logic reside, or the logic to compute shipping costs and select a shipping method?

For invisible "business functions" you can use Enterprise JavaBeans—JavaBeans designed to run in a server environment.

Just as JavaBeans provides a component model for designing the user interface and allows designers who are not necessarily professional programmers to build client programs, Enterprise JavaBeans are reusable components of logic that run on the server. They have no user-interface components—they encapsulate business rules that allow a tool-user to integrate client applications with (typically) a database. Figure 20.3 illustrates how Enterprise JavaBeans fit into an *n*-tier architecture.

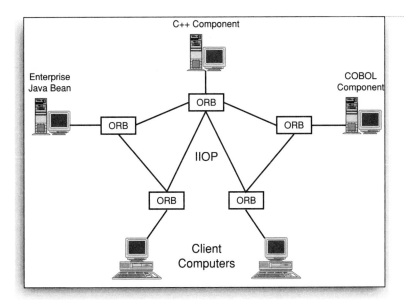

FIGURE 20.3

You can mix Enterprise JavaBeans with components written in other languages if you use CORBA as the basis for communications between them.

One of the greatest benefits of Enterprise JavaBeans is the fact that tool-users will be able to develop custom applications from reusable components without having to have access to or modify the source code. If you *are* a professional programmer, anticipate a market for Enterprise JavaBeans that provides small pieces of specific business functionality.

Just as conventional JavaBeans can be dropped into the BeanBox or a similar container, Enterprise JavaBeans (EJB) need a container. These EJB containers are provided by the "component execution system," a software layer that insulates Enterprise JavaBeans from the operating system. A component execution system might be implemented in

Learn more about Enterprise JavaBeans online

Point your browser to
`http://java.sun.com/products/ejb/white_paper.html` to learn more about the benefits of Enterprise JavaBeans.

Microsoft's Transaction Server could be used as a component execution system

While Microsoft's Transaction Server would make a fine component execution system, Microsoft is one of the few major software companies to show no interest in EJB. Microsoft has its own component architecture—ActiveX—and its own distributed object model—DCOM.

- A Transaction Processing (TP) monitor such as IBM's CICS and Encina, or BEA's Tuxedo.

- A Database Management System (DBMS) such as Oracle, Sybase, or DB2.

- A Web Server such as Netscape's Enterprise server.

By design, Enterprise JavaBeans are portable between component execution systems. You could build an EJB under, say, the Netscape Enterprise Server and sell it to someone who is running in an Oracle environment. Figure 20.4 illustrates a typical component execution system.

FIGURE 20.4

Clients don't interact directly with the Enterprise Bean—they work through an `EJBReference` object provided by the component execution system.

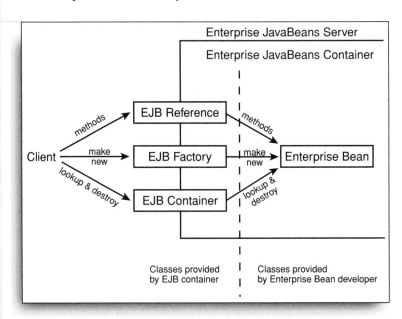

Placing Your Beans on the InfoBus

Learn more about the InfoBus online

Read about the InfoBus at `http://java.sun.com/beans/infobus/index.html`.

As more and more Beans are placed onto a given JVM, the opportunities for collaboration between Beans multiply. Sun and Lotus have cooperated to define a standard called the InfoBus, which supports communications between Beans running on the same JVM.

To communicate with other components, your Bean must implement `InfoBusMember`. When they're ready to communicate, they can call `InfoBus.get()` to get the default InfoBus. (You can also call `get` with a `String` parameter to get a named InfoBus.)

Typically you'll call `get()` to get the InfoBus, and then call `join()` on that InfoBus to connect to the bus. The InfoBus will, in turn, call your component's `setInfoBus()` method to set itself as the current InfoBus.

In your implementation of `setInfoBus()`, you should call the InfoBus's `register()` method, telling it that you're an active component ready to send and receive messages. (When you're done with the bus, you should call `leave()` to unregister and `release()` to unjoin.)

When you `register()` with an InfoBus, the bus becomes a `PropertyChangeListener` on your `InfoBus` property. Now you can place items on the bus by firing `ItemAvailable` messages to the bus. These messages can be broadcast to anyone who is listening, or they can be directed to one or more `InfoBusDataConsumers`. You can also register as an `InfoBusDataConsumer` yourself, so you can exchange data with other components.

The data transferred over the bus is `Transferable`, so you can pass various flavors for use by the `InfoBusDataConsumer`.

TDrugIDInput: An Illustration of an *InfoBusDataProducer*

Suppose you wanted to build a medical application in which components communicate via an InfoBus. You might build a Web page from three components: an input applet, a data access applet, and a spreadsheet, to show the "big picture" of the data, if each of these three applets is an `InfoBusMember` that can communicate via the browser's `InfoBus`.

To input a value such as a drug ID number, you might define the class `TDrugIDInput` as both an `InfoBusMember` and an `InfoBusDataProducer`. The following code illustrates some of the

> **What is a bus?**
>
> In computer hardware, a bus is a set of data paths that connect one hardware component with another. For example, your hard drive communicates with memory and the processor over a bus. The InfoBus is a software analog of these hardware entities.

Get the latest version of the InfoBus

InfoBus 1.0 was designed for use with JDK 1.1. If you're using JDK 1.2, you'll get your best results by using InfoBus 1.1 or later.

InfoBus-specific portions of such a class. In Listing 20.1 the TDrugIDInput could include a field into which the user enters the drug ID number. You could trigger the lookup by including a Button or other control on one of the InfoBusDataConsumer applets to look up the information on the drug identified by the current ID.

LISTING 20.1 *TDrugIDInput:* **An Example of an** *InfoBusDataProducer*

```
1  import javax.infobus.InfoBusMember;
2  import javax.infobus.InfoBusDataProducer;
3
4  public class TDrugIDInput extends Applet implements
5  InfoBusMember, InfoBusDataProducer, ActionListener
6  {
7    private InfoBusMemberSupport fInfoBusHolder;
8    private TSimpleDataItem fData;
9    private String fInfoBusName = null;
10   private String fDataName;
11   private Object fAvailableRevokeInterlock = new Object();
12
13   public  InfoBus getInfoBus()
14   {
15     return fInfoBusHolder.getInfoBus();
16   }
17
18   // other InfoBusMember calls are
19   // delegated in the same manner as getInfoBus()
20
21   public void init()
22   {
23     super.init();
24
25     // 'this' tells the new InfoBusMemberSupport to use this
26     // applet as the source field of all events that it
27     // issues.
28     fInfoBusHolder = new InfoBusMemberSupport( this );
29     fInfoBusHolder.addInfoBusPropertyListener( this );
30
31     // We'll let the applet user specify the name of the
32     // InfoBus in a parameter. If the parameter isn't set,
33     // we'll use the default InfoBus from the browser.
```

```
34      fInfoBusName = getParameter("InfoBusName");
35
36      // Let the applet user specify the name of this data item
37      // and provide a default name if the parameter is not
38      // provided
39      fDataName = getParameter("DataItemName");
40      if (fDataName == null)
41        fDataName = "DrugID";
42    }
43
44
45    // When a data consumer needs a copy of the data
46    // (for example, to initialize or redraw an applet)
47    // it places a request on the InfoBus. InfoBusDataProducers
48    // such as TDrugIDInput listen for this request by
49    // implementing a listener object and adding it to
50    // the list of listeners of the InfoBus.
51    // In this simple example, we'll put the listener into the
52    // applet class; in a more sophisticated example, consider
53    // making the listener a separate class.
54
55    // We'll register this listener in start() and remove it
56    // in stop()
57    public void dataItemRequested ( InfoBusItemRequestedEvent
58                                                     theEvent)
59    {
60      if (fData == null)
61        return;
62      String aString = theEvent.getDataItemName();
63      if ((aString != null) && aString.equals(fDataName))
64      {
65        synchronized (fData)
66        {
67          theEvent.setDataItem(fData);
68        }
69      }
70    }
71
72    public void start()
73    {
```

continues…

LISTING 20.1 **Continued**

```
74    try {
75      if (fInfoBusName != null)
76        fInfoBusHolder.joinInfoBus( fInfoBusName );
77      else
78        fInfoBusHolder.joinInfoBus( this );
79    } catch (InfoBusMembershipException e) {
80      // report an error; thrown if the InfoBus property
81      // is already set
82      . . .
83    }
84    if (fInfoBusName != null)
85    {
86      try {
87        // add event listener to InfoBus
88        fInfoBusHolder.getInfoBus().addDataProducer( this );
89      } catch (StaleInfoBusException) {
90        // report an error; thrown if InfoBus has been
91        // declared inactive
92        . . .
93      }
94    }
95  }
96
97  public void stop()
98  {
99    try {
100     if (fInfoBusName != null)
101       fInfoBusHolder.leaveInfoBus();
102     else
103       fInfoBusHolder.leaveInfoBus();
104   } catch (InfoBusMembershipException) {
105     // report an error; thrown if the InfoBus property
106     // is already null
107     . . .
108   }
109   // revoke our data item and leave the bus
110   synchronized (fAvailableRevokeInterlock)
111   {
112     InfoBus theInfoBus = fInfoBusHolder.getInfoBus();
113     theInfoBus.fireItemRevoked( fDataName, this );
```

```
114        }
115        try {
116          fInfoBusHolder.leaveInfoBus();
117        } catch (PropertyVetoException e) {
118          // ignore; our InfoBus property is
119          // managed by external bean
120        } catch ( InfoBusMembershipException e) {
121          // ignore; thrown only if the InfoBus
122          // was already null.
123        }
124      }
125  }
```

The display applet and spreadsheet would be implemented as
InfoBusDataConsumers; their InfoBus-specific methods would
resemble the methods shown in TDrugIDInput.

TSimpleDataItem: An Illustration of a *DataItem*

The class TSimpleDataItem is an implementation of
ImmediateAccess, an InfoBus interface that defines three ways to
retrieve the data: getValueAsString(), getPresentationString(),
and getValueAsObject().

You can implement these ImmediateAccess methods with a single
line each:

```
public class TSimpleData implements ImmediateAccesss
{
  Integer fValue;
  public TSimpleData()
  {
    fValue = new Integer(0);
  }
  public String getValueAsString()
  {
    return fValue != null ? fValue.toString() : new
➥String("");
  }
  public String getPresentationString(Locale theLocale)
  {
```

What is ImmediateAccess?

ImmediateAccess is a
simple interface that extends
DataItem. All DataItems
are Transferable, so you
can cut, copy, paste, drag, or
drop them, depending upon
what support you've provided
for these features in your
Beans.

```
        // this method is used to prepare a properly formatted
        // String for this locale. We just use the standard
        // String
        return getValueAsString();
    }
    public Object getValueAsObject()
    {
        return fValue;
    }
    public void setValue (ImmediateAccess theNewValue) throws
InvalidDataException
    {
        fValue = theNewValue.clone();
    }
}
```

TSimpleData is Transferable (since it is indirectly derived from DataItem). You should provide a getTransferable() method to provide access to its MIME type, as well as getProperty() and getProducer() methods.

Simple tips to get your InfoBus classes up fast

When you're just starting out with InfoBus-aware classes, you can skip some of the work of making your data items fully compliant with the InfoBus standard. Just return null to getTransferable() and getProperty() and fill them in later. You'll still need to provide a reference to the instance that supplies the item in getProducer().

VIII

Advanced Java

Using the Java Database Connectivity Package

Learn about the relational database model and the Structured Query Language (SQL)

See how to add, modify, and delete records

Find out how to query a table in the database

Learn how to extend a query across more than one table

See how to connect to a relational database from inside a Java program

Understanding JDBC

Although many applications can be written by using just Java and file I/O, a broad class of applications cry out for sophisticated database management. Some of these applications serve information from the database. Others collect information from site users and store it in the database.

Sun offers a package—`java.sql`—that allows your Java program to access relational database management systems (RDBMSs). Through this Java Database Connectivity package, or JDBC, you can connect to a relational database and interact with the database by using the popular database language, SQL.

When the application must capture information about more than one entity, a relational database management system (RDBMS) is usually the right choice. In this section I'll describe RDBMSs and the language used to communicate with them—the Structured Query Language, SQL. In the remainder of this chapter I'll show you how to use JDBC to connect to a database, send SQL statements, and read back the results.

Use relational databases when your objects are heavy with data and light on relationships

Relational databases allow you to store numbers, dates, and character strings directly. Many relational databases also allow you to store large binary objects such as sound or images. I recommend that you consider JDBC and the relational model when your objects are dominated by these kinds of data, rather than by relationships between the data (modeled by references in Java, pointers in C++, and foreign keys in SQL).

Understanding Relational Databases

During the early days of software development, programmers were content to write data to files and read it back again. The languages introduced in those days, such as COBOL, reflect the fact that programmers were organizing data into records directly on the disk. This sort of file, in which all of the information about an application is written to the disk without internal pointers or indexes, is called a *flat file*. You can read and write flat files in Java by using `java.io.InputStream` and its counterpart, `java.io.OutputStream`.

Many simple systems are still built by using a flat file, but flat files can introduce unnecessary complexity and inefficiency when used in sophisticated applications.

When the application must capture information about more than one entity, a relational database management system (RDBMS) is a better choice than a flat file. This chapter describes RDBMSs and how to access them from a Java program.

Most industrial-strength database managers use what is called the relational model of data. The relational model is characterized by one or more relations, more commonly known as *tables* (see Figure 21.1).

In a well-defined database, each table represents a single concept. For example, a book wholesaler may need to model the concept of a book. Each row holds one record—information about a single title. The columns represent the fields of the record—things that the application needs to know about the book, such as the title, the publication year, and the retail price. Every table must have some combination of columns that uniquely identifies each row—this set of columns is called the *primary key*. In most good database designs, the primary key is stored in a single column and serves as an identifying name or number for the record. For the book table, this column could be the book's ISBN.

ISBN	Title	Publication Year	Retail Price	Publisher ID
0-7897-0801-9	Webmaster Expert Solutions	1996	59.99	7897
0-7897-0932-5	Platinum Edition HTML 3.2, Java 1.1	1996	70.00	7897
1-5627-6449-7	The Offical Gamelan Java Directory	1996	29.99	5627
0-7897-1138-9	Special Edition Using Java Script, 2nd	1997	49.99	7897
1-5620-5664-6	Inside Java	1997	55.00	5620
1-5716-9083-2	Java 1.1 Interactive Course	1997	49.99	5716
0-7897-1477-9	Platinum Edition HTML, Java 1.1	1998	59.99	7897
0-7897-1627-5	Using Java 1.2	1998	29.99	7897

FIGURE 21.1

A single table is defined by its columns and keys and holds the data in rows.

Each table may also contain pointers—called *foreign keys*—to other tables by storing the primary key from the other table in its own columns. For example, each book is associated with a publisher by storing the publisher's key in the book record (see Figure 21.2). In the book table, the publisher ID is a foreign key. In the publisher table, the publisher ID is the primary key.

You may not need an RDBMS

Many Java programmers prefer to bypass the complexity of an RDBMS and save their objects directly to a database, particularly when the persistent objects in their application are characterized by relationships between the data, rather than the data itself. You need a Java-compatible Object-oriented Database Management System (ODBMS) to accomplish this task. Visit http://www.odi.com/ for one example of such an ODBMS.

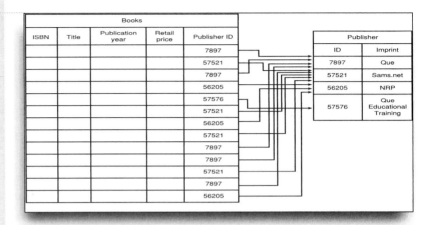

Relational databases are pulled in two competing directions. If
redundancy exists between the tables, there is always a possibility
that the tables may become inconsistent. For example, if the
books table were to include the address of the publisher as well as
the publisher ID, it would be possible for the application to
update the publisher's address in the publisher table but fail to
update the address in the book table.

If a database is divided into many small tables—so that there is
no redundancy—consistency is easily ensured. But if the database is large, a design with several small tables may require many
queries to search through tables looking for foreign keys. Large
databases with little or no redundancy can be inefficient both in
terms of space and performance.

SEE ALSO

➤ *Learn more about* java.io *classes, page 511*

Normalized Relations

Database designers talk about five levels of *normalization*—standards to ensure database consistency. The normal forms are
hierarchical; a database in third normal form satisfies the guidelines for first, second, and third normal forms. Here are the
guidelines that define the five normal forms:

1. *First normal form.* At each row-column intersection, there must be one and only one value. For example, a database in which all of the books published by a given publisher in 1998 are stored in a single row-column intersection violates the rule for first normal form.

2. *Second normal form.* Every non-key column must depend on the entire primary key. If the primary key is *composite*—made up of more than one component—no non-key column can be a fact about a subset of the primary key. As a practical matter, second normal form is commonly achieved by requiring that each primary key span just one column.

3. *Third normal form.* No non-key column can depend on another non-key field. Each column must be a fact about the entity identified by the primary key.

4. *Fourth normal form.* There can be no independent one-to-many relationships between primary key columns and non-key columns. For example, a table like the one shown in Table 21.1 violates the fourth normal form rule: Cities Toured and Children are independent facts. An author who has no children and has toured no cities can have a blank row.

5. *Fifth normal form.* Break tables into the smallest possible pieces in order to eliminate all redundancy within a table. In extreme cases, tables in fifth normal form may consist of a primary key and a single non-key column.

TABLE 21.1 Tables that are not in fourth normal form are characterized by numerous blanks

Author	Children	Cities Toured
Brady	Greg	Seattle
Brady	Cindy	Los Angeles
Brady	Bobby	
Clinton	Chelsea	Washington
Clinton		Los Angeles
Clinton		St. Louis

Don't force your design into fifth normal form

Databases should not be indiscriminately put into fifth normal form. Such databases are likely to have high integrity but may take up too much space on the disk (because many tables have many foreign keys). They are also likely to have poor performance because even simple queries require searches (called *joins*) across many tables.

What's the latest version of SQL?

The SQL standard is controlled by the American National Standards Institute (ANSI) and the International Organization for Standardization (ISO), so it's known as ISO-ANSI SQL. The 1992 version of that standard is voluminous; for most purposes the 1989 version is sufficient. ANSI declared the 1989 standard to be the "ANSI 92 Entry Level" standard (often called ANSI 92-compliant SQL in marketing material).

The best design is a tradeoff between consistency and efficiency. An experienced database designer can help you determine where the site's database belongs on the path between first normal form and fifth normal form.

Using SQL

Some developers with a background in PC applications are more comfortable with database managers like dBase than they are with newer programs like Visual FoxPro or Microsoft SQL Server. Many of the newer or more powerful programs use the Structured Query Language (SQL, pronounced see-quel). SQL was one of the languages that emerged from early work on relational database management systems (RDBMSs). Among RDBMSs, SQL has emerged as the clear winner. Non-relational databases such as ObjectStore, Object Design's object-oriented database, often offer a SQL interface in addition to any native Data Manipulation Language they may support.

Making New Databases and Tables

A typical life-cycle of a database proceeds like the following:

1. The database is created with the SQL CREATE DATABASE statement:

   ```
   CREATE DATABASE bookWholesale
   ```

2. Tables are created with the CREATE TABLE statement:

   ```
   CREATE TABLE books
   (isbn char(10) NOT NULL,
   title char(20) NOT NULL,
   publicationYear datetime NULL,
   retailPrice money NULL))
   ```

3. One or more indexes are created:

   ```
   CREATE INDEX booksByYear ON books \
   (publicationYear)
   ```

   Many RDBMSs support *clustered* indexes. In a clustered index, the data is physically stored on the disk sorted in accordance with the index. A clustered index incurs some overhead when items are added or removed, but it can give exceptional performance if the number of reads is large with respect to the number of updates. Because only one physical arrangement of the table exists on the disk, at most only one clustered index is possible for each table.

SQL also supports the UNIQUE keyword, in which the RDBMS enforces a rule that says no two rows can have the same index value.

4a. Data is inserted into the tables.INSERT INTO books VALUES

('0789716275', 'Using Java 1.2', 1998, 29.99)

Depending on the application, new rows may be inserted often, or the database, once set up, may stay fairly stable.

4b. Queries are run against the database.

```
SELECT title, publicationYear WHERE retailPrice <
40.00
```

For most applications, queries are the principal reason for the existence of the application.

4c. Data can be changed.

```
UPDATE books
SET retailPrice = 59.95
WHERE ISBN='0789762750'
```

4d. Data can be deleted from the tables.

```
DELETE FROM books
WHERE publicationYear < 1990
```

5. Finally, the tables and even the database itself can be deleted when the organization no longer has a need for them.

```
DROP TABLE books
DROP DATABASE bookWholesale
```

When a table is created, the designer specifies the datatype of each column. All RDBMSs provide characters and integers types. Most commercial RDBMSs also support a variety of character types, floating point (also known as decimal type), money, a variety of date and time types, and even special binary types for storing sound, images, and other large binary objects.

The CREATE INDEX syntax is not standard across RDBMSs

Check your RDBMS's reference manuals to see what kinds of indexes are allowed. Those manuals will tell you the exact syntax you need to use to generate those indexes on your system. Since you usually just set up the index once, you may prefer to add the **CREATE INDEX** statements to the batch file that builds your tables, rather than calling it from a Java program through JDBC.

How many indexes do you need?

If the number of queries is high compared to the number of inserts, deletes, and updates, indexes are likely to improve performance. As the rate at which database changes climbs, the overhead of maintaining the indexes begins to dominate the application.

SQL isn't completely portable

The JDBC simply passes your SQL code straight to the database drivers. Be aware that if you use features unique to one vendor, you'll have to recode your SQL if you change to an RDBMS from a different vendor.

Managing Rows with *INSERT, DELETE,* and *UPDATE*

For many Web-based applications, the database is set up with all of the tables before the application is installed. Some applications treat the database as read-only—all of the data is inserted and updated offline. Other applications enable users to insert new records in the tables, delete existing records, or update existing records. The SQL statements INSERT, DELETE, and UPDATE are used for these functions.

Throughout this chapter lines like this INSERT statement are presented to show syntax:

```
INSERT INTO tableName [(columnList)] VALUES(dataList)
```

The portions of the diagram in square brackets ([and]) are optional elements. Portions in *italics* are to be replaced by your own elements and data. The capitalized elements are SQL, which you should copy into your own statements. Where there is more than one option, the options are separated by a vertical bar, |. Where you may repeat an element, the syntax diagram shows an ellipsis, ... (Most SQL interpreters will accept SQL in either upper- or lowercase—by convention SQL commands are usually written in upper case.)

Adding a New Record by Using the *INSERT* Statement

To insert a new record in a table, use the INSERT statement. The syntax is

```
INSERT INTO tableName [(columnList)] VALUES(dataList)
```

Note that you specify the name of the table, the names of the columns into which the data goes, and the data values themselves. If you omit the column list, you must supply values for *each* defined column.

For example, if the books table has columns for the ISBN, title, publication year, and retail price, the following statement populates a new record:

```
INSERT INTO books VALUES('0789716275','Using Java
1.2',1998,29.99)
```

If a column is specified NOT NULL, the SQL interpreter will raise a runtime error if that column is omitted in an INSERT.

If your application enables the user to insert records at runtime, insert code like the following:

```
try {
  if (theTitle == null)
    // If you have many
    // exceptions like
    // this one, consider
    // defining your own
    // exception class.
    throw (
      new Exception(
        "Usage: you must
        ➦supply a value for
        ➦the title"));
    if (theISBN == null)
      throw (
        new Exception(
          "Usage: you must
          ➦supply a value for
          ➦the ISBN."));
    int theRowsAffected =
      theStatement.executeUpdate(
        "INSERT INTO books VALUES(" +
        theISBN + "," + theTitle +
        "," + theYear + "," +
        thePrice + ")");
    // For serious database
    // errors, JDBC will raise
    // a SQLException. The
    // following code is "belt
    // and suspenders" to make
    // sure the insert succeeded.
    if (theRowsAffected != 1)
      throw (new Exception(
        "A database error
        ➦occured."));
} catch (Exception e) {
  // In a GUI-based program,
  // consider displaying this
  // message in a dialog
```

```
// box.
System.err.println(
   e.getMessage());
}
```

to make sure that fields specified NOT NULL cannot be left blank.

To insert just part of a record (leaving the other fields NULL), use a statement like

```
INSERT INTO books (isbn, title) VALUES ('0789716275','Using
Java 1.2')
```

You can also copy part of one table into another. Suppose the database contains a table called TopQueBooks, which is intended to hold high-end books published by Que. You can populate TopQueBooks quickly by saying

```
INSERT INTO TopQueBooks (isbn, title, retailPrice)
SELECT isbn, title, retailPrice
FROM books
WHERE books.publisher = '7897' AND books.retailPrice > 45.00
```

Introducing the *NULL* Value

NULLs are more than just placeholders for missing information. They are a positive statement that a piece of information is unknown. By introducing NULL into SQL, the language designers converted SQL into a three-valued logic language. Statements may be true, false, or unknown (represented by a NULL).

For example, suppose the publicationYear field for a given book in the books table is NULL. The developer runs a query that asks for the retail price of all books whose publication year is greater than 1995. Then the developer runs a query that asks for the retail price of all books whose publication year is less than 1996. Based on these two queries, the developer believes he can compute the average retail price of a book in the database, but the developer is wrong.

SQL's interpretation of those queries is "Show me the retail price of every book for which the publication year *is known* to be greater than 1995" and "Show me the retail price of every book for which the publication year *is known* to be less than 1996."

NULL is not null

NULL, which is part of SQL and means "unknown," is in no way related to null, the Java value meaning "empty." They happen to share the same name.

Get data from the database with a SELECT statement

To implement this query you could use the following SQL code:

```
SELECT retailPrice
from BOOKS
   WHERE
(publicationYear >
          1996 OR

publicationYear
          IS NULL)
```

The SELECT statement is described in detail later in this section.

Books with an unknown publication date are missed by both queries, even though their retail price is known.

NULL is considered to be a statement that a value is unknown. Two occurrences of NULL are never equal—SQL has no reason to assume that one unknown value is the same as another. To write a query that captures data about NULL fields, you should use the IS NULL condition explicitly. Thus, a query can use IS NULL to say, "Show me the retail price of all books for which the publication year is known to be greater than 1996 or for which the publication year is unknown."

Deleting Records with the *DELETE* Statement

A record is deleted with the DELETE statement, which has the general form

```
DELETE FROM tableName [WHERE searchCondition]
```

For example, old books can be cleaned out with the statement

```
DELETE FROM books WHERE publicationYear < 1991
```

Update a Record

If the data in a record is essentially correct but needs some fields updated, you can modify it by using UPDATE:

```
UPDATE tableName SET [columnName=expression
[,columnName=expression][...]] [WHERE searchCondition]
```

Suppose the price on one of the books changes. You can issue the statement

```
UPDATE books
SET retailPrice = '59.99' WHERE isbn = '0789716275'
```

Querying the Database with the *SELECT* Statement

For many databases, CREATES, DROPS, INSERTS, DELETEs, and even UPDATEs occur infrequently. The day-to-day statement that is run against most databases is SELECT. Recall that SQL stands for Structured Query Language. It is SELECT that implements the SQL query. You'll use these queries as the basis for reports you may run against the database. The full syntax for SELECT is

```
1: SELECT [ALL | DISTINCT] selectList
2:   FROM {tableName | viewName }
```

Caution: DELETE is not undoable

Unless the statement is issued inside a transaction (described later in this chapter), the **DELETE** statement is irrevocable. A common mistake is to issue a statement like

```
DELETE FROM books
```

forgetting to specify a **WHERE** clause limiting the **DELETE** to certain records. Without the **WHERE** clause, **DELETE** deletes *all* records in the table.

Caution: Don't forget a WHERE clause

Like **DELETE**, **UPDATE** without the **WHERE** clause operates on *all* records in the table.

```
UPDATE books
Set retailPrice =
'49.99'
```

sets the new price on *all* books in the table—probably not what you intended.

```
3:   [ WHERE searchConditions ]
4:   [ GROUP BY columnName [, columnName][...]]
5:     [ HAVING searchConditions ]
6:   [ORDER BY { columnName ¦ selectListNumber } [ ASC ¦
     DESC ]
7:     [,{columnName ¦ selectListNumber} [ASC ¦ DESC]][...]]
```

While SELECT is the most complex statement in SQL, most of the clauses are optional. Many useful SELECT statements have only the required elements.

Issuing a Simple Query

The simplest SELECT statement asks for all the columns of all the rows of a single table:

```
SELECT * FROM books
```

In this statement, * is a wildcard that stands for all columns. The query could have asked for a subset of the available columns:

```
SELECT title, publicationYear FROM books
```

Specifying the *SELECT* List

The elements of the SELECT list are expressions and may include any of the following:

- Constants
- Column names
- Functions
- Combinations of these elements connected by arithmetic operators and parentheses

Thus, you can write

```
SELECT isbn FROM books
```

or

```
SELECT avg(retailPrice) FROM books
```

or

```
SELECT isbn, title, (retailPrice * 20000 * .75) * .18 FROM
books
```

Each of these lines is a valid SELECT statement.

You can give elements in the SELECT list names that appear in column headings. This technique is often useful when the column headings are cryptic or when the SELECT list includes expressions. For example,

```
SELECT isbn, title, retailPrice, DiscountedPrice =
retailPrice * .85
```

returns a table like the one shown in Table 21.2.

TABLE 21.2 SQL enables the developer to specify the printed name for a column

isbn	title	retailPrice	DiscountedPrice
0789708019	Webmaster Expert Solution	59.99	50.99
1575210703	Creating Web Applets With	39.99	33.99
078970790X	Enhancing Netscape Web Pa	34.99	29.74
(3 rows affected)			

The order in which elements appear in the SELECT list is up to you. If the table is specified with isbn first, then title, publicationYear, and finally retailPrice, it is still perfectly acceptable to say

```
SELECT retailPrice, isbn, title FROM books
```

Identifying Specific Records with *WHERE*

The books table stores several pieces of information about many different books. To limit the query to books meeting certain conditions, add a WHERE clause to the query, as follows:

```
SELECT title, publicationYear FROM books WHERE retailPrice
< 50.00
```

Now only books priced below $50.00 appear on the resulting list.

Although the WHERE clause is optional, it is usually included. By contrast, the remaining clauses and modifiers are somewhat less common.

SQL is a free-form language

Neither Java nor the RDBMS care how a SQL statement is indented nor how many lines it spans. For readability, keep the lines short and indent subordinate clauses. When breaking a clause into its components, leave the Boolean connector on the first line—the connector serves as a reminder that another condition is coming up and makes it less likely during maintenance that your eye will miss the additional information.

Conditions in the WHERE clause may be combined with the Boolean operators AND, OR, and NOT. Thus,

```
SELECT title, publicationYear
FROM books
WHERE retailPrice < 50.00 AND
        publicationYear > 1996
```

is valid SQL and limits the query to those rows that satisfy both the retail price condition *and* the publication year condition.

Sorting the Output with *ORDER BY*

As a matter of style, show all defaults

Even though some keywords, like **ASC**, are the default, it is a good idea to show them explicitly. Later, when you maintain the code, these explicit keywords serve as a reminder of your design decision and are a cue that you can change your mind if needed.

The relational model does not have a built-in concept of "first record" or "last record." If you add a new record right now and then do a SELECT on the table, the new record may be at the top of the list, the bottom of the list, or anywhere in between. If your application needs some kind of ordering, add a date-time stamp or other ordered field and use the ORDER BY clause, like the following:

```
SELECT isbn, title FROM books ORDER BY publicationYear
```

By default, ORDER BY lists the records in ascending order. You can explicitly set the order by using the keywords ASC and DESC.

```
SELECT isbn, title, publicationYear FROM books
ORDER BY publicationYear ASC
```

gives the same output as the default, whereas

NULL sorting is not portable

THE 1986 ISO-ANSI standard specifies that when **NULL**s appear in the column on which you sort, they should be either greater than or less than all non-**NULL** values. If you need to know which end of the list the **NULL**s fall on, check the documentation that comes with your RDBMS.

```
SELECT isbn, title, publicationYear FROM books
ORDER BY publicationYear DESC
```

outputs the list in order from the most recently published book to the oldest.

You can also use ORDER BY for nested sorts. For example,

```
SELECT isbn, title, publicationYear, retailPrice
FROM books
ORDER BY publicationYear, retailPrice
```

orders the list by publication year. Books with the same publication year are ordered by price. A useful output may be to list the books from the newest to the oldest and to list them from the ascending order by price within each publication year.

```
SELECT isbn, title, publicationYear, retailPrice
FROM books
ORDER BY publicationYear DESC, retailPrice ASC
```

Controlling which Records are Listed with *DISTINCT* and *ALL*

A relational database should always be designed so that the primary key is unique. Other columns, however, may have duplicate values. For example, many records in the books table will have a publication year of 1998. If you issue the statement

```
SELECT ALL publicationYear from books
```

you may get

```
publicationYear
- - - -
1998
1998
1995
1997
1997
1992
1998
(7 rows affected)
```

With the keyword ALL (which is the default), you get the values from all records—including any duplicates. Depending on the application, these duplicates may be annoying. To eliminate them, use the DISTINCT keyword:

```
SELECT DISTINCT publicationYear from books
```

The result is

```
publicationYear
- - - -
1998
1995
1997
1992
(4 rows affected)
```

Note that the ALL or DISTINCT keywords, if they are used, must be the first word in the SELECT list. Suppose the database has a table of customers that includes columns city and state. To get a list of states where you do business, write

```
SELECT DISTINCT state FROM customers
```

To get a list of *cities* (including their states) where you have customers, just write

```
SELECT DISTINCT city, state FROM customers
```

SQL then lists the rows where the combination of city and state are unique.

Understanding Aggregates

Until now, the variations of the SELECT statement have dealt with individual rows. SQL provides a set of functions that combine data from more than one row. This set is known as the *aggregate functions*.

For example, to find the average retail price of a book, write

```
SELECT avg(retailPrice) FROM books
```

The result is a single row:

```
- - - - -
49.95
(1 row affected)
```

Some versions of SQL enable you to specify a column heading:

```
SELECT avg(retailPrice) AveragePrice FROM books
```

which produces

```
AveragePrice
- - - -
49.95
(1 row affected)
```

The standard SQL aggregate functions are given in Table 21.3.

NULL may not equal NULL

NULLs are, by definition, unknown values. When comparing values, a NULL in one column does not equal a NULL in another column. But when preparing a DISTINCT list, SQL treats all NULLs alike. One NULL in a column is treated as a duplicate for all other NULLs.

Build your column headings in Java, not SQL

When you use SQL in a Java program, you'll usually want to use a *cursor*—a construct that allows you to easily iterate through the rows returned by a **SELECT** statement. You'll get more control over the appearance of the headings if you use this mechanism to send the results back to the user—don't rely on headings supplied by the RDBMS.

TABLE 21.3 The SQL aggregate functions combine data from more than one row

Function	Effect
SUM([DISTINCT] *expression*)	Total of the (distinct) values in the numeric expression
AVG([DISTINCT] *expression*)	Average of the (distinct) values in the numeric expression
COUNT([DISTINCT] *expression*)	Number of (distinct) non-NULL values in the expression
COUNT(*)	Number of selected rows
MAX(*expression*)	Highest value in the expression
MIN(*expression*)	Lowest value in the expression

Recall that the primary key of a table must be unique and non-NULL, and that the primary key is usually a single column (in databases that conform to second normal form or higher). But SQL does not have any way for you to specify which column contains the primary key. To check a table to ensure that no duplicates have slipped into the primary key, issue a query like

```
SELECT count(DISTINCT isbn), count(*) FROM books
```

This query tells the RDBMS to show the number of non-NULL entries in the column isbn, followed by the number of records in the table. If the two numbers are not the same, either a NULL or a duplicate has found its way into the primary key column and should be eliminated.

You can put a WHERE clause on a SELECT statement that has an aggregate in the SELECT list, but you cannot use an aggregate in the WHERE clause. Thus,

```
SELECT avg(retailPrice) FROM books WHERE publicationYear >
1996
```

gives the average retail price of books published more recently than 1996, but

```
SELECT retailPrice FROM books WHERE avg(retailPrice) > 50.00
```

is incorrect, and gives a syntax error.

When can you use DISTINCT?

Most aggregate functions enable you to use the DISTINCT keyword to specify whether the function should be performed on all rows or only on unique rows. DISTINCT is not illegal on the MAX and MIN functions, but it is not useful. The maximum value is the maximum value, regardless of whether only unique rows are considered.

Don't confuse COUNT and COUNT(*)

Despite the similarity of names, COUNT and COUNT(*) have rather different meanings. COUNT returns the number of rows for which the argument is non-NULL. COUNT(*) counts all rows.

Don't fix problems—prevent them

Queries to find problems in the database after they are entered can be useful in maintenance and troubleshooting, but the best practice is to keep the bad data from being entered in the first place. Knowing how to use Java or your RDBMS to check data before inserting it in the database will help to keep problems out of the database.

The rule of thumb is to use the WHERE clause to pull out the desired records. Then any aggregates in the SELECT list are applied over the selected records.

Building Sophisticated Queries by Using *GROUP BY*

Although it may be interesting to use aggregate functions to gather statistics on the data in the database, the principal use of aggregates is in SELECT queries with the GROUP BY clause. Here's a simple example of how GROUP BY is used:

```
SELECT publisherID, count(title)
FROM books
GROUP BY publisherID
```

The SELECT list contains the grouping column and an aggregate. If seven publishers are represented in the books table, the resulting list has seven rows. Each row contains the publisher ID and the number of non-NULL titles associated with that publisher, like this:

```
publisherID
-----  ----------
57521       4
7897        8
56205       4
57576       1
57169       2
56276       1
56830       1
(7 rows affected)
```

GROUP BY can also be nested. For example,

```
SELECT publisherID, publicationYear, count(title)
FROM books
GROUP BY publisherID
```

yields results like

```
publisherID          publicationYear
-----  ----         ----------
57521  1996              4
7897   1996              6
7897   1995              1
```

7897	1990	1
56205	1996	4
57576	1996	1
57169	1996	2
56276	1996	1
56830	1996	1

(9 rows affected)

GROUP BY is a simple clause, but it can trip up an unwary developer. To avoid problems, remember these rules of thumb:

- Put all of the grouping columns in the SELECT list.

- Only columns can be used for grouping, not expressions.

- Don't use GROUP BY to get multiple levels of summary value—run separate queries and combine them by using Java.

- Don't use GROUP BY without aggregates—DISTINCT gives the same effect and the meaning is clearer.

You may combine aggregates, WHERE, GROUP BY, and ORDER BY clauses freely within the rules given in this section to get the desired effect. Remember to follow the order given in the SELECT syntax declaration: WHERE comes first, GROUP BY, and finally ORDER BY. For example,

```
SELECT publisherID, avg(retailPrice)
FROM books
WHERE publicationYear > 1997
GROUP BY publisherID
ORDER BY 2 ASC
```

In this example, the column number, rather than the name, is used in order to have the results sorted by the average retail price.

Selecting Specific Groups by Using the *HAVING* Clause

You saw earlier that the WHERE clause in the SELECT statement determines which rows are used. The HAVING clause provides the same control for groups. The expressions in the HAVING clause follow the same syntax as those in the WHERE clause.

Include the elements from *HAVING* in the *SELECT* list

Be sure that each element in the **HAVING** clause appears in the **SELECT** list. Not all RDBMSs enforce this restriction, but the results of running a query with a **HAVING** clause element that is not in the **SELECT** list are seldom what you expected.

Here's a simple example with a HAVING clause:

```
SELECT publisherID, avg(retailPrice)
FROM books
WHERE publicationYear > 1995
GROUP BY publisherID
HAVING avg(retailPrice) > 25.00
```

In this query, the HAVING clause restricts the query to show only those publishers whose average retail price is greater than $25.00.

Dealing with *NULL* Values

Recall that the table specification can allow some columns to be NULL, or empty. If you use such a column in a SELECT list, all records with NULL for that column show an empty field. If you use an expression that references a NULL field, the result of the expression is always NULL.

Combining Tables with Joins

Everything that I've said about SQL and RDBMSs up to this point can apply just as well to a flat file. Indeed, a flat file is simply a table that holds everything. All of the examples so far have worked on only one table at a time.

Much of the power of the relational model comes from the fact that you can write queries that cross table boundaries.

Suppose that the books table includes a foreign key publisherID, and the publishers table contains the city and state of each publisher. To list all the books published in New York City, you can write

```
SELECT * FROM books, publishers
WHERE books.publisherID = publishers.ID AND
  publishers.city = 'New York' AND
  publishers.state = 'NY'
```

Joins are implemented with SELECT statements

In SQL, relational joins are expressed by using the SELECT statement, but the join is rather different from a single-table query. A proposal by developers to the standards committee would introduce a JOIN keyword into a future version of SQL to make this distinction clearer.

What distinguishes this statement from the SELECT statements you saw earlier is the presence of more than one table in the FROM clause. A SELECT statement that draws data from more than one table is called a relational *join*. The foreign key in one table is the primary key in another—this special column is called the *join column*.

Relational databases are based on a field of mathematics known as *relational algebra*. Although most databases can be designed without knowing the mathematical theory behind the software, it is important to understand how the database performs a join.

Suppose the books table has 100 entries, each of which contains a publisherID field. Suppose the publishers table has 10 entries, each of which has an ID field. The *Cartesian product* of the two tables is all combinations of rows from the two tables—in this case there are 100X10 ways to combine the rows in the tables. In theory (and under some circumstances, in practice), an RDBMS starts a join by examining all the combined rows in the Cartesian product. Because the SELECTs shown in earlier sections searched only one table, you may be surprised to find that joins take much more time than single-table selects. In this example, the join could take 10 times longer than a query over books and 100 times longer than a query over publishers.

Relational theory recognizes five different types of join:

- Natural join
- Equijoin
- Theta join
- Self-join
- Outer join

Understanding the Natural Join and the Equijoin

A join based on the equality operator is called an *equijoin*. An equijoin that names the join column only once is called a *natural join*. For example,

```
SELECT books.isbn, books.title, books.publisherID
FROM books, publishers
WHERE books.publisherID = publishers.ID
```

is a natural join, but

```
SELECT books.isbn, books.title, books.publisherID, publish-
ers.ID
FROM books, publishers
WHERE books.publisherID = publishers.ID
```

is not (though it is a equijoin).

A NULL in a table can cause a row to be skipped

Remember that NULLs are never equal to each other. If either table in a join has a NULL in a given row, that row is not included in the output. The inventor of much of relational theory, E.F. Codd, argued for a "maybe-join" feature in the relational model that would join NULLs, but that feature is not present in the standard, nor in most implementations of the language.

Using Theta Joins to Build Advanced Queries

Theta joins are joins that use any of the comparison operators:

- Greater than, denoted by >
- Greater than or equal to, denoted by >=
- Less than, denoted by <
- Less than or equal to, denoted by <=
- Equal to, denoted by =
- Not equal to, denoted by != or <>

Joins that are not equijoins are often described informally as a "less-than join," or "greater-than join," and so forth.

For example, suppose that each publisher discounts their books after a certain number of years, but that the specific number of years varies from publisher to publisher. To get a list of discounted titles, you could write

```
SELECT books.isbn, books.title, books.publisherID,
books.publicationYear
FROM books, publishers
WHERE books.publisherID = publishers.ID AND
books.publicationYear >= publishers.cutoffYear
```

Expressing Complex Queries As Self-Joins

Sometimes it is useful to use the join syntax but have the same table on both sides of the join. To make this syntax work, use aliases for both occurrences of the table in the FROM clause, like this:

```
SELECT DISTINCT publishers1.name, publishers1.zip
FROM publishers publishers1, publishers publishers2
WHERE publishers1.city = "Indianapolis" AND
  publishers1.zip = publishers2.zip AND
  publishers1.ID != publishers2.ID
```

This rather odd-looking query tells the RDBMS to make three passes through the Cartesian product of publishers with itself. In the first pass, this query pulls out only those rows that have "Indianapolis" in the city column. In the second pass the query works only with the rows it found on the first pass—those with

"Indianapolis" as their `city`. Finally this query removes from the result the occurrences of the publisher that match itself.

The result is the set of publishers who are based in Indianapolis and have exactly the same zip code. A book wholesaler might use a query such as this to reduce freight rates by finding suppliers who are physically close to each other.

Showing Context by Using Outer Joins

Sometimes you'll want the user to see the results of a join in context. The query

```
SELECT DISTINCT publishers.name, books.publishersID
FROM publishers, books
WHERE publishers.ID = books.publishersID
```

is a conventional join that shows all publishers who have books in the database. The result of this query might resemble the following output:

```
publishers.name        publishersID
-------------------    -----
Que                    7897
(1 rows affected)
```

By changing the comparison to the *outer join* operator, `*=`, the query shows all of the publishers:

```
publishers.name        publishersID
-------------------    -----
Que                    7897
NoBooksOut             NULL
BrandNewPublisher      NULL
(3 rows affected)
```

Building Powerful Queries with Nesting

SQL was originally named the *Structured* Query Language because entire SQL statements can be embedded in other statements. When this is done, the outer statement is known as the *enclosing statement*. If the inner statement is a SELECT, as is commonly the case, it is called a *subquery*.

Subqueries are complex but efficient

Sometimes the intent of a subquery can be captured in a join. When this is possible, the join is preferred because its syntax is likely to be clearer than the subquery.

If it is not possible to frame the query as a join, use the subquery–although the statement may look complex, it is more efficient than the commonly used alternative of issuing a series of queries and passing the results along in Java variables.

Subqueries enable you to frame powerful queries against the database, at the price of some complexity. Subqueries are often difficult to read and sometimes difficult to write.

Here's the syntax for a subquery:

```
SELECT [DISTINCT] selectList
FROM tableList
WHERE [expression {[NOT] IN ¦ comparisonOperator} ¦ [NOT]
EXISTS}
( SELECT [DISTINCT] subquerySelectList
  FROM tableList
  WHERE searchConditions )
```

Here's an example showing why subqueries are useful. Suppose a developer using the books table wants to find all books that cost more than *Using Java 1.2*. Without a subquery, you can run two separate queries:

```
SELECT retailPrice
FROM books
WHERE title = 'Using Java 1.2'
```

This query returns the price, $29.99. Now with that price stored (in a Java variable or even in your head if you are composing the query ad hoc), you run a second query:

```
SELECT title, retailPrice
FROM books
WHERE retailPrice > 29.99
```

These two queries do the job, but at the cost of some complexity. If the query is part of a Java program, you must capture the price from the first query in a variable and deal with any errors from the first query before framing the second query and feeding the variable back in at the right place. Using a subquery, you can frame the same query more efficiently:

```
SELECT title, retailPrice
FROM books
WHERE retailPrice >
(SELECT retailPrice
  FROM books
  WHERE title = 'Using Java 1.2')
```

Subqueries are not just difficult to read and write—they can also be difficult to interpret. RDBMS vendors differ in the restrictions they place on subqueries. Check the documentation that comes with your RDBMS for specific guidance on subqueries.

Comparing Subqueries and Joins

For many subqueries, an equivalent join returns the same answer. For example,

```
SELECT DISTINCT name
FROM publishers
WHERE publishers.ID IN
  (SELECT publisherID
   FROM books
   WHERE publicationYear = 1998)
```

returns the names of publishers who had a book come out in 1998. The same question is asked by this simpler join:

```
SELECT DISTINCT publishers.name
FROM publishers, books
WHERE publishers.ID = books.publisherID
  AND books.publicationYear = 1998
```

Not all subqueries have an equivalent join. Here's a simple variation of the above subquery:

```
SELECT DISTINCT name
FROM publishers
WHERE publishers.ID NOT IN
  (SELECT publisherID
   FROM books
   WHERE publicationYear = 1998)
```

This query asks for the names of publishers who did not have a book published in 1998. The "analogous" join does not ask the same question:

```
SELECT DISTINCT publishers.name
FROM publishers, books
WHERE publishers.ID = books.publisherID
  AND books.publicationYear != 1996
```

This join asks for publishers who have had a book published in a year *other than* 1998—not at all the same question as that asked by the subquery.

When should you use sub-queries?

Remember this rule of thumb: If the intent of a subquery can be expressed by a join, use the join. The join is usually easier to understand and may even outperform the subquery. If there is no equivalent join, use a subquery–the subquery is more efficient than running a series of queries and passing the results along in Java variables.

In most versions of SQL, subqueries may be nested—there is no reason to limit the query to a single subquery. As a practical matter, SELECT statements with many levels of subquery may perform poorly. If such statements appear frequently in the application, you may want to re-examine the underlying design of your database.

Using Correlated Subqueries to Examine Every Row

Most subqueries are easiest to understand by reading them from the inside out. Some queries include what is called a *correlated subquery* or *repeating subquery*. In these queries, the outer query generates a series of rows—each row is then evaluated by the subquery. For example, a subquery introduced by the keyword EXISTS is always a correlated subquery:

```
SELECT DISTINCT name
FROM publishers
WHERE EXISTS
   (SELECT *
    FROM books
    WHERE books.publisherID = publishers.ID
    AND books.publicationYear = 1998)
```

This query may be thought of as sending each row of publishers, one at a time, to the subquery. The subquery looks through books to see if that publisher had a book published in 1998. If it did, the subquery returns a non-NULL value, and the publisher's name appears on the list output by the outer SELECT.

Use * for the SELECT list on the inner query

When a subquery is introduced by EXISTS or NOT EXISTS, the outer statement cares only whether the result of the query is NULL or non-NULL. It is customary to use * for the SELECT list on the inner query because the outer query does not use the specific columns.

Here's another way to construct a correlated query that finds the names of publishers who published books in 1998:

```
SELECT DISTINCT name
FROM publishers
WHERE 1998 IN
( SELECT publicationYear
  FROM books
  WHERE books.publisherID = publishers.ID)
```

Conceptually, the outer query runs through the rows in publish-ers. Each row is sent to the subquery. If you need to duplicate this process manually (which is often useful when troubleshooting a complex query) you can execute just the subquery,

```
SELECT publicationYear
FROM books
WHERE books.publisherID = 'nnnnn'
```

manually substituting the publisher ID. If the result of the subquery is (1998), the IN clause of the outer query succeeds, and the publisher's name appears in the listing.

In practice, RDBMS vendors compete hotly on the basis of their implementations of features like subqueries. A vendor may maintain internal data structures or rely on developer-defined INDEXes to improve the performance of the query. Nevertheless, if you break down the query as shown in this section and it runs correctly when run by hand, it should run the same way when run as a subquery.

Putting It All Together: A Sophisticated Example of *SELECT*

There is nothing complex about putting the various SELECT clauses together, but the size of the query becomes large, and the query may become more difficult to understand. Remember to keep the clauses in the proper order (FROM, WHERE, GROUP BY, and HAVING) and to read subqueries from the inside out (unless the subquery is a correlated query, in which case it should be read from the outside in).

Suppose you extend this example database by adding an authors table. Some books have more than one author, so you should not put a foreign key to authors directly into books or you will not conform to first normal form. Instead, you add an authorsOfBooks table, which has two columns: an author ID and an ISBN (which uniquely identifies each book).

Now take apart this complex query to see what it asks:

```
SELECT DISTINCT name
FROM authors
WHERE authors.ID IN
( SELECT authorsOfBooks.ID
   FROM authorsOfBooks
   WHERE authorsOfBooks.isbn IN
     (SELECT isbn
      FROM books
      WHERE title LIKE "Special Edition Using%") )
```

This query is longer than others in this chapter, but it does not contain any new concepts. The LIKE keyword looks for a pattern embedded in a character field. In a LIKE expression, the % stands for any string of zero or more characters. A - stands for any single characters. Many RDBMS vendors allow * in place of % to be consistent with regular expression syntax from UNIX and other systems.

Although this query has two levels of subqueries, both of which are introduced with IN, they are not correlated subqueries because the subqueries can conceptually be broken down into simple queries and strung together with variables. Begin the analysis of noncorrelated subqueries with the inner query:

```
SELECT isbn
FROM books
WHERE title LIKE "Special Edition Using%")
```

which produces a list of ISBNs.

The next query matches ISBNs in authorsOfBooks with the ISBNs returned from the deepest subquery.

```
SELECT authorsOfBooks.ID
FROM authorsOfBooks
WHERE authorsOfBooks.isbn IN[...]
```

This subquery produces a list of author IDs.

Finally, the outer query looks through the authors table for each author ID, uses it to retrieve the author's name, and outputs the name. If the author has written more than one book that meets the search criteria, DISTINCT ensures that the author's name appears only once on the list.

Establishing a JDBC Connection

Now that you know some SQL you can begin to connect your Java programs to a relational database by using JDBC. The following is a three-step process for communicating with a relational database.

Using JDBC to work with a database

1. Establish a connection between the Java program and the database manager.

2. Send a SQL statement to the database by using a Statement object.

3. Read the results back from the database and use them in your program.

This section shows you how to establish a connection. The next two sections show you how to use the Statement and ResultSet classes.

Working with *DriverManager*

JDBC is designed to work with many different database managers from a variety of vendors. In order to establish a connection with a database the Java runtime environment must load the driver for the specified database. The DriverManager class is responsible for loading and unloading drivers.

Figure 21.3 illustrates the path from your Java code to the database. The DriverManager maintains a data structure that contains the Driver objects themselves as well as information about the Drivers.

DriverManager **works behind the scenes**

As a Java application or applet programmer you won't see much of **DriverManager**. You should know how it works, however. That knowledge will help you troubleshoot connection failures.

FIGURE 21.3
Your program connects to the database through a series of layers.

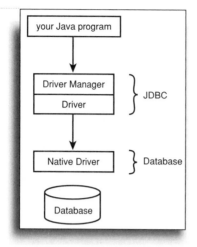

Loading *Drivers*

The DriverManager is responsible for making security checks

The DriverManager maintains a security context for each Driver. The security context defines the environment in which the application is running. When the DriverManager opens or queries a Driver, it checks the security context against the security context of your program to be sure they match.

JDBC Drivers are typically written by a database vendor; they accept JDBC connections and statements from one side and issue native calls to the database from the other.

Some database vendors haven't yet written JDBC drivers, but they have drivers that conform to a Microsoft standard—Open Database Connectivity, or ODBC. If you're working in a Windows environment, chances are your database vendor can provide you with an ODBC driver.

Preloading a *Driver* from the Command Line

To use a JDBC Driver (including the JDBC-ODBC bridge driver) you ask the system to load it. The easiest way to specify Drivers is to set the system property jdbc.drivers. You can preload the JDBC-ODBC bridge driver from the command line by typing:

```
java -Djdbc.drivers=sun.jdbc.odbc.JdbcOdbcDriver
MyApplication
```

Preloading a *Driver* Programmatically

Since the end user, and not the programmer, is usually in control of the command line, you may want to embed the name of the Driver directly into your program. This approach is less flexible—the end user can't easily change to a different version of the database—but is less likely to break in actual use. Use code like this example, which preloads the JDBC-ODBC bridge:

```
try {
  // we don't use 'theDriver' but the compiler requires us
  // to specify a left-hand-side in order to use .class
  Class theDriver = sun.jdbc.odbc.JdbcOdbcDriver.class;
} catch (ClassNotFoundException e) {
  System.err.println("Cannot find JDBC/ODBC driver class.");
}
```

Using the *Connection* Class

Once a Driver has registered with the DriverManger you can use it to connect to a database. Tell DriverManager that you want it to make a new Connection. It will invoke the Driver and return a reference to a Connection to you. You'll need to specify the location of the database, and for many database you'll need a username, and a password. For example, you might write:

```
Connection myConnection = DriverManager.getConnection(
  "jdbc:odbc:myDataSource",
  "admin",
  "password");
```

When DriverManager gets a getConnection() request, it takes the JDBC URL and passes it to each registered Driver in turn. The first Driver to recognize the URL and say that it can connect gets to establish the connection. If no Driver can handle the URL, DriverManager throws a SQLException, reporting "no suitable driver." If you get this error check your Driver documentation to see make sure the Driver has been installed correctly, and to double-check the form of the JDBC URL that you're using.

Recall that SQL statements execute immediately. For many simple queries this behavior is fine, but if you're building a complex multi-statement transaction you may not want to change the database unless all parts of it succeed. For example, suppose you want to add a new book, but you don't want to add the book unless the publisher is already on file. In SQL you use *transactions* to get this sort of *atomic* behavior. This behavior is called atomic because it cannot be split—a transaction either succeeds or it fails, there's no "half-way" state.

What's a JDBC URL?

The first parameter to getConnection() is a JDBC URL that specifies the location of the database—in this case jdbc:odbc:myData Source. The format is

jdbc:*sub-protocol*:*subname*

where *sub-protocol* is the name of the driver set and sub-name is additional information required by this driver set.

You can use the Connection object to manage transactions. By default, your new Connection is set to auto-commit—every statement is instantly committed to the database. To run transactions manually, use the following procedure.

Managing SQL transactions explicitly

1. Use Connection's setAutoCommit() method to disable auto-commit.

2. Issue SQL statements (described later in this chapter).

3a. If you're ready to commit the changes to the database, call commit() on your Connection.

3b. If you decide to abandon all of the statements made since the last commit(), issue a call to rollback().

Using the *Statement* Object

In Chapter 8, "Object-Oriented Design and Programming," we talked about the Factory design pattern. The Connection class is such a Factory: it produces Statement objects. The Factory mechanism is a Connection method called createStatement().

You use a Statement object to hold your SQL statements. When you send a Statement object to the database over the Connection the database runs your SQL and returns a ResultSet. Figure 21.4 illustrates how Statements and ResultSets pass back and forth between your program and the database.

Wrap your Statement methods in a try[...]catch statement

Most Statement methods throw SQLException. Be sure to catch this exception and either fix the problem or show it to the user.

To get a ResultSet write code like this sample:

```
ResultSet theSet =
    theStatement.executeQuery("SELECT * FROM books");
```

If you prefer you can write

```
Resultset theSet;
if (theStatement.execute("SELECT * FROM books"))
    theSet = theStatement.getResultSet();
```

In this version the execute() method returns a Boolean—true if the Statement returned a ResultSet and false if it returned an integer. You can use this method to retrieve multiple ResultSets from a single query.

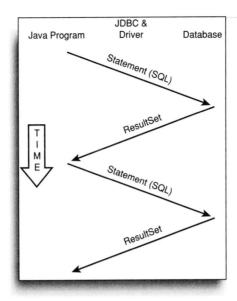

FIGURE 21.4
Use a Statement object to
request a ResultSet from
the database.

If you know your SQL statement will return an integer—something of the form *n* rows affected—you can use this form of
execute:

```
int theRowsAffected =
   theStatement.executeUpdate("UPDATE books
                          SET retailPrice = 59.95
                          WHERE ISBN='0789716275'");
```

As the name implies, this method is often used with SQL UPDATE,
but it's use is not limited to that statement. You might find it
useful with INSERTs and DELETEs as well. You can retrieve this row
count at any time by calling getUpdateCount().

You can get the ResultSet from a Statement by calling
getResultSet(). If the Statement contains more than one
ResultSet you can advance to the next one by calling
getMoreResults. This method returns true if the next result is a
ResultSet and false if the next result is an integer.

**Increase efficiency by using
PreparedStatement**

Many database managers support the concept of a "pre-compiled statement," so that
the work of interpreting the
SQL is only done once.
java.sql provides a sub-class of **Statement** called
PreparedStatement
that can generate such pre-compiled SQL.

Increase efficiency by using CallableStatement

If your database manager supports stored procedures–another way of avoiding recompilation–you can use **CallableStatements**. Just use the **prepareCall()** method to write the method, with question marks ('?') for parameter placeholders. Then use the **getType()** methods (described in the next section, "Handling the Result Set") with integer arguments to retrieve the parameters by number.

Be sure to call next() before you use the ResultSet

In a new **ResultSet** the initial position of the cursor is just "above" the first row. You must call **next()** in order to position the cursor onto the first row.

Retrieving columns by number

Your code will be most readable if you retrieve columns by name. If you want to increase performance slightly, retrieve the columns by number. For example, you can write

```
float thePrice =
theResults.getFloat
(3);
```

Handling the Result Set

The ResultSet class itself functions as a SQL cursor, allowing you to step through the data from a SELECT statement one row at a time. To advance from one row to the next, call next(). next() returns a boolean—you'll get false when there are no more rows in the ResultSet.

Within a row you can read out the contents of the columns from left to right. (Recall that you can use the SELECT to specify which columns you want and how they should be ordered.) Sun has provided getType() methods for all of the primitive types that SQL can store.

For example, you could write

```
1: ResultSet theResults =
2:   theStatement.executeQuery("SELECT title, author,
3:     retailPrice FROM books");
4: while (theResults.next())
5: {
6:   String theTitle = theResults.getString("title");
7:   String theAuthor = theResults.getString("author");
8:   float thePrice = theResults.getFloat("retailPrice");
9:   System.out.println(theTitle + " " + theAuthor + " " +
      ➥thePrice.toString());
10: }
```

When you've finished with the Statement and Connection objects it's good practice to call close() on both. This step will free up resources, often long before the garbage collector would have gotten around to it.

Improving Your Java Program's Performance

Learn why even unoptimized Java code running on old JVMs may be fast enough for most users

Use common-sense techniques to write efficient Java source code

Take advantage of advanced JVM technology

Learn why performance concerns about garbage collection and thread synchronization will become a thing of the past with Project HotSpot

Use the Java Native Interface to add "just enough" native code to smooth out your hot spots

How Fast Is "Fast Enough?"

There's a rule of thumb among Java developers: A JDK 1.0 Java program runs about 20 times slower than an equivalent native application. Before you erase your copy of `javac` in shock, let me ask you a question: is that level of performance a problem? Modern computers are so fast that, in fact, many machines are running the idle loop nearly all of the time. I just spent a few minutes pounding my Windows NT machine fairly hard—opening files, editing text, accessing the Web, and running a Java compile. Figure 22.1 shows the results—the only task I could find that really pounded the CPU was compiling Java. (That's what it was doing as this screen shot was taken, which accounts for the fact that the processor is 78 percent utilized.)

FIGURE 22.1

Most of the time our computers have plenty of idle time.

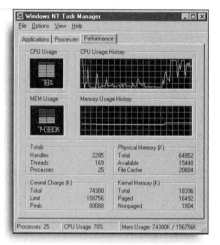

It's better to be slow and right than fast and wrong

For a certain class of software, performance is a major issue. This class is small—much smaller than most people think. For such a project, address performance concerns as part of the design activity. For the rest, concentrate on software quality and tune the code later.

If your applications don't do many computer-intensive tasks—if they're mostly user interface and I/O—you may not get much benefit from code optimization. If your user currently waits three milliseconds for some task to complete, and you can heavily optimize your code so you get that task down to three microseconds, does your user care, or even know?

OK, so maybe I can't convince you that code optimization doesn't matter. Maybe you're writing your next compiler in Java and really need your code to fly. This chapter describes two approaches to increasing your program's performance:

- Writing more efficient Java source code
- Executing Java bytecodes more efficiently

We'll cover the first task in the next section, where we'll talk about what slows Java code down and how to write around it. Later in the chapter, in the sections titled "Taking Advantage of Just-In-Time Compilers" and "Introducing HotSpot," we'll talk about just-in-time compilers and Sun's new JVM, based on Project HotSpot. Finally we'll talk about the possibility of compiling your Java to platform-specific code.

Using Simple Optimizations that Really Work

If you're an experienced programmer, chances are you've developed your own list of "code-tuning" strategies and techniques over the years. Let me share with you my personal favorite: Don't get too concerned about performance until the program works. I have little patience with programmers who brag about how fast their code is but ignore the fact that it doesn't do the job it was designed to do.

I'm not suggesting that you ignore common sense programming techniques until all of the code is perfect. During the design of your methods, you should be thinking about the time- and memory-complexity of your algorithm. If you suspect that performance is going to be critical, be sure to choose an efficient algorithm. After you've designed the code, don't worry about performance again until you've written the code. Then run it and see whether you have a problem or not. If the performance is hopelessly poor, don't worry about fine-tuning the code. You've got to change the hardware, abandon the algorithm, or prepare the customer for a letdown. But if the performance is mostly pretty good, you can concentrate on functional testing first, and then go on to identify and fix the "hot spots."

Don't confuse overall performance with raw code speed

Overall performance is only loosely related to the raw speed of your code, because your program may spend time waiting for user input or other I/O. While you're working on improved performance, you're not working on other issues, such as code quality or new features, both of which may allow the user to get his or her work done more quickly. Get your raw code speed into an acceptable range, and then make tradeoff decisions to decide whether it's better to tweak the speed or work on something else.

Designing for Adequate Performance

During the analysis activity, determine "how fast is fast enough" for this application. You'll use this information later, during code-tuning, to decide when to quit code-tuning and work on other aspects of the product. If you know that this combination of hardware and application is going to demand high performance, consider taking the following steps during design:

- *Consider changing the hardware.* With hardware costs low and getting lower, adding a faster processor, more RAM, or a wider data bus can often give you the performance you need without requiring tricky, hard-to-maintain code.

- *Define a time and memory budget and allocate it to each method.* If every method on every object stays within its budget, the whole system will meet its goals. Identify objects that are having a hard time staying within their budget and target them for redesign (or at least code-tuning).

- *Pay attention to data structures.* A hash table takes a lot of memory but looks up items in a single step. A linked list may require less RAM, but it needs an average of $n \div 2$ steps to find one item in n. A binary tree with a lookup time proportional to $\log_2 n$ may sometimes be a good choice for lookup (though it's difficult to delete items from such a tree).

- *Determine early on whether your program's performance is limited by the speed of the processor, the size of the memory, or the speed of the I/O.* If you spend 90 percent of your time waiting on the hard drive to deliver data, no amount of conventional code-tuning will have a significant impact on performance. (In that case you may want to explore the benefits of a cache, use buffered I/O, or optimize the layout of the data on the hard drive.)

Optimizing Hot Spots in Your Code

Most software follows the "Pareto Principle," also known as the 80/20 rule. Twenty percent of your code often accounts for 80 percent of your performance problems. One study, by Barry

Boehm of TRW ("Industrial Software Metrics Top Ten List," *IEEE Software* 4, no. 9: 84-85), found that 20 percent of a program's routines consume 80 percent of the execution time. Another famous study ("An Empirical Study of FORTRAN Programs" by Donald Knuth, *Software—Practice and Experience* 1:105-33) revealed that less than 4 percent of a program usually accounts for more than 50 percent of its run time.

The following procedure can give a big performance boost to your code.

Optimizing hot spots

1. Once your code passes functional test, run a profiler to tell you where the code is spending most of its time.

2. Make small optimizations and rerun the optimizer. If your optimizations are having the opposite effect than you intended, analyze this behavior and change your code.

3. Continue to profile and optimize until your code meets your performance objectives.

I once wrote a program that ran the blink cycle on some lights. The program was clean, clear, and elegant. It was also way too slow, by a factor of ten. In about an hour, I was able to double the speed. By the end of the day, I doubled the speed again. By the end of the next day, I had doubled the speed yet again. It took me to the end of the week to get code to run fast enough. The point is that simple speed-up is easy—you can get dramatic gains in just a few hours. Massive speed-up may take a bit longer.

Here's a list of obvious time-wasters you should avoid if performance is important:

- *Avoid unnecessary disk I/O*. If your computer has enough memory, don't write to disk files. If your design cries out for external storage, use a `ByteArrayStream` and save the data in memory. As a rule of thumb, RAM is around 1,000 times faster than the hard drive.

Measuring program speed

For some ideas on how to measure the speed of your program, look at the JMark 2.0 benchmark developed by PC Labs. You'll find it online at `http://www.virtual-labs.com/`.

Know what you're measuring

Make sure your profiler measures only the execution time of your program. Some poorly written utilities don't work correctly in a multitasking or multi-user environment—you'll end up optimizing code that is already efficient.

- *Avoid unnecessary screen I/O.* An innocent write to a `java.awt.TextArea` can have a big impact on program performance. In general, command-line I/O is faster than GUI I/O, and no I/O is faster still.

- *Put I/O in its own thread.* When you must do I/O, remember that `reads` and `writes` block. Move the I/O to its own thread, give it lower priority, and make sure it `yield()`s or `sleep()`s each time through the `run()` loop so the user thread doesn't starve.

- *Avoid floating point operations.* If your target machine doesn't have a floating point coprocessor or a floating point processor built into the CPU, floating point operations will be expensive. Look for an alternative, such as fixed-point arithmetic.

- *Stay in real RAM.* Use your operating system utilities to see whether you're paging. UNIX's `vmstat` utility or Windows NT's Task Manager will tell you this. If your program spends most of its time swapping pages, it will never run quickly. If possible, add RAM. Failing that, attempt to redesign the program to use caches more efficiently.

- *Wrap your streams in* `BufferedReader()` *or* `BufferedInputStream()`. In general, any buffer you place between the operating system and your program will serve you well. Similarly, use `BufferedWriter()` or `BufferedOutputStream()` for output.

- *Wherever possible remove common code from loops.* For example, change

```
for (int i=0; i< kLimit; i++)
{
  if (theType == kFirst)
  {
    processTheFirstType( i );
  }
  else
  {
    processTheSecondType( i );
  }
}
```

```
to

if (theType == kFirst)
{
  for (int i=0; i<kLimit; i++)
    processTheFirstType( i );
}
else
{
  for (i=0; i<kLimit; i++)
    processTheSecondType( i );
}
```

This redesigned code avoids doing an unnecessary comparison inside the loop.

- *Eliminate common subexpressions.* Compute it once, save it, and reuse it from the saved copy.

Your hot spots will nearly always include a loop, so anything you can do to simplify the work done in a loop will usually save you time in the long run. Simplifying loops often means moving some work outside the loop and doing it once—a big performance gain, but the code becomes less readable.

Here are some ideas for picking up these gains:

- *Fuse compatible loops.* For example, replace

```
for (int i=0; i< kLimit; i++)
{
  doTheFirstStep( i );
}
for (i=0; i<kLimit; i++)
{
  doTheSecondStep( i);
}
```

with

```
for (int i=0; i< kLimit; i++)
{
  doTheFirstStep( i );
  doTheSecondStep( i );
}
```

Remember that the second and third clauses of a for loop are also "in the loop"

Instead of

```
for (int i=0;
i<myString.length();
i++)
```

write

```
int theLength=myString.
length();
for (int i=0;
i<theLength; i++)
```

Caution: Be careful that the saved value doesn't need to change

If you save a value that depends upon, say, i, and i changes, your saved value is worthless. Be sure common expressions are truly common; rebuild them when necessary.

This redesign eliminates the overhead of the second loop and will usually increase the speed of the program by a few percent.

- *Where possible, eliminate tests in loops.* The following is a loop that searches for a specific value in an array. It has three tests inside each iteration—a test of i and a test of the value in theArray:

```
int i=0;
while (i < theArray.length)
{
  if (theArray[i++] == theDesiredValue)
    break;
}
```

The following version is longer and less readable, but has only a single test:

```
// replace the last element with the desired value.
i=0;
int theLastCell = theArray.length - 1;

// make sure the desired value isn't in the last
➥cell of the array
if (theArray[theLastCell] != theDesiredValue)
{
  // save the value of the last cell, and replace it
  ➥with a sentinel
  int theSavedValue = theArray[theLastCell];
  theArray[theLastCell] = theDesiredValue;
    // now just hunt for the value--one test per
    ➥iteration
  while (theArray[i] != theDesiredValue)
    i++;

  // restore the value of the last cell
  theArray[theLastCell] = theSavedValue;

  // handle the case of the desired value not being
  ➥found
  if (i == theLastCell)
    doDesiredValueNotFound();
```

```
}
  else
    i = theLastCell; // record where the value was
    ➥found
```

- *Replace computationally expensive operations, such as multiplication, with simpler operations, such as addition.* The following code performs several multiplications inside the loop:

```
for (int i=0; i< kLimit; i++)
{
  theArray[i] = i * aValue * anotherValue *
➥stillAnotherValue;
}
```

You can avoid all those multiplications by writing

```
float theIncrement = aValue * anotherValue *
➥stillAnotherValue;
float theRunningTotal = 0;

for (int i=0; i< kLimit; i++)
{
  theArray[i] = theRunningTotal;
  theRunningTotal += theIncrement;
}
```

The second version is less readable; trace it out for yourself and satisfy yourself that `theArray` ends up with the same values in both cases.

In general, you may get a performance boost if you replace

- Multiplication with addition
- Exponentiation with multiplication
- Trigonometric routines with trigonometric identities
- Double-precision floating point numbers with single-precision floating point numbers
- Floating point numbers with fixed-point or integer numbers
- Long integers with shorter integers
- Integer multiplication and division by multiples of two with left and right shift operators

Building multi-dimensional arrays in Java

Java doesn't support multi-dimensional arrays *per se*, but you can get the same effect by building arrays of arrays.

- *Arrange tests in order of likelihood.* If you have to test for three cases and one is far more likely than the other two, place that test first—in most cases you'll avoid the work of two additional tests.

- *Substitute table lookups for complicated expressions.* If you find yourself writing complex if...then expressions deep inside a loop, build a multi-dimensional array outside the loop. Inside the loop, just use the loop indexes to look up the desired value in the array.

- *Use lazy evaluation.* If you need a large table (such as the one described in the previous recommendation) and some values are more common than others, start with an empty table. As you need the value, compute it and leave it in the table. You'll avoid computing all those extra values you never needed.

- *Some versions of the JVM deal with arrays-within-arrays better than others; if you can find a way to solve a problem that involves only a single-dimensioned array, that version may be faster.* On the other hand, if you make your code too Byzantine, you may defeat the compiler's optimizer and end up with a net performance loss (not to mention the loss of readability). Test both ways to be sure.

- *Array accesses can be computationally expensive.* If you're accessing the same element repeatedly, save it in a local variable to avoid hitting the array.

- *If you have to search large, complex data structures repeatedly, build an index.* Such an index may be a candidate for lazy evaluation, described previously in this list.

- *If you have a hot spot that includes an API call, consider whether you may be able to substitute a less expensive API call.* For example, new Date() is noticeably slower than System.currentTimeMillis().

- *If you have a hot spot that includes an API call, consider whether you may be able to substitute a custom method for the API call.* Many API calls are written to handle the general case. You may get a performance boost if you write a routine tailored to your requirements.

If, after you've performed all of the code tuning you can think of, and your hot spots are still keeping your program from running as fast as it needs to, consider recoding those routines in a native language. In Java you can hook in platform-specific libraries by using the Java Native Interface (JNI). We'll look at the JNI later in this chapter, in the section entitled "Evaluating Translation."

Optimizing with Java-Specific Techniques

Much of the delay in Java comes from user interaction. Here are some tips for increasing the performance of your user interface:

- Paint only inside your `clipRect`.

- `repaint()` only when necessary, and only as much as necessary.

- Use Swing components rather than their heavyweight AWT counterparts.

- Avoid the old JDK 1.0 event model. It's slower, and it's deprecated anyway.

- Use layout managers. They're faster, and the results will not depend upon a particular screen size.

- Use double-buffering, or paint containers while they're invisible, and then make them visible.

Remember that `Strings` are immutable—once you make one, you can't change it. If you write

```
String myString = new String();
for (int i=0; i<kLimit; i++)
{
  myString = myString + newComputedString();
}
```

the runtime environment must make a new `String` inside the loop and copy the old version of `myString` to the new version. If you loop enough times and the `Strings` are large enough, you may use up so much memory that the garbage collector runs.

While it's running, the current thread must wait. (But see the comments about the new HotSpot JVM in the section, "Introducing HotSpot"—the garbage collector may no longer be a problem.)

Here's a different approach that avoids having to make and copy all those Strings:

```
StringBuffer myStringBuffer = new StringBuffer();
for (int i=0; i<kLimit; i++)
{
   myStringBuffer.append(newComputedString());
}
return myStringBuffer.toString();
```

If you want to include some debug code, make it depend upon a static final variable. The compiler may be able to eliminate the test and the code, just as the C preprocessor does. Thus, you might write

```
static final boolean kDebugging = false;
. . .
if (kDebugging)
   System.err.println(testValue);
```

When you must call an operation that blocks or that takes a long time, do so in a separate thread so the user interface doesn't appear to freeze. Here's an example where performance doesn't depend on raw code speed, but on good design.

If you're using multiple threads, you must think about synchronization. Synchronization between threads is computationally expensive. While Sun and other vendors have done a great deal to reduce the overhead associated with synchronization, synchronization is still not free. Too much synchronization can be safe, but will exact a performance penalty. (But see the description of HotSpot, coming up later in this chapter—synchronization may become virtually free in the near future.)

When possible, preallocate the StringBuffer

Sun advises that this code will be even faster if you preallocate your **StringBuffer** to about the right size, rather than letting it grow at runtime.

Debunking Optimization Myths

This section lists some "rules of thumb" that either don't work, don't work in Java, or work but are more trouble than they're worth. Some of these myths are based on valid optimizations that worked for first-generation JVMs. Since most JVMs are now using second-generation technology, and Sun's third-generation JVM—HotSpot—is due out before the end of 1998, there is no need for these optimizations anymore.

- *Reducing the lines of code improves the speed or size of the resulting class file.* Not true! The best way to write high-quality class files is to write clear Java, and that usually means that you don't try to cram the entire program into just a few lines.

- *Operation x is probably faster than operation y.* Not necessarily. The actual performance of Java statements depends upon many factors, not the least of which is the JVM on which the bytecodes are running. Don't settle for "probably." Write high quality code, and then go back and measure the product. Finally, tune out hot spots that account for any unacceptable slowdowns.

- *Use* static *and* final *methods to help the compiler optimize.* False! While you may get a small performance gain, you'll lose class reusability. In fact, with HotSpot, Sun reports that there will be no performance gain at all.

- *Write big methods to avoid extra method invocations.* Wrong. In second-generation JVMs (which have JIT compilers) the performance difference is negligible. The same comment applies to the third-generation JVM, HotSpot.

- *Minimize object allocation.* Bad idea. Decreases the readability of your code, and isn't necessary in the third-generation JVM.

JVM's evolution to optimization

The first generation of the JVM was essentially an interpreter, with all the performance problems associated with that technology. The second generation is based on Just-In-Time (JIT) compilation and is part of nearly every Java environment today. The third generation–HotSpot–is based on adaptive optimization and promises to change everything we know about Java optimization.

- *Avoid thread synchronization*. Very bad idea. Decreases the reliability of your code, and isn't necessary in the third-generation JVM. If you avoid using multiple threads altogether, overall performance may suffer.

- *Avoid doing garbage collection*. Wrong. Decreases the reusability of your code, and isn't necessary in the third-generation JVM.

Taking Advantage of Just-In-Time Compilers

Recall from Chapter 1, "What is Java, and Why Is It Important?" that a Just-In-Time (JIT) compiler runs on the end user's machine and is integrated into the JVM. The first time the JIT compiler sees a piece of code, it passes it through to the interpreter in the JVM, but it also compiles it and saves the native code. If the program loops back through this same section and the JIT compiler sees this code again, it doesn't bother to run the interpreter—it just executes the native code.

One way of looking at JIT compilers is to think of them like conventional optimizing compilers—the kind you have in your development environment in most languages—that run on-the-fly. The problem that JIT compilers have is that they don't have much time—they must review the code and generate their native instructions before the next set of bytecodes comes in, or their overall effect will be to hurt performance.

The good news is that, in certain kinds of code, a JIT compiler can give you a 13- to 15-fold increase in performance. That gives you back much of the 20-fold decrease we talked about at the beginning of this chapter. The bad news is that you only get that performance boost in certain parts of the code: loops that include repeated method invocations or simple (C-like) logic. The other speed problems—object allocation, thread synchronization, and garbage collection—remain.

Table 22.1 shows eighteen commercial JDK 1.1-compliant JVMs, twelve of which include JIT compilers. *PC Magazine* performed a review of these environments (reported on page

144–145 of their April 7, 1998 issue). They found that JIT compilers had a significant impact on computationally intensive tasks but gave no real boost to user interface methods such as drawing to the screen.

TABLE 22.1 JIT compilers in Java environments

Operating System	JVM	Version	JIT Compiler
Mac OS 8	Microsoft Internet Explorer	4.0	Yes
Mac OS 8	Mac OS Runtime for Java	2.0	Yes
Windows 95/NT 4.0	Microsoft Internet Explorer	4.0	Yes
Windows 95/NT 4.0	Netscape Communicator	4.04	Yes
Windows 95/NT 4.0	Sun JDK	1.1.5	No
Windows 95/NT 4.0	Sun JDK with Win32 Performance Pack	1.1.5	Yes
Windows 95/NT 4.0	Symantec Visual Café for Java	2.1	Yes
OS/2 Warp 4.0	IBM Java for Warp	1.1.4	Yes
Solaris 2.6	Microsoft Internet Explorer Preview	4.0	No
Solaris 2.6	Netscape Communicator	4.04	No
Solaris 2.6	JDK	1.1.3	Yes
Solaris 2.6	JDK	1.1.5	No
Solaris 2.6	JDK with Native Threads Pack	1.1.5	No

Taking Advantage of Performance Enhancements in JDK 1.2

Recall from Chapter 1 that Sun has been working hard to close the performance gap between Java programs and programs written in a native language. The greatest successes come from the use of the Just-In-Time (JIT) compilers I've just described, but

---

JDK 1.2 includes JIT compilers

In addition to the environments shown in Table 22.1, JDK 1.2 includes JIT compilers for Windows 95, Windows NT, and Solaris.

PC Magazine picks "JVM of the Year"

The 1998 "Editors Choice" for JVM was Microsoft's JVM for Windows. They write, "For the second year in a row, Microsoft has produced the fastest and most reliable Java implementation available." Read more at http://www.pcmag.com/features/java98.

they've also introduced improved performance for multi-threaded programs. JDK 1.2 also offers better memory management than its predecessors.

Understanding Native Thread Support

JDK 1.2 offers native threads in both Windows and Solaris

Sun has used Microsoft's native thread package to good effect. Starting in JDK 1.2, they also offer native threads on the Solaris versions of the JDK.

In Chapter 17, "Concurrent Programming with Threads," we talked about the fact that forking (also known as "spawning"), a new process, is computationally expensive. Switching between threads, and especially synchronizing threads, isn't as expensive as working with processes, but it isn't free, either. Microsoft, Sun, and other operating system vendors have invested heavily in improving the performance of their native threads. Sun gets a performance improvement in the JVM by using these native threads to implement Java threads.

Using Memory Compression for Loaded Classes

Allowing the compiler to compress your `Strings`

In order to take advantage of this new feature, your `Strings` must truly be identical. If you have two or more classes with similar `Strings`, consider making them identical so the compiler can eliminate all but one copy.

Starting in JDK 1.2, constant strings are shared between classes, reducing the memory needs of all classes. Since Java `Strings` are immutable, you don't need to worry about some other class changing your class's `String`.

Enjoying Faster Memory Allocation and Garbage Collection

As programmers have started to take advantage of multithreading, resources shared among threads become the constraining factor in performance. In JDK 1.2 Sun has given each thread some independent memory allocation and garbage collection assets. The effect of this change is a marked improvement in performance for multithreaded programs.

Taking Advantage of Monitor Speedups

As we saw in Chapter 11, "Building the User Interface with the AWT," thread synchronization is critical to correct performance. You synchronize threads by naming an `Object` through which you and the other threads will agree to lock a critical section.

The component of the `Object` on which all parties lock is called the monitor. Sun has improved the performance of the monitor in JDK 1.2, which leads to further speedups for multithreaded code.

SEE ALSO

➢ *Learn more about synchronized threads, page 467*

Getting a Performance Boost from the Native Library JNI Port

In the first section of this chapter, "How Fast Is 'Fast Enough?'," I suggested that you could improve performance by profiling your code and optimizing the hot spots.

Sun has been using that same lesson to improve the performance of Java. Most of an application or applet's time is spent deep inside Sun's code, not out at the level that you and I write. Sun has rewritten their core libraries to use the Java Native Interface (JNI).

Introducing HotSpot

The next generation of JVM from Sun is codenamed Project HotSpot. HotSpot relies on *adaptive optimization* —a two-step process that offers better optimization than even static optimizing compilers offer. The following shows how adaptive optimization works:

1. The JVM profiles the Java program as it runs and finds the critical "hot spots" where the program is spending most of its time.

2. The JVM uses runtime information (not available to a static compiler) as well as traditional optimization techniques in order to optimize the code on-the-fly.

In addition to adding adaptive optimization, Sun's designers included two new features in HotSpot:

- An improved garbage collector
- A performance breakthrough in thread synchronization

Much of the API runs at native speed

Since your program is now running native code when it runs Sun's libraries, your program gets a performance boost. For example, if your program spends 80 percent of its time in the core API libraries, and if, after optimization, Java code runs at one fourth the speed of native code, your overall program will be more than twice as fast as it was before Sun rewrote their libraries.

Sun expects Java to run at the same speed as native code

The combination of adaptive optimization, improved garbage collection, and the breakthrough in thread synchronization means that your users can enjoy the benefits of platform-independent programs in Java without a performance disadvantage relative to platform-specific code. Look for Sun to make HotSpot available for general use by the end of 1998.

Enjoying the Benefits of an Improved Garbage Collector

Traditional garbage collectors run as a low-priority background thread. When memory is low, they must deal with large amounts of data. This process takes time, during which the program must not move any objects. The effect is that the garbage collector locks the threads while it's running, effectively freezing the program.

The garbage collector in HotSpot will have two components. For short-lived objects it will rely on a scavenging mechanism that reclaims objects quickly—usually within a few milliseconds. For longer-lived objects, it will employ incremental collection that doesn't disrupt the running program.

The upshot of these changes is that the cost of garbage collection will fall to nearly zero. The long pauses during garbage collection will be a thing of the past, even if your program manipulates large amounts of data. Sun has told developers, "The user will essentially never see GC pauses again, even when manipulating very large numbers of objects."

Utilizing Sun's Thread Synchronization Advances

In the first generation of JVMs, thread synchronization was very expensive in terms of computing time. JIT compilers can do little to improve synchronization, though second-generation JVMs typically include native thread support, which offers some improvement.

In Project HotSpot, Sun's engineers were able to achieve a breakthrough—a new way of managing thread synchronization that reduces the cost of synchronization to near-zero levels. Sun is now advising users of the HotSpot JVM, "Don't worry about the cost of thread synchronization."

Evaluating Native Translation

Several vendors have introduced translators that compile Java to native binaries. These compilers get a big performance boost from two factors:

- The finished code is binary, so you avoid the overhead of the JVM.
- These static optimizing compilers have much more time than the JIT compilers to look for optimization opportunities.

Java development environments with native translators include:

- CodeWarrior Professional 2.0 from Metrowerks
- JBuilder Client/Server Suite from Borland
- Sun Java Workshop 2.0
- Sybase Power/J Enterprise 2.x
- SuperCede's SuperCede for Java 2.0 Professional Edition
- Symantec's Visual Café for Java 2.x, (Professional Edition or Database Development Edition)

Follow the instructions that come with your development tools to compile your Java code into native code. This section describes the cost and benefits associated with native translation.

Enjoying the Benefits of Native Translation

What is there to like about native translation? Well, speed, mostly. A native application will run about twenty times faster than raw Java. It will run somewhat faster than Java running on a JVM with a JIT compiler, though the performance impact at the user's level may be small.

Furthermore, Java is completely object-oriented (unlike C++, which is *almost* completely object-oriented). Static optimization techniques that work well in traditional programming languages

Why do traditional optimizations not give big performance boosts?

As we've seen throughout this book, object-oriented languages encourage you to write small, highly focused methods rather than big functions. This means that you have a large number of method invocations, which, in an object-oriented language like Java, means dynamic dispatch. This dynamic dispatch is slow and becomes the bottleneck.

don't offer the same benefits when they're applied in an object-oriented environment, so static compilers for Java don't bring you up to quite the same level of performance as you might get from C++. In most cases—especially for large programs—the benefits of staying object-oriented in terms of readability and maintainability far outweigh the performance differences.

Paying the Cost of Native Translation

Most of the benefits of Java have to do with security and portability. (See Chapter 1 for a review of the benefits of Java.) You lose those benefits when you move to a platform-specific language. For example, if you write an applet in Java, it will run on any machine with a JVM. If you convert it to native code, you'll also have to convert it to, say, an ActiveX control or a Netscape browser plug-in.

As you saw in the previous section, the performance difference between Java and native code may evaporate as third-generation compilers and JVMs move into the marketplace. If you have a hot spot that must be optimized, and the methods described at the beginning of this chapter haven't been able to do the job, consider going to native code. For a long-term solution, keep watching Project HotSpot. As the new JVM moves out into the marketplace, you may decide to bring your native methods back into Java.

Using JNI to Optimize Hot Spots

If you're not ready to give up the benefits of Java but you have some hot spots that resist further optimization, consider coding just those methods in a native language such as C++. If you distribute your program (such as an applet) on many different platforms, you'll need to write a different version of the library for each platform, but that impact may be acceptable compared to the impact of distributing the entire executable in native code.

Use the Java Native Interface (JNI) to add a native method to a Java program. By using the JNI, you are guaranteed that your Java binaries (class files of bytecodes plus the native library) will run on any JVM that runs on that platform. Your Java code will continue to take advantages of any improvements Sun and the other vendors make in the JVM—as HotSpot matures, you may consider bringing your native methods back into Java.

SEE ALSO
➤ *Learn more about JNI, page 81*

Making and Using Java Archives

See how Web browsers download applets, and why using JARs streamlines the process

Learn how to make a JAR file using Sun's *jar* utility

See how to digitally sign your JAR so end users can trust your applets

Prepare JAR files for JavaBeans so end users can drop your Beans into their IDE

Learn how to read and write JAR files from inside your program

How Does an Applet Get Downloaded?

When you write simple applets you'll often have only one class and one class file. Your `<APPLET>` can look like the following:

```
<APPLET CODE="TMyApplet.class" WIDTH="200" HEIGHT="200">
</APPLET>
```

But what do you do with sophisticated applets that use many classes, and possibly other files? Before Java 1.1 there was no good solution to this question. Suppose you want to download the applet shown in Figure 23.1. In response to your `<APPLET>` tag your Web browser fetches `http://someServer.com/ TMyApplet.class`. The browser turns that file over to the Java Virtual Machine (JVM) that's built into the browser, which, in turn, performs security checks on the code and then turns it over to the `ClassLoader`. The `ClassLoader` discovers the fact that `TMyApplet` uses `TBar`. Back to the Net it goes, does another fetch from the Web server, and repeats the process. It also discovers that `TMyApplet` needs `TBaz`, so it repeats the process again. Finally it discovers that `TBaz` uses `TQuux`, so it retrieves that class file as well. Now that it has all the code, it discovers that this program wants to download twelve frames of an animation: T1.gif through T12.gif.

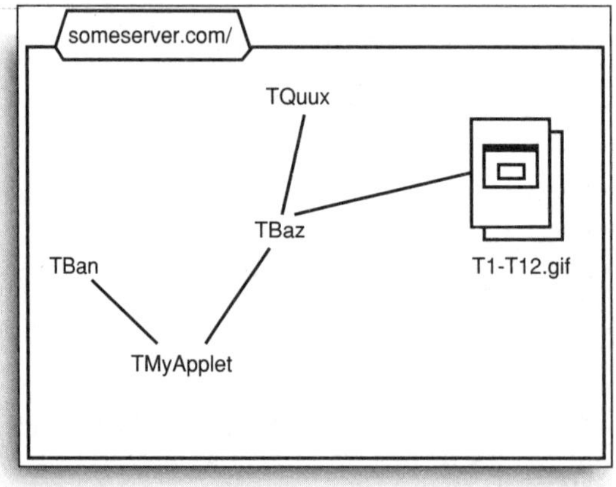

Multiple classes go to multiple class files

Even if you put more than one class in a source file, the compiler will still split them out into separate class files.

"Loose" class files can get lost

Not only is it inefficient to download a series of "loose" class files, it's easy to make a mistake. If someone moves or renames one of the files, users will begin to get mysterious messages about the missing class.

FIGURE 23.1

Sophisticated applets with lots of classes were one of the driving forces behind JARs.

If you know anything about the HyperText Transfer Protocol (HTTP)—the protocol of the Web—you know that it's inefficient to transfer a series of small files. Each transfer sets up a new TCP/IP connection, and then tears it down again. There's considerable overhead associated with each new connection. On some dial-up links it can take nearly a half-second to establish the connection; if your applet needs 16 files, this overhead adds up to about eight seconds, when you might have completed the transfer in about one.

To give you a more efficient way of distributing applets (and, for that matter, applications and JavaBeans), Sun introduced the Java Archive, or JAR, format. You can place all of the files associated with an applet into a JAR file, and write

```
<APPLET CODE="TMyApplet.class"
  ARCHIVE="MyArchive.jar, AnotherArchive.jar"
  WIDTH="200" HEIGHT="200">
</APPLET>
```

This bit of code tells the browser to download the two JARs named. The browser can expect that the components of TMyApplet will all be found in those two JARs. Furthermore, if the browser already has a current copy of one or both of those JAR files in its cache, it may be able to skip the download and display the applet right away. Figure 23.2 illustrates how the class files for TMyApplet are distributed across the two JAR files.

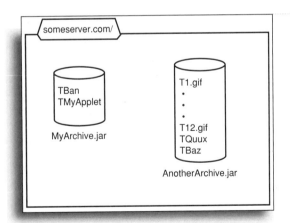

As an applet developer, you get six benefits from JARs:

- Improved download efficiency—Because you only need one HTTP transfer per JAR, instead of one per class file.

Some newer servers have efficient HTTP

If you're running a newer server, you may have a **KEEPALIVE** function that keeps TCP/IP connections intact for a few seconds in case there's a second request from the client, but you shouldn't have to rely upon that feature when you're developing applets.

You can still use loose files

If your applet uses files that aren't in the JAR file, the Web browser will go back to the Web server and look in the current **CODEBASE** directory for the missing files.

FIGURE 23.2

You can store the files of an applet in one or more JAR files.

- Improved file storage—A JAR stores the class files in one compressed file, instead of leaving them "loose" in the directory.

- Improved security—You can sign JAR files digitally, giving the end user a guarantee that the file has not been tampered with since you signed it. If the end user trusts you, he may be willing to give your signed applet access to his hard drive or other sensitive resources.

- Platform independence—JAR files are based on PKZIP, a popular DOS compression utility, but they can be built and stored on any computer platform.

- Backwards compatibility—A JAR file doesn't care what kind of files you put into it. You could take a JDK 1.0 applet and store its class files in a JAR file. As long as the user's browser understands how to read JAR files, he or she will be able to download and run the applet.

- Extensibility—Sun acknowledges that Internet technology in general, and Java technology in particular, is still in a state of flux. It has provided some hooks in the JAR specification for future growth, so that future developers can extend it as demands change.

Understanding .zip Files

How does the JAR format relate to Zip?

The JAR format was introduced in JDK 1.1, and is a specialization of the PKZIP format that has long been popular in the MS-DOS world. In fact, you can use PKZIP and similar tools to work with JAR files, and you can work with .zip files by using Sun's j ar utility.

Figure 23.3 shows WinZip, a Windows utility based on the PKZIP format, displaying the contents of classes.zip. The file classes.zip is distributed as part of JDK 1.2, and is located in the /lib subdirectory of your JDK directory.

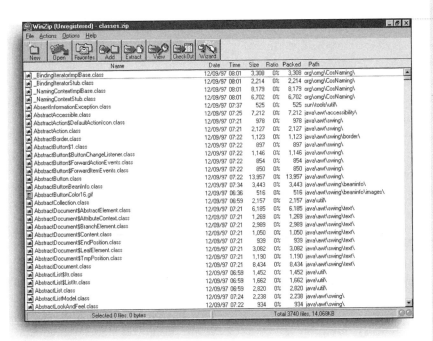

FIGURE 23.3
You can use PKZIP-compatible tools such as WinZip to look at Java archives.

Evolving to JARs

The major difference between conventional .zip files and JAR files is that a JAR file includes a text file called the *manifest file* that contains information about the files in the archive.

There are certain elements that must be included in your manifest file. A manifest file lists the following:

- The version number of the JAR standard under which this archive was built. This number, called Manifest-Version, is required. In JDK 1.2 the Manifest-Version is 1.0.

- The minimum version of JAR required to read this archive. If the user has a version of JAR that is higher than the required minimum, he or she can read JAR extensions. This value, Required-Version, is optional.

Learn about the Java Archive format

Visit http://java. sun.com/products/ jdk/1.1/docs/guide/ jar/jarGuide.html to learn more about the Java Archive format. Read docs/tooldocs/ win32/jar.html (or its Solaris equivalent) to learn about the jar utility.

The jar **utility will write your manifest file**

You don't have to write a manifest file; Sun's jar utility can prepare one for you. If you write your own, you don't have to list every file in the archive. You should write your own if you intend to use the JAR to distribute JavaBeans, so you can specify which files contain JavaBeans.

Digital signatures go in the file entry

If you use digital signatures, that signature will go in the file entry of the archive. We'll talk more about digital signatures later in this section.

- An entry for each file in the archive. You don't need to list all of the files. In fact, the only file that *must* appear is the main class file, and then only if you intend for the contents of the archive to be used as a JavaBean. The entry for the file has two fields: Name, which specifies the name of the file in the archive, and Java-Bean, a Boolean value that tells the user of the archive that this file is associated with a JavaBean.

Here are the complete contents of a simple manifest file:

```
Manifest-Version: 1.0
Name: TMyBean.class
Java-Bean: True
```

Making a JAR

While you can use PKZIP-based tools to make and change JARs, Sun provides a tool specifically designed for the task. This utility is called jar, and they offer versions for all supported platforms.

Suppose you have the directory structure shown in Figure 23.4: several .class files plus an images directory. You could use the jar utility to put all of these into a new JAR file. We'll name it MyApplet.jar.

FIGURE 23.4

This directory contains a typical set of files for an applet or application.

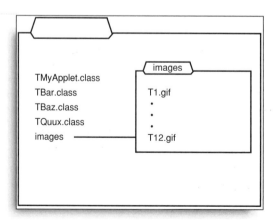

The general format for the jar command line is

```
jar options filenames
```

The first file named in the `filenames` list is the name of the archive. The use of any remaining files named in this list is given in the options list:

- c   Make a new archive.

- m   Use an external manifest file, named as the second file in the `filenames` list.

- M   Do not make a manifest file for this archive.

- t   List the contents of this archive.

- x   Extract the files named in the `filenames` list; if none, extract all of the files in the archive.

- f   Specifies that the archive is named as the first file in the `filenames` list.

- v   Specifies that the utility should produce verbose info mation while it performes the actions described by the other options.

- 0   Stores files in the archive without using compression.

In order to make our new archive, then, we write

```
jar cf MyApplet.jar *.class images/*.gif
```

If you had prepared a manifest file in the text file MyApplet.MF, you would write

```
jar cfm MyApplet.jar MyApplet.MF *.class images/*.gif
```

You can examine a JAR file by using any PKZIP-compatible tool, including the jar utility itself. To get a listing of the files in MyApplet.jar, type

```
jar tf MyApplet.jar
```

Suppose you want to make a copy of a file that's come to you in a JAR file. Use the x option. For example, to read the manifest file out of MyApplet.jar, type

```
jar xf MyApplet.jar MyApplet.MF
```

Why did Sun call this utility jar?

Sun's jar utility is consciously modeled on a UNIX utility called tar (for "tape archiver"). The tar utility is used by UNIX users for building a variety of archives (not just those on tape) in much the same way as PKZIP and WinZip are used by MS-DOS and Windows users.

Options don't require / or -

Unlike other utilities you may be familiar with, jar doesn't require that you use / or - in front of the options.

Remember that package names imply directory names

In Chapter 15, "Understanding Packages," you learned that a package name like com.mcp. que.usingjava12.chap ter15 means that the class file is located in the com/ mcp/que/usingja- va12.chapter15 directory underneath one of the directories named in the CLASS- PATH environment variable. Be sure to place these class files into the proper directory before installing them into the JAR.

Signing Your JARs

We've seen one of the principal uses of JAR files: distributing applets. You can also use JAR files to distribute applications and JavaBeans. We'll look at all three of these uses in the next section, "Using JARs to Distribute Your Programs."

Regardless of what your JAR file contains, there are times when you want to be able to prove to the person using it that you are, indeed, the originator, and that no one has tampered with the contents after you made the JAR. If your JAR contains an applet, this need is particularly critical, because without such proof, applets are left in an untrusted state and will have no access to the hard drive or operating system services on the machine to which they're downloaded.

You can provide this guarantee by *digitally signing* your JAR. In order to understand how to set up a digital signature, you need to understand just a bit about cryptography.

Understanding Public Key Encryption

Many years ago encryption was the province of the military and the diplomats. You kept messages secret by combining the message with a secret piece of information called a *key*. The receiver needed a copy of the key. With the key and the proper equipment anyone could decrypt a message. Figure 23.5 illustrates one of these old systems.

FIGURE 23.5

Old-style encryption systems were based on secret keys.

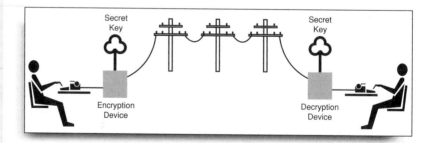

In more recent days cryptographers have invented *public key encryption*. A public key encryption system is based on two pieces of information, or keys. These keys come in pairs—they must be used together. One of these keys is secret, and is kept under tight security by the owner. The other is public, and may be distributed widely. Figure 23.6 illustrates how a public key encryption system works.

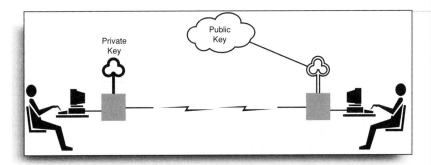

FIGURE 23.6

Public key encryption is based on the fact that no one can read a message that was signed with one key unless he has the other key.

Suppose I want to send you a message (which could be a JAR file) and be able to assure you that the message is really from me and hasn't been tampered with. I'll start by encrypting the message with my private key. Since only I have my private key—I'm being very careful to keep it secret—only I could have produced this encrypted file. My public key is well-known—assume you already have a copy. When you receive my message you attempt to decrypt the message with *my* public key. Remember that these keys work together—only one key can successfully decode a message encrypted by my private key. If you're able to decrypt the message with my public key, you can safely assume that it was signed by me.

There's a flaw in this system. I said that my public key was well-known, and you already have a copy. That's not true—you don't know me all that well, and you probably don't have a copy of my public key. I could send you one by email, but then how could you know that *that* message didn't come from someone impersonating me?

Keep your private key private

You should never send your private key out over the Internet. Most of the time it never even needs to leave your computer. When you generate it, choose a good long (multiword) passphrase no one else is likely to guess, but that you're certain to remember.

Not all public key systems require certificates

While certification authorities and X.509v3 certificates are emerging as the *de facto* standard, other systems are available. Phil Zimmermann's PGP (Pretty Good Privacy) software, for example, is based on a "web of trust," in which you are invited to trust an unknown person because people whom you know and trust either vouch for the unknown person, or vouch for people who vouch for the unknown person, and so on. Learn more about PGP online at `http://www.nai.com/def ault_pgp.asp` and `http://www.pgpi.com/`.

Use `keytool` and `jarsigner` from the command line

Both `keytool` and `jarsigner` are designed to be run from the command line–they're simply wrappers around the Java classes that implement keys, certificates, and signatures. Sun provides a tool for users to use in setting their security policy–called `policytool`–that has a graphical interface.

The solution is to have my public key embedded in a message that is signed by someone we both trust. Such a message is called a *digital certificate*. The current standard and version is X.509 version 3, so these certificates are often called *X.509v3 certificates*. The "someone" we both trust is called a *certification authority*, or CA. If we both work for the same company, or if you trust my employer, I might present a certificate signed by my company CA. If you and I have no other relationship, I might present a certificate signed by a public certification authority such as Verisign (`http://www.verisign.com/`). If you're the trusting sort, you might even accept a certificate I signed myself—a self-certifying certificate.

There's another flaw in this system. Computationally, it's extremely inefficient to encrypt a large file such as a JAR file with a private key. Actual public key encryption systems don't try to do this—instead, they apply an efficient algorithm called a *message digest* algorithm to produce a long number—one that is virtually unique to this message.

One of the most common message digest algorithms is called SHA1; one of the most common public key encryption algorithms is called DSA. In the rest of this section I'll show you how to sign JAR files with an SHA1/DSA-based signature.

In addition to the `jar` utility, you'll need two tools to sign JARs:

- `keytool`　Used to produce public/private keypairs and certificates. For complete documentation on `keytool` see `docs/guide/security/spec/security-spec.doc17.html` in your JDK directory.

- `jarsigner`　Used to actually sign the JARs, based on your certificate. For complete documentation on `jarsigner` see `docs/tooldocs/win32/jarsigner.html` in the JDK directory on your hard drive. (If you're a Solaris user, there's a corresponding file in the `solaris` directory that shows how `jarsigner` works on your machine.)

Here's a step-by-step procedure for signing your JAR files.

Signing a JAR

1. Generate a keypair.

2. Obtain a certificate for your keypair.

3. Distribute your certificate so people will know that you're the person behind the trusted applet.

4. Use your certificate to sign your JAR.

Figure 23.7 illustrates this process.

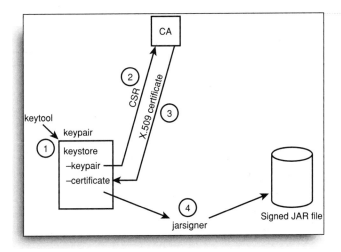

FIGURE 23.7

Use Sun's tools to generate a keypair, request a certificate, install it, and sign a JAR file.

If you've already generated a keypair and obtained a certificate through another means (such as Netscape Navigator and the Netscape Certificate Server or Verisign, Inc.), you can skip the first two steps and go right to `jarsigner`. In the rest of this section we'll assume you're starting from scratch. In the first step we'll generate a keypair and a self-signed certificate. In the second step we'll send off a certificate signing request to the CA of your choice.

Generating a Keypair

Sun provides the utility `keytool` to administer databases of keys and certificates for use by the utility `jarsigner`. You can get basic usage information by typing

```
keytool -help
```

at the command prompt.

Not everyone accepts self-signed certificates

You could use a self-signed certificate to claim you were anyone. Sophisticated users will often ignore such certificates. For serious work on the Internet, consider having your certificate generated by a reputable firm such as Verisign (`http://www.verisign.com/`).

keytool needs more information

There's not enough information in this line for **keytool** to generate a new key. It needs a Distinguished Name, a passphrase for the password itself, and a passphrase for the keystore. It will prompt you for any required fields you fail to specify.

Be sure to escape commas in the Distinguished Name

The X.500 Distinguished Name uses commas to separate the fields. If one of your fields contains a comma, escape it with a \ character.

Where is your keystore?

If you allow **keytool** to put your keys in the default file, it will build a keystore in a file named **.keystore** in your home directory. On a Windows system your "home directory" is the concatenation of the **HOMEDRIVE** and **HOMEPATH** environment variables. If they're not defined or don't constitute a valid path, the keystore is put in the JDK installation directory.

Don't default your Distinguished Name

If you default your Distinguished Name it will prompt you for your state and locality, which are usually unnecessary.

To generate a new key I might type

```
keytool -genkey -alias mike
```

This line tells the `keytool` to generate a new key to be stored under the name `mike`.

When you generate a new keypair you may include the following options:

- `-v`   Produce verbose information.

- `-alias alias`   A common name associated to be associated with this key.

- `-keyalg keyalg`   Specifies the algorithm to be used for generating the key.

- `-keysize keysize`   Specifies the size of the key, in bits.

- `-sigalg sigalg`   Specifies the algorithm to be used for preparing a message digest.

- `-dname distinguishedName`   Your personal Distinguished Name, which usually includes your organization and country.

- `-keypass keypass`   The passphrase for this key. If you don't provide one, you'll be prompted for it. The tool requires that the passphrase be at least six characters long—for better security, make yours much longer than that.

- `-keystore keystore`   The location where the keys will be stored.

- `-storepass storepass`   The passphrase for the keystore.

The default key size is 1024 bits and uses a key algorithm of DSA. Your Distinguished Name should follow the format

```
CN=Common Name OU=Organizational Unit ORG=Organization
C=Country
```

For example, my Distinguished Name is

```
CN=Michael L Morgan OU=Software Engineering ORG=DSE Inc C=US
```

`-alias` refers to a shorter name by which you will know this Distinguished Name. For example, I might write

```
keytool -genkey -alias Mike Morgan
➡-dname CN=Michael L Morgan OU=Software Engineering
➡ORG=DSE Inc C=US
➡-keypass A password for Using Java 1.2
```

By default, keytool wraps the public key into a self-signed X.509v1 certificate (but not the newer X.509v3). The two formats (X.509v1 and X.509v3) are similar—most end users who know the difference won't care whether you're using v1 or v3, but they may hesitate before accepting a self-signed certificate. If you want an X.509v3 certificate you'll have to go to a public Certification Authority such as Verisign or obtain your own Certificate Server.

Obtaining a Certificate

Once you've generated your keypair you need to generate a Certificate Signing Request, or CSR, and send that CSR to the Certificate Authority (CA) of your choice—either a public CA or your own organization's CA.

To generate a CSR type

```
keytool -csr
```

Just as with -genkey, the program will prompt you for any required parameters you omit. You may want to use one or more of the following options:

- -v   Generate verbose output.

- -alias *alias*   Specifies the alias of the key you want to certify. The default is mykey.

- -sigalg *sigalg*   The signing algorithm to be used. The default is DSA with SHA1.

- -file *csr_file*   The file into which the CSR should be written.

- -keypass *keypass*   The passphrase for this key.

- -keystore *keystore*   The file where the keys are stored.

- -storepass *storepass*   The passphrase of the keystore.

javakey is now obsolete

If you've worked with JARs in an earlier release of the JDK you'll have seen a utility called javakey. That program is now obsolete—stick with keytool and jarsigner.

Learn more about CAs online

You can learn how to get your keypair certified by Verisign at http://www.verisign.com/. You'll need to be able to prove that you are who you say you are, and you'll pay a small fee.

To learn more about the Netscape Certificate Server visit http://home.netscape.com/comprod/server_central/product/certificate/index.html.

Finding the beginning and end of your certificate

If your certificate comes by email there may be mail headers and possibly footers on the message. The part of the message you want to copy into a file is the part bounded by "-----BEGIN CERTIFICATE-----" and "-----END CERTIFICATE-----."

Verify all certificates before you install them

Do not use the `-noprompt` option of `keytool`. Require the `keytool` to show you the certificate—satisfy yourself that it's not a forgery. You can call the CA and read them the certificate's message digest (it's called the fingerprint) if you want to be sure.

Install your CA's certificate, too.

Your CA will probably send you a copy of *its* certificate so you can verify the signature on *your* certificate. Install its certificate too, but first, double check its fingerprint to make sure no one has forged its certificate.

After you've generated the CSR, send it to your CA following the instructions they'll give you. (CAs generally accept CSRs by email, though some prefer that you copy the CSR and paste it into an HTML form.) After the CA follows its certificate-signing policy to verify your identify (and, in the case of a commercial CA, after it has received payment) it will issue you a certificate. This certificate may come by email or you may be sent to pick it up at a Web page. Either way, get it into a file by itself and type

```
keytool -import
```

Here are some other parameters for the `import` option that you may find useful:

- `-v`   To get a verbose output
- `-alias` *alias*   The common name of the person associated with this certificate
- `-file` *cert_file*   The name of the file where the certificate is stored

To learn even more about keysigner, point your Web browser to `/docs/tooldocs/win32/keytool.html` in your JDK directory (on a Windows machine). There's an analogous directory for Solaris should you need to learn about the differences between `keytool` on Windows and `keytool` on Solaris.

Distributing Your Certificate

Now that you have a signed certificate, let people know it exists so they can get your public key. They'll use this key to verify messages and applets from you. You might type

```
keytool -export -alias mike -file filename
```

You can also specify a filename in the `-file` parameter. The utility will copy your certificate to the designated *filename*; Distribute that certificate to people who might use your signed applet—they should verify your signature on the certificate before they put a strange applet to work on their machine.

Using *jarsigner* to Sign a JAR File

Once you have a public/private keypair and an X.509 certificate that attests to their authenticity, you're able to digitally sign your JAR files. Sun provides the jarsigner utility for this purpose.

In addition to signing JAR files, jarsigner can also verify the integrity of a signed JAR. Just run it with the -verify option.

The simplest way to use jarsigner is to type

```
jarsigner MyJarFile.jar
```

In this case jarsigner will use the default keystore (.keystore in your home directory) and will prompt you for the passwords to the keystore and the password. jarsigner will also use the default alias, mykey. The output will be written to the file named MyJarFile.jar, overwriting the original file. You can specify more information on the command line:

```
jarsigner -keystore C:\JDK\projects\.keystore -signedjar
➥MySignedJarFile.jar MyJarFile.jar mike
```

tells jarsigner to sign the file MyJarFile.jar by using the certificate associated with the alias mike. The keystore is located at C:\JDK\projects\.keystore. The output is written to MySignedJarFile.jar, and the original file (MyJarFile.jar) is left unchanged.

Working with Encryption from Inside Your Program

You can write Java to do everything we've just done from the command line. Look at the documentation in java.security and its subpackages, java.security.cert, java.security.interfaces, and java.security.spec. These packages provide you with such classes as KeyPairGenerator, Signature, and MessageDigest, and the interface Key.

You can read more about the new JDK 1.2 security architecture in your JDK documentation, at docs/guide/security/spec/security-spec.doc.html.

---

jarsigner works with jar

The version of jarsigner that is distributed with JDK 1.2 can only sign JAR files that have been built with Sun's jar utility.

jarsigner is not compatible with javakey

If you used to use javakey (the forerunner of keytool) you'll have to get a new keypair and certificate. jarsigner has no backwards compatibility with the javakey database.

What does it mean to "sign" a JAR?

When you run jarsigner, it computes a message digest of the JAR file (using either the MD5 or the SHA1 algorithm, depending upon your certificate) and then encodes that message digest by using your private key. It writes two new files—a signature file, with an .SF suffix, and a signature block file (with a .DSA or .RSA suffix)—into the JAR file. The base name used in these two files is based on the alias you used to sign the file.

Using JARs to Distribute Your Programs

The following is a three-step process for preparing your programs to be distributed in JAR files.

Prepare a JAR file for distribution

1. Place all of the files into their proper directories, based on their package names.

2. Use the jar utility to assemble the files into one or more JAR files.

3. Optionally, use jarsigner to digitally sign your JAR.

Use a signed JAR to distribute trusted applets

We've already seen how to specify an archive in the <APPLET> tag. If you intend to run as a trusted applet you should be sure to obtain a proper certificate and sign your JARs.

Distributing Applications by JAR

You can instruct an end user to place your JAR in a specific directory and add that path (including the directory and JAR file) to his CLASSPATH environment variable. When the runtime environment looks for a class, it will behave as though the JAR were expanded and the directories physically existed. Figure 23.8 illustrates this behavior.

FIGURE 23.8

A JAR file in the CLASSPATH is searched just as if it were a top-level directory.

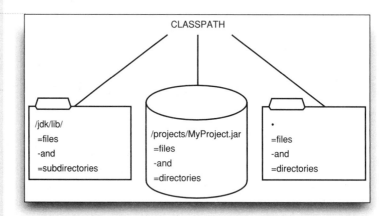

JARs for JavaBeans

One of the most popular uses of JARs is to distribute JavaBeans. Beans are usually used in Integrated Development Environments (IDEs) such as the BeanBox or Visual Café for Java. JARs are the only way to install new Beans into an IDE.

Tell the end user to follow the instructions that came with his or her IDE to see how to install your Beans.

SEE ALSO

➤ *Learn more about JavaBeans, page 539*

➤ *Learn more about the BeanBox, page 549*

➤ *Learn more about installing Beans in Visual Café, page 775*

Working with JARs Programmatically

You can use the JAR format from inside your Java program. If you want to write some data to the hard drive in a convenient compressed format, consider saving it as a JAR. The classes you'll need are in the package java.util.jar.

java.util.jar includes seven classes:

- **Attributes**   Maps attribute values from the manifest file to String values.

- **AttributeName**   A convenience class for working with attribute names. Includes constants for all common attribute names, including MAIN_CLASS, MANIFEST_VERSION, and SIGNATURE_VERSION.

- **JarEntry**   Represents an entry in a JAR file.

- **JarFile**   Used to read or write a JAR file.

- **JarInputStream**   A derived class of java.io.FilterInputStream used to read the contents of a JAR file from any InputStream.

- **JarOutputStream**   A derived class of java.io.FilterOutputStream used to write the contents of a JAR file to any OutputStream.

- **Manifest**   Contains the manifest Attributes as well as manifest entry names and their Attributes.

SEE ALSO

➤ *Learn more about* InputStreams *and* OutputStreams, *page 500*

Testing your JARs

You can test your JARs in the BeanBox before distributing them. If they work in the BeanBox they should work with the commercial IDEs.

Be sure to include a manifest file

If you're using a JAR file to distribute JavaBeans, the JAR file must include a manifest file, and the manifest file must include entries for each Bean (with the Java-Beans property set to True).

Remember the applet security restrictions

Unless your applet is trusted and the end user has granted you permission, you won't be able to read or write the hard drive from an applet. This restriction doesn't apply to applications, of course.

Organizing and Reusing Your Code

Learn how to measure your program's complexity so you can write simpler, more maintainable methods

See how to estimate the development schedule of a project based on lines of code

Organizing Your Code

Java is an object-oriented language; everything you write will be part of an object. *Classes* are templates for objects; they contain data members and methods. The data members may be primitive types, arrays, or references to classes.

Chapter 6, "Methods: Adding Code to Your Objects," began our focus on *methods*—the pieces of code embedded in classes that implement messages sent from one object to another. In Chapter 6 we emphasized methods in their context as class members. In this chapter we'll talk about coding issues.

If you open a Java source file in a text editor and scroll down to a method, you can run your finger down the page to see what the processor will do with your code. In general, you may have three kinds of code:

- Straight-line code, in which control passes from one line to the next

- Branching statements, in which control goes in one direction under one set of circumstances and in other direction under different circumstances

- Iteration statements, in which control loops through the same code repeatedly until some exit condition occurs

In general, code that contains branching and iteration statements is more complex and prone to errors than straight-line code. This first section addresses straight-line code, and introduces a rule of thumb for determining when to convert complex code to straight-line code.

SEE ALSO
➤ *For more information about primitive data types, arrays, and classes, page 106*
➤ *For more information on branching statements, page 142*
➤ *Learn more about iterating, page 152*

Straight-Line Code

Suppose you're writing a medical application and you've come to the section where a new patient is admitted to the hospital. In talking with the hospital staff you determine that admission follows a three-step procedure:

- Gather patient information (including patient's name, name of physician, and a guarantor such as an insurance company).
- Assign the patient to a ward.
- Assign the patient to a bed on the ward.

When you write this code, you'll want to be sure to follow the order used by the hospital staff. Not only is this order more likely to be correct, but you'll find it easier to explain the code to people who are familiar with the manual procedure. Thus, you might write

```
TPatient theNewPatient = new TPatient();
theNewPatient.getPatientInformation();
TWard theWard = THospital.assignWard(theNewPatient);
theWard.assignBed(theNewPatient);
```

In this example `getPatientInformation()` implements the user interface—an admissions clerk gets a screenful of forms and fills them out. `THospital`'s `assignWard()` method looks at the patient record and determines the ward for the patient. (For example, a patient scheduled for a surgical procedure might go to a surgical ward, while a patient in labor would go to the maternity ward.) `assignBed()` allocates a bed for the patient on the assigned ward.

Using Software Metrics

By some estimates, for every hour you spend writing your code, someone will spend seven hours maintaining it. That someone could even be you. If you spend a little time now ensuring that your programs are maintainable, you and your colleagues will thank you for it later.

One of the best ways to assess the maintainability of your code is through the use of software *metrics*. Metrics are a way of estimating something difficult to judge, such as the likelihood of a defect, from something easy to measure, such as the number of lines of code. To too many software engineers, metrics are still an advanced topic, and metrics for object-oriented code have only recently entered the market. Tools to measure common metrics for Java programs are in their infancy. This section describes some of the common object-oriented metrics that are applicable to Java.

As you write straight-line code, you'll find that you need to bring new local variables into existence. You'll write better code (in the sense that you'll make fewer errors and the code will be easier to maintain) if you declare local variables just before you use them. In formal terms you can measure this aspect of the quality of your code by computing each variable's *span* and *live time*.

Minimize Span

Span measures the number of lines of code between the first mention of a variable and the next. If the span is high, there's a good chance that you (or a maintenance programmer) will insert code that inadvertently changes the value of the variable, introducing a defect.

Here's a fragment of Java code that illustrates the span of three variables:

```
int a;
int b;
int c;
b = a + 1;
b = b / c;
```

There are two lines between the declaration of a and the next place where it is used, so a has a span of 2. Similarly, the first pair of statements that mention b has a span of 1, the second pair has a span of 0 (for an average span of 0.5), and c has a span of 1.

You should strive to keep span as low as possible. If the average span of a variable exceeds 20, it's likely that you'll only see a single reference to the variable on your screen at one time, an indication that your code may be difficult to follow.

Use a commercial metric-generating product

Reliable Software Technologies, Inc. (`http://www.rstcorp.com/`) has developed a version of its TotalMetric product that evaluates Java code. Hatteras Software reports that they are working on a similar product. (See `http://www.hatteras.com/oom_h.htm`.)

Free metrics program available

Tim Littlefair at Edith Cowan University has developed a free Java metrics measurement program as part of his graduate work. Visit `http://www.fste.ac.cowan.edu.au/~tlittlef/` to learn more about his project. This page also contains some useful links to other sites about software metrics.

The concept of span is described in more detail in *Software Engineering Metrics and Models* by Conte, Dunsmore, and Shen (Benjamin/Cummings, 1986).

Minimize Each Variable's Live Time

A similar concept to span is a variable's live time. The live time is the number of lines over which the variable is "alive"—that is, the number of lines between the first reference to the variable and the last.

Keep your methods short

If you follow the guideline that methods should typically fit on one screen, they'll naturally have no more than about 20 lines, which will help keep your span low.

The lower the live time and the span, the less likely you'll be to insert an error. If you first introduce a variable in line 10, but you don't use it until line 100, you have a large span and a large live time. During maintenance, a programmer trying to fix a problem with that variable may change code down around line 100, but miss the reference in line 10. If you can change the code so that the span goes down, those kinds of problems tend to go away. Of course, if the live time is high but the span is very low, you're simply using that variable frequently, which doesn't necessarily indicate a problem. It does suggest that the programmer who follows you will have a lot to think about if a problem arises with that variable. You may want to consider encapsulating that code differently to decrease the live time.

The concept of live time is described in more detail in *Software Engineering Metrics and Models*.

Measuring Program Complexity

During the life of a program, simple straight-line code tends to turn into a convoluted mess, with many branches and iterations. Bearing this fact in mind, you should strive to make your initial design simple, so that the product doesn't become overly complex and unmaintainable.

The best way to measure code complexity is with an automated tool. This section shows how to compute complexity by hand with two common metrics: McCabe's Cyclomatic Complexity Metric and Halstead's Complexity Metric. By understanding how complexity is computed, you can avoid complexity while you design and code.

Many researchers who have evaluated numerous metrics have concluded that a weighted average of McCabe's and Halstead's metrics can form an effective basis for estimating the maintainability of a program. They call the composite metric the Maintainability Index (MI).

McCabe's Cyclomatic Complexity Metric

The easiest metric to compute by hand is McCabe's Cyclomatic Complexity Metric. Tom McCabe was one of the first researchers to think about complexity metrics—his landmark paper, "A Complexity Measure," was published in 1976. (See *IEEE Transactions on Software Engineering*, SE-2, no. 4, pages 308 to 320.)

To compute this metric for a Java program, follow this step-by-step procedure for each method.

Computing McCabe's Cyclomatic Complexity Metric

1. Start with 1 for the straight-line path through the routine.

2. Add 1 for each of the following keywords: `if`, `while`, and `for` or the conditional operator `?:`.

3. Add 1 for each of the Boolean operators `&&` and `¦¦`.

4. Add 1 for each case in a `switch` statement, plus one more if the `switch` statement doesn't have a `default` case.

Here's an example:

```
if (((theResult == true) && (theEndTest == true)) ¦¦
    ((theEndTest == false) && (theSwappedEntries >=
        ➥kMaxSwappedEntries)))
...
```

Compute McCabe's metric as follows:

- Straight-line path: 1
- Branching and looping keywords: 1
- Boolean operators: 3
- Switch cases: 0

so the total McCabe's metric for this code fragment is 5.

Consider counting exception-handling code

McCabe's original paper was written decades before exception-handling was invented. For a complete measure of your program's complexity, consider adding 1 for each `throw` statement.

As a rule of thumb, if I am building a piece of code and the McCabe's metric on it is around five or less, I'm happy. As the McCabe's metric climbs past five, I begin to think about ways to simplify the code, possibly by breaking some of the functionality into a private or protected method. When the complexity metric hits ten, it's time to split the method.

The major exception to this rule of thumb is the large dispatch method common in user interfaces. In an application's `main` routine where I'm handling messages from the user interface, a long `switch` statement or a series of `if` statements may be the best way to organize the code.

Several variants of McCabe's metric are used. For example, the extended cyclomatic complexity metric takes decision complexity into account. A decision that depends on five factors is weighted more heavily than one that depends on just one factor.

SEE ALSO

➤ *Learn more about the Boolean operators, page 106*

Halstead's Complexity Metric

Halstead's metric is, well, complex. Whereas McCabe's metric emphasizes structural complexity, Halstead's metric measures logical complexity. To compute Halstead's Complexity Metric you need to first examine the language and decide which tokens are operators and which are operands. For example, in Java (and in C and C++) plus (+) is an operator and a variable such as `theLineCount` is an operand. Once that decision is made, count the following for each method:

n1, the number of distinct operators

n2, the number of distinct operands

N1, the total number of operators

N2, the total number of operands

Based on these four numbers, compute the five metrics shown in Table 24.1.

TABLE 24.1 **Halstead complexity metrics**

Measure	Symbol	Formula
Program length	N	$N = N1 + N2$
Program vocabulary	n	$n = n1 + n2$
Volume	V	$V = N \times \log_2(n)$
Difficulty	D	$D = (n1 \div 2) \times (N2 \div n2)$
Effort	E	$E = D \times V$

Like McCabe's metric, smaller numbers are better. "Difficulty" measures the ability of a routine to be understood. "Effort" is an estimate of the amount of work to be done to code the routine.

The Maintainability Index

Several software metrics experts (including the prestigious Software Engineering Institute) have suggested that a weighted average that includes both McCabe's and Halstead's metrics be used to estimate program maintainability. The specific formula they recommend is called the Maintainability Index, and is computed by:

$$171 - 5.2 \times \ln(aveV) - 0.23 \times aveV(g') - 16.2 \times \ln(aveLOC) - 50 \times \sin(sqrt(2.4 \times perCM))$$

where:

aveV is the average Halstead volume V per module.

aveV(g') is the average extended cyclomatic complexity per module.

aveLOC is the average number of lines of code per module.

perCM is the average percent of lines that are comments.

Higher MI scores suggest that the program is more maintainable.

For example, suppose you have a program in which the methods average 30 lines of code and 10 lines of comment. Suppose that the aveV = 500 and aveV(g') = 10. Then the MI = 81, which is considered to be quite maintainable. The maintainabilty of this code is helped by the low McCabe's complexity. The maintainability could be further improved by simplifying the logic of the methods (which would reduce Halstead's volume metric) and by breaking some of the larger methods into smaller ones (reducing the average LOC per module).

The ReaderDemo and Fibonacci classes from Chapter 5, "Using Branches and Loops," contain good examples for measuring method complexity. You may want to refer back to Listings 5.1 and 5.2 to see how these two classes are written. Figure 24.1 shows the results of checking the static code metrics of both the Fibonacci and the ReaderDemo classes with Reliable Software Technologies's TotalMetric. (ReaderDemo is from Listing 5.1. The Fibonacci code is available in Listing 5.2.) For our purposes, Fibonacci's metric is more interesting because there are three methods in this class. The average McCabe's Cyclomatic Complexity Metric for the three methods of Fibonacci is 4.67, with main() being the worst case at 7. The average Halstead's volume is 421.02, the average number of lines of code per method is 9, and the percent of comment lines is 10 percent, so the Maintainability Index for Fibonacci is a respectable 98.

The Maintainability Index

Learn more about the Maintainability Index from http://www.sei.cmu.edu/technology/str/descriptions/mitmpm.html at the Software Engineering Institute's site.

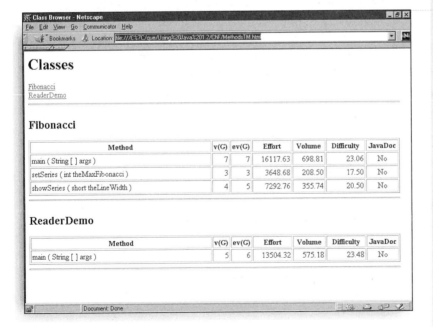

FIGURE 24.1

Strive to keep McCabe's metric, v(G), below 10.

Classes

Fibonacci
ReaderDemo

Fibonacci

Method	v(G)	ev(G)	Effort	Volume	Difficulty	JavaDoc
main (String [ ] args)	7	7	16117.63	698.81	23.06	No
setSeries (int theMaxFibonacci)	3	3	3648.68	208.50	17.50	No
showSeries (short theLineWidth)	4	5	7292.76	355.74	20.50	No

ReaderDemo

Method	v(G)	ev(G)	Effort	Volume	Difficulty	JavaDoc
main (String [ ] args)	5	6	13504.32	575.18	23.48	No

Saving Time and Money with Code Reuse

Barry Boehm, inventor of the Constructive Cost Model (COCOMO) for software cost estimation and author of the classic *Software Engineering Economics* (Prenticc-Hall, 1981), suggests that approximately half of all software development effort is programming. If we can substantially reduce the amount of programming required in our projects, we can substantially reduce the cost of software development.

One of the greatest benefits of object-oriented development is the prospect of code reuse. As we move from our analysis and design activity to the coding activity, we need to look for classes that have already been built, debugged, and tested, and use them as the foundation for our design. This section tells you how to generate opportunities for code reuse.

Estimating Development Cost

Just because you write in Java, don't assume your programs are object-oriented

You'll get to enjoy the benefits of object-oriented development only if you use the object-oriented methods. Much of the information in this section, as well as the techniques described in Chapter 7, "Object-Oriented Analysis: A New Way of Looking at Software," and Chapter 8, "Object-Oriented Design and Programming," will help you write reusable code.

Reused code is not free code. There's a cost associated with finding reusable code, and a cost associated with adapting it for your new purposes. In order to determine whether a particular opportunity for code reuse makes economic sense, you need to estimate the cost two ways—with the reuse, and without it.

Boehm determined that you could develop a reasonable estimate of the amount of labor required to develop a particular piece of software if you knew just 17 factors: the type of product (an embedded system or a standalone piece of software), the number of lines of source code to be delivered, and 15 factors that describe the software product, the development environment, the personnel, and the project. (This technique is called Intermediate COCOMO, and is described in Chapter 8 of *Software Engineering Economics*.)

COCOMO II

More recently Boehm and others have updated his research to take object-oriented methods into account.

Suppose that you're writing an application to help nurses administer medications at the patient's bedside. You observe that the process of administering doses is, essentially, a three-step process:

- Receive medications from the pharmacy into a medication cart.

- Keep track of which medication is where in the cart, until the medication is needed for a patient.

- Give the medication to the patient when it is needed, and record the fact that the dose was given.

By the time you've completed your early design and settled on a software architecture for this project you're able to state the following assumptions:

- You are able to count about 10 classes in your design: a patient, a nurse, a scheduled medication, a PRN medication (given only as needed), a cart, a drawer of the cart, and so forth.

- You estimate that each class will have about ten methods (including `private` and `protected` methods) of about 20 lines of code each, so the total project will have 10×10×20 or 2,000 delivered source lines of code.

- You select an experienced team of analysts and programmers who have worked in this field before.

- You determine that you're willing to pay extra to make sure the software is highly reliable (since a medication error can jeopardize the health of a patient).

Estimating Nominal Person Months

Based on these assumptions you'd like to know how much effort you need to budget to complete the design, coding, and testing of this software. You decide to use COCOMO II's post-architecture cost-estimation model to estimate the level of effort required to complete the project. COCOMO II starts with the following formula:

$$PM_{nom} = A \times Size^B$$

COCOMO II is online

Review Boehm's latest work online, at `http://sunset.usc.edu/COCOMOII/cocomo.html`; this site includes several COCOMO calculators and spreadsheets that you can use to estimate the sizes of your own projects. You can download either the PDF or the PostScript version of the COCOMO II manual from this site.

where PM_{nom} is the nominal number of person-months required, Size is the size of the software in thousands of delivered lines of source code, and A and B are constants. Boehm suggests that 2.45 is a reasonable value for A. B is given by this formula:

$$B = 1.01 + .001 \times \Sigma W_i$$

where W_i are the scores of the five scale factors shown in Table 24.2. PREC denotes precedentedness, FLEX is development flexibility, RESL is architecture/risk resolution, TEAM is team cohesion, and PMAT is a measure of process maturity. (See the COCOMO II User Manual available at http://sunset.usc.edu/COCOMOII/cocomo.html for detailed descriptions of how to calculate each of these factors.)

TABLE 24.2   The scale factors of COCOMO II

Factor	Very Low	Low	Nominal	High	Very High	Extra High
PREC	4.05	3.24	2.43	1.62	0.81	0.00
FLEX	6.07	4.86	3.64	2.43	1.21	0.00
RESL	4.22	3.38	2.53	1.69	0.84	0.00
TEAM	4.94	3.95	2.97	1.98	0.99	0.00
PMAT	4.54	3.64	2.73	1.82	0.91	0.00

Following the guidelines given in the COCOMO II User Manual, and based on your knowledge of the project, the product, and the team, you calculate precedentedness (PREC) as very high (0.81), development flexibility (FLEX) as nominal (3.64), architecture/risk resolution (RESL) as high (1.69), team cohesion (TEAM) as high (1.98), and process maturity (PMAT) as 2 (as calculated from the Key Process Areas in the Software Engineering Institute's Process Maturity Model).

Summing these factors to 10.12, you find B for the project and team to be .99988, and nominal person-months (PM_{nom}) to be 4.9 person-months.

Adjusting the Level of Effort

In COCOMO II Boehm identifies 10 cost drivers that are used to adjust the nominal level of effort up or down. These drivers are shown in Table 24.3, along with their associated values.

TABLE 24.3 The cost drivers of COCOMO II

Factor	Very Low	Low	Nominal	High	Very High	Extra High
RELY	.75	.88	1.00	1.15	1.39	
Required software reliability						
DATA		.93	1.00	1.09	1.19	
Database size (compared to program size)						
CPLX	.75	.88	1.00	1.15	1.30	1.66
Product complexity						
RUSE		.91	1.00	1.14	1.29	1.49
Required reusability						
DOCU	.89	.95	1.00	1.06	1.13	
Documentation match to life-cycle needs						
TIME			1.00	1.11	1.31	1.67
Execution time constraint						
STOR			1.00	1.06	1.21	1.57
Main storage constraint						
PVOL		.87	1.00	1.15	1.30	
Platform volatility						
ACAP	1.50	1.22	1.00	.83	.67	
Analyst capability						
PCAP	1.37	1.16	1.00	.87	.74	
Programmer capability						
PCON	1.24	1.10	1.00	.92	.84	
Personnel continuity						
AEXP	1.22	1.10	1.00	.89	.81	
Applications experience						

continues...

TABLE 24.3 **Continued**

Factor	Very Low	Low	Nominal	High	Very High	Extra High
PEXP	1.25	1.12	1.00	.88	.81	
Platform experience						
LTEX	1.22	1.10	1.00	.91	.84	
Language and tool experience						
TOOL	1.24	1.12	1.00	.86	.72	
Use of software tools						
SITE	1.25	1.10	1.00	.92	.84	.78
Multi-site development						
SCED	1.29	1.10	1.00	1.00	1.00	
Required development schedule						

Just as he does with the scaling factors, Boehm's handbook gives us clear guidelines for calculating the value of each of these factors on our project, product, and team. The factors are multiplied with each other—we find that the overall adjustment factor is 0.53.

By multiplying this adjustment factor by PM_{nom} you come up with a more realistic estimate of the effort required: 2.6 person-months.

Estimating Schedule

Most experienced software engineers are familiar with the "mythical man-month" described in Frederick Brooks' classic *The Mythical Man-month* (Addison-Wesley, 1975). This principle suggests that if you have a level-of-effort estimate, such as the one produced by COCOMO, you cannot exchange people for time with impunity. You cannot assume, for example, that a project that requires an estimated 3.0 person-months could be done by one person over three months or by twelve people in a week. Boehm acknowledges this point and suggests the following formula for calculating the schedule:

$$TDEV = [A \times PM^{(0.33 + 0.2 \times (B - 1.01))}] \times {}^{SCHED\%}/_{100}$$

B is calculated as before; Boehm uses A = 2.66 to compute the schedule. SCHED% is the percentage by which the schedule must be compressed (or expanded) to meet the required development schedule. Thus, if our initial estimate is that the development schedule is uncompressed, our 2.6 person-month project has a natural schedule of

$$\text{TDEV} = 2.66 \times 2.6^{(0.33 + 0.2 \times 0.99988 - 1.01))} \times {}^{100}\!/_{100}$$

or 3.6 months.

This equation suggests that, for a small project such as this, we would do well to staff the project at about a 71% level.

Reusing Classes by Inheritance

Inheritance captures the "is a" relationship. For every class you should have as a goal finding some more abstract class that is already implemented (or at least designed). Derive your class from that base class. Add new data or methods that pertain only to the derived class, and override methods from the base class that work differently in the derived class. (Often you can write a method in the derived class that calls the base class's method of the same name.)

In designing the TPatient class, you first determine that a patient is a person. From another project you find a person class. That class includes several data fields and methods, including the following:

Use abstract base classes

Since a base class is an abstraction, you'll usually want to derive from classes that have been declared `abstract`.

- `String primary_personname`
- `int marital_status_code`
- `int_military_branch_of_service_code`
- `String military_rank_name`

Figure 24.2 shows that class in Together/Professional, a software design tool from Object International, Inc. (You can visit its Web site at `http://www.oi.com/`.) Object International has also developed Together/Java, a Java-specific design tool.

FIGURE 24.2

You can reuse existing classes by inheriting from them.

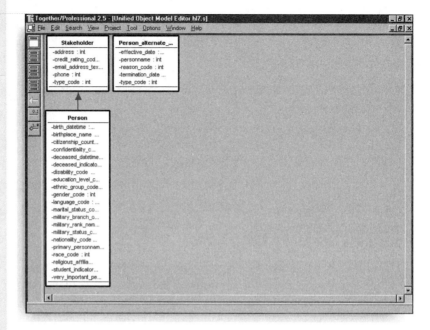

Finding reusable designs

The **person** class shown in Figure 24.3 is derived from Health Level 7 (HL7), a cooperative effort of the medical community to share information among different hospital systems. You can learn more about HL7 online at `http://dumccss.mc.duke.edu/standards/HL7/hl7.htm`.

After reviewing this person class, you decide to use it as the basis for your TPatient class. If the person class were implemented in Java, were named TPerson, and were stored in the package EDU.duke.mc.hl7, you would write

```
import EDU.duke.mc.hl7.TPerson;
public class TPatient extends TPerson
{
    ...
}
```

Before you've ever written a line of code in TPatient, your patient already knows how to be a person—he or she has a name, a marital status, a military status (and possibly a rank), and other attributes common to people and applicable to patients.

SEE ALSO

➤ *Learn more about* abstract *classes, page 162*

Reusing Classes by Encapsulation

When you inherit a class from a base class, you are asserting that the derived class "is a" kind of the base class. A patient is a kind of person, an elephant is a kind of animal, a car is a kind of vehicle, and so forth.

Sometimes "is a" is the wrong kind of relationship between two entities. Instead, "has a" may be more appropriate. In the course of your analysis you may find that a patient has:

- A guarantor—An insurance agency or other organization responsible for payment.
- An employer.
- A next of kin.
- A patient service order—For example, a dietary order, an order for a medication, or an order for physical therapy.
- A financial transaction—The patient may make a payment against his or her bill.

You'll want to pay particular attention to the *cardinality* of the relationship between two classes. For example, a patient may have only one guarantor or employer, but could have many service orders or financial transactions. When the relationship is one-to-many, consider implementing the relationship by using a *container* class. For example, an instance of TPatient might contain a reference to a TGuarantor, a TEmployer, a TNextOfKin, a set of TPatientServiceOrders, and a list of TFinancialTransactions.

Cost Savings from Reuse

Boehm's examination of software engineering research suggests that code reuse is a mixed blessing. The time spent reviewing possible reusable components and understanding how they work negatively impacts the overall schedule. If you consider reuse, you may have to pay that penalty even if you don't end up reusing any code. Good coding techniques, object-oriented methods, and the use of modern tools such as javadoc all help reduce the amount of time required for a Java programmer to consider reusing existing code, but they don't reduce the time to zero. Boehm's formula for estimating the impact of code reuse is based on the following seven factors:

- ASLOC   The number of lines of source code to be adapted.
- DM   The percentage of the design to be adapted.
- CM   The percentage of the code to be adapted.
- IM   The percentage by which the integration effort changes (compared to the integration plan without reuse).
- SU   A "software understanding" factor, based on well-defined factors such as structure, application clarity, and self-descriptiveness, all described by Boehm in the COCOMO II handbook. SU is expressed as a penalty percentage of the reused code—the easier the code is to understand, the lower the penalty.
- AA   An "assessment and assimilation" factor chosen based on the degree to which the module selected for reuse is "reuse-friendly."
- UNFM   A factor determined by the degree to which the programmer is unfamiliar with the code being adapted.

Boehm suggests that we calculate the amount of savings due to code reuse by the following process.

Calculating savings

1. Compute the amount of modification (AAF), by totaling $0.4DM + 0.3CM + 0.3IM$.

2a. If AAF is less than or equal to 0.5, compute the equivalent source lines of code by this equation:

$$ESLOC = (ASLOC[AA + AAF(1 + 0.02 \times SU \times UNFM)]) \div 100$$

2b. If AAF is greater than 0.5, compute the equivalent source lines of code by this equation:

$$ESLOC = (ASLOC[AA + AAF + SU \times UNFM]) \div 100$$

ASLOC is the size of the component being modified, in terms of logical lines of code.

We can then divide the effective source lines of code (ESLOC) by 1000 to identify thousands of lines of code saved, and apply that savings back into the original COCOMO II equations.

Suppose we've discovered classes in our HL7 library that are similar to the receive, store, and distribute functions required in the nursing application. The modified component is about 2,000 lines of code. We determine that the percentage of the design being adapted (DM) is 50%, the percentage of the code being adapted (CM) is 40%, and the reduction in integration effort (IM) is 20%, so the amount of modification (AAF) is 26.12%. We determine that the code is clear and well-documented—the software understanding factor (SU) is 10%—and that our analysts and programmers are completely familiar with it—the unfamiliarity factor (UNFM) is 0.0. We also find that we're able to locate suitable methods and classes with only a simple search—the assessment and assimilation factor (AA) is 2, the best possible score. We choose the formula on line 2a, giving

$$ESLOC = (ASLOC[AA + AAF(1 + 0.02 \times SU \times UNFM)]) \div 100$$

or

$$ESLOC = (2000[2 + 26.12(1 + 0.02 \times 10 \times 0.0)]) \div 100$$

so $ESLOC = 562$.

Subtracting this value of the effective source lines of code (ESLOC) from the SLOC count used to compute the original effort, we find that the number of person-months required (PM) is only 1.87 person-months. Through reuse, we've reduced our labor cost by over 28% on this relatively small project. This savings may easily translate to several thousand dollars. We get the added benefit that this reuse saves over a week on the development schedule—we get schedule compression (if we need it) without paying the penalty of a compressed schedule.

Finding Internal Sources of Code Reuse

One of the best (and often overlooked) opportunities for reuse is the current project. As you proceed through the design, look for ways to generalize the class so that it applies to other aspects of the design. For example, you may be able to share code between the nursing package (which emphasizes receiving a medication from the pharmacy, storing the medication on the ward, and distributing it to a patient) and the pharmacy storeroom package (which receives a medication from a drug wholesaler, stores it in the storeroom, and distributes it to the wards).

In addition to the obvious cost savings, you get three benefits from internal reuse:

- Your analysts and programmers are already familiar with the code, so the unfamiliarity factor (UNFM) is likely to be low.

- You can take the time now, during development, to make sure the class is reusable and well-documented, improving the assessment and assimilation (AA) and software understanding (SU) on this and future projects.

- Because the code will be used in more than one part of the design, you can often afford to have your analysts and programmers put some extra effort into improving the quality of this code, increasing the overall quality of the product.

If you've taken steps to keep your classes general and have been careful to provide good documentation, you have the beginnings of a good class library. Be sure to take time to fully document the source code and Java package before you put the code into the library. That way you'll enjoy improved UNFM, AA, and SU on future projects.

If your Web server supports a search engine, you'll be able to search the HTML documentation of all your code.

Consider using Netscape Enterprise Server as your Web server—it has a built-in search engine—or use the Netscape Catalog Server to build a taxonomy of packages. Both servers are part of Netscape's Suitespot package, described online at `http://search.netscape.com/comprod/server_central/index.html`.

Reusing Code from the JDK

Some of the most powerful and general classes have been developed by Sun, and are included in the JDK. Sun is also developing

---

Use `javadoc` to enforce your documentation standards

Prepare templates for the kind of information you'd like to maintain on every package, class, and method. Include this information in `javadoc` comments. Then make it your practice to run `javadoc` before any class or package is checked into your configuration control system, and place the resulting documentation on an in-house Web site.

additional libraries. As these libraries mature and move out of beta, many of them will be added to the JDK. You can find pre-release versions of these libraries on the Java Developer Connection (JDC) site `http://developer.javasoft.com/`. Figure 24.3 shows a few of the products available through JDC's early-access program.

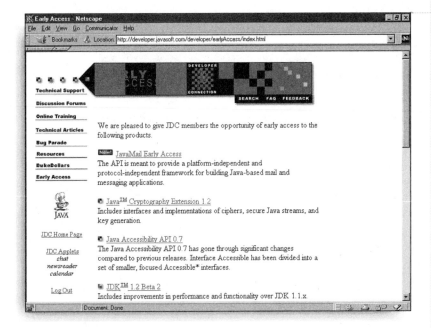

FIGURE 24.3

Join the Java Developer Connection to get early access to libraries and tools from Sun.

For a complete picture of the class libraries in JDK 1.2, see *Java 1.2 Class Libraries Unleashed* (Sams, 1998).

Using Third-Party Class Libraries

Many of the companies that have offered class libraries in C++ are developing a version of their product in Java. Third-party products can be costly—evaluate their quality in terms of understandability (SU) and the degree of work necessary to find an applicable class or method (AA). If the product is new, or if your programmers and analysts have not had experience with it before, take that fact into account in computing the unfamiliarity factor (UNFM). Use COCOMO II or a similar method to compute the estimated benefit of using the product, and compare that benefit with the cost.

There are numerous class libraries available over the Internet, many available at no charge. Some are samples of larger libraries; others are complete projects being released by companies as a promotion. A query to your favorite search engine for Java class libraries will produce results similar to the ones in Table 24.4.

TABLE 24.4   **Third-party class libraries**

Product	Description	Source
CoCoBase	Database access middleware	http://www.thoughtinc.com
CinnaMoney	Secure financial calculations	http://www.thoughtinc.com
Nutmeg	Collection classes	http://www.thoughtinc.com
VanillaSearch	Regular expression matching	http://www.thoughtinc.com
CoCOBaseFree	Free local persistant-objects	http://www.thoughtinc.com
SimpleText	Free flat-file JDBC database	http://www.thoughtinc.com
Neural Network Components		http://rfhs8012.fh-regensburg.de/~saj39122/jfroehl/diplom/e-index.html
ILOG JViews	2D Graphics	http://www.ilog.com/html/products/visualization/jviews.htm
JDAP	Lightweight Directory Access Protocol	http://www.ncware.com/home/jdap/
GEF	Graph Editing Framework	http://www.ics.uci.edu/pub/arch/gef/
JHLClassBrowser	Especially the SubComponent class library	http://www.easynet.it/~jhl/apps/jclass/ClassBrowser.html

Product	Description	Source
Objective Blend	Graphical user interface	http://www.stingsoft.com/
Objective Grid/J	Spreadsheet-like grid support	http://www.stingsoft.com/
JTools	Foundational tools from a classic toolmaker	http://www.rwave.com/
JDBTools	Database integration tools	http://www.rwave.com/
JMoney	Financial objects	http://www.rwave.com/
JWidgets	Graphical user interface	http://www.rwave.com/
JChart	Add charts to your interface	http://www.rwave.com/
JGL	Collection classes	http://www.objectspace.com/jgl/

While you don't need source code to reuse classes, if you're using a non-standard compiler (perhaps to get a performance boost), you should consider getting the Java source so you can recompile the classes.

Find Java class libraries

The `http://www.developer.com/directories/pages/dir.java.programming.libraries-body.html` frame of the massive Gamelan site lists several hundred class libraries. You should also visit `http://www.jars.com/javasearch.html` and search the Java Applet Rating Service's repository. Search for "class library" and add additional terms to narrow your search to find libraries of interest to you.

You don't need source code

Unlike many other languages, you can reuse object-oriented code without having the source code. You can inherit from a class or make an instance for encapsulation with just the Java `.class` file. (You'll want to be sure to have good documentation, though, so you don't waste your time looking for the right class and method.)

Introduction to Programming

Learn how hardware and system software affect your Java program

Discover how to use Java statements to implement loops, conditionals, recursion, and sophisticated data structures

Find out why "algorithms plus data structures equal programs"

See how programming fits into the bigger picture of software engineering

Learn what standardized processes can do to lower your software development costs and increase the quality of your code

A Software Engineer's Primer on Computer Fundamentals

This appendix is about computer science—the academic discipline behind programming. In this appendix we'll talk about computer hardware, operating systems, and compilers. We'll also talk about the tasks of programming itself. Finally, we'll talk about the "bigger issues"—how programming fits into software engineering, and the role of process in programming.

Over my twenty-odd years in the software industry, it's been my privilege to teach many people to program. I've taught both in academic settings and in industry—enough to know that I cannot make you a programmer in this one appendix. If you're new to programming, I recommend that you use this chapter as a starting point in your study of Java. You can use Java as a first language—this appendix includes many references back to the various chapters of this book. Take every opportunity to write programs and constantly improve your skills and your style. If you have the opportunity, sign up for a course in programming. I recommend you skip any course that promises to teach you a specific language—even Java. You can get plenty of language information from books like this one. Look for a course that teaches the principles of programming. Many of those principles are described in this appendix.

You may also find a good introductory programming text helpful.

In order to understand the discipline of programming, look at what computer science is, and isn't:

- *Computer science is not computer literacy.* As important as it is in today's world to have some knowledge of word processors, spreadsheets, and databases, computer science goes much farther than those topics. Just as being able to drive a car doesn't make you an expert mechanic, so being able to use a computer doesn't make you a computer scientist.

Texts suitable for introductory programming courses

If you teach a course in introductory programming, or would like to use material suitable for such a course, consider *An Introduction to Java Programming* (Que E&T, 1998). This book covers much of the same material covered here, but aims for an introductory audience who typically have the help of a qualified instructor.

- *Computer science is a branch of mathematics.* The branch that deals with the study of *algorithms.* Algorithms are a series of steps—a procedure—that solve some problem. Closely related to algorithms are *data structures*—complex descriptions of the relationships between data.

- *Computer science is science—like chemistry or physics.* Like those sciences, we believe that there are principles in our field that transcend a particular machine or piece of software that we may be working on today. Unlike those sciences, we've only had a few decades to discover those principles.

- *Computer science is an art.* Although we try to develop processes for much of what we do, there is a creative component to much of our work—especially software design.

- *Computer science is engineering—the implementation of solutions based on science.* Engineers in any field transform abstract ideas into models of a solution. As computer scientists—and, in particular, as Java programmers—we construct object-oriented models of the application domain and implement those models in Java.

- *Computer science is interdisciplinary.* As much as the popular media seeks to represent us as "geeks" and social misfits, tucked away in our own little world and not thinking about anything other than our computers, nothing could be farther from the truth. A successful computer scientist must be knowledgeable about the application domain, and must be able to communicate with professionals in that domain. In my career in computers, I've worked alongside civil, mechanical, and electrical engineers, military strategists, pilots, air traffic controllers, nurses, doctors, and pharmacists, just to name a few such professionals.

Computer science as a profession

Academic programs in computer science are accredited by the Computing Sciences Accreditation Board (CSAB) in the U.S. CSAB offers a detailed definition of the profession of computer science at `http://www.cse.fau.e du/~roy/csab97/comp _sci_profession. html`.

Understanding Computer Hardware

As a programmer you're writing software to run on some computer. While you may not design the computer system itself, you'll write better code and be able to make it operational more quickly if you understand something of how the underlying layers of hardware and software work. The remainder of this section describes the hardware, operating system, and compiler that make it possible for your program to run.

The term *hardware* refers to the physical components of the computer system—the processor, the memory, the hard drives, and other electrical and mechanical items. Figure A.1 shows the hardware of a typical computer system. "Software," of course, includes the programs we write, as well as supporting programs such as the operating system, the compiler, and, in the case of Java, the Java Virtual Machine.

FIGURE A.1

A computer system includes hardware—the processor, the memory, and other peripherals—as well as software to manage these resources.

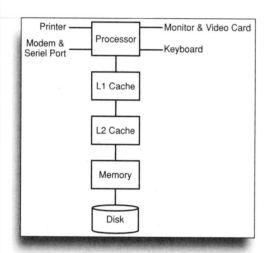

Working with the Processor

At the heart of the computer is the processor—the piece of the computer responsible for actually carrying out the instructions in our software. Larger or older machines implement the processor with several integrated circuits (ICs). Newer and smaller machines often use only a single high-density IC (often called a "chip") for the processor. Such machines are called *microprocessors*. If you're running a Windows machine, you probably have a microprocessor made by (or at least compatible with those made by) Intel, such as the 486, the Pentium, or the Pentium II. If you use one of the newer Macintoshes, you have a PowerPC microprocessor. The newest UNIX machines made by IBM also use the PowerPC, while those made by Sun use the

SPARC processor. (In fact, UNIX is a highly portable operating system—there's a version of UNIX available for almost any processor you might name.)

As you'll see in Chapter 1, "What is Java, and Why Is It Important?" a *compiler* translates human readable programs into binary machine instructions. These instructions are stored on the hard drive. When your program is loaded, much of your program—sometimes all of it—is copied from the hard drive into memory. When the processor runs your program, it calls for these instructions, one at a time, and executes them. Figure A.2 illustrates this process.

Processors are often called "CPUs"

You'll often hear the processor called a "central processing unit" or CPU.

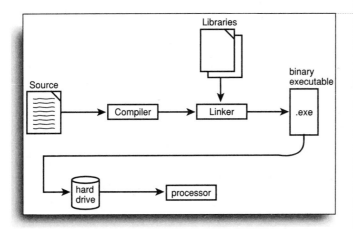

FIGURE A.2
A non-Java compiler converts human-readable source code to binary instructions.

When you write Java, the Java compiler translates your source code into Java bytecodes—the machine instructions of the Java Virtual Machine (JVM). The bytecodes are stored in a class file. The JVM runs directly on top of your computer's processor; the JVM, in turn, executes the instructions in your class file. Figure A.3 illustrates a Java compiler and JVM in action.

Working with Registers

As your program runs, the processor needs to keep some of the values in your program readily accessible. Most processors can access main memory—your computer's RAM—in a few millionths of a second, but it may take many milliseconds (thousandths of a second) to read a value from the hard drive.

For this reason the compiler will try to keep frequently used values as close to the processor as possible—at least in memory, and possibly in a section of very fast memory called the *cache*. An L2 cache is physically located right next to the processor—it can deliver instructions quickly. An L1 cache is built right into the processor IC. It can deliver instructions at blinding speed, but it only has room for a few instructions at a time. The fastest memory is a tiny amount of memory called the *registers*. Registers are part of the processor itself and are used as working storage when the program is running.

FIGURE A.3

A Java compiler generates bytecodes for the Java Virtual Machine.

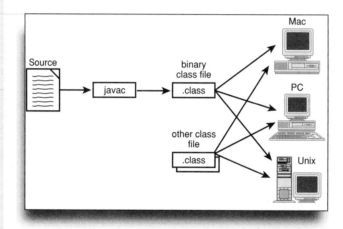

Figure A.4 illustrates this design of faster and faster memories.

Understanding the Stack

Suppose your program is running and comes to an instruction that tells it to call a subprogram (known in some languages as a "function" or "procedure," and known in Java as a method). For example, you may have written

```
int theInt = fibonacci(3);
```

telling the processor to stop running the main program for a moment and switch to the method called "fibonacci." In fact, you've told the processor that it should pass a value to fibonacci()—the number "3." When fibonacci() finishes, it will return control to the calling program, and will return a value—for example, 2 (the third number in the Fibonacci series).

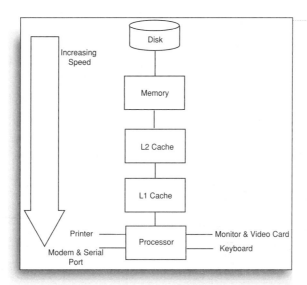

FIGURE A.4

Computer engineers keep the small, fast (and expensive) memory closest to the processor.

In order to pass values between the calling program and the sub-program, the processor uses a piece of memory called the *stack*. The stack is so-called because it resembles a stack of plates such as you might find in a cafeteria—one of those spring-loaded affairs that always presents the top plate to you. When you call a subprogram such as `fibonacci()`, the processor "pushes" the parameter of `fibonacci()`—3—onto the stack and transfers control to `fibonacci()`. `fibonacci()` pops the stack, retrieving the parameter. (It retrieves as many parameters as it has *formal arguments*—the number of parameters listed in the subprogram's definition.) Then it pushes its *return address* onto the stack. The return address is the location in the main program from which the subprogram was called. Then `fibonacci()` begins to run. When it's done, it pops the stack to get its return address, pushes its *return value* onto the stack, and transfers control back to the return address. The calling routine will retrieve the return value by popping the stack. Figure A.5 illustrates this process.

Storing Data in Memory

Farther out from the processor, beyond the L1 and L2 cache, lies the rest of memory. While not as fast as the cache, this memory typically responds with a value in just a few

---

What is the Fibonacci series?

Every element of the Fibonacci series (starting with the third element) is the sum of the two numbers before it. The series starts with 1, 1. Thus, the first 10 Fibonacci numbers are 1, 1, 2, 3, 5, 8, 13, 21, 34, and 55.

microseconds—a few millionths of a second. Think of memory as millions upon millions of individual locations, each of which holds eight *bits*, or binary digits. Each bit holds either a zero or a one, so the entire location—called a *byte*—can hold 2^8 or 256 different items.

While each byte has an address, most computers don't let you access it. They require that you access memory on word boundaries, where a typical word is 16- or 32-bits.

In Java (and most other languages), you organize memory by assigning values to variables.

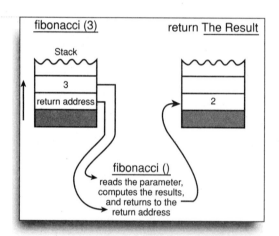

Storing Data on the Hard Drive

You've already seen that your Java class file is a file on the hard drive. If your hard drive is like mine, you have thousands of stored files, threatening to overflow it. Most languages give you a mechanism to read and write these files. In Java, you can read and write the hard drive by using the stream objects found in the package `java.io`.

SEE ALSO

➤ *Learn more about streams, page 500*

Untrusted applets cannot read or write the hard drive

Untrusted applets are the exception to this rule—they cannot access anyone's hard drive, as a security precaution.

Communicating with the Network

The slowest but largest storage available to the processor is the server(s) on the network. Whether you store files on a local file server or a Web server on the Internet, your programs should not neglect this important resource.

Java programs connect to the network through *sockets*, which are part of the java.net package.

SEE ALSO

➤ *Learn more about sockets, page 516*

Understanding Operating Systems

In addition to your hardware, your computing environment is defined by the *operating system*. The operating system is the software responsible for allocating the computer's resources to all of the competing software in the system.

Using the Operating System to Allocate Resources

Even on a single-user computer such as a PC, there are plenty of competitors for system resources. In Chapter 17, "Concurrent Programming with Threads," you'll see an example in which my single-user Windows NT machine is running a couple dozen different software processes. The operating system—in that case, Windows NT—is responsible for making sure that each process gets its fair share of processor time, memory, and hard drive space. The operating system must also make sure that one process cannot interfere with another. On a multiuser system such as UNIX, the operating system is responsible not only for allocating resources to competing processes, but to competing human users as well.

Allocating Processor Time with Scheduling Algorithms

Most operating systems allocate processor time with some variation of the "round-robin" scheduling algorithm. The operating system maintains a list of processes that want to run. Every so often—usually many thousands of times a second—the processor

Preemptive multitasking systems are usually multithreaded

If you're running Java on a preemptive multitasking system, you can usually expect to find a good multithreading mechanism, so that each process can be divided into threads. If the operating system isn't multithreaded, the JVM implements threads on its own. Learn more about threads in Chapter 17.

Some operating systems allow shared memory

Some operating systems, such as UNIX, allow two processes to share a portion of memory as one mechanism for InterProcess Communication (IPC). Such IPC must be built into the two processes—it cannot happen by accident, nor can a malicious process force access to another process's memory.

preempts the current process and allows the next process on the list to run. After a fraction of a second (called a *time slice*) that process is preempted, and so on. Very soon the original process is allowed to run again. The effect is that each process "thinks" that it has a single processor to itself. Windows NT and UNIX are preemptive multitasking systems.

Some older operating systems allow multiple processes, but each process must explicitly yield in order for the next process on the list to run—the operating system is not able to preempt a process. Such systems are called cooperative multitasking systems. The old Mac OS version 7 is one such system.

Real-time operating systems (RTOSs) are designed so real-world processes that cannot be interrupted can have the processor for as long as they need. Such processes must yield the processor as quickly as they can in order to avoid blocking other processes. Most of these operating systems use some sort of priority system to decide which process is allowed to preempt which. To learn more about a typical RTOS, visit the QNX Web site at http://www.qnx.com/. A growing number of RTOSs support the Java Virtual Machine.

Allocating Memory

In addition to scheduling processes, the operating system grants requests for memory. In most modern operating systems, each process runs in its own protected block of memory (called an *address space*). No process can read or write the memory in another process's address space.

As with any resource, it's possible for the operating system to run short of physical memory. Many operating systems support *virtual memory*—an extension of the address space onto the hard drive. Recall from our discussion about hardware that hard drives are about 1000 times slower than physical RAM—if the processor had to load instructions directly from the hard drive, the program would slow to glacial speed. Instead, the operating system tries to anticipate the needs of each process and copies blocks of memory (called pages) from the hard drive into physical RAM before the process needs them.

Understanding the Directory Structure

The operating system also manages access to the hard drives, typically by organizing the files into directories. As you'll see in Chapter 18, "Communicating in Java: Streams and Sockets," the naming conventions used for files and directories are platform-specific. In Java, you can "wrap" this platform-specific information inside a `File` object and write the rest of your program in a platform-independent style.

Using I/O Services

The computer system is usually connected to many peripheral devices, such as modems, scanners, printers, and tape drives. The operating system (OS) manages access to these resources. For example, on a multiuser system, the OS can't just grant the printer to anyone who wants it—the result would be scrambled print jobs when two users tried to print at once. Instead, most operating systems today use a *print spooler*—a program that sends jobs to the printer one at a time.

The operating system also controls access to the network. Many computer systems include one or more Network Interface Cards (NICs) that connect the machine to a Local Area Network, or LAN. (Many networks connect to the Internet from the LAN.) A program must ask the operating system to open a connection to the network. In Java you can open a `Socket` object, defined in the package `java.net`.

SEE ALSO

➤ *Learn more about the* `Socket` *class, page 516*

Working with the Compiler

In addition to the hardware and the OS, you need to be aware of the capabilities and limitations of your compiler. In the case of Java, the term "compiler" is extended to include the JVM. You'll seldom have control over the JVM that the end user selects, but you should be aware of the strengths and weaknesses of the major versions, including the ones in Netscape Communicator and Microsoft Internet Explorer, as well as the one distributed in the JDK and the Java Runtime Environment (JRE).

Encourage end users to use the Run Everywhere plug-in

The JVMs supplied by Netscape and Microsoft differ in several important respects; neither is fully compliant with the Sun standard. Sun has released a plug-in called Run Everywhere that installs Sun's JVM into both Netscape Communicator and Microsoft Internet Explorer.

Choosing a Compiler Based on Compile-Time

Whether you compile with Sun's `javac` or with a compiler from an IDE, you'll be interested in the compile time. Several reviews suggest that Symantec's Java compiler—part of Visual Café for Java—is among the fastest in the industry. See Appendix E, "Building Java Applets in an IDE," to learn more about Visual Café for Java.

Using an Optimizing Compiler

Some of the better compilers are able to rearrange the output that they generate from your code in order to optimize performance. These compilers are called (naturally enough) optimizing compilers.

Sun has suggested that many popular optimizing techniques are less effective with object-oriented code than they are with traditional languages. Sun believes that the best optimizing compilers will run in the runtime environment, where they have access to complete runtime information. For Java, that means that the optimizer should be part of the JVM.

For this reason Sun is building a powerful adaptive optimizer into their next generation of the JVM, codenamed HotSpot. You can learn more about HotSpot and other techniques for optimizing Java in Chapter 22, "Improving Your Java Program's Performance."

Working with Language Standards

One measure of a compiler's quality is the degree to which it correctly handles the language itself. With many languages, the keywords and syntax are standardized by the American National Standards Institute (ANSI). Java isn't an ANSI standard yet—the definition is still controlled by Sun. You can judge a compiler and JVM by how well they compile and run standard Java.

You'll find an annotated version of the keywords and syntax of Java in Appendix D, "Java Language Reference."

Interpreting Error Messages

Another measure of the quality of a compiler is the degree to which its error messages help you pinpoint a problem in your code. For example, while the Symantec compiler mentioned earlier is fast, its error messages are not always as clear as those produced by javac. For day-to-day work, you may choose to use Visual Café, but be prepared to drop out of that program and run javac and java from the command line if you're having a problem chasing down an error.

See Chapter 16, "Testing and Debugging Java Code," to learn more about ways to see what's going wrong in your program.

Applying Literate Programming

Some expert programmers have observed that we, as an industry, don't prepare very good documentation. If we do prepare it, we often don't keep it up-to-date. Most experienced maintenance programmers understand this, so they won't even read design documents—they'll always go straight to the source code.

These same experts have noticed that good programmers *do* maintain the source code—often including the comments in the source code—and have started an initiative called *literate programming*. In literate programming the programmer is encouraged to document the source code with a particular comment style. The literate programming system includes a parser that looks for that style and extracts the documentation into a stand-alone documentation file. In Java, you can use the javadoc utility to maintain your documentation in this way.

SEE ALSO
➤ *Learn more about JavaDoc, page 418*

Building Programs

Niklaus Wirth, the computer pioneer who invented the programming languages Pascal and Modula-2, is fond of saying that "algorithms plus data structures equal programs." His statement is more true in object-oriented programming than anywhere else in computer science, since the definition of an object is that it is the combination of algorithms (in the form of methods) and data structures (in the form of the class and instance data members).

You can learn more about the object-oriented methods in Chapter 7, "Object-Oriented Analysis: A New Way of Looking at Software," and Chapter 8, "Object-Oriented Design and Programming." In this section we'll concentrate on those elements that Java has in common with other procedural languages: syntax, algorithms, and data structures.

Using Language Basics: What Are You Typing?

Before we can even think about algorithms and data structures, we need to take a moment to notice what we're typing. When we write a line like

```
int theInterest = thePrincipal * 0.1;
```

what, exactly, are we typing? This section describes the basics of the tokens that make up a programming language such as Java.

Defining Identifiers

We use character strings called *identifiers* to name variables, classes, methods, and the other entities in the program. In general, an identifier must start with an alphabetic character, but may include numbers in the subsequent characters.

In this book we use certain naming conventions. For example, local variables—those made inside a method and only used there—and parameters—values passed into a method from the outside—are given names that start with a and the, while class and instance variables—variables that are built into the object—are given names that start with f.

These conventions are purely for our convenience as programmers—the compiler doesn't care what we call our variables. For example, many programmers have adopted what is known as the "Hungarian" method—the first character or two of every variable name tells you the data type of the variable. In that system, the integer that holds the value of the principal in a financial transaction might be named iPrincipal.

In Java (and many other modern programming languages) identifiers are case-sensitive. `theInterest` and `TheInterest` are two different variables. Needless to say, you should avoid using identifiers in your program that differ only in their capitalization—you're certain to use the wrong one at the wrong time somewhere in your code.

Working with Data Types and Operators

I've alluded to the fact that identifiers can name variables, which store values used by the program. If I write

```
int thePrincipal = 1000;
int theInterest = thePrincipal * 0.1;
```

I can reasonably expect the variable `theInterest` to hold the value 100 after this code executes. The variables themselves—`thePrincipal` and `theInterest`—are integers. They hold whole numbers. If I had wanted to keep track of the fractional part of these numbers, I could have stored them as `floats` or even `doubles`, which give 32-bits and 64-bits of storage, respectively.

Recall that all of the computer's memory is organized around bytes and words. Variables come in a variety of sizes, from bytes and 2-byte integers to huge 64-bit floating point numbers. The data types supported directly by the language are called *primitive types*.

You can learn about Java's primitive types and the operators that you can use to manipulate them in Chapter 4, "Understanding Java Data Types and Operators."

Using Constants and Literals

Not only can you write variables, you can also write down literal numbers. Just a moment ago I wrote

```
int theInterest = thePrincipal * 0.1;
```

Java interprets the characters `0.1` as a floating-point number (since it has a decimal point in it) and uses it accordingly in the calculations. Appendix D shows how you can represent other types and number bases in Java.

Another meaning of "magic number"

Among UNIX experts (often called wizards) there's another definition of "magic number." Many versions of UNIX store special data at the beginning of a binary file to indicate the file type to utilities. You can see these numbers by dumping the file with the **od** command and use these numbers by running the **file** command.

Use naming conventions for your constants

Make sure you give constants distinctive names so you don't confuse them with variables. I've used the convention that constants start with a **k**. The JDK authors at Sun make all of their constants uppercase, so they'd write **INTEREST**. The exact convention doesn't matter as much as the fact that, by using it, you cue yourself that you aren't allowed to change that value in the program.

Usually you should avoid using literals in the body of your code. In the principal-and-interest example, what happens if the interest rate (0.1) changes? You or some other programmer is going to have to hunt down every instance of 0.1, make sure that this instance is being used as interest, and then change it to the new value. The practice of using literal numbers is discouraged—veteran programmers refer to them disparagingly as *magic numbers*.

A better approach is to store values like this interest rate in a named *constant*. Unlike a variable, a constant cannot have its value changed at runtime. Nearly all computer languages give you some way of declaring that an identifier refers to a constant rather than a variable—in Java you declare the identifier to be static and final. Thus, I can write

```
static final float kInterest = 0.1;
```

Library Functions

In any programming language, if you have variables, literals, constants, and the operators to work with them, you have enough to write some useful programs. Most programmers would prefer not to have to rebuild every function from scratch. Once you've written some code, you'd like to reuse it without having to resort to copy and paste.

The solution in nearly all languages is to encapsulate that code as some sort of subprogram. Some languages call these functions or procedures, others call them subroutines. In Java they're called methods, and they're part of a class of objects.

You get a tremendous jump-start in your program by using methods that have already been written for you by Sun or others. You can use any method in the Java Application Programming Interface (API) to help you write your program. You can also buy libraries of classes from third parties; each such library defines an API. Of course, you'll often want to reuse your own code—Java encourages you to place your code into *packages* for this reason.

Most of this book describes the API that is part of JDK 1.2. You can apply the principles described in this book to learn about any class libraries you may buy. You can learn more about packages, including how you can write your own, in Chapter 15, "Understanding Packages." If you write a good package, you may find that others want to use it. You can distribute your class files and documentation in a Java Archive, or JAR file. Learn more about the JAR format in Chapter 23, "Making and Using Java Archives."

Writing Algorithms

Computer science is about solving problems. If you're using the object-oriented methods to solve a problem, you begin by looking for classes of objects—then you explore how those classes relate to one another. Finally, you identify the data stored in each class and the operations each class needs to carry out.

In the medical example that we use throughout this book, you might begin by identifying classes such as "nurse," "patient," "dose," and "medication." You might conclude that the relationship between a dose and a medication is such that a dose includes a specific, physical instance of a medication. You might find that a nurse gives a dose to a patient. Figure A.6 illustrates these classes. In each class node, the top compartment contains the name of the class, the middle compartment lists any public data members, and the bottom compartment lists the public methods associated with the class.

Further uses of the middle and bottom compartments

As you elaborate your design, you can add private and protected data members and methods to the middle and bottom compartments, respectively. When you do, you can use special symbols in your **CASE** tool to denote the access restrictions. For example, in the Unified Modeling Language (UML), a key is used to denote a protected member, and a padlock denotes private members.

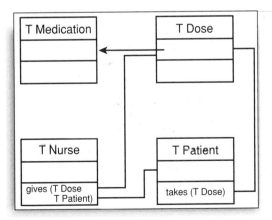

FIGURE A.6

When you use object-oriented methods, you describe the application domain in terms of classes and objects.

How to write methods

In Java, the only place to put code is inside classes, and most of that code will go inside methods. For example, you might write

```
public class TNurse {
  public static void-
main() {
    ...put method code
here...
  }
  public void getDose()
{
    ...put method code
here...
  }
}
```

The methods in these classes are examples of subprograms (also known as procedures or functions in other languages). To design good programs, you must become expert in developing the algorithms within each method, as well as the algorithms that span methods and classes.

This section describes the details of coding methods—what some people call "programming in the small." To learn more about software analysis and design—"programming in the large"—read Chapters 7 and 8. You'll also learn more about programming in the small in Chapter 6, "Methods: Adding Code to Your Object," and Chapter 24, "Organizing and Reusing Your Code."

Viewing Procedures as Subprograms

Java belongs to the class of computer languages called *procedural languages*. In a procedural language you, the programmer, are responsible for coding the procedure—the steps by which the computer will solve the problem. Most modern computer languages, including BASIC, COBOL, C, C++, and Ada, are procedural. A handful of languages, notably Prolog, are *non-procedural*—you give the computer a series of facts, and then state a problem. The computer figures out a solution by itself. (While it sounds great, in practice non-procedural languages cannot solve most real-world problems.)

In procedural languages such as Java, your task is to divide the proposed solution into subprograms. You may want to continue to divide the problem into smaller pieces, perhaps distributed across many objects. Your goal is to hide details of your solution inside the lowest-level subprograms, so that higher levels look like they're working in a very high-level language that is specific to your application domain. When you're done, code the detailed algorithms for the methods of each object in Java.

When you write subprograms, you specify the parameters to be passed from the calling routine with *formal parameters* in the subprogram. As a trivial example, you might write:

```java
public class TDemo
{
  static public void main(String argv[])
  {
    int aNumber = 2;
    System.out.println("The square of " +
        aNumber + " is " + square(aNumber));
  }
  private int square(int theNumber)
  {
    return theNumber * theNumber;
  }
}
```

Inside the method `square` the formal parameter is the `int` named `theNumber`. The actual parameter called on line 7 is `aNumber`, a variable local to the calling routine.

As you design your solution, look for ways to reuse existing code—either your own programs, third party libraries, or the Java API itself. As you'll see in Chapter 24 the benefits of code reuse are tangible.

Using Conditional Expressions

Conditional expressions include such Java statements as `if`, `if...else`, and `switch...case`.

Your Boolean expressions evaluate to `true` or `false`. Often they'll include some kind of comparison operator. For example,

```java
a < 7
iloops >= kLimit
```

and

```java
aNumber > 14 && done == false
```

Indent inside your conditional statements

You should develop an indenting style that works for your conditionals. For example, I often write

```java
if (boolean)
  doThis();
else
{
  doThatPart1();
  doThatPart2();
  if (anotherBoolean)
    doThatPart3();
}
```

Notice that each clause in the conditional is indented two spaces from the preceding level to make this code easier to read.

Check your understanding of Java

What would be the value of x and y in the following code if x is initially 381.5?

```java
float y;
if (x >= 0.0)
  if (x < 1000.00)
  {
    y = 2 * x;
    if (x <= 500))
      x /= 10;
  }
  else
    y = 3 * x;
else
  y = abs(x);
```

Since x is greater than zero and less than 1000 (and less than 500), the lines

```java
y = 2 * x;
```

and

```java
x /= 10;
```

are executed, so y is set to 763 and x is set to 38.15.

are all valid Boolean expressions. Learn more about conditional statements in Java and Boolean expressions in Chapter 5, "Using Branches and Loops."

SEE ALSO

➤ *Learn more about conditional expressions, page 142*

Working Within Loops

Frequently, you will need to repeat an operation more than once. This repetition is accomplished by looping and may take one of three forms:

- *Looping for a fixed number of iterations.* Implemented in Java by the for loop. Usually you'll use a for loop with some counter; each time through the loop the for loop checks the counter against some limit. If you haven't reached the limit, you increment the counter.

- *Testing the loop's conditions before entering an iteration (known as a pretest or entrance-controlled loop).* In Java, implement a pretest loop with the while statement.

- *Testing the loop's conditions after an iteration (known as a posttest or exit-controlled loop).* In Java, you can use do...while to implement a post-test loop.

You can learn the details of the for, while, and do...while statements in Chapter 5.

Note that you can often nest loops to great effect. Later in this appendix, we'll talk about a fixed-size data structure called the array—you'll often use a for loop to work your way through an array. If you build complex data structures, such as arrays of arrays, you can use nested for loops to explore the contents of the data structure. Just be careful that your code doesn't become so complex that you can't maintain it easily.

To increase the readability of your programs, I recommend that you indent the body of a loop two or more spaces. For example, you might write:

```java
while (!done)
{
  processNextNode(theDataStructure, theCurrentNode);
```

```
    for (int i=0; i<kLimit; i++)
        theArray[i] = processArrayCell(theArray[i]);
    done = isDone(theDataStructure);
}
```

Unless you're deliberately designing an infinite loop, loops should always have a stopping condition. If you're using a `for` loop, the iteration stops when the middle clause of the `for` loop is no longer `true`. In `while` and `do...while` loops, the loop exits when the condition in the `while` statement becomes `false`.

You can use conditional statements to break out of a loop early. Just execute the `break` statement. You can even `break` to a label, allowing you to get out of nested iterations quickly.

To improve readability of your programs, every subprogram should have a single entrance point and a single point of exit. Avoid calling `return` from the middle of a loop. Instead, you might write something like this bit of code:

```
public boolean loopAwhile()
{
    boolean theResult = true;
    for (int i=0; i<kLimit; i++)
    {
        doProcessSomething();
        if (isLooksLikeItsDone)
        {
            theResult = generateTheResult();
            break;
        }
    }
    return theResult;
}
```

SEE ALSO
➤ *Learn more about looping,* page 153

Applying Recursion

Many problems look complex until you realize that there's a *recursive* solution. Recursion is a mechanism by which a subprogram (such as a Java method) calls itself. Here's an example, solved first the hard way—without recursion.

Check your understanding of Java

What is the output of the following code:

```
for (int i=3; i<9;
i++)

    System.out.print-
ln("*");
```

The loop starts with `i=3` and ends when `i=8`, so it runs six times and prints six asterisks (each on a separate line).

Suppose you wanted to generate all possible combinations (mathematically, they're called permutations) of three colors: red, green, and blue. You might start with an array to hold the color names. (We'll talk more about arrays later in this section. An array is a variable that can hold more than one value, indexed by some integer.)

```
static final int kNumberOfColors = 3;
String[] theColors = new String[3];
theColors[0] = "red";
theColors[1] = "green";
theColors[2] = "blue";
for (int i=0; i<kNumberOfColors; i++)
  for (int j=0; j<kNumberOfColors; j++)
    if (j != i)
      for (int k=0; k<kNumberOfColors; k++)
        if ((k != j) && (k != i))
          System.out.println(
            theColors[i] + ":" +
            theColors[j] + ":" +
            theColors[k]);
```

This solution works, but it isn't reusable. If someone changes the problem slightly—say, adding a fourth color—I have to make substantial changes to this code.

The secret of recognizing an opportunity for recursion is to recognize a problem that has two solutions. One solution is simple, and the other, which is not so simple, is based on the simple solution. Listing A.1 shows a simple solution to the "Towers of Hanoi" problem. This problem, based on an ancient Vietnamese legend, is illustrated in Figure A.7. The task is to move all of the disks on pillar A to pillar C, one at a time, while making sure that you never put a disk on top of a smaller disk.

In the simplest case—only one disk—the program just moves the disk from pillar A to pillar C. If there are two disks, move the first disk to pillar B. Then move the second disk to pillar C and move the first disk from B to C.

In the not-so-simple case where there are three disks, use the N=2 procedure to move the first two disks to pillar B, then move the third disk to pillar C. Finally, use the N=2 procedure again to move the first two disks from B to C (using pillar A as the intermediate stop).

In the general case of N disks, use the simpler case (N–1 disks) to move the disks from A to B. Then move the one remaining disk from A to C and use the N–1 case again to move the remaining disks from B to C.

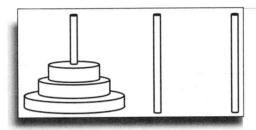

FIGURE **A.7**

The Towers of Hanoi problem requires that you move all of the disks from one pillar to another, one at a time, without changing the relative order of the disks.

LISTING A.1   **THanoi.java—This class handles Tower of Hanoi problems of any size up to an arbitrary limit**

```
1  public class THanoi
2  {
3    private void move(int n, char source, char destination,
       ➥char intermediate)
4    {
5      if (n == 1)
6        System.out.println("Move disk from " + source +
         ➥" to " + destination + ".");
7      else
8      {
9        move ( n - 1, source, intermediate, destination);
10       System.out.println("Move disk from " + source +
         ➥" to " + destination + ".");
11       move ( n - 1, intermediate, destination, source);
12     }
13   }
14   public static void main(String argv[])
15   {
16     try
17     {
18       if (argv.length < 1)
```

continues…

LISTING A.1 **Continued**

```
19        throw (new NumberFormatException());
20        int theSize = Integer.parseInt(argv[0]);
21        if (theSize <=0)
22          throw (new NumberFormatException());
23        move (theSize, 'A', 'C', 'B');
24      } catch (NumberFormatException e) {
25        System.out.println("Usage: THanoi size");
26        System.out.println("    where size >= 1.");
27      }
28    }
29  }
```

Learn why this example works

Although even the relatively small case of n=3 takes a while to explain, it is important that you take the time to understand why each step works as it does. Recursion is a powerful technique—in this case we've solved a fairly complex problem with a method that requires just four executable lines of code.

Run this example in the debugger

To understand recursive programs you may find it useful to run this program in a debugger or to insert a line like

```
System.out.println
("move(" + n + ", " +
source + ", " +
➥destination + ", " +
intermediate + ");");
```

between line 4 and line 5 to help you keep track of what the program is working on.

To illustrate, suppose we call THanoi 3 from the command line. The program calls move(3, 'A', 'C', 'B');—move three disks from pillar A to pillar C, using pillar B as an intermediate stop. Since n is not 1, the if statement in line 5 leads to move(2, 'A', 'B', 'C'); move two disks from A to B, using C as an intermediate. But 2 isn't 1 either, so move() calls itself recursively again: move(1, 'A', 'C', 'B');. This time the program prints the directions

```
Move disk from A to C.
```

because of line 6. Now move(1, 'A', 'C', 'B'); returns, so the program prints

```
Move disk from A to B.
```

because of line 10 and calls move(1, 'C', 'B', 'A'); from line 11. Now the program prints

```
Move disk from C to B.
```

from line 5 and the n=2 case returns. The program now prints

```
Move disk from A to C
```

in response to the n=3 case's line 10, then calls move(2, 'B', 'C', 'A') from line 11 to finish the n=3 case. This next n=2 call causes move() to call move(1, 'B', 'A', 'C'); followed by the println() in line 10, followed by move(1, 'A', 'C', 'B');, so the user sees

```
Move disk from B to A

Move disk from B to C

Move disk from A to C
```

solving the problem.

Reusing Algorithms

Many programmers find that up to half of their work goes not into writing code but into designing new algorithms. If you can build an algorithm library, you'll have designs that you can reuse.

As I've already mentioned in this appendix, your choice of algorithm is determined in part by your choice of data structure, and vice versa. For a comprehensive treatment on basic data structures see the second section of *The Art of Computer Programming* (Vol. 1). The section on lists has an excellent discussion on garbage collection, one of the more important capabilities (and limitations) of the Java Virtual Machine.

Building Data Structures

Recall that Niklaus Wirth believes that "algorithms plus data structures equals programs." Data structures are the framework upon which your data is hung. The data itself is stored in variables of primitive types such as ints, booleans, and chars. The data structures store the relationships between these variables.

Primitive Types

Java includes integer and floating point numbers as well as Strings and booleans. Use these types as the basis for your variables (which hold your data) as well as literals and constants.

See Chapter 4, "Understanding Java Data Types and Operators," for details on the primitive types

References and Pointer Variables

In languages such as Pascal, C, and C++ you can implement "pointer variables." These special variables point to a memory location. You can store data there or retrieve the contents of the location. Unfortunately, you can also use these powerful tools to

Recursion is not free

While recursion is often the most natural way to express an algorithm, it may not be computationally efficient. I recommend you start with recursion whenever the algorithm is naturally recursive, but be prepared to optimize the recursion away if necessary. See Chapter 22, "Improving Your Java Program's Performance," to learn more about optimizing techniques.

Read more about algorithms in Knuth

One of the best sources for algorithms is Donald Knuth's classic *The Art of Computer Programming*. This three-volume work (a fourth volume is due out in 1998) describes fundamental algorithms and data structures, seminumerical algorithms, searching, and sorting. If you continue in programming and have occasion to ask an experienced programmer about an algorithm, one of the most common pieces of advice you'll hear is "Look it up in Knuth."

corrupt data. In some operating systems it's possible for your program to actually interfere with other programs running on the same machine. The use of pointer variables is a necessary evil in most languages.

Java has been carefully designed to eliminate visible pointers while still giving you the power to access other objects. Instead of giving you a pointer (that you might change), Java gives you a *reference* to an object. A reference is just like a pointer except that it is "attached" to a particular object. You're free to detach it, and to reattach it to some other object in your program. But you cannot point it to an arbitrary location that might be controlled by some other program.

For example, you can write

```
Button fButton;
```

You now have a reference to a button, but you don't have the object itself. To make a new object—a process called *instantiation*—you can now write

```
fButton = new Button("OK");
```

Later, if you choose to write

```
fButton = new Button("OK");
Button fAnotherButton = new Button("Cancel");
fAnotherButton = fButton;
```

the program will obligingly point the fAnotherButton reference to the button object that is pointed to by fButton. Figure A.8 illustrates the arrangement of the references before and after fAnotherButton is reassigned.

JDK 1.2 includes new kinds of references

As you review your JDK 1.2 documentation, you'll find new kinds of references, including "weak references." Don't worry about this information while you're learning to program. You won't need to use these special kinds of references until you've had more experience.

FIGURE A.8

If you point an existing reference at an existing object, the reference changes and the reference's old object is abandoned.

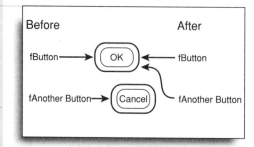

By eliminating pointer arithmetic, Java's designers went a long way toward reducing programming errors.

Building Your Own Types

We've talked throughout this book about building your own classes and objects. A class is simply a user-defined type. You can use it to store data members from the primitive types or other user-defined types.

Using Arrays

Sometimes you have a fixed number of items, and you'd like to be able to refer to them by index inside one big variable. The solution is to use an array. You can declare an array of either primitive data types or your own type, though all of the array must contain the same type. For example, to get an empty array that has a capacity of 100 integers, write

```
int[] myArray = new int(100);
```

As I pointed out earlier in this appendix, loops—especially for loops—are the most common way to access an array. As you begin to associate algorithms and data structures, think of loops and arrays working together. for loops and arrays have a natural connection: for loops are often used to iterate over a fixed number of objects, and arrays are often limited by the choice that was made for them when you initialized the system.

SEE ALSO

➤ *Learn more about arrays, page 121*

Collections and Other Dynamic Data Structures

Unlike conventional arrays, *dynamic data structures* can be resized at runtime. Dynamic data structures, also known as *collections*, are often packaged as a class with search and sort methods. For example, JDK 1.2 includes a series of new collection classes. One of the most popular collections, java.util.Hashtable, has methods containsKey() and containsValue() that do direct lookups in the Hashtable.

What happened to fAnotherButton's last Button?

If you've had any experience in C or C++, you may think that the code that reassigned fAnotherButton has a bug—it doesn't delete the button that was originally assigned to fAnotherButton. That's a feature, not a bug. If that reference was the last reference to this Button, the garbage collector will reclaim that storage automatically the next time it comes by.

You can make arrays of objects, too

You're not limited to primitive types when you make arrays. You can make arrays of your own types—objects. You can also use arrays as a type of data member *inside* a class definition.

The linked list is particularly efficient in adding and deleting nodes

Use the linked list when the number of requests for adds and deletes that your data structure will receive exceeds the number of searches.

Searches are easy in binary trees

Searches are particularly easy in binary trees, but it may be computationally expensive to add and delete items and keep the tree sorted. Use a binary tree when your program must spend a lot of time searching the data structure, but adds and deletes are less frequent.

Building Your Own Data Structures

In addition to the collection classes provided in the JDK API, you can implement your own dynamic data structures. Figure A.9 illustrates these common data structures:

- Linked list—A series of nodes in which each node is connected to the next by a pointer or reference.
- Queue—A first-in, first-out (FIFO) data structure. There are two access points, usually called "front" and "rear." New data items are added at the rear, and the data item that is about to be processed is removed from the front.
- Stack—A last-in, first-out (LIFO) data structure. Items are added and removed at the top.
- Binary tree—A hierarchical data structure in which each node has at most two "daughter" nodes. The nodes in binary trees are often stored in sorted order.
- Graph—A general data structure characterized by bidirectional links. In a graph, any node may be connected to any other node.

FIGURE A.9

Become familiar with the most common data structures in order to build better programs.

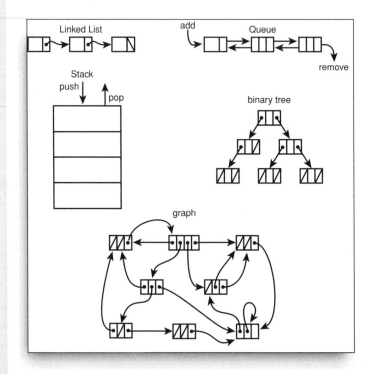

Assembling Programs

Algorithms plus data structures equal programs. You can put together basic techniques, such as recursion, and basic data structures, such as binary trees, to implement useful programs. This section shows how you might combine algorithms and data structures to sort.

Building a Sorting Program

If someone unfamiliar with computer science were given an array of n items and asked to sort it, they might come up with the following algorithm (written here in structured English):

```
Initialize a counter, i, to zero
Initialize a Boolean variable, switched, to true
While (i < n - 2) and switched = true
  Set switched to false
  Increment i
  For j = 0 to n - i - 1
    if theArray[j] > theArray[j + 1]
      Exchange these entries
      Set switched to true
```

Suppose you started with this array:

0: Apple

1: Pear

2: Banana

3: Orange

In this case n is 4, so i will run from 0 to 2. During the first while iteration, j will also run from 0 to 2. In the first comparison (in line 7), "Apple" is not greater than "Pear," so the two elements are not switched. When j is 1, line 7 compares "Pear" and "Banana" and exchanges them.

When j is 2, line 7 compares "Pear" and "Orange." (Remember that "Pear" has already been exchanged with "Banana.") "Pear" and "Orange" are exchanged, and the for loop ends.

Because switched has been set to true, the while loop begins again. This time each of the elements is found to be correctly sorted; since switched is set to false, the while loop exits.

This algorithm is known as the *bubble sort*, since smaller elements "bubble up" from the bottom. The bubble sort is a simple algorithm, well suited for arrays (which are available in nearly every computer language). It's also horribly inefficient.

The bubble sort consists of two nested loops. The outer loop controls a series of (increasingly shorter) passes through the array. The inner loop compares the elements a pair at a time and exchanges them as necessary. Thus the computer-time required to complete the sort is proportional to the square of the number of elements in the array (n).

Analyzing Programs

When computer scientists are called upon to design a program, they must often compare two or more algorithms to see which is the most efficient. The standard method for reporting the time required for an algorithm to run is called *big-O notation*. In big-O notation you show a function of n that is proportional to the time required for the algorithm to run.

The following procedure determines the big-O function of an algorithm.

Determining the big-O function of an algorithm

1. Ignore any steps in the algorithm that don't include loops.

2. Estimate the number of run-time steps required to complete the loops, as a function of n. Express the number of steps as a sum of the form.

   $f_1(n) + f_2(n) + . . . + f_{[k}(n)$

3. Arrange the terms of this sum in order of their relative size. (For example, n^3 dominates n_2. Drop all of the terms except the dominant term. (Table A.2 shows which functions dominate which.)

4. Use only the dominant term as the big-O function of the algorithm.

Big-O notation is independent of processor speed

Note that big-O notation is not an attempt to measure the speed of a program on a particular machine or to estimate how long it will take to run on a particular data set. Big-O notation shows how an algorithm will perform when compared with other algorithms on the same data, and on the same system.

TABLE A.2 **Which functions dominate in big-O analysis?**

Function		Function	Comments
n	dominates	$log_a(n)$	a is often 2
n $log_a(n)$	dominates	n	a is often 2
n^m	dominates	n^k	when m > k
a^n	dominates	n^m	for any a > 1 and m

Let's use this technique on the bubble sort. We start our analysis at the first loop, in line 3. We'll run the outer loop n-2 times, and the inner loop n - i - 1 times each time we go through the outer loop. In the worst case (when the loop is completely backwards) the time required is proportional to

n(n - 1)/2

or

1/2 X (n^2 - n)

While the number of inner loops is constantly getting smaller as the program runs, it's clearly on the order of n^2—and that's what big-O analysis is all about: establishing an order of magnitude.

Compare the performance of the bubble sort with other sorting algorithms shown in Table A.3.

TABLE A.3 **These run times assume an input of size 10^6, a constant of proportionality of 1, and a machine speed of one operation per microsecond**

Sorting algorithm	Time-analysis, in big-O notation	Run time
Bubble sort	$O(n^2)$	11.5 days
Selection sort	$O(n^2)$	11.5 days
Insertion sort	$O(n^2)$	11.5 days
Shell sort	$O(n(log_2(n))^2)$	14 minutes
Quick sort	$O(nlog_2(n))$	21 seconds
Radix sort	$O(n)$	1 second

Use big-O analysis for memory as well as time

When you analyze a program, look at its use of memory as well as computer time. Often the use of memory will climb as the program becomes more computationally efficient. You can use big-O notation to report memory utilization just as you do for time.

Why not use radix sort all the time?

You may be wondering, if the radix sort is so efficient, why isn't it the only sort algorithm used? The radix sort can use significantly more memory than the other algorithms shown here and requires that all of the data elements have the same length. Furthermore, the constant of proportionality of this O(n) algorithm is such that, for some sets of data, a less efficient algorithm may actually complete faster.

These and other sorting algorithms are documented in most introductory programming books. Of course, you can always look them up in Knuth! (They're in volume 3 of *The Art of Computer Programming*.)

Programming in Context

You can implement some components while you design others

Whether you wait for all of the components to be designed before you attempt to code any of them depends upon your organization's development methodology.

Programming is only one of the many activities associated with building software. Most software engineering activities begin when you try to understand the requirements that the customer and the end user have for the software—a process called *analysis*. Once you understand the requirements, you design a software solution. You should complete the design of a software component before you attempt to code it.

This section describes *software engineering*, the engineering discipline concerned with the development of computer software. This section concludes with a discussion of *process*—the step-by-step procedures that you and your organization have decided to use to build software.

Understanding Software Engineering

As you gain experience in programming you'll want to extend your skills. Many analysts and designers started their careers as programmers and then moved into areas where they worked closely with customers and end users. Several chapters of this book will help you build these skills in a Java environment.

Capturing User Requirements with Analysis Techniques

Strictly speaking, analysis is language-neutral. In some cases you may not have even chosen the implementation language when you begin your analysis. If you're thinking about using Java, however, you should consider using an object-oriented analysis methodology. Chapter 7, "Object-Oriented Analysis: A New Way of Looking at Software," provides you with an overview of these techniques.

Designing Your Program

Top-level, or architectural, design is concerned with how the major components of the software fit together. As you proceed in your design tasks you'll move from architectural design to increasingly detailed design, until you're designing the methods of the classes of which your objects are made.

Learn about object-oriented design in Chapter 8. Read Chapter 6 for more information about writing methods in Java. Chapter 24 gives even more information about how to ensure that your code is readable, maintainable, and reusable.

Writing Your Program

Remember that algorithms plus data structures equal programs. Most of this book, of course, is about Java programming. Use Chapter 4 to learn about Java's primitive data types. Chapter 5 introduces you to basic Java statements. Chapter 9, "Increasing Program Sophistication by Using Interfaces," and Chapter 10, "Simplifying Code with Exceptions," teach you some techniques that will improve your programs.

Testing Your Program

There are many ways to ensure that your program is operating correctly. You should consider using code walkthroughs, inspections, and reviews. The one aspect of software engineering you should never neglect, however, is test.

See Chapter 16 to learn more about testing your program.

Maintaining Your Finished Software

By some estimates your organization will spend seven dollars to maintain your software for every dollar it spends to build it. With ratios like that you must be sure your code is as readable and maintainable as you can make it. Your maintenance activities will fall into three classes:

- *Removing latent defects.* When you (or a user) discover a latent defect—a bug—you must identify the failing code and repair it.

- *Keeping up with other software.* Your program runs in an environment that includes an operating system, a Java Virtual Machine, a compiler, and possibly other software such as a database. As other vendors update their products, you may need to change your program.

- *Product improvement.* From time to time customers and end users may suggest improvements or new features. That's good news—the only software that people want to see improved is software that they're using. If possible, spend most of your software maintenance budget in this area.

Understanding the Importance of Process

In some organizations each analyst, designer, programmer, and tester performs his or her duties as they see fit. If a particular project is blessed with a skilled development team, the software is delivered on-time, on-budget, and meets the requirements. If a project has people who use less effective techniques, the quality of the software suffers.

In an effort to bring the software development process under control, many software engineers and software development organizations are attempting to define standard ways of performing analysis, conducting design, and writing and testing code. These standardized approaches are known as *processes*.

Watts Humphrey and his team at the Software Engineering Institute (part of Carnegie-Mellon University) have characterized software organizations into five levels, based on the degree to which the organization has standardized their processes. Level 1 organizations have little or no reliance on process—every person in the software development organization proceeds as he or she thinks best, leading to inconsistent results. As the organization moves up levels of the Capability Maturity Model (CMM) they become increasingly focused on using, documenting, and improving processes.

SEE ALSO
➤ *Learn more about the Capability Maturity Model, page 172*

Organizations at the higher levels of the CMM enjoy lower costs and higher quality

Organizations at higher levels on the CMM are able to develop software on a more consistent schedule and budget. Often the effect of continuous process improvement is that the schedules become shorter, the required budgets come down, and the quality of the software improves. See the 1995 article by H. Saiedian and R. Kuzara entitled "SEI Capability Maturity Model's Impact on Contractors," *IEEE Computer_28* (1), pages 16-25, for details on these improvements.

Java for C++ Programmers

B

Learn how Java's strong typing differs from C and C++

Learn why Java's syntax will seem familiar to C++ programmers

---

Java doesn't have C++'s *const* keyword; learn the Java idiom for constants

---

Like C++, Java supports runtime exceptions

Even though Java doesn't come with a preprocessor, you may still find uses for the C preprocessor

Building on the Strengths of C++

Recall from Chapter 1, "What Is Java, and Why Is It Important?" that the designers of Java were experienced C++ programmers. They built on the strengths of this highly successful language. This appendix reviews the major elements of C++ that have been adopted in Java.

Strong Typing

C++ starts out as a strongly typed language, but by using casting, a programmer can completely circumvent the strong typing. A C++ programmer can write

```
Airplane* myAirplane = (Airplane*) &myTruck;
```

A programmer can use casting to write some silly code. Responsible programmers use casting to get around certain language limitations. Java acknowledges the utility of strong typing, and limits the places where casts may be used. For example, Java will allow you to cast an integer to a short, but if the integer stores a number that's too big for the short, you'll corrupt the data when you lose the high-order bytes.

When you're working with objects you should write explicit conversion methods to allow you to build one object out of another, rather than trying to just cast the object. For example, if you really wanted a flying truck you could write an `Airplane` constructor that used a `Truck` as its model. Then you could say:

```
Airplane myFlyingTruck = new Airplane(myTruck);
```

Programmers familiar with object-oriented methods often speak of up-casting and downcasting to distinguish between two different directions of cast.

Upcasting

Suppose you are working in an application that has a hierarchy similar to the one shown in Figure B.1.

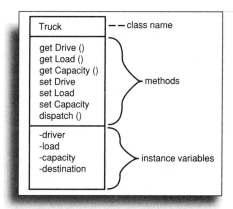

FIGURE B.1

With polymorphism you can substitute a derived class for its base class.

Java, C++, and most other object-oriented languages support a concept known as *polymorphism*, which simply means that you can use any class in place of its parent class. Thus, if we write a RepairShop class that has a method doQuarterlyMaintenance(Vehicle theVehicle), doQuarterlyMaintenance() will accept any Vehicle, including a Truck, a Airplane, or a Locomotive.

This technique of passing an object as though it were an instance of its parent class is called *upcasting*, since class diagrams are usually drawn with the parent toward the top. Upcasting is safe because the calling function only expects the behavior of a Vehicle. Although Truck, Airplane, and Locomotive each support more functionality than the simple Vehicle class, they can all do anything that is expected of any Vehicle.

You can explicitly tell the compiler to cast by placing the name of the destination class in parentheses. Thus, in Java you can write

```
Vehicle theVehicle = (Vehicle) theTruck;
```

C++ supports a similar syntax; this code would pass through a C++ compiler without error.

Downcasting

Upcasting is always safe, since every object inherits the full interface of its parent. The opposite process, *downcasting*, is not always safe. For example, if you write

```
Truck theTruck = (Truck) theVehicle;
```

and the object referenced by theVehicle was originally a Truck, all is well. But if the object referenced by theVehicle is really an Airplane, this code is in serious trouble.

In C++ you must take special precautions to ensure that downcasts work. In Java every cast is checked. If the types are not compatible, the code will throw a ClassCastException that you can use for error processing.

Object-Oriented

Like C++, Java directly supports object-oriented programming. For the most part, even the syntax is identical. For example, C++ allows you to specify more than one method with the same name—they differ only in the type of parameters they take. This technique, called *overloading*, allows you to simplify some pieces of code. Java and C++ both allow overloading in the same way.

Note that C++ allows you to overload both methods and operators. In Java you can only overload methods. (The Java built-in operators + and += are used both for integers and for strings, but they're a special case.)

There is one other difference you may find useful. In C++ you can have as many class hierarchies as you like—rather like a forest of trees. In Java, all classes implicitly descend from one master class, called Object. The C++ design leads to a problem—if you want to write a container class such as a stack or a queue, you must explicitly specify the objects your container will contain. Thus, you might have to write one queue for Trucks and another for Flowers. (C++ programmers get around this problem by using a relatively cumbersome mechanism called templates.) Java programmers can choose to write a single class for each kind of container, and declare that it contains Objects.

See Chapter 7, "Object-Oriented Analysis: A New Way of Looking at Software," and Chapter 8, "Object-Oriented Design and Programming," for a review of the object-oriented methods as they apply to Java.

Constructors

In C++ you, the programmer, write one or more constructors that the run-time system uses to bring instances of your classes into existence. You can always recognize a constructor—it has the same name as the class it constructs. For example, the zero-argument constructor for class `Truck` is `Truck()`.

In Java you may choose not to write a constructor. If you don't supply any constructors, Java will supply a zero-argument constructor for you.

If you're coming to Java from C++, you may be surprised to learn that there are no copy-constructors. (Copy-constructors are used in C++ to make a "deep copy" of an object that copies all of its internal structure.) The reason you don't need a copy constructor is that objects are always passed by reference. If you write a method for class `Truck`

```
void dispatch(Destination theDestination)
{
    ...
}
```

and then call it

```
Truck myTruck = new Truck();
Destination theCityOfChicago = new Destination(41.83,
87.75);
myTruck.dispatch(theCityOfChicago);
```

the `dispatch` method gets the actual object `theCityOfChicago`, not just a copy of it.

If you need the equivalent of a copy-constructor, use the Java `clone()` mechanism to make a local copy of the argument.

Destructors

In C++, you, the programmer, are responsible for deleting instances of classes when you're done with them. If you don't delete them, they can add up to make a "memory leak." When memory is filled up, your application may not work correctly.

Where'd my constructor go?

A common frustration among new Java programmers is the "disappearing constructor" problem. If you don't supply any constructors, Java will supply the zero-argument constructor for you, but as soon as you write even a single constructor, Java stops supplying the default constructor. If your class needs a zero-argument constructor (and most do) you must now write it explicitly.

The fact that C++ programmers have to manage memory explicitly has led to many subtle programming defects (and not a few memory leaks). To solve this problem, the designers of Java added a *garbage collector*. The garbage collector periodically runs through memory looking for objects that no one is using. When it finds them, it reclaims their memory.

C++ programmers usually write an explicit function for each class called the *destructor*. You can always spot a destructor—it has the same name as the class, but starts with a tilde (~). For the most part, Java programmers are free to ignore the issue of destructors. Sometimes, however, you may want to ensure that certain code is called when the garbage collector releases the memory associated with an object. You do this by writing a method called `finalize()`. When the garbage collector is about to delete an object, it will call `finalize()` for you.

In any class that requests resources (such as internal objects), consider defining a "cleanup" method. When you're done with an object, call the cleanup method. In `finalize()`, just check to be sure the object has been cleaned up, and call `cleanup()` if it's needed.

Inheritance

Both C++ and Java allow inheritance (though the syntax differs). When one class is listed as a descendant of another, the child class inherits all `public` and `protected` methods and instance variables of the parent.

C++ supports the concept of *multiple inheritance*, in which a class belongs to more than one class hierarchy. Java doesn't have multiple inheritance, but gives you much the same effect through *interfaces*. (Interfaces are described in Chapter 9, "Increasing Program Sophistication by Using Interfaces.")

To tell Java that class A is a kind of class B, use the keyword `extends`. For example, you might write

```
public class Truck extends Vehicle
{
    ...
}
```

Helping the garbage collector along

Depending upon the system it's running on, a Java applet or application may not run the garbage collector often. You'll write clearer code, and it may run a bit faster, if you explicitly clean up after yourself just as you'd do in a C++ application.

In object-oriented methods the parent class is referred to as the *base class*, and the child class is referred to as the *derived class*. Inside the class definition you can refer to the base class as super.

In C++ you call the base class's constructor explicitly from an initialization list in the derived class's constructor. In Java the syntax is different, but the effect is the same. If you wish to initialize any members of the base class, you must do so before you begin initializing members of the derived class. Here's a comparison between the two methods.

In C++ you might write

```
Truck(int theCapacity) :
  Vehicle (theCapacity)
{
  ...
}
```

while in Java you would say

```
Truck (int theCapacity)
{
  super(theCapacity);
  ...
}
```

C++ supports a complex mechanism by which the inheritance itself may be considered public, private, or protected. For example, a C++ programmer might write

```
class MyDerivedClass : private MyBaseClass
```

In Java all inheritance is public. If you would write

```
class MyDerivedClass extends MyBaseClass
```

in Java, you would write

```
class MyDerivedClass : public MyBaseClass
```

to get the same effect in C++.

A Java derived class cannot restrict access to a member any further than the restriction in the base class. Thus, if the base class Vehicle has a public member named dispatch, the derived class Truck cannot change dispatch to be protected or private.

In both C++ and Java you can declare a class to be abstract. An abstract class cannot be instantiated—some of its methods are incomplete. Use an abstract class as the base class for a concrete class that "fills in" the incomplete methods.

Many designers consider it poor form to derive a concrete class from another concrete class. They recommend that you abstract the common elements from the base class to form a new base class (which is abstract). Thus, if you plan to instantiate both Truck and FlatbedTruck, split Truck into two classes: AbstractTruck and GeneralTruck. Then write

```
public class GeneralTruck extends AbstractTruck
{
   . . .
}
```

and

```
public class FlatbedTruck extends AbstractTruck
{
   . . .
}
```

C++ has a keyword virtual that tells the compiler that a derived class may override a method. Java gets the same effect with a different keyword. The Java keyword final tells the compiler that a particular method will *not* be overridden. The Java default is that methods can be overridden (equivalent to the C++ virtual); you may get a slight efficiency gain if you declare some small methods as final, because the compiler may choose to expand them inline.

Inner Classes

In C++ you can place one class definition inside another, although there's no advantage to this technique. (It has the effect of hiding the inner class, but you can use C++ namespaces to do the same thing.)

In Java if you place one class definition inside another, the inner class maintains a reference (called outer) to the outer class. The inner class has full access to members of the outer class, just as though those methods and instance variables belonged to the inner class.

Inline Methods

In C++ there are ways (such as the `inline` keyword) to suggest to the compiler that a method be expanded inline, rather than compiled as a subroutine. Inline functions are faster than subroutines, though they take up more room.

In Java you make the same suggestion by using the `final` keyword.

Familiar Syntax

If you're a C++ programmer, there are whole sections of Java programs that you'll recognize immediately. Java control statements such as `for`, `while`, `do`, and `if` can pass through a C++ compiler without error. Upon closer examination you'll find a few differences. Some of them simplify the language (compared to C++) or make the files easier to read. This section will talk about three "almost-like-C++" features of the language:

- Primitive data types
- Comments
- Access specifiers

You can learn about Java's control structures in Chapter 5, "Using Branches and Loops."

Primitive Data Types

Like C++, Java supports primitive data types. Unlike C++, the size of these data types is fixed in the language standard, so you don't have to worry about whether your `int`s are 16-bit or 32-bit. In Java these types are

- `boolean` Defined to be one bit wide
- `char` An unsigned 16-bit type, designed to hold Unicode characters
- `byte` A signed 8-bit integer in two's complement representation
- `short` A signed 16-bit integer in two's complement representation

- `int`   A signed 32-bit integer in two's complement representation
- `long`   A signed 64-bit integer in two's complement representation
- `float`   Single-precision (32-bit) floating point numbers based on the *IEEE Standard for Binary Floating-Point Arithmetic*, ANSI/IEEE 754-1985
- `double`   Double-precision (64-bit) floating point numbers, also based on the ANSI/IEEE 754-1985 standard

Table B.1 shows the maximum and minimum values of these primitive types.

TABLE B.1   Java primitive types

Type	Minimum Negative Value	Maximum Negative Value	Minimum Positive Value	Maximum Positive Value
`boolean`	N/A	-1	N/A	0
`short`	-32,768	-1	0	32,767
`char`	N/A	N/A	0	65,525
`int`	-2,147,483,648	-1	0	2,147.483,647
`long`	-9,223,372,036,854,775,808	-1	0	9,223,372,036,854,775,807
`float`	-3.40282347e+38	-1.40239846e-45	1.40239846e-45	3.40282347e+38
`double`	-1.7976931348623157e+308	-4.94065645841246544e-324	4.94055645841246544e-324	1.7976931348623157e+308

Note that the absolute value of the minimum negative number in the integer types (`byte`, `short`, `int`, and `long`) is one greater than the absolute value of the maximum positive number. Java uses *two's complement* notation to store negative integers, which can lead to some surprising results if you're working with integer at the bit level.

What special numbers does IEEE 754 support?

In addition to the minimum and maximum values shown for floats and doubles in Table B.1, the ANSI/IEEE 754-1985 standard also supports four values that represent special numbers:

- Negative infinity
- Zero
- Positive infinity
- Not a number

Here's an example. Suppose you want to represent the number -2 in a byte. In binary, +2 is `0000 0010`. If the Java designers had elected to use one's complement notation, we could just flip all the bits and get `1111 1101`. Unfortunately, one's complement notation has an unfortunate side-effect: it results in two zeros: `0000 0000` and `1111 1111`. To solve this problem the Java designers selected two's complement notation, in which the computer subtracts one from the positive number and then flips every bit. Thus -2 is formed by starting with 2, subtracting 1 to get `0000 0001`, and then flipping every bit to get `1111 1110`.

The surprising result I spoke of is the fact that the sign bit—the high-order bit in the integer—is repeated down to the most significant bit. This phenomenon is known as *sign extension*. In writing Java applets and applications you may sometimes have occasion to use the right-shift operator, >>. This operator moves all of the bits in the integer from left to right one place, and replicates the sign bit to fill the high-order bit position. There's a different operator, >>>, that replaces the high-order bit with a zero. (Some documentation refers to >>> as the logical right-shift operator, and to >> as the arithmetic right-shift operator.)

If you haven't worked with non-European languages before, you may not be familiar with Unicode. Unicode is a 16-bit character encoding standard; with Unicode you can represent over 65,000 different characters. It is necessary because many Asian languages are based on character sets with thousands of characters. Unicode incorporates the older standard, the American Standard Code for Information Interchange (ASCII). If you only need to work in ASCII, use the Unicode-ready char type, and set the high-order byte to zero. That way your application will be ready for other languages besides English.

We'll examine Unicode in more detail later in the section titled "Overcoming the Limitations of C++."

SEE ALSO

➤ *Learn more about Java's primitive data types, page 106*

Be careful when casting chars to shorts

While both chars and shorts occupy 16 bits, be careful about casting chars to shorts. A char is an unsigned 16-bit type intended to support Unicode character data, and can represent over 65,000 characters. If you cast a char that is being used to store a Unicode character to a short, you may corrupt the data because the high-order bit will be lost.

Comments

Java supports both kinds of C++ comments:

```
// This line is a comment
```

and

```
/*
    This section is commented out. Typically you
    use this comment style to insert a paragraph
    or list of information.
 */
```

You can also use comments to build package and class documentation, through a Sun tool called `javadoc`.

SEE ALSO

➤ *Learn more about* `javadoc`, *page 33*

Access Specifiers

You'll recall from the "Write Once, Run Anywhere" section in Chapter 1 that classes can be arranged into packages. You'll also recall that classes have methods that allow objects to send messages to one another. Sometimes it's convenient to include private methods to simplify the design of other methods. You can specify which classes are allowed to use which methods by placing *access specifiers* on the method declaration.

C++ and Java have almost identical lists of access specifiers. The Java access specifiers are

- `public`   Access is allowed from any object
- `protected`   Access is allowed by any instance of the class, any descendant, and any other class in this package
- `private`   Access is allowed only by instances of the class

Note that Java's `protected` access is slightly different from C++'s `protected` access—Java's `protected` access allows access from the rest of the package, somewhat like C++'s `friend` access.

If you don't include an access specifier, access is allowed to any member of the class or any other object in the same package. This level of access is roughly equivalent to the C++ `friend` specifier.

You can use access specifiers on instance variables just like you can on methods. For example, to ensure that outside classes cannot read or set the Boolean variable `checked`, write

```
private boolean checked;
```

If you keep your instance variables `private`, write accessor methods (`get`, `set`, and `is`) if other classes need to read them or set them. For example, you might write

```
public boolean isChecked()
{
    return checked;
}
```

Note, too, that in C++ you place the access specifier on a block of declarations. In Java you must place an access specifier on each declaration.

Declaring Constants

Way back in the days of C, programmers used the C preprocessor to replace some string (such as SIZE) with a constant (such as 80). The problem with this approach was that it wasn't type-safe. If you had the misfortune to use SIZE some place where 80 wasn't appropriate, the compiler might not catch it.

C++ introduced the `const` keyword. Now you can specify a variable of a particular type, and use `const` to tell the compiler that variable cannot be changed. Thus, in C++ you might write

```
const short kLineSize = 80;
```

Java continues this theme, though the syntax is different. In Java you can write

```
static final short SIZE = 80;
```

The `static` keyword says that this variable belongs to the class, not to the instance. Since the value of the variable will not be changed, there's no need to keep a copy in each instance.

The `final` keyword tells the compiler that derived classes may not override the value of this variable. The remainder of the line states that the variable named SIZE is, in fact, a `short` with a value of 80.

Restricting access to instance variables

Most designers agree that giving `public` access to an instance variable is a bad idea. If you ever decide to change the internal representation of the data, your change could break other classes.

Most of the time you should specify your instance variables as `private`.

Should static final variables be `private`?

Sun often makes static final variables (which are used as constants) publicly accessible. For example, `Calendar.YEAR` is `public`. Other designers prefer to keep even constants `private`, and require the programmer to use an accessor method. Use whichever approach works best for your design.

How do you name a constant?

The compiler doesn't much care what you name your variables, but designers tend to adopt naming conventions to make it easier to read the design documents and code. In Java, it's customary to give constants a name that is all caps (such as SIZE).

Runtime Type Identification

Both C++ and Java allow you to identify a class's type at runtime. For example, if you have a Java object named theObject you can write

```
theObject.getClass().getName()
```

to get the name of the object's class.

You might want to use runtime type identification when you are getting ready to downcast an object, so you know what sort of object you're dealing with.

Error Control Through Exceptions

There was a time when most programs had two separate missions, interlaced in the code. One mission was to do whatever the program was supposed to do. The other was to catch problems that arose while the program was running.

Here's an example: a simple program that attempts to open a file and print out the contents. The language is pseudocode.

```
FileHandle theHandle = openFile (myFile);
if (theHandle == openFailed)
  tellUser("Cannot open myFile.");
else
{
  String aString;
  short theCount;
  Status theStatus;
  theCount = readFile (theHandle, aString);
  if (theCount != 0 && theHandle != EOF && theCount !=
readFailed)
    do
    {
      theStatus = print(aString);
      theCount = readFile (theHandle, aString);
    } while (theCount != 0 && theHandle != EOF && theCount
➥!= readFailed && theStatus != printFailed);
    close(theHandle);
}
```

Notice what the programmer has had to do here. Almost every other line is concerned with handling some kind of failure. This design makes it difficult for the programmer to keep the original objective in mind and is prone to error. In Java (and the latest versions of C++), the programmer could write the same program this way:

```
FileHandle theHandle;
try
{
  theHandle = openFile (myFile);
  String aString;
  short theCount;
  do
  {
    theCount = readFile (myFile, aString);
    theStatus = print(aString);
  } while (true);
}
catch (fileOpenException)
{
 tellUser("Cannot open myFile.");
}
catch (fileReadException)
{
 tellUser("Cannot read myFile.");
}
catch (fileEmptyException, fileEOFException,
printFailedException)
{
  close(theHandle);
}
```

Notice how much clearer this code is. The first section (the try block) contains the essence of the program itself. Code in the try block lives in an ideal world in which nothing ever goes wrong.

If something does go wrong in the try block, it simply throws a special object called an exception and transfers control to the corresponding catch block. The catch block contains a list of exceptions that can be caught and policy on how to handle each exception. For example, if the file cannot be opened or read, this catch block complains to the user. When the file becomes empty, or the file system returns EndOfFile (EOF), or if the string cannot be printed, the catch block simply closes the file and exits.

In Java you can also supply a finally block. Any code in the finally block will be executed after all the trying and catching is over. Typically you'll use the finally block to do any cleanup you need to do, such as closing files or freeing system resources.

Overcoming the Limitations of C++

C++ is a wonderful language, but, like anything made by humans, it is not perfect. Over the years C++ programmers have come with a long list of features they'd like to see in the language (or, occasionally, capabilities they'd like to see removed). The designers of C++ have extended the language when they could, but they couldn't make some changes since those changes would have broken existing code.

With the introduction of Java, there was no existing code to break. The Java designers started with the C++ model and added or deleted features to improve the language. Java is still a young language, so the process of refining the language and the standard libraries is still ongoing. Nevertheless, it is fair to say that in many ways Java is a better C++ than C++.

The following sections describe some of the improvements that led to Java.

Default Initialization

Continue to initialize your variables

Even though Java will take care of initialization for you, your code will be clearer if you continue to specify the initialization explicitly.

One of the most common C++ errors is to attempt to dereference an uninitialized pointer. In most C++ environments such an attempt will force the program to crash, though sometimes the behavior can become erratic. In Java, object references (the equivalent to pointers) are always initialized to null. If the programmer fails to initialize the reference and attempts to use it, the runtime environment will throw an exception.

Likewise, primitive data types are initialized to a known value. For example, integers are initialized to 0 and floats are initialized to 0.0.

Preprocessor Directives

Many language designers have considered the old C preprocessor (which is still a part of C++) to be something of a kludge—an imperfect solution that was tolerated for the sake of efficiency. Many of the common uses of the preprocessor, such as defining constants and inline functions (as macros), have a C++ equivalent that is generally considered to be superior to the preprocessor (if only because they are type-safe).

One major use of the preprocessor in C++ is to build alternate versions of a product. It's not uncommon to see code like this:

```
#ifdef UNIX
...do things the UNIX way
#elif defined(MACOS)
...do things the Macintosh way
#else
...do things the Windows way
#endif
```

Since Java is platform-independent, this important use of the preprocessor is not required in Java. Consequently, the Java designers decided to dispense with the preprocessor entirely.

In C and C++, it is common to use the preprocessor directive #include to refer to header (.h) files. In Java there are no header files—all classes are defined in the same file in which they are declared. Often, however, you'll want to arrange classes in some kind of hierarchy. Java supports packages to reflect this hierarchy. You tell one class where to find members of other classes by referring to the package's path. To simplify your code, you'll often use the import statement at the top of your file to tell Java to which packages you are referring.

You can still use CPP

Nearly all versions of the C preprocessor (CPP) allow you to invoke the preprocessor on any file. If you want to use the CPP on your Java (for example, to handle #ifdef DEBUG directives) write a rule in your makefile that makes .java files out of some other source (such as .j) by passing it through the CPP.

Native Unicode

Three generations of programmers have grown up on ASCII—the American Standard Code for Information Interchange. Over the years users whose first language was not American English have found ways to adapt to ASCII, or to work around it by using special encodings. ASCII is a 7-bit standard—it encodes 2^7 or 128 characters. In most applications ASCII characters are stored in a byte—an 8-bit container. Developers have found creative ways to use the additional 128 characters that can be represented in a byte. These encodings allow alphabetic languages such as the European languages, Turkish, Hebrew, and Russian (with its Cyrillic alphabet) to be represented in systems otherwise designed for American English.

Many Asian languages, such as Chinese, Japanese, and Korean, do not use alphabets. They use a large set of ideographs—one per word. There is no way to encode these thousands of symbols in an 9-bit character set, since 2^8 is only 256. Until recently, the solution was to require people who read and write those languages to adapt their language to the English character set of ASCII, but now there's a better approach. With Unicode, characters are represented in 16 bits. Since 2^{16} is 65,535, Unicode's developers hope to have enough room for virtually every alphabetic or ideographic symbol used in Earth's languages.

Unicode is the native encoding for Java, as well as for newer operating systems such as Windows NT. You can learn more about Unicode from the Unicode Consortium at
`http://www.unicode.org/`.

No Global Names

C++ is an object-oriented language, but it still shows its C roots. The `main()` routine in a C++ program is not part of any object. Similarly, you can declare global objects and functions. In fact, you can pass most C programs, which are not object-oriented, through a C++ compiler, and get perfectly good results.

Java differs from C++ in this respect: Java is a completely object-oriented language. There are no global functions. There is no global data. Everything is in an object. In fact, to write a Java application, you pick one class to be the "starting point" and define a main() method in that class. When the Java interpreter launches the application, it starts in the designated class by calling the main() method. Everything else in the application is called from that instance of main().

SEE ALSO

➤ *Learn why every class should have a* main() *method, page 438*

Run-Time Bounds Checking on Arrays

In C++, arrays are implemented by a bit of pointer magic. Most efficient array access is done with some form of pointer arithmetic. It's easy for the programmer make a mistake and accidentally read or write outside the bounds of the array. The C++ runtime environment doesn't know about the array—only about the underlying pointers—so it makes no attempt to stop or warn the programmer about the error.

In Java, arrays are true objects. All arrays have a method length that specifies their size. If you should exceed the allocated size of an array and attempt to read or write outside the array, you'll get an out-of-bounds exception.

The Generic Collection Library for Java

Over the years that C++ has been in use, C++ programmers felt a need for a standard library of collection classes. Since collection classes (also called container classes) are useful generic classes, and need efficient algorithms for methods such as search() and sort(), programmers clamored for a library of collection classes to be included with C++ compilers. The C++ community responded with the Standard Template Library (STL), which now ships with many popular compilers.

Java doesn't yet have the equivalent of an STL, but one company—ObjectSpace—has written a set of packages that might be considered standard one day. Their package is called the Generic Collection Library for Java, but is abbreviated JGL

What's a collection class?

Collection classes are classes that hold objects from other classes. A list, a map, or a set are all examples of collections. You might build a list of ints, a map of Trucks, or a set of Loads.

Try out the JGL

Download the JGL from
`http://www.object-space.com/jgl/` and try it out for yourself. It's free, and it's powerful enough to use in real-world applications.

for historical reasons. ObjectSpace reports that ten major vendors have already licensed the JGL and will include it in their Integrated Development Environment (IDE).

On the other hand, you may decide to stick with the JDK. Sun is moving in the direction of including more container classes in the JDK.

SEE ALSO

➤ *Learn about the new container classes in JDK 1.2, page 33*

Java Resources

Finding Resources Online

Programming may sometimes seem a lonely profession—many of our working hours are spent interacting with a machine rather than with people. Nevertheless, there are thousands of people available to help you learn Java and become familiar with the advanced capabilities of various Java packages. This appendix examines some of the more important online resources:

- Sun Microsystems—As the developer of Java, Sun offers a rich set of online tutorials and downloadable tools as well as opportunities for continuing education and certification.

- IBM—Big Blue was among the first in line to support Java. It offers an innovative online tutorial to help you get started.

- Netscape Communications Corporation—Netscape adopted Java into Navigator, making the language a success on the Internet overnight. Netscape's DevEdge site and subscription service will keep you posted on applet development.

- Java Applet Rating Service—JARS is among the most important independent Java resources; its charter goes far beyond what its name implies.

- User groups—Locally and nationally, users band together to understand and use Java.

Macmillan Computer Publishing's Java Resources

Macmillan Computer Publishing is the world's largest publisher of computer books (including the Que book you're reading right now). You can explore Macmillan's Java resources online by visiting the main Resource Center page at: `http://www.mcp.com/resources`. From there, choose the link titled Programming. From the Programming Resource Center page, follow the Java Resource Center link.

- Discussion groups—Whether you read a weekly newsletter or participate in the daily deluge from Usenet, there are plenty of people ready to talk with you about Java.

- Commercial products—Microsoft's Visual J++ is one of the best known Java development environments, but it is by no means alone.

Sun Resources

As the developer and greatest champion of Java, it's only natural that Sun Microsystems would offer a rich set of resources to help you use the language. This section describes the resources Sun makes available to the general public, and those that are aimed at developers.

Public Resources

The first place you should turn online to learn about Java is `http://java.sun.com/`. This site, operated by JavaSoft, is the starting point for all of Sun's public resources that support Java users and developers.

From the JavaSoft home page you can follow links to press releases, product information, and galleries of applets and applications. Be sure to follow the Map link at the top of the page—it leads to a sophisticated Java-based navigation system called MAPA, shown in Figure C.1.

Java Developer Connection

If you're developing Java applets and applications, you should subscribe to Sun's Java Developer Connection, or JDC. Point your browser to `http://developer.javasoft.com/`. You'll need to sign up, but membership is free. Once in, you have the opportunity to get prerelease versions of the JDK and various Java tools. You'll also find online tutorials on various aspects of Java programming.

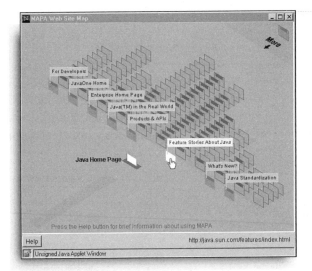

FIGURE C.1

MAPA gives you a fast way to navigate the JavaSoft site.

JavaSoft Programs for Developers

If you're writing Java programs as anything other than a hobby, chances are you'd appreciate some marketing help from Sun. Sun offers a wide range of marketing programs that can help you build name recognition and customer confidence. It also has collateral materials on its Web site to help answer your customers' and investors' question: "Why Java?"

With the growing popularity of Java, it is inevitable that many people with only a passing knowledge of Java will try to present themselves as Java programmers. As a professional programmer, you can benefit from credentials that show that you've taken the time to learn your subject. Java offers two certification programs to help you test your knowledge.

Certified Java Programmers are persons who have passed a test (available at local Sylvan testing centers) on Java and the JDK.

Certified Java Developers are certified Java programmers who have passed an additional test as well as a practical demonstration of their programming skills.

Sun will help your business grow

Learn about Sun's programs at `http://java.sun.com /marketing/` to help your business grow.

Become a Sun-certified Java programmer

Learn more about Sun's certification programs from Sun Educational Services at `http://suned.sun.com /suned/template.html ?file=Certification/ java.`

Gamelan

The single largest showcase of Java technology is at
`http://www.gamelan.com/`. That address takes you to
`http://www.developer.com/directories/pages/dir.java.html`, the
Java directory of Developer.com. This site is sponsored by Sun
and contains links to applets, applications, Java-related documents, and Java-related Web sites. Categories include the following:

- Arts and entertainment
- Business and finance
- Commercial Java
- Educational
- Games
- How-to and help
- Java-enhanced sites
- Tools and utilities
- JavaBeans
- Miscellaneous
- Multimedia
- Network and communications
- Programming in Java
- Publications
- Special effects

IBM

IBM is a strong Java supporter; you can find its resource site at
`http://www.ibm.com/java/`. IBM offers versions of the JDK for
major IBM platforms, including OS/2, the RS/6000, and the
AS/400. It also offers a variety of Java development tools,
including a version of its popular VisualAge line that generates
Java. If you work on an IBM platform you should visit this site.

Take an online course from IBM

IBM has developed a free multimedia course called Intro to Java. You'll
find it at
`http://www.ibm.com/`
`java/education/intro/`
`courseoptions.htm`. Be sure
to give feedback after you finish the
course. You might also enjoy the
course on building an applet, at
`http://www.ibm.com/`
`java/education/`
`buildapplet/`.

Netscape Resources

Java is one of Netscape's core technologies—a collection it calls
the Netscape Open Network Environment, or Netscape ONE.
All current versions of Netscape Navigator support Java. You can
also write Java servlets that run on Netscape's SuiteSpot servers.

If you're developing applets or if you use Java on a Netscape server, you need to visit `http://developer.netscape.com/one/java/index.html`. You'll also find an excellent collection of technical papers describing specific ways to use Java. Netscape's site is second only to Sun's in technical depth. Bookmark it and return there frequently.

Java Applet Rating Service

From its name you might guess that the Java Applet Rating Service (JARS) rates applets—and you'd be right. But JARS does much more. In addition to rating Java applets, it also lists JavaScript, PERL, ActiveX, and VRML resources. It lists news stories about Java. It also sponsors discussions about Java, an online newsletter about Java, and an extensive Web site. Visit this site at `http://www.jars.com/`.

User Groups

Sometimes it's useful to get together with other Java programmers for the kind of networking that doesn't require wires. At the national and international level, you can join Java-SIG, the special interest group of the Sun user group. In most parts of the U.S. and many other countries, local Java user groups (JUGs) meet to discuss various aspects of the language. These user groups are a good way to find out about local resources. Does your local college offer a course in Java? Are you looking for people with Java skills to help you on a project? Visit the local JUG to meet the people in your area who are interested in Java.

Find a local Java user group

The Java-SIG maintains a list of local JUGs at `http://java.sun.com/aboutJava/jug/user-groups.html`. If you don't find a group in your area, keep checking this page—it's updated regularly. If you still don't find a local JUG, consider starting one of your own. Put up a notice in local newsgroups. Chances are you'll get a positive response.

Java Lobby

Some lobbyists lobby Congress; others work at the state level. The Java Lobby works where it can do the Java community the most good—in the halls of developers and licensees. Its mission statement says that "[t]he main purpose of the Java Lobby is to represent the needs and concerns of the Java developer and user community to the companies and organizations who have influence in the evolution of Java."

If you're interested in helping the Java Lobby or just want to learn more, visit `http://www.javalobby.org/` to read its "who we are" and "what we stand for" statement. Membership is free.

Discussion Groups

If you have questions about Java or a specific Java tool or package, chances are someone online has an answer. If you're working with Java, you should subscribe to one or more of the Usenet newsgroups that discuss the language. You might also want to subscribe to some of the mailing lists and electronic newsletters described in this section.

comp.lang.java and Its Kin

Point your newsreader to `comp.lang.java`, the basic Usenet newsgroup for Java users and developers. Figure C.2 shows a typical set of messages.

FIGURE C.2

Review the messages in `comp.lang.java` every few days to see what's new in the Java community.

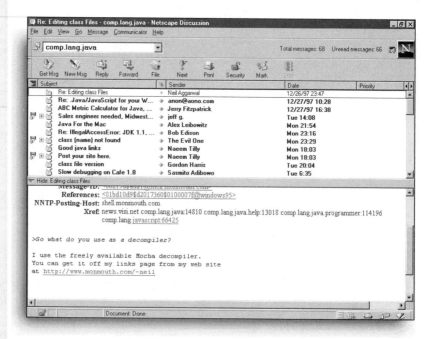

There are 13 newsgroups under `comp.lang.java` in the Usenet hierarchy:

- `comp.lang.java.advocacy`   Discussion about the merits (and lack thereof) of various aspects of Java

- `comp.lang.java.announce`   Announcements of interest to Java developers

- `comp.lang.java.api`   Discussion about the Java API

- `comp.lang.java.beans`   Discussion of the JavaBeans component API

- `comp.lang.java.databases`   Discussion of Java-SQL interfaces such as JDBC and Java-based databases such as jDB

- `comp.lang.java.gui`   Discussion of the user-interface components in the AWT and JFC

- `comp.lang.java.help`   Help for end users (not programmers) trying to install and run Java programs

- `comp.lang.java.javascript`   Mostly about JavaScript

- `comp.lang.java.machine`   Technical issues on Java other than issues related directly to the language itself

- `comp.lang.java.misc`   Miscellaneous topics

- `comp.lang.java.programmer`   Discussion of the Java language

- `comp.lang.java.security`   Discussion of the Java security model and its implementations

- `comp.lang.java.softwaretools`   Discussion of IDEs and other tools for writing Java

For the latest on the HotJava browser, you may also want to explore `alt.www.hotjava`.

DejaNews

If you read every message in every Java newsgroup on Usenet, you'll never have time to write Java programs. A better approach is to pick one or two newsgroups that represent your interests and use DejaNews (`http://www.dejanews.com/`) to research specific needs. For example, you can point your Web browser to

Read the FAQs

To learn more about the `comp.lang.java` newsgroups, read their Frequently Asked Questions list at `http://sunsite.unc.edu/javafaq/javafaq.html`. For a broader list of resources, visit Café au Lait at `http://sunsite.unc.edu/javafaq/`.

http://www.dejanews.com/home_sf.shtml to set up a filter for messages that have been posted to comp.lang.java in the last year that deal with runtime type identification.

Non-Usenet Discussions

You need a newsreader

You need a newsreader in order to read newsgroups. Newsreaders are included in popular browser packages such as Netscape Communicator. Sun also offers one (written as a Java applet).

Many organizations host newsgroups on their own servers. These newsgroups don't circulate (as those on Usenet do), but they're just as accessible as a Web page.

If you're a member of Sun's Java Developer Connection (JDC) you can read the DukeDollars newsgroups at http://developer.javasoft.com/developer/toolbar.shtml. The DukeDollars program rewards JDC members for answering questions. This approach makes it likely that your questions will be answered in a timely manner. For details, see http://developer.javasoft.com/developer/DukeDollars/dukedollars.shtml.

Figure C.3 shows Sun's Java newsgroups as viewed through the GroupReader applet.

FIGURE C.3

The Sun Java newsgroups are only open to JDC members, but anyone may join for free.

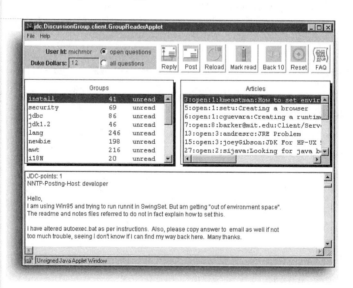

Mailing Lists

One of Java's most popular (and busiest) electronic discussions doesn't take place on Usenet—it's based on email. It's called the `java-interest` list. To subscribe, send email to `majordomo@java.sun.com`; put the words **subscribe java-interest** in the body of your message. You can post messages by sending them to `java-interest@java.sun.com`.

Commercial Development Environments

If you already have the JDK and a good editor, why would you want anything else? For one thing, your editor probably doesn't know anything about Java. Many developers believe they develop better code in less time if they work in an *Integrated Development Environment* such as those offered by Microsoft, Symantec, Borland, and Sun.

While Microsoft's J++ is one of the best known Java development environments, Microsoft's competitors have not let this opportunity slip past them. Borland and Symantec, makers of competing C++ development tools, also offer Java development environments. Sun also has a competing product, Java Workshop.

Which IDE is best? Who's to say? In a 1997 Users' Choice contest sponsored by Developer.com (the folks who maintain the Gamelan site), the three winners were Symantec's Visual Café for Java, Borland's JBuilder, and IBM's VisualAge for Java. These three products got almost identical scores. (Microsoft's Visual J++ came in fifth, behind Metrowerks' CodeWarrior Professional and ahead of Sun's Java Workshop.) Read the detailed results at `http://www.developer.com/news/userschoice/n_usersframe.html`.

Microsoft's Visual J++

Microsoft has been wildly successful with its Visual line of programming products, including Visual Basic and Visual C++. When Java emerged as an important standard, Microsoft was well-suited to move into the marketplace with a Java version of

---

Sun's mailing lists are gated to Usenet

Sun lists its mailing lists on its Web site: `http://java.sun.com/mail.html`. If you subscribe to the `comp.lang.java` discussion group, you can skip the Sun mailing lists. Sun routes all messages on the mailing list to the newsgroup.

Still more mailing lists

There are several dozen mailing lists that discuss various aspects of Java. Visit `http://sunsite.unc.edu/javafaq/mailinglists.html` to see a description of each.

Start your search at Yahoo!

Visit Yahoo! for a list of companies offering Java development environments and other tools. Their Java page (`http://www.yahoo.com/Business_and_Economy/Companies/Computers/Software/Programming_Tools/Languages/Java/`) is particularly useful.

Macintosh users, take note!

While most IDEs are only available on Windows, Symantec Café and Sun's Java Workshop run on either the Macintosh or Windows.

Is Visual J++'s output really Java?

There remains some doubt about Microsoft's commitment to the Java standard. By its own admission, it has added functionality to the Java API and deleted some standard methods. In October 1997 Sun filed suit against Microsoft, asking the court to prevent Microsoft from using the Java logo until its version of Java conforms to the standard.

You can follow the news of the lawsuit at `http://java.sun.com/aboutJava/info/index.html`. Microsoft's response is at `http://www.microsoft.com/visualj/prodinfo/lawsuit.htm`.

its C++ compiler. Independent market research firm Market Decisions, Inc., reports that about half of all Java developers use Visual J++.

With its most recent releases of Visual J++, Microsoft no longer claims to be producing 100% Pure Java. Instead, it offers Windows Foundation Classes (WFC) that ties Java directly to the Windows platform. If you plan to use Java as a Windows application development environment rather than for its cross-platform capabilities, check out the WFC. To learn more about the debate between Microsoft and Sun, read the *San Jose Mercury News* article "Microsoft Escalates Battle on Java," which is online at `http://www.sjmercury.com/business/top/033098.htm`.

Figure C.4 shows Visual J++ 6.0 in action. Note the WFC components instead of the JFC on the left side of the figure. If you choose to use the WFC rather than the JFC, your applets and applications are not portable to a non-Microsoft environment.

FIGURE C.4

Unlike other Java IDEs, the newest Visual J++ doesn't work with the JFC.

Visit Microsoft

Learn more about Microsoft's family of Java products at its Web site: `http://www.microsoft.com/visualj/`.

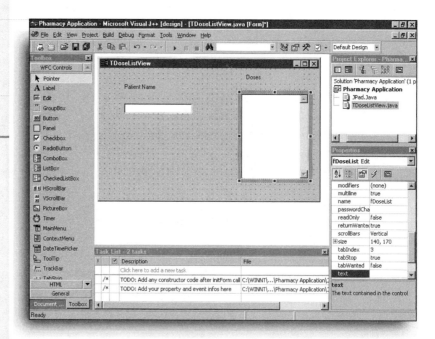

Symantec Visual Café for Java

In the Java market, Symantec is one of Microsoft's strongest competitors. Symantec observes that Microsoft J++ is "a slightly updated version of their C++ development environment with a few Java tools and wizards added." It points to the fact that many tools available in the Visual tool palette are not supported in the Microsoft Java wizard. Symantec also observes that Java's standard layout managers are not supported in J++. Figure C.5 shows Visual Café at work.

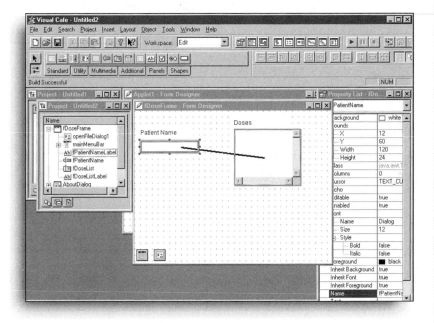

FIGURE C.5

Visual Café allows you to connect event sources to event listeners without typing any code.

SEE ALSO
➤ *Learn about the graphical components of the Java user interface, page 274*
➤ *Learn about layout managers, page 289*

Symentec points to its highly integrated Café as evidence that it is fully committed to Java. Its Web site lists features that help it stand apart from Visual J++, as well as other competitors.

Visit `http://cafe.symantec.com/` to learn more about Café or to download a trial version.

Borland JBuilder

Most professional developers are familiar with Borland C++, the strongest competitor to Microsoft's Visual C++. Now Borland is attempting to beat Microsoft's Visual J++ with Borland JBuilder. You can get a feel for JBuilder by downloading a self-running tutorial from the Web site. Figure C.6 shows one step of this tutorial. Learn more about JBuilder at

http://www.borland.com/jbuilder/.

FIGURE C.6

You'll spend most of your time in the AppBrowser window when using JBuilder.

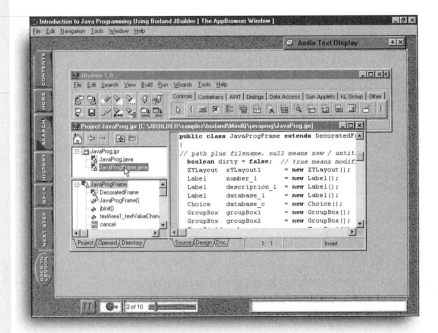

IBM's VisualAge for Java

IBM offers one of the most successful Java IDEs. You can get a feel for the product by downloading the trial edition. VisualAge has many of the same features as Visual Café from Symantec, yet its user interface is somewhat cleaner. Figure C.7 shows VisualAge's Composition Editor, where you can assemble the user interface visually.

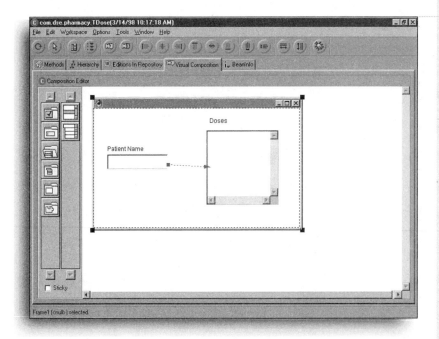

FIGURE C.7

Like Visual Café, you can identify interactions between components in VisualAge for Java
by drawing a line from one
component to the other.

You can get more information about IBM's VisualAge for Java
family of products at `http://www.ibm.com/ad/vajava/`.

SuperCede by Asymetrix

Asymetrix offers a low-cost product—SuperCede—with many of
its competitors features. Figure C.8 shows the visual design window of SuperCede. Learn more about this product at
`http://www.asymetrix.com/sales/info_scjava.html`.

Special offer on SuperCede

If you're just learning to pro-
gram you may appreciate the
tutorial nature of *Sam's Teach
Yourself Java 1.1 Programming
in 24 Hours* (Sams.net, 1997).
You can get that book and
SuperCede in one box as Java
Starter Kit 3.0 from Macmillan
Digital Publishing.

FIGURE C.8

SuperCede is a good choice if
you need a Java-aware editor
and layout tool.

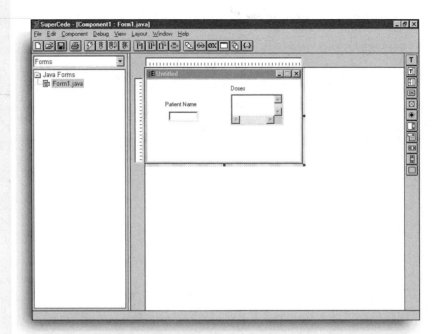

FIGURE C.8

SuperCede is a good choice if
you need a Java-aware editor
and layout tool.

Java Language Reference

D

Learn the reserved words of Java, including eleven words reserved for future use

See how to specify literals and variables in all of Java's primitive data types as well as in classes and arrays

Get a concise list of the syntax of the major Java statements

Refer to a cross-reference of this book organized around these language elements

Language Issues

Many Java language references are written for compiler designers who need to know how to parse a programmer's source code and turn it into bytecodes. This appendix is different—it's designed for use by programmers, and serves as a quick reference to the major features of the language. You can use this appendix to direct you into the chapters where these topics are dealt with in more depth.

In addition to knowing the Java language itself, you need to know the APIs of the JDK and any third-party packages you use. Refer to the documentation that comes from Sun and other vendors for the most up-to-date API documentation.

Reserved Words

The Java language reserves 57 words for special use by the compiler. You may not use these words as variable names, class names, or for any purposes other than those intended by the language designers. Not all of these words are currently implemented in the language. The reserved words are the following:

- `abstract` Indicates that a class or method is not implemented. It must be implemented in a subclass in order for the class to be instantiated. See Chapter 6, "Methods: Adding Code to Your Objects."

- `boolean` A primitive type defined to hold `true` or `false`. See Chapter 4, "Understanding Java Data Types and Operators."

- `break` Break out of a loop (or to a specified label). See Chapter 5, "Using Branches and Loops."

- `byte` A signed 8-bit integer primitive data type (see Chapter 4).

- `case` Used with the `switch` statement to select blocks of code (see Chapter 5).

- `catch` Used with `try` to handle exceptions. See Chapter 10, "Simplifying Code with Exceptions."

- `char` An unsigned 16-bit primitive data type designed to hold Unicode characters. (see Chapter 4).

The JDK documentation is on your hard drive

If you followed the procedure recommended in Chapter 3, "Getting Started Fast," you installed the JDK documentation in the `/docs` directory underneath the JDK root directory. Use your Web browser to explore that documentation.

`byvalue` is reserved

`byvalue` is reserved for future use.

`cast` is reserved

`cast` is reserved for future use.

`const` is reserved

`const` is reserved for future use.

- `class` Used to declare a new type of object (see Chapter 6).

- `continue` Pass control from the inside of a loop back to the top (or to a specified label) (see Chapter 5).

- `default` Used in a `switch` statement to specify the block of code to execute if no `case` matches the switch value (see Chapter 5).

- `do` Initiate a `do-while` loop (see Chapter 5).

- `double` A 64-bit floating-point primitive data type (see Chapter 4).

- `else` Used with `if` statements to specify an alternate branch (see Chapter 5).

- `extends` Used to indicate that a class or interface is derived from another class or interface. See Chapter 7, "Object-Oriented Analysis: A New Way of Looking at Software."

- `final` When used with a variable, specifies that the variable holds a constant value. When used with a method, indicates that subclasses may not override the method (see Chapter 4).

- `finally` Used with `try` and `catch` to specify a block of code that will always be executed, regardless of any exceptions that may be thrown (see Chapter 10).

- `float` A 32-bit floating-point primitive data type (see Chapter 4).

- `for` Used as part of the `for`-loop statement (see Chapter 5).

- `if` Used to test a Boolean expression select a path of execution (see Chapter 5).

- `implements` Used to indicate that a class implements one or more interfaces. See Chapter 9, "Increasing Program Sophistication by Using Interfaces."

- `import` Allows the programmer to reference other classes without fully specifying the package name. See Chapter 15, "Understanding Packages."

- `instanceof` Determines whether an object is an instance of a particular class or implements a particular interface.

- `int` A 32-bit signed integer primitive data type (see Chapter 4).

`future` is reserved

`future` is reserved for future use.

`generic` is reserved

`generic` is reserved for future use.

`goto` is reserved

`goto` is reserved for future use.

`inner` is reserved

`inner` is reserved for future use.

- `interface`   Defines a Java interface, which resembles a completely abstract class (see Chapter 9).

- `long`   A 64-bit signed integer primitive data type (see Chapter 4).

- `native`   Used to indicate that a method has been implemented in a platform-specific language such as C++ (see Chapter 3).

- `new`   Used to construct new objects (see Chapter 3).

- `null`   Used to indicate that a reference doesn't refer to anything (see Chapter 3).

- `package`   Places a file in a specified Java package (see Chapter 15).

- `private`   An access specifier that makes a method or variable accessible only within the class in which it is declared (see Chapter 3).

- `protected`   An access specifier that makes a method or variable accessible only to the class in which it is declared, subclasses of that class, and other classes in that package (see Chapter 3).

- `public`   An access specifier for classes, interfaces, method, and variables. A `public` class is accessible throughout the program. A `public` method or variable is accessible wherever its class is accessible (see Chapter 3).

- `return`   Returns control (and, optionally, a value) from a method to the calling routine (see Chapter 3).

- `short`   A 16-bit signed integer primitive data type (see Chapter 4).

- `static`   Specifies that a method or data member applies to the class as a whole, rather than to a specific instance (see Chapter 3).

- `super`   Within a method or constructor, refers to this class's base class (see Chapter 7).

- `switch`   Begins a statement (which also includes `case` and `default`) that selects one block of code based on a switch value (see Chapter 5).

operator is reserved

`operator` is reserved for future use.

outer is reserved

`outer` is reserved for future use.

rest is reserved

`rest` is reserved for future use.

- `synchronized`   Used to indicate critical methods or sections of code. See Chapter 17, "Concurrent Programming with Threads."

- `this`   Within a method or constructor, refers to this instance (see Chapter 7).

- `throw`   Generates an exception (see Chapter 10).

- `throws`   Serves to specify any exceptions that may be thrown by a method (see Chapter 10).

- `transient`   Indicates that a member variable is not part of an object's persistent state, and should not be written to persistent storage (as is done, for example, during serialization). See Chapter 13, "Designing for a JFC Interface."

- `try`   Begins a block of code that may generate an exception. Must be matched with one or more `catch` statements, a `finally`, statement, or both (see Chapter 10).

- `void`   Indicates that a method has no return value (see Chapter 3).

- `volatile`   Informs the compiler that a variable may change asynchronously and without action by the program.

- `while`   Initiates a `while` loop (see Chapter 5).

var is reserved

`var` is reserved for future use.

Comments

You can embed multiline comments in your source files by using `/*[...]*/`:

```
/*
This is a
multiline
comment.
*/
```

Anything you place between double-slashes (`//`) and the end of the line will be ignored:

```
// This line is a comment
for (int i=0; i<theMax; i++) // this line has a for loop and
                    // a comment
```

Use tagged paragraphs with javadoc comments

You can add additional information to your javadoc documentation by using tagged paragraphs–a special keyword preceded by an "at sign" (@). See Chapter 15 for details.

You can use javadoc to extract special comments from your source code. javadoc comments begin with /**:

```
/**
  Javadoc will associate
  this comment with the
  class which follows.
  */
public class TDemo
```

SEE ALSO

➤ *Learn more about* javadoc, *page 419*

Primitive Data Types, Classes, Interfaces, and Arrays

All data in Java is stored in instance variables or class variables— except when it's stored in primitive data types. This section shows you how to specify data literals and variables. See Chapter 4 to learn more about primitive data types.

Literals

Table D.1 shows how to generate specific types of literal.

TABLE D.1   How Java interprets literals

To make a literal	Write	Example
Integer	*number*	1234
Long	*number* l or *number* L	1234567890L
Hexadecimal integer	0x*number*	0xFF
Octal integer	0*number*	077
Double	*number.number* or *.number*	12.34
Float	*number*f or *number*F	12.34F
Double	*number*d or *number*D	12.34D
Signed	+*number* or –*number*	–6

To make a literal	Write	Example
Exponent	*numberenumber* or *numberEnumber*	1.2E3
Single character	`'character'`	`'j'`
Character string	`"characters"`	`"abcxyz"`
Empty string	`""`	`""`
Backspace	`\b`	`\b`
Tab	`\t`	`\t`
Line feed	`\n`	`\n`
Form feed	`\f`	`\f`
Carriage return	`\r`	`\r`
Double quote	`\"`	`\"`
Single quote	`\'`	`\'`
Backslash	`\\`	`\\`
Unicode character	`\uNNNN`	`\u0013`
Boolean	`true` or `false`	`true`

Variable Declaration

In general you declare variables by writing

```
type variablename
```

For example, you can make a new 32-bit integer named `myInteger` by writing

```
int myInteger;
```

You can also initialize variables to a specific value. For example, you can specify that `myInteger` starts with the value 123:

```
int myInteger = 123;
```

Table D.2 shows you how to specify variables for all of Java's primitive data types.

Learn more about primitive data types

See Chapter 4 for more information on primitive data types.

TABLE D.2   **How to specify data types**

To make a data type	Write	Example
Integer	byte or short or int or long *varname*	int myInt
Float	float or double *varname*	float myFloat
Unicode char	char *varname*	char myChar
Boolean	boolean *varname*	boolean myBool
Multiple variables	*type varname*, *varname*, *varname*	int i, j, k

Operators

Following are the operators Java supports on numeric and Boolean data.

- Addition   *arg* + *arg*
- Subtraction   *arg* - *arg*
- Multiplication   *arg* * *arg*
- Division   *arg* / *arg*
- Modulus   *arg* % *arg*
- Less than   *arg* < *arg*
- Greater than   *arg* > *arg*
- Less than or equal to   *arg* <= *arg*
- Greater than or equal to   *arg* >= *arg*
- Equal   *arg* == *arg*
- Not equal   *arg* != *arg*
- Logical AND   *arg* && *arg*
- Logical OR   *arg* ¦¦ *arg*
- Logical NOT   !*arg*
- Bitwise AND   *arg* & *arg*
- Bitwise OR   *arg* ¦ *arg*
- Bitwise XOR   *arg* ^ *arg*
- Left-shift   *arg* << *arg*

- Right-shift   `arg >> arg`
- Zero-fill right-shift   `arg >>> arg`
- Complement   `~ arg`
- Casting   `(type)something_of_another_type`
- Instance of   `arg instanceof class`
- Conditional   `test ? trueOp : falseOp`

Variable Assignment

Java supports both prefix and postfix increment and decrement. It also allows you to combine some operators with assignment.

- Assignment   `variable = value`
- Postfix increment   `variable++`
- Postfix decrement   `variable--`
- Prefix increment   `++variable`
- Prefix decrement   `--variable`
- Add and assign   `variable += value`
- Subtract and assign   `variable -= value`
- Multiply and assign   `variable *= value`
- Divide and assign   `variable /= value`
- Modulus and assign   `variable %= value`
- AND and assign   `variable &= value`
- OR and assign   `variable |= value`
- XOR and assign   `variable ^= value`
- Left-shift and assign   `variable <<= value`
- Right-shift and assign   `variable >>= value`
- Zero-fill, left-shift, and assign   `variable <<<= value`

Classes and Objects

With the exception of primitive data types, all data in Java is stored in classes and their instances (called objects). See Chapter 4 for more information on instance and class variables.

Postfix operators return the original value of the variable

When you apply a postfix operator the operator returns the value of the variable before it increments (or decrements) the value. Thus,

```
temp = 1;
System.out.println
➥("The result is " +
➥temp++ + ".");
```

returns

"The result is 1."

Prefix operators return the changed value of the variable

When you apply a prefix operator the operator returns the value of the variable after it increments (or decrements) the value. Thus,

```
temp = 1;
System.out.println
➥("The result is " +
➥++temp + ".");
```

returns

"The result is 2."

How do combined operators work?

The add and assign operator (+=) has the effect of adding the operand to the variable. Thus,

i += 3;

has the same effect as

i = i + 3;

The other operators combined with assign, such as -= and *=, work the same way.

Learn more about classes and interfaces

Learn more about class design in Chapter 7 and Chapter 8, "Object-Oriented Design and Programming." Learn about interfaces in Chapter 9.

Learn more about classes and objects

See Chapter 3 for an overview of classes and objects. Chapter 7 will give you a broader foundation on this subject.

Declaring Classes and Interfaces

You declare a class by writing

```
class classname block
```

You can also apply zero or more of the following modifiers to a class declaration.

- final   No subclasses
- abstract   Cannot be instantiated
- public   Accessible outside package
- [...]extends *NameOfSuperclass*   Defines a base class
- [...]implements *NameOfInterfaces*   Declares that the class implements one or more interfaces (separated by commas)

Accessing Data Members and Methods

The following list shows the special operators that apply to classes.

- new *className*();   Make a new instance
- new *className*(arg, arg, arg[...]);   Make a new instance with parameters
- new *type*(arg, arg, arg[...]);   Make a new instance of an anonymous class
- *Primary*.new *type*(arg, arg, arg[...]);   Make a new instance of an anonymous class
- *object.variable*   Instance variable
- *object.classvariable*   Class variable
- *ClassName.classvariable*   Class variable
- *object.method()*   Instance method (no args)
- *object.method*(arg, arg, arg[...])   Instance method
- *object.classMethod*(arg, arg, arg)   Class method
- *ClassName.classMethod()*   Class method (no args)
- *ClassName.method*(arg, arg, arg[...])   Class method

Arrays

Read more about arrays

Chapter 4 includes a section on understanding arrays.

You can declare arrays of primitive data types, objects, or arrays.

- `type varname[...]`   Array variable
- `type[...] varname`   Array variable
- `new type[numberOfElements]`   New array object
- `new type[...] {initializer}`   New anonymous object
- `arrayName[index]`   Array element
- `arrayName.length`   Length of array

Java Statements

Nicholas Wirth, the inventor of the Pascal programming language and an expert in program design, asserts that "Algorithms plus data structures equals programs." You use Java statements to implement algorithms. See Chapter 5 for an overview of loops and conditions. Chapter 6 describes how to assemble statements into methods. Chapter 24, "Organizing and Reusing Your Code," shows how to assemble larger pieces of code into reusable components.

Loops and Conditionals

While you can accomplish many interesting things with straight-line code, the real power of programming comes from loops and conditionals. Chapter 5 gives you in-depth information on this topic. The following is a summary list of the loop and conditional statements that Java supports.

- Conditional   `if (test) block`
- Conditional with else   `if (test) block else block`
- switch to a case (on integer or char types):
  ```
  switch (test) {
    case value : statements
    case value : statements

    . . .

    default : statement
  }
  ```

- for loop   for (*initializer*; *test*; *change*)
- while loop   while (*test*) *block*
- do loop   do *block* while (*test*)
- Break out of switch or loop   break or break *label*
- Continue loop   continue or continue *label*
- Labeled loops   *label*:

Constructors

The basic constructor format is

className() *block*

or

className(*type parameterName*, *type parameterName*, . . .)
block

You can also specify access control: public, protected, or private.

Methods

To write a method, write

returnType methodName() *block*

or

returnType methodName(*type parameterName*, *type*
parameterName, . . .) *block*

You can place the following keywords before the method definition:

- abstract   "Placeholder" to be implemented in a derived
  class
- static   Class method
- native   To be implemented in platform-specific language
- final   Cannot be overridden in subclass
- synchronized   Only allow one thread in the method at a
  time
- public, private, or protected   Access specifiers

Inside a method or constructor body the following keywords are available:

- `this`   Refers to the current object
- `classname.this`   Refers to an inner class object
- `super`   Refers to the base class
- `super.methodName()`   A method of the base class
- `this(. . .)` Calls this class's constructor
- `super(. . .)`   Calls the base class's constructor
- `type.class`   Returns the class object for the type
- `return` or `return value`   Returns control to the calling routine

Importing

You can always fully specify the package for each variable or method. To improve readability (and save some typing) you may prefer to import a class or an entire package.

- `import package.className`   Imports a single class
- `import package.*` Imports all `public` classes in package
- `package packageName`   Classes in this file belong to this package

Guarding

You can guard code against intrusion by other threads by writing

```
synchronized ( object ) block
```

This code will wait for a lock on the *object* before executing the *block*.

Chapter 17 describes `synchronized` and the related API.

You can guard your code from throwing exceptions by writing

```
try block
catch (exceptionName exceptionVariable) block
```

Read more on methods

See Chapter 6 for more information on this subject.

Learn more about the `import` statement

See Chapter 16, "Understanding Packages," for more information on the `import` statement.

Read more about exceptions

See Chapter 10 for more information on exceptions.

You can also write

```
try block
catch (exceptionName exceptionVariable) block
finally block
```

If you use `finally` you can optionally delete `catch`.

Building Java Applets in an IDE

Learn why professional programmers use Integrated Development Environments

Build an empty applet in Symantec's Visual Café to see what Java Visual Café generates

Add components to the applet and watch the growing user interface in the source code

Build a complete applet with a sophisticated layout and an event listener

Learn how to add Swing components to the Visual Café Component Palette

A Tour of Visual Café

The examples in this book have concentrated on "brute force" coding—writing every line of Java with a simple text editor such as WordPad. This technique is appropriate when you are learning Java, because it helps you understand what every line of code does.

As a professional programmer someone is paying for every minute of your time—you owe it to them to be as productive as you can. One productivity aid is to use an Integrated Development Environment, or IDE. Visual Café for Java, from Symantec, is one such IDE. In this chapter you'll look at how applets built in Visual Café differ from those you built by hand back in the first few chapters of this book.

SEE ALSO

➤ *Learn more about IDEs, page 743*

In the next section you'll use Visual Café to build an "empty" applet, without ever writing a line of code. Then you'll examine the code generated by Visual Café to see how its Java compares with something you'd write yourself. In the next two sections after that you'll repeat the process—first, with a simple "Hello, World"-style applet, and then with a more substantial applet—approaching something that you might actually use on a Web site.

Using the Form Designer Window

When you open a new, empty applet project in Visual Café you'll see the windows shown in Figure E.1, with the Form Designer window in the center. In this configuration you can drag components from the Component Palette to the Form Designer. Visual Café for Java takes care of inserting the code for that JavaBean into the applet's file.

Learn more about Visual Café

Visual Café is loaded with features—far more than this appendix can show. You can read about the product and download a trial version (which runs on the Macintosh) at `http://cafe.symantec.com/`. For an in-depth tutorial read *Teach Yourself Visual Café 2 in 21 Days* (Sams.net, 1997).

Why Visual Café?

As you saw in Appendix C, "Java Resources," there are over a half-dozen serious contenders in the Java IDE market—most have an entry level version with a street price under $100. Visual Café is one of the most popular of these products, and it has plenty of features. However, you can replicate all of the exercises in this chapter in whatever commercial IDE you happen to use.

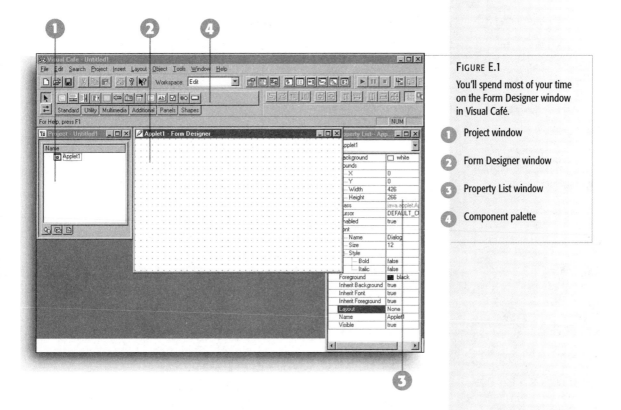

FIGURE E.1

You'll spend most of your time on the Form Designer window in Visual Café.

1 Project window

2 Form Designer window

3 Property List window

4 Component palette

Working with the Component Palette

See Figure E.2 for a closeup of the Component Palette, with the Standard tab showing. The components on the Standard tab strongly resemble the components from the AWT library. If you have Visual Café, take some time to familiarize yourself with each of these tabs. Move the mouse over the component—it will show you the name of the component.

To add a new component to the form, click the component in the Component Palette and draw it onto the Form Designer.

Do you want to disable layouts?

By default, the Java layout manager is disabled. If you want to use a layout manager you should specify it in the applet's property list, described later.

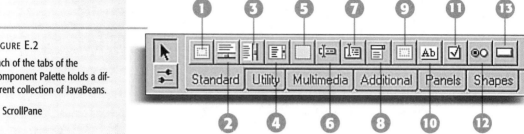

FIGURE E.2

Each of the tabs of the Component Palette holds a different collection of JavaBeans.

1. ScrollPane

2. Horizontal Scrollbar

3. Vertical Scrollbar

4. List

5. Canvas

6. TextField

7. TextArea

8. Choice

9. Pane

10. Label

11. Checkbox

12. Radiobutton

13. Button

Working with Properties

Figure E.3 shows the Form Designer after I've drawn a few components on it. There's a label, a button, and a text field. I've selected the text field—you'll note that the Property List for the textField appears in the Property List window. You can edit all of the properties from this list. When you're done, be sure to save all of the files in your project.

Building the Empty Applet

This appendix describes how I built one specific applet, for use in the medical application described throughout this book. Use this section as a guide to show you how you can build your own applets. You can also use the code generated by Visual Café for Java as a starting point for applets you build by hand.

Building the Applet

Start by launching Visual Café. To make a new, empty applet, follow this three-step procedure.

Making an empty applet with Visual Café

1. Close any open projects—If there's a project open, close it by selecting the Project Window, and then choose Close Form Designer from the File menu. Now make a new, empty project by choosing File, New Project. You should see a window similar to the one shown in Figure E.4.

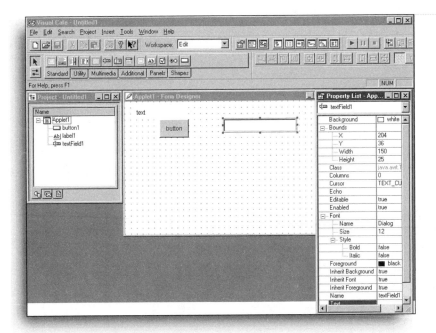

2. Make a new "Basic Applet" project—You'll see several alternative project templates, each designed to build a different kind of Java program:

- Basic Java Bean—This template will get you started building a new component.

- Empty Project—This template contains no objects; use it when you want to completely customize your program.

- Basic Application—This template contains a `Frame`, an `AboutDialog`, and a `QuitDialog`. The `Frame` contains a menu bar and an Open File dialog box.

- Basic Applet—This template contains an empty applet.

For this example we're making an applet, so choose the "Basic Applet" template and click the OK button.

Even more templates available

Visual Café is available in three versions: Web development, Professional, and Database Development. If you have the Professional edition you'll have three more templates: Basic Win32 Dynamic Link Library, Basic Win32 GUI Application, and Basic Win32 Console Application. If you have the Database Development edition you'll have all of the templates in the Professional edition, plus dbAWARE Template Wizard and dbAware Project Wizard.

Making a project folder

Visual Café has a folder named Projects in its main directory. I recommend that you make a new folder inside Projects for each different application, applet, or JavaBean you develop. If your project grows large, break it up by grouping the files into subordinate folders.

3. Save the project to its own folder—Within a few seconds Visual Café makes a copy of the Basic Applet file—it's named Applet1.java. Save the project, which includes the Applet1.java file, to a new directory by selecting the Project window, and then choosing Save from the File menu. Figure E.5 shows the Project window right after you've completed the Save. (I've switched the window to the File tab and expanded it so you can see the characteristics of the file. I also opened the Imports folder so you can see what Visual Café is including for you.)

FIGURE E.4

Visual Café will write some of your code for you if you choose one of the templates.

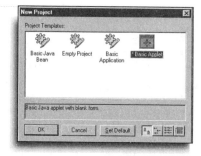

FIGURE E.5

For easier deployment keep all of the files for one project inside one folder.

Be sure to use Save All

The first time you save a project, Visual Café saves all of the files in the project. After this first Save, Visual Café only saves the project file itself—you must choose Save All in order to save all of the files in the project.

This new applet doesn't do much, but it is a complete applet. You can compile it and run it, all from inside Visual Café. Choose Project, Execute to run the applet. When you choose Execute, Visual Café will run the code that is generated through its own compiler—you can choose to use Sun's compiler in Project Options, but Symantec's is noticeably faster. Visual Café also generates an HTML file with an `<APPLET>` tag. Then it loads the HTML file into AppletViewer to display the applet.

Figure E.6 shows the empty applet running in AppletViewer.

Examining Visual Café's Code

If you go to the project folder and examine the file named Applet1.java, you'll see the code shown in Listing E.1. If you prefer, you can view this code inside Visual Café by switching the Project window to the Files tab and double-clicking Applet1.java. Visual Café includes a Java-aware editor—keywords are shown in blue and the text is correctly indented.

Don't get rid of `javac` quite yet

While Sun's compiler is slower than Symantec's, the error messages are of higher quality. If you're troubleshooting a tough problem and the error message in Visual Café seems less than enlightening, go to the command prompt and compile the project under `javac`.

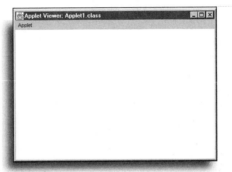

FIGURE E.6
Without writing any code, you already have a simple applet with a menu.

LISTING E.1 **Applet1.java—Code generated by Visual Café as part of the basic applet template**

```
1  /*
2      A basic extension of the java.applet.Applet class
3  */
4
5  import java.awt.*;
6  import java.applet.*;
7
8  public class Applet1 extends Applet
9  {
10     public void init()
11     {
12        // Take out this line if you don't use
```

Changing the HTML file and viewer

As your applet moves closer to deployment you may prefer to have Visual Café load your own HTML file rather than the one it generated. You may also prefer to use a Web browser rather than AppletViewer. You can change these options from the Project Options dialog.

continues…

LISTING E.1 Continued

```
13  symantec.itools.net.RelativeURL or
14  symantec.itools.awt.util.StatusScroller
15        symantec.itools.lang.Context.setApplet(this);
16
16        // This code is automatically generated by Visual Cafe
          when you add
18        // components to the visual environment. It instantiates
          and initializes
19        // the components. To modify the code, only use code
          syntax that matches
20        // what Visual Cafe can generate, or Visual Cafe may
          be unable to back
21        // parse your Java file into its visual environment.
22        //{{INIT_CONTROLS
23        setLayout(null);
24        setSize(426,266);
25        //}}
26      }
27
28      //{{DECLARE_CONTROLS
29      //}}
30  }
```

Recall from Chapter 3, "Getting Started Fast," that the runtime environment calls an applet's `init()` method when the applet is instantiated on a Web page. In this case `init()` does three things:

- Calls a Symantec library routine
- Turns the layout manager off
- Sets the applet to a specific size.

Symantec has included a complete API reference in their help system. To see what `symantec.itools.lang.Context.setApplet(this)` is all about choose Help, Java API Reference. Choose the Symantec API Packages line from the resulting window, and select the `symantec.itools.lang` package. You can double-click the line or click the Display button to open the documentation. From the Class Index window that results, choose Context; navigate down to the setApplet() method, and read the documentation. You'll learn that the Context class is used in conjunction with symantec.itools.net.RelativeURL to keep track of the program's codebase so that relative URLs can be generated correctly. If you don't need this capability, just comment out the symantec.itools.lang.Context.setApplet(this) line.

After the comment you see the line

```
setLayout(null);
```

Recall from Chapter 11, "Building the User Interface with the AWT," that every AWT container has a default layout manager. Class Applet is a kind of Panel; the default layout manager for Panel is FlowLayout. By default, Visual Café disables this layout manager and takes over direct control of component positioning.

There are many reasons you might want to leave the layout manager on. To set the layout manager without editing the code, select the Form Designer window. The Property List window will display the properties of Applet1. (Of course, at this point there's nothing else in the applet to display.)

Toward the bottom of the property list you'll find a property called Layout. By default Visual Café has set Layout to None. This is why you saw setLayout(null); in the generated code. Click the word None—you'll see a list of layout managers. Choose whichever layout manager you prefer. Figure E.7 shows this property on the property list.

The last line of the generated code reads:

```
setSize(426,266);
```

This line calls the Applet's setSize() method, which is inherited from java.awt.Component. The size itself is taken from Applet1's Bounds property. Open Bounds by clicking the small plus sign next to it—you'll see an origin (X and Y are both zero), a Width, and a Height. As you resize the Form Designer window you'll see the Width and Height change.

Caution: Applets without a layout manager may not look good

Layout managers were designed so that applets could run on many different sized monitors and in different GUIs and still look good. When you turn off the layout manager and take direct control over the positioning, you take the risk that someone with a different sized monitor may see overlapping components, or components may disappear off the side of the screen.

Specify the layout options

Some layout managers accept parameters. For example, if you choose FlowLayout you'll see a plus sign appear to the left of the Layout property. Click it to open the node and access the layout properties.

FIGURE E.7

By default, Visual Café sets the layout manager to `null`.

Make sure the `<Applet>` tag matches the `Width` and `Height`

Recall from Chapter 3 that the `<APPLET>` tag contains the `WIDTH` and `HEIGHT` attributes that are actually used by the browser. Visual Café has set the `WIDTH` and `HEIGHT` for you in the "autogen" HTML file. If you write your own `<APPLET>` tag, you should copy the `WIDTH` and `HEIGHT` from the `setSize()` method or the `Bounds` property into your `<APPLET>` `WIDTH` and `HEIGHT` attributes.

Hello, World–Café Style

Now add some components to your applet. Applet1 isn't a very descriptive name for an applet— change it to HelloApplet. You can do this by clicking the name in the Object tab of the Project window, and typing the new name, or by changing the `Name` property in the Property List for `Applet1`.

Adding a component is a three-step process.

Adding a component to an applet

1. Select the component in the appropriate tab of the Component palette. The Standard tag roughly corresponds to the most popular components in the AWT. Other components from the API are found on Utility and Additional tabs. These tabs also support classes developed by Symantec, such as the BorderPanel on the Panel tab.

2. Draw the component onto the Form Designer window.

3. Use the Property List window to set the `Name`, `Text`, or other properties.

Add a "Hello, World!" label to your applet. The `Label` component is listed under the Standard tab of the Component palette. Figure E.8 shows this component on the Standard tab.

FIGURE E.8

Choose the Label component from the Standard tab of the Component palette.

With the Label component selected, draw the component onto the Form Designer. If you've left the applet's Layout property at the default—None—the component will assume whatever size and location you draw it. If you've specified a layout manager, the component will assume a size and location consistent with the rules of that layout manager.

As long as the component is selected, its property list will be visible in the Property List window. Set the Name to fHelloLabel and the Text to "Hello, World!" While you're on the property list, go ahead and set the Font and Style properties to whatever suits you. I set mine to 18-point Helvetica with Bold and Italics both true. I also set the Foreground to blue. I left Inherit Background true, so the default Applet background—white—remains in effect on the label. I also set the Alignment to CENTER. Figure E.9 shows the finished applet.

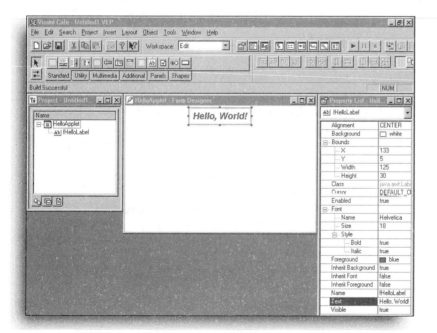

FIGURE E.9

Use the property list to quickly set the component's properties.

The Form Designer makes the changes as you change the property list, so there's not much point in running this applet. To generate the code without executing the applet, choose, Project, Build Applet (or press F7 on a Windows platform).

Listing E.2 shows the code generated for this applet. New or changed lines are highlighted **in boldface type**.

LISTING E.2 *HelloApplet.java*–**Simple applet written entirely by Visual Café**

```
1   /*
2       A basic extension of the java.applet.Applet class
3   */
4
5   import java.awt.*;
6   import java.applet.*;
7
8   public class HelloApplet extends Applet
9   {
10      public void init()
11      {
12          // Take out this line if you don't use
13  symantec.itools.net.RelativeURL or
14  symantec.itools.awt.util.StatusScroller
15          symantec.itools.lang.Context.setApplet(this);
16
17          // This code is automatically generated by Visual Cafe
            when you add
18          // components to the visual environment. It
            instantiates and initializes
19          // the components. To modify the code, only use code
            syntax that matches
20          // what Visual Cafe can generate, or Visual Cafe may
            be unable to back
21          // parse your Java file into its visual environment.
22          //{{INIT_CONTROLS
23          setLayout(new FlowLayout(FlowLayout.CENTER,5,5));
24          setSize(392,241);
25          fHelloLabel = new java.awt.Label("Hello, World!",
26  Label.CENTER);
```

```
27          fHelloLabel.setBounds(133,5,125,30);
28          fHelloLabel.setFont(new Font("Helvetica", Font.BOLD|
29 Font.ITALIC, 18));
30          fHelloLabel.setForeground(new Color(255));
31          add(fHelloLabel);
32          //}}
33      }
34
35      //{{DECLARE_CONTROLS
36      java.awt.Label fHelloLabel;
37      //}}
38 }
```

Compare this listing to one you wrote by hand, such as the HelloPlus.java shown in Listing 11.3. In both programs you have a `Label` declaration (though you put yours at the top and Visual Café put it at the bottom, after `init()`). In this program you made the `Label` data member private; Visual Café allows their data members to keep the default access specifier, which allows programs throughout this package to read this data member.

Apart from those two relatively minor differences, Visual Café generated almost the same code as you did—but Visual Café did it far more quickly, and is far less likely to make an error.

SEE ALSO

➤ *See the hand-written* `HelloPlus` *(Listing 11.3), page 274*

Building an Interactive Applet in Visual Café

Figure E.10 illustrates an applet you'd like to write. The plan is to have the user choose a medication from the list on the left, and have it appear in the list on the right. In this way a physician could build a set of orders for the patient, and then have it sent off to the pharmacy.

Editing source code

Whenever possible, make your changes visually rather than by modifying source code. When you must add code to the source files, stay out of the code blocks that are regenerated by Visual Café. These blocks begin with `//{{` and end with `//}}`.

FIGURE E.10

In any applet designed for real use, sketch out a design before you begin implementation.

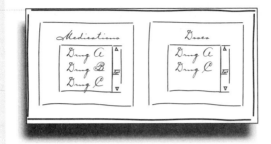

A real-world applet

To make this applet truly useful for physicians, you should continue to develop it. Consider adding buttons to make it possible to remove items from the list on the right, and a Commit button that allows the user to send the finished list to the pharmacy.

Open a new project in Visual Café; call it Sample Applet. Change the applet Layout to GridLayout and specify one row with two columns. Give the applet a name—I've called mine TAddDose.

Constructing the Left Panel

Into this applet place BorderPanels—it's on the Panels tab of the Component Palette. Since you want different-sized components in this panel, set the Layout of the new BorderPanel to GridBagLayout. Now add a Label and a List to the new panel. Set the fonts and styles to whatever you consider attractive. I made my label 18-point bold italic Dialog, and left the font and style of the List at the default values. You should also give each component a name. I named these two components fMedicationLabel and fMedication, respectively. I set the Text of fMedicationLabel to Medication and the Items of the List to a list of medications. For now, I just used one real medication to make sure I got the size right. Later I can go in with a list of medications from the pharmacy, or, better still, I could design this class to load from a server.

Now get the proportions right on these two components. Select the Label and open its GridBagConstraints property. Specify the GridX and GridY to be 0, 0, since this cell is to appear as the first cell of the first (and only) column. Set the GridWidth to 1, and the GridHeight to –1—that's the numeric equivalent of GridBagConstraints.RELATIVE. Leave the two Weights set to 0.0, the Anchor to CENTER, and the Fill to NONE. This combination helps keep the Label small.

Now select the List. Here are the settings I used for this component:

- GridX—0
- GridY—1
- GridWidth—1
- GridHeight—0 (equivalent to GridBagConstraints.REMAINDER)
- WeightX—1.0
- WeightY—1.0
- Anchor—CENTER
- Fill—BOTH

Feel free to adjust the Insets on these components to whatever you think is aesthetically pleasing; I left all of mine at 0.

SEE ALSO
➤ *Learn more about the* GridBagLayout, *page 289*

Constructing the Right Panel

Now add a second BorderPanel to the applet. Add a Label and set its text to Doses. Name that label fDosesListLabel. As you did with the Label in the first panel, set the Font and Style to whatever you find attractive.

Now add a TextArea to the right-hand panel. Name it fDoseList. Set the Layout of the panel to GridBagLayout. Set the GridBagConstraints of the Label and the TextArea to be the same as the ones you used on the Label and the List in the left-hand panel. Your screen should now resemble Figure E.11.

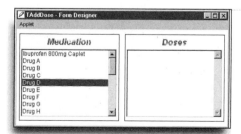

FIGURE E.11

You've implemented this applet with two panels, each of which contains two components in a GridBagLayout.

Set the Editable property to false—you don't want users to be able to change the doses on the list to arbitrary values.

Making the *TextArea* Listen to the *List*

Here's a feature that isn't found in every IDE: Visual Café's Interaction Wizard. Select the Interaction Wizard from the tool-bar—Figure E.12 shows you where it is. With the Interaction Wizard selected, drag a line from the List in the left panel to the TextArea in the right.

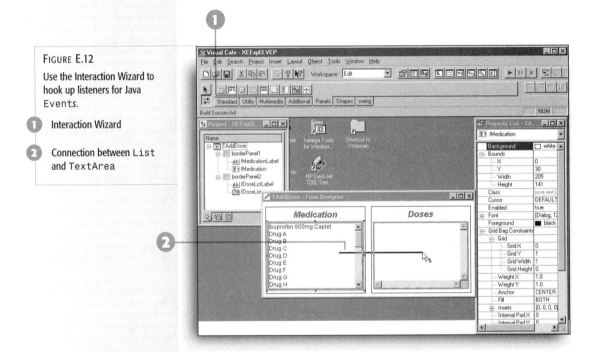

FIGURE E.12

Use the Interaction Wizard to hook up listeners for Java Events.

1 Interaction Wizard

2 Connection between List and TextArea

Now the Wizard opens and asks you for the specifics of the interaction. Figures E.13 and E.14 show the two screens of the Wizard. The list at the top—Start An Interaction for "fMedication"—is asking for the name of the Event to listen for. The second field—Select the Item You Want to Interact With—names the listener. Set the first field to ItemEvent and the second to fDoseList.

The third field is named Choose What You Want to Happen. In this field you specify an action from a list of common actions. Choose Append String to TextArea. Now click the Next button to move to the second screen of the Wizard.

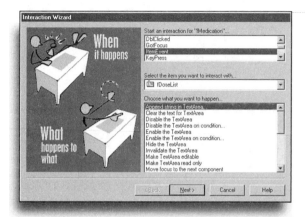

FIGURE E.13

On the first Interaction Wizard screen, specify when the interaction happens, and what happens to what.

Because you chose Append String to TextArea, the Wizard asks for you to identify the string. Choose Another Item: fMedication in the top field, and Get the Current Item Text in the second field. Now click the Finish button, and the Wizard will write your code for you.

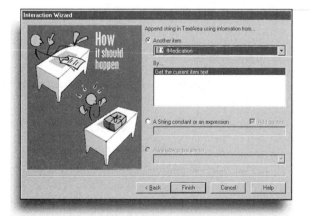

FIGURE E.14

The second Interaction Wizard screen specifies details about the interaction.

A Test Run of the New Applet

Save all your files frequently

As with any application, it's a good practice to save your files frequently. You can click the Save button in the toolbar to save the currently select-ed window, or choose Save all from the File menu.

So far you've written an applet with a fairly complex layout and some simple interaction, and haven't touched a line of source code (though knowing about layout managers, events, and other language and API issues is clearly useful when working with an IDE). Now let's see what you've built.

Choose Execute from the Project window. Visual Café compiles the source code it has been generating and runs the applet. Click a few medications in the left-hand pane and observe the effect in fDoseList. Figure E.15 shows the applet at work.

FIGURE E.15

This version of the applet copies medications from the list on the left to the list on the right.

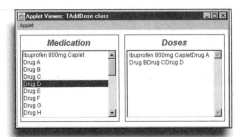

The good news is that the applet layout is correct and the inter-action seems to work just fine. The bad news is that there's a defect in the append logic. You're appending the String from fMedication, but failed to add a newline character ('\n'), so all of the text in fDoseList is on the same line. Fix that defect by edit-ing the source code.

To make a change to an existing interaction, perform the follow-ing steps.

Changing an existing interaction

1. Open the Class Browser window.

2. Locate the class that serves as the event receiver—in this example, that's TAddDose.

3. In the Members list, locate the method that Visual Café has written for you—in this example, it's named fMedication_ItemStateChanged.

4. Finally, edit the source code that appears in the bottom pane.

Using this procedure, open `fMedication_ItemStateChanged` and find the line that reads

```
fDoseList.append(fMedication.getSelectedItem());
```

Change it to read

```
fDoseList.append(fMedication.getSelectedItem() + "\n");
```

Now close the Class Browser, do a Save All, and Execute the Project. Figure E.16 shows the finished applet in action.

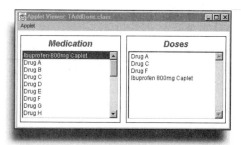

FIGURE E.16
You fixed the defect by adding the newline.

Figure E.17 shows what the second screen of the Interaction Wizard would have looked like if you had used the Interaction Wizard to specify the newline.

Doing it right the first time

If you had thought of it at the time, you could have put the newline in when you used the Interaction Wizard.

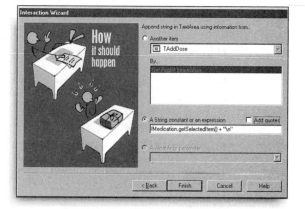

FIGURE E.17
You can add a tiny bit of code right in the Interaction Wizard.

Examining the Source Code

By using Visual Café you have built a moderately sophisticated applet without any significant amount of coding. While other applets (or further extensions to this one) may require more work with the source code, clearly using an IDE is a great way to save time in developing your Java programs.

In this section we'll review the source code Visual Café generated. This source is shown in Listing E.3. I've added a bit of white space to make the code more readable.

Always double-check the source

Even when you're using a good IDE, I recommend you always look over the source before you release your program. You may find some code you'd like to improve, or you may discover a coding technique you didn't know before.

LISTING E.3 TAddDose—By using an IDE, you can generate many lines of Java code quickly

```
1   /*
2       A basic extension of the java.applet.Applet class
3    */
4
5   import java.awt.*;
6   import java.applet.*;
7
8   import symantec.itools.awt.BorderPanel;
9   public class TAddDose extends Applet
10  {
11      public void init()
12      {
13          // Take out this line if you don't use
14  symantec.itools.net.RelativeURL or
15  symantec.itools.awt.util.StatusScroller
16          symantec.itools.lang.Context.setApplet(this);
17
18          // This code is automatically generated by Visual
19          Cafe when you add
20          // components to the visual environment. It
21          instantiates and initializes
22          // the components. To modify the code, only use code
23          syntax that matches
24          // what Visual Cafe can generate, or Visual Cafe may
25          be unable to back
26          // parse your Java file into its visual environment.
27          //{{INIT_CONTROLS
28          setLayout(new GridLayout(1,2,0,0));
29          setSize(453,197);
30
```

```
31        borderPanel1 = new symantec.itools.awt.BorderPanel();
32        GridBagLayout gridBagLayout;
33        gridBagLayout = new GridBagLayout();
34        borderPanel1.setLayout(gridBagLayout);
35        borderPanel1.setBounds(0,0,226,197);
36        add(borderPanel1);
37
38        fMedicationLabel =
39          new java.awt.Label("Medication",Label.CENTER);
40        fMedicationLabel.setBounds(48,0,108,30);
41        fMedicationLabel.setFont(new Font("Dialog",
42                                Font.BOLD|Font.ITALIC, 18));
43        fMedicationLabel.setForeground(new Color(255));
44        GridBagConstraints gbc;
45        gbc = new GridBagConstraints();
46        gbc.gridx = 0;
47        gbc.gridy = 0;
48        gbc.gridheight = -1;
49        gbc.fill = GridBagConstraints.NONE;
50        gbc.insets = new Insets(0,0,0,0);
51        ((GridBagLayout)borderPanel1.getLayout()).setConstraints(
52                                        fMedicationLabel,
        gbc);
53        borderPanel1.add(fMedicationLabel);
54
55        fMedication = new java.awt.List(0,false);
56        fMedication.addItem("Ibuprophen 800mg Caplet");
57        fMedication.addItem("Drug A");
58        fMedication.addItem("Drug B");
59        fMedication.addItem("Drug C");
60        fMedication.addItem("Drug D");
61        fMedication.addItem("Drug E");
62        fMedication.addItem("Drug F");
63        fMedication.addItem("Drug G");
64        fMedication.addItem("Drug H");
65        fMedication.addItem("Drug I");
66        fMedication.addItem("Drug J");
67        fMedication.addItem("Drug K");
68        fMedication.addItem("Drug L");
69        fMedication.addItem("Drug M");
70        fMedication.addItem("Drug N");
```

continues…

LISTING E.3 Continued

```
71        fMedication.addItem("Drug O");
72        fMedication.addItem("Drug P");
73        fMedication.addItem("Drug Q");
74        fMedication.addItem("Drug R");
75        fMedication.addItem("Drug S");
76        fMedication.addItem("Drug T");
77        fMedication.addItem("Drug U");
78        fMedication.addItem("Drug V");
79        fMedication.addItem("Drug W");
80        fMedication.addItem("Drug X");
81        fMedication.addItem("Drug Y");
82        fMedication.addItem("Drug Z");
83        fMedication.setBounds(0,30,205,141);
84        gbc = new GridBagConstraints();
85        gbc.gridx = 0;
86        gbc.gridy = 1;
87        gbc.gridheight = 0;
88        gbc.weightx = 1.0;
89        gbc.weighty = 1.0;
90        gbc.fill = GridBagConstraints.BOTH;
91        gbc.insets = new Insets(0,0,0,0);
92        ((GridBagLayout)borderPanel1.
          getLayout()).setConstraints(
93                                                fMedication,
          gbc);
94        borderPanel1.add(fMedication);
95
96        borderPanel2 = new symantec.itools.awt.BorderPanel();
97        gridBagLayout = new GridBagLayout();
98        borderPanel2.setLayout(gridBagLayout);
99        borderPanel2.setBounds(226,0,226,197);
100       add(borderPanel2);
101
102       fDoseListLabel = new java.awt.Label("Doses",
          Label.CENTER);
103       fDoseListLabel.setBounds(68,0,68,30);
104       fDoseListLabel.setFont(new Font("Dialog",
          Font.BOLD¦Font.ITALIC, 18));
105       fDoseListLabel.setForeground(new Color(255));
106       gbc = new GridBagConstraints();
107       gbc.gridx = 0;
108       gbc.gridy = 0;
```

```
109        gbc.gridheight = -1;
110        gbc.fill = GridBagConstraints.NONE;
111        gbc.insets = new Insets(0,0,0,0);
112        ((GridBagLayout)borderPanel2.getLayout()).
           setConstraints(
113                                              fDoseListLabel,
           gbc);
114        borderPanel2.add(fDoseListLabel);
115
116        fDoseList = new java.awt.TextArea("",0,0,
117                             TextArea.
           SCROLLBARS_VERTICAL_ONLY);
118        fDoseList.setEditable(false);
119        fDoseList.setBounds(0,30,205,141);
120        gbc = new GridBagConstraints();
121        gbc.gridx = 0;
122        gbc.gridy = 1;
123        gbc.gridheight = 0;
124        gbc.weightx = 1.0;
125        gbc.weighty = 1.0;
126        gbc.fill = GridBagConstraints.BOTH;
127        gbc.insets = new Insets(0,0,0,0);
128        ((GridBagLayout)borderPanel2.getLayout()).
           setConstraints(
129                                         fDoseList,
           gbc);
130        borderPanel2.add(fDoseList);
131        //}}
132
133        //{{REGISTER_LISTENERS
134        SymItem lSymItem = new SymItem();
135        fMedication.addItemListener(lSymItem);
136        //}}
137    }
138
139    //{{DECLARE_CONTROLS
140    symantec.itools.awt.BorderPanel borderPanel1;
141    java.awt.Label fMedicationLabel;
142    java.awt.List fMedication;
143    symantec.itools.awt.BorderPanel borderPanel2;
144    java.awt.Label fDoseListLabel;
145    java.awt.TextArea fDoseList;
146    //}}
```

continues…

LISTING E.3 **Continued**

```
147
148    class SymItem implements java.awt.event.ItemListener
149    {
150        public void itemStateChanged(java.awt.event.
           ItemEvent event)
151        {
152            Object object = event.getSource();
153            if (object == fMedication)
154                fMedication_ItemStateChanged(event);
155        }
156    }
157
158    void fMedication_ItemStateChanged(java.awt.event.
       ItemEvent event)
159    {
160        // to do: code goes here.
161
162        //{{CONNECTION
163        // Append string in TextArea... Get the current
           item text
164        fDoseList.append(fMedication.getSelectedItem()+"\n");
165        //}}
166    }
167 }
```

Deleting *symantec.itools.lang.Context.setApplet(this)*

As you saw earlier in this chapter, in the section entitled
"Building the Empty Applet," Visual Café always includes the
line

```
symantec.itools.lang.ContextsetApplet(this);
```

Since you're not using Symantec's `RelativeURL` or `StatusScroller`
classes, you can comment out this line or remove it entirely.

Exploring *init()*

`init()` opens with the call to `setLayout()` to set up the
`GridLayout` you specified, and a call to `setSize()`. Remember to
use this size in your `<APPLET>` tag—that's where the browser will
look when it sets up your applet.

Note that `borderPanel1` is an instance of a Symantec class: `symantec.itools.awt.BorderPanel`. You can look up the API for any Symantec class by choosing Help, Java API Reference.

Figure E.18 shows an alternative design based on `BorderPanel`'s `setLabel()` method.

Once the `BorderPanel` is in place, you see first the `Label` and then the `List` being built and added. Note that Visual Café uses the actual integers for `GridBagConstraints` constants. If you prefer, you can replace

```
gbc.gridheight = -1;
```

with

```
gbc.gridheight = GridBagConstraints.RELATIVE;
```

Similarly, in the section that builds and adds `fMedication` you can replace

```
gbc.gridheight = 0;
```

with

```
gbc.gridheight = GridBagConstraints.REMAINDER;
```

Improve the user interface

If you examine the documentation for `BorderPanel` you'll find that BorderPanel supports a `setLabel()` method. If you prefer you can simplify the design by removing the two `Label`s and using `setLabel()` to annotate the `BorderPanel`s.

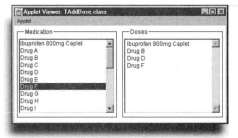

FIGURE E.18
You can simplify the layout by removing the `Label`s and using `BorderPanel`. `setLabel()` in their place.

The second half of `init()` adds `borderPanel2`, `fDoseListLabel`, and `fDoseList`. These sections strongly resemble their counterparts from the left-hand panel; you can make analogous changes here if you like.

At the end of `init()` you see two lines that are used to implement the listener on `fMedication`:

```
SymItem lSymItem = new SymItem();
fMedication.addItemListener(lSymItem);
```

This construct is familiar—it's the standard pattern you learned in Chapter 11. But what, exactly, is a `SymItem`? Visual Café includes a definition of that class later down the page.

SEE ALSO

➤ *To learn more about listeners and events, see page 274*

Making the Data Members *private*

Each of the data members is declared in a short section just after `init()`. If you prefer, you can move this section to the top of the class, where you're used to seeing it. Just be sure you move the lines

```
//{{DECLARE CONTROLS
```

and

```
//}}
```

along with any text between them. Those lines are used by Visual Café, and should be moved with the block in any code you intend to maintain through Visual Café. You might also want to switch the access specifier from the default (which is no explicit specifier) to `private`. Just remember that anything inside the `//{{` and `//}}` delimiters is subject to be overwritten the next time Visual Café generates code, so you may want to check this section and reset the access specifiers before each release.

Understanding Class *SymItem*

`SymItem` is an inner class implementation of `java.awt.event.ItemListener`. It includes just one method: `itemStateChanged()`. That method asks the `ItemEvent` for the name of the event's source; if the source is `fMedication` the method calls `fMedication_ItemStateChanged()`, which is defined next.

Examining the *fMedication_ItemStateChanged()* Method

The last method Visual Café has written for us is `fMedication_ItemStateChanged()`. As you just saw, it is called by the listener. It has one line:

```
fDoseList.append(fMedication.getSelectedItem()+"\n");
```

Recall that most of this line was written by the Interaction Wizard; you added the additional new line as part of your debugging process.

Making the Swing JARs Available to Café

Some versions of Visual Café don't have Swing installed by default, but you can always add Swing components (or any other JAR of JavaBeans) to the Component Palette. Choose Window, Component Library to open the Component Library window. Examine the library to see if the components you want are already installed. If they are, just drag the folder icon to the Component Palette.

To add a new JAR to the component library, follow this procedure.

Adding a JAR to the component library

1. Make sure the Component Library window is open.

2. Choose Insert, Component into Library.

3. Navigate to the directory that holds your JAR—Symantec includes swing.jar in the JFC directory.

4. Select the JAR file and click the Open button, or double-click the JAR file.

JFC available in Symantec's Update Center

If your version of Visual Café doesn't have the JFC classes visit `http://www.symantec.com/domain/vc4java.html` and follow the links to the Update Center for your version of the product. Symantec offers optional files such as jfc.bin in the Update Center.

Glossary

Abstract Windowing Toolkit (AWT) A collection of Java graphical user-interface modules provided by Sun with the Java Developers' Kit. Usually abbreviated AWT.

actor Stereotype of a class that interacts with the software under development. Typical actors are human users and other software systems. *See also: UML*

adaptive optimization A two-step process introduced by Sun in the Project HotSpot JVM; it promises to offer better optimization than static optimizing compilers offer.

address space A processor or program's range of possible addresses.

adapter A convenience class that handles only one kind of event.

adapter A design pattern used to convert the interface of a class into another interface that clients expect. The Adapter pattern lets classes work together even though they may have incompatible interfaces.

aggregate function In SQL, a function such as "average" (avg) that combines data from more than one row.

algorithm A series of steps—a procedure—that solves some problem.

American Standard Code for Information Interchange The most common encoding system, which maps characters to numbers in the range 0 to 127. Usually abbreviated *ASCII*. ASCII is a subset of the American National Standards Institute (ANSI) encoding, which provides extended characters such as math symbols and non-English characters in the range 128 to 257. Microsoft Windows uses the ANSI encoding.

analysis The process of understanding the requirements that the customer and the end user have for the software.

API *See* Application Programming Interface.

applet A Java program that runs with the help of another program (typically a Web browser).

application domain *See* problem domain.

applications Standalone Java programs. Contrast with *applet*.

Application Programming Interface A set of functions provided by a library developer to give the programmer access to a specific set of features. Often abbreviated API.

arguments *See* parameters.

array A static data structure that places one type of data in contiguous "cells." Contrast with *hash table* and *tree*. *See also: data structure*

ASCII *See* American Standard Code for Information Interchange.

assistive technology Hardware and software products that allow people with disabilities to use computers.

atomic A property of transactions, specifying that they either succeed or fail, there's no "half-way" point. *See also: transaction*

AWT *See* Abstract Windowing Toolkit.

balking rendezvous A task rendezvous that returns immediately if the other task is not available. *See also: rendezvous*

base class The parent class in an "is-a" relationship. "Mammal" could be a base class for "dog." *See also: derived class*

The JDK contains an API

The Java Developers' Kit contains an extensive API to Sun's packages. Download the JDK from `http://java.sun.com/`.

JDK 1.2 supports assistive technology

The latest version of Java contains provisions to support assistive technology. Learn more at `http://java.sun.com/products/jfc/accessibility/doc/index.html`.

Boolean Having only two possible values, such as on and off, 0 and 1, or `true` and `false`. Based on Boolean algebra, developed by the English mathematician George Boole.

browser *See* Web browser.

bubble sort A simple sorting algorithm often used to illustrate programming techniques.

byte codes Instructions for the *Java Virtual Machine*, generated by the Java compiler and stored in the class file. *See also: Java Virtual Machine*

byte-code verifier Routines in the *Java Virtual Machine* that ensure that the instructions in the class file do not violate certain security restrictions. *See also: Java Virtual Machine* and *JavaSecurity*

cache Any repository (of data or instructions) used to speed up access. A cache may be located on a proxy server or a client machine to speed up Web access, or between a processor and the hard drive to speed up program execution.

call by reference A way of passing parameters to a subroutine in which a pointer or reference to the item itself is passed, so that the subroutine can read and change the referenced item.

call by value A way of passing parameters to a subroutine in which a copy of the item is passed; modifications to the copy do not affect the original item.

callback A method that allows an object of one class to tell an object of another class where to find it.

cardinality In analysis, the number of instances that participate in an association or aggregation relationship.

Cartesian product All combinations of rows from two tables.

CASE *See* Computer-aided Software Engineering.

casting Overriding a type of the object; coercing an object of one type into a different type. *See also: upcasting* and *downcasting*

certificate The combination of a public key, identifying information, and a certification authority's signature. *See also: X.509v3 certificate*

Obtain your own X.509v3 certificate

You can obtain a personal or server certificate from Verisign. Contact `http://www.verisign.com` for details.

Certification Authority A person or organization that signs certificates.

character A symbol that represents information, or the encoding of that symbol in a computer. Letters of the alphabet, numbers, and punctuation are common characters. *ASCII* is a common encoding system. *See also: ASCII*

class A template for objects, typically modeled from real world entities.

class loader The portion of the Java runtime environment responsible for finding class files and loading them onto the *Java Virtual Machine*. The class loader also enforces various security restrictions. *See also: Java Virtual Machine*

client Software typically associated with an end user; client software does its work in collaboration with a *server*. *See also: server*

collection Data structures that facilitate rapid access and/or updates. *See also: data structure, set, list*, and *map* as typical collection classes

color space A coding system that defines the colors available in a computer program. For example, the color space used in the Hypertext Markup Language (HTML) is RGB—it allocates one byte for red, one for green, and one for blue.

compiler Software responsible for converting human-readable source code to machine-readable instructions. The Java compiler converts Java source into *byte codes* for use by the *Java Virtual Machine*. *See also: byte codes* and *Java Virtual Machine*

component A portion of an application, which can be assembled together later to make the finished program. *See also: component-based software engineering*

component-based software engineering The technology that allows vendors to build visual programming environments, so that end users can assemble the finished application from components. *See also: component*

Computer-Aided Software Engineering The practice of designing software with the help of computerized tools.

constant A value used in a computer program that is guaranteed not to change at runtime. The guarantee is often enforced by the compiler. In Java, constants are declared `static final`.

container In user-interface design, an object that holds the *components* (such as buttons, sliders, and text fields). *See also: component* and *widget*

container class A Java *container*, derived from `java.awt.Container`. *See also: container*

controller The portion of a Model-View-Controller design that changes the data in the model. *See also: model* and *view*

correlated subquery *See* repeating subquery.

cursor A SQL construct that allows you to easily iterate through the rows returned by a `SELECT` statement.

critical section A section of code that is protected so that only one thread or process can be executing it at any given moment.

daemon A process or thread designed to run in the background, independent of any user interface.

data structure A software construct (in memory or on the hard drive) that holds data and the logical relationships between that data. See, for example, *array*, *hash table*, and *tree*.

deadlock A condition in which two or more software entities become mutually blocked, each waiting for a resource that has been seized by the other.

delegation event model A way of communicating events that was introduced by Sun in JDK 1.1. When using the delegation event model, each component has one or more *listeners* listening for a specific event type. *See also: listener*

derived class The child class in an "is-a" relationship. "Dog" could be a derived from the class "mammal." *See also: base class*

device space A coordinate space that applies to a specific graphical output device. *See also: user coordinate space* and *image space*

digital certificate *See certificate and X.509v3 certificate.*

digital signing A mechanism by which an unforgable electronic "signature," typically based on an *X.509v3 certificate*, is added to a document. This signature assures recipients that the document has not been altered after it was signed. *See also: X.509v3 certificate*

double-buffering A technique to eliminate the flickering in an animation by preloading the image into memory.

downcasting Passing an instance as though it were an instance of a derived class. Usually considered unsafe, and may be blocked by the Java compiler. *See also: derived class, casting,* and *upcasting*

dynamic data structures A data structure whose size can be expanded or reduced at runtime. *See also: data structure*

enclosing statement The outer statement of a SQL statement that has been embedded in another statement.

enumeration A mechanism that allows access to the elements of a collection in an orderly fashion, even when the collection itself may be unordered. *See also: collection*

ephemeral port A port that is used as a temporary communications mechanism, often to reply to a request that has come in through a *well-known port. See also: well-known port number*

exception An event that occurs during the execution of a program that disrupts the normal flow of instructions.

exponent The power in a floating-point number. For example, the number 123.4 may be represented as a mantissa of 1.234 with a base-10 exponent of 2. *See also: floating-point number* and *mantissa*

extension A group of Java packages (typically stored in a JAR file) that implement an API that extends the Java platform. *See also: Application Programming Interface* and *Java Archive*

event A message signifying an important occurrence, usually from the environment outside of the software.

flat file A file in which all of the data about one entity is written into a single record, without internal pointers or keys. Contrasts with the tables used in relational databases. *See also: relational algebra*

floating-point number A number that can have its decimal point in any position. Internally, the computer usually stores these numbers using scientific notation, so that the number of digits of precision (the *mantissa*) is separate from the *exponent*. For example, .234 X 2^4 is a floating-point number equal to 3.744. *See also: mantissa* and *exponent*

focus The user's attention on a *GUI* control such as a button or text field, as indicated by a mouseclick, keypress, or similar user action.

fork In the UNIX operating system, to split a process into two processes. *See also: spawn*

formal parameters The names used inside a subroutine for the subroutine's parameters. *See also: parameters*

framework A reusable design expressed as a set of abstract classes and a particular pattern of collaboration.

functional cohesion In software theory, a measure of the relatedness of functions in a module. "Relatedness" is defined in terms of the application domain. In object-oriented software, high functional cohesion is a characteristic of well-designed classes.

garbage collector In Java, the mechanism by which the memory associated with unused objects is reclaimed and freed.

glyph Integer codes used by Fonts that represent pieces of the graphical representation of characters.

Graphical User Interface A human-computer interface such as Microsoft Windows, the Mac OS, or the X Windowing System, which relies upon a high-resolution display, a graphical pointing device such as a mouse, and a set of on-screen controls (often called *widgets*) which the user manipulates directly. Usually abbreviated *GUI*. *See also: widget*

GUI *See* Graphical User Interface.

hardware The physical aspects of a computer system, such as the processor, hard drive, or printer.

hashtable A highly efficient data structure that can look up most entries in just one step. *See also: data structure*, *array*, and *tree*

heap   The portion of memory that is allocated and deallocated in chunks, which have nothing to do with function calls. The heap typically grows from the opposite end of the *address space* to the *stack*. *See also: address space* and *stack*

heavyweight components   Java user-interface classes that do their work through peer objects. *See also: lightweight components*

IDE   *See* Integrated Development Environment.

image space   The local coordinate system where the bounding rectangle of an image is computed. *See also: device space* and *user coordinate space*

input method   A method for mapping keys on the standard Western keyboard to the ideographic symbols commonly used in some Asian languages.

instance   A software object made from a *class*. For example, you might have a class *Aircraft* but a fleet of fifteen *Aircraft* instances. *See also: class*

integer   A whole number, either positive or negative, with no fractional part.

Integrated Development Environment   A visual development tool in which a program may be built, run, and debugged.

interface   In Java, a mechanism for telling the compiler that you intend that a specific set of methods be defined in certain classes. (Those classes are then defined to "implement" the interface.) *See also: multiple inheritance*

Interface Definition Language   The language used by the Common Object Request Broker Architecture (CORBA) to describe the services offered by a class. *See also: Object Request Broker*

Inter-Process Communication   In operating systems, the methods by which one process can send data or synchronize with another.

invariant   Assertions about a class's internal state. In general, client classes should never be able to see the invariant being violated.

JAR   *See* Java Archive.

jarsigner A tool provided by Sun that allows developers to digitally sign JAR files. *See also: digital signing* and *Java Archive*

Java Archive A file that contains Java components (such as class files) and, optionally, supporting resources (such as sounds and images). The contents of the Java Archive file are often described by an embedded manifest file. *See also: manifest file*

Java Native Interface A method developed by Sun that allows Java methods to be implemented in a native language such as C or C++.

Java Runtime Environment Software provided by Sun that allows Java programs to run on a user's machine. The Java Runtime Environment (JRE) includes the Java Virtual Machine (JVM). *See also: Java Virtual Machine*

Java Virtual Machine The Java interpreter that executes the *byte codes* on a particular platform. *See also: byte codes*

`JavaSecurity` The portion of the Java API that allows an applet programmer to request access to restricted system resources. *See also: Application Programming Interface* and *applet*

JNI *See* Java Native Interface.

join In *relational algebra*, the mechanism by which two or more tables are combined to present a single representation of an entity. *See also: join column* and *relational algebra*

join column In a relational *join*, the table column whose value must appear in both tables. *See also: join* and *relational algebra*

key In *relational algebra*, a value (usually unique) that identifies a record in a table. *See also: relational algebra*

key In cryptography, the value used to encrypt and decrypt a message or to digitally sign a message. *See also: digital signing*, *certificate*, and *X.509v3 certificate*

keytool A utility provided by Sun that allows a user to generate a public/private keypair. This keypair may serve as the basis for an X.509v3 certificate (generated by a Certification Authority) or a self-generated X.509v1 certificate. Either *certificate* may be used for *digital signing*. *See also:* `certificate`, `digital signing`, *X.509v3 certificate*, and *Certification Authority*

lightweight components Java user-interface classes that are not tied to the peer objects of the native operating system. *See also: heavyweight components*

list A dynamic collection class that can efficiently be updated (by adding or removing elements). A list has a natural order and allows duplicates. *See also: collection, map*, and *set*

listener An interface designed to receive a specific type of event from a specific component.

literate programming The practice of embedding design information in comments in the source code, and using a special utility to extract those comments into design documentation. Sun's javadoc utility makes literate programming possible in Java.

live time The number of lines over which a variable is "alive"— that is, the number of lines between the first reference to the variable and the last.

loose typing In a programming language, the practice of allowing the programmer to easily convert objects of one sort to objects of another. *See also: strong typing*

magic numbers The disparaged practice of placing literals (often numbers) directly into the program, instead of storing them as *constants*. *See also: constants*

manifest file A text file within a JAR file that contains information about the files in the archive.

mantissa The value in a floating-point number. For example, the number 123.4 may be represented as a mantissa of 1.234 with a base-10 exponent of 2. *See also: exponent* and *floating-point number*

map An unordered *collection class* that allows duplicates. *See also: collection class, list*, and *set*

message digest algorithm An *algorithm* that accepts a stream of characters (such as a message) as input and outputs a numeric "fingerprint" that is virtually unique to the message. *See also: digital signing* and *algorithm*

method In object-oriented design, a function that is associated with a *class*. *See also: class*

metrics Ways of measuring some process. For example, debugged source lines of code per day might be one measure of programming productivity.

microprocessor A computer processor implemented on a single chip.

middleware Software that provides an interface between the user interface and the database. Middleware is often used to encapsulate the rules of business logic in an application.

mitre limit In `java.awt.BasicStroke`, the minimum distance that two lines must approach each other before the `JOIN_MITRE` style will join them.

model The portion of a Model-View-Controller design that holds the data. *See also: view* and *controller*

model in object-oriented design, a representation of the real world in software abstractions called classes and the relationships between them. *See also: class* and *Unified Modeling Language*

multiple inheritance The practice (permitted in languages such as C++ but not in Java) of deriving a class from more than one *base class*. *See also: base class* and *derived class*

multiprocessing In operating systems, the ability to run two or more independent programs, commonly on a single processor (through *multitasking*). *See also: multitasking* and *process*

multitasking In operating systems, the capability to run two or more tasks on the same processor so that they appear to be running at the same time. *See also: task*

non-procedural language A computer language such as Prolog in which the programmer does not need to specify an *algorithm*. *See also: procedural language* and *algorithm*

n-tier architecture A system design in which clients, servers, and the database may be distributed across many different machines. *ORBs* are often used to implement n-tier architectures. *See also: ORB*

namespace A mechanism by which the names in one program cannot be mistaken for or interfere with the names in another program.

null The Java value meaning "empty." *See: NULL*

NULL The SQL value meaning "unknown." *See: null*

Object Request Broker A software object that allows client software to obtain a reference to a remote server object, typically through the Internet Inter-ORB Protocol (IIOP). *See also: Interface Definition Language*

opaque In object-oriented design, the internal structure is invisible to outside objects.

operating system Software responsible for allocated computer system resources to users (including processes). UNIX, Windows NT, and Mac OS are all examples of operating systems.

ORB *See* Object Request Broker.

package Java's name for a class library.

parameters Values or objects passed between a subroutine and a calling routine. *See also: call by value* and *call by reference*

peer objects Graphical components displayed by the native operating system (such as Windows 95) that communicate directly with Java components in the Abstract Windowing Toolkit (AWT). *See also: Abstract Windowing Toolkit*

plug-in A platform-specific program designed to be called by a Web browser. Often used to display information that cannot be displayed by the browser itself.

pluggable look and feel A feature of *Swing* components that allows the end user to change from one defined look and feel to another at runtime. *See also: Swing*

pointer A variable that holds the address of another software entity.

policytool A Sun utility that allows an administrator to specify the security policy to be followed by Java programs on a specific machine.

polymorphism In object-oriented design, the ability to use a derived class in place of its base class. For example, a programmer might write a speak() method for class Mammal. A Dog, a Cow, and a Cat are all derived from Mammal and can all speak(), though their voices are quite different.

primitive type In Java, a data type that is not an object. Primitive types include *characters, integers, floating-point numbers*, and *Booleans. See also: character, integer, floating-point number*, and *Boolean*

print spooler In an operating system, software that allows users to share a printer. The spooler accepts more than one print job and sends them to the printer, one document at a time.

private methods In object-oriented design, a *method* that is not accessible outside of the class in which it is defined. *See also: method* and *class*

problem domain The application area for a given piece of software. For example, Microsoft Word addresses the horizontal problem domain of word processing, while a commercial logistics application might address the vertical application of warehouse management. Also known as an application domain.

procedural language A computer language such as C, Pascal, or Java, in which the programmer must specify an *algorithm* for solving the problem. *See also: non-procedural language*

process A defined procedure designed to be followed by workers. For example, a software development company might use a specific process for conducting peer reviews of code.

process An instance of a running program. For example, if you start up two copies of the Java interpreter, you have two Java Virtual Machine processes running on your computer.

protected rendezvous A task *rendezvous* in which one task will throw an exception if the other task is not ready to communicate. *See also: rendezvous*

pseudocode Design documentation that describes the workings of a program in structured English (or some other language) rather than a computer language.

Learn more online

The key patents for public key encryption are held by RSA Data Security, also known as RSADI. Learn more about this technology from their Web site, `http://www.rsa.com`.

public key encryption An encryption system based on a pair of keys, one of which is kept private while the other is distributed widely.

Reader In Java, an input stream that returns Unicode `chars` rather than `bytes`. *See also:* `Writer` and *stream*

realtime system A computer system that interacts with the outside world on the basis of deadlines. For example, a computer controlling a chemical process may need to respond to events within a few seconds. *See also: event*

recursion The ability of a subroutine to call itself, either directly or indirectly.

reflection The process of examining classes and objects at runtime. Sun provides the `java.lang.reflect` package to support reflection.

registers In a processor, memory to support a small number of working variables. *See also: microprocessor*

regression test A test to ensure that software is still working correctly after some part has been changed.

relational algebra The mathematical theory underlying relational databases, in which records are divided across tables and may be assembled in response to a *join*. *See also: join*

rendezvous A point at which two tasks meet, typically to synchronize or to exchange data.

Remote Method Invocation A Java mechanism for allowing programs on one machine to run methods on objects on a different machine. *See also:* method

return value A value or object returned from a subroutine to a calling routine.

rendering The mechanism by which images or other graphical objects are made to appear on a device such as the computer monitor.

repeating subquery A query where the outer query generates a series of rows, where each row is evaluated by the subquery.

Request for Comment The most common way of disseminating a standard in the Internet community. Usually abbreviated *RFC*.

RFC *See* Request for Comment.

RMI *See* Remote Method Invocation.

return address The memory location from which a subroutine was called. The return address is typically saved on the *stack*. *See also: stack*

round-robin scheduling A multitasking scheduling algorithm that allocates one time slice to every process that is ready to run. *See also* multiprocessing, multitasking, time slice, and process.

sandbox A set of security restrictions designed to keep Java applets from accessing system resources.

schema The layout of a database, showing which fields are associated with each table (in a relational database) or object (in an object-oriented database).

screen magnifier An *assistive technology* that allows an end user to increase the size of the objects on the screen. *See also: assistive technology*

screen reader An *assistive technology*, primarily for the blind, that converts text on the screen to spoken output.

Secure Sockets Layer A protocol developed by Netscape Communications Corporation and released to the Internet community that uses public key encryption to protect transmissions going across the Internet. *See also: public key encryption*

Security Manager A part of the Java Virtual Machine responsible for enforcing security rules and policies. *See also*: *Java Virtual Machine* and *security policy*

security policy A set of rules contained in an external configuration file that specify who is authorized to access which system resource. *See also: Security Manager* and *policytool*

semaphore A software construct often used to protect *critical sections*. *See also: critical section*

Obtain RFCs by FTP

You can download RFCs from the Internic FTP server, `ftp://ds.internic.net/rfc`. Check their login message; they offer mirror sites around the world, including two in North America.

Java's security information available online

Visit `http://java.sun.com/security/` to read about the security features of Java.

serialization The practice of writing objects to a stream and reading them back again.

server Software, often running on a centralized machine, that supports a number of *clients*. Client software contacts the server, obtains some service (such as information) and returns the results of that service to the end user. *See also: client*

set An unordered *collection class* that does not allow duplicates. *See also: list* and *map*

shared class A *class* whose *instances* may be shared by more than one *process*. *See also: class, instance,* and *process*

shell In UNIX, a command interpreter.

sign extension The practice of copying the sign bit from the high-order bit to every bit down to the most significant bit of the data.

signature The combination of a method's name, parameters, and keywords such as the return type and access specifier.

software engineering The branch of engineering concerned with the analysis, design, implementation, test, and maintenance of computer programs.

span The number of lines of code between the first mention of a variable and the next.

spawn In Microsoft Windows NT and other operating systems, to make a new process. *See also: fork*

SQL *See* Structured Query Language.

sRGB A proposed standard Red-Green-Blue (RGB) *color space. See also: color space*

SSL *See: Secure Sockets Layer*

stack The portion of memory that is allocated in response to function calls. It stores subroutine parameters, return addresses, and local variables. The stack typically grows from the opposite end of the *address space* from the *heap*. *See also: address space* and *heap*

Learn about sRGB online

The sRGB color space model is under review by the World Wide Web Consortium. Read about it at `http://www.w3.org/pub/WWW/Graphics/Color/sRGB.html`.

static In object-oriented design, of or pertaining to the class as a whole, rather than an instance. *See also: instance* and *class*

stream Data in the process of being input to or output from a program.

strong typing In a programming language, the practice of prohibiting the programmer from converting objects of one sort to objects of another. *See also: loose typing*

structure An approach to software design that emphasizes the decomposition of the problem into functions, and the assembly of functions into modules. Includes structured analysis, structured design, and structured programming.

Structured Query Language The most common language for accessing relational databases. Commonly called *SQL* and pronounced "sequel."

subquery The inner SELECT statement of a nested *SQL* statement. *See also: Structured Query Language*

Swing Sun's code name for a family of lightweight graphical components. The Swing components are included in the Java Foundation Classes, or JFC. *See also lightweight components.*

task The basic unit of execution in an operating system—a single-threaded process. *See also: thread*

thread A "lightweight process" that can be started and used more quickly than a process that has been started by *fork* or *spawn*. *See also: fork*, *spawn*, and *process*

thread, green Threads that are implemented entirely within the JVM. *See also: thread*

thread, native Threads that rely upon the native operating system. *See also: thread*

timed rendezvous A rendezvous that times out if the other task is not ready when the timer expires. *See also: rendezvous*

time slice In a multiprocessing operating system, a short period of time during which the processor is dedicated to a particular task. *See also: task* and *round-robin scheduling*

transaction An atomic interaction between an actor and a system. *See also: atomic* and *actor*

transient A characteristic of a data member, meaning that the value of the data member does not need to be saved when the class is serialized. See also *serialization.*

tree A data structure that maintains order naturally. *See also: data structure, array,* and *hash table*

Trojan horse Programs that pretend to be useful applications, but carry out some hidden (and generally malicious) operation.

two's complement The notation that Java uses to store negative integers.

UML *See* Unified Modeling Language.

Learn more about UML online

Rational Software maintains an online UML resource center at
`http://www.rational.com/uml/index.shtml`.

Unified Modeling Language The *de facto* standard notation used in object-oriented software analysis and design, based on work by Grady Booch, James Rumbaugh, and Ivar Jacobson.

upcasting Passing an instance as though it were an instance of a base class. *See also: base class, casting,* and *downcasting*

user coordinate space A common coordinate space that is transformed to device space when required during rendering. *See also: device space, image space,* and *rendering*

user space *See: User Coordinate Space*

view The portion of a Model-View-Controller design that displays data. *See also: model* and *controller*

virus A program that attaches itself to other programs or media (such as floppy disks) and, as part of its function, copies itself. A virus is programmed to deliver some payload, often mischievous, but sometimes malicious.

virtual memory In operating systems, a portion of the hard drive reserved for "overflow" memory. Virtual memory is used to make the computer's physical memory appear larger than it actually is, at some cost to performance.

waiting rendezvous A task that waits indefinitely.

Web browser Software that allows a user to connect to a Web server by using the Hypertext Transfer Protocol (HTTP). Microsoft Internet Explorer, Netscape Navigator, and Sun's HotJava are all popular Web browsers.

Web spoofing The practice of designing a Web site that appears to belong to one organization but really belongs to another.

well-known port number A published 16-bit number used as the "address" of a standard TCP/IP service.

widget In user-interface design, a component such as a button or slider with which the user may interact.

Writer In Java, an output stream that sends Unicode chars rather than bytes. *See also:* Reader and *stream*

X.509v3 certificate The current generation of the standard for *certificates. See also: certificate*

Find the well-known port numbers online

The well-known port numbers are listed in the "Assigned Numbers *RFC,*" RFC 1340. You can download any RFC from `ftp://ds.internic.net/rfc/`. Check the login message when you connect to their server; they list mirror sites throughout the world, including two in North America.

Index

digital signatures

SQL (Standard Query Language)

Special Edition Using Java 1.2

Joe Weber

The programmer's tutorial/reference on Java 1.2 that contains detailed descriptions of Sun's Java 1.2 standards, APIs, class libraries, and programming tools.

Covers other relevant Sun, Microsoft, and OMG technologies for Java and ActiveX, including CORBA, Java IDL, JavaBeans, and Enterprise JavaBeans.

Provides Web Developers with tools to make information on their sites easily accessible to users and tips to make the tools more efficient.

Contains over 20,000 lines of documented Java code that show programmers the details of building sophisticated Java applications. Contains all the tools necessary to get started: a CD-ROM of JavaScript Code, Java applets, style sheets, and templates.

$49.99 U.S.	*Accomplished*	
$71.95 CAN	*1,200 Pages*	
0-7897-1529-5	*PUB 7/98*	

Java 1.2 Unleashed

Jamie Jaworski

Extensive coverage of the latest Java 1.2 technologies. Ideal for the intermediate- to expert-level user, this guide explores the new Java extensions and APIs, JavaBeans, JavaOS, and other new Java-based technologies; guides the reader in using JDBC to gain database connectivity; teaches effective programming strategies and application development, and investigates Java security. Using expert tips, advice, and real-world examples, this comprehensive guide and reference is ideal for readers wanting to master professional-level programming with Java.

$49.99 U.S.	*Accomplished – Expert*	
$71.95 CAN	*1,200 Pages*	
1-57521-389-3	*PUB 8/98*	

JFC Unleashed

This programmer's tutorial helps the reader understand how to build client and server applications utilizing all the features of the new Java Foundation Classes.

Extensive use of code samples demonstrates how to put each feature to use.

Complete coverage of the Swing Toolkit, Pluggable Look and feel, and Drag and Drop.

$39.99 U.S.	*Accomplished – Expert*
$57.95 CAN	*800 Pages*
0-7897-1466-3	*PUB 9/98*

Java 1.2 Class Libraries Unleashed

Serves as a nuts-and-bolts, code-level book for programmers who want to use Java Class Libraries.

Examines specifications, major vendors' libraries, compilers, and SDKs.

Shows readers how to use and create class libraries to meet their personalized needs.

$49.99 U.S   *Accomplished – Expert.*

$71.95 CAN   *1,200 Pages*

0-7897-1292-X   *PUB 8/98*

Using Visual J++ 6

Using Visual J++ 6 is a task-based reference that uses clear organization, step-by-step tasks, abundant code samples, and new cross-indexing techniques to teach Visual J++. This book covers all aspects of using Visual J++ to build a wide range of Java applets and applications, ActiveX objects, COM/DCOM objects, and more. The book also covers some of the more advanced features of the Java 1.2 language.

Using Visual J++ 6 accomplishes these goals by anticipating the needs of the user, providing strong navigation and accessibility to the content. This book provides a powerful price/content value proposition versus other books in the marketplace.

$29.99 U.S.   *Beginner - Intermediate*

$42.95 CAN   *800 Pages*

0-7897-1400-0   *PUB 8/98*

Sams Teach Yourself Visual J++ 6 in 21 Days

This easy-to-use tutorial teaches you everything you need to know about Visual J++ 6.

Hands-on practical approach and well-documented code examples ensure that readers understand and learn Visual J++ programming techniques.

This book is an excellent companion to the #1 Java tutorial *Sams Teach Yourself Java 1.2 in 21 Days.*

$29.99 U.S.   *Beginner - Intermediate*

$42.95 CAN   *600 Pages*

0-672-31351-0   *PUB 9/98*

Mitchell Waite Signature Series: Data Structures and Algorithms in Java

Not filled with obtuse mathematics and difficult proofs, *MWSS: Data Structures and Algorithms in Java* removes the mystique from DS&A. It does this in two ways. First, the text is written in a straightforward style, making it accessible to anyone. Second, unique new Java demonstration programs, called "Workshop Applets," are provided with the book. These Workshop Applets provide interactive "moving pictures" that the user can control and modify by pressing buttons. The book's text describes specific operations the user can carry out with these Workshop Applets, and the applets then reveal the inner workings of an algorithm or data structure.

49.99 U.S.	*Accomplished – Expert*
$71.95 CAN	*600 Pages*
1-57169-095-6	*PUB 8/98*

Add to Your Library Today with the
Best Books for Java Technologies

ISBN	Quantity	Description of Item	Unit Cost	Total Cost
0-7897-1529-5		Special Edition Using Java 1.2	$49.99	
0-57521-389-3		Java 1.2 Unleashed	$49.99	
0-7897-1466-3		JFC Unleashed	$39.99	
0-7897-1292-X		Java 1.2 Class Libraries Unleashed	$49.99	
0-7897-1400-0		Using Visual J++ 6	$29.99	
1-672-31351-0		Sams Teach Yourself Visual J++ 6 in 21 Days	$29.99	
1-57169-095-6		Mitchell Waite Signature Series: Data Structures and Algorithms in Java	$49.99	
		Shipping and Handling: See information below.		
		TOTAL		

Shipping and Handling: $4.00 for the first book, and $1.75 for each additional book. If you need to have it NOW, we can ship product to you in 24 hours for an additional charge of approximately $18.00, and you will receive your item overnight or in two days. Overseas shipping and handling adds $2.00. Prices subject to change. Call between 9:00 a.m. and 5:00 p.m. EST for availability and pricing information on latest editions.

201 W. 103rd Street, Indianapolis, Indiana 46290

1-800-428-5331 — Orders   1-800-882-8583 — FAX   1-800-858-7674 — Customer Service